AIR CARRIER OPERATIONS

FOURTH EDITION

MARK J. HOLT & PHILLIP J. POYNOR

Assisted by:
Andrea Georgiou, PhD, and Caitlin Lyons

AVIATION SUPPLIES & ACADEMICS, INC.
NEWCASTLE, WASHINGTON

Air Carrier Operations
Fourth Edition
by Mark J. Holt and Phillip J. Poynor

Aviation Supplies & Academics, Inc.
7005 132nd Place SE
Newcastle, Washington 98059
asa@asa2fly.com | 425-235-1500 | asa2fly.com

© 2022 Mark J. Holt and Phillip J. Poynor

See the ASA website at asa2fly.com/aircr for additional information, updates, and regulatory changes related to this book.

All Rights Reserved. No part of this publication may be reproduced, stored in a retrieval system, or transmitted in any form by any means, electronic, mechanical, photocopy, recording, or otherwise, without the prior written permission of the copyright holder. While every precaution has been taking in the preparation of this book, the publisher, Mark J. Holt, and Phillip J. Poynor assume no responsibility for damages resulting from the use of the information contained herein.

None of the material in this book supersedes any operational documents or procedures issued by the Federal Aviation Administration, aircraft and avionics manufacturers, flight schools, or the operators of aircraft.

URLs appearing in this book are active at the time of publication, but site content may have since changed, moved, or been deleted.

Fourth edition published 2022, third edition published 2020, and second edition published 2016 by Aviation Supplies & Academics, Inc. First edition published 2002 by Blackwell Publishing.

ASA-AIR-CR4
ISBN 978-1-64425-260-4

Additional formats available:
eBook EPUB ISBN 978-1-64425-262-8
eBook PDF   ISBN 978-1-64425-263-5
eBundle   ISBN 978-1-64425-261-1

Printed in the United States of America
2026 2025 2024 2023 2022   9 8 7 6 5 4 3 2 1

Front cover photos—Main image: ©iStock.com/southerlycourse. Small images (clockwise from top left): Angelo Giampiccolo/Shutterstock.com; ©iStock.com/InkkStudios; ©iStock.com/atosan; Pierre-Yves Babelon/Shutterstock.com; ©iStock.com/richterfoto; ©iStock.com/JazzIRT.
Back cover—Phillip Poynor photo credit: Captain Craig O'Mara, NASA Research Pilot.

Library of Congress Cataloging-in-Publication Data:
Names: Holt, Mark J., author. | Poynor, Phillip J., author.
Title: Air carrier operations / Mark J. Holt & Phillip J. Poynor.
Description: Fourth edition. | Newcastle, Washington : Aviation Supplies & Academics, Inc., [2022] | Includes bibliographical references and index.
Identifiers: LCCN 2022025314 (print) | LCCN 2022025315 (ebook) | ISBN 9781644252604 (trade paperback) | ISBN 9781644252628 (epub) | ISBN 9781644252635 (pdf) | ISBN 9781644252611
Subjects: LCSH: Aeronautics, Commercial. | Airlines--Management. | Aeronautics, Commercial—Law and legislation—United States.
Classification: LCC TL552 .H65 2022 (print) | LCC TL552 (ebook) | DDC 387.7068—dc23/eng/20220812
LC record available at https://lccn.loc.gov/2022025314
LC ebook record available at https://lccn.loc.gov/2022025315

CONTENTS

Preface to the Fourth Edition   vi
Acknowledgments   ix
About the Authors   x
Abbreviations   xi

Introduction   1
1   What Is an Air Carrier?   7
2   Operations Specifications: Development and Application   21
3   Airline Organization: Required Management Positions   39
4   Operating Manuals: Requirements and Development   51
5   Part 121, Subpart M: Airman and Crewmember Requirements   63
6   Part 121, Subpart N: Training Programs and Part 121, Subpart O: Crewmember Qualifications   81
7   Air Carrier Flight and Duty Time Limitations   95
8   Airplanes Used in Part 121 Operations   133
9   Airworthiness Requirements   155
10   Instrument and Equipment Requirements   169
11   Dispatching and Flight Release Rules   189
12   Part 121, Subpart T: Flight Operations   215
13   Part 121, Subpart V: Records and Reports and Part 135, Subpart B: Recordkeeping Requirements   241
14   Maintenance   257
15   Selected Part 121 Appendices and Part 120   269

Appendix: Answers to Chapter Exams   287
Glossary of Terms   307
Bibliography   337
Index   339

PREFACE TO THE FOURTH EDITION

I confess that in 1901, I said to my brother Orville that man would not fly for fifty years.
—**Wilbur Wright**, 1908

What's New in the Fourth Edition?

This fourth edition of *Air Carrier Operations* includes an overall update and necessary revisions to address FAA regulatory changes made since the publication of the third edition. Specifically, new sections cover the Pilot Records Improvement Act and the FAA's creation of a new 14 CFR Part 111 Pilot Records Database. This edition also includes a discussion on the recent allowance for a single-engine type rating and offers a review of type ratings, class, and category definitions. With updates throughout the book and the addition of new material, this text continues to provide students and professionals with the essential information pertinent to today's air carrier operations. Now, let's take a look at how to get the most out of the fourth edition of this textbook.

Getting the Most Out of This Text

Air Carrier Operations is an entry-level text that introduces the student to the significant regulatory environment impacting airline operations. Although it is primarily intended for use in an air carrier flight operations course, it can be easily adapted for use in a flight dispatcher course, as part of a general air carrier operations management course, or in independent study by an aviation manager seeking a better understanding of air carrier operations. This book is intended primarily for use in university-level courses and for independent study by airline pilot or dispatcher candidates and aviation managers. At this juncture in their career development, they have been exposed to very little of the restrictive regulations that make up modern airline operations. Whether Part 121 airline or Part 135 charter operator, these companies live or die by their compliance with the applicable Federal Aviation Regulations, or FARs (14 CFR). Surprisingly, aviation students are largely unexposed to the layers of regulations in a Part 61 flight-training program or, at best, minimally exposed to them in a Part 141 pilot school.

The purpose of this book, therefore, is to examine the multitude of regulations governing an air carrier. It will focus primarily on Part 121 air carriers, though we necessarily discuss portions of Parts 25, 110, 117, 119 and relevant portions of Parts 135, 91, and 61 of the FARs. We approach this discussion assuming that the student has some background in piloting or maintenance and has been exposed to introductory courses in aviation. These introductory courses are often found in the freshman or sophomore year and have titles such as General Aeronautics or Introduction to Aviation and are often conducted as a private pilot ground school. Due to the nature of air carrier operations, a large portion of this text focuses on instrument flight rules (IFR) flight operations. Consequently, we recommend that flight students complete the instrument rating before undertaking study of this book.

We do not attempt to explain every regulation in all of its nuances. Rather, we try to paint a mosaic that explains as much the *why* as it does the *what*, leaving the student with a clear understanding of why some of the complex rules are as they are. For this reason, we don't quote excessively from the regulations. Where actual regulation text is provided in the book, it is called out in a different font style for easy identification (with any paraphrased text placed in brackets and italicized). We do try to give the appropriate reference so the student may read it on his or her own, and ***it is essential*** that the student do this as part of the study of this book. Therefore, the student should acquire a copy of the current FARs that includes at a minimum 14 CFR Parts 1, 61, 91, 110, 117, 119, 121, and 135. These are available from ASA, online at *faa.gov*, and in various forms from other aviation publishers, including in a subscription format.

When we reference a regulation in the text, it is important that students reference a copy of the regulations and ***read the text*** of that rule at the same time the explanation is read. That way, they get not only the "big picture" from our text but also the detail and wording from the actual regulation. If there is ever a conflict between our statement of the rule and the actual rule, obviously the rule governs. In addition to learning about that particular rule, students will also develop the skills needed to properly read and interpret the FARs. This is a skill that will surely be needed as students progress further along in their professional careers.

This book is designed to assist students in their first serious foray into the FARs by explaining what something means and why it is done, and then allowing students to get the full meaning of the rule by reading it on their own. At the conclusion of the book, students will have been exposed to the entirety of 14 CFR Part 121 and collateral parts of the FARs. We don't expect an expert level of understanding after one pass through this text. It is reasonable to expect at the conclusion of this book that students should have an appreciation of the variety of regulatory issues involved in air carrier operations and be able to identify the appropriate and applicable regulations pertaining to them. The students should then be able to read the regulations and apply them with an understanding of what is required. With this in mind, it is suggested that any testing in a course based on this text be open book with respect to use of the Federal Aviation Regulations.

We intend this book to be useful as a review or introduction of Part 121 regulations to the airline pilot candidate. Whether the pilot is going for an employment interview or starting an initial training class with a 121 carrier, this book can provide a quick study so the pilot will be better prepared. In recent times due to changes in the hiring process, pilots are going to the airlines with a minimum of 750 to 1,500 flight hours but relatively little to no experience in operations other than flight instruction (or military piloting background). Yet at the same time, design of the initial training programs more or less still assume that pilots have been exposed to this material somewhere. Increasingly, that is not true. Pilots that have not gone through collegiate training programs (e.g., many military pilots or civilian flight school trained pilots) have probably never seen most of the material in this book. This book can enable the pilot to get a head start on the interview process or initial training class. Such pilots should pay particular attention to Chapters 2, 8, 9, 10, 11, and 12 as these chapters are most directly related to the operational issues likely to be asked about in an interview or addressed in the indoctrination and initial training programs.

As pilots, we understand the angst that you may be feeling about your aviation future as a result of the 2020 COVID-19 pandemic and the awful conditions that created in the aviation field (and many, many other segments of society and industry). That may create a considerable sense of indecision and doubt as to whether pursuing an aviation career is still a good idea. If you do have doubts about whether continuing toward an aviation career is wise, we thought it might be helpful to give you some encouragement and things to consider.

The aviation industry is one of the most regulated industries in the world. It is also one of the most challenging, but also rewarding, fields in which a person can engage. It seems that every time we think we have it all down pat, some major event happens that forces the industry and its employees to, yet again, adapt to unfamiliar circumstances. Now, as *Air Carrier Operations* goes to press, is such a time. Flight operations carry on under very challenging conditions while managers and planners address the challenges of recovery.

Under difficult circumstance, people begin to pick up the pieces, start recovering, and then begin to strive to achieve even greater heights. The days start to brighten. Through creativity and hard work, commerce begins to recover. Slowly, things start to grow again. Creativity has time to blossom and, as always, the doers will rise to the challenges of their profession. This process is found in virtually all fields of endeavor. It's not always easy, but for the young person just embarking on a career in aviation, it will be a seminal moment in time.

As a little background, I (Poynor) was the owner of a large flight training and charter company in New York and watched in utter horror as the towers fell on 9/11 about 30 miles distant. In a matter of minutes, the airport was shut, not to reopen for about two months and then much restricted as to use for the training fleet of airplanes—the great majority of our business. It seemed like my aviation career was pretty much ended. But, in reality, it opened a whole different world of aviation to me. Now, after nearly 50 years in the industry, I have had aviation adventures of all kinds, taught aviation in colleges and to individuals, bought and sold airplanes, and, yes, flown them for training and charter.

The point? If you have read this far, you very obviously still desire a career in aviation—as a pilot, a dispatcher, an aviation entrepreneur or something of your own making. With the 2020 pandemic damaging the world economy and all the rest, you may be feeling, like I did, that there is no hope for an aviation career. Here is advice from an "old timer": if aviation was the career you dreamed of before recent events, follow your heart and dreams. Things really do tend to smooth out and improve over time. What you thought you would be doing in aviation might be how you spend your time, but, remember, things you haven't even dreamt of might be hiding in your future as well.

As for those of you reading this text as a college student, let me give you a tremendous insight I got from a sophomore student in New York after 9/11. He came by my office for discussion and guidance about where things were going to go and if he had a career. After telling him something like what I shared above, he thought a few seconds and came up with a truly inspirational thought:

> I was worried about 9/11 keeping me from getting a job, but then I realized: ***I'm not ready for a job.*** I still have two years of school and then finishing flight training. *This actually **gives me an advantage because I can study now and then be qualified when hiring returns.***

That was exactly how it played out.

Organization of the Text

In organizing this text, we decided, for ease of correlation to the FARs, to follow the general layout of the subparts to 14 CFR Part 121. Within the subparts, we intentionally do not attempt to present the rules in numerical order. In some cases that might make sense, but in many others the flow of the material in the FARs is confusing and misleading. We have tried to reorganize the material so that related rules are discussed at the same time. We want the reader to be able to put the disjointed pieces together and grasp the interrelationships that so often exist in the FARs. For this reason, each chapter pretty much stands on its own. If you are especially interested in a particular area (operational rules, for example), you can go directly to Chapter 12, which covers Subpart T, Operations. Again, for the most part, you can start your journey through this book at any point and end it at any point and still get the full value of the effort expended.

At the end of each chapter you will find a brief summary and list of important terms. The summary gives a condensed view of the chapter and helps you identify important ideas. The list of important terms is organized in alphabetical order and will help in the review of the material to facilitate study for the end-of-chapter exam questions.

If an unfamiliar term is used in the text, check the glossary. We have included a greatly expanded and extensive glossary of new terms that are introduced in the book. If you don't find the term in our glossary, another place you can try is the FAA Pilot/Controller Glossary found in the *Aeronautical Information Manual* (AIM), which is widely available from ASA as well as online at faa.gov. Finally, a symbol that may not be familiar to some readers is the "§" symbol. This is used in legislation and legal documents as an abbreviation for the word "section."

ACKNOWLEDGMENTS

The authors would like to thank, first and foremost, the aviation professionals who were kind enough to assist us in our efforts through the years since publication of the first edition of *Air Carrier Operations* in 2002.

Greg N. Brown, aviation author, photographer, and always cheerful and supportive friend provided the catalyst by connecting Mark Holt and Phillip Poynor to start the ball rolling on the original project and offered his design and graphic arts expertise in the production of a number of the figures in the text. Rusty Bell, an industry expert and consultant on airline operations and control was there from the beginning as we went about creating this text.

We would especially like to thank Captain "Billy" Walker and Captain Al Spain, both retired from JetBlue Airways, and Captain Athena Pettit, now retired from American Airlines, who contributed their expertise in so many areas. We especially thank Captain Dave Young of Delta Airlines for allowing us access and use of company flight, maintenance, and operations specifications manuals. As always, any errors contained herein are entirely the responsibility of the authors.

Others who contributed inspirational and moral support include Becky Holt and a number of undergraduate students and faculty through the years who have used the previous editions of the book and offered their feedback on the contents.

Once again, our special thanks to Dave English for allowing us the use of the snippets that begin each chapter. These come from his wonderfully whimsical books of great quotations of flight, *Slipping the Surly Bonds* and *The Air Up There*. These quotations truly help lighten and enliven what can otherwise be a pretty mind-numbing subject, and Dave's books and materials are real treasures. We encourage you to check out all of his aviation publications at www.DaveEnglish.com.

Finally, thanks to Jackie Spanitz and the great staff at ASA in working closely with us, prodding when needed, and always encouraging. Our special thank you for a job well done goes to our editors.

Each of these kind folks contributed their valuable time, knowledge, support, and encouragement of our goal to produce the best and most appropriate materials for pilots striving to learn and achieve at the top rung on the commercial aviation ladder—employment as a pilot at a major air carrier.

ABOUT THE AUTHORS

Mark J. Holt, a captain for a major airline, soloed at age sixteen and has logged over 22,000 hours in more than 40 years of flying. He holds an ATP pilot certificate with Boeing 757/767, Airbus 319/320/321, and BAE Jetstream 41 type ratings, as well as a Flight Engineer Turbojet certificate (L1011 aircraft). His professional aviation career includes extensive flight and ground school instruction experience and service as a check airman for a large regional airline. He also co-authored *The Turbine Pilot's Flight Manual*.

Phillip J. Poynor, JD, is the FAA/Industry 2001 National Flight Instructor of the Year. He also was awarded the National Air Transportation Association Excellence in Pilot Training Award and the New York State University Chancellor's Award for Excellence in Teaching. He has been captain qualified on Part 135 air carriers and taught courses in Air Carrier Operations, Advanced Systems, and Aviation Safety at three major aviation universities. He is an attorney with practice limited to aviation matters and was a staff attorney at a major international airline.

The authors appreciate and gratefully acknowledge the editorial assistance and contributions to this edition provided by:

Andrea Georgiou, PhD (General Psychology), is an associate professor and coordinator of the Flight Dispatch Program at Middle Tennessee State University. She holds an FAA Aircraft Dispatcher Certificate.

Caitlin Lyons is an Aircraft Dispatcher at a major airline and works in its training department. Caitlin holds Private Pilot Single Engine Land and Sea certificates with an instrument rating.

ABBREVIATIONS

AC	Advisory Circular
ACARS	Aircraft Communications Addressing and Reporting System
ACS	Airman Certification Standards
AD	Airworthiness Directive
ADF	automatic direction finder
ADI	attitude director indicator
ADS-B	Automatic Dependent Surveillance–Broadcast
AFGS	automatic flight guidance system
AFM	airplane flight manual
ALD	available landing distance
AMOC	alternative method of compliance
AOA	angle of attack
APU	auxiliary power unit
AQP	Advanced Qualification Program
ARC	Aviation Rulemaking Committee
ARINC	Aeronautical Radio, Incorporated
ARTS	Aircrew Records Tracking System
ASDA	accelerate/stop distance available
ASR	airport standby reserve (flight crew)
ATC	air traffic control
ATD	aviation training device
ATIS	Airport Terminal Information Service
ATP	Airline Transport Pilot
ATP-CTP	Airline Transport Pilot–Certification Training Program
AURTA	Airplane Upset Recovery Training Aid
CAA	Civil Aviation Authority
CAB	Civil Aeronautics Board
CAMP	continuous airworthiness maintenance program
CAP	continuous analysis process
CASE	Coordinating Agencies for Suppliers Evaluation
CASS	Cockpit Access Security System *or*
CASS	continuing analysis and surveillance system
CAST	Commercial Aviation Safety Team
CDFTRS	Crewmember Duty and Flight Time Record System
CDL	configuration deviation list
CFM	company flight manual
CFR	Code of Federal Regulations
CL	centerline lights
CMP	Configuration Maintenance and Procedures Document
CRM	crew resource management
CTP	Certification Training Program
CVR	cockpit voice recorder
DA/DH	decision altitude/decision height
DFDR	digital flight data recorder
DHS	Department of Homeland Security
DME	distance measuring equipment
DMI	deferred maintenance item
DO	director of operations
DOT	Department of Transportation
DRM	dispatcher resource management
EAD	Emergency Airworthiness Directive
EAP	employee assistance program
EFB	electronic flight bag

ETA	estimated time of arrival
ETOPS	Extended Twin Engine Operation
FAA	Federal Aviation Administration
FCC	Federal Communications Commission
FCM	flight crew member
FCOM	flight crew operations manual
FDAR	flight deck access restriction program
FDM	flight data monitoring
FDP	flight duty period
FDR	flight data recorder
FFS	full flight simulator
FIS-B	Flight Information Service–Broadcast
FL	flight level
FMC(S)	flight management computer (system)
FMS	flight management system
FOM	flight operations manual
FOQA	flight operational quality assurance
FP	flying pilot
FRMS	fatigue risk management system
FSB	Flight Standardization Board
FSDO(s)	Flight Standards District Office(s)
FSTD	flight simulation training device
FTD	flight training device
GLS	GPS-based landing system
GMM	general maintenance manual
GMT	Greenwich Mean Time
GOM	general operations manual
GPS	Global Positioning System
GPWS	ground proximity warning system
GSC	ground security coordinator
HAA	height above airport
HAT	height above terrain
HAZMAT	hazardous materials training
HGS	heads-up guidance system
HIRL	high intensity runway lights
IAS	indicated airspeed
ICAO	International Civil Aviation Organization
ICATEE	International Committee for Aviation Training in Extended Envelopes
IFR	instrument flight rules
IFSD	in-flight shutdown
ILS	instrument landing system
IMC	instrument meteorological conditions
INFO	Information for Operators
INS	inertial navigation system
IOS	instructor operating station
JAA	Joint Aviation Authorities
LAHSO	land and hold short operations
LCR	long call reserve (flight crew)
LDA	localizer directional aid
LOA	letter of authorization
LOC/BC	localizer back course
LOC-I	loss of control in-flight
LOFT	line oriented flight training
LRCS	long-range communication system
LRNS	long-range navigation system
MDA	minimum descent altitude
MDR	master differences requirements
MEA GAP	gap or break in navigation signals at the minimum enroute altitude
MEL	minimum equipment list
MIS	maintenance irregularity summary report
MLS	microwave landing system
MMEL	master minimum equipment list
MNPS	Minimum Navigation Performance Standards
MRO	maintenance repair organization
MRO	medical review officer
MRR	maintenance reliability report
MSL	mean sea level
MTOW	maximum takeoff weight
NAMNPS	North Atlantic Minimum Navigation Performance Standards
NAVAIDS	navigation aids
NDB	nondirectional beacon
NFP	non-flying pilot
NOTAMs	Notices to Air Missions
NPRM	notice of proposed rulemaking
NTSB	National Transportation Safety Board
NWS	U.S. National Weather Service
OEI	one engine inoperative
OEM	original equipment manufacturer
OMB	Office of Management and Budget
OSHA	Occupational Safety and Health Administration
PA	public address system
PANS-OPS	Procedures for Air Navigation Services—Aircraft Operations
PAR	PRD Airman Record
PBE	protective breathing equipment
PED	personal electronic device
PF	pilot flying
PIC	pilot-in-command
PM	pilot monitoring
PMI	principal maintenance inspector
POI	principal operations inspector

PRD	pilot records database	**SVT**	single visit training
PRIA	Pilot Records Improvement Act	**TAF**	terminal area forecast
PTS	Practical Test Standards	**TAs**	traffic alerts
RAs	resolution advisories	**TAWS**	terrain awareness and warning system
RAP	reserve availability periods	**TC**	type certificate
R-ATP	restricted privileges Airline Transport Pilot	**TCAS**	traffic alert and collision avoidance system
RCLM	runway centerline markings	**TERPS**	Terminal Instrument Procedures
RNAV	area navigation	**TIS-B**	Traffic Information Service–Broadcast
RNP	required navigation performance	**TOCWS**	takeoff configuration warning system
RP	responsible person	**TODA**	takeoff distance available
RTO	rejected takeoff	**TSA**	Transportation Security Administration
RVR	runway visual range	**U.S.C.**	United States Code
RVV	runway visibility value	**ULR**	ultra long-range operation
SAFO	Safety Alert for Operators	**UTC**	Universal Coordinated Time
SATCOM	satellite communications system	**VFR**	visual flight rules
SCR	short call reserve (flight crew)	**VNAV**	vertical navigation equipment
SD	security directive	**VOR**	VHF omnirange
SDF	simplified directional facility	**VOR/DME**	VHF omnidirectional range/distance measuring equipment
SIC	second in command		
SIGMET	significant meteorological information	**VORTAC**	VHR omnirange radio/tactical air navigation
SM	statute mile		
SMS	safety management system	**WAT**	weight-altitude-temperature
SNPRM	supplemental notice of proposed rulemaking	**WOCL**	window of circadian low

INTRODUCTION

Airplane travel is nature's way of making you look like your passport photo.
—Vice President Albert Gore

Before we begin our study of air carriers and their governing operations specifications, we need to review the history of the agency that has the authority to regulate and oversee all aspects of American civil aviation.

The Federal Aviation Administration (FAA)

Historical Origin

The modern age of powered flight began in 1903, when Orville Wright made the first sustained, powered flight on December 17 in an airplane he and his brother, Wilbur, built. The next few decades witnessed a flurry of aviation activity as a number of new and improved aircraft designs from around the world entered service.

During World War I, aircraft production increased dramatically to meet the increased demand for airplanes from military air forces on both sides of the conflict. Most significant was the development of more powerful motors, enabling aircraft to reach speeds more than twice the speed of pre-war aircraft. More power made it possible to build ever larger aircraft.

Though the airplane proved its worth as a military weapon during World War I, attempts to turn the airplane into a successful commercial endeavor ended in failure. The single exception was the delivery of mail by air—airmail. The U.S. government pushed to establish a postal airmail service across the continental United States. By the mid-1920s, the U.S. Post Office had a fleet of airplanes flying millions of letters annually. This postal flying proved the economic feasibility of airmail. The U.S. Congress then decided to transfer the delivery of airmail to the private sector.

The Contract Air Mail Act of 1925

The **Contract Air Mail Act of 1925** was the first step towards the development of an air carrier industry by allowing the postmaster to contract with private airlines to deliver mail. The initial airmail contracts went to small companies that would grow and go on to pioneer developments in the air carrier industry for decades to come. Also in 1925, a presidential board was created to recommend a national aviation policy. The board recommended that the government establish a regulatory authority to set federal safety standards for civil aviation. The need for such an authority had been recognized for years; however, the numerous bills introduced to the United States Congress attempting to create one were unsuccessful. The air carrier industry activity that began because of the Air Mail Act was minimal, yet this activity, along with requests from industry for federal aviation safety regulations, prompted legislative proposals for an **Air Commerce Act**.

The Air Commerce Act of 1926

The **Air Commerce Act of 1926** charged the Secretary of the Department of Commerce with the responsibility of fostering air commerce, issuing and enforcing air traffic rules, certifying pilots and aircraft, and operating and maintaining air navigation aids. The Act became the cornerstone of the federal government's regulatory authority over civil aviation by establishing a new Aeronautics Branch of the Department of Commerce. This Aeronautics Branch concentrated on functions such as safety rulemaking and the certification of pilots and aircraft.

Bureau of Air Commerce, 1934

Over the next decade, air travel developed from what could be considered a risky endeavor into a crucial mode of transportation for people and products. In 1934, the Aeronautics Branch was renamed the **Bureau of Air Commerce**. As commercial flying increased, the Bureau requested that a group of airlines establish the first air traffic control centers in the United States. In 1936, it was decided that the Bureau of Air Commerce should take over responsibility for controlling en route air traffic, and it began to expand the air traffic control (ATC) system which became its most demanding civil aviation responsibility.

The Federal Register Act of 1935

In 1934, the Supreme Court agreed to hear a case (unrelated to aviation), in which the federal government was trying to enforce an agency regulation against an industrial company. The government later realized that there had been a technical, though inadvertent, revocation of the very regulation in question. Needless to say, the government was very embarrassed by this, and on July 26, 1935, Congress passed the **Federal Register Act of 1935**, requiring all federal regulations to be compiled and published in the *Federal Register*.

This Act was further amended in 1937 to provide for the codification of regulations instead of simply compiling and publishing them. A codification board was established, and it decided the overall structure of the new **Code of Federal Regulations (CFR)**, and assigned the various agencies their own titles. The **Federal Aviation Regulations (FARs)**, as we know them today, are now part of **Title 14 of the Code of Federal Regulations: Aeronautics and Space**. The Federal Register Act established that all federal regulations be codified into a Code of Federal Regulations.

The Civil Aeronautics Act of 1938

In 1938, as a result of a nationally recognized need to improve the disastrous air safety record of the airline industry, the **Civil Aeronautics Act of 1938** was enacted. This Act transferred the federal civil aviation responsibilities from the Department of Commerce to a newly formed **Civil Aeronautics Authority (CAA)**. The CAA was given the additional authority to issue air carrier route certificates and to regulate airline fares. In 1940, President Roosevelt signed a law that divided the CAA into the **Civil Aeronautics Board (CAB)** and the **Civil Aeronautics Administration (CAA)**.

The CAB was given the authority and responsibility for economic and safety regulation and for accident investigations. The CAA was given the responsibility for air traffic control, airman and aircraft certification, safety enforcement, and airway development.

The Federal Aviation Act of 1958

After World War II, the success and rapid growth of air commerce, aviation technology, and the increasing public demand for air services caused the aviation industry to become more complex than the antiquated CAA was able to handle. In addition, with the introduction of jet airliners into service and several horrific midair collisions in 1956 and 1957, the public became concerned about aviation safety issues. For this reason and to address the lack of aviation infrastructure funding, Congress enacted the **Federal Aviation Act of 1958**.

The Act transformed the CAA into an independent agency and renamed it the **Federal Aviation Agency (FAA)**. The FAA was given both the CAA responsibilities of developing and maintaining a federal system of air navigation and air traffic control, *and* the safety and rulemaking functions of the CAB.

The Modern Federal Aviation Administration (FAA)

In 1966, Congress passed legislation authorizing the creation of a cabinet-level department that would combine all the major federal transportation responsibilities. It was also believed that the nation's transportation systems could be managed better by a single department. This new **Department of Transportation (DOT)** officially began operations on April 1, 1967. As part of the new DOT organizational structure, the Federal Aviation Agency was given a new name, the **Federal Aviation Administration**. As part of the reorganization of the FAA, a new, independent accident investigation authority was created: the **National Transportation Safety Board (NTSB)**. The NTSB became the federal government's primary accident investigation agency for not just aviation, but all methods of transportation: highway, rail, marine and pipeline.

On July 5, 1994, the Federal Aviation Act, along with many other transportation-related regulations, was recodified into the format we use today. On that date, the Federal Aviation Act was rescinded and recodified into **Title 49 of United States Code (49 U.S.C.)**. Title 49 of the USC is the code that governs the role of all modes of transportation in the United States.

In this text we will spend most of our time with what we informally call the Federal Aviation Regulations (or FARs), regulations which govern today's aircraft and air carriers. However it is worth noting that **Title 49 of USC, Section 40101**, describes seven basic responsibilities of the FAA, which are summarized below.

1. Assigning, maintaining, and enhancing safety and security as the highest priorities in air commerce.
2. Regulation of air commerce to best promote its development and safety and to fulfill national defense requirements.
3. Promotion, encouragement, and development of civil aeronautics.
4. Control of the use of navigable United States airspace and the regulation of both civil and military operations in that airspace in the interest of the safety and efficiency.
5. Consolidation of air navigation facility research and development, as well as the installation and operation of those facilities.
6. Development and operation of a common air traffic control and navigation system for military and civil aircraft.
7. Providing assistance to law enforcement agencies in the enforcement of laws related to regulation of controlled substances, to the extent consistent with aviation safety.

(49 U.S.C. §40101[d]: Policy)

Since the Air Commerce Act of 1926, we have seen an incredible improvement in the design and capabilities of aircraft. At the same time, we have also seen the steady evolution of the regulatory structure that supports them. Today the Federal Aviation Administration is empowered by the U.S. Congress to promote aviation safety, and issue and enforce regulations dictating the minimum standards of manufacturing, operating and maintaining aircraft. The FAA also certifies airmen and the airports that serve air carriers.

So far, we've familiarized ourselves with the history of the agency that has the authority to regulate and oversee all aspects of civil aviation the United States. Now let's review a list of FARs that are directly or indirectly related to the governing of air carriers. The following list is made up of those parts you will most likely encounter during the course of your aviation career.

Title 14 of the Code of Federal Regulations (CFR) Related to Air Carriers

Part 1: Definitions and Abbreviations

Part 1 is a glossary of definitions and abbreviations of terms used in the Federal Aviation Regulations. Additional definitions may be found in the text of specific regulations.

Part 21: Certification Procedures for Products and Parts

Part 21 lists the requirements of and the procedures for obtaining type certificates, supplemental type certificates, airworthiness certificates, and import and export approvals.

Part 23: Airworthiness Standards for Normal, Utility, Acrobatic, and Commuter Category Airplanes

Part 23 specifies the airworthiness standards for the issue of type certificates, and changes to those certificates, for airplanes in the normal, utility, acrobatic, and commuter categories. The normal, utility, and acrobatic categories are limited to airplanes that have a seating configuration (excluding pilot seats) of nine or less and a maximum certificated takeoff weight of 12,500 pounds or less. The commuter category is limited to multi-engine airplanes that have a seating configuration (excluding pilot seats) of 19 or less and a maximum certificated takeoff weight of 19,000 pounds or less. The main difference between these categories is the types of flying maneuvers they are allowed to perform. Section 23.3 lists the maneuvers and limits each category is legal to perform.

Part 25: Airworthiness Standards for Transport Category Airplanes

The airworthiness standards for transport category aircraft are found in Part 25. This part contains the standards for issuing of type certificates, and changes to those certificates, for transport category airplanes. Transport category airplanes are airplanes for which a type certificate is applied for under Part 21 (Certification Procedures for Products and Parts) in the transport category and that meet the transport category airworthiness requirements. Multi-engine airplanes with more than 19 seats or a maximum takeoff weight greater than 19,000 pounds must be certificated in the transport category.

Part 39: Airworthiness Directives

Despite the best efforts of manufacturers' product design and certification testing, unanticipated failures can and do occur. When this happens the FAA issues **airworthiness directives (ADs),** which are legally enforceable regulations to correct an unsafe condition in an aircraft, engine, propeller, part, or appliance. An airworthiness directive contains measures which become effective and must be accomplished within certain periods of time to preserve the aircraft's airworthiness and restore an acceptable level of safety. An **emergency airworthiness directive (EAD)** is an airworthiness directive issued when an unsafe condition exists that requires immediate action by an aircraft owner or operator. EADs become effective upon receipt of notification.

Part 43: Maintenance, Preventive Maintenance, Rebuilding, and Alteration

This part provides the standard for maintaining the hundreds of thousands of civilian aircraft registered in the United States.

Part 61: Certification of Pilots, Flight Instructors, and Ground Instructors

Part 61 pertains to the certification of pilots, flight instructors, and ground instructors. 14 CFR Part 61 prescribes the eligibility, aeronautical knowledge, flight proficiency, and training and testing requirements for each type of pilot certificate issued.

Part 65: Certification of Airmen Other Than Flight Crewmembers

This part prescribes the requirements for issuing the following certificates and associated ratings and the general operating rules for the holders of those certificates and ratings:

   a. Air traffic control tower operators
   b. Aircraft dispatchers
   c. Mechanics
   d. Repairmen
   e. Parachute riggers

Part 67: Medical Standards and Certification

Part 67 establishes the medical standards and certification procedures for issuing medical certificates for airmen and for remaining eligible for a medical certificate.

Part 91: General Operating and Flight Rules

Part 91 is broad in scope and provides general guidance in the areas of general flight rules, visual flight rules (VFR), instrument flight rules (IFR), aircraft maintenance, and preventive maintenance and alterations.

Part 110: General Requirements (for Air Carrier and Related Operations)

Part 110 provides definitions applicable to various types of air carrier operations and other kinds of commercial operations. Many of the regulatory terms we mention in this text can be found in Part 110.

Part 111: Pilot Records Database

Part 111 prescribes regulations for the use of an electronic Pilot Records Database (PRD). This part contains the statutory requirements to facilitate the creation and sharing of pilot records among air carriers and other operators in an electronic data system managed by the FAA.

Part 117: Flight and Duty Limitations and Rest Requirements for Flightcrew Members

This part covers the flight and duty limitations and rest requirements for all flight crewmembers and certificate holders conducting passenger operations under Part 121 of this chapter.

Part 117 also applies to all operations directed by Part 121 certificate holders under Part 91, other than subpart K (Fractional Ownership Operations), of this chapter if any segment is conducted as a domestic passenger, flag passenger, or supplemental passenger operation.

Part 119: Certification of Air Carriers and Commercial Operators

Part 119 applies to each person operating or intending to operate a civil aircraft as an air carrier or commercial operator in air commerce. If common carriage is not involved, Part 119 applies in operations of U.S. registered civil airplanes with a seat configuration of 20 or more passengers, or a maximum payload capacity of 6,000 pounds or more.

Part 120: Drug and Alcohol Testing Program

Part 120 applies to air carriers and operators certificated under Part 119 of this chapter authorized to conduct operations under Part 121 or Part 135 of this chapter.

This part is also applicable to all contracted air traffic control facilities and all operators as defined in 14 CFR §91.147 (passenger carrying flights for compensation or hire).

In addition, Part 120 applies to all individuals who perform, either directly or by contract, a safety-sensitive function listed in subpart E or subpart F of this part. This includes full-time, part-time, temporary, and intermittent employees regardless of the degree of supervision. The safety-sensitive functions are:

a. Flight crewmember duties
b. Flight attendant duties
c. Flight instruction duties
d. Aircraft dispatcher duties
e. Aircraft maintenance and preventive maintenance duties
f. Ground security coordinator duties
g. Aviation screening duties
h. Air traffic control duties
i. All Part 145 repair station certificate holders who perform safety-sensitive functions and elect to implement a drug and alcohol testing program under this part
j. All contractors who elect to implement a drug and alcohol testing program under this part

Part 121: Operating Requirements of Domestic, Flag, and Supplemental Operations

This part prescribes rules governing the domestic, flag and supplemental operations of each person who holds an air carrier certificate or operating certificate under Part 119.

Part 125: Certification and Operations: Airplanes Having a Seating Capacity of 20 or More Passengers or a Maximum Payload Capacity of 6,000 pounds or More; and Rules Governing Persons on Board Such Aircraft

Part 125 prescribes rules governing the operations of U.S.-registered civil airplanes that have a seating configuration of 20 or more passengers or a maximum payload capacity of 6,000 pounds or more when common carriage is *not* involved.

Part 129: Operations: Foreign Air Carriers and Foreign Operators of U.S.-Registered Aircraft Engaged in Common Carriage

Rules governing the operation within the United States of each foreign air carrier holding permits issued by the U.S. Department of Transportation are found in Part 129.

Part 129 also describes the rules governing operations of U.S.-registered aircraft solely outside of the United States and operations of U.S.-registered aircraft operated solely outside the United States in common carriage by a foreign person or foreign air carrier.

Part 135: Operating Requirements of Commuter and On Demand Operations and Rules Governing Persons On Board Such Aircraft

Part 135 prescribes the rules governing the commuter or on-demand operations of each person who holds or is required to hold an air carrier certificate or operating certificate under Part 119.

Part 136: Commercial Air Tours

Part 136 applies to each person operating or intending to operate a commercial air tour in an airplane or helicopter and, when applicable, to all occupants of the airplane or helicopter engaged in a commercial air tour.

Part 141: Pilot Schools

This part covers the requirements for issuing pilot school certificates, provisional pilot school certificates, and associated ratings, and the general operating rules applicable to a holder of a certificate or rating issued under Part 141.

Part 142: Training Centers

Part 142 lists the requirements governing the certification and operation of training centers. It provides alternative methods to accomplish training required by a number of other parts of the FARs—especially those related to large airplanes, airlines, charter operations and fractional ownership flying.

Part 145: Repair Stations

This part describes how to obtain a repair station certificate. It also contains the rules a certificated repair station must follow related to its performance of maintenance, preventive maintenance, or alterations of an aircraft, airframe, aircraft engine, propeller, appliance, or component part to which Part 43 applies. It also applies to any person who holds, or is required to hold, a repair station certificate issued under this part.

Part 147: Aviation Maintenance Technician Schools

Part 147 prescribes the requirements for issuing aviation maintenance technician school certificates and associated ratings and the general operating rules for the holders of those certificates and ratings.

Advisory Circulars (ACs)

An advisory circular is a publication offered by the Federal Aviation Administration to provide guidance for compliance with airworthiness regulations. The advisory circular system was developed in 1962 to provide a single, uniform, agency-wide system to deliver advisory material to pilots, mechanics, aviation industry participants, the aviation community, and the public. While, as we've discussed, airworthiness directives are legally enforceable rules, advisory circulars offer instead guidance on what the FAA considers are best policies and procedures for aviation operations.

The subjects of advisory circulars typically involve aircraft, airports, flight schools, pilots, operations, or maintenance personnel. The FAA issues advisory circulars for various reasons from offering policy guidelines to specific safety precautions (eg. notifying pilots of an equipment malfunction or a pertinent rule change).

Summary

This completes the list of the specific parts of the FARs that you will most likely encounter during the course of your aviation career. This large array of materials can be intimidating at times. However, it would in fact be unlikely that someone would need to know all of these sections of the FARs for any single job or area of employment. Depending upon your interests, some sections may well be of more interest than others. Materials included in this text were primarily chosen for their applicability to a commercial airline pilot or dispatcher, or managers of those employee groups. For further research, we recommend using The Office of the Federal Register's online version of the Code of Federal Regulations, the **e-CFR**, which is normally updated within two days after changes that have been published in the *Federal Register* become effective.

Next, in Chapter 1, we will answer the question: What is an air carrier?

Important Terms in the Introduction

advisory circulars (ACs)
Air Commerce Act of 1926
airworthiness directive (AD)
Bureau of Air Commerce
Civil Aeronautics Act of 1938
Civil Aeronautics Administration (CAA)
Civil Aeronautics Authority (CAA)
Civil Aeronautics Board (CAB)
Code of Federal Regulations (CFR)
Contract Air Mail Act of 1925
Department of Transportation (DOT)
e-CFR
emergency airworthiness directive (EAD)
Federal Aviation Act of 1958
Federal Aviation Administration (FAA)
Federal Aviation Agency (FAA)
Federal Aviation Regulations (FARs)
Federal Register Act of 1935
National Transportation Safety Board (NTSB)
Title 14 of the Code of Federal Regulations: Aeronautics and Space
Title 49 of United States Code (49 U.S.C.)
Title 49 of USC, Section 40101

CHAPTER 1
WHAT IS AN AIR CARRIER?

You cannot get one nickel for commercial flying.
— **Inglis M. Uppercu**
Founder of the first American airline to last more than a couple of months

As we begin this study of air carriers we first need to answer the deceptively simple question: What are **air carriers**? What do they do? How are they different from us flying around in our training airplanes or perhaps our private aircraft? These are the questions we seek to answer in this chapter. We also will introduce the parts of the Federal Aviation Regulations (14 CFR) that apply to air carriers. These regulations will then form the basis for study of the rest of the book.

What Is an Air Carrier?

To understand what is meant by the term "air carrier," first we must understand what is meant by "term of art." Then we can understand the phrase "air carrier" as a term of art. A term of art is simply a term that has a meaning beyond that understood by the layman. That is, it has a special meaning within the context of the trade in which it is used. To understand the term "air carrier" we need to look back at several hundred years of British common law theory and principles to understand the concept of carriage. *Black's Law Dictionary* defines **carriage** as

> …Transportation of persons either for pleasure or business,…drawn over the ordinary streets and highways of the country.

In other words, carriage was the simple act of carrying or transporting persons. This concept has been expanded through the centuries to include carrying or transporting both persons and goods. Early in the development of the concept of carriage, it was discerned that there are different types or levels of carriage. If you take your computer in your car to be repaired, is that carriage? If you take your friend's computer in your car to be repaired, is that carriage? What if you take your friend to the computer repair shop to pick up the repaired computer, is that carriage? More important, is there any legal difference between these examples?

Private vs. Common Carriage

As British culture developed from a completely agrarian base to more of a centralized and industrial base, the law began to recognize that there were differences in carriage based on the differences in what was being done. In the law of **torts**, which is the law of compensating for civil wrongs, the law developed the concept of **duty to care**. Duty to care is essentially the level of responsibility that a person (or company) has toward others to protect them from harm. As an example, older common law carved out a number of differing levels of duty depending upon the relationship between the people involved and the circumstances surrounding their interaction.

For example, what responsibility do you have toward my car and me if I park it in the lot at your mall? Is that different from the responsibility you have toward my car and me if I park it in your driveway to attend a party at your house? Further, is that different from the responsibility you have to my car and me if I park it in your pay parking lot? Finally, what if I deliver it to your employee (say a valet in a restaurant) and he or she parks it? Is the responsibility changed? In such situations, British (and later American) common law drew distinctions among these transactions. The law said that in the first example, you have a gratuitous bailment with little (but some degree of) duty to care. A **bailment** is simply where you have handed something that you have a right to possess over to someone else to hold or keep for you. A **gratuitous bailment** is one in which the receiving party derives no benefit from holding the property. He or she is essentially just doing a favor. This concept proceeds along a continuum until in the last two examples the law would hold that you have a **bailment for hire** and therefore a much higher duty to care. Our common law heritage is wonderful at drawing arcane distinctions between very slightly differing sets of facts. In modern times, many courts have eliminated these distinctively different standards of care with respect to bailments, but with respect to carriage the arcane lines of care are still deeply drawn in the sand.

With respect to carriage, the distinction drawn was first between **private carriage** and **public carriage**. Private carriage is that carriage arranged between two parties—the carrier and the carried (or between some other small number of parties and the carrier). In this case, the carrier is simply carrying this small number of persons or property, and it may be *gratuitous* (meaning there is no compensation exchanged for the carriage) or it may be *for hire* (which means money *or some other medium of exchange* has changed hands). So in the examples above where you were taking your friend or your friend's computer to the repair shop, you have an example of private carriage. If you received no money or other tangible rewards, then you have a *gratuitous private carriage*. On the other hand, if you received money or tangible (or in some cases even intangible) rewards for the carriage, then you have *private carriage for hire*.

Public carriage, on the other hand, implies a willingness to deal with many people who have a need to have something or someone taken someplace. Although it is possible some good Samaritan might do this for free, it is much more likely that the concept of public carriage will apply to someone that is engaging in the business of carrying people or things in hopes of making a dollar. Therefore, we will speak only of *public carriage for hire*. Note that it is not necessary that the person make money off of the transportation alone for it to be carriage for hire. What if I owned a resort in a very remote location and, as a service to my guests, provided air transportation into and out of the resort? Would that be public carriage for hire or gratuitous public carriage? FAA and NTSB decisions have held that this is public carriage for hire.

Again, looking at this example as a continuum, what lies further out than the above example of the resort operator? What if there was a resort area with many resorts (such as Aspen, Colorado) and you saw an opportunity to make money by starting a bus line (or an airline) to take anyone who wishes from Denver to Aspen. This willingness to take anyone as a public carrier for hire has now moved you the highest level, that of the **common carrier**. *Black's Law Dictionary* defines a common carrier as

> …those that undertake to carry all persons (or cargo) indifferently who may apply for passage, so long as there is room and there is no legal excuse for refusal.

In other words, the *common carrier* is a person or company who will carry anyone so long as they have the money to pay the fare (tariff). General indicators of **common carriage** include

- **holding out** to the public of willingness to
- perform **carriage of all comers** (persons or goods)
- from **place to place**
- for **compensation or hire**.

We've dwelt at length on the distinctions between private and common carriage. What difference does it make? The difference is in the liability that the law places on the carrier. Private carriage has some liability. For example, if you injure someone and it can be proved that you were negligent, the injured party may recover damages against you for injuries that you caused. However, if someone were injured in your car through no fault of yours, recovery from you in a lawsuit would be quite difficult to impossible.

On the other hand, as a common carrier, your *duty to care* is much higher. Our common law background has held you to a much higher standard of care that approaches that of an **insurer**. What is an insurer? An insurer is someone who has responsibility to make sure or secure, to guarantee, to ensure safety to anyone covered by that policy. This is done by financial compensation for loss. An insurer is completely responsible financially for the liability for breeches of safety and security of anyone with whom it has a contract. In analogous fashion, a common carrier is nearly totally responsible for the safety and security of the passengers and freight in its care.

Why is the duty to care so high for a common carrier? Again, the origins are found in the early British common law cases. To understand, picture yourself back in that agrarian British society. Bandits roam the highways (highwaymen). Travel is by horse or stagecoach. In that environment, passengers were truly put at the complete disposal of the carrier. Other than perhaps packing a weapon, passengers could not protect themselves from the various travails and dangers that might lurk along the highways in the course of traveling. Each traveler *had to rely* on the protection of the carrier and its agents. The law therefore placed this responsibility squarely on the shoulders of the carrier. This concept has continued to modern times and forms the conceptual basis for the regulation of the public transportation industries.

Our common carriers, be they taxicabs, buses, trains, boats, or airplanes, are held to the highest standard of care found in tort law. They are virtually insurers of the safety and security of the passengers who entrust their lives and property to the carriers every day. In addition to the responsibility that the civil law (through the torts system) places on the common carrier, the government at its various levels seeks to assure that the common carrier recognizes and lives up to this extraordinary level of duty to care. This is done through any number of regulations under the local, state, and federal regulatory and administrative law systems. For aviation, this takes the form of federal regulation of air carriers by the Federal Aviation Administration, found primarily in Title 14 of the **Code of Federal Regulations (CFR)** (14 CFR), **Parts 1, 61, 63, 65, 91, 110, 117, 119, 121, 135 and 145.**

FAA Tests for Common Carriage

(If it looks like a duck and quacks like a duck…)

Earlier in this section we introduced the four tests to determine common carriage. These are essentially the tests the FAA uses in determining if an individual or company is acting as a common carrier (that is, as an air carrier).

Holding Out to the Public of Willingness to Carry

To be considered a common carrier, the carrier must *hold itself out to the public*. That is, it must let the public know that it is available for carriage. Advertising is not the only way a carrier may hold out to the public, but it is probably the most common way of doing so. Flyers, notices, and newspaper, television, and radio ads certainly each qualify as a holding out. However, word of mouth, promotions and public appearances by the carrier or its agents stating the willingness of the carrier to carry people or goods are also considered a holding out.

Perform the Carriage of All Comers

We previously discussed that one of the early definitions of common carrier included a willingness to transport anyone. A common carrier is interested in carrying anyone; a private carrier is interested only in limited carriage. There are a number of types of private carriers. One example is a corporate aircraft operated for only one corporation. Another example includes operators that carry automobile parts from the parts manufacturers to the assembly plants. In this case the carrier serves only one contract, namely the carmaker operating the assembly plant.

So, how many contracts may an operator have and remain in private carriage? There is no hard and fast rule, but in FAA Advisory Circular 120-12A, *Private Carriage versus Common Carriage of Persons or Property* (1986), which relates to carriage in large aircraft, the FAA has stated that if an operator is operating as many as three contracts, it will be held to be private carriage. Conversely, the advisory circular says that as few as 18 to 24 contracts are considered to be common carriage. What about four or five contracts? Well, at present, that issue has not been definitively decided, but anyone considering operating more than three private carriage contracts is doing so at considerable peril of being held to the common carriage standards.

From Place to Place

This of course is central to the idea of carriage; that is, you actually take people or goods someplace other than where you started. That's why sightseeing rides aren't generally viewed as common carriage. In a sightseeing flight, no one is carried anyplace.

For Compensation or Hire

Common carriage requires that the person providing the service be hired to provide the service. If there is no hiring, then it is gratuitous private carriage and does not become subjected to regulation as a common carrier. However, hiring can have some very unusual considerations. The first example: "I'll pay you a hundred bucks to take me to Altoona" clearly includes transportation (carriage) for hire ($100). It's an "exchange thing."

You give me transportation; I'll give you money. Nearly everyone would understand this to be transportation for hire. But what about the following example?

You, an aspiring airline pilot and broke flight student, want to get flight time. You know a lot of your fellow students like to ski, so you put a sign in your dorm bulletin board that reads

> *WANTED: Skiers to share expenses of flights to ski country. Will take you and one friend to Sugarbush Mountain, Vermont, any weekend. Your share: $100 each. Call Bella at…*

We will see that this will probably be held to constitute common carriage under the Federal Aviation Regulations (FARs). This is one of the many ways small operators can run afoul of the regulations in Part 135 and be found to be common carriers. Students often ask, "But how would the FAA catch this?" The enforcement action for this kind of activity normally arises out of one of two situations: a post-accident/incident investigation, or an FAA ramp check at a popular tourist/visitor destination airport. Our concern isn't so much about how you might get caught as it is making sure you understand and are able to comply with the regulations.

FAR Implications of Common Carriage

Before beginning a discussion of the ramifications of regulations on common carriage, we need to look at the structure of the Federal Aviation Regulations. Most commonly referred to as "FARs," they are actually Title 14 of the Code of Federal Regulations (14 CFR). You may have seen references such as 14 CFR §61.105. A pilot would probably refer to this as "Part 61, Section 105," or even more simply as FAR 61.105. 14 CFR is broken down into a number of "parts" such as *Part 61: Pilots and Flight Instructors* or *Part 91: Operating Rules*.

Figure 1-1 illustrates the relationship between multiple parts of the FARs that must be considered in operations of an air carrier. 14 CFR Part 91 is applicable to all operators of any kind of aircraft. The other parts in Figure 1-1 modify, supplement, define or replace the Part 91 general requirements for air carriers. As you can imagine, this creates a set of very stringent requirements for air carriers to manage.

We will begin with a discussion of 14 CFR Part 1: Definitions. Part 1 doesn't define common carrier. That is a term of art carried down through years of British and American common law. It does define air carrier:

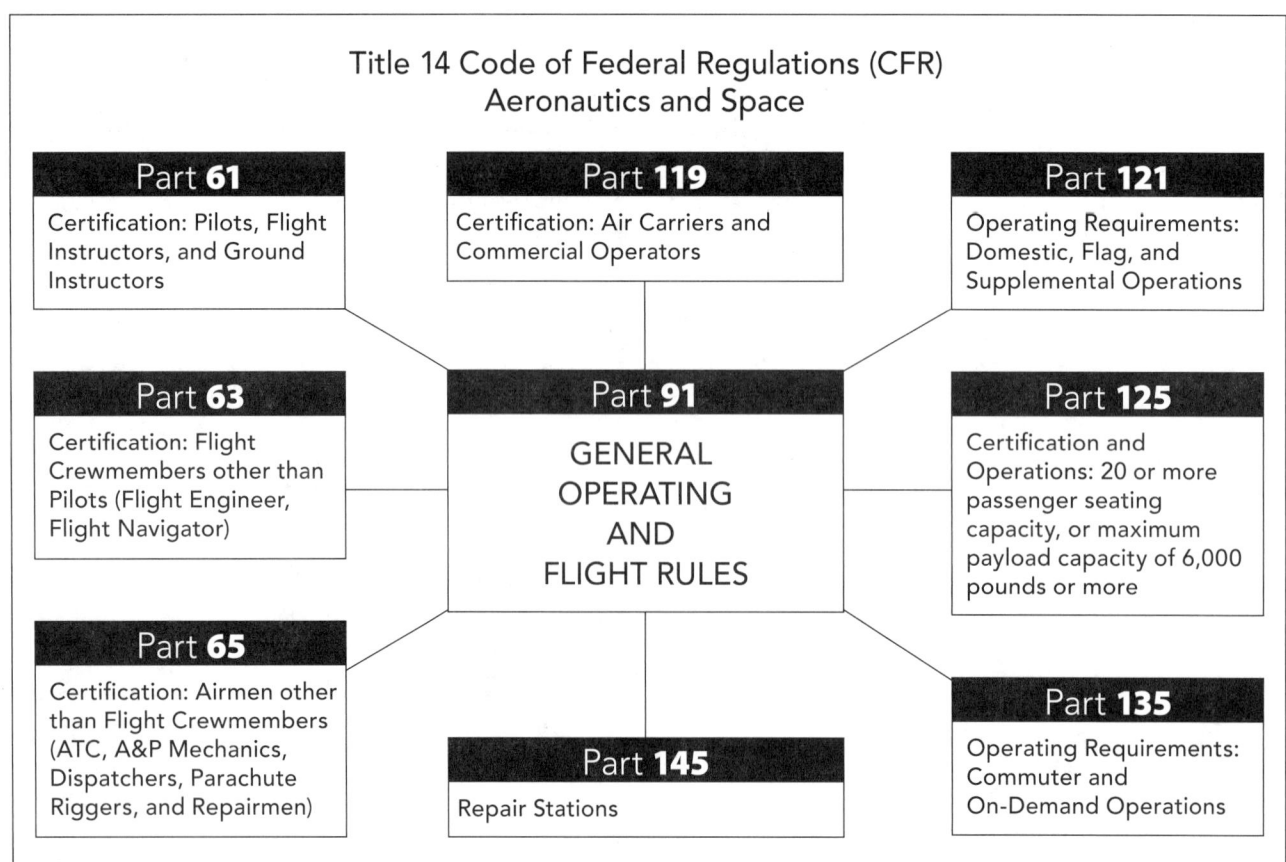

Figure 1-1. Putting the "Parts" Together.

Air carrier means a person who undertakes directly by lease, or other arrangement, to engage air transportation. *(14 CFR §1.1)*

This begs the question: What is **air transportation**?

Air transportation means interstate, overseas, or foreign air transportation or the transportation of mail by aircraft. *(14 CFR §1.1)*

This is somewhat circular in reasoning but basically says that if you are carrying people in interstate, overseas, or foreign transportation or if you are carrying any mail (even intrastate), you are providing air transportation as far as the FARs are concerned. So, if you are doing these things, you are an air carrier.

A third definition we need to understand is that of **commercial operator**.

Commercial operator means a person who, for compensation or hire, engages in the carriage by aircraft in air commerce of persons or property, other than as an air carrier or foreign air carrier.... Where it is doubtful that an operation is for "compensation or hire," the test applied is whether the carriage by air is merely incidental to the person's other business or is, in itself, a major enterprise for profit. *(14 CFR §1.1)*

Why do we care about all these fine points? Simply put, we care because we need to have the knowledge to comply with all of the appropriate regulations. For any of this to apply, we must first find that the proposed operation is common carriage. If it isn't, Parts 121, 135 and the other air carrier-related parts don't apply. We would first apply the four point test. What about our example from above of advertising for skiers? This is the four point **test for common carriage**:

1. Holding out? *Yes, the sign.*
2. Transport persons or property? *Yes, that's why you advertised.*
3. From place to place? *Yes, home airport to Vermont.*
4. Carriage for compensation? *Yes, you are being paid.*

So applying this test to the example, you have a common carriage situation; now what? Some of you who are pilots are probably saying to yourselves, "Wait a minute. I know Part 61 allows a private pilot to 'share expenses' of a flight. I'll just change the $100 to a pro rata share and then this is ok to do." 14 CFR §61.113 addresses this point.

14 CFR §61.113—Private Pilot Privileges and Limitations: Pilot in Command [1]

(a) Except as provided in paragraphs (b) through (h) of this section, no person who holds a private pilot certificate may act as pilot in command of an aircraft that is carrying passengers or property for compensation or hire; nor may that person, for compensation or hire, act as pilot in command of an aircraft. . . .

(c) A private pilot may not pay less than the pro rata share of the operating expenses of a flight with passengers, provided the expenses involve only fuel, oil, airport expenditures, or rental fees.

On the surface, this seemingly allows you to perform this flight. However, the facts we assumed still seem to indicate a common carrier. The dilemma is that the FAA will look at this and see common carriage. One of the tests they will use to determine whether or not it is common carriage is what is sometimes referred to as the **independent interest** test. That means that for Section 61.113 and its expense-sharing provision to apply, you as the pilot would have to have an independent interest in going on this trip even if the "paying passenger" were to cancel at the last minute. Would you still go to Sugarbush Mountain if two hours before departure the passenger said he had an unexpected assignment to do and couldn't go skiing this weekend? If not, that is a strong indicator that this is not a sharing of expenses situation, but rather an exercise of common carriage.

One of the authors is an avid fan of his college football team, the Texas Tech Red Raiders. (Guns Up!) Since owning a flight school and teaching college he has flown his Piper Seneca from New York out to Columbus (twice, to watch his team lose to Ohio State), to

---
[1] Although 14 CFR §61.113 is titled "Private Pilot Privileges and Limitations," it has significant application to Commercial (and even Airline Transport) pilots. When a pilot is performing an operation that doesn't require the privileges of a higher certificate, the pilot uses the privileges of the lower certificate. Even though those privileges aren't specifically spelled out under the higher certificate Privileges and Limitations section, the pilot may use any of the privileges of a lower certificate. A commercial pilot who wants to use the "expense sharing" authority must use the provisions of Section 61.113.

Raleigh-Durham (to watch them lose to North Carolina State), to Athens, Georgia (to watch them lose to Georgia), to Happy Valley (to watch them lose to Penn State) (and to others he's too ashamed to mention). Finally, he trekked to Arizona and watched them beat Air Force in the Copper Bowl. Flying back that evening to Texas, it was very mellow; Tech had won, the clear night sky over the southern Rockies was beautiful, the peaks were snow-covered, life was good. Then it occurred to him. He had spent more money flying his airplane all over the country watching Texas Tech try to win a football game than he had spent going to Texas Tech! That's dedication and probably a little insanity.

But the point is, what do you think? If he had placed an ad asking for someone to accompany him to a game and share expenses, would he have gone had that person backed out at the last minute? Well, nearly every one of these trips was made by the author alone, so clearly he would have. A cancellation would not have affected his decision to bear the full costs of the trip. The FAA would say that he had an independent interest in making the trip. That would take him out of common carriage and allow him to use the relief provision of Section 61.113(c) and have a pro rata sharing of expenses with any other football fans that might like to come along. But if, like in the case of the skiing trip, he cancelled at the loss of the passenger, the FAA would probably hold this type of flight to be covered under the common carriage rules.[2] So what? What difference does it make?

The short answer is: it makes a huge difference. When conducting flights for compensation or hire, the FARs set forth two general types of requirements. The first is a requirement that the pilot hold at least a commercial pilot certificate; this is necessary for the *pilot to be compensated or hired*. Many aspiring airline pilots upon receipt of their commercial certificate rush right out and put up ads just like we described. In the New York area, it's very common to see ads for flying to ski areas or the summer resort islands around Cape Cod. Their thinking is, "I'm now a commercial pilot so I can finally charge money to carry passengers for hire." In fact, 14 CFR §61.133 would seem to support that point of view:

14 CFR §61.133—Commercial Pilot Privileges and Limitations

(a) *Privileges*
 (1) *General.* A person who holds a commercial pilot certificate may act as pilot in command of an aircraft—
  (i) Carrying persons or property for compensation or hire, provided the person is qualified in accordance with this part and with the applicable parts of this chapter that apply to the operation; and
  (ii) For compensation or hire, provided the person is qualified in accordance with this part and with the applicable parts of this chapter that apply to the operation.

What is the difference between (i) and (ii)? On the surface, they may appear to mean the same thing. But, a closer look reveals that (i) covers passengers paying (compensating or hiring the aircraft) regardless of whether the pilot gets paid; (ii) covers the pilot being paid, regardless of whether the passengers are paying for the trip.

So if you have a commercial pilot certificate, you're all set to start charging, right? Well, not so fast. Notice that Section 61.133 simply says that you, the pilot, may act as pilot-in-command of the aircraft. But, both (i) and (ii) have that little clause at the end that nobody pays much attention to that says:

> ...in accordance with this part and with the applicable parts of this chapter that apply to the operation. *(14 CFR §61.133[a][1][2])*

What is the significance of this clause? Simply stated, it means that if you are otherwise found to be a common carrier and not entitled to the sharing expenses provision of Section 61.113(c), you need to have an air carrier certificate to comply with those pesky "applicable parts of this chapter that apply to the operation." Note that there is significant flying that only requires a commercial pilot certificate but that is not common carriage, and therefore does not require an operating certificate.

---

2 The only authority in the FARs for sharing expenses in this manner is found in 14 CFR §61.113. If the pilot is receiving money from a passenger to take him someplace in an airplane that is not owned or leased by the passenger, there are only two ways this can be done in compliance with the regulation: (1) Have an operating certificate and commercial pilot certificate or (2) use the expense-sharing provisions of Section 61.113. The expense-sharing provision is applied extremely narrowly by FAA. If you plan on doing a shared expenses flight, you should be absolutely certain that you are familiar with and understand the limitations in Section 61.113. This book does not provide a complete explanation of what is and is not allowed when using the expense-sharing provisions. If you plan to do any such expense shared flights, you are cautioned to obtain, read and understand any applicable FAA General Counsel opinions from the FAA website or resources such as the Aircraft Owners and Pilots Association (AOPA).

This includes flying for things such as traffic watch, fish spotting, commercial aircraft ferrying and the like. But if your compensated flying includes carrying anything (people or property) for hire, you must comply with those pesky "applicable parts" mentioned above.

What parts are those?

Meet 14 CFR Parts 110, 117, 119, 121, and 135. These provisions of the FARs set up the requirements to hold air carrier certificates if you are an air carrier (a common carrier) as previously defined and discussed. Section 61.133 only addresses the issue of whether you may pilot the aircraft when used for carriage for compensation or hire. There is a second, unrelated requirement, which is independent of the pilot question. That requirement examines the need to hold an operator's certificate. If you are conducting flights carrying passengers or cargo for compensation or hire and the company (or you) don't hold the required *air carrier operating certificate*, you are committing multiple, major FAR violations.

The requirement to have an operating certificate is found in 14 CFR Part 119.

14 CFR §119.1—Applicability

(a) This part applies to each person operating or intending to operate civil aircraft—
   (1) As an air carrier or commercial operator, or both, in air commerce; or
   (2) When common carriage is not involved, in operations of U.S.-registered civil airplanes with a seat configuration of 20 or more passengers, or a maximum payload capacity of 6,000 pounds or more.

Section 119.5(g) sets forth the specific requirements for air carriers to obtain a certificate and operations specifications prior to initiating service.

(g) No person may operate as a direct air carrier or as a commercial operator without, or in violation of, an appropriate certificate and appropriate operations specifications.

Therefore, if it is your intent to operate as either a commercial operator or direct air carrier (see definitions in 14 CFR §1.1 and 14 CFR §110.2) you must first obtain the appropriate certificate and operations specifications. But how do we know what kind of certificate is needed? That is, do we need to operate under Part 135 or Part 121? The answer to this question is found by looking in Subpart B, specifically 14 CFR §119.21 and the definitions of Section 110.2.

Section 119.21, paragraph (a), says an operator must conduct its operations under Part 121 if it is a domestic operation, a flag operation, or a supplemental operation, while commuter operations and on-demand operations fall under Part 135. These terms are all defined in Section 110.2. The following are simplified explanations of each of the terms.

A **domestic operation** is any *scheduled* operation that is operated entirely within the 48 contiguous United States. This includes those flight legs of an international trip that are entirely within the 48 contiguous United States. For example, the Los Angeles to New York leg of a Los Angeles–New York–London flight would be a domestic operation. These are flights that are conducted in sophisticated aircraft. This includes turbojets, airplanes with more than nine passenger seats, or airplanes with a payload capacity in excess of 7,500 pounds.

A **flag operation** is any *scheduled* operation that operates between any point within Alaska or Hawaii and any point outside of Alaska or Hawaii; between any point within the 48 contiguous United States and any point outside the 48 contiguous United States; or between two points that are completely outside the 50 United States. As with domestic operations, these are also flights that are conducted in sophisticated aircraft. This includes turbojets, aircraft with more than nine passenger seats, and aircraft with a payload capacity in excess of 7,500 pounds.

A **supplemental operation** is one that conducts charter-type (nonscheduled) operations. That is, the place and time of departure and arrivals are negotiated between the operator and the customer. These operations don't operate on a fixed schedule. The distinction between on-demand and supplemental has to do with the size of the aircraft used. A supplemental operator uses aircraft having more than 30 seats and/or aircraft with more than 7,500 pounds payload capacity.

A **commuter operation** is one that conducts scheduled operations (five or more round trips per week) in non-turbojet aircraft that have nine or fewer passenger seats and a payload capacity of 7,500 pounds or less.

An **on-demand operation** can be either scheduled operations or non-scheduled operations. **Scheduled on-demand operations** utilize airplanes, other than turbojets, with nine or fewer passenger seats *and* a 7,500-pound or less payload capacity, or any rotorcraft, used in scheduled passenger-carrying operations with a frequency less than five round trips per week on at least one route between two or more points according to the published flight schedules. **Nonscheduled on-demand**

operations utilize airplanes with 30 or fewer passenger seats *and* a 7,500 pound or less payload capacity, or any rotorcraft.

To recapitulate, if an operation is a domestic, flag, or supplemental operation, then the carrier must hold a Part 121 certificate (14 CFR §119.21[a][1, 2, or 3]). If it is a commuter or on-demand operation, then the carrier must hold a Part 135 certificate (14 CFR §119.21[a][4,5]).

Most of the balance of this book will explore the ins and outs of Part 121 applicable to domestic, flag, and supplemental operators: 14 CFR §119.21(a)(1) through (a)(3). We will occasionally contrast a Part 135 rule with a Part 121 rule, but the focus of the book will be Part 121. Here's a brief description of each:

Part 135—Operating Requirements: Commuter and On Demand Operations and Rules Governing Persons on Board Such Aircraft.

14 CFR §135.1 Applicability.

(a) This part prescribes rules governing—
  (1) The commuter or on-demand operations of each person who holds or is required to hold an Air Carrier Certificate or Operating Certificate under part 119 of this chapter.

Part 121: Operating Requirements: Domestic, Flag, and Supplemental Operations

§121.1 Applicability.
This part prescribes rules governing—

(a) The domestic, flag, and supplemental operations of each person who holds or is required to hold an Air Carrier Certificate or Operating Certificate under part 119 of this chapter.
(b) Each person employed or used by a certificate holder conducting operations under this part including maintenance, preventive maintenance, and alteration of aircraft.

Part 121, Subpart A—General
(14 CFR §121.1 through §121.15)

This subpart of Part 121 sets forth the very basics of what is applicable to a domestic, flag, or supplemental carrier. Section 121.1 is used to determine the applicability of Part 121 to various persons and activities. The obvious application of Part 121 to domestic and flag carriers and their employees and contractors is stated. Also covered is the not-so-obvious application of the drug and alcohol testing provisions of Part 121 to nonstop sightseeing flights in small aircraft that cover less than 25 miles from the departure airport. This section also extends coverage of Part 121 to the persons (passengers) aboard Part 121 aircraft.

We mentioned earlier that if you operate an aircraft in operations that require an air carrier certificate but you don't possess one, you are committing major, multiple violations of the FARs. To see how this works, take a look at Section 121.4 (or 135.7 for commuter and on-demand operators). These rules, entitled Applicability of Rules to **Unauthorized Operators**, provide that in this case, the FAA will treat your operation *as if you had a certificate* and then violate you for all of the provisions applicable to a certificate holder. Since there are literally hundreds of provisions and each violation has a significant potential civil penalty ($11,000 at the time of publication), even a single flight could result in potential fines in the millions of dollars as well as certificate action against any airmen involved in the operation. It pays to know if your proposed operation requires a Part 121 or a 135 certificate.

Another question that arises in regard to flag operations (or certain domestic operations at foreign airports—e.g., Canada and Mexico) is what rules are followed in the other country? 14 CFR §121.11 covers that rule by stating that you must follow local air traffic and airport rules except if the Part 121 rule is more restrictive and may be followed without violating the local rules. Conversely, a foreign carrier operating in the United States is not subject to Part 121 rules but is required to follow our air traffic and general operating rules. Fortunately, International Civil Aviation Organization (ICAO) rules significantly standardize these operational and air traffic rules, but a pilot must pay particular attention to the local rules when operating in foreign airspace as they may differ from U.S. rules.

Part 121, Subpart E—Approval of Routes: Domestic and Flag Operations
(14 CFR §121.91 through §121.107)

Unlike flying under Part 91, a domestic or flag carrier can't simply fly anywhere it wishes to fly. Subpart E provides the basis for certificating the routes of the carrier. This certification process looks at the adequacy of airports and other facilities and then approves those routes and airports for use. A basic concept is that domestic and flag carriers can only use approved routes and facilities in Part 121 operations. Sections 121.93 and 121.95 set up the requirements for route approvals and Section

121.97 sets the requirements for airport approvals. Some of the significant items for approval of airports are airport safety and security; runway, clearway, and stopway information; displaced thresholds; obstacles; instrument procedures; and special information. This information must be maintained and distributed by the carrier to the appropriate personnel.

Part 121 air carriers must have the ability to communicate with their aircraft at any point on the route structure. This is to ensure that the carrier retains **operational control** of the aircraft at all times. We will discuss operational control later in the text, but for now it's the concept that the carrier, not the crew, is the final determinant of how the aircraft is operated. Certainly that is done in consultation with the pilot-in-command, but ultimately, decisions regarding how the aircraft is operated are decisions of the carrier, not the individual pilot. Of course, the pilot-in-command retains emergency authority to deal with situations that require immediate decisions. Section 121.99 establishes the communications requirements for being able to contact an aircraft at any point on the route structure in a rapid and reliable fashion. This system must be independent of any system operated by the U.S. government (e.g., flight service or air traffic control networks).

Part 121 carriers (except supplemental operations) perform their flight planning in a function called **dispatch**. Dispatch is a department in the airline that is responsible for all flight planning and control. A dispatcher is a certificated airman and works with the crew and other departments such as maintenance and meteorology to ensure compliance with all operational rules. Section 121.107 sets forth the requirements for flag and domestic operators to have adequate numbers of conveniently located dispatch centers to ensure proper operational control of each flight. Section 121.101 sets forth the requirements to have sufficient weather reporting facilities to ensure reports and forecasts for the operation. Domestic carriers must use either U.S. National Weather Service (NWS) forecasts and reports or forecasts and reports prepared by a source approved by the NWS. Flag carriers must use sources approved by the **Administrator** (of the FAA).

Approved by the Administrator

That's the first (but certainly not the last) time the phrase "approved by the Administrator" appears in this book. Does this term mean the Administrator has to look at every carrier's weather service and approve it? Clearly the Administrator would be a busy person if that were the case. When the FARs refer to "approval by the Administrator" (or similar phrases), this means approval by the Administrator *or a person who has been delegated authority to issue the approval by the Administrator*. In most operational areas including flight operations and maintenance, that means the approval has been delegated to the **Flight Standards** organization of the FAA. The Associate Administrator for Flight Standards (AFS-1) in Washington, D.C., heads this organization. He or she delegates authority to flight standards policy offices and to the regional flight standards organizations, which in turn delegates the authority to local **Flight Standards District Offices (FSDOs)**. These are the offices you may have had contact with if you are a pilot or student pilot. They control certification of pilots and enforcement of operational regulations. At an airline, each carrier is assigned a **principal operations inspector (POI)** and a **principal maintenance inspector (PMI)**. These inspectors have overall responsibility for surveillance of the carrier and ensuring compliance of the carrier with all regulations.

Finally, Section 121.105 requires that the carrier have adequate numbers of servicing and maintenance facilities available to it for the necessary and proper servicing of the aircraft in its operations.

Part 121, Subpart F—Approval of Areas and Routes: Supplemental Operations
(14 CFR §121.111 through §121.127)

Subpart F of Part 121 covering supplemental operations is similar to Subpart E for domestic and flag operations in that it specifies the routes and areas of operations. Since charter departure and destination airports are negotiated between the airline and customer, they don't operate as much according to a set schedule/route as do domestic or flag carriers. Therefore, the FAA also approves *areas of operations* for supplemental carriers.

The major distinction between flag and domestic carriers and supplemental carriers is seen in the area of operational control. As discussed earlier, flag and domestic operators are required to conduct dispatch of their aircraft. That is, the flight crew and the certificated dispatcher must agree before every flight how the flight is to be conducted, and deviations from the plan during flight must, generally speaking, be agreed upon as well. Looking at Section 121.125, we can see that supplemental operators don't need to dispatch their aircraft; rather, they must provide for **flight following**. Flight following is significantly different from dispatching in several ways. First, dispatching requires the use of certificated airmen holding a dispatcher's certificate. Section 121.127(b), covering flight following requirements, merely requires that the supplemental carrier show that the persons performing the function of operational control be able to perform their required duties. That is, the carrier, not the FAA certificate, determines the fitness of the operational control personnel. Supplemental operators must perform operational control but need not dispatch their aircraft. That means the pilot-in-command solely determines the suitability for flight and has ultimate responsibility for all planning decisions.

To support this method of operations, the FAA requires that the carrier have adequate facilities to properly maintain operational control of the aircraft. That control can be performed in a number of different ways. The supplemental carrier is left to its own devices to determine how, under its operational need, it can meet the operational control requirements. This system is the flight following system described in 14 CFR §§121.125 and 121.127. The purpose of this system is to keep the managers of the operation informed as to the safe progress and needs of the carrier's flights so that those personnel can maintain operational control.

Summary

This chapter has examined the relationship between the common law concept of common carriers and the very high duty to care. We have seen how that has been translated into a federal regulatory structure to ensure that U.S. air carriers are operated so as to achieve that very high duty to care. The FAA requires that carriers specifically implement the various provisions of the FARs so as to ensure compliance. This is done through a document called **operations specifications**, and these specifications are the subject of the next chapter.

Important Terms in Chapter 1

14 CFR Part 1
14 CFR Part 61
14 CFR Part 63
14 CFR Part 65
14 CFR Part 91
14 CFR Part 110
14 CFR Part 117
14 CFR Part 119
14 CFR Part 121
14 CFR Part 135
14 CFR Part 145
Administrator
air carrier
air transportation
bailment
bailment for hire
carriage
carriage of all comers
Code of Federal Regulations (CFR)
commercial operator
common carriage
common carrier
commuter operation
compensation or hire
dispatch
domestic operation
duty to care
flag operation
flight following
Flight Standards
Flight Standards District Office (FSDO)
gratuitous bailment
holding out
independent interest
insurer
nonscheduled on-demand operations
on-demand operation
operational control
operations specifications
place to place
principal maintenance inspector (PMI)
principal operations inspector (POI)
private carriage
public carriage
supplemental operation
test for common carriage
torts
unauthorized operator

Chapter 1 Exam

1. The concept of common carriage is derived from:
   a. U.S. Federal Aviation Regulations
   b. U.S. federal statutes
   c. British common law
   d. state statutes

2. Private carriage is distinguished from common carriage primarily by
   a. the lack of an exchange of money for transportation (carriage).
   b. the amount of money charged for the transportation (carriage).
   c. contracts between parties as opposed to contracts between individuals.
   d. transportation (carriage) of only one or a very small number of parties.

3. Which of the following is not an element of common carriage?
   a. Having a license or certificate
   b. Performing carriage for anyone (persons or goods)
   c. From place to place
   d. For compensation or hire

4. Holding out to the public would include:
   a. Advertising
   b. Flyers in a campus student union
   c. Statements on a web page
   d. All of the above

5. In analyzing a situation in which a private pilot is accused of acting illegally as a common carrier, the FAA will, among other tests, look to see if the pilot
   a. was paid only for the fuel, oil, and aircraft rental.
   b. had an independent interest in taking the trip.
   c. had a commercial pilot certificate.
   d. used his or her personal aircraft or paid money for a rental aircraft.

6. As a commercial pilot, acting individually and without further certificates, you may
   a. charge a hunter to take him to the deep north woods of Alaska.
   b. charge a fellow student half of the costs to take him home to visit his girlfriend.
   c. charge a gas company to perform pipeline aerial spotter patrols.
   d. charge an acquaintance to take her to the Atlantic City casinos.

7. A company must operate under 14 CFR Part 121 if it is:
   a. a domestic operation.
   b. a commuter operation.
   c. an on-demand operation.
   d. None of the above.

8. A company operating turbo-propeller aircraft with 8 passenger seats and a payload of 7,000 pounds three times a week between Los Angeles and Mexico City on a scheduled basis would need to hold
   a. domestic operating certificate.
   b. a flag operating certificate.
   c. a supplemental operating certificate.
   d. a Part 135 operating certificate (which allows on-demand operations).

9. Assume you were found to be operating as an on-demand air carrier but didn't have an operating certificate. The potential penalty for this would be an $11,000 fine for
   a. each flight conducted for compensation or hire.
   b. conducting flights without a certificate.
   c. each provision of Part 135 applicable to each flight conducted.
   d. you wouldn't be fined; you would be required to obtain a certificate before continuing and your pilot certificate could be suspended.

10. Operational control is the concept that:
    a. The carrier, not the crew, is the final determinant of how the aircraft is operated.
    b. The carrier knows where all of its aircraft are and relies on the crew to advise it of what they intend to do.
    c. The crew, acting for the carrier, determines how best to operate the flight.
    d. The pilot-in-command is solely responsible for the conduct of the flight.

11. A supplemental operation is one that
    a. conducts charter-type (nonscheduled) operations using aircraft having more than 30 seats and/or with more than 7,500 pounds payload capacity.
    b. conducts charter-type (nonscheduled) operations using aircraft having less than 30 seats and/or with less than 7,500 pounds payload capacity.
    c. supplements a scheduled air carrier operation with five or more round trips per week in a turbojet aircraft that is operated entirely within the 48 contiguous United States.
    d. supplements a (nonscheduled) air carrier operation in a turbojet aircraft that is operated entirely within the 48 contiguous United States.

12. A commuter operation is one that
    a. conducts nonscheduled on-demand operations (five or more round trips per week), in supplemental non-turbojet aircraft that have no more than 19 passenger seats and a payload capacity of 12,500 pounds or less.
    b. conducts scheduled operations (five or more round trips per week) in non-turbojet aircraft that have nine or fewer passenger seats and a payload capacity of 7,500 pounds or less.
    c. conducts scheduled operations (five or more round trips per week) in turbojet or turboprop aircraft that have a passenger capacity of 19 or less passengers.
    d. None of the above.

13. A flag carrier must use weather sources approved by
    a. the individual exercising operational control for the air carrier.
    b. the person in charge of flight operations.
    c. the National Weather Service (NWS).
    d. the Administrator of the FAA.

14. Part 121 air carriers must have the ability to communicate with a flight crew
    a. from report time until the flight is finally dispatched for takeoff, just in case issues arise that might affect the actual dispatch of the flight.
    b. through an approved system operated by the government (e.g., flight service or air traffic control networks).
    c. at any point in the route structure in a rapid and reliable fashion.
    d. only when the pilot-in-command exercises emergency authority.

15. A flight follower differs from an aircraft dispatcher in that:
    a. A flight follower is a certificated airman who works with the flight crew and other departments to ensure compliance with all operational rules.
    b. A flight follower has more stringent duty and rest requirements than an aircraft dispatcher
    c. A flight follower is not required to be a certificated airman.
    d. None of the above.

CHAPTER 2
OPERATIONS SPECIFICATIONS: DEVELOPMENT AND APPLICATION

Federal Aviation Regulations are worded either by the most stupid lawyers in Washington, or the most brilliant.

—anonymous

In Chapter 1 we saw how, historically, air carriers were held to the highest standard of care and, as a result, a large body of federal regulatory authority developed to ensure that they perform to that high standard. We saw that they are subject to regulation in 14 CFR Parts 110, 117, 119, 121, 135, and others. This chapter will cover the FAA's requirement for carriers to formulate a plan and a document to identify *exactly how* they will comply with a wide variety of regulations. This process results in the creation of an **operations specifications (ops specs)** document. This is simply the document created by the carrier and FAA wherein the carrier specifically explains (or identifies) how it will conduct operation of its aircraft in accordance with the FARs.

Part 119—Certification: Air Carriers and Commercial Operators

The study of air carrier rules must begin with 14 CFR Part 119. What is the purpose of Part 119 anyway? The FAA instituted Part 119 in 1996 to further bring the air carriers of both Part 121 and Part 135 under the umbrella of "*One Level of Safety*." Prior to that date, regional airlines (19 seats or less) operated under Part 135, which at that point was much less restrictive, while aircraft larger than that were operated under the most restrictive provisions found in Part 121. One Level of Safety was a major effort by the Air Line Pilots Association and other pilot labor groups (unions) that was picked up by the FAA; it sought to have a completely uniform set of operating rules for all scheduled air carriers *regardless of the size of the aircraft*.

We introduced some sections of Part 119 in Chapter 1. Now we will examine the specific requirements for a carrier to obtain, maintain, and conduct its operations in accord with its operations specifications. 14 CFR §119.33 establishes the specific requirement that Part 121 and Part 135 **direct air carriers**[1] be United States citizens (including corporate "citizens"), obtain an **air carrier certificate**, and develop and maintain operations specifications. These operations specifications must contain "the authorizations, limitations, and procedures under which each kind of operation must be conducted." Figure 2-1 shows the "decision tree" that is created by 14 CFR Part 110, which sorts common carriage operators and private carriers for hire using large aircraft into Part 121 "airline," Part 125 "commercial operators," or Part 135 commuter and on-demand. (*Note*: "Commuter" here has a specific, defined meaning that is different from common usage when people say they will seek employment at "a commuter airline" and the like.)

___
1 *Direct air carrier* is defined 14 CFR §110.2 as a person who provides or offers to provide air transportation and who has operational control over the functions performed in providing that transportation.

22 AIR CARRIER OPERATIONS

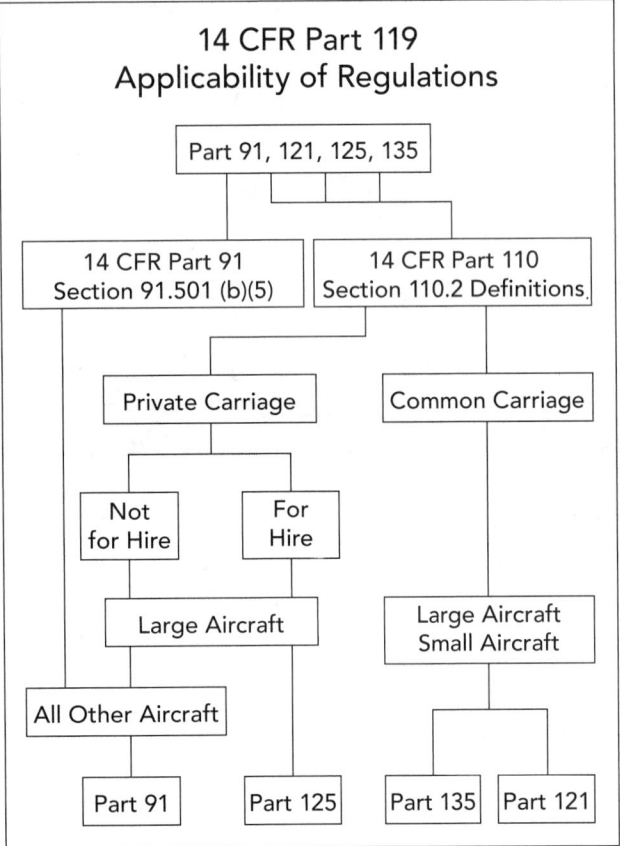

Figure 2-1. Applicability of regulations to different types of operators.

Operations Specifications

Once it has been determined that a proposed operation (or series of operations) requires an air carrier certificate, we must then move our attention to either 14 CFR Part 121 or Part 135. These parts prescribe the rules to be followed by commercial operators, air carriers operating large aircraft (Part 121) or small aircraft (Part 135). These parts of the FARs establish specific rules for air carriers that are substantially more restrictive than 14 CFR Part 91: General Operating and Flight Rules. All operators of all aircraft must comply with the general rules of 14 CFR Part 91. Then, Part 121 or Part 135 adds additional rules that apply exclusively to the certificated, direct air carriers.

Prior to the implementation of Part 119, the FARs recognized the substantially different operating capabilities and environments that existed for large and small aircraft. With the implementation of Part 119, the dividing line between Part 135 and Part 121 operations was moved to considerably smaller aircraft. As seen in Chapter 1, domestic and flag operators must comply with Part 121, while commuter and on-demand operators must comply with Part 135. All of these operators must have operations specifications. In a somewhat similar approach, other non-air carrier operators are required to have documents similar to ops specs. "Fractional share" operations, 14 CFR Part 91 Subpart K, require the operator to have management specifications ("M specs"). Part 141 flight school operators must have training specifications ("training specs"), and certain large airplanes (aircraft with 20 or more seats or a payload of greater than 6,000 pounds) that are not operated under Part 121 or Part 135 are required to have letters of authorization ("LOAs"). (Figure 2-2.)

Standard FAA Operations Specifications Templates

FAA templates are used to create a document an air carrier, owner, or flight school operator may use to explain (or identify) how it will conduct the operation of its aircraft in accord with Federal Aviation Regulations.

Operations performed under 14 CFR Parts 121, 125, 135, 142, 145 utilize a document designated by the FAA as:

Operations Specifications (Ops Specs)

Operations performed under 14 CFR Part 91K Fractional Owners and Operators utilize a document designated by the FAA as:

Management Specifications (M Specs)
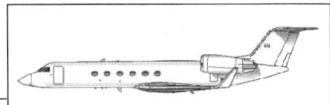

Operations performed under 14 CFR Part 141 Pilot Flight Schools utilize a document designated by the FAA as:

Training Specifications (Training Specs)

Operations performed under 14 CFR Part 91 and Part 125 M Operators (Continued Airworthiness and Safety Improvements) utilize a document designated by the FAA as:

Letters of Authorization (LOA)
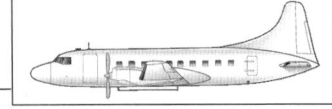

Figure 2-2. Ops specs, management specs, training specs, and letters of authorization (LOA).

As previously discussed, 14 CFR §119.33 states that a person may not operate as a direct air carrier unless that person obtains operations specifications that prescribe the authorizations, limitations, and procedures under which each kind of operation must be conducted. Section 119.7 tells us specifically what the operations specifications must contain:

(a) Each certificate holder's operations specifications must contain—
  (1) The authorizations, limitations, and certain procedures under which each kind of operation, if applicable, is to be conducted; and
  (2) Certain other procedures under which each class and size of aircraft is to be operated.

Since each operator must have a set of operations specifications, what must go into them? The answer to this question is found in 14 CFR §119.49, Contents of Operations Specifications. This provision breaks down the contents of the ops specs into three categories, depending upon what type of carrier is involved. Section 119.49(a) covers domestic, flag, and commuter carriers; Section 119.49(b) covers supplemental carriers; and Section 119.49(c) establishes the requirements for on-demand operations. While these requirements are similar in nature, there are differences between the different classes of carriers.

Let's look at domestic, commuter, and flag carriers as an example.

14 CFR §119.49—Contents of operations specifications.

(a) Each certificate holder conducting domestic, flag or commuter operations must obtain Operations Specifications containing all of the following:
  (1) The specific location of the certificate holder's principal base of operations…
  (2) Other business names under which the certificate holder may operate. [DBA or "Doing business as"]
  (3) Reference to the economic authority issued by the Department of Transportation, if required.
  (4) Type of aircraft, registration markings, and serial numbers of each aircraft authorized for use, each regular and alternate airport to be used in scheduled operations, and, except for commuter operations, each provisional and refueling airport.
     (i) [All the items in (4) may be kept current on a list, which is incorporated by reference into the ops specs.]
     (ii) The certificate holder may not conduct any operation using any aircraft or airport not listed.
  (5) Kinds of operations authorized.
  (6) Authorization and limitations for routes and areas of operations.
  (7) Airport limitations.
  (8) Time limitations, or standards for determining time limitations, for overhauling, inspecting and checking airframes, engines, propellers, rotors, appliances and emergency equipment.
  (9) Authorization for the method of controlling weight and balance of aircraft.
  (10) Interline equipment interchange requirements, if relevant.
  (11) Aircraft wet lease information required by §119.53(c).
  (12) Any authorized deviation and exemption granted from any requirement of this chapter.
  (13) An authorization permitting, or a prohibition against, accepting, handling, and transporting materials regulated as hazardous materials in transport under 49 CFR parts 171 through 180.
  (14) Any other item the Administrator determines is necessary.

That summarizes the content of the operations specifications (or ops specs). But, what are ops specs? In a very real sense, they are nothing more than the carrier telling the FAA how it intends to comply with the requirements of the Federal Aviation Regulations. FAA Order 8900.1 of the Flight Standards Information Management System (volume 3, chapter 18, section 1, paragraph 3-678) explains it well:

Within the air transportation industry there is a need to establish and administer safety standards to accommodate many variables. These variables include a wide range of aircraft; varied operator capabilities; the various situations requiring different types of air transportation; and the continual, rapid changes in aviation technology.

It is impractical to address these variables through the promulgation of safety regulations for each and every type of air transport situation and the varying degrees of operator capabilities. Also, it is impractical to address the rapidly changing aviation technology and environment through the regulatory process. Safety regulations would be extremely complex and unwieldy if all possible variations and situations were addressed by regulation. Instead, the safety standards established by regulation should usually have a broad application that allows varying acceptable methods of compliance.

The ops specs provide an effective method for establishing safety standards that address a wide range of variables. In addition, ops specs can be adapted to a specific operator's class and size of aircraft and type and kind of operation. Operations specifications can be tailored to suit an individual operator's needs. Only those authorizations, limitations, standards, and procedures that are applicable to an operator need to be included.

Perhaps the best way to understand the concept of ops specs is to look at a sample template of a Part 121 jet carrier's ops specs outline (for Aeromech Airways Corporation). Specific detailed examples of the provisions will be given in the text.

U.S. Department of Transportation Federal Aviation Administration
Operations Specifications

Table of Contents

Operating Certificate

Part A: General

Part B: Enroute Authorizations, Limitations, and Procedures

Part C: Airplane Terminal Instrument Procedures and Airport Authorizations and Limitations

Part D: Maintenance

Part E: Weight and Balance

U.S. Department of Transportation Federal Aviation Administration
Operations Specifications

Table of Contents

PART A: General

	HQ CONTROL DATE	EFFECTIVE DATE	AMENDMENT NUMBER
1. Issuance and Applicability	04/09/12	03/16/13	1
2. Definitions and Abbreviations	03/30/12	02/16/13	2
3. Airplane Authorization	02/01/12	03/16/13	1
4. Summary of Special Authorizations	11/20/11	02/21/14	8
5. Exemptions and Deviations	07/19/09	12/04/09	3
6. Management Personnel	02/10/14	12/01/14	2
7. Other Designated Persons	02/10/14	12/01/14	2
8. Operational Control	04/28/13	03/16/14	1
9. Airport Aeronautical Data	04/29/13	03/16/14	1
10. Aeronautical Weather Data	04/29/13	03/16/14	1
11. Approved Carry-on Baggage Program	01/11/13	03/16/14	1
12. Part 121 Domestic Operations to Certain Airports Outside the 48 Contiguous States	01/11/13	03/16/14	2
22. Approved Exit Seat Program	05/08/11	03/16/14	1
23. Authorization to Use an Approved Procedure for Determining Operations During Ground Icing Conditions	02/10/12	03/16/14	1
25. Approved Computer-based Record Keeping System	04/23/11	03/16/14	1
27. Land and Hold Short Operations	08/11/14	02/16/15	2
30. Part 121 Supplemental Operations	11/05/14	03/16/15	1
31. Authorized to Make Arrangements with Training Centers, Air Agencies, and/or Other Organizations for Certificate Holder Training	12/04/14	03/16/15	1
447. Emergency Airworthiness Directives (AD) Notification Requirements for U.S.-Registered Aircraft	12/31/11	03/16/15	0

Print Date: 12/13/2014
CERTIFICATE NO.: YENA761K
Aeromech Airways Corporation

U.S. Department of Transportation Federal Aviation Administration
Operations Specifications

Table of Contents

PART B: En Route Authorizations, Limitations, and Procedures

	HQ CONTROL DATE	EFFECTIVE DATE	AMENDMENT NUMBER
31. Areas of En Route Operation	02/01/14	03/16/14	1
32. En Route Limitations and Provisions	02/09/14	03/16/14	1
34. IFR Class I En Route Navigation Using Area Navigation Systems	03/27/13	03/16/14	1
35. Class I Navigation in the U.S. Class A Airspace Using Area or Long-Range Navigation Systems	07/01/13	03/16/14	1
36. Authorized to Conduct Class II Navigation Using Long-Range Navigation Systems (LRNS)	12/04/13	03/16/14	1
45. Extended Overwater Operations Using a Single Long-Range Communication System	12/09/13	08/09/14	0
50. Authorized Areas of En Route Operations	09/12/12	08/09/13	2

Print Date: 02/09/2014
CERTIFICATE NO.: YENA761K
Aeromech Airways Corporation

U.S. Department of Transportation Federal Aviation Administration
Operations Specifications

Table of Contents

PART C: Airplane Terminal Instrument Procedures and Airport Authorizations and Limitations

		HQ CONTROL DATE	EFFECTIVE DATE	AMENDMENT NUMBER
51.	Terminal Instrument Procedures	08/02/13	03/16/14	1
52.	Basic Instrument Approach Procedure Authorizations: All Airports	08/02/13	03/16/14	1
53.	Straight-in Category I Approach Procedures Other than ILS, MLS, or GPS and IFR Landing Minimums: All Airports	08/02/13	03/16/14	1
54.	Limitations and Provisions for Instrument Approach Procedures and IFR Landing Minimums	08/02/13	03/16/14	1
55.	Alternate Airport IFR Weather Minimums	08/02/13	03/16/14	1
56.	IFR Takeoff Minimums, Part 121 Airplane Operations: All Airports	08/02/13	03/16/14	1
61.	Flight Control Guidance Systems for Automatic Landing Operations Other Than Categories II and III	08/02/13	03/16/14	1
63.	Published RNAV Instrument Approach Operations Using an Area Navigation System	01/13/14	03/16/14	1
69.	Turbojet Airplane Takeoff Operations with Tailwind Components of 10 Knots or Less	12/04/10	03/16/14	1
70.	Airports Authorized for Scheduled Operations	07/28/1	05/01/15	9
71.	Autopilot Engagement After Takeoff and During Initial Climb for Auto Flight Guidance System (AFGS) Operations	11/06/13	03/16/14	1
73.	IFR Approach Procedures Using Vertical Navigation (VNAV)	08/27/13	03/16/14	1
74.	Category I, ILS, MLS, or GLS Approach Procedures and IFR Landing Minimums: All Airports	08/02/13	03/16/14	1
75.	Category I IFR Landing Minimums: Circle-to-Land Approach Maneuver	08/02/13	03/16/14	1
76.	Category I IFR Landing Minimums: Contact Approaches	08/02/13	03/16/14	1
77.	Terminal Visual Flight Rules, Limitations, and Provisions	11/09/13	03/16/14	1
78.	IFR Lower than Standard Takeoff Minimums 14 CFR Part 121 Airplane Operations: All Airports	11/19/13	03/16/14	1

Print Date: 01/19/2014
CERTIFICATE NO.: YENA761K
Aeromech Airways Corporation

U.S. Department of Transportation Federal Aviation Administration
Operations Specifications

Table of Contents

PART D: Maintenance

	HQ CONTROL DATE	EFFECTIVE DATE	AMENDMENT NUMBER
72. Aircraft Maintenance: Continuous Airworthiness Maintenance Program: (CAMP) Authorization	08/15/13	03/27/14	4
76. Short-Term Escalation Authorization	08/15/13	03/16/14	2
83. Short-Term Escalation Authorization for Parts Subject to Overhaul Requirements	04/01/13	03/16/14	3
84. Special Flight Permit with Continuous Authorization to Conduct Ferry Flights	04/01/13	03/16/14	2
85. Aircraft Listing	02/06/13	05/01/14	14
89. Maintenance Time Limitations Section	08/15/13	04/06/14	3
90. Coordinating Agencies for Suppliers Evaluation (CASE)	08/15/13	03/31/14	0
91. Arrangements with Other Organizations to Perform Substantial Maintenance	08/15/13	01/02/14	2
95. Minimum Equipment List (MEL) Authorization	08/15/13	03/16/14	2

Print Date: 08/15/2013
D085-1
CERTIFICATE NO.: YENA761K
Aeromech Airways Corporation

U.S. Department of Transportation Federal Aviation Administration
Operations Specifications

E096.	Weight and Balance	HQ Control: 01/29/14
		HQ Revision: 01b

The following procedures have been established to maintain control of weight and balance of the certificate holder's aircraft operated under the terms of these specifications (identified below) and to ensure that these aircraft are loaded within the gross weight and center of gravity limitations.

    a. Procedures by which either actual or approved average passenger and crew weights may be used are in the operator's weight and balance control program.

    b. Procedures by which either actual or approved average baggage weights may be used are in the operator's weight and balance control program.

    c. The actual passenger and baggage weights shall be used in computing the weight and balance of charter flights and other special service involving the carriage of special groups.

    d. All aircraft shall be weighed in accordance with the procedures for establishing individual or fleet aircraft weights outlined in the operator's weight and balance control program.

    e. The following loading schedules and instructions shall be used for routine operations:

Aircraft M/M/S/	Type of Loading Schedule	Loading Schedule Instructions	Weight and Balance Control Procedures
A-320-232	Computer	FCOM—Vol. 2 (data) Vol. 3 (procedures) SOM—Chapter 17	Aeromech Weight and Balance Manual, Revision 00 dated 12/03/99

Document references by volume, chapter, etc.

Print Date 02/11/2001
CERTIFICATE NO.: YENA761K
Aeromech Airways Corporation

Ops Specs Contents Explained

Now that you have seen the table of contents and a sample section of this carrier's ops specs, let's take a closer look at what they contain. An air carrier's ops specs contain all the material needed to comply with 14 CFR §119.49(a). They are broken down into five subchapters:

A. General
B. En Route Authorizations, Limitations, and Procedures
C. Airplane Terminal Instrument Procedures and Airport Authorizations and Limitations
D. Aircraft Maintenance
E. Weight and Balance Control Procedures

The following description of the table of contents and the material contained therein lays the foundation for the discussion in the rest of the text. Note that Section E: Weight and Balance Control Procedures is a single ops specs section, so we have included the entire section as an example of what one looks like.

Operations Specifications Table of Contents

Part A: General

Issuance and Applicability
This section of the ops specs contains a discussion of who the carrier is, business names, principal place of business, certificate number, and similar items.

Definitions and Abbreviations
This portion contains definitions of certain aeronautical terms used in an air carrier's operations specifications, such as Category I instrument approach, certificate holder, and operational service volume (of a NAVAID).

Airplane Authorization
This section lists the *types of aircraft* that the FAA has approved for use by the carrier.

Summary of Special Authorizations
The summary lists the special authority that the carrier may or may not have. Typical issues would include operational authority such as domestic operations to certain foreign airports (e.g., Caribbean islands or Canada), lower than standard takeoff minimums under Part 121, ferry flight, minimum equipment list usage, North Atlantic operations (NAT/OPS), and extended operations (ETOPS). The ops specs will clearly spell out if the carrier either has or is prohibited from using these special authorizations.

Exemptions and Deviations
Any carrier may apply for exemptions (waivers) from the requirements of the FARs. If these exemptions have been granted, they will be listed under the exemptions and deviations section. These exemptions would be specific to that carrier. For example, Aeromech Airways has been granted the "People's Express" exemption (to be discussed in Chapter 11), which allows it to disregard the qualifiers in the terminal aerodrome forecast in certain circumstances.

Management Personnel
This is a listing of the required management positions and the name of each person filling that position. This section also specifically lists which management position is responsible for application and modification of various sections of the ops specs for the company. In chapter 3 we will explore the specific management personnel requirements.

Other Designated Persons
This section lists other persons that, while not specifically spelled out by the FARs, are still essential to the company. Examples are who you would serve with process in the event of a lawsuit or other legal action, and who is authorized to apply for and receive operations specifications for the carrier.

Operational Control
This is a very important issue with the FAA. The FAA wants to know exactly who is in control of planning and operation of company aircraft and how that control is exercised. This is a major conceptual difference between Part 91 operations and Part 121 or Part 135 operations. As an air carrier, operation of a flight is a collaborative process and the company retains the right (and responsibility) to direct the planning and operation of the flight.

Airport Aeronautical Data
This covers the kind of regular and provisional or refueling airports to be used. Usually, the list of specific airports will be contained in the company operations manual or flight manual and will be incorporated by reference into the ops specs. On scheduled flights, the company may only operate into those airports listed. Another important issue covered in this section of the ops specs is how performance analysis charts will be produced and distributed for each runway at each airport. This takeoff and landing data is runway-specific for a Part 121 carrier and is usually contained in the aircraft or operating manuals.

Aeronautical Weather Data
What source of official weather data does the carrier intend to employ? How is it going to be disseminated to affected personnel? What procedures are in effect to ensure all of this happens in a timely manner?

Approved Carry-on Baggage Program
If the company intends to allow carry-on baggage, it must describe how that system will work. How will it ensure that bags will fit in the allocated space?

Part 121 Domestic Operations to Certain Airports Outside the 48 Contiguous States
Under certain circumstances, carriers are permitted to use the domestic rules of Part 121 even though the operation meets the requirements of flag operations. For example, most flights to Canada may be permitted to operate under domestic rules. However, before a carrier may do this, it must list in the ops specs the city pairs (routes) on which it will use the domestic rules.

Approved Exit Seat Program
The company must spell out how it will comply with the FAA requirement to have able-bodied persons seated next to emergency exits. These people must be given the opportunity to decline to assist in the event of an evacuation. If a passenger seated in the emergency exit row is unable or unwilling to assist in the event of an evacuation, the company must have a procedure allowing the passenger to be reseated prior to aircraft movement.

Authorization to Use an Approved Procedure for Determining Operations During Ground Icing Conditions
The company must state how it will comply with required deicing and anti-icing requirements of the FAA, including how it will compute holdover times.

Approved Computer-Based Record Keeping System
The company must address how it will keep the records required by Part 121. It will spell out if computers are to be used, how audits will be performed, where and how backups will be maintained, and other similar items.

Land and Hold Short (LAHSO) Operations
If the company is authorized to conduct LAHSO operations, the specific runway configurations that may be used will be listed in the ops specs. This may include incorporation by reference to the Chart Supplement U.S. (previously called *Airport/Facility Directory* or *A/FD*). This section also contains the technical details as to how the LAHSO operations are to be conducted.

Part 121 Supplemental Operations
If the carrier is authorized to conduct nonscheduled (supplemental) operations, this section will specify the geographic area where these operations are permitted. It will state that the carrier may conduct supplemental operations at its regular airports using domestic or flag rules as applicable.

Authorized to Make Arrangements with Training Centers, Air Agencies, and/or Other Organizations for Certificate Holder Training
The air carrier may be authorized to use other airlines or private providers such as Flight Safety International, SimuFlite, CAE or other Part 142 simulator training facilities to conduct its required training program. If so, the details are spelled out in the ops specs.

Emergency Airworthiness Directives (AD) Notification Requirements for U.S.-Registered Aircraft
This section spells out the procedure to be followed in the event the FAA issues an emergency airworthiness directive applicable to the carrier's airplanes. Further, it identifies exactly who is responsible for processing the AD after receipt from the FAA and who is to acknowledge receipt of the AD to the issuing FAA office.

Part B: En Route Authorizations, Limitations, and Procedures

Areas of En Route Operation
IFR operations on and off airways are defined along with the operational criteria that must be used to operate off airway. This includes the use of Class I navigation (navigation within the service volume of the navigation aid) and Class II navigation (navigation outside the service volume of the navigation aid), if authorized.

En Route Limitations and Provisions
This section establishes that the carrier's aircraft will be operated in a manner that assures the position may be reliably fixed sufficiently to comply with air traffic control. If operating using Class II navigation, the aircraft must be able to reliably fix its position at least once an hour.

IFR Class I En Route Navigation Using Area Navigation Systems
If the carrier is authorized to use any form of area navigation, (VOR/DME RNAV, RNAV RNP, GPS, INS, FMCS, etc.), it will be spelled out in this section. In addition, the ops specs will identify exactly which equipment is authorized for use for Class I navigation.

Class I Navigation in U.S. Class A Airspace Using Area or Long-Range Navigation Systems (LRNS)

If the carrier is authorized to conduct operations in U.S. Class A airspace, using any form of long-range navigation equipment, as discussed above, it will be stated here.

Authorized to Conduct Class II Navigation Using Long-Range Navigation Systems (LRNS)

If the carrier seeks to perform navigation using multiple long-range navigation systems, that will be authorized in this section. In addition, the section will specify in which Class II airspace it is authorized to be used. For example, it may not be authorized to be used in the North Atlantic Minimum Navigation Performance Standards (NAT MNPS) airspace or in international operations with required navigation performance (RNP) navigation specification (RNP 4 or RNP 10).

Extended Overwater Operations Using a Single Long-Range Communication System

The operator may be authorized to conduct extended overwater operations with only a single long-range communications system. This provision will establish what equipment is authorized to be used and the geographic areas where the single system is permitted.

Authorized Areas of En Route Operations

This section identifies the specific areas where the carrier is authorized to conduct enroute operations. For example, this carrier is permitted to operate in the western Atlantic Ocean outside of MNPS airspace and in the 48 contiguous United States and the District of Columbia.

Part C: Airplane Terminal Instrument Procedures and Airport Authorizations and Limitations

Terminal Instrument Procedures

This section establishes the authority under which an approach must have been issued in order for the carrier to use it. For example, this carrier must use approaches that are developed by the carrier (and approved by the FAA), approved U.S. Part 97 civil approaches, approved U.S. military approaches, or foreign approaches approved under either ICAO PANS-OPS (procedures for air navigation services—aircraft operations) or the JAA JAR-OPS-1 document of the European Joint Aviation Authorities (JAA).

Basic Instrument Approach Procedure Authorizations: All Airports

The air carrier lists all of the approaches that are approved by the FAA for use by the carrier.

Straight-in Category I Approach Procedures Other than ILS, MLS, or GPS and IFR Landing Minimums: All Airports

This section describes the lowest operational minimums applicable to the carrier's operations. It also lists the penalties paid (in terms of minimums) for inoperative equipment. Examples from this section of the operations specifications are discussed in more detail in Chapters 11 and 12.

Limitations and Provisions for Instrument Approach Procedures and IFR Landing Minimums

A low time captain may fall into the category of "high minimums" captain. That means the FAA raises the approach minimums over the published minimums until such time as the captain has sufficient experience to no longer be considered a high minimums captain. This section establishes the increases to the approach minimums and also requires additional runway to be available under certain conditions for high minimums captains.

Alternate Airport IFR Weather Minimums

The carrier may use **standard alternate (weather) minimums** or **derived alternate minimums** in its operations. A derived alternate minimum is a method of determining alternate airport weather minimums other than by the standard alternate minimums required by Part 91. For example, see 14 CFR §91.169(c), which requires that an airport have forecast weather of 600 foot ceiling and 2 miles visibility for a precision approach or 800 foot ceiling and 2 miles visibility for a nonprecision approach in order to list the airport as a required alternate airport. If the carrier wishes to use derived alternate minimums, then the approved method for determining the alternate minimums must be given.

IFR Takeoff Minimums, Part 121 Airplane Operations: All Airports

Part 91 establishes IFR takeoff visibility minimums for Part 121 and Part 135 operators (e.g., see 14 CFR 91.175[f]). The company may be authorized to conduct **reduced minimums takeoffs**. If so, the method of computing the amount of reductions and the applicable conditions will be given.

Flight Control Guidance Systems for Automatic Landing Operations Other than Categories II and III

Modern flight management equipment often permits automatic approach and landing to be performed even on Category I approaches. If this is permitted for this carrier, the terms and conditions allowing it will be spelled out in this section. It will require specific training for the crew before they are permitted to use the automatic landing capability of the aircraft.

Published RNAV Instrument Approach Operations Using an Area Navigation System

If the carrier is permitted to perform RNAV approaches (including FMCS), it will be detailed here. The crew must be specifically trained on how to use this equipment.

Turbojet Airplane Takeoff Operations with Tailwind Components of 10 Knots or Less

If the approved airplane flight manual (AFM) allows for tailwind takeoffs, it may be approved. The limits placed on this will include a maximum tailwind component of 10 knots.

Airports Authorized for Scheduled Operations

The carrier will list airports it intends to use for operations. This includes regular, refueling, provisional and alternate airports. A regular airport is one it intends to serve with scheduled service. A refueling airport is one to which aircraft may be dispatched only for the purposes of refueling. A provisional airport is one that is used to provide scheduled service to a community when the regular airport serving that community is unavailable. An alternate airport is one at which the carrier's aircraft may land if a landing at the intended airport becomes impractical.

Autopilot Engagement After Takeoff and During Initial Climb for Auto Flight Guidance System (AFGS) Operations

This provision allows the pilot to engage the autopilot at a lower than standard altitude. Parts 121, 125, and 135 normally require that the autopilot not be engaged below 500 feet. However, if the system is fully operational and the crew trained, it may engage the autopilot below 500 feet with this ops specs provision.

IFR Approach Procedures Using Vertical Navigation

If the carrier has vertical navigation equipment (VNAV), this provision allows it to conduct nonprecision approaches using the VNAV for vertical guidance.

Category I, ILS, MLS, or GLS Approach Procedures and IFR Landing Minimums: All Airports

This section sets minimums for this type of approach and outlines what equipment and limitations are applicable to the carrier.

Category I IFR Landing Minimums: Circle-to-Land Approach Maneuver

This provision limits the use of circling approach procedures to a minimum of 1,000 foot ceiling and 3 miles visibility (or higher published minimums). This is common for air carriers to limit circling approaches to VFR conditions.

Category I IFR Landing Minimums: Contact Approaches

The carrier cannot conduct contact approaches unless the pilot in command has received special training in the procedures to be used.

Terminal Visual Flight Rules, Limitations, and Provisions

The carrier is authorized to conduct visual approach procedures and charted visual flight procedures within Class B, C, and D airspace and in some Class E airspace.

IFR Lower than Standard Takeoff Minimums, 14 CFR Part 121 Airplane Operations: All Airports

Part 91 sets minimum visibilities for instrument departures. Standard takeoff minimums are 1 statute mile for two-engine aircraft and ½ statute mile for aircraft with three or more engines. These values can be substantially reduced with training and certain equipment, such as runway lighting available.

Part D: Aircraft Maintenance

Aircraft Maintenance: Continuous Airworthiness Maintenance Program (CAMP) Authorization

The basic FARs require commercial aircraft to be maintained according to 100 hour inspection. In most airline environments this is very impractical, as the aircraft would be set down for extended times on a regular basis. Continuous airworthiness allows the maintenance tasks to be broken into much smaller pieces and performed a bit at a time at each layover or overnight stay. This may be authorized by ops specs.

Short-Term Escalation Authorization
Even with the continuous airworthiness inspections described above, the carrier may face a problem where a check is due but the aircraft is needed for operations. In this case, the carrier is permitted to exceed a "weekly" check by 1 day and an "A" check by 50 flight hours.

Short-Term Escalation Authorization for Borrowed Parts Subject to Overhaul Requirements
In the world of airline maintenance, aircraft are often found in remote locations with inoperative equipment that must be fixed prior to further flight. If the carrier doesn't have the spare part, in many cases it may borrow the part or equipment from another carrier. Different carriers sometimes have different intervals for overhauling various parts, so it is possible that your carrier borrows a part from another carrier that is within the other carrier's overhaul interval but beyond your carrier's overhaul interval. In that case, you may be permitted to use the borrowed part for a period of time pursuant to this provision.

Special Flight Permit with Continuous Authorization to Conduct Ferry Flights
In Part 91 operations, if an aircraft is unairworthy but still safe to fly, it is possible to obtain a special flight permit (ferry permit) that allows the operator to ferry the aircraft to a facility where repairs may be made or maintenance performed. To do this, the operator needs to secure the permit from a Designated Engineering Representative or FAA Maintenance Inspector. This ops specs provision is sort of an open ended ferry permit that doesn't require individual application for each permit, but rather allows the carrier to make the determination that it is permissible to fly.

Aircraft Listing
Typically, this section will incorporate by reference a list containing the specific airplanes (N-numbers) to be used. That way, if the list changes, all copies of the ops specs would not have to be amended. Instead, only this referenced list would need to be changed.

Maintenance Time Limitations Section
In this section, the carrier is required to specify the time intervals for its maintenance. The time intervals (or limitations) will be addressed in the maintenance manual(s).

Coordinating Agencies for Suppliers Evaluation
This provision allows the carrier to use CASE (Coordinating Agencies for Suppliers Evaluation) as a means of qualifying a vendor for services, parts, and materials to satisfy the requirements of 14 CFR §121.373. As will be discussed in Chapter 14, the carrier may not delegate its responsibility for complying with the quality control requirements, but it may use the services of another agency to perform the work.

Arrangements with Other Organizations to Perform Substantial Maintenance
As with training, the carrier may utilize the services of another carrier or air agency to perform certain maintenance tasks. These maintenance providers must be identified and approved in the ops specs along with the limitations placed on the use of these firms.

Minimum Equipment List (MEL) Authorization
The basic rule is that an airplane with *any* inoperative equipment is unairworthy. This would be impossible to deal with in the real world of airline flying because things break all the time. With the redundancy of equipment, broken equipment doesn't necessarily mean unsafe aircraft. A carrier is permitted to establish a program where the aircraft manufacturer and carrier develop a document called a minimum equipment list. This document must be approved in the ops specs and it allows the carrier to operate with certain items (or combinations of items) inoperative.

Part E: Weight and Balance Control Procedures
(See example E096 Weight and Balance, page 29)

Weight and Balance Control Procedures
This provision sets the company's procedures for determining passenger weights, aircraft weight, baggage weights, and so forth, for the purpose of calculating weight and balance prior to flight.

Ops Specs Preparation Process
All of the above material will be contained (in detail) in the ops specs once the FAA issues them. How do the ops specs get produced in the first place? The FAA uses an automated process of producing ops specs. At the Part 135 on-demand air carrier level, the carrier's first point of contact is with the local Flight Standards District Office (FSDO). The FSDO personnel use the FSIMS program to assist the carrier in getting ops specs prepared. This process begins with a series of discussions with the FSDO operations inspector assigned the case, wherein the proposed operation is outlined in detail.

These discussions address issues such as reduced minimums, waivers, limitations, and operational control. As a result of that meeting and follow-up meetings, computer-generated ops specs are produced by the FAA.

If the start-up carrier is going to be a Part 121 domestic, flag, or commuter carrier, the process is similar to that of Part 135 except that the initial meeting is with a representative of the FAA national certification team. They will meet with representatives of the company, evaluate their needs, and set limitations on the operations. Again, computer-generated ops specs are produced and become the guiding document for the company's operations.

Maintenance of Operations Specifications

Once ops specs have been approved and the carrier begins operations, it must maintain the document at its principal base of operations (14 CFR 119.43[a]). This is the formal or official copy that is available to any FAA operations inspector. In addition, the carrier must insert pertinent sections of its ops specs into its manual(s). It must clearly identify the sections as coming from the ops specs and indicate that, therefore, compliance is mandatory. The carrier has the further obligation to ensure that each employee affected by the ops specs is kept informed as to his or her responsibility under the ops specs.

Duration of Operations Specifications

14 CFR §119.61 states that, generally speaking, once the ops specs are issued, they remain effective until they are surrendered by the holder, or suspended or revoked in an action by the FAA. Other things can also affect the validity of the ops specs. For example, if the holder does not conduct the kind of operations approved for a period of 30 days (for domestic, flag, and commuter carriers) and fails to follow the procedures of Section 119.63 upon resumption of service, the ops specs are no longer valid. Amending the ops specs renders the amended sections invalid.

Before we complete this discussion, there are a few odds and ends to cover in Part 119.

Obtaining the Air Carrier Certificate

We earlier mentioned the air carrier certificate in passing. A carrier must have an air carrier certificate to operate. Prior to deregulation of the airline industry in 1978, this certificate was issued primarily in the sense of an economic "franchise" to conduct business and then a safety evaluation as to fitness to conduct air operations. It required approval of the Civil Aeronautics Board prior to the carrier going to the FAA for the operating certificate. Since deregulation, this step is no longer required for domestic flights. (International flights/routes are a different matter and are subject to treaty agreements and approvals by the affected governments.) Today, holding an operating certificate shows that the carrier has been found "fit" by the FAA to conduct air carrier operations. It's a safety issue, no longer an economic issue, for domestic operations.

14 CFR §119.37 spells out the contents of the air carrier certificate and §119.39 provides the criteria the FAA will use to determine whether or not to issue an air carrier certificate. To be issued the certificate, the carrier must be in compliance with the requirements of Part 119 and must have shown that it is properly and adequately equipped and able to conduct safe operations under Part 121 or Part 135. Application for the certificate may be denied if the FAA finds that the carrier is not so equipped or that it held a previous air carrier certificate that was revoked. Additionally, if the carrier attempts to employ a person in a key management position who held a similar position in a carrier whose certificate was revoked, or if the owners are found to be previous owners of a revoked certificate holder, the FAA may deny the certificate.

Deviation Authority

In some cases, it is desirable to conduct a certain operation although compliance with Parts 119, 121, or 135 would preclude such operations. The FARs provide some relief in this event. 14 CFR §119.55 provides that in some cases the carrier may obtain permission to operate while not in compliance with the FARs in order to perform operations under a military contract. 14 CFR §119.57 likewise provides that in some cases the carrier may obtain permission to operate while not in compliance with the FARs in order to perform operations during an emergency. This permission is called **deviation authority** and is obtained upon application to the FAA and compliance with Section 119.55 or Section 119.57.

Summary

In this chapter we have discussed the regulatory framework imposed on the carrier that assures compliance with the Federal Aviation Regulations. This includes the preparation and approval of operations specifications. We have seen that through operations specifications the FAA requires air carriers to formulate a plan and a document to identify exactly how the carrier will comply with a wide variety of federal regulations. We've also examined the five subchapters that make up the standard FAA "template" for an air carrier's operations specifications:

Operations specifications:

Part A: General
Part B: En Route Authorizations, Limitations, and Procedures
Part C: Airplane Terminal Instrument Procedures and Airport Authorizations and Limitations
Part D: Aircraft Maintenance
Part E: Weight and Balance Control Procedures

In the next chapter, we will explore the organizational and managerial structure of an air carrier.

Important Terms in Chapter 2

air carrier certificate
derived alternate minimums
deviation authority
direct air carriers
operations specifications (ops specs)
reduced minimums takeoff
standard alternate minimums

Chapter 2 Exam

1. The purpose of operations specifications (or ops specs) is for the company to
   a. identify to the FAA and itself how it will specifically comply with various provisions of the FARs.
   b. identify to the employees how the company will accomplish certain operations.
   c. identify for operational management how it is to manage the carrier.
   d. None of the above.

2. The FAA instituted which part in 1996 to further bring air carriers of both Parts 121 and 135 under the umbrella of "One Level of Safety"?
   a. 14 CFR Part 110
   b. 14 CFR Part 117
   c. 14 CFR Part 119
   d. 14 CFR Part 120

3. Operating under 14 CFR Part 121
   a. eliminates the carrier's requirement to comply with Part 91.
   b. requires only that the carrier comply with Parts 119 and 121.
   c. requires the carrier to comply with Part 91 as well as Part 121 unless the requirements under Part 121 are more stringent than the Part 91 requirements.
   d. None of the above.

4. Ops specs must contain which of the following:
   a. Authorizations
   b. Limitations
   c. Certain procedures
   d. All of the above

5. Where is the required content of operations specifications for a commuter or on-demand operator found?
   a. 14 CFR Part 25
   b. 14 CFR Parts 121 and 135
   c. 14 CFR Part 119
   d. 14 CFR Part 135

6. Which of the following is *not required* to be in a domestic carrier's ops specs?
   a. Names and addresses of the five largest shareholders
   b. Registration markings of each aircraft
   c. Other business names under which the carrier may be operating
   d. Any authorized deviations or exemptions granted by the FAA

7. Production of ops specs are now automated by the FAA through the use of what amounts to a punch card system. By doing this, the FAA intends that the ops specs of each carrier be
   a. identical to other carriers of the same size.
   b. standard in form and language but tailored to suit the individual, specific needs of each carrier.
   c. completely up to the carrier what procedures it wants to include.
   d. None of the above.

8. If you were a ramp service supervisor for Aeromech Airlines, where would you look to find the loading instructions (procedures) for how to load a particular A-320-232 aircraft? (Refer to Aeromech Ops Specs E096.)
   a. Aeromech's ops specs
   b. Volume 2 of the flight crew operations manual (FCOM)
   c. Volume 3 of the flight crew operations manual (FCOM)
   d. Aeromech Weight and Balance Manual revision 00

9. The starting point for a new Part 121 domestic carrier in setting up ops specs is to
   a. first contact a representative of the national certification team.
   b. first contact a representative of the regional certification team.
   c. first contact a representative of the local FSDO certification team.
   d. first contact the principal operations inspector assigned to that carrier.

10. A copy of the ops specs must be maintained by the carrier at
    a. all locations where it conducts business.
    b. all locations where crew bases are located.
    c. its general counsel's office.
    d. its principal base of operations.

11. A domestic, flag or commuter carrier's ops specs are valid
    a. for 1 year from date of issue.
    b. for 2 years from date of issue.
    c. until the carrier fails to conduct the kind of approved operation for 30 days and doesn't give the FAA 5 days' notice before resuming operations.
    d. permanently, once issued.

12. A domestic carrier must get an air carrier certificate prior to operations. This is
    a. an economic approval required by the Civil Aeronautics Board.
    b. an economic approval required by DOT.
    c. a safety issue required by international treaty.
    d. a safety issue required by the FAA.

CHAPTER 3
AIRLINE ORGANIZATION: REQUIRED MANAGEMENT POSITIONS

This is a nasty, rotten business.
—**Robert Crandall**
Former CEO and President of American Airlines

In this chapter the organizational structure of air carriers operating under FAR Parts 121 or 135 is examined in detail. Obviously, airlines come in all sizes and shapes. There are Part 121 carriers operating a single turbojet aircraft and Part 135 carriers operating dozens of airplanes. Likewise, Part 121 carriers may have hundreds of aircraft in their fleets and a Part 135 operation may consist of a single Cessna Skyhawk. With this wide variation in size and complexity, airlines need the flexibility to organize in pretty much whatever manner is required for their operations. However, having said that, it is important to understand that the FAA is quite concerned with the issue of establishing specific responsibilities with specific people at an airline. For that reason, 14 CFR §119.65 and the sections following it provide specific guidance as to *required management positions*.

First, the FAA specifies the minimum management positions a carrier must have in order to obtain and maintain a certificate. These requirements are spelled out separately for Part 121 and Part 135 air carriers.

Required Management Positions Under 14 CFR Part 121

Part 121 requirements are found in 14 CFR §119.65. The regulations mandate five specific management positions for a Part 121 air carrier. They are

- director of safety,
- director of operations,
- chief pilot,
- director of maintenance, and
- chief inspector.

These positions are the only required positions in a Part 121 air carrier. Of course, an airline probably couldn't function with only these positions, but the FAA leaves the non-safety related positions to the discretion of the individual airline. Larger airlines may have hundreds of management positions ranging from president and chief executive officer (CEO) to positions in marketing, finance, accounting, planning, sales, and ramp service. All of these additional positions may or may not be used as the airline sees fit; however, the five positions listed above must be filled. Note that Section 119.65(b) does allow the carrier to use a different number of, or title for, the positions if the carrier can show that it can perform the operation with the *highest degree of safety* (note the old common law carryover). Section 119.65(c) requires that the titles (or approved equivalent titles) be set forth in the operation specifications.

14 CFR 119.65

(b) The Administrator may approve positions or numbers of positions other than those listed in paragraph (a) of this section for a particular operation if the certificate holder shows that it can perform the operation with the highest degree of safety under the direction of

fewer or different categories of management personnel due to—
  (1) the kind of operation involved;
  (2) the number and type of airplanes used; and
  (3) the area of operations.
(c) The title of the positions required under paragraph (a) of this section or the title and number of equivalent positions approved under paragraph (b) of this section shall be set forth in the certificate holder's operations specifications.

(14 CFR §119.65[b] and [c])

The next question that must be addressed is what training, background, or experience the people that fill these positions must have. The answer to this question is actually found in two different sections of the FARs. First, generalized requirements are found in 14 CFR §119.65(d)(1) through (3). This sets forth requirements such as:

(1) Be qualified through training, experience and expertise;
(2) To the extent of their responsibilities, have a full understanding of the following materials with respect to the certificate holder's operation—
  (i) Aviation safety standards and safe operating practices;
  (ii) 14 CFR Chapter I (Federal Aviation Regulations);
  (iii) The certificate holder's operations specifications;
  (iv) All appropriate maintenance and airworthiness requirements of this chapter (e.g., parts 1, 21, 23, 25, 43, 45, 47, 65, 91, and 121 of this chapter); and
  (v) The manual required by §121.133 of this chapter; and
(3) Discharge their duties to meet applicable legal requirements and to maintain safe operations.

[14 CFR §119.65[d]]

Further, in the operations manual required by 14 CFR §121.133, the carrier must state the duties, responsibilities, and authority of the required management personnel. The names of the specific individuals assigned to these positions as well as their business addresses must be listed. If there are changes in the personnel (or position vacancies), the FAA must be notified within 10 days.

Beyond these general requirements, the regulations go on to require specific background and experience for these positions. These requirements are found in Section 119.67, and are summarized below along with the typical duties and responsibilities of each position.

Director of Operations (DO)
(Part 121 Operations)

The position of **director of operations** must be filled by a pilot experienced in the type of operations the carrier conducts. He or she must be an airline transport (ATP) rated pilot who has had three or more years of experience in a supervisory or managerial position within the last six years. This experience must include managing or supervising a function that exercised operational control over operations conducted with large airplanes (unless the carrier uses only small airplanes, in which case the experience may be in either large or small airplanes).

If this is the first time this person has held the position of director of operations with any company, then he or she must have at least three years' experience within the last six years as pilot-in-command of a large airplane (unless the carrier uses only small airplanes, in which case the experience may be in either large or small airplanes). If the person has previously served in the capacity of director of operations, then the three years of pilot-in-command experience may have been obtained at any time in the past.

The director of operations typically has the following duties and responsibilities:

- Provides operational control of all flight operations
- Directs and supervises chief pilot, director of inflight, and flight operations personnel
- Develops the budget for flight operations
- Ensures proper training of all required personnel and is responsible for the quality of training output
- Reviews contract services quality and performance and ensures proper ground handling services
- Supervises the collection and storage of flight/load manifest and weight and balance data
- Has authority to employ, discipline, reward, or terminate air carrier employees

Chief Pilot
(Part 121 Operations)

To serve in the position of **chief pilot**, a person must hold an ATP certificate with type ratings for at least one of the aircraft operated by the certificate holder. He or she must have had at least three years of experience as pilot-in-command of large airplanes (unless the carrier uses only small airplanes, in which case the experience may be in either large or small airplanes). As with the DO position, this experience must have been obtained within the previous six years if this is the first chief pilot position held by that person. If the person has held other chief pilot positions, the experience may have been obtained at any time.

The chief pilot typically has the following duties and responsibilities:

- Supervises all of the air carrier's pilots
- Directs and supervises all pilot recruitment, interviewing, testing, and final selection of pilots; also responsible for arranging FAA required pre-employment pilot background check
- Supervises the director of training, director of flight standards, and check airman staff and is responsible for the training and checking of all pilots
- Directs and coordinates crew scheduling, crew tracking, and crew reroute departments in setting pilot scheduling policy
- Participates in continual flight operations budget process

Director of Maintenance (DM)
(Part 121 Operations)

The candidate for **director of maintenance** must be a certificated mechanic with both airframe and powerplant ratings. He or she must have at least one year of experience in returning aircraft to service. This means making the determination that the aircraft is airworthy and complies with all applicable regulations after maintenance or repairs. The person must have had at least one year of experience in a supervisory capacity under either 14 CFR §119.67(c)(4)(i) or (ii), and three years' total experience within the previous six years maintaining large aircraft (10 or more seats) or repairing airplanes in a certificated airframe repair station that is rated to maintain airplanes in the same category and class of airplane as the certificate holder is using.

The director of maintenance typically has the following duties and responsibilities:

- Manages all company maintenance activities
- Establishes and supervises maintenance control department
- Directs maintenance planning, scheduling, and aircraft routing to meet maintenance requirements
- Oversees any contract maintenance activities
- Sets standards of performance for maintenance technicians and other personnel assigned to the maintenance department
- Has responsibility for dictating work rules, job standards, and job description for all maintenance personnel

Chief Inspector
(Part 121 Operations)

The **chief inspector** must have held a mechanic certificate with airframe and powerplant ratings for at least 3 years. In addition, the chief inspector must have had at least three years of maintenance experience on different types of large airplanes (10 or more seats), one year of which was as a maintenance inspector, and have one year's experience in a supervisory capacity maintaining the same category and class of aircraft as is to be used by the certificate holder.

The chief inspector typically has the following duties and responsibilities:

- Conducts internal and external maintenance audits and maintains a record of all audits in accordance with standard policies and procedures
- Evaluates and recommends approval or rejection of contract overhaul/repair facilities
- Supervises the scheduling and conduct of all maintenance training
- Oversees fueling, deicing, and general aircraft familiarization training and inspections prior to any new station opening
- Supervises all company inspectors and auditors in the performance of their duties
- Ensures all work performed on company aircraft conforms with the approved company maintenance manual and all applicable federal regulations

Director of Safety
(Part 121 Operations)

Note that 14 CFR §119.67 does not have any specific experience requirements for this position. Therefore, only the general requirements of 14 CFR §119.65(d) are applicable to the **director of safety**.

The director of safety typically has the following duties and responsibilities:

- Conducts safety reviews of all functions including public safety, security, maintenance, and flight operation
- Accomplishes annual internal safety audits and investigations in accordance with company policies and procedures
- Attends National Transportation Safety Board (NTSB), FAA, Air Transport Association, and other industry safety meetings and seminars as authorized or directed by the CEO
- Oversees communications between the company and the FAA regarding inspection results, safety reviews, and enforcement actions
- Participates in the use of flight data recorder/engine monitoring information to develop safety programs or recommend safety improvement actions
- Conducts routine surveillance and inspections throughout the company's route system
- Conducts regulatory and safety training for company managers and maintenance and flight operations supervisors

In the event the carrier wishes to propose a candidate for one of these positions who does not have the requisite experience, there is a relief provision contained in 14 CFR §119.67(e). This provision allows a request for a deviation to be made to the Manager of the Air Transportation Division (AFS-200) in the case of the DO or chief pilot, or to the Manager of the Aircraft Maintenance Division (AFS-300) in the case of the DM or chief inspector position.

Required Management Positions under 14 CFR Part 135

Part 135 requirements are found in 14 CFR §119.69. These regulations mandate only three specific management positions for a Part 135 air carrier:

- Director of operations
- Chief pilot
- Director of maintenance

The generalized requirements for a Part 135-mandated management position are very similar to those required under Part 121. Section 119.69 requires that the manager:

(1) Be qualified through training, experience and expertise;
(2) To the extent of their responsibilities, have a full understanding of the following material with respect to the certificate holder's operation—
 (i) Aviation safety standards and safe operating practices;
 (ii) Definitions found in 14 CFR Chapter I (Federal Aviation Regulations);
 (iii) The certificate holder's operations specifications;
 (iv) All appropriate maintenance and airworthiness requirements of this chapter; and
 (v) The manual required by §135.21 of this chapter; and
(3) Discharge their duties to meet applicable legal requirements and to maintain safe operations.

(14 CFR §119.69[d])

The specific requirements for these three positions are found in 14 CFR §119.71. These requirements are summarized below along with the typical duties and responsibilities of each position.

Director of Operations (DO)
(Part 135 Operations)

If the pilots-in-command on this operation are required to have an airline transport pilot certificate, the director of operations must hold an ATP certificate. If the operation only requires a commercial pilot certificate, the DO must hold a commercial pilot certificate. If the operation requires an instrument rating, the DO must hold an instrument rating. Further, he or she must have at least three years' supervisory or managerial experience within the last six years in a position that exercised operational control over either Part 121 or Part 135 operations. If this is the first-time appointment to a DO position, the person must have three years' experience in the last six years as pilot-in-command of an aircraft operated under Part 121 or Part 135. If the person has previously held a DO position, the pilot-in-command experience may have been obtained at any previous time.

The director of operations typically has the following duties and responsibilities:

- Supervises the chief pilot and other employees as directed by the president
- Ensures that all flight operations are conducted safely and in compliance with all Federal Aviation Regulations, operations specifications, and company policies

- Has authority to act for the certificate holder, including the signing of FAA correspondence and operations specifications
- Communicates with the FAA Flight Standards District Office and the National Transportation Safety Board; files all required reports and documents
- Devises revisions to this manual as needed, submits the proposed revisions to the FSDO, receives confirmation from the FSDO that the revisions are acceptable, and then distributes those revisions to all manual holders
- Schedules aircraft availability, including scheduling the aircraft for required inspections
- Coordinates with the director of maintenance the timely correction of mechanical irregularities and discrepancies
- Hires and fires flight personnel
- Manages the minimum equipment list (MEL) program

Chief Pilot
(Part 135 Operations)

If the pilots-in-command on this operation are required to have an airline transport pilot certificate, the chief pilot must hold an ATP certificate. If the operation only requires a commercial pilot certificate, the chief pilot must hold a commercial pilot certificate. If the operation requires an instrument rating, this person must hold an instrument rating. Further, the chief pilot must have three years' experience as pilot-in-command under either Part 121 or Part 135 within the last six years or, if he or she has previous experience as a chief pilot, the experience may have been obtained at any previous time.

The chief pilot typically has the following duties and responsibilities:

- Reports to the director of operations
- Supervises flight crew personnel
- Conducts or supervises all training activities of flight crew personnel
- Advises the director of operations regarding the training of flight crew personnel
- Assists the director of operations in formulating and coordinating operations policies, and coordinates operations and training
- Ensures that all aircraft are properly equipped for applicable operations
- Disseminates information to all crewmembers pertaining to routes, airports, Notices to Air Missions (NOTAMs), navigation aids (NAVAIDS), company policies, and regulations
- Maintains proficiency as pilot-in-command
- Supervises scheduling of flight crewmembers, including assigning pilot-in-command duties
- Prepares and maintains proficiency records, pilot files, flight schedules, duty time records, reports, and correspondence pertaining to flight operations activities
- Submits all reports regarding flight personnel to the director of operations
- Keeps the aircraft copies of the air carrier's operations manual current
- Ensures that all flight crew personnel are certified and supervised according to the requirements specified in the Federal Aviation Regulations

Director of Maintenance (DM)
(Part 135 Operations)

The director of maintenance must hold a mechanic certificate with airframe and powerplant ratings. In addition, this person must have either three years' experience within the past six years maintaining aircraft as a certificated mechanic including experience in the same category and class as the certificate holder, or three years' experience within the last three years repairing aircraft in a certificated repair station including one year returning aircraft to service.

The director of maintenance typically has the following duties and responsibilities:

- Is responsible for all maintenance and inspection personnel and signing of Part D (Aircraft Maintenance section) of the operation specifications
- Ensures that company aircraft are maintained in an airworthy condition
- Ensures that all inspections, repairs, and component changes are accomplished in accordance with manufacturers' or FAA-approved procedures
- Ensures compliance with maintenance procedures, airworthiness directives, service bulletins, service letters, and applicable Federal Aviation Regulations
- Ensures all maintenance technicians are trained and current on the types of aircraft for which approved

- Ensures that all maintenance technicians are certified and supervised according to the requirements specified in the Federal Aviation Regulations
- Coordinates with maintenance contracting agencies when maintenance activities are being performed on company aircraft
- Provides the director of operations with the current airworthiness status of the aircraft and the forecast down times to facilitate maintenance scheduling and ensure timely deferral or correction of aircraft discrepancies
- Maintains a close liaison with manufacturer's representatives, parts supply houses, repair facilities and the FAA
- Makes available to maintenance personnel the necessary overhaul manuals, service bulletins, service letters, airworthiness directives, applicable sections of this manual, and any other required technical data
- Maintains all necessary work records and logbooks, including certification in the aircraft permanent maintenance records that the aircraft is approved for return to service
- Maintains the weight and balance records for all aircraft
- Completes the required maintenance reliability report (MRR) and maintenance irregularity summary (MIS) reports and submits them to the director of operations for forwarding to the FAA

Operational Control

In reviewing the requirements for several of the positions, note that the FAA wants the person in those positions to have had experience in exercising operational control of the air carrier. What is this concept of operational control? 14 CFR §1.1 defines **operational control** as "the exercise of authority over initiating, conducting, and terminating a flight." Operational control is exercised through both active and passive means. **Active control** consists of making those tactical decisions and performing those actions necessary to operate a specific flight, such as crew scheduling, accepting charter flights from the public, reviewing weather and NOTAMs, and flight planning. **Passive control** consists of developing and publishing policies and procedures for operational control personnel and flight crew to follow in the performance of their duties and ensuring adequate information and facilities are available to conduct the planned operation.

This concept of operational control is a crucial one in air carrier operations. It is one of the key distinctions in the difference between air carrier operations and private carriage under Part 91. Operational control means that someone other than the pilot-in-command is involved in the decision making as to whether a flight starts, how it is conducted, and how and where it terminates. The pilot-in-command retains emergency authority to act independently, but under routine operations, the flight is conducted under control and through consensus with the appropriate authority within the company. The required management positions of chief pilot and director of operations require previous exercise and experience in the application of the concept of operational control.

The scope of operational control varies with the type of operation authorized. In accordance with company policy, the major responsibility for operational control is with the director of operations. When operating as an air carrier, the director of operations may delegate the active control of flight to the pilot-in-command (PIC) or other persons but always retains full responsibility (Refer to FAA Notice 8900.4, "Guidance for Operations Specifications"). The persons delegated to exercise active operational control are usually termed **flight dispatchers** (or just **dispatchers**) (Part 121) and **flight followers** (Part 121 or 135). In Part 121 operations, the function is typically called "dispatch," and in Part 121 (supplemental operations) and part 135 operations it is typically called **flight following**.

Within a flight dispatching system, the air carrier is required to be able to establish direct radio contact with a flight while en route.

> Each certificate holder conducting domestic or flag operations must show that a two-way communication system…is available over the entire route. The communications [system]…[must] provide reliable and rapid communications under normal operating conditions between each airplane and the appropriate dispatch office, and between each airplane and the appropriate air traffic control unit. (14 CFR §121.99)

The **flight following** system may be divided into two distinct categories: the flight release system (used by Part 121 supplemental air carriers and commercial operators) and the flight locating system (used by Part 135 operators). Within the flight following system, the carrier is not required to be able to establish direct radio contact with a flight while en route. However, if a carrier uses the flight release system, it is required to maintain a suitable means of communication between the flight follower and the PIC at each point of departure.

Operational control includes, but is not limited to, the performance of the following:

- Ensuring that only those operations authorized by the operations specifications are conducted
- Ensuring that only crewmembers trained and qualified in accordance with the applicable regulations are assigned to conduct a flight
- Ensuring that crewmembers are in compliance with flight, duty, and rest requirements when departing on a flight
- Designating a pilot-in-command (PIC) for each flight
- Providing the PIC and flight control personnel access to the information necessary for the safe conduct of the flight (such as weather, NOTAMs, airport information)
- Specifying conditions under which flights may be released (weather minimums, flight planning, aircraft airworthiness, aircraft loading, and fuel requirements)
- Ensuring that each flight has complied with the conditions specified for release before it is allowed to depart
- Ensuring that when the conditions specified for release cannot be met, the flight is cancelled, delayed, or rerouted
- Monitoring the progress of each flight and initiating timely actions when the flight cannot be completed as planned, including diverting or terminating a flight

Other Management Positions

This chapter is concerned with the *required* managerial positions within an air carrier. However, in order to put them into perspective, it might help to look at the typical organizational arrangements of a variety of carriers. Figure 3-1 shows an example of a major international (flag) airline, and Figure 3-2 shows a small regional airline.

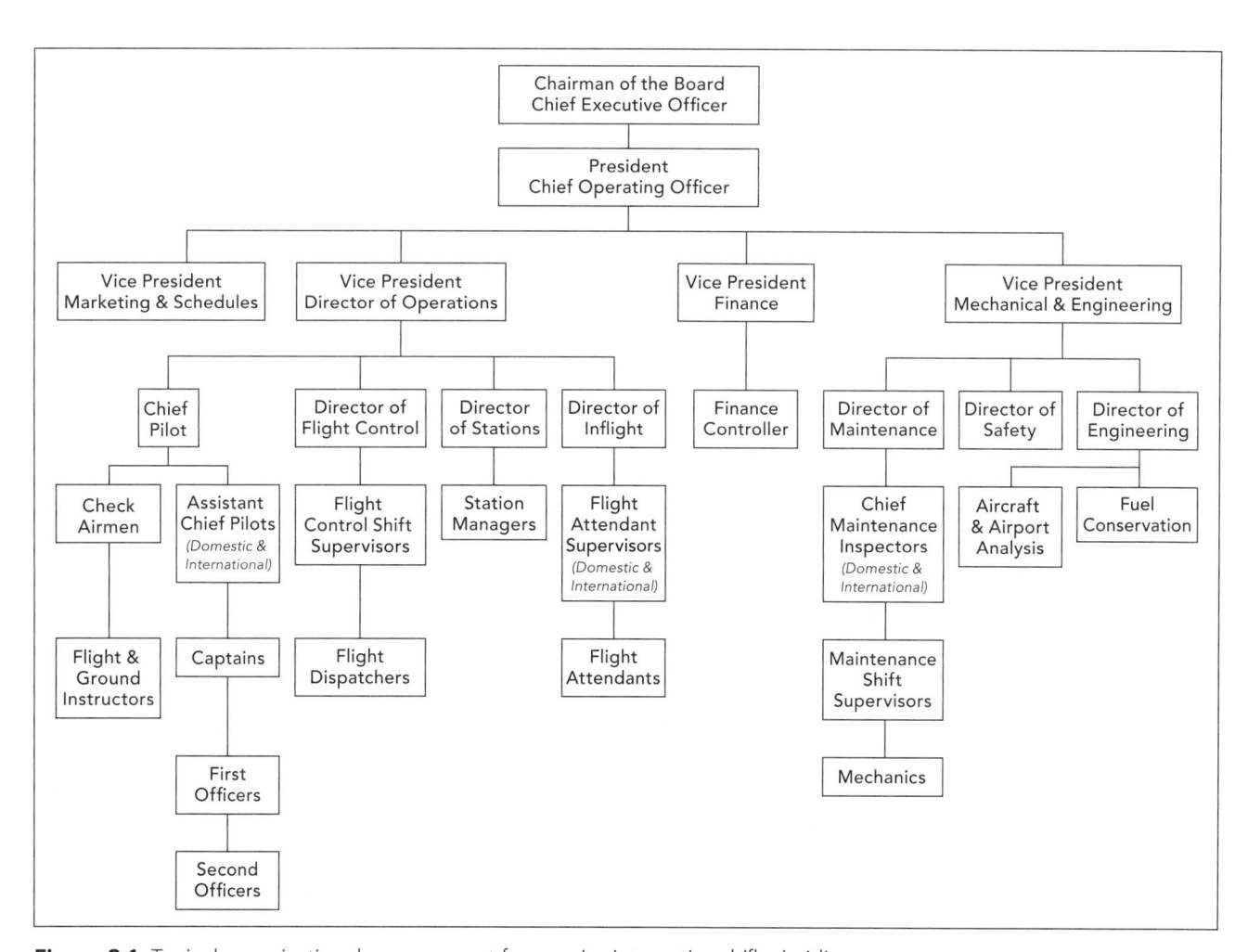

Figure 3-1. Typical organizational arrangement for a major international (flag) airline.

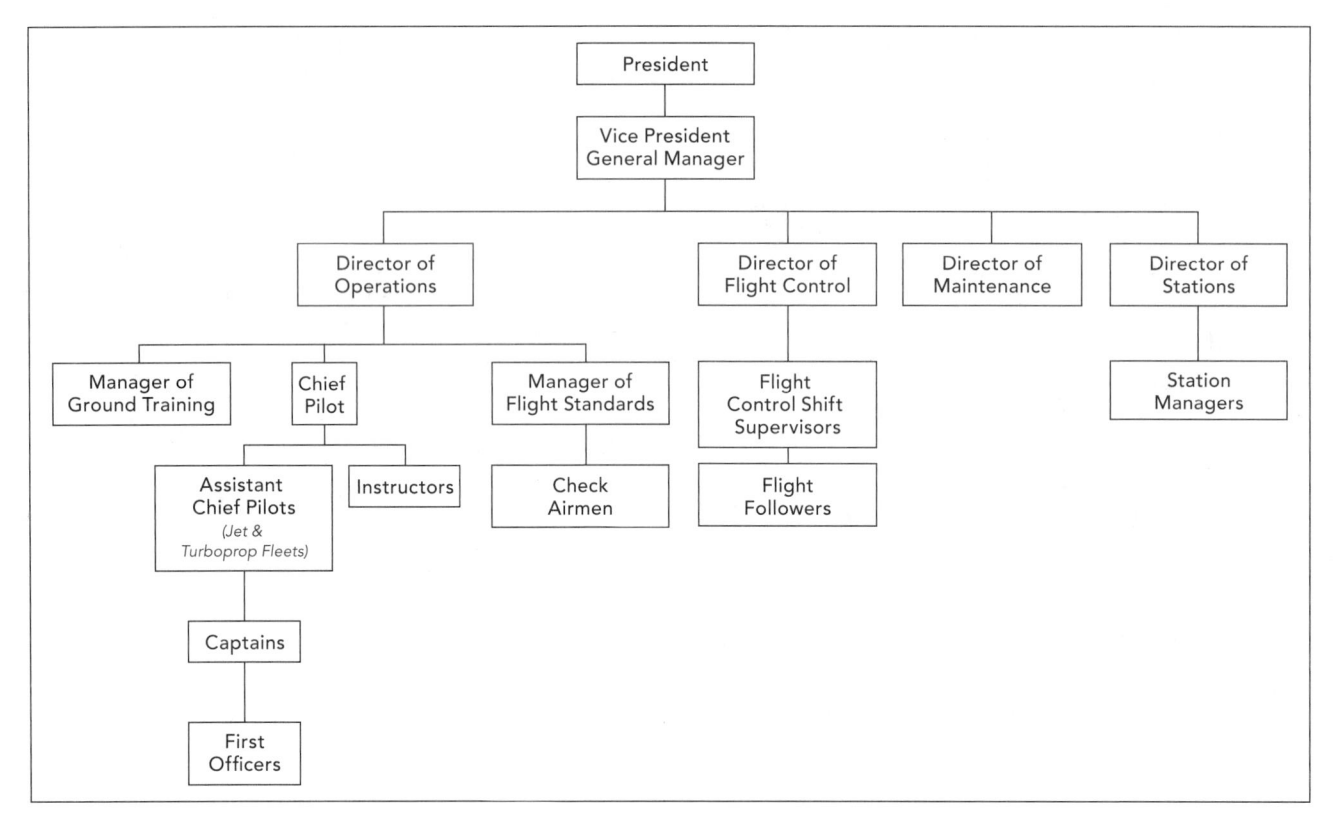

Figure 3-2. Typical organizational arrangement for a small regional airline.

There are many more positions than those required by the FARs. For a smoothly functioning airline, all of these positions must integrate and work well together. That is the role of the chief operating officer (COO). Typically, this person will hold the title of president. In a large company, this position will usually be separate from that of **chief executive officer (CEO)**. The **chief operating officer (COO)** is responsible to the chairman of the board and the board of directors of the company. The CEO's primary duties are maintaining the relationship between the air carrier and the board of directors of the company and overseeing senior financial matters such as lender relations, shareholder concerns, and representation with senior regulatory agencies. This position is responsible for the operation of all aspects of the company, not just the airline operations.

Below this level in the organization, there are as many variations in management structure as there are airlines. Each one has its own unique way of organizing and managing its affairs. Some trends seen over the years include placing all operational departments such as flight operations, maintenance, operational control, and in-flight service under a single department. The idea is that one strong operational leader can force the departments to work together smoothly. Unfortunately, many times this position has been filled by a flight-related person (usually a pilot) who was too often insensitive to the non-flight issues.

A solution to this dilemma that is sometimes used is to break off maintenance and in-flight services into separate organizational departments reporting, ultimately, to the COO. There are numerous organizational strategies, and it is not uncommon for a carrier to reorganize these functions every few years in an effort to keep them from becoming bogged down or mired in tradition. However, whenever organizational changes take place, the carrier must be sensitive to the required managerial positions and make certain that the requirements of FARs are complied with at all times.

An important department within the airline is the dispatch center, which may also be called the flight control or flight following department. This department serves to specifically implement the concept of operational control. **Dispatch** has the responsibility to plan the details of each specific flight and maintain communications with the flight at all times to keep it apprised of such things as weather, NOTAMs, and operational limitations. The dispatchers, along with the pilots and mechanics, hold a certificated position. Even though there is not a required position of head dispatcher, the FAA does mandate the presence of the dispatch function.

The **flight control** department (used in Part 121 operations) or the flight following department (common in Part 135 operations) can be thought of as the nerve center of the tactical operation of the airline. This is where aircraft routings and scheduling, equipment substitutions, and cancellations are all brought together to create the minute-by-minute plan for running the airline. This department responds to the real-world assaults on the nice neat schedules that the scheduling department has published for the month. The scheduling department develops the "perfect plan," while the folks in flight control make that plan work in an imperfect world. Flight control personnel are neither licensed (although they often come from the dispatcher ranks) nor required by the FAA. Therefore, the company may organize this important function to suit its needs. However, it will be closely scrutinized in its ability to provide and maintain operational control of the airline.

Flight control/flight following or dispatcher duties typically are as follows:

- No aircraft will be released unless it is in airworthy condition. However, an aircraft may be released with inoperative or missing components in accordance with the minimum equipment list (MEL). Consideration must be given to the number of MEL items in effect on any aircraft so that flight crew management is not compromised.
- The flight controller or flight follower will coordinate dispatch and release of 14 CFR Part 121 or Part 135 operations and monitor 14 CFR Part 91 operations (e.g., ferry flights). They will be responsible for adherence to all applicable federal and company regulations and policies and will keep the captain fully informed of all flight, traffic, and airport conditions pertinent to the safety and completion of the flight.
- The flight controller or flight follower is responsible for solutions to operational problems, caused by cancellations, delays, diversions, and mechanical interruptions.
- Each flight controller or flight follower on duty will remain on duty until each flight released by him has terminated or until properly relieved by another flight follower.
- A flight controller or flight follower will check with crew scheduling, as required prior to releasing any flight, checking that the flight crew is within their legal rest, duty, and flight time limitations.
- The flight controller or flight follower is responsible for flight planning, release generation, and flight following of each flight within his or her jurisdiction.
- The flight controller or flight follower will maintain a current summary list of all inoperative or missing components on company aircraft.
- All aircraft departing a station for the purpose of revenue flight must be authorized by an approved flight controller or flight follower.
- Flight controllers or flight followers must ensure flights may only be released to an airport if the appropriate weather reports and forecasts or combination thereof indicate that the destination and alternate weather conditions at the estimated arrival time at each airport will be at or above authorized landing minimums.
- No flight may depart unless both the captain and the flight controller or flight follower are thoroughly familiar with the reported and forecast weather and have considered all factors and conditions. The captain and flight controller/flight follower will signify their responsibility by signing the flight release for Part 121 or Part 135 flights. The flight controller or flight follower will provide the captain the following information immediately prior to each flight:
  - All available weather reports and forecasts or subsequent changes thereto affecting the proposed flight
  - All current NOTAMs for origination, destination, and alternate airports, plus any enroute abnormalities that might affect the proposed flight
  - All significant meteorological information (SIGMETs) or convective SIGMETs affecting the proposed route of flight
  - Advisories of all anticipated adverse changes in the weather phenomena affecting the proposed flight

- All inoperative or missing components on the aircraft to be flown and any restrictions that may apply; any irregularities of facilities and services, even though a NOTAM has not been issued
- Anticipated or known traffic delays
- Field condition reports and braking action reports that might adversely affect the operation
- Forecasts or reported icing conditions that exist, including the intensity thereof
- Any information not discussed above, but having an adverse effect on a safe operation

Summary

This chapter has examined the organizational and managerial structure of 14 CFR Part 121 and Part 135 air carriers. We've discussed the minimum management positions the FAA requires in order to obtain and maintain a certificate and the experience required for personnel filling those positions. In the next chapter, we will see that the FAA requires a description of the air carrier's operational structure to be contained in the operations manual or the general operating manual.

Important Terms in Chapter 3

active control
chief executive officer (CEO)
chief inspector
chief operating officer (COO)
chief pilot
director of maintenance (DM)
director of operations (DO)
director of safety
dispatch
flight control
flight dispatcher (or dispatcher)
flight follower
flight following
operational control
passive control

Chapter 3 Exam

1. As per the Part 121 requirements found in 14 CFR §119.65, what five specific management positions are required for a Part 121 air carrier?

    a. Director of maintenance, director of quality assurance, chief pilot, director of operations, and chief counsel

    b. Director of safety, director of operations, chief pilot, director of maintenance, and chief inspector

    c. Director of operations, chairman of the board of directors, director of inflight, chief pilot, chief inspector

    d. Chief pilot, chief inspector, director of maintenance, director of safety, and director of inflight

2. As per the Part 135 requirements found in 14 CFR §119.69, what three specific management positions are required for a Part 135 air carrier?

    a. Director of safety, director of maintenance, and chief pilot

    b. Director of operations, director of safety, and director of maintenance

    c. Director of inspections, chief pilot, and director of maintenance

    d. Director of operations, chief pilot, and director of maintenance

3. If an air carrier conducts any operations in which the pilot-in-command is required to hold an airline transport certificate, what two required management positions, for both Part 121 and Part 135 air carriers, must be filled by a pilot holding an air transport pilot certificate (ATP)?

    a. Chief pilot and chief inspector
    b. Chief pilot and director of safety
    c. Director of operations and chief pilot
    d. Chief director and chief pilot

4. What minimum required management positions (Part 121) must be filled by a mechanic holding an airframe and powerplant certificate (A&P)?

    a. Director of maintenance and chief inspector
    b. Chief inspector, director of safety, and director of maintenance
    c. Director of maintenance, director of operations, and chief inspector
    d. Director of maintenance and director of safety

5. What required management position is responsible for the overall *operational control* of an air carrier's flight?

    a. Chief pilot
    b. Director of operations
    c. Pilot-in-command
    d. Director of inflight

6. Which department of an air carrier serves to specifically implement the concept of operational control?

    a. The dispatch center, flight control or flight following center
    b. The in-flight tactical center
    c. The maintenance control center
    d. The director of operations office

7. The director of safety is required to hold which FAA certificates?

    a. Air transport pilot certificate (ATP) and airframe and powerplant certificate (A&P)
    b. ATP only
    c. A&P only
    d. None

8. 14 CFR Part 1 defines *operational control* as

    a. ensuring only crewmembers trained and qualified in accordance with the applicable regulations are assigned to conduct a flight.
    b. ensuring each flight has complied with the conditions specified for release before it is allowed to depart.
    c. the exercise of authority over initiating, conducting, and terminating a flight.
    d. designating a pilot-in-command.

9. Which best describes the concept of operational control?

    a. The pilot-in-command must, at all times, ensure that the flight is operated in accord with all applicable regulations.
    b. The dispatcher must, at all times, keep the flight informed as to changing weather and anticipated flight conditions.
    c. Under routine operations, the flight is conducted under control and through consensus with the appropriate authority within the company. In emergency situations, it is conducted in this manner to the extent possible, subject to the captain's emergency authority.
    d. None of the above.

10. What is the role of active flight control in an airline?

    a. Active flight control is part of the maintenance organization that oversees and repairs flight control automation equipment.
    b. Active flight control is the part of the airline organization that oversees the tactical operation of the airline.
    c. Active flight control is the planning part of the airline that develops monthly and quarterly operational plans.
    d. Active flight control is the same thing as crew scheduling.

CHAPTER 4
OPERATING MANUALS: REQUIREMENTS AND DEVELOPMENT

Everything in the company manual—policy, warnings, instructions, the works—can be summed up to read, "Captain, it's your baby."
—anonymous

The FARs seek to ensure that everyone involved in a safety-critical function has a detailed description or explanation of how that function is to be performed. This begins with the requirements for the specific management positions, as discussed previously in Chapter 3. Those positions set specific responsibilities upon specific people within the carrier. By doing this, the FAA knows exactly who is accountable for the operational areas of the carrier. The next issue is how to "get the word out," and this is done by requiring specific manuals to be prepared, distributed, and updated continually. The carrier must do this to comply with both its ops specs and the FARs.

The manual requirements of 14 CFR Part 121 are set forth in Subpart G. The manual requirements of 14 CFR Part 135 are set forth in Sections 135.21 and 135.23.

Approval of Manuals

The required manuals must be reviewed and approved by the operator's FAA principal operations inspector (POI) or other FAA inspector assigned to the air carrier. The inspector reviews the manuals to determine whether they comply with all current Federal Aviation Regulations. The inspector also ensures the manuals contain operating policies and procedures in enough detail that the operator's personnel can properly carry out the policies or procedures for which they are responsible with the *highest degree of safety*. The FAA encourages its inspectors to offer guidance and advice to air carriers in the crafting of their manuals. However, the actual production of an acceptable manual is the sole responsibility of the air carrier.

Manual Requirements: 14 CFR Part 121

14 CFR §121.131 requires all certificate holders to prepare and maintain a number of manuals.

14 CFR §121.133 requires each certificate holder to prepare and keep current a manual for the use and guidance of flight, ground operations, and management personnel in conducting its operations.

14 CFR §121.135 describes, in detail, the contents required to be in the manual.

- Flight operations for flight personnel
- Ground operations for ground service personnel
- Management policy and procedures for management personnel

With the widespread use of tablet computers by air carriers over the last few years, the FAA has issued a legal interpretation in which it clarified that an electronic version of a manual is satisfactory. This interpretation also clarified that if a manual is provided in electronic form, the certificate holder must provide sufficient technological resources to permit crewmembers "to review effectively the applicable portions of the manual while performing their duties." Whether on paper, a tablet, microfilm, microfiche or computer, the system used must be approved by an appropriate Flight Standards District office (FSDO) *or* by a Certificate Holding District Office (CHDO). Previously, approvals had to be made by the specific FSDO that maintained the carrier's file. If one FSDO is backlogged, it is now authorized to send the file to a different FSDO for review and approval for that carrier. The FSDO providing that assistance is then referred to as the CHDO for that specific application.

14 CFR §121.135 sets forth items required to be in the manual. Section 121.135(a)(1) says it all:

(a) Each manual required by §121.133 must—
  (1) Include instructions and information necessary to allow the personnel concerned to perform their duties and responsibilities with a high degree of safety.
  (2) Be in a form that is easy to revise;
  (3) Have the date of last revision on each page concerned; and
  (4) Not be contrary to any applicable Federal regulation and, in the case of a flag or supplemental operation, any applicable foreign regulation, or the certificate holder's operations specifications or operating certificate.

To achieve this, the FAA reviews the air carrier's operations manual to ensure these instructions contain clear descriptions of the duties and responsibilities for each type of employee group (i.e., mechanic, flight crew, management personnel, etc.).

The FARs also require that the manual be in an easy-to-revise form, have a date of revision printed on each page, and be consistent with the regulations and the carrier's ops specs. In order for the employee or FAA representative to quickly determine whether the manual is current, each manual should contain a revision control log (Figure 4-1) or similar section. Each revision is numbered, dated, and logged in the revision control page.

The manual must also contain a description of the types and kinds of operations the air carrier is authorized to conduct. In addition, the operations manual must contain information on the authorized areas of enroute operations in which the air carrier is approved to operate. This must include the types of aircraft authorized, required flight crew staffing, and specific enroute and instrument approach procedures authorizations and requirements.

While the FARs only require the air carrier to produce a single manual, the carrier is permitted to break the manual down into "sub-manuals." That is, the required information doesn't have to be all in one volume or publication, which would yield an unwieldy publication and work against its general usage. 14 CFR §121.135(b) sets forth the exact information that must be in each manual or manual part:

14 CFR §121.135—Manual contents.

(b) The manual may be in two or more separate parts, containing together all of the following information, but each part must contain that part of the information that is appropriate for each group of personnel:
  (1) General policies.
  (2) Duties and responsibilities of each crewmember, appropriate members of the ground organization, and management personnel.
  (3) Reference to appropriate Federal Aviation Regulations.
  (4) Flight dispatching and operational control, including procedures for coordinated dispatch or flight control or flight following procedures, as applicable.
  (5) En route flight, navigation, and communication procedures, including procedures for the dispatch or release or continuance of flight if any item of equipment required for the particular type of operation becomes inoperative or unserviceable en route.
  (6) For domestic or flag operations, appropriate information from the en route operations specifications, including for each approved route the types of airplanes authorized, the type of operation such as VFR, IFR, day, night, etc., and any other pertinent information.
  (7) For supplemental operations, appropriate information from the operations specifications, including the area of operations authorized, the types of airplanes authorized, the type of operation such as VFR, IFR, day, night, etc., and any other pertinent information.
  (8) Appropriate information from the airport operations specifications, including for each airport—
    (i) Its location (domestic and flag operations only);
    (ii) Its designation (regular, alternate, provisional, etc.) (domestic and flag operations only);
    (iii) The types of airplanes authorized (domestic and flag operations only);
    (iv) Instrument approach procedures;

Revision Log						10 Nov 15
Revision Number	**Revision Date**	**Revision Number**	**Revision Date**	**Revision Number**	**Revision Date**	
1	10 Feb 07					
2	20 Apr 07					
3	3 Sept 07					
4	29 Jan 08					
5	11 May 08					
6	22 DEC 08					
7	1 FEB 09					
8	8 Jun 09					
9	17 Oct 09					
10	7 Mar 10					
11	15 Mar 10					
12	30 Aug 10					
13	9 SEPT 10					
14	1 JAN 11					
15	9 Jan 11					
16	12 Feb 11					
17	15 FEB 11					
18	3 Mar 11					
19						
20						
21						
22						

Figure 4-1. Revision control log.

  (v) Landing and takeoff minimums; and
  (vi) Any other pertinent information.
(9) Takeoff, en route, and landing weight limitations.
(10) For ETOPS, airplane performance data to support all phases of these operations.
(11) Procedures for familiarizing passengers with the use of emergency equipment, during flight.
(12) Emergency equipment and procedures.
(13) The method of designating succession of command of flight crewmembers.
(14) Procedures for determining the usability of landing and takeoff areas, and for disseminating pertinent information thereon to operations personnel.
(15) Procedures for operating in periods of ice, hail, thunderstorms, turbulence, or any potentially hazardous meteorological condition.
(16) Each training program curriculum required by §121.403.
(17) Instructions and procedures for maintenance, preventive maintenance, and servicing.

(18) Time limitations, or standards for determining time limitations, for overhauls, inspections, and checks of airframes, engines, propellers, appliances and emergency equipment.

(19) Procedures for refueling aircraft, eliminating fuel contamination, protection from fire (including electrostatic protection), and supervising and protecting passengers during refueling.

(20) Airworthiness inspections, including instructions covering procedures, standards, responsibilities, and authority of inspection personnel.

(21) Methods and procedures for maintaining the aircraft weight and center of gravity within approved limits.

(22) Where applicable, pilot and dispatcher route and airport qualification procedures.

(23) Accident notification procedures.

(24) After February 15, 2008, for passenger flag operations and for those supplemental operations that are not all-cargo operations outside the 48 contiguous States and Alaska,
   (i) For ETOPS greater than 180 minutes a specific passenger recovery plan for each ETOPS Alternate Airport used in those operations, and
   (ii) For operations in the North Polar Area and South Polar Area a specific passenger recovery plan for each diversion airport used in those operations.

(25) (i) Procedures and information, as described in paragraph (b)(25)(ii) of this section, to assist each crewmember and person performing or directly supervising the following job functions involving items for transport on an aircraft:
   (A) Acceptance;
   (B) Rejection;
   (C) Handling;
   (D) Storage incidental to transport;
   (E) Packaging of company material; or
   (F) Loading.
  (ii) Ensure that the procedures and information described in this paragraph are sufficient to assist the person in identifying packages that are marked or labeled as containing hazardous materials or that show signs of containing undeclared hazardous materials. The procedures and information must include:
   (A) Procedures for rejecting packages that do not conform to the Hazardous Materials Regulations in 49 CFR parts 171 through 180 or that appear to contain undeclared hazardous materials;
   (B) Procedures for complying with the hazardous materials incident reporting requirements of 49 CFR 171.15 and 171.16 and discrepancy reporting requirements of 49 CFR 175.31
   (C) The certificate holder's hazmat policies and whether the certificate holder is authorized to carry, or is prohibited from carrying, hazardous materials; and
   (D) If the certificate holder's operations specifications permit the transport of hazardous materials, procedures and information to ensure the following:
     (1) That packages containing hazardous materials are properly offered and accepted in compliance with 49 CFR parts 171 through 180;
     (2) That packages containing hazardous materials are properly handled, stored, packaged, loaded, and carried on board an aircraft in compliance with 49 CFR parts 171 through 180;
     (3) That the requirements for Notice to the Pilot in Command (49 CFR 175.33) are complied with; and
     (4) That aircraft replacement parts, consumable materials or other items regulated by 49 CFR parts 171 through 180 are properly handled, packaged, and transported.

(26) Other information or instructions relating to safety.

(c) Each certificate holder shall maintain at least one complete copy of the manual at its principal base of operations.

(14 CFR §121.135)

An air carrier will typically develop a series of manuals tailored to its particular needs covering this information and more. The FAA allows wide latitude in the organization of an air carrier's manuals. Some common manual titles in use at many air carriers are described below.

The Airplane Flight Manual, Company Flight Manual, or Flight Crew Operations Manual

The **airplane flight manual** (AFM) is prepared by the manufacturer and approved by the FAA Aircraft Certification Office under the provisions of 14 CFR 21.5. 14 CFR §§121.141, 135.81(c) and 91.31(b) require, at a minimum, an FAA-approved AFM to be kept by the carrier. The AFM is designed to give the crew all of the operational and performance information it needs in order to operate the aircraft. In the case of Part 121 operators, the certificate holder shall carry *either* an approved airplane flight manual *or* it may elect to create and carry the manual required by Section 121.133, *if* it contains the information required to be contained in the applicable airplane flight manual. This is simply an AFM developed by, or for, a specific operator.

This alternative manual to the AFM is sometimes called the **company flight manual** (CFM). If the certificate holder elects to carry a CFM in lieu of an AFM, it may revise the operating procedures sections and modify the presentation of performance data from the applicable airplane flight manual. These revised operating procedures and modified performance data presentations must be approved by the Administrator and clearly identified as meeting the airplane flight manual requirements. The AFM/CFM includes the necessary information on aircraft systems, aircraft limitations, specific procedures (e.g., normal and abnormal checklists), techniques, and operating methods by which a specific aircraft should be operated. It must contain, at a minimum, all of the procedures required by the AFM and must include enough procedural details to allow a flight crew to operate the aircraft to the highest level of safety.

The current trend is away from using company flight manuals in favor of using the manufacturer's AFM and manufacturer's suggested operating procedures combined in a manual the FAA calls a **flight crew operations manual** (FCOM).

Note that this AFM/CFM manual requirement is separate and distinct from the rest of the **flight operations manual** required in 14 CFR §121.133. However, Section 121.141 does allow for all of the information to be placed in one book. It is, as we've discussed, far more common for carriers to give the flight crews two separate manuals along with approach and enroute procedure charts. These two manuals would be the flight operations manual (FOM) required in 14 CFR §121.133 and the airplane flight manual or company flight manual (AFM or CFM) required in 14 CFR §121.141.

General Operations Manual

The **general operations manual** (GOM) is prepared by the air carrier and includes flight operations material not related specifically to a particular aircraft's operation. 14 CFR §121.135 specifies topics that must be addressed in the air carrier's GOM. The GOM contains clear descriptions of the types of operations the air carrier is authorized to conduct. The GOM includes information such as policies, procedures, and guidance necessary for flight operations personnel to perform their duties with the highest degree of safety. The information in this manual is not aircraft or fleet specific but covers the entire airline operation. Information and policies pertaining to passenger handling, the carriage of dangerous goods, safety training, and general company "housekeeping" information (i.e., employee appearance standards, jumpseat policy, and important company phone numbers) can all be found in the GOM. When the air carrier operates a wide variety of aircraft types, the FAA prefers the flight operations procedures common to all of the air carrier's aircraft be published in the GOM as opposed to in a particular aircraft's company flight manual.

General Maintenance Manual

The **general maintenance manual** (GMM) is prepared by the air carrier or aircraft manufacturer and covers the airworthiness information for a particular model of aircraft. The GMM contains policies and procedures for an air carrier's technical operations organization (i.e., mechanics, inspectors, and engineering support personnel) so they may provide safe and reliable aircraft, powerplants, and other components for daily flight operations.

Management Policy and Procedures Manual

The third major area of guidance required by 14 CFR §121.133 is for management policy and procedures, which are generally placed in the **management policy and procedures manual**. This manual provides instruction and guidance for the myriad of "behind the scenes" things that must be done in any organization to keep it functioning smoothly and effectively. This manual can include issues ranging from how the accounting for the airline will be organized, to whether zebras may be carried as live freight. In short, it covers the functioning of the complex organization of the many divisions and departments that are needed behind the scenes to run the airline but that are not structured within the operational frameworks of flight operations, ground (airport) operations, or maintenance. It is primarily used by the staff and support organizations in administering the business aspects of the carrier.

Access and Distribution of Manuals

In order to facilitate the FAA's ability to inspect an air carrier, each carrier must keep at least one complete copy of the manual(s) at its principal base of operations (14 CFR §121.135[c]).

14 CFR §121.137(a)(3) further requires an air carrier to provide to representatives of the Administrator duplicate manual(s), which will be kept at the FAA certificate-holding district office. These manuals must be complete and current at all times. The manuals are to be used by the FAA to review any procedures or incidents at the carrier. In addition to these copies, the carrier must set up a publication and distribution system that ensures that each employee who may require the information in the manual either has a manual or has access to the manual. This distribution system must be spelled out, indicating exactly who has to physically possess a manual (for example, pilots must have a flight crew operations manual, while mechanics must have a maintenance manual available to them while performing their work).

14 CFR §121.137(a) states that the carrier must distribute the manual and its updates to appropriate ground operations and maintenance personnel and flight crewmembers. The carrier must also furnish a complete manual (or collection of manuals) to the specific representatives of the FAA assigned to that carrier.

14 CFR §121.137(b) then further requires that each person assigned to hold a manual must keep it up to date with the changes and additions and have it accessible while performing his or her assigned duties.

In the case of the maintenance manuals, these are very often kept in some type of storage retrieval system such as microfilm, microfiche, or computer files. Given the detail of the maintenance diagrams and instructions, this is really the only feasible way to keep these manuals. 14 CFR §121.137(c) provides specific relief to the carrier to develop an alternative means of distributing the maintenance manual. It only requires approval of the Administrator, which, practically speaking, means the principal maintenance inspector (PMI) or maintenance inspector (MI) assigned to the carrier.

Because by the nature of their operations supplemental carriers don't operate to the same locations on a repetitive basis, 14 CFR §121.139 requires them to have a copy of the entire manual aboard the aircraft for use by the contract personnel at those locations. Further, if the carrier maintains the maintenance manual in a form other than a paper manual, it must carry an appropriate reading device with the aircraft. This ensures that the personnel at remote locations will have the ability to read all parts of the manuals when performing their tasks.

Manual Requirements: 14 CFR Part 135

14 CFR §135.21 makes the requirements to prepare and maintain manuals applicable to all Part 135 air carriers *except those employing only one pilot*. Section 135.23 sets forth the specific form the manuals must take. First, they must contain, at a minimum, the following major provisions:

- *flight operations* for flight personnel
- *ground operations* for ground service personnel
- *maintenance procedures* for maintenance personnel

The requirements for preparing and distributing the manual are very similar to those required by Part 121 except that the regulations recognize that the size of the operation may be so limited that safety may be met by allowing some other method of distributing the manuals. By and large, the manual design and preparation will be the same for Part 121 and 135 manuals.

14 CFR §135.23 also spells out the specific contents of the manual. While these requirements are similar to those in Part 121, there are some differences, the most significant of which is the reliance on the pilot-in-command to perform many different functions. The small size of many Part 135 air carriers dictates that the pilot-in-command must wear many different "hats" (e.g., flight attendant, flight dispatcher, maintenance coordinator, etc.). Following are the items that the manual must contain as specified in 14 CFR §135.23.

14 CFR §135.23—Manual contents.

(a) The name of each management person required under §119.69(a) of this chapter who is authorized to act for the certificate holder, the person's assigned area of responsibility, the person's duties, responsibilities, and authority, and the name and title of each person authorized to exercise operational control under §135.77;

(b) Procedures for ensuring compliance with aircraft weight and balance limitations and, for multiengine aircraft, for determining compliance with §135.185;

(c) Copies of the certificate holder's operations specifications or appropriate extracted information, including area of operations authorized, category and class of aircraft authorized, crew complements, and types of operations authorized;

(d) Procedures for complying with accident notification requirements;

(e) Procedures for ensuring that the pilot in command knows that required airworthiness inspections have been made and that the aircraft has been approved for return to service in compliance with applicable maintenance requirements;

(f) Procedures for reporting and recording mechanical irregularities that come to the attention of the pilot in command before, during, and after completion of a flight;

(g) Procedures to be followed by the pilot in command for determining that mechanical irregularities or defects reported for previous flights have been corrected or that correction has been deferred;

(h) Procedures to be followed by the pilot in command to obtain maintenance, preventive maintenance, and servicing of the aircraft at a place where previous arrangements have not been made by the operator, when the pilot is authorized to so act for the operator;

(i) Procedures under §135.179 for the release for, or continuation of, flight if any item of equipment required for the particular type of operation becomes inoperative or unserviceable en route;

(j) Procedures for refueling aircraft, eliminating fuel contamination, protecting from fire (including electrostatic protection), and supervising and protecting passengers during refueling;

(k) Procedures to be followed by the pilot in command in the briefing under §135.117;

(l) Flight locating procedures, when applicable;

(m) Procedures for ensuring compliance with emergency procedures, including a list of the functions assigned each category of required crewmembers in connection with an emergency and emergency evacuation duties under §135.123;

(n) En route qualification procedures for pilots, when applicable;

(o) The approved aircraft inspection program, when applicable;

(p) (1) Procedures and information, as described in paragraph (p)(2) of this section, to assist each crewmember and person performing or directly supervising the following job functions involving items for transport on an aircraft:
  (i) Acceptance;
  (ii) Rejection;
  (iii) Handling;
  (iv) Storage incidental to transport;
  (v) Packaging of company material; or
  (vi) Loading.
 (2) Ensure that the procedures and information described in this paragraph are sufficient to assist a person in identifying packages that are marked or labeled as containing hazardous materials or that show signs of containing undeclared hazardous materials. The procedures and information must include:
  (i) Procedures for rejecting packages that do not conform to the Hazardous Materials Regulations in 49 CFR parts 171 through 180 or that appear to contain undeclared hazardous materials;
  (ii) Procedures for complying with the hazardous materials incident reporting requirements of 49 CFR 171.15 and 171.16 and discrepancy reporting requirements of 49 CFR 175.31.
  (iii) The certificate holder's hazmat policies and whether the certificate holder is authorized to carry, or is prohibited from carrying, hazardous materials; and
  (iv) If the certificate holder's operations specifications permit the transport of hazardous materials, procedures and information to ensure the following:
   (A) That packages containing hazardous materials are properly offered and accepted in compliance with 49 CFR parts 171 through 180;

(B) That packages containing hazardous materials are properly handled, stored, packaged, loaded and carried on board an aircraft in compliance with 49 CFR parts 171 through 180;
(C) That the requirements for Notice to the Pilot in Command (49 CFR 175.33) are complied with; and
(D) That aircraft replacement parts, consumable materials or other items regulated by 49 CFR parts 171 through 180 are properly handled, packaged, and transported.

(q) Procedures for the evacuation of persons who may need the assistance of another person to move expeditiously to an exit if an emergency occurs; and
(r) If required by §135.385, an approved Destination Airport Analysis establishing runway safety margins at destination airports, taking into account the following factors as supported by published aircraft performance data supplied by the aircraft manufacturer for the appropriate runway conditions—
  (1) Pilot qualifications and experience;
  (2) Aircraft performance data to include normal, abnormal and emergency procedures as supplied by the aircraft manufacturer;
  (3) Airport facilities and topography;
  (4) Runway conditions (including contamination);
  (5) Airport or area weather reporting;
  (6) Appropriate additional runway safety margins, if required;
  (7) Airplane inoperative equipment;
  (8) Environmental conditions; and
  (9) Other criteria affecting aircraft performance.
(s) Other procedures and policy instructions regarding the certificate holder's operations issued by the certificate holder.

(14 CFR §135.23)

Periodic Review of Manuals

An air carrier's POI is responsible for developing a plan to periodically review an operator's manual system. The periodic review of manuals is necessary because of the constantly changing aviation regulatory environment and the possibility of changes in the air carrier's flight operations. Each POI is directed to inspect at least one portion of an air carrier's manual system annually, with the entire manual system being reviewed over a period of one to three years.

Operational Control

In reviewing the requirements for an air carrier's operating manual, the FAA wants to see that a carrier's operational control procedures are included. Remember, 14 CFR §1.1 defines operational control as *"the exercise of authority over initiating, conducting, and terminating a flight."* The FAA requires the air carrier's operating manual to thoroughly describe the procedures, duties, and responsibilities of pilots and operational control personnel. The FAA also requires the general operating manual to include flight dispatching or flight following procedures as discussed in Chapter 3. Specifically, the FAA requires policies for handling late flights, adverse weather conditions, and procedures for discontinuing a flight when confronted with unsafe conditions to be clearly described in the air carrier's general operating manual. Finally, the operations manual must describe the relationship between flight dispatchers, maintenance coordinators, crew schedulers, and flight crew.

A thorough discussion of manuals would not be complete without looking at the latest technology being used to access and display all that printed data: electronic flight bags.

Electronic Flight Bag (EFB)

From the earliest days of aviation, pilots have relied upon paper manuals and charts to safely operate and navigate their way around the globe. Flight crew operating manuals, maintenance manuals, and performance manuals, not to mention thousands of pages of navigational charts and maps, added up to a hundred pounds of paper sitting in every cockpit of an air carrier's fleet. With the advent of the tablet computer and its use as an **electronic flight bag** (EFB), all this paper is now a thing of the past.

In FAA Advisory Circular (AC) 120-76C, *Guidelines for the Certification, Airworthiness, and Operational Use of Electronic Flight Bags*, the FAA defines an EFB as "An electronic display system intended primarily for flight deck or cabin crew member use that includes the hardware and software necessary to support an intended function. EFB devices can display a variety of aviation data or perform basic calculations (e.g., performance data, fuel calculations, etc.)." The EFB eliminates the need for paper and other reference materials often found in the pilot's carry-on flight bag, hence the name. An EFB can perform basic flight planning calculations and display a variety of digital documentation, including navigational charts, operations manuals, systems manuals and aircraft checklists. Many EFBs include a moving map navigation display for both enroute navigation and ground taxi operations, which greatly improves the flight crew's situational awareness. Additionally, the once burdensome task of completing navigation and company manual revisions that flight crews and other airline personnel performed on a sometimes daily basis is now done automatically by the EFB, so every manual or navigational chart is kept continuously up-to-date. Another benefit with EFB use is the almost instantaneous capability to communicate operational information with an air carrier's entire employee group that may be dispersed across the globe.

Electronic flight bags can be either an **installed EFB** or **portable EFB** (e.g., a tablet or personal electronic device [PED]).

Installed EFB

Installed EFBs are "hard-wired" (installed in the aircraft) and considered part of the aircraft, and therefore would be covered by the aircraft's airworthiness approval. Installed EFBs are fully certified as part of the aircraft avionics system and are integrated with aircraft systems such as the FMS and GPS. Not only do installed EFBs display such things as the aircraft flight manual, flight crew operating manual, and aircraft position on navigational and taxi charts, but they are also able to display an aircraft's position on navigational approach charts, depict real-time weather, and perform many complex flight planning tasks.

Portable EFB

The portable EFB is the most common form in use today. Typically, the portable EFB is mounted in the cockpit using suction cups or another type of mount (e.g., kneeboard). The FAA requires the EFB to be easily removable from its mounting device without the use of tools, and it must not block emergency egress out of the cockpit. Portable EFBs must be secured to a certified mount in order to be allowed use in all flight phases. Many portable systems are very capable. Some even include a GPS and are able to display the aircraft's position on navigational charts. The main advantage of the portable EFB over the installed EFB is cost. The typical portable EFB costs around $500 dollars while an installed EFB may cost as much as $25,000 or more.

Regardless of whether an air carrier uses an installed or portable EFB, the FAA requires that at least two operational EFBs be available in the cockpit in order to go to a completely **paperless cockpit**—that is, remove all paper manuals and aeronautical charts, checklists, or other data required by the operating rules. In addition, the design of the EFB must ensure that no single failure or common mode error may cause the loss of required aeronautical information. In AC 120-76C, the FAA has published EFB guidance for certificated air carriers on the installation and development of EFB training programs and making the transition to a completely paperless cockpit.

Summary

In this chapter, we've discussed the manual requirements set forth in 14 CFR §§121.133 and 135.21. These are the FAA requirements that each operator prepare and keep current a general operations manual or series of manuals containing guidance for use by ground and flight personnel during the conduct of the air carrier's operations. These manuals must be in an easy-to-revise form and be consistent with the regulations and the carrier's ops specs. Finally, each carrier must keep at least one complete copy of the manual(s) at its principal base of operations and provide duplicate manual(s) to representatives of the Administrator, which will be kept at the FAA certificate-holding district office.

In the next chapter, we will look at the airman and crewmember certificate requirements for Part 121 and Part 135 air carriers.

Important Terms in Chapter 4

airplane flight manual (AFM)
company flight manual (CFM)
Certificate Holding District Office (CHDO)
electronic flight bag (EFB)
flight crew operations manual (FCOM)
general maintenance manual (GMM)
general operations manual (GOM)
installed EFB
management policy and procedures manual
paperless cockpit
portable EFB

Chapter 4 Exam

1. When a Part 121 carrier is preparing the required operational manuals, how would you suggest that it proceed?
    a. Since the carrier is responsible for the preparation of the manual, it should assemble a team, develop the manual and, when complete, submit it to the FAA.
    b. It should acquire a copy of another air carrier's manual and duplicate the provisions for that airline.
    c. The carrier should contact the FAA office that it will deal with and work collaboratively with the assigned inspectors.

2. Where would a Part 121 pilot or dispatcher look to find the procedures to use in planning a flight that is forecast to have icing and very turbulent weather conditions?
    a. The flight operations manual required by 14 CFR §121.133
    b. The FAA-approved AFM required by 14 CFR §21.5
    c. The operational planning manual required by 14 CFR §121.133

3. Which manuals are required to be carried aboard an air carrier aircraft operated under Part 121?
    a. The airplane flight manual or company flight manual and the ground operations manual
    b. The airplane flight manual or company flight manual and the pilot's emergency procedures handbook
    c. The airplane flight manual or company flight manual and the certificate holder's Section 121.133 manual parts pertaining to flight operations

4. What manuals are required to be aboard a Part 121 air carrier aircraft engaged in supplemental operations?
    a. The AFM or CFM and the entire 14 CFR §121.133 manual including all of its subparts
    b. The AFM or CFM and the Section 121.133 manual concerning flight operations
    c. The AFM or CFM and the ground operation manual

5. Which manual must be used by a Part 121 carrier to provide ground service crews the necessary information about procedures to use for a particular ground operational situation such as refueling an aircraft with passengers aboard?
    a. The carrier's AFM or CFM
    b. The general operations manual
    c. No manual is required. These issues may be covered in operational bulletins posted throughout the facility.

6. Where must an air carrier maintain a complete copy of the Section 121.133 manual(s)?
    a. At each operational station (airport) where the company operates
    b. At the carrier's principal base of operations
    c. At the corporate offices

7. What process is used to ensure that any given manual is properly maintained and contains up-to-date information?
    a. Whenever revisions are made to any procedure, a new manual is issued.
    b. The manual(s) must contain a revision control page that shows the applicable effective dates of every page.
    c. The entire manual(s) is/are periodically reprinted with all current information.

8. Which manual must be issued in paper form?
    a. The flight operations manual
    b. The ground operations manual
    c. The maintenance manual
    d. None of the above

9. If a Part 121 supplemental carrier has issued its maintenance manual using microfiche or a computer file format and must carry it on the aircraft, what must also be carried aboard the aircraft?

   a. A compatible reading device that produces a legible image of the maintenance information and instructions

   b. A contact number for remote maintenance station personnel to contact the carrier's maintenance department

   c. A backup paper copy of the manual to be used in case the microfiche or computer file is corrupted

10. Operational control of a flight refers to

    a. exercising the privileges of pilot-in-command of an aircraft.

    b. the specific duties of any required crewmember.

    c. exercising authority over initiating, conducting or terminating a flight.

11. Which manual would contain guidance on passenger handling policies?

    a. General maintenance manual

    b. Airplane flight manual or company flight manual

    c. Ground operations manual

    d. Airman's information manual

12. When is a Part 121 supplemental air carrier required to carry a maintenance manual on board the aircraft?

    a. Any time the aircraft is carrying passengers on a "live" revenue flight.

    b. Whenever an Air Carrier Safety Inspector deems a particular aircraft has fallen below a certain maintenance reliability threshold also known as the "Mendoza Line," which increases the probability of a maintenance irregularity occurring in the near future.

    c. There is no requirement for a Part 121 supplemental or Part 135 air carrier to carry a maintenance manual.

    d. Supplemental air carriers are required to have a copy of the entire manual aboard the aircraft for use by the contract personnel at those locations. By the nature of supplemental operations, these air carriers don't operate to the same locations on a repetitive basis, so this ensures a manual will be accessible to maintenance personnel.

CHAPTER 5
PART 121, SUBPART M: AIRMAN AND CREWMEMBER REQUIREMENTS

You can always tell when a man has lost his soul to flying. The poor bastard is hopelessly committed to stopping whatever he is doing long enough to look up and make sure the aircraft purring overhead continues on course and does not suddenly fall out of the sky. It is his bound duty to watch every aircraft within view take off and land.

—**Ernest Gann,** Fate Is the Hunter

We now turn our attention to the requirements that the FAA places on Part 121 carriers in regard to mandatory staffing for certain safety-critical functions. These provisions are primarily intended to ensure standardization in company operations as they relate to the various activities of operating complex, transport aircraft.

14 CFR §121.381 covers applicability and is really quite simple: this subpart applies to all Part 121 carriers, no exceptions.

Next, in Section 121.383 the FAA states that if a position requires the person filling it to have a particular certificate, then the carrier is responsible for ensuring that the person actually has the required certificate and that it is current for performing the tasks required of that crewmember or airman. What positions require an airman certificate?

- Cockpit crewmembers,
- Dispatchers, and
- Mechanics

An FAA-certificated airman must fill each of these positions. You might have noticed that flight attendants do not appear on this list. While flight attendants are not considered certificated airman, **flight attendants** must hold a **certificate of demonstrated proficiency** issued by the FAA. This certificate is similar in size and appearance to airman certificates. We will discuss the certificate of demonstrated proficiency later in this chapter.

Cockpit crewmembers, dispatchers and mechanics are required to carry these certificates on their person while engaged in operations (performing the tasks) that require the certificate (121.383[a][2]). In addition, he or she must be qualified for the operation for which he or she is to be used. What does this mean? Simply that all required training, qualification, and recentness of experience requirements have been met. The FAA has the right to ensure that all personnel are properly certificated, so Section 121.383(b) requires the airman to present any required certificate(s) to any representative of the Administrator.

While we are on the subject of airman certificates, let's take a look at the **Fair Treatment for Experienced Pilots Act** (enacted in December 2007), which changed the mandatory retirement age for airline pilots from age 60 to age 65. Known as the **age 65 rule**, this was probably one of the most contentious FAR changes in decades. The revised FAR can be found in Section 121.383(d). This rule, quite simply, prohibits the use of pilots in Part 121 operations after they reach the age of 65 years old. The original age 60 rule had been in effect since 1959. So, depending on where you were in your career in 2007, this change was either the greatest thing since sliced bread or the most onerous rule change on the books. Airline management and younger pilots were typically in favor of the old age 60 rule. Management liked the old rule in part because it ensured pilot seats were filled by more junior *(read lower paid)* pilots. Younger pilots tended to like the age 60 rule because it created movement in the seniority list. Older pilots, on the other hand, saw themselves being forced out of their profession right at their peak. They saw professionals in other career fields just hitting their stride at age 60 and being allowed, as required by federal law, to work to at least age 70. Pilots, however, were forced to retire upon reaching their sixtieth birthday.

There had been a number of unsuccessful attempts to raise the retirement age in the past; however, several issues finally aligned to give those seeking to raise the age limit enough evidence to create the political will to do so. The three most important issues were:

1. In November 2006, the International Civil Aviation Organization (ICAO) raised its retirement limit to age 65. Raising the limit in the United States would align it with Canada, the United Kingdom, Japan, Australia and a host of other nations.
2. There was no medical rationale to support forcing pilots to retire at age 60. In fact, medical and safety studies showed that an increase in the retirement age was justified. For example, average life expectancy had increased by 10 years since the original rule was implemented in 1959.
3. Airline bankruptcies after the 9/11 terrorist attacks resulted in both the destruction of airline pilot pensions and pay cuts of close to 50 percent for many pilots. It was hoped that allowing the pilots to work longer would help them recover financially.

For these and other regulatory reasons (age discrimination lawsuits) and economic reasons (impending pilot shortage), the age 60 retirement age was raised to age 65.

So what about the pilots who had already retired before the law was changed but had yet to reach age 65? Unfortunately, for a few thousand U.S. airline pilots, the law was not retroactive so they were not reinstated to their old positions with their former airline. However, airlines did have the option to rehire those pilots who were under age 65. The rehiring of pilots was not mandatory and was the decision of each individual airline. If rehired, these pilots started at the bottom of the seniority list! As you might imagine, there weren't many takers.

Composition of Flight Crews, Part 121 Operators

To really understand the rules in Subpart M regarding **composition of flight crews**, you need to know a little of the historical background of why we staff airplanes as we do. In the early days of commercial aviation (1920s and early 1930s), airline equipment was flown single pilot (often out in the cold and the rain, but that's another story). With the advent of the first generation all-metal airliners (such as the Boeing 247 and the Douglas DC-3) in the mid-1930s, designers built the cockpits around two pilots. Tradition held that the captain was a virtual god on the airplane and the copilot not much more than a flunky to assist with unpleasant tasks like loading bags and assisting boarding. It was a number of years before operators of this class of equipment really incorporated their copilots into the operation in any meaningful way.

With the development of more complex transport equipment (e.g., the Douglas DC-4 and DC-6 and the Lockheed Constellations), the copilot became more integral in the operations. These aircraft were much more complex, and the designs practically required the involvement of both crewmembers for the successful and safe operations of the airplanes. By the end of the World War II period, two-pilot operations were pretty well accepted on the world's airlines.

The DC-6s were originally built for two-pilot crews. However, the rules changed after a series of accidents in the immediate postwar period highlighted a fact that would later become part of the concept of the crew resource management philosophy. That is, a review of these accidents revealed that when mechanical problems occurred on flight decks of two-member-crew airliners of the DC-6's complexity, the crew members quickly became involved in trying to solve the mechanical/systems problems, and that seriously distracted them from their primary task of flying the airplane safely. The response to this was to require a **flight engineer** (FE) for the DC-6 series of aircraft and later-certificated aircraft of a similar size, weight, and complexity. Beginning in the late 1940s, all four-engine aircraft and larger aircraft were required to have flight engineers during "overwater" operations and when the gross weight of an aircraft exceeded 80,000 pounds.

The early jets (Boeing 707, Douglas DC-8, Convair 880, Boeing 727) all were certificated with three-person crews—two pilots and one flight engineer. This was taken as standard until Douglas sought to certificate its DC-9-10 aircraft. During development of this *light jet,* Douglas sought to deliberately keep the gross weight under the 80,000 pound limit that had been placed as the threshold for requiring flight engineers to be part of the crew. Initially the ramp weight of the DC-9-10 was to be 78,500 pounds; however, during the final development of the DC-9-10, the ramp weight topped out at well over 80,000 pounds. Douglas successfully lobbied the CAA (predecessor to the FAA) to discard the 80,000-pound, three-pilot limit during certification of the DC-9-10. The DC-9 was then successfully certificated for only two pilots in 1965. This began a long period of discussion and disagreement between the airlines and their pilot unions over the acceptability of a very complex aircraft being flown with two-pilot crews. Many unions simply refused to fly it. Delta Air Lines was one of the first companies to get its union (ALPA) to accept the two-pilot concept. The DC-9-10 began service with Delta in February of 1965. Once that wall came down in 1965, Boeing also sought certification of a two-pilot jet. Their model, the Boeing 737, was based on the overall fuselage of the B-707/727 series of aircraft but included substantially improved flight controls and automation. Boeing argued that the weight of the aircraft was irrelevant as to whether two or three crewmembers operated the aircraft. Rather, Boeing successfully argued, the determining factor should be the complexity of operations and whether two or three crewmembers were required for safe operations. After a protracted period of hostility between the unions and the companies (some early B-737s were actually delivered with a "flight engineer" position, although there was little for the flight engineer to do!), the 737s were certificated with a two-member crew. At least one airline had a catchy name for the third 737 crewmember seated on the jumpseat; he was called a "GIB," or *Guy in Back.*

Since the late 1960s, each aircraft has been certificated on its own merit, not by an arbitrary weight limitation. The last three-member crew aircraft certificated in the United States were the three widebodies delivered in the early 1970s. These include the B-747 Classic (100/200 models), the Lockheed L-1011, and the Douglas DC-10. All aircraft certificated in the United States since then have been with a two-pilot (no flight engineer) crew.

Now, with that backdrop, 14 CFR §§121.385–121.389 make sense. Section 121.385 states that for all Part 121 operations, the operations must be conducted with two pilots. Further, the company must designate one pilot as pilot-in-command (PIC) and the other as second-in-command (SIC). If the aircraft certification requires a flight engineer, one person can't be used as both a pilot and the flight engineer. If an FE is required, the crew is then at least three people. Finally, Section 121.385(d) spells out the requirements for backup positions. If the airplane certificate requires a flight engineer, then one of the other crewmembers must be trained to perform the emergency functions of the flight engineer. This provision specifically does not require the other person to be qualified in the position, merely trained in performing the basic functions of the position should the flight engineer become incapacitated.

Flight Crewmember Qualifications and Pre-Employment Screening

As the result of several high-profile Part 121 accidents, most notably Colgan Flight 3407 near Buffalo, New York, in February 2009, a number of significant changes were made to the ways airlines conducted their operations and training. **Public Law (PL) 111-216** (Airline Safety and Federal Aviation Administration Extension Act of 2010), **Section 216—Flight Crewmember Screening and Qualifications**, greatly expanded the air carrier's responsibility and requirements for pre-employment screening to determine a prospective pilot employee's background, training, and skill level. The FAA was directed by Congress to conduct a rulemaking proceeding to require Part 121 air carriers to develop and implement means and methods for ensuring that flight crewmembers have proper qualifications and experience—specifically, to require carriers to ensure that prospective flight crewmembers undergo comprehensive pre-employment screening. This would include an assessment of the skills, aptitudes, airmanship, and suitability of each applicant for a position as a flight crewmember in terms of functioning effectively in the air carrier's operational environment.

The reason for this requirement is vague because U.S. airlines have been world leaders in terms of pre-screening and assessment of pilot knowledge, skills and capabilities. However, it is true that the previous training model assumed much of the pilot evaluation was during initial pilot training, not pre-employment.

A major change required by the act was largely unprecedented. That is, rather than relying on the administrative agency's expertise in establishing operational rules, Congress asserted its power to set the minimum licensing requirements for employment as an airline pilot. Prior to the act, the minimum qualification needed to fly as a first officer in Part 121 operations was a commercial certificate with an instrument rating. Congress mandated that an air carrier pilot have an airline transport pilot (ATP) certificate. Congress allowed for a transition period for the FAA to develop these rules, but if new rules were not promulgated by the FAA within three years of law's enactment, the law would impose this requirement directly. Further, Congress mandated that the FAA impose a requirement that a pilot applicant must have "appropriate multi-engine flight experience" and the FAA would determine what that level of experience would be.

The Pilot Records Improvement Act of 1996

The **Pilot Records Improvement Act (PRIA)** was enacted in 1996 following a number of U.S. air carrier accidents attributed to pilot error in the previous ten years. NTSB investigations found that although the pilots involved in these accidents had a history of poor performance, current employers were not aware of this because the pilots' backgrounds were not fully investigated. PRIA was enacted to ensure a pilot's background was thoroughly investigated by hiring air carriers and air operators before allowing a pilot to conduct commercial flights. Under PRIA, a hiring employer could not place a pilot into service until obtaining and reviewing the last five years of a pilot's background and other safety-related records.

PRIA allowed a company hiring a pilot to request FAA records including verification of the medical certificate, pilot certificate, or any other authorized certificate held by a pilot. This also included accident and incident information and FAA enforcement information. Additional records included the National Driver Register, the pilot's employment history, and even training records.

In 2010, various amendments were made to PRIA designed to improve access and availability of pilot records. Specifically, Congress required the FAA to create an electronic **pilot records database (PRD)**.

Pilot Records Database

In 2021, the FAA adopted final regulations for the use of an electronic PRD (Figure 5-1). This resource facilitates the gathering and sharing of pilot records among the FAA and air carriers and other aircraft operators holding out to the public. The PRD, managed by the FAA, replaces PRIA as a means to access and investigate a pilot's background. Unlike PRIA records, the PRD allows direct, uninterrupted access to pilot records in order for prospective employers to quickly make more informed hiring decisions. The main improvement of the PRD over PRIA is it provides electronic responses to information requests within moments, while PRIA information retrieval could takes days or weeks.

A new regulatory Part was established, 14 CFR Part 111, prescribing the rules governing the use of the PRD. Part 111 applies to operators holding an air carrier or operating certificate issued in accordance with Part 119, and authorized to conduct operations under Part 121, 125, or 135. Part 111 also applies to fractional ownership programs issued in accordance with Subpart K of Part 91, passenger carrying "air tour" flights for compensation or hire, and corporate flight departments.

Accessing the Pilot Records Database

The FAA manages access to the PRD and user activity within the PRD. The following individuals are eligible to request access to the PRD:

- **Responsible Person (RP)** is the individual legally responsible for all company activities in the PRD. Only the FAA PRD administrator approves the RP in accordance with 14 CFR §111.15. All other authorized users, excluding pilot accounts, are approved by each operator's RP. Only certain individuals can qualify as the RP depending on the type of operator.
- **Authorized User** is an individual employed by an air carrier or operator that has been assigned access rights to the PRD on behalf of the employer by the responsible person. Authorized Users can view, download and print airman records. These access rights are approved and managed by the RP.
- **Proxy** is a person designated by a responsible person to access the PRD on behalf of the applicable company hiring pilots.

Various types of pilot records are available in the PRD. These include:

1. Name and current address.
2. Airman certificate information.
3. Medical certificate class, limitations, and date of issuance (if applicable).
4. Enforcement history (if applicable).
5. Accident/incident history (if applicable).
6. Previous aviation employers (if entered by the airman into the PRD).
7. Date of last National Driver Registry request (if entered by the airman into the PRD).

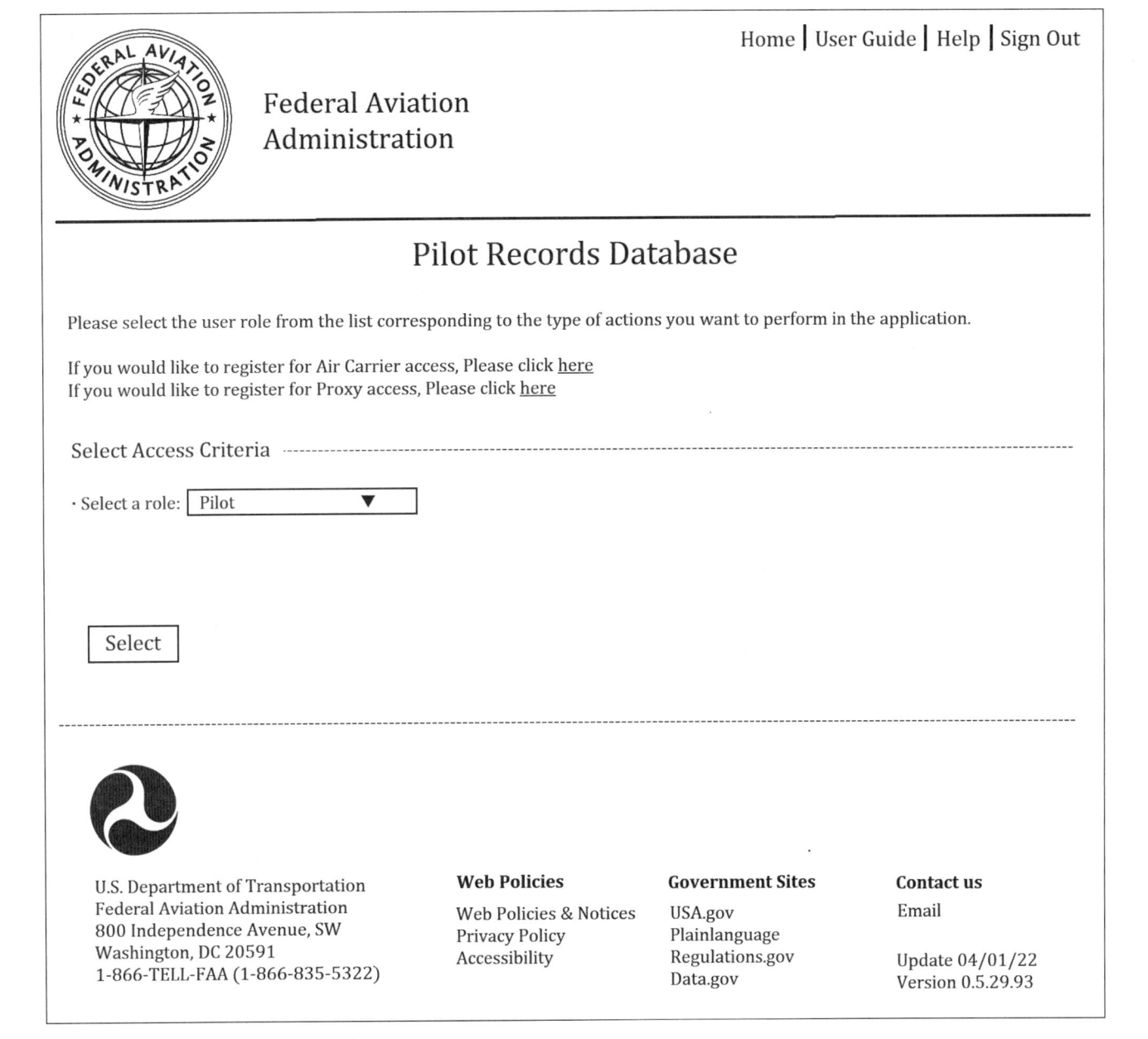

Figure 5-1. The Pilot Records Database website.

The Pilot's Role in the PRD Process

A Commercial, ATP, or Remote Pilot Certificate holder actively seeking employment must first register on an FAA website to access the PRD. Once a pilot has access to their **PRD Airman Record (PAR)**, the pilot is then responsible for ensuring his or her employment history is up-to-date and accurate. The pilot must then grant consent to reviewing entities (i.e., prospective employers). The pilot also controls PRD accuracy regarding employer-generated records in their PAR.

It is important to note that PRD is only intended for those Commercial or ATP Certificate holders actively seeking employment. As such, in order to use PRD a pilot must:

1. Hold a FAA Commercial, ATP, or Remote Pilot Certificate.
2. Hold a valid FAA medical certificate.

Only these appropriately certificated pilots who seek employment as a pilot are granted access into and authorized to use the PRD. While a pilot is actively seeking employment it is necessary for the pilot to review and ensure their employment history is accurate. A pilot is required to list all previous operators who employed them as a pilot for the last five years in accordance with 14 CFR §111.310. This list even includes employers where a pilot may have begun training, but did not finish. Keep in mind that previous employers may have entered records related to a pilot whether or not the pilot listed them in their history. That is why it is important for a pilot to review their records carefully for completeness and accuracy.

In order for prospective employers to view a pilot's PAR, the pilot must grant consent to that specific operator in accordance with 14 CFR §111.120. The pilot is also given an opportunity to see the records exactly as they will be displayed to the prospective employer. The pilot can then decide how many days (30, 45, or 60) the PAR is available and can revoke access to the PAR at any time.

Pilots should carefully review all records provided in the PRD before granting consent to a prospective employer. Because the PRD is not the authoritative record source of the information and displays key information from the original records, pilots should initiate corrections or disputes to have the records corrected by the FAA or original sources (e.g., former employers, National Driver Registry, etc.). If a pilot finds inaccuracies or wishes to dispute a record entered by a source other than the FAA, that pilot should initiate a request for correction of the PRD record in accordance with 14 CFR §111.320.

Also, it is important to note the PRD is only *required* for newly hired pilots. In a situation where a pilot returns from a break in performing flightcrew member duties (e.g., furloughed, loss of medical certificate, or other extended absence), an additional PRD request is not required by Part 111. However, an employer may choose to check the PRD for information entered during the period of extended leave.

The Air Carrier's Role in the PRD Process

14 CFR §111.105 requires each operator holding an air carrier or operating certificate issued under Part 119 and authorized to conduct operations under Parts 121, 125, 135, or corporate flight departments and air tour operators to evaluate all relevant information available in the PRD prior to allowing an individual to enter service as a pilot. Additionally, air carriers and other operators are required by §111.205 to report certain records about individuals employed as pilots to the PRD. These records include:

1. Drug and alcohol testing records.
2. Training, qualification, and proficiency records.
3. Final disciplinary action records.
4. Final separation from employment records.
5. Verification of motor vehicle driving record search and evaluation.

If an air carrier or other operator discovers or is informed of an error in information contained in the PRD, the method of correcting reported information and/or dispute resolution of pilot records is covered in 14 CFR §111.250 (Table 5-1).

Pilot Records Privacy

In an effort to protect a pilot's privacy, 14 CFR §111.30(c) requires each person who accesses the PRD to retrieve a pilot's records to protect the confidentiality of those records and the privacy of the pilot of whose records they pertain.

> **14 CFR §111.30—Prohibited access and use.**
>
> (a) No person may access the database for any purpose other than the purposes provided by this part.
> (b) No person may share, distribute, publish, or otherwise release any record accessed in the database to any person or individual not directly involved in the hiring decision, unless specifically authorized by law or unless the person sharing or consenting to share the record is the subject of the record.
> (c) Each person that accesses the PRD to retrieve a pilot's records must protect the confidentiality of those records and the privacy of the pilot as to those records.

Pilots are the only ones who can consent to grant access of their PAR to a prospective employer. A company can't search the PRD for a specific pilot without that pilot's approval for that particular company, and in the time period chosen by the pilot.

In order to ensure air carriers and other air operators are only using the database for the purposes provided by Part 111, the FAA will conduct random audits of the application and its usage by air carriers and operators to ensure the PRD is being used in accordance with its regulations.

Pilot Records Removal

How long does the FAA maintain pilot records in the PRD? According to 14 CFR §111.40, pilot records are maintained in the database for the life of the pilot. The

Table 5-1. Pilot Records Database record reporting by operator.

	Drug and alcohol records in accordance with Part 120 (§111.20(a))	Training, qualification, and proficiency records (§111.225)	Final disciplinary action records (§111.230)	Records concerning separation of employment (§111.235)	Verification of motor vehicle driving record search and evaluation (§111.240)
Parts 121 and 135: §111.200(a)(1)	Yes	Yes	Yes	Yes	Yes
Part 125: §111.200(a)(1)	No	Yes	Yes	Yes	Yes
Part 91K: §111.200(a)(2)	No	Yes	Yes	Yes	No
Air tour §91.147: §111.200(a)(3)	Yes	Yes (may be reported on request)	Yes (may be reported on request, exceptions apply, see §111.215(b)(1))	Yes (may be reported on request, exceptions apply, see §111.215(b)(1))	No
Operators described in §111.1(b)(4): §111.200(a)(4)	No	Yes (may be reported on request)	Yes (may be reported on request, exceptions apply, see §111.215(b)(1))	Yes (may be reported on request, exceptions apply, see §111.215(b)(1))	No
Public aircraft operators (§111.1(b)(5)): §111.200(a)(5)	No	Yes (may be reported on request)	Yes (may be reported on request, exceptions apply, see §111.215(b)(1))	Yes (may be reported on request, exceptions apply, see §111.215(b)(1))	No
Trustee in bankruptcy: §111.200(a)(6)	As required by operator circumstances	As required by operator circumstances	As required by operator circumstances	As required by operator circumstances	As required by operator circumstances

PAR may be deleted once the FAA has received a certified copy of the pilot's death certificate. This gives new meaning to the saying "this will go on your permanent record."

Airline Transport Pilot (ATP) Certification

Having set the pre-employment licensing requirement higher (at the ATP level instead of commercial pilot level), Congress then mandated, in Public Law 111-216, **Section 217—Air Transport Pilot Certification**, that the FAA significantly raise the bar on standards for obtaining the airline transport pilot certificate.

Section 217 of the law imposed significant new requirements on aspiring airline (and other) pilots with respect to obtaining the ATP certificate. The first change is not so much a change in the certification requirements, but a change in how the qualifications of the certificate are obtained. ICAO requirements for an internationally valid ATP certificate were already set at 1,500 flight hours.

Historically, flight time requirements for employment have largely been a function of supply and demand. So depending upon the time period involved, airlines have hired new pilots with varying levels of flight times and experience—sometimes low flight times and other times very high. For example, during the late 1960s, most major carriers were actually advertising and hiring pilots with "no experience necessary—will train," with a college degree as the only real requirement. This is still the preferred method of employment in a number of countries around the world.

During the 1980s and early 1990s with large drawdowns of the military aviation establishment and, therefore, a surplus of professional pilots available for hire, de facto hiring standards were as high as 4,500 hours (or higher) at some airlines. The opposite was true during the 1960s when a first officer required only 250 hours (for a commercial pilot certificate) and again in the late 1990s when flight time minimums dropped to about 500 hours. Therefore, not surprisingly, in times of high demand and low supply such as the 1960s or late 1990s, a person could be hired with little to no flight experience beyond that required for certification. Then, when certificated as a commercial pilot, that person could build flight experience with the employer airline. Depending on the carrier, pilots would obtain the ATP either as part of normal training on the particular aircraft they were assigned to or when upgrading to captain. That all changed with Section 217 of PL 111-216.

Section 217 of PL 111-216 requires that in order to receive an ATP certificate, an individual must have *sufficient flight hours*, as set by the FAA, to enable him or her to function effectively in an air carrier operational environment. Additionally, to receive ATP certification, the individual must have received *flight training, academic training or operational experience* that will prepare the pilot minimally to:

- function effectively in a multipilot environment;
- function effectively in adverse weather conditions (including icing conditions);
- function effectively during high altitude operations;
- adhere to the highest professional standard; and
- function effectively in an air carrier operational environment.

Congress granted the FAA discretion in setting the number of flight hours for the ATP certificate. They were required to be at least 1,500 hours and include a very nebulous stipulation that the FAA set sub-minima of hours for specific kinds of flight experience. For example, Congress mandated that the total flight hours required include flight hours in difficult operational conditions that may be encountered by an air carrier to prepare a pilot to operate safely in such conditions. The requirement for a minimum flight time of 1,500 hours for an ATP certificate was strongly challenged by the University Aviation Association, a number of colleges and universities that conduct flight training, as well as the large pilot training academies. As a result of this input, a provision was added to the law that allowed the FAA some discretion in establishing lower flight time minima for the ATP certificate.

The FAA was allowed to grant to specific academic training courses that provide more extensive education and training than the minimum required for the ATP to be credited toward the required flight time. In other words, the FAA is permitted to reduce the 1,500-hour minimum for specific academic courses that it found to enhance safety more than just complying with the flight hour requirement.

Finally, Section 217 of PL 111-216 required the FAA to consider the recommendations of an expert panel that was to review the training hours that had been imposed by Section 209 of the law. Section 209 required that the FAA study and make recommendations about the training and qualification standards and requirements of Part 121 and Part 135 air carriers.

Pilot Certification, Qualification and Training Requirements for Air Carrier Operations

Public Law 111-216 generated a number of changes to the FAA's certification, qualification and training requirements for current and aspiring airline pilots. These changes fall into three general areas:

- It requires training to the airline transport pilot (ATP) certificate level prior to employment at an air carrier, instead of to the commercial pilot certificate level as previously required.
- It requires additional training in order to receive the ATP certificate itself.
- It requires the carrier to provide additional training in its own programs.

Section 216 of the Act focused on the initial, pre-employment qualifications of air carrier pilots, and directed the FAA to issue a rule that would require all pilots serving in Part 121 domestic, flag, and supplemental air carrier operations to hold an ATP and a type rating for the aircraft to be flown. That means to be a first officer for a U.S. Part 121 airline, a person must hold an ATP certificate, or a newly-created **"restricted" ATP (R-ATP) certificate**. Prior to this law, only the captain (pilot-in-command) in Part 121 operations was required to hold an ATP. For decades, the minimum regulatory requirements to be hired as a first officer (second-in-command) for a Part 121 air carrier was to hold a commercial certificate, which was a minimum of 250 hours of flight time. This could be reduced even further to 190 hours for pilots attending FAA Part 141 approved flight schools.

Section 217 of the Act mandated the FAA to modify 14 CFR Part 61, Certification of Pilots, by changing the ATP certification requirements to *"better prepare a pilot to function effectively in a multi-pilot environment, in adverse weather conditions, during high altitude oper-*

ations, and in an air carrier environment, as well as to adhere to the highest professional standards." Here, Congress focused on whether newly hired airline pilots have sufficient flight-hour experience in difficult operational conditions that might be encountered in air carrier operations. The law stated that the minimum total flight hours to be qualified for an ATP certificate shall be at least 1,500 flight hours. So as before, the FAA required a pilot to be 23 years of age and have 1,500 hours total time as a pilot to qualify for an ATP certificate.

Pilots with fewer than 1,500 flight hours may, however, qualify for the aforementioned "restricted" R-ATP certificate beginning at 21 years of age if they are a military-trained pilot, or have a bachelor's or associate's degree with an aviation major from an approved, accredited institution. Students considering a course of training and expecting the lower flight hour allowance should confirm that the institution has the **letter of authorization (LOA)** from the FAA as allowed by 14 CFR §61.169. This authorization allows the institution to certify its graduates to take the FAA ATP Knowledge and Practical Tests with less than the required 1,500 total flight hours. Students pursuing this option should be sure to obtain this authorization certificate and retain it for their tests.

The R-ATP certificate is also available to pilots who are at least 21 years of age who obtain their certificates and ratings through non-structured general aviation flight training with 1,500 hours of flight time. This restricted-privileges ATP certificate allows a pilot to serve as first officer (second-in-command) in domestic, flag, and supplemental operations not requiring more than two pilot-flight crewmembers.

Congress gave the FAA the discretion to allow different flight hour requirements for a restricted privilege ATP certificate with an airplane category multi-engine class rating or type rating. This enables a pilot to obtain an ATP certificate with reduced total flight time as a pilot based on academic experience. Let's take a look at 14 CFR §61.160 to see how the FAA implemented this directive from Congress.

Section 61.160(a) allows military-trained and qualified pilots to get their ATP with 750 hours of total flight time and the remaining requirements found in paragraph (a). For a graduate of a four-year institution with an aviation program who has received a commercial certificate and instrument rating from a Part 141 program affiliated with that institution and who meets the remaining requirements of §61.160(b), an ATP certificate can be achieved after 1,000 hours. Similarly, a graduate who holds an associate's degree with an aviation major and meets the remaining requirements of §61.160(c) will be able to hold an R-ATP with a total time of 1,250 hours.

This rule created one significant change to the eligibility requirements for an ATP certificate with an airplane category multi-engine class rating or an ATP certificate obtained concurrently with a type rating. In either of these cases, to receive an ATP certificate with a multi-engine class rating, a pilot must now have 50 hours of multi-engine flight experience and must have completed a newly created and FAA-approved **Airline Transport Pilot Certification Training Program (ATP CTP)**. For the 50 flight hours of multi-engine experience, a maximum of 25 hours of training in a full flight simulator (FFS) representing a multi-engine airplane may be credited toward the flight time requirement if the training was accomplished as part of an approved training course in Part 121, 135, 141, or 142. A flight training device (FTD) or aviation training device (ATD) may not be used to satisfy this requirement. This new training program includes academic coursework and training in a flight simulation training device. These requirements will ensure that a pilot has the proper qualifications, training, and experience before entering an air carrier environment as a pilot flight crewmember. Table 5-2 shows the ATP certificate requirements compared to the Restricted ATP (R-ATP) certificate requirements. Once a pilot with an R-ATP meets all the hour requirements for an ATP Certificate, the applicant must request that the FAA issue a new unrestricted ATP Certificate.

Previously, as a first officer was only required to be a commercial pilot, he or she only needed to hold a second-class medical certificate. So the question arose about the class of medical that would be required of an ATP-rated first officer. Since a first officer who happened to hold an ATP was only required to exercise the commercial privileges of that certificate, he or she could fly with just a second-class medical certificate. This rule retains the second-class medical certification requirement for first officers (SIC) in most Part 121 operations even though they now must hold an ATP certificate. A first-class medical certificate is required for first officers (SIC) in a Part 121 flag or supplemental operation that requires three or more pilots. For pilots who have reached their sixtieth birthday, a first-class medical is also required when serving as a required pilot flight crewmember in Part 121 operations. The qualifications required to serve as PIC and SIC are summarized in Table 5-3.

Table 5-2. ATP vs. R-ATP Qualifications

ATP

Airline Transport Pilot certificate (ATP) with an airplane category and multiengine class rating.

- Must be at least 23 years old
- Hold a commercial pilot certificate with instrument rating
- Must have successfully completed an ATP Certification Training Program (CTP) prior to taking the ATP knowledge test
- Pass the ATP knowledge test and practical test
- Have at least 1,500 hours total time as a pilot
- Have a minimum of 50 hours in class of airplane

R-ATP

Airline Transport Pilot certificate with restricted privileges (R-ATP) (restricted to serving as SIC in Part 121 operations with multengine class rating only).

- Must be at least 21 years old
- Hold a commercial pilot certificate with instrument rating
- Must have successfully completed an ATP Certification Training Program (CTP) prior to taking the ATP knowledge test
- Pass the ATP knowledge test and practical test
- Have at least:
  - 1,500 total time as a pilot; or
  - 1,250 hours total time as pilot and an associate's degree with an aviation major; or
  - 1,000 hours total time as pilot and a bachelor's degree with an aviation major; or
  - 750 hours total time as military-trained pilot

Table 5-3. Captain (PIC) vs. First Officer (SIC) Qualifications

To serve as Captain (PIC) in Part 121 operations, a pilot must:

- Hold an ATP certificate with appropriate aircraft type rating; and
- Hold a first class medical certificate;
- Have a minimum of 1,000 flight hours in air carrier operations as a First Officer (SIC) in Part 121 operations, or as Captain in Part 135 turbojet, commuter, or 10 or more passenger seat operations, or any combination of these.

To serve as First Officer (SIC) in Part 121 air carrier operations, a pilot must:

- Hold an ATP certificate with type rating for aircraft flown; or
- Hold a R-ATP and type rating for aircraft flown; and
- Hold at least a second class medical certificate.

To serve as First Officer (SIC) in flag or supplemental operations requiring three or more pilots, a pilot must:

- Hold an ATP certificate with appropriate aircraft type rating; and
- Hold a first class medical certificate.

FAA Advisory Circular 61-138 discusses the creation of the Airline Transport Pilot Certification Training Program (ATP CTP). The ATP CTP is a prerequisite for the FAA's highest certificate and includes training in aerodynamics, automation, adverse weather conditions, air carrier operations, transport airplane performance, professionalism, and leadership and development. It is designed to bridge the widely recognized knowledge gap that exists between a pilot who holds a commercial pilot certificate and a pilot operating in an air carrier environment. An ATP CTP graduation certificate from an authorized training provider is now a requirement to take the aeronautical knowledge test for the ATP certificate. 14 CFR §61.156 (see also AC 61-138) sets forth the required subject areas and minimum curriculum outline, as required by Public Law 111-216, shown below. (Note: When approved by the FAA, the 40,000-pound weight requirement may be waived.)

(a) *Academic training.* The applicant for the knowledge test must receive at least 30 hours of classroom instruction that includes the following:
  (1) At least 8 hours of instruction on aerodynamics including high altitude operations;
  (2) At least 2 hours of instruction on meteorology, including adverse weather phenomena and weather detection systems; and
  (3) At least 14 hours of instruction on air carrier operations, including the following areas:
    (i) Physiology;
    (ii) Communications;

                (iii) Checklist philosophy;
                (iv) Operational control;
                (v) Minimum equipment list/
                    configuration deviation list;
                (vi) Ground operations;
                (vii) Turbine engines;
                (viii) Transport category aircraft
                    performance;
                (ix) Automation, navigation, and flight
                    path warning systems.
        (4) At least 6 hours of instruction on
            leadership, professional development, crew
            resource management, and safety culture.
    (b) *FSTD training.* The applicant for the knowledge
        test must receive at least 10 hours of training
        in a flight simulation training device qualified
        under part 60 of this chapter that represents a
        multiengine turbine airplane. The training must
        include the following:
        (1) At least 6 hours of training in a Level C or
            higher full flight simulator qualified under
            part 60 of this chapter that represents
            a multiengine turbine airplane with a
            maximum takeoff weight of 40,000
            pounds or greater. The training must
            include the following areas:
                (i) Low energy states/stalls;
                (ii) Upset recovery techniques; and
                (iii) Adverse weather conditions,
                    including icing, thunderstorms, and
                    crosswinds with gusts.
        (2) The remaining FSTD training may be
            completed in a Level 4 or higher flight
            simulation training device. The training
            must include the following areas:
                (i) Navigation including flight
                    management systems; and
                (ii) Automation including autoflight.
    (c) *Deviation authority.* The Administrator may
        issue deviation authority from the weight
        requirement in paragraph (b)(1) of this section
        upon a determination that the objectives of the
        training can be met in an alternative device.

(14 CFR §61.156)

Composition of Flight Crews, Part 135 Operators

The composition of flight crew for Part 135 operators is covered in Section 135.99(a) and states that the minimum required flight crew component is ultimately determined by the approved aircraft operating limitations or aircraft flight manual. However, a two-pilot minimum flight crew requirement for all aircraft with 10 or more passenger seats is mandated by Section 135.99(b). In other words, aircraft with 10 or more passenger seats must have a pilot-in-command and a pilot who is second-in-command. For aircraft with less than 10 passenger seats, it is legal under certain circumstances to fly with only one pilot. An aircraft equipped with less than 10 passenger seats may be flown under Part 135 without a second-in-command under the following conditions:

- The aircraft is equipped with an operative approved autopilot system and the use of that system is authorized by the appropriate operations specifications. *(14 CFR §135.105[a])*
- The pilot-in-command must have at least 100 hours PIC time in the make and model of aircraft to be flown and have met all other applicable requirements of this part. *(14 CFR §135.105[a])*
- The certificate holder must apply for an amendment of its operation specifications to authorize the use of an autopilot system (which must be capable of controlling all three axes) in place of a second-in-command. *(14 CFR §135.105[b] and [c][1])*
- The certificate holder demonstrates, to the satisfaction of the Administrator, that operations using the autopilot system can be conducted safely and in compliance with this part. *(14 CFR §135.105[c][2])*
- The aircraft is not operated in a Category II operation. *(14 CFR §135.111)*

Flight Navigator

Forget about it. **Flight navigators** haven't been used on U.S. commercial airliners in years. As far back as the mid-1970s, Trans World Airlines was down to one navigator who worked in management. 14 CFR §121.389 provides two alternatives for operating. A company may use a navigator or **specialized navigation equipment**. While navigators still exist and are used on occasions such as ferry flights with inoperative navigation equipment, this is a real rarity. Virtually all aircraft are operated under the specialized navigation equipment provision. The cost considerations make it much more efficient to invest several million dollars per aircraft in specialized navigation equipment and not have the recurring costs of labor of real, live navigators. Interestingly, some pilot contracts still paid "navigation pay" to the pilots well into the late 1990s. When the navigators came off airliners beginning in the late 1950s, some pilot unions were able to negotiate that since the pilots were doing the navigation (using the specialized navigation equipment), they should be paid extra for performing the task.

Flight Attendant Requirements and Responsibilities

Certificate of Demonstrated Proficiency

In the fall of 2003, Congress established a flight attendant certification requirement as part of the **Vision 100—Century of Aviation Reauthorization Act**. The Act required that after December 11, 2004, no person could serve as a flight attendant aboard an aircraft of an air carrier unless that person held a **certificate of demonstrated proficiency** issued by the FAA. Previous to the enactment of this Act, flight attendants were not certificated by the FAA. The Act defines a flight attendant as an individual who works in the cabin of an aircraft that has 20 or more seats and is used by a Part 121 or Part 135 air carrier to provide air transportation. The FAA will not issue a certificate of demonstrated proficiency to any flight attendant that does not meet this definition.

Surprisingly, flight attendants are not required to carry the certificate while in performance of their duties. If requested, flight attendants shall present their certificate to the FAA, the National Transportation Safety Board, or another federal agency within a reasonable period of time after the date of request. The FAA policy for "a reasonable period of time" is 15 days. The Act distinguishes between this certificate and an airman certificate. This certificate is not an airman certificate as specified in Title 49 of the United States Code (49 U.S.C.), Section 44703; it is a separate kind of certificate as specified in 49 U.S.C., Section 44728.

Flight Attendant Staffing

While flight attendants are required on board the aircraft for safety reason, the airlines have developed the position into one that is perceived by the public as primarily a customer service function. However, the FAA requirement for flight attendants is primarily to assist passengers in emergencies and their presence is particularly important in helping with the emergency evacuation of the aircraft. As we will discuss further in the next paragraph, the FAA requires passenger-carrying aircraft to be evacuated in 90 seconds or less. For this reason, 14 CFR §121.391 provides minimum staffing levels of flight attendants for Part 121 carriers. Part 135 staffing levels are briefly addressed in Section 135.107 and state simply that aircraft having seating configurations of more than 19 seats must have a flight attendant crewmember on board the aircraft. These minimums have nothing to do with customer service. They are there to ensure safety standards can be met in emergency situations.

The formula for **flight attendant minimum staffing levels** is quite simple. It is shown in Table 5-4.

Note that Section 121.391 covers *seating capacity*, not passengers. So if an aircraft is certificated with 127 seats, but only 43 passengers are aboard a flight, how many flight attendants are required? Three are required because of the 127-seat capacity.

When a manufacturer designs and certificates a new model of aircraft with more than 44 seats, it must demonstrate to the FAA that it can do an emergency evacuation of the airplane in 90 seconds. This is demonstrated with a "generic" airplane. However, 14 CFR §121.291 also requires that *each airline* must do an **emergency evacuation demonstration** as well. This is to prove that the airline can evacuate its aircraft as configured by that airline in 90 seconds or less. Installed equipment, seating configurations, and so forth may hinder the evacuation, so the airline must demonstrate its ability. Section

Table 5-4. Flight attendant minimum staffing levels

Seating Capacity	Minimum Requirements
From 10 seats to 19 seats: 　less or equal to 7,500 lb. payload capacity 　more than 7,500 lb. payload capacity	 0 flight attendants 1 flight attendant
From 20 to 50 seats	1 flight attendant
From 51 to 100	2 flight attendants
Over 100 seats	1 additional flight attendant for each unit (or part of a unit) of 50 seats

121.391(b) states that if the carrier had to put on flight attendants in excess of the formula discussed above in order to meet the evacuation tests, then the increased number becomes the minimum number of flight attendants required for that airline. This is so important that Section 121.391(c) requires that the number of extra flight attendants required must be set forth in the carrier's ops specs.

We'll see in Chapter 7 that the flight attendant duty period limitations also affect required staffing. For example, a flight attendant's duty period is normally limited to a scheduled duty day of 14 hours. This, however, may be extended to between 14 and 16 hours if the carrier assigns an extra flight attendant to the flight; 16 to 18 hours if the carrier assigns two extra flight attendants to the flight; and 18 to 20 hours if three extra flight attendants are assigned to the flight.

For the reasons we've discussed, Section 121.391(d) sets forth the requirements that flight attendants be uniformly distributed about the aircraft and be located near the emergency exits in order to provide the most effective egress of passengers in event of an emergency evacuation, and also requires that during taxi flight attendants be in their seats with belts and harnesses fastened except as necessary to carry out duties related to the safety of the aircraft and its occupants.

Passengers on Board: During Through Stops

The FAA is concerned about the safety of passengers on the aircraft at all times, not just the time the aircraft is under way. For this reason, when passengers remain aboard the aircraft at through stations, someone must be nearby and available to assist the passengers in an emergency evacuation, if required. Normally, this will be a flight attendant. If the full complement, that is the **minimum number of flight attendants required for dispatch**, remains aboard, then passengers may be boarded or deplaned with the engine running. What if the stopover is also a crew change station? That is, the passengers are continuing on to another destination and are not deplaning, but the flight attendants are laying over, completing a trip, or are assigned to another flight. In this case, during boarding and deplaning of through flights, either the full complement of flight attendants must remain on board or, alternatively and with limitations, one-half the FAA minimum number of flight attendants (rounded down, minimum one) required for dispatch must be on board the aircraft (Table 5-5).

Also, Section 121.393 allows that instead of a flight attendant, a non–flight attendant may be available on board to assist in emergencies. If the aircraft does not require flight attendants (as a result of 121.391[a]), or the carrier chooses, it may substitute a non–flight attendant (e.g., station gate agent) to perform these evacuation duties. That person must be qualified (trained) in emergency evacuation procedures, must be identified to the passengers, and must be on or nearby the aircraft. In addition, the engines must be shut down and at least one floor-level door must remain open to provide a route for deplaning.

Note that the responsibility of each person who is assigned a task in the emergency evacuation plan must be spelled out in the manual provided to the crews. This assignment of tasks must consider issues such as what happens if a crewmember is incapacitated or can't reach a portion of the cabin.

Table 5-5. Flight attendant staffing requirements (for typical aircraft seating capacities)

Aircraft Type	Number of Flight Attendants Required for:	
	Minimum Dispatch	En Route Stopovers
E175, E190, CR700, CR900 (>50 to <100)	2	1
A319/320, B717, B737-700, MD80/MD88 (>100 to <150)	3	1
A321, B737-800, B757-200, MD90 (>150 to <200)	4	2
B767-300 (>200 to <250)	5	2
A330 (>250 to <300)	6	3
B777-300 (>300 to <350)	7	3
B747-800 (>350 to <400)	8	4
A380 (>400 to <450)	9	4

Dispatchers

As discussed in Chapter 3, an aircraft dispatcher is an individual holding an FAA aircraft dispatcher certificate. Part 121 flag and domestic operators must employ aircraft **dispatchers** who exercise certain operational control functions over an air carrier's flight. These functions include the flight planning of each specific flight and maintaining communications with the flight at all times to keep its flight crew apprised of things such as weather, NOTAMs, operational limitations, and so on. Air carriers must ensure these aircraft dispatchers are supplied with the necessary information to plan, conduct, and control flight operations. Part 121 supplemental and Part 135 operators are not required to use FAA-certified aircraft dispatchers. Each Part 121 carrier conducting either domestic or flag operations must provide enough qualified aircraft dispatchers to ensure proper operational control over each flight (14 CFR §121.395).

Emergency Evacuation Duties

To complete Part 121 Subpart M, we'll visit emergency evacuation duties covered in Section 121.397. Simply put, an air carrier must, for each type and model of airplane, make sure every required crewmember is assigned specific duties to be performed in an emergency or a situation requiring emergency evacuation. These FAA-approved duties must be described in the air carrier's operations specifications and approved by the FAA. Finally the air carrier must demonstrate that these duties are *realistic, can be practically accomplished, and will meet any reasonably anticipated emergency including the possible incapacitation of individual crewmembers or their inability to reach the passenger cabin because of shifting cargo in combination cargo-passenger airplanes.*

Summary

In this chapter we have covered airmen and crewmember requirements for Part 121 operations. These operations must have certificated airmen including pilots, copilots, and—if required by the aircraft type certificate—flight engineers aboard the aircraft. Flight attendants are required to be aboard the aircraft in minimum numbers; they are not certificated airmen, but must have been awarded a certificate of demonstrated proficiency from the FAA. The number of flight attendants required in order to evacuate all occupants of the aircraft in 90 seconds or less determines the flight attendant minimum staffing level. Additionally, certificated airmen are required to fill positions of dispatchers (except for supplemental carriers) and mechanics. Pilots are limited by regulation to working only until their sixty-fifth birthday, while there is no age limit on other airman certificates including flight engineers.

In the next chapter, we will examine the required training programs for pilots, flight attendants, dispatchers, and mechanics.

Important Terms in Chapter 5

age 65 rule
Airline Transport Pilot Certification Training Program (ATP CTP)
certificate of demonstrated proficiency
composition of flight crews
dispatchers
emergency evacuation demonstration
Fair Treatment for Experienced Pilots Act
flight attendant
flight attendant minimum staffing levels
flight engineers
flight navigators
letter of authorization (LOA)
minimum number of flight attendants required for dispatch
Pilot Records Improvement Act of 1996 (PRIA)
Pilot Records Database (PRD)
Public Law 111-216, Section 216—Flight Crewmember Screening and Qualification
Public Law 111-216, Section 217, Air Transport Pilot Certification
Restricted ATP (R-ATP)
specialized navigation equipment
Vision 100—Century of Aviation Reauthorization Act

Chapter 5 Exam

1. What positions in an air carrier require an FAA airman certificate?
    a. Captain, first officer and flight follower
    b. Flight crew, flight attendants, and mechanics
    c. Cockpit crewmembers, dispatchers, and mechanics
    d. Captain, chief executive officer, and dispatchers

2. Which air carrier personnel are required to carry an FAA airman certificate on his/her person when performing the tasks which require the certificate?
    a. Cockpit crewmembers, flight attendants, and mechanics
    b. Mechanics, captains, first officers, head flight attendant, and dispatchers
    c. Cockpit crewmembers, dispatchers and mechanics
    d. Cockpit crewmembers, dispatchers, and chief operating officer

3. What is the mandatory retirement age for all pilots in Part 121 operations?
    a. No person may serve as a pilot on an airplane engaged in operations under Part 121 if that person has reached his/her sixtieth birthday.
    b. No person may serve as a pilot on an airplane engaged in operation under Part 121 if that person has reached his/her sixty-second birthday.
    c. No person may serve as a pilot on an airplane engaged in operations under Part 121 if that person has reached his/her sixtieth-fifth birthday.
    d. No person may serve as a flight engineer on an airplane engaged in operations under Part 121 if that person has reached his/her sixtieth birthday.

4. What is the minimum pilot crew operating under Part 121?
    a. 1
    b. 2
    c. 3
    d. 4

5. To be employed as a pilot by a Part 121 air carrier, what pilot certificate must you hold?
   a. A commercial pilot certificate with an instrument rating only
   b. A restricted airline transport pilot certificate with an instrument rating only
   c. An airline transport pilot certificate only
   d. Either a restricted airline transport pilot certificate or an airline transport pilot certificate

6. What is the minimum flight hours needed to obtain a restricted airline transport pilot certificate?
   a. 1,250 hours only
   b. 1,000 hours only
   c. 750 hours only
   d. Depending upon where the training was obtained, (a), (b) or (c) may be correct.

7. What is the minimum pilot crew operating an aircraft with an approved and authorized autopilot under Part 135 in a Category I operation?
   a. 1
   b. 2
   c. 3
   d. 4

8. If an aircraft operated in Part 121 is certificated with 275 seats, but only 249 passengers are aboard for a particular flight, how many flight attendants are required?
   a. 7
   b. 6
   c. 5
   d. 4

9. How many flight attendants are required for an aircraft that has a payload capacity of less than 7,500 pounds and is equipped with 19 passenger seats?
   a. 3
   b. 2
   c. 1
   d. 0

10. During boarding and deplaning of originating and terminating flights, the FAA requires how many flight attendants be on board the aircraft?
    a. Two less flight attendants than the minimum number of flight attendants required for dispatch.
    b. One less flight attendant than the minimum number of flight attendants required for dispatch.
    c. The FAA minimum number of flight attendants required for dispatch must be on board the aircraft during boarding and deplaning.
    d. The FAA minimum number of flight attendants required for a stopover must be on board during boarding and deplaning.

11. Flight attendants are required to carry a FAA certificate of demonstrated proficiency on his/her person when performing their job functions.
    a. True
    b. False

12. Which act raised the mandatory retirement age for Part 121 airline pilots to age 65?
    a. The Air Commerce Act
    b. The Federal Register for Older Americans Act
    c. The Fair Treatment for Experienced Pilots Act
    d. The Older Pilots Retirement Prevention Act

13. To apply for a restricted airline transport pilot (R-ATP) certificate, an applicant must
    a. be at least 21 years old and hold a commercial pilot certificate with an instrument rating.
    b. be at least 23 years old and hold a commercial pilot certificate.
    c. be at least 23 years old and have at least 1,500 hours total time as pilot.
    d. be at least 21 years old and have at least a private pilot license.

14. To apply for an air transport pilot (ATP) certificate, an applicant must
    a. be at least 21 years old and hold a commercial pilot certificate, with an instrument rating.
    b. be at least 23 years old and hold a commercial pilot certificate.
    c. be at least 23 years old and hold a commercial pilot certificate with an instrument rating.
    d. be at least 21 years old and have at least a private pilot license.

15. To serve as a first officer (SIC) in Part 121 air carrier operations, a pilot must
    a. hold an ATP certificate, with type rating for the aircraft flown; and hold at least a second-class medical certificate.
    b. hold an R-ATP certificate, with type rating for the aircraft flown; and hold at least a second-class medical certificate.
    c. hold at least a commercial pilot certificate; and hold a first-class medical certificate.
    d. both (a) and (b) are correct.

16. Who is responsible for ensuring a PRD airman record is up-to-date and accurate?
    a. The Federal Aviation Administration.
    b. An airline or employer.
    c. Each pilot is responsible for their own record.

CHAPTER 6
PART 121, SUBPART N: TRAINING PROGRAMS AND PART 121, SUBPART O: CREWMEMBER QUALIFICATIONS

What can you conceive more silly and extravagant than to suppose a man racking his brains, and studying night and day how to fly?

—**Will Law**, *A Serious Call to a Devout and Holy Life XI,* 1728

The FARs impose very stringent regulations in order to assure the highest duty to care by air carriers on the training that airmen, crewmembers, and others must receive. In addition, a complex set of proficiency check and recurrent training requirements are imposed on air carriers. We now turn our attention to what these two subparts of the FARs require of air carriers.

Part 121, Subpart N: Training Programs

14 CFR Part 121, Subpart N, defines the type of training programs that are required of Part 121 carriers, the requirements for the instructors and check airmen to be used in the program, and program-specific syllabi for the various types of training that are required. 14 CFR §121.400 makes the training program requirements applicable to all Part 121 air carriers and defines a number of terms that are used in the training regulations. Some of these important terms are covered below.

For the purpose of the training regulations, airplanes are broken down into three categories: reciprocating powered (piston engine, propeller driven) airplanes, turbopropeller airplanes, and turbojet (pure jet) airplanes. The first two categories (piston and turboprop) are **Group I airplanes**, and the last category (jet aircraft) are **Group II airplanes**. These definitions will be important in determining what specific training is required and the minimum (or programmed) hours of instruction required for various types of required training.

Section 121.400 goes on to define some of the different types of training found in Part 121:

- **Initial training** is the training required for crewmembers and dispatchers who have not qualified and served in the same capacity on another airplane of the same group at that carrier.
- **Transition training** is the training required for crewmembers and dispatchers who have qualified and served in the same capacity on another airplane in the same group at that carrier.
- **Upgrade training** is the training required for crewmembers who have qualified and served as second-in-command or flight engineer on a particular airplane type, before they serve as pilot-in-command or second-in-command, respectively, on that airplane at that carrier.
- **Differences training** is the training required for crewmembers and dispatchers who have qualified and served on a particular type airplane, when the FAA determines that additional training is necessary before a crewmember serves in the same capacity on a particular variation of that airplane at that carrier.

- **Requalification training** is the training required for crewmembers previously trained and qualified at that carrier, but who have become unqualified due to not having had the recurrent training required under 14 CFR §121.427 or not having taken the proficiency check required by §121.441.

Carriers are required by 14 CFR §121.401 to establish training programs that provide all of the training and checking required by **Part 121 Appendix E (Flight Training Requirements)** and **Appendix F (Proficiency Check Requirements)**. These appendices are quite interesting, especially to the pilot or flight engineer, in that they lay out exactly what material must be trained, how it is to be trained (e.g., simulator, flight training device, or airplane), and who must receive what training. Any pilot who is embarking on Part 121 training (especially initial training) should review Appendix E to see what will be required in the training program. Other types of training required include the following:

- **Flight attendant training**. 14 CFR §121.401 doesn't just apply to pilots and flight engineers. Dispatchers are specifically named in this Section. Flight attendants are included by use of the term "crewmembers" as opposed to "flight crewmembers," and their training is spelled out in Sections 121.421 and 121.427.
- **HAZMAT training**. Anyone who is assigned duties for the carriage of hazardous or magnetic materials must be trained in HAZMAT procedures (see 14 CFR §121.1003, Hazardous Materials Training: General). This training is included as part of other training courses so as to ensure that all applicable employees have received training in marking, identifying, handling, and storing hazardous materials.
- **Recurrent training** ensures each crewmember or dispatcher is adequately trained and currently proficient with respect to the type of airplane he or she is crewing or dispatching (14 CFR §121.427).
- **Crew resource management (CRM) training** and **dispatcher resource management (DRM) training**. 14 CFR §121.404 requires that each crewmember or dispatcher receive crew or dispatcher resource management training. CRM/DRM training focuses on the interrelationships between crewmembers, dispatch, maintenance, the FAA, and other agencies. It is especially designed to help crewmembers learn to communicate effectively and to use all available resources when dealing with in-flight problems or emergencies.

The training programs are required to keep meticulous records to show that all required persons have been trained in accord with the training program. These records are used for many purposes. First, they are used to show compliance with required training program content. That is, they show that the syllabus of training was followed. Next they show that the crewmember, dispatcher, or other required person has actually received the training in the required time frame.

On that point, note that 14 CFR §121.401(b) allows the actual recurrent training or proficiency check accomplishment date to be a month early or a month late and still count as having been accomplished as required. For example, if you (a second-in-command pilot) completed your initial training on a piece of equipment last July, you would be due recurrent training, by virtue of §121.433(c), next July. The FAR recognizes that this may be highly impractical or impossible. Due to scheduling problems, operating requirements, simulator availability, and so forth, the carrier simply may not be able to schedule you for recurrent training next July. July is referred to as your **base month**. Section 121.401(b) allows the training to be accomplished a month before the base month, during the base month, or in the month after the base month. These months are sometimes called base month early or grace month late.

Note that there potentially is a big trap waiting for you here! What happens if you were due for recurrent training in July, but for the reasons given above, the carrier assigns you to an August recurrent training class (say, August 28 and 29) and you continue flying your August schedule, which is allowed by operation of Section 121.401(b)? Come August 27 you become quite ill with the flu and can't leave your house for a week. At the end of that week (early September), are you legal to fly? Clearly you are not because you have not completed your recurrent training during your base month or **grace month**. That is the easy part. Now, what about your August flying? Was it legal? Well, it was while you were doing it in the month of August. By operation of 14 CFR §121.401(b), you could continue to fly. However—and this is a big however—once August passed without your having completed the required recurrent training, *any flying you did in August has become illegal!* If flying takes you into the grace month, it is imperative that you and the carrier ensure that the training is completed in that grace month. If you complete your recurrent training during the grace period, that does not extend your base month. In the example above in which your base month was July, it remains July even if you completed recurrent training in August.

Conduct of Training

Part 121 training can only be conducted by one of two entities. To conduct required training, the company must either be a Part 121 air carrier certificate holder or hold a **14 CFR Part 142 Flight Training Certificate**. If either another certificate holder or a Part 142 certificate holder is to conduct the training, the FAA must authorize this. Section 121.402 allows this training to be contracted out as described.

Curriculum

The FAA requires that the training program be well structured and approved. 14 CFR §121.403 sets forth the requirements for the certificate holder to prepare and keep current a training **curriculum** for each type of airplane and each crewmember or dispatcher. This curriculum must specify things such as the content of the course, the training devices and pictorials to be used, the maneuvers to be taught, and the number of **programmed hours** (or **reduced programmed hours**) (see §121.400[c][5]) that are approved.

Approval of the training program is required and the requirements for that are set forth in Section 121.405. Each program must receive initial approval from the FAA before it may be used in a certificate holder's operation. After the program has been implemented and is being executed, the FAA reviews it and notes any deficiencies in the program. These deficiencies must then be corrected once they are brought to the carrier's attention.

Training Facilities

Carriers are required to have adequate ground and flight training facilities for the conduct of training, and must have enough flight and simulator instructors and check airmen to do the required work (14 CFR §121.401[a][2]). Any training devices or simulators that are used as part of the course of training by virtue of Section 121.409 or are allowed in checking/training activities found in Subpart O or Appendices E or F must be specifically approved both as to the device and as to the course (14 CFR §121.407).

Furthermore, note that 14 CFR §121.407(c) allows an approved simulator to be used to meet the in-flight training requirements for both the airplane recency of experience requirements of §121.439 and the proficiency check requirements of §121.441. In other words, with an approved simulator, these elements of training need not be performed in the aircraft. But Section 121.407 goes even further. In Section 121.407(d), the FAA requires that the **low-altitude windshear flight training program** be conducted in a simulator and not in an aircraft. This is not only because it is virtually impossible to simulate these conditions but also because to do so would be extremely dangerous in an airplane.

A carrier may have a training course for performing the proficiency checks under Section 121.441. This course may utilize flight simulators or flight training devices. The carrier must design the course so that it includes at least four hours of training at the pilot controls of the airplane simulator as well as proper preflight and post flight briefings. The course may be designed either to perform the training required by Appendix F or may be used to provide **line-oriented flight training (LOFT)**. The requirements for these programs are listed in 14 CFR §121.409. Notice that §121.409(c) allows for the reduction of programmed hours of flight training for certain pilot and flight engineer training programs.

Training Requirements for Check Pilots/Check Airmen

Check pilots (that term is slowly replacing the current term, "**check airmen**," in FAA guidance and regulations) are an air carrier or training center's employees, approved by the FAA, that actually perform the required flight checks at the conclusion of a course of training. 14 CFR §121.411 defines two different types of check airman:

(1) A check airman (airplane) is a person who is qualified, and permitted, to conduct flight checks or instruction in an airplane, in a flight simulator, or in a flight training device for a particular type airplane.
(2) A check airman (simulator) is a person who is qualified to conduct flight checks or instruction, but only in a flight simulator or in a flight training device for a particular type airplane.

(14 CFR §121.411[a])

In order to perform as a check airman (airplane), the person must hold the certificates required to serve as either pilot-in-command or flight engineer (as appropriate) on the airplane on which he or she is instructing. Furthermore, he or she must be qualified on the operation for that carrier. This would include such things as initial and recurrent training, proficiency checks, recency of experience, and so on. That person would also have had to complete the check airman training specified in Section 121.413. Since this person is authorized to serve aboard an aircraft, the person must hold a medical certificate. If not serving as a required flight crewmember, then he or she would only need to hold a third-class medical certificate. If serving as either second-in-command or pilot-in-command, the check airman must hold either a second-class or a first-class medical certificate, as appropriate.

As the name suggests, a simulator check airman is only authorized to conduct training or flight checks in a simulator, while an airplane check airman may conduct training or checks in an airplane, a simulator, or a flight training device (121.411[a]).

The requirements to perform duties as a check airman (simulator) are very similar to the check airman (airplane) except there is no requirement to hold a medical certificate or to have met the recency of experience requirements of Section 121.439 (three landings and takeoffs in 90 days). Since this person will not be performing functions in an airplane, there is no requirement to actually be current on the operation.

Training Requirements for Air Transportation Flight Instructors

As with the check airmen, Part 121 specifies the required training for the two types of flight instructors used for Part 121 training, namely airplane and simulator flight instructors. 14 CFR §121.412 allows a flight instructor (airplane) to instruct in airplanes, simulators, or flight training devices, while a flight instructor (simulator) may only instruct in simulators or flight training devices. Section 121.412(b) establishes requirements for the flight instructor (airplane) that are very similar to those for the check airman. The only substantial difference is that the flight instructor (airplane) doesn't need to be approved by the FAA. Rather, the instructor only needs to be trained by the carrier. Section 121.414 lays out the training requirements for flight instructors, airplane and simulator.

Training Flow

Beginning with 14 CFR §121.415, the regulations spell out exactly what training is required for a pilot during any phase of his or her career. The first training a new crewmember or dispatcher receives is **basic indoctrination ground training** (or **indoc**). This training must consist of at least 40 programmed hours (unless reduced) and includes things such as duties and responsibilities of crewmembers or dispatchers, FARs, ops specs, and company manuals. At the conclusion of indoctrination, the crewmember moves on to initial training.

Initial training is the portion of the training that is detailed in 14 CFR §121.419 for ground training for pilots and flight engineers, §121.424 for flight training for pilots and flight engineers, §121.421 for flight attendants, and §121.422 for dispatchers. For pilots and flight engineers, this training must include general topics such as dispatch or release procedures; weight and balance; runway limitations for takeoff or landing; meteorology; ATC systems, procedures, and phraseology; navigation systems and procedures; communications procedures; visual cues used in instrument approaches; crew resource management (CRM) initial training; and other instruction as necessary to ensure competence (14 CFR 121.419[a][1]).

Pilots and flight engineers then proceed to the second half of initial ground training, commonly called "systems" training. Here, the pilots are assigned classes based upon the specific make and model of airplane to be flown. Topics required by Section 121.419(a)(2) include a general description of the airplane; performance characteristics; engines and propellers; major components; major airplane systems; severe weather training; operating limitations; fuel consumption and cruise control; flight planning; normal and emergency procedures; and the approved airplane flight manual.

Section 121.419(c) sets the programmed hours of instruction for initial ground training as follows:

(c) Initial ground training for pilots and flight engineers must consist of at least the following programmed hours of instruction in the required subjects specified in paragraph (a) of this section and in §121.415(a) unless reduced under §121.405:
  (1) Group I airplanes—
      (i) Reciprocating powered, 64 hours; and
      (ii) Turbopropeller powered, 80 hours.
  (2) Group II airplanes, 120 hours.

(d) Initial ground training for pilots who have completed the airline transport pilot certification training program in §61.156 must consist of at least the following programmed hours of instruction in the required subjects specified in paragraph (b) of this section and in §121.415(a) unless reduced under §121.405:
  (1) Group I airplanes—
    (i) Reciprocating powered, 54 hours; and
    (ii) Turbopropeller powered, 70 hours.
  (2) Group II airplanes, 110 hours.
(e) Compliance and pilot programmed hours.
  (1) Compliance with the requirements identified in paragraphs (a)(2)(xi) and (a)(2)(xii) of this section is required no later than March 12, 2019.
  (2) Beginning March 12, 2019, initial programmed hours applicable to pilots as specified in paragraphs (c) and (d) of this section must include 2 additional hours.

(14 CFR 121.419)

At the successful conclusion of initial ground training, pilots and flight engineers proceed to flight training under the provisions of Section 121.424. This training is governed by the training program outline found in Appendix E of Part 121. It also must include the certificate holder's low-altitude windshear flight training program and as we discussed earlier, per 14 CFR §121.424(b)(1), windshear maneuvers and procedures must be performed in a simulator in which the maneuvers and procedures are specifically authorized to be accomplished.

Flight attendant initial training is specified in Section 121.421 and includes topics such as authority of the pilot-in-command, passenger handling, and CRM. Airplane-specific flight attendant training includes a general description of the airplane, especially as it relates to emergency procedure, evacuation, or ditching; communications with passengers and crew; and proper use of galley equipment and environmental controls such as cabin heat and ventilation. Section 121.421(c) sets the programmed hours of instruction for initial ground training of flight attendants as follows:

- Group I piston airplanes—8 programmed hours
- Group I turboprop airplanes—8 programmed hours
- Group II airplanes (jets)—16 programmed hours

Dispatcher initial training is specified in Section 121.422 and includes topics such as use of communications systems; meteorology; NOTAMs, NAVAIDs, and publications; joint dispatcher and pilot responsibilities; airport characteristics; prevailing weather and sources of weather information; ATC and instrument approach procedures; and DRM initial training. Then, like pilots and flight engineers, dispatchers receive airplane-specific training. Section 121.422(a)(2) requires training in topics such as a general airplane description, which emphasizes operating and performance characteristics; navigation equipment; instrument approach and communication equipment; emergency equipment and procedures; flight operation procedures including severe weather avoidance and escape procedures; weight and balance; basic airplane performance dispatch requirements and procedures; flight planning and fuel requirements; and emergency procedures including government notification. Section 121.422(c) sets the programmed hours of instruction for aircraft dispatchers as follows:

- Group I piston airplanes—30 programmed hours
- Group I turboprop airplanes—40 programmed hours
- Group II airplanes (jets)—40 programmed hours

Other required training that is typically accomplished during initial training includes the HAZMAT training of 14 CFR §121.433(a), the crewmember emergency training of §121.417, and the CRM/DRM training required in §121.404.

All of the above training requires a competency check at the end of the course of training. That is, there is a comprehensive "final exam." It often is broken into a series of exams during the course of training. For pilots and flight engineers, it will include a checkride in the simulator and, in many cases, also in the aircraft. For pilots and flight engineers, at the conclusion of initial training and the checkride, the next step is to move on to the initial operating experience (IOE) required by Section 121.434.

Part 121, Subpart O: Crewmember Qualifications

14 CFR Part 121, Subpart O, prescribes crewmember qualifications for all Part 121 operations and those Part 135 certificate holders conducting operations that require two pilots. This means even those conducting commuter operations under Part 135 are governed by the aircraft type certification rules contained in Part

121 Subpart O. These crewmember qualifications cover training requirements, operating experience requirements, required certificates, pilot pairing limitations, and recency of experience requirements.

Initial Operating Experience

Once the pilot or flight engineer has been trained on the aircraft, the regulations (14 CFR §121.434) require a period of supervised flying for the purpose of consolidation of knowledge, known as **initial operating experience (IOE)**. This is a period of time that the new crewmember (new to the operation, not necessarily the company) flies while under the direct supervision of a qualified check pilot.

In the case of a new captain (pilot-in-command), that person will legally be second-in-command of the aircraft since that is the position in which he or she is fully qualified. The check pilot will legally be pilot-in-command and ultimately responsible for the conduct of the flights. During a captain's IOE, the new captain will sit in the left seat and make all of the decisions for the operation of the flight. Only in the event the new captain is about to make a serious error of judgment or violate the FARs will the check airman (pilot-in-command) exert his or her authority over the flight. In the case of a captain's initial or upgrade training, an FAA operations inspector—not just a company check airman—must observe at least one leg of the IOE, including one takeoff and one landing.

In the case of a new second-in-command (copilot), the copilot is legal to fly as second-in-command. The copilot will sit in the right seat and perform all of the duties of a second-in-command under the watchful eye of the check captain (pilot-in-command). The check captain is performing the evaluation of the second-in-command in this case.

In the case of a flight engineer, a check engineer will be aboard the airplane and is the legal flight engineer. The IOE engineer will sit at the panel and operate the flight under the supervision of the check engineer.

14 CFR §121.434 requires minimum experience hours and cycles (takeoffs and landings). The pilot operating experience minimum requirements for initial training are as follows:

- Group I piston airplanes—15 hours of operating experience
- Group I turboprop airplanes—20 hours of operating experience
- Group II airplanes (jets)—25 hours of operating experience

In each case, the experience must include at least four cycles, with at least two cycles actually being flown by the person being checked. The FAA does place more importance on flight cycles as opposed to flight hours in Section 121.434(f). These times may be reduced by one hour for each takeoff and landing above the minimum of four required. The times may be reduced a maximum of 50 percent. In other words, the minimum reduced hours for a Group I propeller airplane would be 7.5 hours and 12 takeoffs and landings, Group I turboprop minimum reduced hours would be 10 hours and 14 takeoffs and landings, and Group II minimum reduced hours would be 12.5 hours and 17 takeoffs and landings.

Line Operating Flight Time

Our new pilot or copilot is almost finished. At the conclusion of IOE, he or she may fly with a "regular" pilot (i.e., not a check airman). However, the FAA wants to see that the new pilot gets substantial experience in a relatively short period of time. This period is known as **line operating flight time** (not to be confused with line-oriented flight training, or LOFT). This is also for the purpose of further consolidation of knowledge. Section 121.434(g) requires that each pilot who is new to the equipment obtain 100 hours of flight time on that equipment within 120 days of completing the type rating checkride or final proficiency check on the aircraft during training. If this experience is not met, Section 121.434(h)(4) allows the time to be extended to 150 days if the pilot completes refresher training. If this isn't done or the time period exceeds 150 days, the pilot must undergo a new proficiency check.

Flight attendants must also undergo IOE. 14 CFR §121.434(e) requires a five-hour period of IOE under the supervision of an authorized supervisor.

Other Training and Checking

Once a new copilot completes the 100 hours of consolidation of knowledge, he or she may perform as a regular crewmember. The next training/checking event in a pilot's career is likely to be annual recurrent training. 14 CFR §121.433(c) requires **annual recurrent ground and flight training**. (Note that dispatchers and flight attendants also require annual recurrent ground training and a competence check.) The content of recurrent training programs for pilots, flight engineers, and flight attendants is spelled out in 14 CFR §121.427, which also specifies the minimum program times for the recurrent training (Table 6-1). The training is essentially a

Table 6-1 Recurrent ground training programmed hours

	Pilots and Flight Engineers	Flight Attendants	Aircraft Dispatchers
Group I piston airplanes	16 hours	4 hours	8 hours
Group I turboprop airplanes	20 hours	5 hours	10 hours
Group II airplanes (jets)	25 hours	12 hours	20 hours

"refresher course" of the material that was covered in the initial training program, and the objective is to ensure that crewmembers continue to be knowledgeable of, and proficient in, their specific aircraft type and crew position.

Recurrent training also offers air carriers the opportunity to introduce crewmembers to changes in company operating procedures and to emphasize new developments in training that reflect changes in the operating environment (e.g., fatigue issues, LAHSO [land and hold short] operations, precision monitored approaches, new FAA regulations, etc.).

The next most likely event in our flight engineer or copilot's career is likely to be a move (in the same capacity) to another (bigger) airplane. This is because at most companies, such a move means an increase in pay because of the larger airplane. When that happens, what training is required of the pilot? Assuming that the airplane group is the same, the pilot would need transition training.

Transition Training

As stated in 14 CFR §121.400(c)(2), transition training is the training provided to a crewmember who is changing airplanes to serve in the same capacity on another airplane of the same group. So, a 737 copilot who is moving on to the A330 as a copilot would require transition training. The contents of the ground training course are defined in Section 121.419 and are the same as for initial training. The flight training portion of transition training is spelled out in Section 121.424. At the conclusion of this training, the pilot would have to go through IOE and 100 hours of consolidation of knowledge for this aircraft.

The next career step would be for the flight engineer to become a copilot, or a copilot to become a captain. If the crewmember has never served on this airplane before, they would be required to complete initial training for that status for that aircraft. On the other hand, if the crewmember has served on that particular airplane, they would only be required to complete upgrade training.

Upgrade Training

Once again, 14 CFR §§121.419 and 121.424 are the applicable regulations for ground and flight training. Each pilot upgrade training course the carrier develops would have to meet these minimum standards as far as content and, if specified, programmed hours.

Proficiency Checks

Once pilots or flight engineers are qualified on an operation and continue to fly, the regulations require that they be monitored fairly frequently as to training and proficiency. 14 CFR §121.441 requires that all captains receive a **proficiency check** every 12 months and an intermediate proficiency check or course of simulator training within the last 6 months. These are commonly referred to as "PCs" or "6 checks." Second-in-command pilots and flight engineers need to undergo either a proficiency check or line-oriented simulator training every 24 months and a proficiency check and any other simulator course within 12 months. The content of the proficiency check is spelled out in Part 121 Appendix F.

Line Checks

In addition to all of the "school house" training and checking that the pilot-in-command is subjected to, pilots must also undergo routine evaluation of their flying skills while operating live line flights. These checkrides, known as **line checks**, are conducted in the normal course of business by company check airmen and consist of observations of one or more legs over a typical part of the certificate holder's route. Section 121.440 requires that captains receive these checkrides at least once every 12 months; they are therefore referred to as **annual line checks**.

Recency of Experience

The concept of **recency of experience** should be familiar to all pilots as it is very similar to 14 CFR §61.57, which was introduced to them very early in their student pilot days. While not technically a training or checking requirement, 14 CFR §121.439 specifies that a pilot must have performed at least three takeoffs and landings as a pilot within the last 90 days. If this recency of experience requirement is not met, the pilot may requalify either in an airplane (although not in line operations) or in a simulator. If the recency has expired, the pilot must meet the specific requirements of Section 121.439(b) and (c). These provisions require that the takeoffs and landings meet certain criteria such as the failure of the most critical engine and ILS approaches to minimums. Further, to use the visual simulator for currency, the pilot must have had at least 100 hours in the airplane.

You might be asking yourself, how could a regular line pilot working a full schedule not be able to perform at least three takeoffs and landings as a pilot within the last 90 days? Actually becoming "non-current" is more common than you might think. For instance, international pilots flying with augmented flight crews might have as many as four pilots onboard the flight. In this case, it is not possible for pilots to perform a takeoff or landing during a typical international trip. Generally it is the captain (the most senior captain if there is more than one) who decides which pilot will get which leg; this is usually dictated by who might need currency on takeoffs or landings. Also, there are flights in which one crewmember performs the takeoff, while another crewmember performs the landing. In these types of flight operations, it is fairly common for an international pilot to perform only one or two takeoffs and landings per month. So recency of experience is an issue these pilots keep a close eye on. Another group of pilots who may find it difficult to maintain recency are those serving on the management side of the company's operation. For a large airline, these pilots can range from the vice president of flight operations, to the various chief pilots, on down to the dozens of pilots who serve as assistants in various duties in support of the line pilots. The same can be said for any full-time pilot union leadership or committee position holders. Their duties might keep them away from actual line flying for a considerable amount of time. If pilots become "non-current," then they must perform "three bounces" (three takeoffs and landings) in either the simulator or a real aircraft.

Flight engineers have a recency of experience requirement imposed by 14 CFR §121.453 that requires them to have met the **50 in 6 requirements**. This means that they must have at least 50 hours of flight engineer time in the same make/model aircraft within the preceding 6 months.

An aircraft dispatcher also must complete a type of recency of experience. 14 CFR §121.463 requires a dispatcher to have observed, within the preceding 12 calendar months, flight operations from the flight deck for at least 5 hours in one of the types of aircraft in each group to be dispatched. This requirement may be reduced to a minimum of 2½ hours by the substitution of one additional takeoff and landing for an hour of flight. This requirement may also be satisfied by observation of 5 hours of simulator training for each airplane group in one of the simulators approved under §121.407 for the group. However, if the requirement is met by the use of a simulator, no reduction in hours is permitted.

Route and Airport Qualifications

Route and airport qualifications require that the carrier establish a system for disseminating information to each pilot concerning the routes and airports to be served by that pilot. 14 CFR §121.443 requires that the captain be route qualified and airport qualified. This entails having provided the following information to each crewmember: weather characteristics appropriate to the season; navigation facilities; communications procedures including visual aids; kinds of terrain and obstructions; minimum safe flight levels; en route, terminal area, departure, holding, and authorized instrument approach procedures; congested areas and physical layout of the terminal areas in which the pilot will operate; and NOTAMs for the en route, departure, arrival phases and any alternate airports.

Special Airport Qualifications

In addition to these general requirements, there are **special airport qualifications** for those airports designated by the FAA as special airports. 14 CFR §121.445 requires that each pilot-in-command operating IFR in conditions where visibility is less than 3 statute miles and the ceiling is less than 1,000 feet below the minimum enroute altitude or minimum obstruction clearance altitude into a special airport to have made an actual entry into that airport within the last 12 months or have qualified using pictorial means to train for the unusual circumstances affecting that airport. Pictorial means is simply a group of pictures and instructional pages describing the peculiarities of operations to and from a particular airport. The most common reasons for the FAA to designate an airport as a special airport are precipitous terrain, congested or unusual airspace, obstructions or complex arrival or departure procedures, or a combination or any of these.

Some special airports can be so difficult to operate in and out of that each pilot-in-command may be required to fly with a check airman or specially qualified captain or first officer to give "on-the-job-training" when flying to these difficult airports for the first time, or if it has been more than 12 months since the pilot has last flown to that airport. Once a pilot has received this special airport training, they will remain current as long as they have flown to that particular airport at least once in the preceding 12 months. In some rare cases, an airline may decide to allow only check pilots or specifically trained pilots to fly to a certain airport.

Of the hundreds of airports a professional pilot may fly to over the course of a career, only a few dozen or so might be special airports. So maintaining currency and keeping accurate records is a must. Typically, an air carrier uses a computer file to help pilots keep track of their special airport qualifications. When a pilot nears the 12 month limit, a message is sent to the pilot warning them of the need to review the pictorial training for a special airport or try to fly a trip to that particular special airport. Only when the pilot either self-certifies having completed the pictorial training or actually flies to the special airport will the electronic warning message be removed from the pilot's computer file.

Pairing Limitations

As a result of several serious accidents where one or more of the flight crewmembers had limited experience in the type of aircraft, the FAA has implemented rules limiting who can fly with whom and under what conditions. In establishing these **pairing limitations**, 14 CFR §121.438 first looks at the experience of the second-in-command.

If the second-in-command has less than 100 hours in type (in a Part 121 operation) and the pilot-in-command is not a check airman, the pilot-in-command must make all takeoffs and landings:

1. at special airports (see above);
2. if visibility is less than ¾ statute mile;
3. if runway visual range (RVR) is less than 4,000 feet;
4. if runways are contaminated (snow, slush, water, etc.);
5. if braking action is reported as less than good;
6. if the reported crosswind component is in excess of 15 knots;
7. if windshear is reported in the vicinity of the airport; or
8. in any other condition where the PIC determines it is prudent to exercise his or her prerogative.

Secondly, Section 121.438(b) limits pairing a low time captain with a low time first officer. One of the two must have more than 75 hours in type under Part 121. Some minor exemptions are available that recognize a new piece of equipment or a domicile where the airplane has never been operated by that particular air carrier.

Advanced Qualification Program (AQP)

Another type of training program was created in the 1980s and has transformed recurrent training in the airline industry. The **advanced qualification program (AQP)** is a type of voluntary training program that offers air carriers an alternative to the traditional Part 121 and Part 135 crewmember training and checking requirements. Although AQP is a voluntary program, the FAA Flight Standards Service encourages air carriers to participate. The development of the AQP was the result of a cooperative relationship between the FAA and U.S. air carriers and had its beginnings back in 1987. The FAA and U.S. air carriers sought to develop an improved training program that recognized the dramatic changes in the capabilities of simulators and other computer-based training devices in the training and qualification of flight crews. This working relationship between the FAA and U.S. carriers led to a list of recommendations that eventually became the framework for Special Federal Aviation Regulation 58 (SFAR 58) and Advisory Circular (AC) 120-54A. These documents authorized the use of advanced qualification programs. AC 120-54A describes AQP this way: *"AQPs are systematically developed, continuously maintained, and empirically validated proficiency-based training systems."* The AQP is, simply, a redesign of traditional air carrier training and checking programs to better suit the requirements of new aircraft and the capabilities of modern training methods.

SFAR 58 and AC 120-54A contain the requirements that air carriers must fulfill to gain approval of an AQP for qualifying, training, certifying, and checking the competency of pilots, flight attendants, and aircraft dispatchers as well as instructors and evaluators who are required to be trained or qualified under 14 CFR Parts 121 and 135. AQP is founded on the principle that the content of training and checking requirements should be directly driven by the requirements of the job. Under the AQP, each air carrier develops its own **proficiency**

objectives and submits them to the FAA for approval. A proficiency objective is a statement describing the behavior a crewmember must demonstrate to be able to successfully perform a task. Once approved by the FAA, these proficiency objectives become regulatory requirements for that particular carrier. An obvious advantage is that this allows air carriers to develop a training program that better suits their needs.

AC120-54A discusses how an AQP can be crafted to use scenario-based training and evaluation. Most accidents are caused by a chain of errors that build up over the course of a flight and which, if undetected or unresolved, result in a final precipitating error. Traditional training programs, with their maneuver-based training and evaluation, artificially segment simulation events in such a way as to prevent the realistic buildup of the error chain. Under AQPs, training and evaluation events are scenario-based, simulating more closely the actual flight conditions known to cause most fatal carrier accidents.

Another advantage of the AQP is that the FAA is authorized to approve significant differences from traditional training requirements if it can be shown these differences will achieve an equivalent or better level of safety. For instance, the FAA allows development of a **single-visit training program**. A single-visit training program allows air carriers to place all flight crewmembers in the same recurrent training cycle (i.e., annual check). The single-visit training program is a comprehensive program that integrates all of the elements of training and checking. A single-visit training program is thought to provide for more realistic training and checking for flight crews in a single annual visit to a training facility than was accomplished under the traditional 6 month visit. Traditionally the pilot-in-command received flight training and/or proficiency checks every 6 months; under AQP single-visit training programs, this is done either on an annual basis or some other approved timetable (e.g., every 9 months). A single-visit training program requires exemptions to 14 CFR §121.433(c)(1)(iii); §121.441(a)(1); §121.441(b)(1); and Part 121, Appendix F.

Generally, an AQP differs from traditional regulatory requirements in terms of the characteristics shown in Table 6-2.

Flight Operational Quality Assurance (FOQA)

Although **flight operational quality assurance (FOQA)** is not technically a training or checking requirement, it does provide a means for measuring the effects of flight crew training directly on line operations. FOQA, also known as **flight data monitoring (FDM)**, is a program air carriers use to collect and analyze digital flight data of actual line aircraft operations. The capability to monitor physical aircraft performance in extensive detail was made possible with the arrival of digital flight data computers. Air carrier FOQA programs actually began with European air carriers, primarily British Airways and SAS. Over a 10-year period, the FAA and U.S. air carriers had been monitoring the European carriers' successful digital flight data recording and analysis programs in the hope of developing a similar program in the United States. Many major airlines are now implementing FOQA programs with their newer aircraft fleets. The primary goal

Table 6-2 Traditional Part 121/135 programs vs. AQP training and checking

Traditional Part 121 Training and Checking	AQP Training and Checking
Mandatory compliance by air carriers governed by the appropriate provisions of Parts 121 and 135.	Participation is *voluntary*.
Training and checking of each crewmember on an individual basis.	Training and checking performed on a crew-oriented basis.
LOFT and CRM are "nonjeopardy" training events.	LOFT training is evaluated; CRM evaluation factors are used.
Carriers maintain training records of final results only.	Carriers submit de-identified data on each evaluation point for each trainee.
Evaluation period is fixed at 12 months	Evaluation period can be adjusted as crew performance warrants.
Simulator training is not required.	Simulator training must be utilized.

of these FOQA programs is to identify significant performance trends before they become accidents.

Most of the FOQA programs are concerned with the detection and reporting of exceedances and other identifiable special events (e.g., in-flight engine shutdown, flap overspeed, engine temperature exceedance, etc.). This data is collected and analyzed for trends. After years of research on the relationship between collected flight data and specific crew qualification standards, the FAA and participating air carriers have been able to develop distinct measurements of crew performance that are thought to be more objective than those applied in traditional training programs (refer to Appendix II of FAA AC 120-82, *Flight Operational Quality Assurance*, for a full list of recorded events).

FOQA data collection is now being used in conjunction with the AQP and has revolutionized air carrier training. Separately, FOQA and AQPs are valuable, but when combined they provide complementary approaches to ensuring training effectiveness. FOQA provides a means for measuring the effects of flight crew training directly on line operations through the collection and analysis of digital flight data. FOQA also affords air carriers the capability to measure the effectiveness of their training programs in directly improving line operations.

Unfortunately, FOQA data collection programs have become a somewhat contentious issue for flight crews, airline management, and the FAA over the last decade. Flight crews and air carriers, for obvious reasons, would like to make certain FOQA data is not used for detection of company policy or FAR violations. The FAA to its credit has agreed, for now, to use only "de-identified" data to monitor for safety trends.

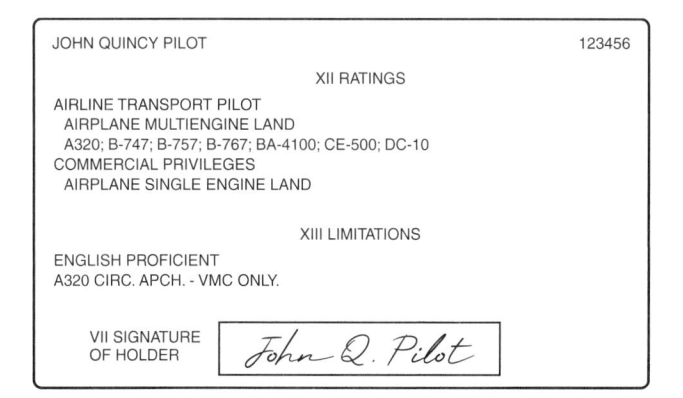

```
JOHN QUINCY PILOT                              123456
                    XII RATINGS
AIRLINE TRANSPORT PILOT
   AIRPLANE MULTIENGINE LAND
   A320; B-747; B-757; B-767; BA-4100; CE-500; DC-10
COMMERCIAL PRIVILEGES
   AIRPLANE SINGLE ENGINE LAND
                    XIII LIMITATIONS
ENGLISH PROFICIENT
A320 CIRC. APCH. - VMC ONLY.

   VII SIGNATURE        John Q. Pilot
   OF HOLDER
```

Figure 6-3. FAA pilot license with numerous type ratings.

Type Ratings

A **type rating** is an FAA authorization stating an airman's particular privileges and limitations (e.g., circling approach allowed in VMC only) pertaining to certain aircraft types listed directly on a pilot's license. Such qualification requires additional training beyond the scope of the initial license and aircraft class training. Requirements for a type rating are spelled out in 14 CFR §61.31(a) (Figure 6-3).

A type rating is required to act as PIC of any turbojet-powered aircraft or any large aircraft. Large aircraft are defined in 14 CFR §1.1 as those of more than 12,500 pounds maximum certificated takeoff weight. Pilots flying piston-engine or turboprop aircraft are, therefore, only affected by the takeoff weight requirement. That is, piston-engine and turboprop aircraft require a type rating if their maxiumum certificated takeoff weight exceeds 12,500 pounds. Examples of piston-engine aircraft requiring a type rating range from the Ford Trimotor to the venerable DC-3. Examples of turboprop aircraft requiring a type rating range from the larger King Airs to the Embraer Brasílias to the ATR 42 and 72.

> **14 CFR §61.31—Type rating requirements, additional training, and authorization requirements.**
>
> (a) Type ratings required. A person who acts as a pilot in command of any of the following aircraft must hold a type rating for that aircraft:
> (1) Large aircraft (except lighter-than-air).
> (2) Turbojet-powered airplanes.
> (3) Other aircraft specified by the Administrator through aircraft type certificate procedures.

Specific requirements for attaining an aircraft type rating are found in paragraphs 14 CFR §61.31 and §61.63(d). Which cover such things as type rating requirements, authorization requirements, additional aircraft training and ratings (other than for ratings at ATP certification level).

You may be surprised to learn an aircraft type rating may cover multiple models or variants of aircraft. A few popular examples of this include the type ratings for the ATR 42 and 72, Boeing 757 and 767, Airbus 318, 319, 320, and 321, and Cessna's diverse line of Citation CE-500 models among many others. These type ratings allow PIC operations in all models covered in the type rating. Sometimes the differences between these models are minor, sometimes they may be extensive. When a type rating covers multiple aircraft models the term **common type rating** is used to describe this authorization.

Typically, both turbojet aircraft and aircraft with a MTOW of 12,500 pounds or more require two pilots at the controls. Therefore, in most cases, aircraft requiring a minimum flight crew of two pilots also requires a type rating. However, there are a number of aircraft certified for single-pilot operation. Pilot's wishing to earn single-pilot privileges must earn a separate **single-pilot aircraft type rating**. Specific requirements for a single-pilot type rating may be found in 14 CFR §61.63(f), multiengine airplane with a single-pilot station.

A single-pilot aircraft type rating lets you fly turbojet airplanes such as an Embraer Phenom 100 or Phenom 300, Cessna Citation Mustang, Cessna Citation 500-series airplanes, or a number of other light jets without a second pilot (i.e., second-in-command, first officer, or copilot).

Summary

The air transport industry has probably the most extensive and demanding training and retraining requirements of any field of endeavor. Training programs for pilots, flight attendants, dispatchers, and, as we'll see in Chapter 14, mechanics are mandated in minute detail by the FAA and must be strictly adhered to by the carriers and their employees. Pilots should be familiar with all of the required training because they share joint responsibility with carriers to ensure that the training has been performed. The same holds true for the other certificated airmen. The specific equipment and procedures training required for cockpit crewmembers is spelled out in Appendices E and F of Part 121, and crewmembers should familiarize themselves with these requirements prior to initiating training.

In the next chapter, we will discuss the flight and/or duty time limitations for pilots, flight engineers, navigators, flight attendants and dispatchers.

Important Terms in Chapter 6

14 CFR Part 121 Appendix E—Flight Training Requirements
14 CFR Part 121 Appendix F—Proficiency Check Requirements
14 CFR Part 142 Flight Training Certificate
50 in 6 requirements
advanced qualification program (AQP)
annual line check
annual recurrent ground and flight training
base month
basic indoctrination ground training (indoc)
check airman (or check pilot)
common type rating
crew resource management (CRM) training
curriculum
differences training
dispatcher initial training
dispatcher resource management (DRM) training
flight attendant training
flight data monitoring (FDM)
flight operational quality assurance (FOQA)
grace month
Group I airplanes
Group II airplanes
HAZMAT training
initial operating experience (IOE)
initial training
line check
line operating flight time
line-oriented flight training (LOFT)
low-altitude windshear flight training program
pairing limitations
proficiency check
proficiency objectives
programmed hours
recency of experience
recurrent training
reduced programmed hours
requalification training
route and airport qualifications
single-pilot aircraft type rating
single-visit training program
special airport qualifications
transition training
type rating
upgrade training

Chapter 6 Exam

1. For the purpose of the training regulations, airplanes are broken down into three categories of aircraft called
   a. Group I, Group II, and Group III.
   b. piston aircraft, turbofan aircraft, and turbojet aircraft.
   c. piston aircraft, turboprop aircraft, and turbojet aircraft.
   d. Group A, Group B, and Group C.

2. What type of training would be required for crewmembers that have qualified and served in the same capacity on another airplane in the same group?
   a. Programmed training
   b. Differences training
   c. Initial operating training
   d. Transition training

3. What type of training ensures each crewmember or dispatcher is adequately trained and currently proficient with respect to the type of airplane that person is crewing or dispatching?
   a. Special qualification training
   b. Theater training
   c. Recurrent training
   d. Indoctrination training

4. If a pilot completes initial training as second-in-command (first officer) on a piece of equipment in March for an air carrier not using AQP, when would be the latest this pilot could complete recurrent training?
   a. Recurrent must be completed by the end of March of the next year.
   b. Recurrent must be completed before the first of March of the next year.
   c. Recurrent must be completed before the end of April of the next year.
   d. Recurrent must be completed before the end of September of the same year.

5. Who may conduct the required Part 121 training?
   a. Any authorized Part 141 flight school or the Part 121 training center.
   b. Either the Part 121 certificate holder or a company holding a Part 142 flight training certificate may conduct the required training.
   c. Either a Part 141 flight school or Part 142 flight training center may conduct the required training.
   d. Only a company holding a Part 142 flight training certificate.

6. What is the recency of experience requirement for a flight engineer?
   a. A flight engineer must have at least 50 hours of flight engineer time in the same make/model aircraft within the preceding 6 months.
   b. A flight engineer must have at least 50 hours of flight engineer (turbojet) time in Group II aircraft within the preceding 6 months.
   c. A flight engineer must have at least 50 hours of flight engineer time in the same make/model aircraft within the preceding 120 days.
   d. A flight engineer must have at least 100 hours of flight engineer time in the same make/model aircraft within the preceding 6 months.

7. No person may serve as a pilot-in-command unless that pilot has received a line check within
   a. the preceding 6 calendar months.
   b. the preceding 24 calendar months.
   c. the preceding 120 days.
   d. the preceding 12 calendar months.

8. When the visibility is below what value must the pilot-in-command make all takeoffs and landings when flying with a second-in-command who has less than 100 hours in the type of airplane to be flown?
   a. When the visibility is below the standard takeoff minimums of 1 statute mile or RVR 5,000 FT
   b. When the visibility is below ¾ statute mile or RVR 4,000 FT for the runway to be used
   c. When the visibility is below ½ statute mile or RVR 1,800 FT for the runway to be used
   d. When the visibility is below published Category I landing minimums

9. How many hours is an aircraft dispatcher required to observe flight operations from the flight deck within the preceding 12 calendar months? May observing simulator training satisfy this requirement?
   a. 5 hours, reducible to 2½ hours by the substitution of additional takeoff and landing for an hour of flight; yes
   b. 12 hours; not reducible, no
   c. 10 hours; not reducible, no
   d. 5 hours, reducible by 1 hour by the substitution of each additional takeoff and landing; no

10. How often must a pilot serving as pilot-in-command satisfactorily complete a proficiency check if that pilot's airline does not utilize an AQP single-visit training program?
    a. Within the preceding 24 calendar months
    b. Within the preceding 6 calendar months; also must complete a special airport qualification
    c. Must complete a proficiency check every 12 calendar months
    d. Within the preceding 12 calendar months; must also complete either simulator training or a proficiency check within the preceding 6 calendar months

11. Which of the following is an example of a type rating limitation?
    a. Single-engine land.
    b. Cessna 182 Skylane.
    c. Circling approach—VMC only.

CHAPTER 7
AIR CARRIER FLIGHT AND DUTY TIME LIMITATIONS

*I want to die like my grandfather did, peacefully in his sleep.
Not screaming in terror like his passengers.*

—anonymous

This chapter will cover one of the more contentious areas of the Federal Air Regulations; that is, the issue of what constitutes an appropriate and safe working day and an appropriate and safe rest period. First, we will cover 14 CFR Part 117, which prescribes the flight crew's **flight and duty time limitations** for *passenger carrying* airlines. Then we will focus our attention on Part 121, Subparts Q, R, and S, for certificate holders conducting **all-cargo operations**. 14 CFR Part 121, Subpart Q, covers limitations for flight crews in **domestic operations** while Subpart R covers limitations for flight crews in **flag operations**. 14 CFR Part 121, Subpart S, covers limitations for flight crews in **supplemental** (non-scheduled) **operations**. Finally, we will cover the duty and rest times for dispatchers and flight attendants for both domestic and flag, which are found in 14 CFR Part 121, Subpart P. Through the flight and duty time limitations found in these different sections, the FAA attempts to balance the rest needs of flight crews, flight attendants and dispatchers with the cost and scheduling needs of the companies that employ them.

HR 5900 and Public Law 111-216—Also Known as 14 CFR Part 117

On January 3, 2014, the federal government instituted a major overhaul of airline pilot certification, training standards, pilot rest and flight time/duty time regulations. The catalyst for this change was the 2009 crash of Colgan Air Flight 3407 in Buffalo, New York. This accident gained the attention of the public and Congress, especially when the investigation began to focus on the issues of pilot fatigue, quality of training, and experience levels of the Colgan Air pilots. An aviation rulemaking committee (ARC) was convened by the FAA to make recommendations on updating existing FAA regulations. The committee was tasked with providing a forum for the U.S. aviation community to discuss and make recommendations on how the FAA should modify its own flight and duty time regulations as well as Airline Transport Pilot (ATP) certifications standards. The aviation rulemaking committee consisted of members representing aviation safety organizations and airline trade and labor associations.

Because the Colgan crash received so much attention, and with the hope of preventing future accidents, on August 1, 2010, President Obama signed into law the **Airline Safety and Federal Aviation Administration Extension Act (49 USC 40101)**, known as H.R. 5900 (H.R. indicates House of Representatives). This Act resulted in some new laws **(such as Public Law 111-216)** and regulation changes (a new Part 117 and changes to Part 121), directly affecting the scheduling of flight crews. The passage of Pub. L. 111-216 acknowledged the need to finally make the major changes to aviation safety regulations that the National Transportation Safety

Board (NTSB), pilot unions, and various aviation safety advocates had been recommending for decades. Surprisingly, various versions of the final regulations had been circulating around the industry for almost twenty years. In fact, the International Civil Aviation Organization (ICAO) had adopted virtually identical flight and duty time rules a few years prior to Pub. L. 111-216.

The Airline Safety and Federal Aviation Administration Extension Act outlines many revised requirements for the improvement of airline safety. In Chapter 5 we discussed those changes dealing with flight crewmember screening, required qualifications, and air transport pilot certification. In this chapter, we will examine one of the most important sections of the Act: Section 212—Pilot Fatigue.

Pilot Fatigue

Section 212 of the Act first mandated that the FAA initiate rulemaking on flight and duty times, founded on the best available scientific information, which had to specify limitations on the hours of flight and duty time allowed for pilots while addressing problems relating to pilot fatigue. Further, in developing the new regulations, the FAA was required to consider issues such as the time of day of the flights in a duty period, the number of flight segments, the number of time zones crossed, and the impact of functioning in multiple time zones or on different daily schedules. In doing this, Congress mandated the FAA to consider previous research, prior recommendations of the NTSB and NASA, as well as international standards related to biological issues such as fatigue, sleep, circadian rhythms, and sleep and rest needs.

Other mandated flight and duty time issues that the FAA was to consider were alternative procedures to facilitate alertness in the flight deck; crew scheduling and attendance policies and practices; sick leave; the effects of commuting; the means of commuting; and the length of the commute. The FAA was also to consider issues related to medical screening and treatment of pilots, and the environments in which pilots would obtain rest. In addition, the FAA was authorized to consider any other matters the Administrator believed appropriate to the intent of the rulemaking.

The second requirement of Section 212 is that each Part 121 air carrier must submit a **fatigue risk management plan** for its pilots that is acceptable to the FAA. This plan must contain the following:

- The current flight time and duty period limitations of the carrier,
- A plan to provide adequate rest (a rest scheme) that is consistent with the flight time and duty period limitations that enables the management of pilot fatigue, and
- A program of annual training to increase awareness of fatigue, the effects of fatigue on pilots, and countermeasures to be employed to combat fatigue.

In addition, the carrier must develop a method of continually assessing the effectiveness of the fatigue management plan in improving alertness of pilots and mitigating performance errors. This is to be a continuous process that reinforces early improvements to the plan.

The third component of Section 212 is the requirement that the FAA in conjunction with the National Academy of Sciences conduct a study of the effects of commuting on pilot fatigue and report its findings to the Administrator. In conducting the study, the National Academy of Sciences was directed to consider:

- the prevalence of pilot commuting in the commercial air carrier industry, including the number and percentage of pilots who commute;
- all relevant information relating to commuting by pilots, including distances traveled, time zones crossed, time spent, and methods used;
- research that has been conducted on the impact of commuting on pilot fatigue, sleep, and circadian rhythms;
- the commuting policies of commercial air carriers (including passenger and all-cargo air carriers) as to pilot check-in requirements, sick leave policy and use, and fatigue policies of the carriers;
- papers and other materials that were the result of the FAA's June 2008 symposium entitled "Aviation Fatigue Management Symposium: Partnerships for Solutions"; and
- FAA, ICAO and other international policies and guidance regarding commuting.

Upon completion, the study's findings were to be submitted along with any recommendations for regulatory or administrative actions the FAA should consider regarding pilot commuting. The FAA was to then consider the findings of the report and, as it found appropriate and based upon scientific data, update the flight and duty time regulations.

From Law to Regulation

Section 212 of the Act directed the FAA to create new regulations, based on recommendations of the aviation rulemaking committee, that addressed the issues of pilot fatigue. As stated by the FAA in the *Federal Register* Notice of Final Rule for Part 117:

> The rule recognizes the universality of factors that lead to fatigue in most individuals and regulates these factors to ensure that flightcrew members in passenger operations do not accumulate dangerous amounts of fatigue. Fatigue threatens aviation safety because it increases the risk of pilot error that could lead to an accident... The new requirements eliminate the current distinctions between domestic, flag and supplemental passenger operations. The rule provides different requirements based on the time of day, whether an individual is acclimated to a new time zone and the likelihood of being able to sleep under different circumstances.

With that in mind, we will now take a look at the new FAA flight-time/duty-time (FT/DT) regulations crafted in response to Section 212 of the new law.

Flight and Duty Time Regulations

The 2010 rule, which runs more than 400 pages, created a new FAR section—**14 CFR Part 117**—which is intended to address the factors that lead to fatigue in most pilots and to regulate flight time and duty time to ensure pilots in passenger-carrying operations receive the proper rest. The FAA used the knowledge gained from numerous fatigue studies to develop regulations that "mitigate" the effects of fatigue. The proposed rule considered issues such as workload demands, the number of takeoffs and landings (segments) per duty period, **circadian rhythms** (wake/sleep cycles), crossing of time zones, crew complements, and **ultra-long-range (ULR) operations**, as well as the fatigue brought on by being in a different bed every night. Part 117 also requires the development of a **fatigue risk management system (FRMS)** and training for all passenger-carrying airlines. An FRMS includes a training plan that educates airline pilots, crew schedulers, dispatchers and other airline employees in fatigue mitigation measures. Before discussing the FRMS in more detail, let's first dig into Part 117.

14 CFR Part 117—Flight and Duty Limitations and Rest Requirements: Flightcrew Members

In 2014 the FAA implemented a major regulatory rewrite of the Flightcrew duty time and rest provisions. This rewrite, **14 CFR Part 117**, introduced several new science-based terms and concepts such as **window of circadian low, physiological night's rest**, and **fatigue risk management system** in addition to redefining a number of existing concepts. First, let's examine who is covered under 14 CFR §117.1.

Applicability

14 CFR §117.1—Applicability.

(a) This part prescribes flight and duty limitations and rest requirements for all flightcrew members and certificate holders conducting passenger operations under part 121 of this chapter.

(b) This part applies to all operations directed by part 121 certificate holders under part 91, other than subpart K, of this chapter if any segment is conducted as a domestic passenger, flag passenger, or supplemental passenger operation.

(c) This part applies to all flightcrew members when participating in an operation under part 91, other than subpart K of this chapter, on behalf of the part 121 certificate holder if any flight segment is conducted as a domestic passenger, flag passenger, or supplemental passenger operation.

(d) Notwithstanding paragraphs (a), (b) and (c) of this section, a certificate holder may conduct under part 117 its part 121 operations pursuant to 121.470, 121.480, or 121.500.

Part 117 simplifies the applicability of FT/DT regulations in a big way. These new rules are applicable to all types of passenger-carrying Part 121 operations. For example, Part 117 also covers those operations performed under Part 91 by Part 121 air carriers or flight crewmembers if any segment is conducted as a domestic, flag, or supplemental passenger-carrying operation (e.g., tail-end ferry flight). Prior to Part 117, there were different rules for scheduled, non-scheduled, domestic, supplemental and international operations. It was confusing, archaic, and long overdue for a change.

While Section 117.1 simplifies the applicability, you may have noticed one glaring omission: Surprisingly, the new rules cover only the FT/DT and rest requirements for flight crewmembers and certificate holders conducting "passenger-carrying" operations under Part 121. All-cargo carrying air carriers will continue to operate under the limits of Part 121.

Why the difference between passenger-carrying and all-cargo carrying airlines? During any FAA rulemaking process, the Department of Transportation and the Office of Management and Budget are required to conduct a cost-benefit analysis of all proposed regulations. It was determined during this process that "the cost of implementing Part 117 to the cargo industry would be more than the societal benefits the public was willing to pay for." As a result, all-cargo carrying airlines operate under the decades-old Part 121 flight and duty time limitations and are not affected by Part 117.

Definitions

Looking at 14 CFR §117.3—Definitions, you will see many terms and concepts probably familiar to you; however, many of these terms have been redefined to reflect the specifics of Part 117 and to better align the definitions to ICAO standards. Let's take a closer look at some of these definitions.

> **§117.3—Definitions.**
>
> In addition to the definitions in §§1.1 and 110.2 of this chapter, the following definitions apply to this part. In the event there is a conflict in definitions, the definitions in this part control for purposes of the flight and duty limitations and rest requirements of this part.
>
> **Acclimated** means a condition in which a flightcrew member has been in a theater for 72 hours or has been given at least 36 consecutive hours free from duty.

In other words, a flight crewmember who is adjusted to the local time zone is considered to be *acclimated* to that time zone. For FAA purposes, a pilot is considered adjusted to the new local time zone by having been in a theater for at least 72 hours or having been given at least 36 hours free from duty. If the flight crewmember is not adjusted to the local time zone, he or she is considered to be unacclimated. This is a new concept and is closely related to the term *theater*, which we'll define later in this section.

Airport/standby reserve means a defined duty period during which a flightcrew member is required by a certificate holder to be at an airport for a possible assignment.

Augmented flightcrew means a flightcrew that has more than the minimum number of flightcrew members required by the airplane type certificate to operate the aircraft to allow a flightcrew member to be replaced by another qualified flightcrew member for in-flight rest.

Calendar day means a 24-hour period from 0000 through 2359 using Coordinated Universal Time or local time.

Certificate holder means a person who holds or is required to hold an air carrier certificate or operating certificate issued under part 119 of this chapter.

Deadhead transportation means transportation of a flightcrew member as a passenger or non-operating flightcrew member, by any mode of transportation, as required by a certificate holder, excluding transportation to or from a suitable accommodation. All time spent in deadhead transportation is duty and is not rest. For purposes of determining the maximum flight duty period in Table B of this part, deadhead transportation is not considered a flight segment.

Duty means any task that a flightcrew member performs as required by the certificate holder, including but not limited to flight duty period, flight duty, pre- and post-flight duties, administrative work, training, deadhead transportation, aircraft positioning on the ground, aircraft loading, and aircraft servicing.

Fatigue means a physiological state of reduced mental or physical performance capability resulting from lack of sleep or increased physical activity that can reduce a flightcrew member's alertness and ability to safely operate an aircraft or perform safety-related duties.

Fatigue risk management system (FRMS) means a management system for a certificate holder to use to mitigate the effects of fatigue in its particular operations. It is a data-driven process and a systematic method used to continuously monitor and manage safety risks associated with fatigue-related error.

Fit for duty means physiologically and mentally prepared and capable of performing assigned duties at the highest degree of safety.

Flight duty period (FDP) means a period that begins when a flightcrew member is required to report for duty with the intention of conducting a flight, a series of flights, or positioning or ferrying flights, and ends when the aircraft is parked after the last flight and there is no intention for further aircraft movement by the same flightcrew member. A flight duty period includes the duties performed by the flightcrew member on behalf of the certificate holder that occur before a flight segment or between flight segments without a required intervening rest period. Examples of tasks that are part of the flight duty period include deadhead transportation, training conducted in an aircraft or flight simulator, and airport/standby reserve, if the above tasks occur before a flight segment or between flight segments without an intervening required rest period.

Flight duty period is a new concept: it is simply the time span from the start or report time of the FDP until the end of the FDP at block-in or release time. Under the old Part 121 and Part 135 rules, pilots could regularly work a 16-hour duty day. The time of day or number of legs was not taken into consideration whatsoever; it was possible to work 16 straight hours and fly 10 legs, whether you started at 6 a.m. or 6 p.m.

As you might expect, flight crews have been complaining about this for decades. Just imagine that if a pilot was on a normal circadian cycle, woke up at 6 a.m., and had a 7 p.m. report time, it is conceivable the pilot might be awake and on duty until 11 a.m. the next morning. That's some 29 hours! Sleep studies have shown a person who has been awake for over 16 to 20 hours approaches a level of performance degradation equivalent to a blood alcohol content of .06 to .08 percent—hardly an acceptable level of performance. Also, studies have shown the more fatigued the pilot is, the harder it is for that pilot to determine his or her own level of fatigue. This can lead some crewmembers to overestimate their individual performance capabilities.

Home base means the location designated by a certificate holder where a flightcrew member normally begins and ends his or her duty periods.

Lineholder means a flightcrew member who has an assigned flight duty period and is not acting as a reserve flightcrew member.

Long-call reserve means that, prior to beginning the rest period required by §117.25, the flightcrew member is notified by the certificate holder to report for a flight duty period following the completion of the rest period.

Physiological night's rest means 10 hours of rest that encompasses the hours of 0100 and 0700 at the flightcrew member's home base, unless the individual has acclimated to a different theater. If the flightcrew member has acclimated to a different theater, the rest must encompass the hours of 0100 and 0700 at the acclimated location.

In other words, a physiological night's rest must have a rest time period of at least 10 hours that entirely overlaps the period from 0100 hours to 0700 hours in the pilot's reference time zone.

Report time means the time that the certificate holder requires a flightcrew member to report for an assignment.

Reserve availability period (RAP) means a duty period during which a certificate holder requires a flightcrew member on short call reserve to be available to receive an assignment for a flight duty period.

Reserve flightcrew member means a flightcrew member who a certificate holder requires to be available to receive an assignment for duty.

Rest facility means a bunk or seat accommodation installed in an aircraft that provides a flightcrew member with a sleep opportunity.

(1) *Class 1 rest facility* means a bunk or other surface that allows for a flat sleeping position and is located separate from both the flight deck and passenger cabin in an area that is temperature-controlled, allows the flightcrew member to control light, and provides isolation from noise and disturbance.

(2) *Class 2 rest facility* means a seat in an aircraft cabin that allows for a flat or near flat sleeping position; is separated from passengers by a minimum of a curtain to provide darkness and some sound mitigation; and is reasonably free from disturbance by passengers or flightcrew members.

(3) *Class 3 rest facility* means a seat in an aircraft cabin or flight deck that reclines at least 40 degrees and provides leg and foot support.

The importance of classifying onboard rest facilities is new to Part 117 and is discussed in detail in FAA Advisory Circular 117-1, *Flightcrew Member Rest Facilities*. This classification of facilities is used to determine the maximum flight duty period limits. The FAA has used a common-sense approach to flight duty limits; that is, the better the onboard crew rest facility, the longer the allowed flight duty period.

Also, now might be a good time to briefly discuss the scheduling of inflight rest periods. First of all, inflight rest periods are not allowed during the takeoff or landing phases of flight. An inflight rest period can only be scheduled during the cruise phase of flight. Most airlines define "cruise flight" as beginning from the top-of-climb for the initially filed cruise altitude to the top-of-descent, which commences the initial descent into the destination terminal area. Many rest facilities are not even certificated for crewmember occupation during takeoffs and landings due to safety (emergency egress) issues.

Generally speaking, most airlines require flight crewmembers to return to their various stations on the flight deck for the last hour of flight. This gives the pilot time to become fully alert, helping to mitigate the effects of sleep inertia (i.e., "that groggy feeling").

Rest period means a continuous period determined prospectively during which the flightcrew member is free from all restraint by the certificate holder, including freedom from present responsibility for work should the occasion arise.

While this may be a familiar term, *rest period* is now used in conjunction with the terms *sleep opportunity time* and *physiological night's rest*. Rest period may be thought of as the time span between the release from the previous flight duty period to the report time of the next flight duty period. Part 117 states that flight crewmembers must be given no less than a 10-hour continuous period free from duty. This is a much-needed two-hour increase over the Part 121 rest requirement rules. Under Part 117, a rest period must further allow for a minimum of 8 hours of uninterrupted sleep opportunity time in a ground rest facility. While Part 121 has a standard 9-hour rest period, reducible to 8 hours, Part 117 does not allow the 10-hour rest period to be reduced. We will discuss the Part 121 all-cargo operations rest rules later in this chapter.

Scheduled means to appoint, assign, or designate for a fixed time.

Short-call reserve means a period of time in which a flightcrew member is assigned to a reserve availability period.

Split duty means a flight duty period that has a scheduled break in duty that is less than a required rest period.

Split duty is a new term but one that most airline flight and cabin crews will recognize under such dubious names as high-speed overnight, a standup-overnight or standup, an illegal overnight, or a continuous-duty overnight (CDO).

Suitable accommodation means a temperature-controlled facility with sound mitigation and the ability to control light that provides a flightcrew member with the ability to sleep either in a bed, bunk or in a chair that allows for flat or near flat sleeping position. Suitable accommodation only applies to ground facilities and does not apply to aircraft onboard rest facilities.

Theater means a geographical area in which the distance between the flightcrew member's flight duty period departure point and arrival point differs by no more than 60 degrees longitude.

A pilot's theater is considered to be any location within 60 degrees of the *acclimated* pilot's beginning reference point (i.e., where the acclimated pilot begins his or her trip assignment). (Figure 7-1.) A pilot is considered to

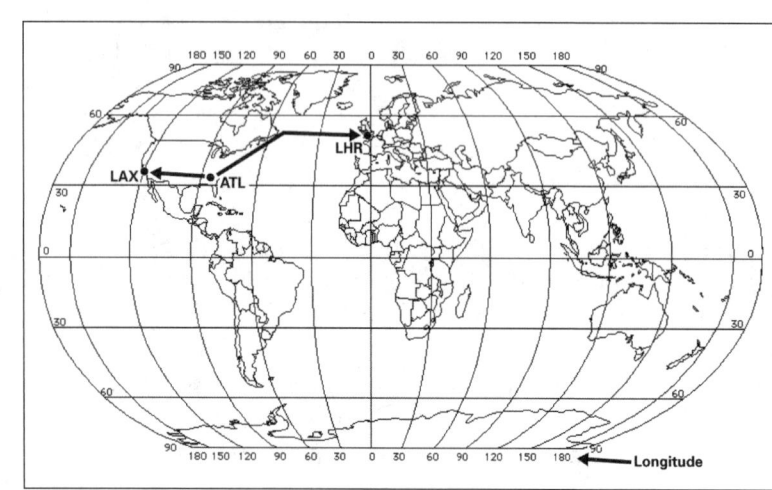

Theater

A geographical zone 60 degrees longitude wide relative to the flight duty period departure point.

A flightcrew member exits a theater after terminating a flight duty period more than 60 degrees east or west from the flight duty period's departure point where the flightcrew member was last acclimated.

Atlanta to Los Angeles is in the same theater with a 34-degree difference in longitude. Altanta to London-Heathrow exits the theater with a 84-degree difference.

Figure 7-1. Theater with reference to a flight duty period.

have changed theater if the ending reference point of the FDP is more than 60 degrees longitude from the pilot's beginning reference point. Keep in mind a pilot is not considered to have changed theater if, for example, the pilot flies more than 60 degrees longitude on leg one, but then returns to a point within 60 degrees of the pilot's beginning reference point on leg two during the same flight duty period.

Domestic flight crews who mainly fly in the continental 48 United States, Central America or the Caribbean will always remain acclimated because they never leave the U.S. domestic theater. The distance between West Coast and the East Coast is less than 60 degrees longitude. However, even though a person remains acclimated to the U.S. domestic theater, they are still affected by time zones. For instance, if you are an Atlanta (ATL)-based flight crewmember flying to Los Angeles (LAX), there is a three-hour time difference to consider. When computing flight duty period start time (after the minimum 10-hour rest period) you would use ATL time, not LAX time.

If we look at an international flight (Figure 7-2) that leaves the U.S. theater (i.e., travels more than 60 degrees), flying from ATL to Rome, Italy (FCO), the flight leaves ATL around dinner time and arrives in FCO in time for breakfast. The flight crew has a 24-hour layover and then flies FCO to ATL. What time zone does the flight crew use to determine the next flight duty period start time: FCO or ATL? In this example, the flight crew has not been in theater for 72 hours or received at least a 36-hour rest period, so they would have to use ATL time when computing the next flight duty period start time.

> **International vs. Domestic Flying**
> Under Part 117, there is no difference between international and domestic flying. All rules apply to all flying.

Figure 7-2. International vs. domestic flying.

Unforeseen operational circumstance means an unplanned event of insufficient duration to allow for adjustments to schedules, including unforecast weather, equipment malfunction, or air traffic delay that is not reasonably expected.

Window of circadian low means a period of maximum sleepiness that occurs between 0200 and 0559 during a physiological night.

Referring to Figure 7-3, the pilot's *window of circadian low* (WOCL) is based on the pilot's reference time zone.

> **Part 117 Nighttime Operations**
> **Physiological Night's Rest** must have a rest period that entirely overlaps the period from **0100** to **0700** hours in the pilot's reference time zone.
> **Window of Circadian Low** means a period of maximum sleepiness that occurs between **0200** and **0559** hours during a physiological night.
> **Night Duty** is any part of a flight duty period that falls from **2200** to **0500** hours local time. (Impacts **Split Duty** utilization.)

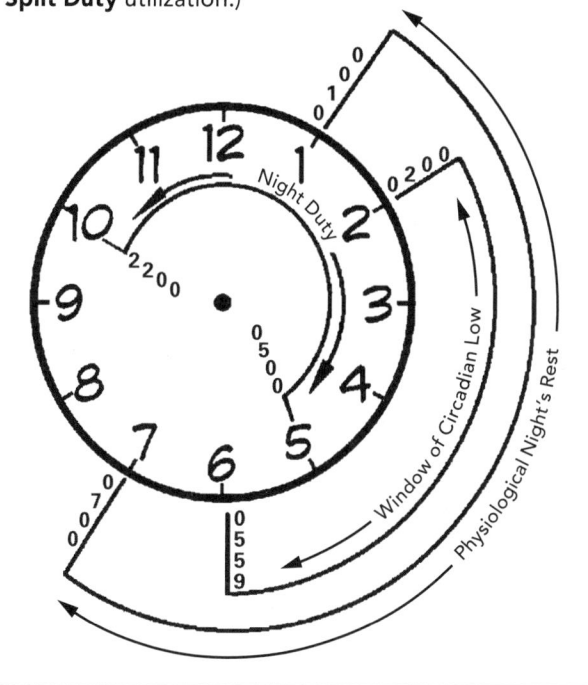

Figure 7-3. Part 117 Nighttime operations—definitions.

Fitness for Duty

Section 117.3 defines *fit for duty* as "physiologically and mentally prepared and capable of performing assigned duties at the highest degree of safety." Section 117.5(d) then requires each flight crewmember to not only report for any flight duty period rested and prepared to perform assigned duties, but must state this on the flight dispatch release. Due to the typical airline's 24-hours-a-day, 7-days-per-week operations, fatigue is the most common culprit for a flight crewmember not being fit for duty. The primary cause of fatigue in the airline industry is lack of sleep.

> **14 CFR §117.5—Fitness for duty.**
>
> (a) Each flightcrew member must report for any flight duty period rested and prepared to perform his or her assigned duties.
> (b) No certificate holder may assign and no flightcrew member may accept assignment to a flight duty period if the flightcrew member has reported for a flight duty period too fatigued to safely perform his or her assigned duties.
> (c) No certificate holder may permit a flightcrew member to continue a flight duty period if the flightcrew member has reported him or herself too fatigued to continue the assigned flight duty period.
> (d) As part of the dispatch or flight release, as applicable, each flightcrew member must affirmatively state he or she is fit for duty prior to commencing flight.

The FAA devotes an entire advisory circular to the subject of fitness for duty. Advisory Circular (AC) 117-3, *Fitness for Duty*, describes fatigue as characterized by a general lack of alertness and degradation in mental and physical performance. Fatigue manifests in the aviation context not only when pilots fall asleep on the flight deck during flight, but perhaps more importantly, during the task-critical takeoff and landing phases of flight. Reported fatigue-related events have included procedural errors, unstable approaches, lining up with the wrong runway, landing without clearances, and poor decision making.

In AC 117-3, the FAA discusses the three types of fatigue: transient, cumulative, and circadian:

(1) **Transient fatigue** is acute fatigue brought on by extreme sleep restriction or extended hours awake within 1 or 2 days.
(2) **Cumulative fatigue** is fatigue brought on by repeated mild sleep restriction or extended hours awake across a series of days.
(3) **Circadian fatigue** refers to the reduced performance during nighttime hours, particularly during an individual's "window of circadian low" (WOCL) (typically between 2:00 a.m. and 05:59 a.m.).

Also included in AC 117-3 is a discussion of the symptoms of fatigue: Symptoms of fatigue that are most common include:

- Measurable reduction in speed and accuracy of performance
- Lapses of attention and vigilance
- Delayed reactions
- Impaired logical reasoning and decision-making, including a reduced ability to assess risk or appreciate consequences of actions
- Reduced situational awareness
- Low motivation

In Section 117.5(b), we see the FAA places a "joint responsibility" for the flight crewmember's fitness on the certificate holder and each flight crewmember. This makes sense; in order for the flight crewmember to report for a flight duty period properly rested, the certificate holder must provide the flight crewmember with a meaningful rest opportunity allowing the flight crewmember to get the proper amount of sleep. Likewise, it is incumbent on the flight crewmember to use the provided rest opportunity to actually attempt to sleep, instead of using the time to do other things.

Fatigue Risk Management System

As part of Public Law 111-216, Congress mandated a fatigue risk management system (FRMS) for all passenger-carrying airlines and they have developed these plans based on FAA guidance materials.

> **14 CFR §117.7—Fatigue risk management system.**
>
> (a) No certificate holder may exceed any provision of this part unless approved by the FAA under a Fatigue Risk Management System that provides at least an equivalent level of safety against fatigue-related accidents or incidents as the other provisions of this part.
> (b) The Fatigue Risk Management System must include:
>   (1) A fatigue risk management policy.
>   (2) An education and awareness training program.
>   (3) A fatigue reporting system.
>   (4) A system for monitoring flightcrew fatigue.
>   (5) An incident reporting process.
>   (6) A performance evaluation.

FAA Advisory Circular 120-103, *Fatigue Risk Management Systems for Aviation Safety*, defines a fatigue risk management system as "a management system for a certificate holder to use to mitigate the effects of fatigue in its particular operations."

14 CFR §117.7 allows the airlines to develop their own method of "mitigating" fatigue based on science and using continuously monitored data that is validated by the FAA. A certificate holder seeking to exceed a

limitation in Part 117 would do so only under an FAA authorization. This alternate method must demonstrate a safety level at least equivalent to Part 117 regulations.

For example, an airline might decide to use additional regulatory components, such as time zones crossed or whether travel is eastbound or westbound, in constructing their flight duty period charts. Most airlines with international operations maintain that traveling east causes more problems for flight crews than traveling west because the body clock has to be advanced, which has been found to be harder than delaying it. Traveling west causes fewer problems and it has been found that seeking exposure to light is usually sufficient to help the body stay awake. This can be incorporated into a flight time duty time chart and over time might be used to allow an airline to exceed a limitation in Part 117, with FAA approval.

This is similar in concept to the FAA-approved interval/tasking maintenance programs, which are developed by the individual airlines using maintenance tracking data. This tracking data becomes the basis upon which the airlines develop their own individual maintenance programs.

A fatigue risk management system functions as a repetitive performance improvement process that leads to continuous safety enhancements by identifying and addressing fatigue factors across time and changing physiological and operational circumstances. The aim is to manage, monitor, and mitigate the effects of fatigue to improve flight crewmember alertness and reduce performance errors. The FAA may authorize a certificate holder to apply an FRMS to any part or to all of its operation, provided that the certificate holder demonstrates an effective alternate method of regulatory compliance that meets or exceeds the safety standards dictated in Part 117.

Fatigue Education and Awareness Training Program

Section 117.9 requires each Part 121 certificate holder to develop, implement, biennially update, and maintain an FAA-approved fatigue education and awareness training program. This type of program provides training for pilots and other airline employees (e.g., dispatchers, flight crew schedulers, and those exercising operational control) to help them recognize the effects of fatigue and its many causes. Part 117 requires airlines to train pilots on an annual basis about the potential effects of long duty days, multiple leg duty periods, commuting, lifestyle, sleep fundamentals, and other fatigue-related issues.

14 CFR §117.9—Fatigue education and awareness training program.

(a) Each certificate holder must develop and implement an education and awareness training program, approved by the Administrator. This program must provide annual education and awareness training to all employees of the certificate holder responsible for administering the provisions of this rule including flightcrew members, dispatchers, individuals directly involved in the scheduling of flightcrew members, individuals directly involved in operational control, and any employee providing direct management oversight of those areas.

(b) The fatigue education and awareness training program must be designed to increase awareness of:
   (1) Fatigue;
   (2) The effects of fatigue on pilots; and
   (3) Fatigue countermeasures

(c) (1) Each certificate holder must update its fatigue education and awareness training program every two years and submit the update to the Administrator for review and acceptance.
   (2) Not later than 12 months after the date of submission of the fatigue education and awareness training program required by (c)(1) of this section, the Administrator shall review and accept or reject the update. If the Administrator rejects an update, the Administrator shall provide suggested modifications for resubmission of the update.

Recommended fatigue education and awareness training program elements and subject areas can be found in FAA Advisory Circular 117-2, *Fatigue Education and Awareness Training Program*.

Flight Time Limitation

To review the definition of flight time found in 14 CFR Part 1, *Definitions and Abbreviations*:

Flight time is pilot time that commences when an aircraft moves under its own power for the purpose of flight and ends when the aircraft comes to rest after landing.

This definition remains unchanged by the new Part 117. For augmented flight crews (3–4 pilot crews), it is important to note that flight time includes any time the crewmember is onboard the aircraft, whether on the flight deck or in the onboard rest facility.

14 CFR §117.11—Flight time limitation.

(a) No certificate holder may schedule and no flightcrew member may accept an assignment or continue an assigned flight duty period if the total flight time:

   (1) Will exceed the limits specified in Table A of this part if the operation is conducted with the minimum required flightcrew.

   (2) Will exceed 13 hours if the operation is conducted with a 3-pilot flightcrew.

   (3) Will exceed 17 hours if the operation is conducted with a 4-pilot flightcrew.

There are a few U.S. air carriers who have routes that exceed 17 flight hours (e.g., Dallas Fort Worth to Hong Kong = 17h05m). The FAA has approved these operations on a case-by-case basis. Due to the growing number of air carriers flying ultra-long-haul routes, it is possible this limit may be raised in the future to over 20 hours.

Table 7-1 shows **Table A** from 14 CFR Part 117. The flight time limits in Table A can be summarized even more simply as nine (9) hours maximum flight time with a report time of between 0500–1959, and eight (8) hours maximum flight time at any other report time, 2000–0459.

Table 7-1. Part 117, Table A—Maximum flight time limits for unaugmented operations

Time of Report (Acclimated)	Maximum Flight Time (Hours)
0000–0459	8
0500–1959	9
2000–2359	8

The FAA does give air carriers some relief from the maximum flight time limits in 14 CFR §117.11(b) by allowing the flight crew to continue to fly to the next destination or alternate airport, as appropriate. In other words, the FAA doesn't expect a flight crew nearing a particular maximum flight time limit to land at the nearest suitable airport.

(b) If unforeseen operational circumstances arise after takeoff that are beyond the certificate holder's control, a flightcrew member may exceed the maximum flight time specified in paragraph (a) of this section and the cumulative flight time limits in 117.23(b) to the extent necessary to safely land the aircraft at the next destination airport or alternate, as appropriate.

(14 CFR §117.11[b])

Cargo Carriers not Subject to Part 117

One key difference between passenger-carrying (Part 117) and all-cargo carrying airlines covered under Part 121 is the concept of scheduling limitations versus actual limitations. We will discuss later in this chapter that Part 121 flight time limitations (applicable to cargo airlines) are not actual limitations, but rather "scheduling" limitations. We will discuss what happens if the flight schedule goes "non-routine" due to weather or other delays. Under the Part 121 rules, it is legal to begin a leg even though you might know that the next leg's historic block time will put you over, for example, the eight hours of flight time in a twenty-four-hour period for an unaugmented domestic flight crew. However, using Part 121 rules, if a flight crewmember is legal to start a trip, they are considered legal to finish the scheduled trip rotation—this is known simply as the "legal to start, legal to finish" rule. 14 CFR §121.471 is written this way in an effort to avoid "stranding" flight crewmembers and their passengers at an outstation somewhere with no backup crew in reserve to get the flight back to the hub airport, in cases in which the crew flies over their legal limit due to some unforeseen delay (e.g., weather).

For passenger-carrying airlines that are now governed by Part 117, "legal to start, legal to finish" is no longer applicable. Unlike Section 121.471, all Part 117 flight time limits are both scheduling and actual limits. So unlike the old rules, extension of flight time limits may not be made prior to takeoff.

In order to ensure the airline scheduling planners utilize flight crew scheduling patterns based on reasonably attainable schedules, the FAA imposes in Section 117.11(c) mandatory reporting requirements any time a flight time limit has been exceeded. Also included here is the requirement to inform the FAA what corrective actions will be taken to avoid flight time limitation overages in the future.

(c) Each certificate holder must report to the Administrator within 10 days any flight time that exceeded the maximum flight time limits permitted by this section or §117.23(b). The report must contain a description of the extended flight time limitation and the circumstances surrounding the need for the extension.

(14 CFR §117.11[c])

The new flight time limitations are straightforward and can be summarized simply (Table 7-2). Unaugmented flight crews are limited to a maximum flight time of 8 hours if the report time is between the hours of 2000 to 0459. The maximum flight time for a trip with a report time between the hours of 0500–1959 has been extended to 9 hours. For augmented operations of 3 or 4 pilots: 3-pilot crews are limited to 13 hours, and 4-pilot crews are limited to 17 hours in a flight duty period. Again these limits are "hard" limits based on the actual flight times not "scheduled."

Table 7-2. Daily flight time limits for unaugmented and augmented crews

Maximum Flight Time Limits for **Unaugmented** Operations

9 hours for flights with a report time* between 0500 and 1959

8 hours for flights with a report time* between 2000 and 0459

Acclimated time zone

Maximum Flight Time Limits for **Augmented** Operations

13 hours for three-pilot operations

17 hours for four-pilot operations (longer flights by FAA approval)

Flight Duty Periods

Unaugmented Operations

Section 117.13 discusses flight duty periods (FDP) for unaugmented operations and refers to "Table B" (reproduced here in Table 7-3).

14 CFR §117.13—Flight duty period: Unaugmented operations.

(a) Except as provided for in §117.15, no certificate holder may assign and no flightcrew member may accept an assignment for an unaugmented flight operation if the scheduled flight duty period will exceed the limits in Table B of this part.
(b) If the flightcrew member is not acclimated:
 (1) The maximum flight duty period in Table B of this part is reduced by 30 minutes.
 (2) The applicable flight duty period is based on the local time at the theater in which the flightcrew member was last acclimated.

FAA Table B is fairly intuitive: enter the table on the left side and select the time of start or report time (based on the pilot being *acclimated* to the current theater where the report is occurring). That means a pilot beginning an FDP when acclimated to a theater encompassing the FDP starting point should use the local time of that FDP starting point. However, if that FDP starting point is within 60 degrees longitude of his or her home base, the pilot should use his or her home base time.

Table 7-3. Part 117, Table B—Flight duty period for unaugmented operations

Scheduled Time of Start (Acclimated Time)	Maximum Flight Duty Period (hours) Limits for Lineholders Based on Number of Operations Flight Segments						
	1	2	3	4	5	6	7+
0000–0359	9	9	9	9	9	9	9
0400–0459	10	10	10	10	9	9	9
0500–0559	12	12	12	12	11.5	11	10.5
0600–0659	13	13	12	12	11.5	11	10.5
0700–1159	14	14	13	13	12.5	12	11.5
1200–1259	13	13	13	13	12.5	12	11.5
1300–1659	12	12	12	12	11.5	11	10.5
1700–2159	12	12	11	11	10	9	9
2200–2259	11	11	10	10	9	9	9
2300–2359	10	10	10	9	9	9	9

If the pilot reports for the trip in an unacclimated state, then according to §117.13(b)(1), the pilot must reduce the corresponding maximum flight duty period by 30 minutes from the value found in Table B. Also, if the pilot is not acclimated to the theater where the flight duty period began, then the pilot should use the local time at the location where he or she most recently began a series of flight duty periods in an acclimated state.

Split Duty

Split duty periods are two night duty periods which contain a duty break in between, and may only be used for unaugmented flight crews (Figure 7-4). The scheduled duty break must take place in a ground rest facility and must allow for at least 3 hours of rest. Travel time to and from the rest facility is not included in the 3-hour rest period. The flight duty period both before or after the duty break may not exceed the limitations computed from Table B. Furthermore, the combined flight duty period and the time spent resting during the duty break may not exceed 14 hours.

14 CFR §117.15—Flight duty period: Split duty.

For an unaugmented operation only, if a flightcrew member is provided with a rest opportunity (an opportunity to sleep) in a suitable accommodation during his or her flight duty period, the time that the flightcrew member spends in the suitable accommodation is not part of that flightcrew member's flight duty period if all of the following conditions are met:

(a) The rest opportunity is provided between the hours of 22:00 and 05:00 local time.
(b) The time spent in the suitable accommodation is at least 3 hours, measured from the time that the flightcrew member reaches the suitable accommodation.
(c) The rest opportunity is scheduled before the beginning of the flight duty period in which that rest opportunity is taken.
(d) The rest opportunity that the flightcrew member is actually provided may not be less than the rest opportunity that was scheduled.
(e) The rest opportunity is not provided until the first segment of the flight duty period has been completed.
(f) The combined time of the flight duty period and the rest opportunity provided in this section does not exceed 14 hours.

14 CFR §117.15 is an optional regulation that benefits both the air carriers and their pilots in several ways. First, by utilizing a split duty period, the air carrier is allowed a longer flight duty period than that afforded in FAA Table B. Secondly, by allowing a flight crewmember to get some sleep during the night, a split duty period addresses the main problem of performance degradation created by working during a window of circadian low (WOCL) after getting low-quality daytime sleep.

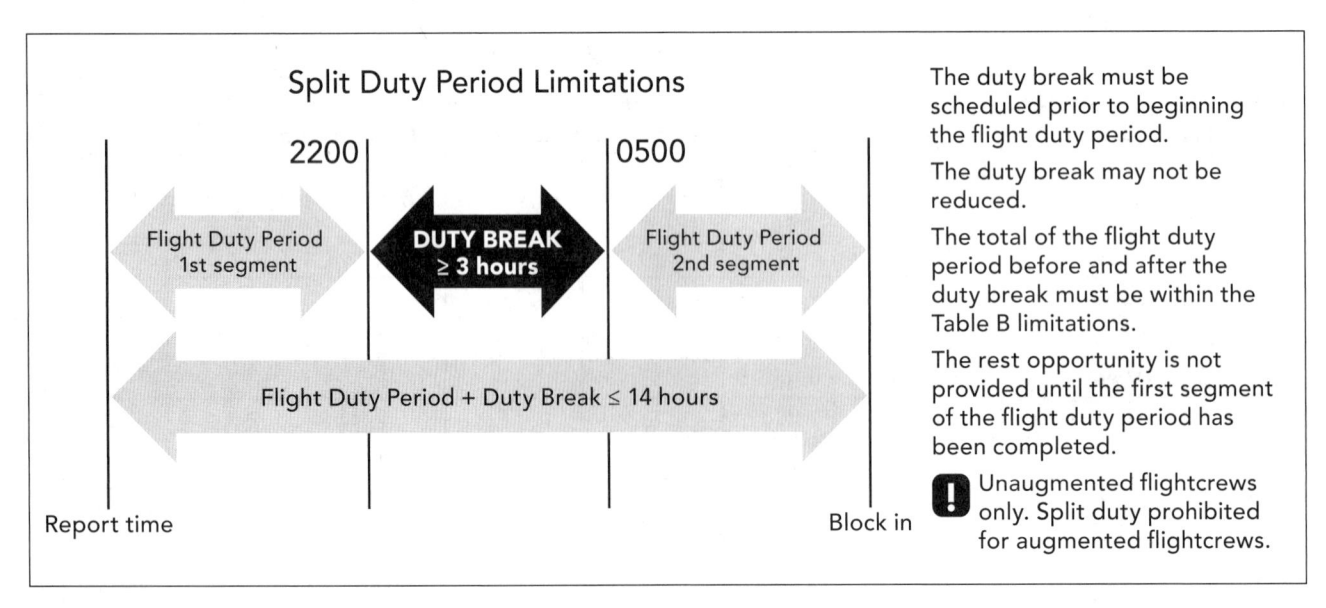

Figure 7-4. Split duty period limitations.

Augmented Flight Crew

Section 117.17 discusses flight duty periods for augmented flight crews and refers to **FAA Table C** (reproduced in Table 7-4).

14 CFR §117.17—Flight duty period: Augmented flightcrew.

(a) For flight operations conducted with an acclimated augmented flightcrew, no certificate holder may assign and no flightcrew member may accept an assignment if the scheduled flight duty period will exceed the limits specified in Table C of this part.

As with Table B, Table C (Table 7-4) uses an "acclimated" start or report time (based on the pilot being acclimated to the current theater where the report is occurring). FAA Table C also has the same duty period penalty if the flight crew reports for work in an "unacclimated" state. That is, the flight duty period limit is reduced an additional thirty minutes from the value found in FAA Table C.

What is different about FAA Table C is the flight crew complement (3 or 4 pilots), and class of onboard rest facility are taken into consideration. It makes sense that the maximum flight duty periods would be higher with a 4-pilot crew complement as opposed to a 3-pilot crew (more pilots equals less hours in a control seat). Also, we would expect the flight crew to get better-quality rest with a higher class of onboard rest facility. Therefore, Class 1 rest facilities have longer maximum allowable flight duty periods than Class 2 rest facilities. A Class 2 also has a higher maximum duty day than a Class 3 rest facility.

Table 7-5. Additional flight duty period limitations for augmented crews

3 flight segments per flight duty period maximum

120 consecutive minutes made available for in-flight rest of the pilot flying (PF) during last half of the flight duty period

90 consecutive minutes made available for the in-flight rest of the pilot monitoring (PM)

14 CFR §117.17 (continued)

(b) If the flightcrew member is not acclimated:
  (1) The maximum flight duty period in Table C of this part is reduced by 30 minutes.
  (2) The applicable flight duty period is based on the local time at the theater in which the flightcrew member was last acclimated.

(c) No certificate holder may assign and no flightcrew member may accept an assignment under this section unless during the flight duty period:
  (1) Two consecutive hours in the second half of the flight duty period are available for in-flight rest for the pilot flying the aircraft during landing.
  (2) Ninety consecutive minutes are available for in-flight rest for the pilot performing monitoring duties during landing.

(d) No certificate holder may assign and no flightcrew member may accept an assignment involving more than three flight segments under this section. [See Table 7-5.]

(e) At all times during flight, at least one flightcrew member qualified in accordance with §121.543(b)(3)(i) of this chapter must be at the flight controls.

(14 CFR §117.17)

Table 7-4. Part 117, Table C—Flight duty period for augmented operations.

Scheduled Time of Start (Acclimated Time)	Maximum Flight Duty Period (hours) Based on Rest Facility and Number of Pilots					
	Class 1 Rest Facility		Class 2 Rest Facility		Class 3 Rest Facility	
	3 Pilots	4 Pilots	3 Pilots	4 Pilots	3 Pilots	4 Pilots
0000–0559	15	17	14	15.5	13	13.5
0600–0659	16	18.5	15	16.5	14	14.5
0700–1259	17	19	16.5	18	15	15.5
1300–1659	16	18.5	15	16.5	14	14.5
1700–2359	15	17	14	15.5	13	13.5

Extensions

While flight time limitations are actual limitations and not allowed to be extended prior to takeoff, 14 CFR §117.19 allows for the extension of flight duty periods (Table 7-6) if unforeseen operational circumstances arise prior to takeoff. Section 117.19(a)(1) allows for a maximum flight duty extension of 2 hours. However, in order to be allowed to extend a flight duty period by 2 hours, no extension over 30 minutes of the scheduled flight duty period limitations may have occurred in the previous 168 hours (i.e., previous seven 24-hour periods). Also at least a 30-hour rest period must have been given since the previous flight duty period extension greater than 30 minutes. But if there has been a flight duty period extension greater than 30 minutes in the previous 168 hours or there has not been at least a 30-minute rest period, then the maximum flight duty extension is 30 minutes.

Table 7-6. Flight duty period extensions

There are three types of flight duty period extensions:

<30 minutes over maximum flight duty period:

- Does not require permission from flight crew.
- There is no compensatory penalty.
- There is no FAA reporting requirement.

Before take-off and >30 minutes over maximum flight duty period:

- Flight duty period extensions before take-off require flight crew consent.
- Flight duty period extensions >30 minutes must be reported to the FAA within 10 days.

After take-off and >30 minutes over maximum flight duty period:

- Flight duty period extension after take-off does not require flight crew consent as long as it occurs due to something that could not have been accurately forecast by the certificate holder.
- Flight duty period extensions >30 minutes must be reported to the FAA within 10 days.

Flight duty period extensions >30 minutes are allowed only once between the weekly 30-hour rest periods required by 14 CFR 117.25(b).

§117.19 Flight duty period extensions.

(a) For augmented and unaugmented operations, if unforeseen operational circumstances arise prior to takeoff:
  (1) The pilot in command and the certificate holder may extend the maximum flight duty period permitted in Tables B or C of this part up to 2 hours. The pilot in command and the certificate holder may also extend the maximum combined flight duty period and reserve availability period limits specified in §117.21(c)(3) and (4) of this part up to 2 hours.
  (2) An extension in the flight duty period under paragraph (a)(1) of this section of more than 30 minutes may occur only once prior to receiving a rest period described in §117.25(b).
  (3) A flight duty period cannot be extended under paragraph (a)(1) of this section if it causes a flightcrew member to exceed the cumulative flight duty period limits specified in 117.23(c).
  (4) Each certificate holder must report to the Administrator within 10 days any flight duty period that exceeded the maximum flight duty period permitted in Tables B or C of this part by more than 30 minutes. The report must contain the following:
    (i) A description of the extended flight duty period and the circumstances surrounding the need for the extension; and
    (ii) If the circumstances giving rise to the extension were within the certificate holder's control, the corrective action(s) that the certificate holder intends to take to minimize the need for future extensions.
  (5) Each certificate holder must implement the corrective action(s) reported in paragraph (a)(4) of this section within 30 days from the date of the extended flight duty period.
(b) For augmented and unaugmented operations, if unforeseen operational circumstances arise after takeoff:
  (1) The pilot in command and the certificate holder may extend maximum flight duty periods specified in Tables B or C of this part to the extent necessary to safely land the aircraft at the next destination airport or alternate airport, as appropriate.

(2) An extension of the flight duty period under paragraph (b)(1) of this section of more than 30 minutes may occur only once prior to receiving a rest period described in §117.25(b).

(3) An extension taken under paragraph (b) of this section may exceed the cumulative flight duty period limits specified in 117.23(c).

(4) Each certificate holder must report to the Administrator within 10 days any flight duty period that either exceeded the cumulative flight duty periods specified in §117.23(c), or exceeded the maximum flight duty period limits permitted by Tables B or C of this part by more than 30 minutes. The report must contain a description of the circumstances surrounding the affected flight duty period.

The FAA stresses that the term "extension" is intended to mean the span of time from the flight duty period table limit to a flight crew's maximum extension (up to 2 hours). That means in order to extend the FDP limits found in FAA tables B and C:

1. The PIC must concur with any FDP extension. This concurrence may not be automatically applied simply because the flight crew attested they were *fit for duty* at the beginning of the FDP (a common misconception).
2. The *fitness for duty* acceptance only qualifies as PIC concurrence of an FDP extension if the need to extend the FDP is known by the PIC at the time the flight crewmember attests fitness for duty at the beginning of the FDP and the extension is 30 minutes or less. For extensions greater than 30 minutes, the PIC must be contacted and approve of the extension.

Reserve

"Accumulated" flight duty period limitations affect the flight duty period extension limits and this is covered in 14 CFR §117.23, but before starting that discussion let's examine what Part 117 says about pilots on reserve status.

Here's a review of a few of the definitions concerning reserve assignments found in Section 117.3:

Airport/standby reserve means a defined duty period during which a flightcrew member is required by a certificate holder to be at an airport for a possible assignment.

Long-call reserve means that, prior to beginning the rest period required by §117.25, the flightcrew member is notified by the certificate holder to report for a flight duty period following the completion of the rest period.

Reserve availability period means a duty period during which a certificate holder requires a flightcrew member on short call reserve to be available to receive an assignment for a flight duty period.

Reserve flightcrew member means a flightcrew member who a certificate holder requires to be available to receive an assignment for duty.

Short-call reserve means a period of time in which a flightcrew member is assigned to a reserve availability period.

14 CFR §117.21 is the specific section dealing with reserve status:

§117.21 Reserve status.

(a) Unless specifically designated as airport/standby or short-call reserve by the certificate holder, all reserve is considered long-call reserve.

(b) Any reserve that meets the definition of airport/standby reserve must be designated as airport/standby reserve. For airport/standby reserve, all time spent in a reserve status is part of the flightcrew member's flight duty period.

(c) For short call reserve,
  (1) The reserve availability period may not exceed 14 hours.
  (2) For a flightcrew member who has completed a reserve availability period, no certificate holder may schedule and no flightcrew member may accept an assignment of a reserve availability period unless the flightcrew member receives the required rest in §117.25(e).
  (3) For an unaugmented operation, the total number of hours a flightcrew member may spend in a flight duty period and a reserve availability period may not exceed the lesser of the maximum applicable flight duty period in Table B of this part plus 4 hours, or 16 hours, as measured from the beginning of the reserve availability period.
  (4) For an augmented operation, the total number of hours a flightcrew member may spend in a flight duty period and a reserve availability period may not exceed the flight duty period in Table C of this part plus 4 hours, as measured from the beginning of the reserve availability period.

(d) For long call reserve, if a certificate holder contacts a flightcrew member to assign him or her to a flight duty period that will begin before and operate into the flightcrew member's window of circadian low, the flightcrew member must receive a 12 hour notice of report time from the certificate holder.

(e) A certificate holder may shift a reserve flightcrew member's reserve status from long-call to short-call only if the flightcrew member receives a rest period as provided in §117.25(e).

Section 117.21 codifies in the regulations some changes in the legal interpretation of duty time rules that have occurred over the last decade. For instance, prior to 2000, the airline industry did not consider the time spent "sitting" reserve as duty time. A pilot was not thought to be "on duty" until he or she reported for a duty assignment. That meant if a pilot woke up at 6 a.m. and went on reserve status at 8 a.m. for a 16-hour reserve availability period, crew scheduling could call the pilot at midnight and keep that pilot on duty and flying until 4 p.m. This was how reserve pilots were treated unless they worked under a contract with stricter rules. That all changed with a document written in November 2000, popularly called the **Whitlow letter**.

The Whitlow letter was written by James Whitlow, a former Deputy Chief Counsel at the FAA. The letter was written in response to some questions posed by an American Airlines captain regarding duty and rest rules for pilots on reserve status. These questions apparently arose as a result of changes in American Airlines' pilot reserve system in use at that time.

In the letter, Mr. Whitlow elaborated on the official interpretation of flight time and duty time regulations for pilots on reserve status. Furthermore, Mr. Whitlow decreed that a reserve pilot must be given the same look-back rest rules prior to a flight as a normally scheduled line pilot. (Note: **"look-back" rules** mean that a flight crewmember must look back over the previous daily, weekly, monthly or yearly time periods to verify cumulative flight time limits have not been exceeded, and/or proper amounts of rest have been received.) As we mentioned earlier, prior to this interpretation, if a pilot began a reserve period at home, he or she was not technically on duty until he or she reported for a duty assignment. This was a major change for the industry.

The Whitlow letter was the first step in the process of implementing more realistic, scientifically based sets of flight time and duty time rules. Part 117 continues this trend. Section 117.21 significantly clarifies the question of how to handle the calculation of duty periods for reserve status pilots. For example, a flight crewmember in reserve status and "on call" during an assigned reserve availability period can only be scheduled for a flight duty period that, for unaugmented operations, ends either (1) 16 hours after the beginning of the reserve availability period, or (2) at the Table B limit plus 4 hours; or for augmented operations, at the Table C limits plus 4 hours (Table 7-7). These new rules are significant because prior to the Whitlow letter (and subsequently Part 117), the FAA had never regulated reserve periods.

What this all means is that a reserve flight crewmember is given more of a rest opportunity under Part 117 than is available to a reserve flight crewmember under Part 121. A long-call reserve pilot must receive at least a 10-hour rest period before reporting for any trip. A short-call reserve pilot during his or her reserve availability period may be required to report for a trip on short notice (usually 1–2 hours' notice). If a short-call reserve pilot is not assigned a trip, the reserve availability period is considered that flight crewmember's duty period and it may not be more than 14 hours. Once a reserve availability period is complete, another reserve availability period cannot begin until the pilot has a minimum of a 10-hour rest period.

Table 7-7. Reserve pilot limitations

The maximum total time spend on short-call plus a flight duty period:

Unaugmented operations:

16 hours *or* the maximum flight duty period found in Table B plus 4 hours, whichever is less

Augmented operations:

The maximum flight duty period found in Table C plus 4 hours

Additional Reserve Pilot Limitations:

14 hours maximum short-call availability period

10 hours rest required to shift a pilot from long-call to short-call reserve status

Cumulative Flight Time Limitations

A significant focus of Part 117 is the adoption of new look-back cumulative limits for both flight time (Table 7-8) and flight duty periods (Table 7-9). Notice some subtle changes to the somewhat familiar flight time limits, in that they are rolling limits; that is, they do not reset with the beginning of a new month or year. In other words, the actual flight hour limits will be controlled by the number of flight hours allowed within a given duty period. The Part 121 rules have a limit of hours flown within a calendar month. The new rules in Part 117 reduce that to hours flown in a rolling twenty-eight days. The Part 121 limit of 1,000 hours of block in a calendar year has been modified in Part 117 so that the 12 months is no longer a calendar year, but a rolling 12 months.

§117.23 Cumulative limitations.

(a) The limitations of this section include all flying by flightcrew members on behalf of any certificate holder or 91K Program Manager during the applicable periods.
(b) No certificate holder may schedule and no flightcrew member may accept an assignment if the flightcrew member's total flight time will exceed the following:
   (1) 100 hours in any 672 consecutive hours or
   (2) 1,000 hours in any 365 consecutive calendar day period.
(c) No certificate holder may schedule and no flightcrew member may accept an assignment if the flightcrew member's total Flight Duty Period will exceed:
   (1) 60 flight duty period hours in any 168 consecutive hours or
   (2) 190 flight duty period hours in any 672 consecutive hours.

Table 7-8. Cumulative flight time limitations

Daily:

Maximum Flight Time Limits for **Unaugmented** Operations:

    9 hours for flights with a report time* between 0500 and 1959

    8 hours for flights with a report time* between 2000 and 0459

Maximum Flight Time Limits for **Augmented** Operations:

    13 hours for three-pilot operations

    17 hours for four-pilot operations (longer flights by FAA approval)

                      Acclimated Time Zone

Monthly:

    100 flight hours per a rolling 672-hour period (28 x 24-hour periods)

Yearly:

    1,000 flight hours per a rolling 365-calendar-day period

Table 7-9. Cumulative flight duty period limits

Weekly:

    60 hours per a rolling 168-hour period (7 x 24-hour periods)

Monthly:

    190 hours per a rolling 672-hour period (28 x 24-hour periods)

Cumulative Flight Duty Period limits may not be extended prior to takeoff.

Unlike the Flight Duty Periods found in Tables B and C, Cumulative Flight Duty Periods may only be extended when unforeseen operational circumstances occur after takeoff.

Remember, no more "legal to start, legal to finish."

There are only three cases where the cumulative limits restricting the amount of flight time and/or flight duty time may be exceeded:

1. Section 117.11(b) allows a flight crewmember to exceed cumulative flight time limits for unforeseen operational circumstances that may arise after takeoff.
2. Section 117.19(b) allows a flight crewmember to exceed cumulative flight duty period limits for unforeseen operational circumstances that may arise after takeoff.
3. Section 117.29(b), which we will discuss shortly, permits emergency and government sponsored operations to exceed the cumulative flight time and flight duty period limits if these operations operate under the exemptions provided by Section 119.57, "Obtaining deviation authority to perform an emergency operation."

In both case (1) and (2), the limits are allowed to be exceeded only to the extent necessary to safely land the aircraft at either the next destination airport or the alternate airport.

Rest Period

For passenger-carrying operations, 14 CFR §117.25 replaces the §121.471 requirement of 24 hours rest in a seven-calendar-day period, known simply as "24-in-7." As previously discussed, this is a "rolling" 168-consecutive-hour period (i.e., seven 24-hour periods), not calendar days. To summarize, "30-in-168" means that prior to beginning a reserve availability period or flight duty period, a pilot must have received 30 consecutive hours free from any duty within the preceding 168-hour period immediately prior to the start of a reserve availability period or flight duty period.

14 CFR §117.25—Rest period.

(a) No certificate holder may assign and no flightcrew member may accept assignment to any reserve or duty with the certificate holder during any required rest period.
(b) Before beginning any reserve or flight duty period a flightcrew member must be given at least 30 consecutive hours free from all duty within the past 168 consecutive hour period.
(c) If a flightcrew member operating in a new theater has received 36 consecutive hours of rest, that flightcrew member is acclimated and the rest period meets the requirements of paragraph (b) of this section.
(d) A flightcrew member must be given a minimum of 56 consecutive hours rest upon return to home base if the flightcrew member: (1) Travels more than 60° longitude during a flight duty period or a series of flight duty period, and (2) is away from home base for more than 168 consecutive hours during this travel. The 56 hours of rest specified in this section must encompass three physiological nights' rest based on local time.

Paragraph (d) could be termed the "long haul pilot's recovery rest period." It states that if a pilot travels more than 60 degrees longitude in a trip that lasts 168 hours or more, that pilot must be given at least 56 hours of consecutive rest following release from the trip. This rest must overlap three full physiological nights (i.e., 0100 to 0700) based on local time.

(e) No certificate holder may schedule and no flightcrew member may accept an assignment for any reserve or flight duty period unless the flightcrew member is given a rest period of at least 10 consecutive hours immediately before beginning the reserve or flight duty period measured from the time the flightcrew member is released from duty. The 10 hour rest period must provide the flightcrew member with a minimum of 8 uninterrupted hours of sleep opportunity.

(14 CFR §117.25)

This paragraph replaces the confusing requirements of 14 CFR §121.471—which includes, as we'll see later, such terms as "reduced rest" and "compensatory rest"—with a simple "10 hours before beginning" requirement. That is, before beginning a reserve availability period or flight duty period, a pilot must have received a minimum of 10 hours of rest with at least an 8-hour uninterrupted period of sleep opportunity.

(f) If a flightcrew member determines that a rest period under paragraph (e) of this section will not provide eight uninterrupted hours of sleep opportunity, the flightcrew member must notify the certificate holder. The flightcrew member cannot report for the assigned flight duty period until he or she receives a rest period specified in paragraph (e) of this section.

(g) If a flightcrew member engaged in deadhead transportation exceeds the applicable flight duty period in Table B of this part, the flightcrew member must be given a rest period equal to the length of the deadhead transportation but not less than the required rest in paragraph (e) of this section before beginning a flight duty period.

(14 CFR §117.25)

In crafting the rest requirements in Section 117.25 (Table 7-10), the FAA did away with the entire notion of "reduced rest" and compensatory rest. The airlines are now required to provide their flight crews with a 10-hour rest opportunity prior to commencing a duty period that includes flying. While the 10-hour rest period may include the amount of time it takes to get to or from a flight crewmember's house or hotel room, the actual amount of time required for a sleep opportunity may not be reduced below 8 hours. In addition, the length of continuous time off during a 7-day period has been extended from 24 hours under the existing Part 121 rules to 30 hours. Additional time off is required for individuals who may be unacclimated because of flying between different theaters.

Table 7-10. Rest limitations

10 consecutive hours (non-reducible) minimum crew rest period providing a minimum of 8 uninterrupted hours of sleep opportunity before beginning a reserve or flight duty period.

30 consecutive hours free from duty per rolling 168 hour period (7 x 24-hour periods). The "30 in 7" rule.

56 consecutive hours rest upon returning to home base if a flight crewmember has travelled more than 60 degrees longitude during a flight duty period or a series of flight duty periods that require the flight crewmember to be away from home base for more than 168 consecutive hours. This rest must encompass three physiological nights' rest based on local home base time.

"Rest after Deadhead" A flight crewmember who has been deadheaded over the allowable flight duty period limit found in Table B, using the column in the chart that corresponds to the number of deadhead segments, the pilot must be given a rest period equal to the length of the deadhead transportation (but not less than ten hours) before beginning another flight duty period.

Consecutive Nighttime Operations

Here the FAA places limits on the consecutive amount of nighttime flying a pilot is allowed to do. These limits focus on mitigating the cumulative fatigue caused by repeated nighttime flying. Scientific studies used in the formulation of Part 117 have shown deteriorating performance after the third consecutive nighttime flight duty period, for flight crewmembers who worked night shifts during their window of circadian low and slept during the day. However, these same studies have shown that if a sleep opportunity is provided during each nighttime flight duty period, that sleep opportunity may allow flight crewmembers to perform safely for up to five consecutive nights. Based on the results of these scientific tests, the FAA determined a 2-hour nighttime sleep opportunity each night does improve pilot performance sufficiently to allow up to 5 nights of consecutive nighttime operations (Table 7-11).

14 CFR §117.27—Consecutive nighttime operations.

A certificate holder may schedule and a flightcrew member may accept up to five consecutive flight duty periods that infringe on the window of circadian low if the certificate holder provides the flightcrew member with an opportunity to rest in a suitable accommodation during each of the consecutive nighttime flight duty periods. The rest opportunity must be at least 2 hours, measured from the time that the flightcrew member reaches the suitable accommodation, and must comply with the conditions specified in §117.15(a), (c), (d), and (e). Otherwise, no certificate holder may schedule and no flightcrew member may accept more than three consecutive flight duty periods that infringe on the window of circadian low. For purposes of this section, any split duty rest that is provided in accordance with §117.15 counts as part of a flight duty period.

Table 7-11. Consecutive nighttime operations limits

Maximum number of consecutive flight duty periods allowed which overlap the window of circadian low (WOCL):

> **5** if the pilot is given a two-hour rest period in a suitable accomodation during each flight duty period
>
> **3** if no rest periods are provided

Emergency and Government Sponsored Operations

14 CFR §117.29 applies to air carrier operations conducted under contract with the U.S. government and agencies. This covers flight operations that require flying into or out of war zones, politically sensitive areas, or remote areas that do not have the rest facilities required under Part 117. These operations range from an emergency situation, moving armed troops for the U.S. military Air Mobility Command (AMC), to conducting humanitarian relief or State Department missions.

14 CFR §117.29—Emergency and government sponsored operations.

(a) This section applies to operations conducted pursuant to contracts with the U.S. Government and operations conducted pursuant to a deviation under §119.57 of this chapter that cannot otherwise be conducted under this part because of circumstances that could prevent flightcrew members from being relieved by another crew or safely provided with the rest required under §117.25 at the end of the applicable flight duty period.

(b) The pilot-in-command may determine that the maximum applicable flight duty period, flight time, and/or combined flight duty period and reserve availability period limits must be exceeded to the extent necessary to allow the flightcrew to fly to the closest destination where they can safely be relieved from duty by another flightcrew or can receive the requisite amount of rest prior to commencing their next flight duty period.

(c) A flight duty period may not be extended for an operation conducted pursuant to a contract with the U.S. Government if it causes a flightcrew member to exceed the cumulative flight time limits in §117.23(b) and the cumulative flight duty period limits in §117.23(c).

(d) The flightcrew shall be given a rest period immediately after reaching the destination described in paragraph (b) of this section equal to the length of the actual flight duty period or 24 hours, whichever is less.

(e) Each certificate holder must report within 10 days:
  (1) Any flight duty period that exceeded the maximum flight duty period permitted in Tables B or C of this part, as applicable, by more than 30 minutes;
  (2) Any flight time that exceeded the maximum flight time limits permitted in Table A of this part and §117.11, as applicable; and
  (3) Any flight duty period or flight time that exceeded the cumulative limits specified in §117.23.

(f) The report must contain the following:
  (1) A description of the extended flight duty period and flight time limitation, and the circumstances surrounding the need for the extension; and
  (2) If the circumstances giving rise to the extension(s) were within the certificate holder's control, the corrective action(s) that the certificate holder intends to take to minimize the need for future extensions.

(g) Each certificate holder must implement the corrective action(s) reported pursuant to paragraph (f)(2) of this section within 30 days from the date of the extended flight duty period and/or the extended flight time.

Section 117.29 covers two categories of operations that are affected: U.S. government contracts and operations conducted pursuant to a deviation issued by the Administrator under §119.57. 14 CFR §119.57 authorizes an air carrier to deviate from the requirements of Parts 121 and 135 to perform emergency operations:

14 CFR §119.57—Obtaining deviation authority to perform an emergency operation.

(a) In emergency conditions, the Administrator may authorize deviations if—
  (1) Those conditions necessitate the transportation of persons or supplies for the protection of life or property; and
  (2) The Administrator finds that a deviation is necessary for the expeditious conduct of the operations.

(b) When the Administrator authorizes deviations for the operations under emergency conditions—
  (1) The Administrator will issue an appropriate amendment to the certificate holder's operations specifications; or
  (2) If the nature of the emergency does not permit timely amendment of the operations specifications—
    (i) The Administrator may authorize the deviation orally; and
    (ii) The certificate holder shall provide documentation describing the nature of the emergency to the certificate-holding district office with 24 hours after completing the operation.

This emergency authority is issued on a case-by-case basis during an emergency situation, as determined by the Administrator. Section 117.29 further requires each certificate holder to report, within 10 days, any flight time or flight duty period limitations that were exceeded during the emergency and government sponsored operations.

All-Cargo Operations

At the beginning of this chapter, we discussed how passenger-carrying airlines operate under Part 117 flight and duty time regulations while all-cargo airlines operate under the less stringent Part 121 regulations. This exemption of cargo airlines from the higher level of safety standards now required of passenger-carrying airlines is termed "the cargo carve-out" or the "great freight debate." At issue in this debate is the fact that flight crews flying the same types of aircraft, to the same locations, carrying some of the same cargo, are treated differently. They are treated differently because the DOT and the FAA believed "the cost of implementing Part 117 to the cargo industry would be more than the societal benefits the public was willing to pay for." As a result, cargo-carrying airlines are not affected by Part 117. However, it is important to acknowledge that excluding cargo pilots from the protections afforded by Part 117 flight and duty time limitations is understandably a confusing and contentious matter for the flight crews of all-cargo operators.

Having now dispensed with some of the politics of the issue, let's discuss the 14 CFR Part 121 subparts covering the most common flight and duty time limitations for all-cargo operations. For Part 121 certificate holders conducting all-cargo operations, the certificate holder is allowed by the FAA to operate under the provisions prescribed in Part 121, Subparts Q, R, and S, as applicable. 14 CFR Part 121, Subpart Q, covers limitations for pilots in **domestic all-cargo operations**, while Subpart R covers limitations for pilots in **flag all-cargo operations**. 14 CFR Part 121, Subpart S, covers limitations for pilots in **supplemental** (nonscheduled) **all-cargo operations**. Duty and rest times for dispatchers and flight attendants for both domestic and flag are covered in Subpart P.

There are a couple of important points to remember when discussing Part 121 flight time limitations. First, unlike Part 117, Part 121 limitations are based primarily on the amount of **scheduled flight time**, not **actual flight time**. We will illustrate this important difference in this chapter by presenting a few examples. The FAA chooses to use scheduled flight time as opposed to writing regulations based on actual time in an effort to offer some schedule flexibility to the air carrier. This schedule flexibility allows air carriers to continue to operate a flight even though events beyond the control of the air carrier cause a pilot's flight time to exceed the scheduled limitations. As discussed earlier in this chapter, the FAA allows this in order to avoid "stranding" passengers, aircraft, and pilots at some intermediate location.

Secondly, while the FAA allows air carriers to use scheduled flight time as opposed to actual flight time during a pilot's workday, it does require the scheduled flight time to be reasonable. For example, if a flight between two city pairs consistently takes 2:30 hours, then the air carrier is expected to use the historic block time for that particular type of aircraft. 14 CFR §121.541 covers both domestic and international (flag) operations:

> In establishing flight operations schedules, each certificate holder conducting domestic or flag operations shall allow enough time for the proper servicing of aircraft at intermediate stops, and shall consider the prevailing winds en route and the cruising speed of the type of aircraft used. This cruising speed may not be more than that resulting from the specified cruising output of the engines.

Finally, compliance with these flight and duty time limitations carries a dual responsibility from the company and the pilot. Notice the wording in 14 CFR §121.471(a), Flight Time Limitations and Rest Requirements:

> No certificate holder conducting domestic operations may schedule any flight crewmember and no flight crewmember may accept an assignment for flight time in scheduled air transportation or in other commercial flying if that crewmember's total flight time in all commercial flying will exceed… [those limitations set down in this regulation].

The FAA imposes this dual responsibility of compliance on the air carrier and the pilot as a check-and-balance mechanism. Also, there may be instances when a pilot has performed some other *commercial flying* (i.e., charter flying, banner towing, etc.) without the knowledge of the air carrier. In basic terms, a pilot may not fly any **commercial flying** if that commercial flying plus any flying in air transportation will exceed any flight time limitation set forth in domestic, flag or supplemental regulations (14 CFR §121.489, 14 CFR §121.517).

Let's look at the calendar year, monthly, weekly, and hourly flight and duty limitations.

Subpart Q: Flight Time Limitations and Rest Requirements: Domestic All-Cargo Operations

14 CFR Part 121, Subpart Q, applies to domestic all-cargo operations except for two exceptions carved out in Section 121.470. The most significant exception is granted for Part 121 operators of smaller aircraft (payload capacity of 7,500 pounds or less) who are permitted to choose to comply with Subpart Q or the slightly less restrictive provisions of Part 135. The other exception applies to operations conducted entirely within the states of Alaska or Hawaii with aircraft having a payload capacity of more than 7,500 pounds. These operators are permitted to operate under the flag rules found in 14 CFR Part 121, Subpart R.

Domestic all-cargo flight crew flight time limitations are set out in 14 CFR §121.471. The first limitations are self-explanatory and limit the pilot's flying on an annual, monthly, weekly, and daily basis. These limits are:

- Calendar year—1,000 flight hours maximum
- Calendar month—100 flight hours maximum
- 7 consecutive calendar days—30 flight hours maximum
- Between rest periods—8 flight hours maximum

The annual, monthly, and weekly (called **30 in 7**) limits are pretty self-explanatory, as all use a calendar-day basis for determining compliance with the regulations. The 8 hours between required rest periods is a lot trickier in application and raises a number of basic questions.

First of all, what does the FAA define as "rest"? 14 CFR §121.471(e) clarifies the term **rest period**. The FAA has determined rest to mean a continuous period of time a flight crewmember is free from *all* duty requirements. These duty requirements include answering the phone, pager, or email or in any way remaining in contact with the company for the reason of being available for assignment if the need arises. Also, time spent deadheading to or from a duty assignment may not be considered a rest period (14 CFR §121.471[f], Domestic All-Cargo Operations; 14 CFR §121.491, Flag All-Cargo Operations; and 14 CFR §121.519, Supplemental All-Cargo Operations).

Most air carriers operate flights between different time zones. With regard to flight and duty limitations, what time zone is used in this case? While this is addressed in Part 117, it is not under Part 121 operations.

Fortunately for the cargo flight crew, the FAA flight and duty limitations are absolute; that is, the air carrier may not use "creative time zone scheduling" to work around the duty time limitations. For this reason, the FAA allows the company to choose the time zone, but whatever time zone the company decides to use for the crewmember must be used throughout the computation of the entire duty period. This could be the time zone of the pilot's base, or Universal Coordinated Time without regard to what time zone the pilot actually enters.

How does the FAA define **flight time** for the purposes of flight limitations? It is defined as the moment the aircraft begins to move under its own power for the purposes of flight until the moment the aircraft comes to a complete stop at a gate, ramp area, or elsewhere at the landing airport (14 CFR Part 1—Definitions).

Finally, what does the FAA define as a **duty period**? 14 CFR §121.471(b) explains that a duty period begins from the first flight duty assignment and continues until that duty period is broken by a minimum rest period. Until that duty period is broken by a rest period, the pilot may not be *scheduled* for more than 8 hours of flight time. That is, the rule is a **"look-back" rule**. The rest periods required to break the duty period are

(1) 9 consecutive hours of rest for less than 8 hours of scheduled flight time *[within the last 24 hours]*.
(2) 10 consecutive hours of rest for 8 or more but less than 9 hours of scheduled flight time *[within the last 24 hours]*.
(3) 11 consecutive hours of rest for 9 or more hours of scheduled flight time *[within the last 24 hours]*.

(14 CFR §121.471[b])

These rules are applied by looking at the end of *each* flight segment and then looking back 24 hours. A crewmember must be able to determine that a legally scheduled rest period *began* within the last 24 hours. For example, assume the schedule shown below:

Report time:　　　0700Z
(beginning of the pilot's duty period)
Departure time:　　0800Z
Arrival time:　　　1150Z　　Flight time = 3:50 hours

Departure time:　　1545Z
Arrival time:　　　1900Z　　Flight time = 3:15 hours
Release time:　　　1915Z

What is the longest flight this pilot may be assigned? Total flight time since 0800Z = 7:05. Therefore, the pilot may only be assigned for an additional 0:55 minutes of flight time before receiving a required rest period. What rest period would be required? If the pilot's last assignment was 0:54 minutes or less, then he or she would have flown less than 8 hours and that would then require a rest period of 9 consecutive hours. Remember, by saying the carrier may not assign the pilot *any duty* during the rest period, it means that the required preflight *report times* and post-flight *release times* may not be counted as part of the rest period.

These report and release times are the time periods, before and after the actual flight time, that the pilot spends briefing for the flight and completing required company paperwork such as payroll sheets and chart and manual revisions. While the FAA hasn't defined what length these periods of time are, preferring to leave that to the collective bargaining process (union contract), it has taken action to declare as insufficient report (pre-flight) times of only 30 minutes and release times of only 10 minutes. The test will be one of reasonableness. That is, is the time allotted reasonable for the tasks being required of the pilot? The minimum required pre-flight tasks are spelled out in 14 CFR §91.103, Preflight Action. The generally accepted times are 1 hour for preflight duties and 15 minutes for post-flight duties.

The contentiousness on this issue comes from the pilot perspective of wanting rest time to be "pillow time"—that is, time actually spent in a hotel room, in bed. Frequently, the crew bus ride to the hotel, check-in, dinner, early morning preparation, and breakfast can reduce the amount of sleep actually possible to only 5 or 6 hours. The companies, on the other hand, have a real concern in terms of schedules and costs. After a few accidents whose causes were partly attributed to fatigue, there was finally enough political will to change the decades-old flight and duty time regulations. However, as we've mentioned earlier, the change was only for the passenger-carrying portion of the airline industry.

Now let's look at an example that uses Paragraph 121.471(b)(2). Assume the pilot has done no other flying for several days and then encounters the following schedule.

Report time:	0700Z	
Departure time:	0800Z	
Arrival time:	1150Z	Flight time = 3:50 hours
Departure time:	1215Z	
Arrival time:	1530Z	Flight time = 3:15 hours
Release time:	1545Z	

What is the earliest clock time that the pilot may be assigned to a flight of 1:25? When added to the previous flight time, 1:25 will give a total of 8:30 for this pairing. That falls into the provision of subparagraph (b)(2) in that it is 8 or more hours but less than 9 hours scheduled flight time, so it requires 10 consecutive hours of rest. Allowing for report/release time, this could result in the following schedule:

Report time:	0700Z	
Departure time:	0800Z	
Arrival time:	1150Z	Flight time = 3:50 hours
Departure time:	1215Z	
Arrival time:	1530Z	Flight time = 3:15 hours
Release time:	1545Z	
Rest		Rest = 10:00 hours
Report time:	0145Z	
Departure time:	0245Z	
Arrival time:	0410Z	Flight time = 1:25 hours

What if instead of wanting to add a flight of 1:25, we had wanted to assign a flight of 2:00 to the original schedule? In this case, the scheduled time of 2:00 when added to the previous flight time will give a total of 9:05 for this pairing. That falls into the provision of subparagraph (b)(3) in that it is more than 9 hours scheduled flight time, so it requires 11 consecutive hours of rest. Allowing for report/release time, this could result in the following schedule:

Report time:	0700Z	
Departure time:	0800Z	
Arrival time:	1150Z	Flight time = 3:50 hours
Departure time:	1215Z	
Arrival time:	1530Z	Flight time = 3:15 hours
Release time:	1545Z	
Rest		Rest = 11:00 hours
Report time:	0245Z	
Departure time:	0345Z	
Arrival time:	0545Z	Flight time = 2:00 hours

These examples cover the circumstances in which a single minimum rest period is given. In airline operations, the schedules or *trip pairings*, as they are known, typically go on for 3 or 4 days. In this circumstance, the required minimum rest periods may be reduced if at a later time a longer rest period is granted. 14 CFR §121.471(c) covers these contingencies.

Paragraph 121.471(c)(1) says a minimum 9 hour rest period may be reduced to 8 hours if no later than 24 hours after the commencement of the reduced rest period the pilot is given a 10 hour rest period. So, going back to our original example, normally this schedule would require a 9 hour minimum rest:

Report time:	0700Z	
Departure time:	0800Z	
Arrival time:	1150Z	Flight time = 3:50 hours
Departure time:	1545Z	
Arrival time:	1900Z	Flight time = 3:15 hours
Release time:	1915Z	

9 hour minimum rest would mean report no earlier than 0415Z.

However, this could be reduced to 8 hours (with a 0315Z report) if, no later than 1915Z on the second day, the pilot is given a 10 hour minimum rest:

Report time:	0700Z	
Departure time:	0800Z	
Arrival time:	1150Z	Flight time = 3:50 hours
Departure time:	1545Z	
Arrival time:	1900Z	Flight time = 3:15 hours
Release time:	1915Z	

8 hour reduced rest commencing at 1915Z—Pilot may return to duty (report) at 0315Z at the earliest.

Report time:	0315Z	
Departure time:	0415Z	
Arrival time:	0615Z	Flight time = 2:00 hours
Departure time:	1230Z	
Arrival time:	1400Z	Flight time = 1:30 hours
Departure time:	1600Z	
Arrival time:	_____?	Flight time = _____?

What is the longest flight that this crew may be assigned? That is, what is the latest possible scheduled arrival time? First, we see that since the last assigned break, the pilot has flown 3:30. Paragraph 121.471(a)(4) states that a pilot may not be scheduled for more than 8:00 hours since the last required rest period. Using this rule, the pilot could be scheduled for an additional 4:30 hours, which would bring the total hours up to 8:00.

However, since the pilot had a reduced rest period at the last required rest and that was reduced using Paragraph 121.471(c)(1), a 10-hour compensatory rest period must be started no later than 24 hours after the last rest period began. The last rest period began at 1915Z, so this pilot must be released no later than 1915Z. Given a release period of 15 minutes, the arrival time must be scheduled no later than 1900Z. Therefore, the longest flight the pilot may be scheduled for is 3:00 hours, which results in an arrival time of 1900Z and a release time of 1915Z. The earliest next *report time* would then be 10 hours later at 0515Z.

Paragraphs 121.471(c)(2) and (c)(3) work exactly the same way except that (c)(2) allows a 10-hour rest period to be reduced to 8 hours if an 11-hour rest period is scheduled to commence no later than 24 hours after the start of the reduced rest period. Paragraph (c)(3) allows an 11-hour rest period to be reduced to a minimum of 9 hours (note the time difference) if a 12-hour rest period is scheduled to commence no later than 24 hours after the start of the reduced rest period.

Finally, the question arises: What happens if the schedule goes "nonroutine"? Paragraph 121.471(g) covers this by stating that if a flight normally terminates at its scheduled time but, because of weather or other delays, goes nonroutine, then the pilot is not considered to be in violation of the minimum rest period if it was otherwise scheduled legally. In other words, if the crewmember was legal to start a trip segment, then he or she is legal to finish regardless of how long the flights take. Neither the carrier nor the crewmember will be penalized with a violation if a normally scheduled flight goes longer than planned. The pilot simply gets more fatigued!

Let's look at an example of a scheduled flight day that becomes nonroutine: A crewmember is scheduled to fly four, 1-hour 59-minute flight segments totaling 7 hours 56 minutes. Due to air traffic control and flight delays, the first three segments have totaled 7 hours. Is the crewmember legal to fly the last leg of the day even though the total flying time between rest periods will be more than 8 hours? Yes, the pilot is legal to fly the last segment because FAA flight time limitations are placed on *scheduled* flight time only, not actual flight time. The crewmember was legal to begin the trip assigned that day; that crewmember is therefore legal to finish the trip as long as duty day limitations are not exceeded.

Now let's look at an example of a scheduled flight day that becomes nonroutine and the company decides to alter the pilot's schedule midday: A crewmember is scheduled to fly four, 1-hour 59-minute flight segments totaling 7 hours and 56 minutes. Due to air traffic control and weather delays, the actual flight time for the first three segments has totaled 7 hours. At the completion of the third segment, the crew scheduling department advises the crewmember that he or she has been rerouted or *rescheduled* to fly a shorter, 1-hour 30-minute flight. Surprisingly, this would not be a legal trip even though the flight time in this example is less than the originally scheduled day. This is because any time a trip is *rescheduled*, you must examine the *actual* flight time since the last rest period. Because the crewmember had already flown 7 hours, that pilot may only be rescheduled to fly an additional 1-hour flight segment.

Maximum Time "On Duty"

Now that we've examined maximum flight time regulations, let's look at what limitations are placed on a pilot's **duty day**. As we mentioned earlier, a pilot must always be able to "look back" 24 hours and find at least an 8-hour rest period. For this reason, the maximum duty day can never exceed 16 *actual* duty hours in a 24-hour period. (Figure 7-5.) This means that pilots must be certain when departing on each flight segment that they will be able to be released from duty before the 16-hour duty limit. A pilot must look at weather, ATC delays such as ground stops, or any known holding that may be anticipated. If any of these factors may cause a crewmember to exceed the 16-hour duty day, then the aircraft must not leave the gate. If you have already left the gate but because of an unanticipated ground stop you have been delayed and now calculate you will exceed the 16-hour duty day limitation before reaching your destination, you will not be legal to finish the trip and must return to the gate.

To determine required rest periods, take into account all of your scheduled flying in a 24-hour "lookback" window surrounding the rest period you are about to start. Check to see if you are scheduled to fly more than 8 hours of flying in the 24-hour window before the completion of any flight leg.

Scheduled Flight time within 24 hours	Normal Rest	Minimum Reduced Rest	Minimum Required Compensatory Rest (to begin no later than 24 hours after the commencement of the reduced rest period)
Less than 8:00 hours	9:00 hours	8:00 hours	10:00 hours
8:00 hours to 8:59	10:00 hours	8:00 hours	11:00 hours
9:00 hours or more	11:00 hours	9:00 hours	12:00 hours

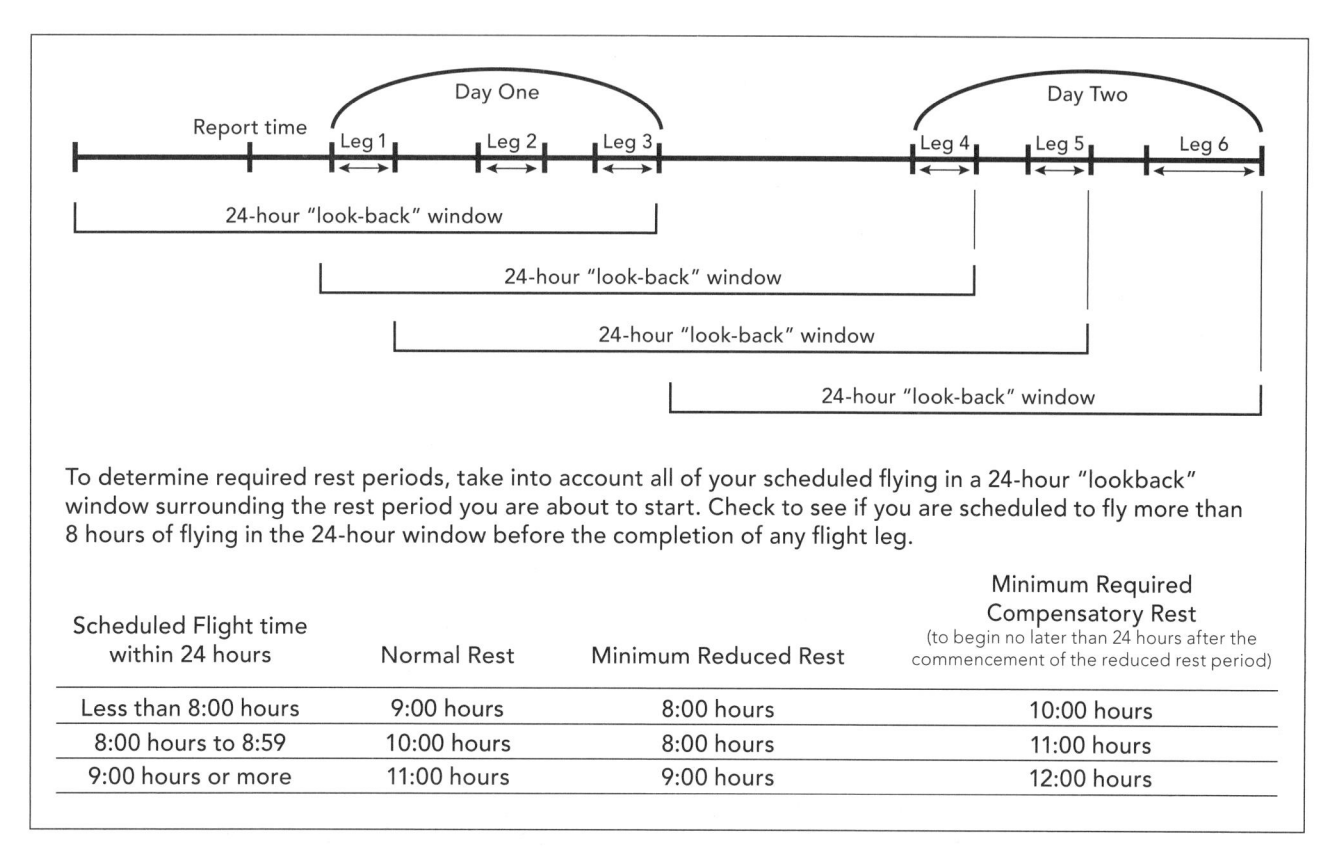

Figure 7-5. The 24-hour "look-back" window and required rest periods.

Before we leave the domestic all-cargo rules, let's look at Paragraph 121.471(d). This is sometimes referred to as the **1 in 7 rule**. It requires the carrier give the pilot 1 day (24 consecutive hours) free from all duty in each 7-day period. Recently, the FAA has changed its view on how this rule is to be interpreted. The issue is reserve pilots who are on call each day.

Before 1999, the view was that if at any time the company could look backward and find a 24-hour period in which the pilot had not flown, it could count that as the 24-hour period free from all duty. A reserve pilot could therefore "sit" reserve for more than 6 calendar days at a stretch. (Note carefully the wording of 121.471[d].) In the summer of 1999, the FAA issued a policy statement that beginning in December 1999, it would apply an interpretation of this rule that says the 24-hour period must be planned into the pilot's schedule—*looking forward*. That is, if a reserve pilot was required to be available to answer the telephone, then he was not free from all duty; therefore, a break from flying, *per se*, did not constitute a period free from all duty. This meant the air carrier was required to place 24-hour rest periods on a reserve pilot's future weekly or, as is most common, monthly schedule.

This was a major change from the way scheduling had been performed and it soon became evident many more pilots would be needed to "sit" reserve. This meant air carriers would have to hire more pilots. The carriers were given until December 1999 to work out with their pilot unions how it would be applied. By November 1999, all major domestic carriers had applied for and been granted a waiver from this provision until sometime in 2000 to work out a mutually acceptable method of compliance. This was done without public comment (i.e., from the pilot unions). As you can imagine, since they were not consulted on this issue, the pilot unions were not happy with the FAA's handling of the exemption applications of the airlines.

Eventually, after this reserve system was implemented, most pilots appeared to like the Part 121 reserve rest requirements. However, there were some complaints. The most common complaint made by some pilots is that the reserve rest requirement implemented in 1999 does not allow the flexibility of scheduling large blocks of reserve days in a row. Some pilots, such as pilots who commute from another city to "sit" reserve in their domicile, prefer to schedule large blocks of reserve days together so they can spend larger blocks of time at home and keep the number of days spent commuting to and from work to a minimum.

Subpart R: Flight Time Limitations: Flag All-Cargo Operations

Flag or international all-cargo flight operations are flights flown to destinations outside the 48 contiguous states, including to or from Alaska and Hawaii. Like domestic all-cargo flight time limitations, flag all-cargo flight time limitations are for *scheduled* flight time, while rest requirements are based on *actual hours flown*. Flag flight time limitations and regulations, because of the long routes flown in international operations, are considerably different for Part 121 flag operators. 14 CFR §121.480 makes the section applicable to flag all-cargo operators operating with a payload capacity of more than 7,500 pounds. Those aircraft with a payload capacity of 7,500 pounds or less have the option to operate under Part 121 or the slightly less restrictive rules of Part 135.

Two-Pilot Crews

Flight time limitations for flag all-cargo operations flight crews are set out in 14 CFR §121.481. The first flag limitations are self-explanatory and limit the pilot's flying on an annual, monthly, weekly, and daily basis. Notice, however, that there are a few differences in the wording of some of the flight time limitations; for instance, the domestic 1,000 flight hours in any calendar year limitation has been changed to 1,000 flight hours in any *12-calendar-month period*.

The flag operation limits are

- 12 calendar months—1,000 flight hours maximum
- 1 calendar month—100 flight hours maximum
- 7 consecutive calendar days—32 flight hours maximum
- 24 consecutive hours—8 flight hours maximum *(without a rest period)*

When a two-pilot crew is operating the flight, it may be scheduled for up to 8 hours in a 24 hour period (14 CFR §121.481[a]). If this crew is scheduled to fly more than 8 hours in a 24-consecutive-hour period, then it must be given a rest period prior to exceeding 8 hours. This rest period must be of at least twice the scheduled flight time, but no less than 8 hours rest. That is, it takes a minimum rest period of 8 hours to break a duty period. At the conclusion of the flying in excess of 8 hours in a 24-hour period, Paragraph 121.481(c) requires the pilot to receive a rest period of at least 18 hours free from all duty.

Would the following schedule be legal for a flag crew?

Report time:	1900Z
Departure time:	2000Z
Arrival time:	0100Z Flight time = 5:00 hours
Release time:	0115Z

Rest	Rest = 8:00 hours

Report time:	0915Z
Departure time:	1015Z
Arrival time:	1530Z Flight time = 5:15 hours
Release time:	1545Z

This would *not* be a legal pairing because while the crew gets 8:00 hours rest (which exceeds the basic minimum), the rest period must also equal or exceed twice the number of hours flown since the last rest. In this case, the first leg was a 5-hour flight, so the rest period must be at least 10 hours. The earliest the crew could be required to report would be 1115Z. Their maximum legal schedule would then be as follows:

Report time:	1900Z
Departure time:	2000Z
Arrival time:	0100Z Flight time = 5:00 hours
Release time:	0115Z

Rest	Rest = 10:00 hours

Report time:	1115Z
Departure time:	1215Z
Arrival time:	2015Z Flight time = 8:00 hours
Release time:	2030Z

How long does the next rest period have to be? At the end of this trip at 2015Z, we look back 24 hours and see that the pilot has flown 12:45 during the period 2015Z on day one and 2015Z on day two. On day one he or she flew from 2015Z until 0100Z (4:45 hours) and on day two he or she flew from 1215Z to 2015Z (8:00 hours) for a total of 12:45. Therefore, according to Paragraph 121.481(c), the pilot must receive a minimum of 18 hours rest. Therefore, the minimum rest period would result in a pairing on the third day of:

Release Time:	2030Z

Rest	Rest = 18:00 hours

Report Time:	1430Z
Departure Time:	1530Z
Arrival Time:	2330Z Flight time = 8:00 hours
Release Time:	2345Z

Flight time limitations and rest requirements for a two-pilot crew are summarized in Table 7-12.

Table 7-12. Flag flight time limitations and rest requirements (two-pilot crew)

Time Period	Flight-Time Aloft	Duty-Time Limitation	Rest Requirement
12 calendar months	1,000 hours		
1 calendar month	100 hours		
7 consecutive days			24 consecutive hours of rest
24 consecutive hours	Maximum of 8 hours *scheduled* without an intervening rest period	Maximum total time on duty is 16 hours in any 24 hour period	
	More than 8 hours	Maximum total time on duty is 16 hours	A rest period twice the number of flight hours since the preceding rest period. *8 hours minimum rest*
	More than 8 hours—*Actual*	Maximum total time on duty is 16 hours	18 hours of rest

Two Pilots Plus One Additional Flight Crewmember

Recognizing that the long international flights have unique needs, 14 CFR §121.483 provides a relief valve for operating flights in excess of 8 hours and up to 12 hours duration. In order to avail the carrier of the use of this provision, the carrier must put on a relief pilot in the form of "an additional crewmember." In this case, the limiting factors are 12 hours flight time in a 24-hour period, 20 flight hours in a 48-hour period, and 24 flight hours in a 72-hour period. At the end of these duty periods, a pilot must be given at least 18 hours free from all duty. The total flight hour limitations for two pilots plus one relief crewmember are as follows:

- 12 calendar months—1,000 flight hours
- 90 consecutive days—300 flight hours
- 30 consecutive days—120 flight hours

Notice that with the additional crewmember and, as we'll see below, with three pilots plus one additional flight crewmember, the 30 in 7 (domestic) or 32 in 7 (flag) limitation is removed.

Three (or More) Pilots Plus One Additional Flight Crewmember

14 CFR §121.485 provides relief for really long haul flights such as the transpacific flights operating from the United States to China, Japan, or Australia. It is available for flights in excess of 12 hours. In this case, the airplane must be crewed with at least three pilots and one additional flight crewmember. First, the carrier has to schedule its flights so as to provide "adequate rest periods on the ground for each pilot who is away from his base." Next, the airplane must have adequate sleeping quarters in the form of bunks or an isolated set of first-class seats that are somewhat removed from the cabin commotion. Then, upon the pilot's return to his or her base, the carrier must give a rest period that is at least twice the number of hours flown since the pilot's last rest period at *his or her base*.

These crews are limited in terms of total hours of service as follows:

- 12 calendar months—1,000 flight hours
- 90 consecutive days—350 flight hours

14 CFR §121.487(b) covers the pilot who is not regularly assigned to one of these types of crews for the entire month. For example, the pilot may fly part of the month as part of a two-pilot-plus-one-crewmember crew and part of the month as part of a two-pilot crew. In that case, the monthly maximums are given in Paragraph 121.481(e), namely, 100 hours in the calendar month. The quarterly and annual limitations of a pilot who is scheduled for more than 20 hours in augmented crews will be found in Paragraphs 121.483(c)(2) and (3), namely 300 hours in 90 days and 1,000 hours in 12 calendar months.

14 CFR §121.489 provides that in calculating a pilot's flight time limits, a carrier must include not only the flying done for it but also *any other commercial flying*. In other words, if the pilot has any other flying job (e.g., civilian), that flight time must be considered in determining the flight limitations under 14 CFR §§121.483 and 121.485. Military reserve or guard flying *is not counted toward the flight time limits*.

14 CFR §121.491 further spells out that deadhead time (time spent traveling on an airplane as a passenger) does not count as rest time.

Flight Engineers and Navigators

Flight and duty limitations for flight engineers and navigators are briefly mentioned in 14 CFR §121.493. If only *one* flight engineer or one navigator is required, then the air carrier must use the flight time limitations for *two pilots and one additional flight crewmember* (14 CFR §121.483). For any flight operation requiring more than one flight engineer or more than one navigator, the air carrier must use the flight time limitations for *three or more pilots and an additional flight crewmember* (14 CFR §121.485).

Subpart S: Flight Time Limitations: Supplemental All-Cargo Operations

This subpart applies to *nonscheduled* or *supplemental domestic* and *supplemental overseas and international* all-cargo flight operations for aircraft having a payload capacity of greater than 7,500 pounds. Flight time limitations for *supplemental operations* are covered in 14 CFR §121.503 and are similar to flag flight time limitations with some interesting differences.

- Calendar year—1,000 flight hours maximum
- 30 consecutive days—100 flight hours maximum
- Between rest periods—8 flight hours maximum

Notice that the standard calendar month limitation used in domestic and flag operations has been changed to read *in any 30 consecutive days*. Also, flight time limitations have been relaxed to allow an air carrier to exceed the 8-flight-hour maximum between rest periods by up to 2 hours. To be allowed to exceed the 8-hour maximum, the flight must be a transcontinental nonstop flight (not overseas). The aircraft must have an operative pressurization system at the beginning of the flight, and the flight crew must consist of at least two pilots *and* a flight engineer (14 CFR §121.503[f]).

Two-Pilot Crews

When a two-pilot crew is operating the flight, it may be scheduled to fly more than 8 hours in a 24 hour period (14 CFR §121.505[a]). If this crew is scheduled to fly more than 8 hours in a 24-consecutive-hour period, then it must be given a rest period prior to exceeding 8 hours. This rest period must be at least twice the scheduled flight time, but no less than 8 hours. Therefore, as we mentioned in the previous FAR subparts, it takes a minimum rest period of 8 hours to break a duty period.

The duty day limitation for a two-pilot crew is similar to the domestic duty day limitation. A pilot may not be on duty more than 16 hours in any consecutive 24-hour period (14 CFR §121.505[b]). Flight time limitations and rest requirements for a two-pilot crew are summarized in Table 7-13.

Let's consider a 3-day trip scheduled to the maximum allowable flight and duty time limitations for a two-pilot crew under supplemental operations.

Report time:	0700Z	
Departure time:	0800Z	
Arrival time:	1300Z	Flight time = 5:00 hours
Release time:	1315Z	
Rest		Rest = 10:00 hours
Report time:	2315Z	
Departure time:	0015Z	
Arrival time:	0815Z	Flight time = 8:00 hours
Release time:	0830Z	

In this case, how long does this rest period have to be? At the end of the trip at 0815Z, we look back 24 hours to 0815Z on day one and see that the pilot has flown 12:45 hours during the period 0815Z on day one to 0815Z on day two. On day one he or she flew from 0815Z until 1300Z (4:45 hours) and on day two he or she flew from 0015Z to 0815Z (8:00 hours) or a total of 12:45. Therefore, according to Paragraph 121.503(b), the pilot must receive a minimum of 16 hours rest. For this reason, the minimum rest period would result in a pairing on the third day of:

Release time:	0830Z	
Rest		Rest = 16:00 hours
Report time:	0030Z	
Departure time:	0130Z	
Arrival time:	0930Z	Flight time = 8:00 hours
Release time:	0945Z	

Three-Pilot Crews

For three-pilot crews in supplemental operations, we begin to see the FAA distinguish between **flight deck duty** time and **duty aloft time**. No pilot may be scheduled for more than 8 hours *flight deck duty time* or 12 hours *aloft* in any 24 consecutive hours (14 CFR §121.507[a]). In addition, when a three-pilot crew is flying in supplemental operations, the maximum duty day is extended 2 hours for a maximum of 18 hours in any 24-hour period (14 CFR §121.507[b]).

Table 7-13. Supplemental flight time limitations and rest requirements (two-pilot crew)

Time Period	Duty-Time Aloft	Duty-Time Limitation	Rest Requirement
Calendar year	1,000 hours		
30 consecutive days	100 hours		
7 consecutive days			24 consecutive hours of rest
24 consecutive hours	Maximum of 8 hours—*scheduled*	Maximum total time on duty is 16 hours in any 24 hour period	
	More than 8 hours	Maximum total time on duty is 16 hours	A rest period twice the number of flight hours since the preceding rest period. *8 hours minimum rest*
	More than 8 hours—*Actual*	Maximum total time on duty is 16 hours	16 hours of rest

Four-Pilot Crews

For a crew of four pilots, the maximum flight and duty time limitations have been extended still more. No pilot may be scheduled for more than 8 hours *flight deck duty time* or 16 hours *aloft* in any 24 consecutive hours (14 CFR §121.509[a]). Also, when a four-pilot crew is flying in supplemental operations, the maximum duty day has been extended another 2 hours for a maximum of 20 hours in any 24-hour period (14 CFR §121.507[b]).

Flight Engineers and Navigators

Supplemental flight and duty limitations for flight engineers and navigators are covered in 14 CFR §121.511. If only *one* flight engineer or *one* navigator is required, then the air carrier must use the flight time limitations found in 14 CFR §121.503 and §121.505. For any flight operation requiring more than one flight engineer or more than one navigator, the air carrier must use flight time limitations: four pilot crews (14 CFR §121.509).

Subpart S: Flight Time Limitation for Supplemental Overseas and International All-Cargo Operations

For overseas and international supplemental all-cargo operations, 14 CFR §121.513 gives an air carrier the option to comply with the more restrictive domestic supplemental regulations (14 CFR §§121.503–121.511) or to use the following flight and duty time limitations:

- 12 calendar month period—1,000 hours aloft

Notice the 1,000 hours in a calendar year limitation found in the supplemental domestic limitations has been changed to read in any 12 calendar month period. Also, the limitation is based on 1,000 hours aloft, not just the time the pilot spends up front in the pilot seat.

Two Pilots and One Additional Crewmember

With a crew of two pilots and one additional crewmember (e.g., flight engineer or navigator), the supplemental limitations, covered in 14 CFR §121.521, are as follows:

- 24 hour period—12 hours aloft
- 30 consecutive days—120 hours aloft
- 90 consecutive days—90 hours aloft

Additionally, an air carrier is required to give a pilot 18 hours of rest for the following times aloft:

- 20 or more hours in a 48-consecutive-hour period
- 24 or more hours in a 72-consecutive-hour period

Three (or More) Pilots and Additional Crewmembers as Required

14 CFR §121.523 covers ultra long-haul flight and duty limitations and contains some interesting additional limitations. For ultra long-range flying, or flights in excess of 12 hours, another pilot is required. Adding the third pilot, with the additional crewmembers, allows the air carrier to fly routes in excess of 12 flight hours. Instead of limiting the flight time aloft to 12 hours as in the two-pilot limitation, the FAA limits the *flight deck duty time*. Just as we've seen with flag ultra long-range operations, supplemental ultra long-range operations require the air carrier to schedule its flights so as to provide "adequate rest periods on the ground for each pilot who is away from his or her base." Next, the airplane must have adequate sleeping quarters in the form of bunks or an isolated set of first-class seats that are somewhat removed from the cabin commotion. Then, upon the pilot's return to his or her base, the carrier must give a rest period that is at least twice the number of hours flown since the pilot's last rest period *at his or her base*. The Section 121.523 limitation is

- 90 consecutive days—350 hours aloft

With a flight crew consisting of three or more pilots, the maximum continuous duty is extended to 30 hours! The FAA defines continuous duty as the time from report time to the time the pilot is released for at least a 10 hour rest *on the ground*. If the flight crew is on continuous duty for more than 24 hours, they must be given 16 or more hours of rest on the ground after the last flight scheduled for that duty period (14 CFR §121.523[c]).

Deadhead time aloft in excess of 4 hours requires that at least one-half of that time aloft be considered duty time if the flight crew is required to deadhead before the start of any flight duty. This limitation is waived if the flight crew is given at least 10 hours of rest on the ground before beginning any flight duty (14 CFR §121.523[d]).

Once a pilot has returned to his or her domicile, the air carrier is required to give the pilot a rest period of at least twice the total number of hours the pilot was aloft during the entire previous trip since first reporting at that domicile (14 CFR §121.523[e]).

Part 121 Fatigue Risk Management System (FRMS)

As we discussed in 14 CFR §117.7, a fatigue risk management system (FRMS) is an optional approach to current FAA regulations. A certificate holder seeking to exceed a limitation listed in Part 121, Subparts Q, R, or S, would do so under an FAA authorization. An FRMS is largely developed as an alternative method of compliance to the current FAA limitations based upon objective performance standards. A certificate holder may be authorized to apply an FRMS to any part or to all of its operation, provided that the certificate holder demonstrates an effective alternative method of compliance. All three subparts discussed in this section (Subparts Q, R, and S) include the same FRMS paragraph at the end of their respective part.

Fatigue risk management system.

(a) No certificate holder may exceed any provision of this subpart unless approved by the FAA under a Fatigue Risk Management System.
(b) The Fatigue Risk Management System must include:
   (1) A fatigue risk management policy.
   (2) An education and awareness training program.
   (3) A fatigue reporting system.
   (4) A system for monitoring flightcrew fatigue.
   (5) An incident reporting process.
   (6) A performance evaluation.

(14 CFR §121.473, §121.495, §121.527)

FAA Advisory Circular 120-103 defines a fatigue risk management system as "a management system for a certificate holder to use to mitigate the effects of fatigue in its particular operations."

Subpart P: Flight Attendant Duty Period Limitations and Rest Requirements: Domestic, Flag, and Supplemental Operations; Aircraft Dispatcher Qualifications and Duty Time Limitations: Domestic and Flag Operations

Flight Attendant Duty Time Limitations

Flight duty time limitations for flight attendants (both domestic and flag) are found in 14 CFR §121.467. The concept of the duty period for flight attendants is a little different than it is for flight crews. Their duty period is not flight duty (measured from block out to block in) as for pilots, but rather is the total time spent "at work" between reporting for duty involving flight time and being released from duty. Therefore, the ground layovers are included in the calculation of flight attendant duty time (14 CFR §121.467[a]). The basic flight attendant duty period limitation is 14 hours. If given 14 hours or less duty time, the carrier need only provide at least 9 consecutive hours of rest (14 CFR §121.487[b][1]). As with a pilot, this rest period may be reduced to a minimum of 8 hours if a compensatory rest period of 10 hours is provided.

The duty period limitation may be extended to between 14 and 16 hours if the carrier assigns an extra flight attendant to the flight; 16 to 18 hours if the carrier assigns two extra flight attendants to the flight; and from 18 to a whopping 20 hours if three extra flight attendants are assigned to the flight. Also, to schedule a flight from 18 to 20 hours, the flight must take off or land at a point outside the 48 contiguous United States and the District of Columbia. If these extended duty

Table 7-14. Flight attendant duty limitations and rest requirements

Number of Flight Attendants (FAs)	Scheduled Duty Period	Rest	Reduced Rest	Compensatory Rest**
FAA minimum staffing (refer to 121.391)	14 hours maximum	9 hours	8 hours	10 hours
Minimum staffing plus one extra FA	14–16 hours maximum	12 hours	10 hours	14 hours
Minimum staffing plus two extra FAs	16–18 hours maximum	12 hours	10 hours	14 hours
Minimum staffing plus three extra FAs	18–20 hours maximum*	12 hours	10 hours	14 hours

*Scheduled duty period includes one or more flights that land or take off outside the 48 contiguous states and the District of Columbia.
**Compensatory rest must begin within 24 hours after the beginning of the reduced rest period.

periods are used, the rest requirements are increased accordingly. A flight attendant must receive at least 24 consecutive hours free from all duty in each 7 consecutive day period. Table 7-14 summarizes flight attendant duty limitations and rest requirements.

As an alternative to these provisions, Paragraph 121.467(c) states that the carrier may apply to flight attendants the same Part 117 rules that are applied to the flight crew. To do this, the carrier must state the procedures in its general operations manual. These procedures must apply to all flight attendants used in the certificate holder's operation. Surprisingly, one portion of Part 117 does not apply to flight attendants: if you look at Paragraph 121.467(c) you'll see that onboard rest facilities are not required for flight attendants.

Aircraft Dispatcher Duty Time Limitations

Dispatcher duty time limitations are found in 14 CFR §121.465. These apply to domestic or flag operations. First, the dispatcher must begin each shift so as to allow time to become thoroughly familiar with the existing and anticipated weather conditions along the route of flight for all aircraft he or she is dispatching. The dispatcher must remain on duty until each airplane he or she has dispatched has completed its flight or gone beyond his or her jurisdiction, or until the dispatcher is relieved by another qualified dispatcher. Except for emergency situations, the carrier may not schedule the dispatcher for duty in excess of 10 consecutive hours. If a dispatcher is scheduled for duty in excess of 10 consecutive hours in a 24-consecutive-hour period, that dispatcher must be given a rest period of at least 8 hours at or before the end of the 10 hours on duty. Further, the dispatcher must be relieved of all duty with the carrier for at least 24 consecutive hours in any 7-consecutive-day period or the equivalent thereof in any calendar month. Table 7-15 summarizes dispatcher duty time limitations.

Table 7-15. Aircraft dispatcher duty time limitations.

Scheduled Duty Period	Rest
Less than or equal to 10 hours in a 24 hour period	Normal rest equals remainder of the 24 hour period
More than 10 hours in a 24 hour period	8 hours rest commencing at or before the end of 10 hours of duty

No certificate holder conducting domestic or flag operations may schedule a dispatcher for more than 10 consecutive hours of duty. (14 CFR §121.465 [b]).

Summary

Air carriers and their pilots, flight attendants, and flight dispatchers share the responsibility for conducting flight operations at the highest level of safety. Both flight crews and air carriers are responsible for ensuring that flight and duty time limitations are not exceeded. Pilots have the responsibility to take advantage of the opportunity for rest and report for their assignments well rested and ready for duty. Air carriers have the responsibility to conduct their operations at the highest level of safety. This includes establishing the appropriate scheduling practices that provide pilots with adequate rest. Preventing the degradation of alertness and performance caused by fatigue is a shared responsibility that brings shared benefits in terms of increased safety, better working conditions, and greater overall operational efficiencies.

In the next chapter, we will discuss the requirements imposed upon the air carrier aircraft used in 14 CFR Part 121 operations.

Important Terms in Chapter 7

1 in 7 rule
14 CFR Part 117
30 in 7 rule
acclimated
actual flight time
Airline Safety and Federal Aviation Administration Extension Act (49 USC 40101)
airport/standby reserve
all-cargo operations
augmented flight crew
calendar day
certificate holder
circadian fatigue
circadian rhythms
commercial flying
consecutive nighttime operations
cumulative fatigue
cumulative flight time limitations
deadhead transportation
domestic all-cargo operations
domestic operations
duty
duty aloft
duty day
duty period
fatigue
fatigue risk management plan
fatigue risk management system (FRMS)
fitness for duty
flag all-cargo operations
flag operations
flight and duty time limitations
flight deck duty
flight duty period (FDP)
flight duty period extensions
flight time
home base
lineholder
long-call reserve
"look-back" rule
physiological night's rest
Public Law 111-216
report time
reserve availability period
reserve flight crewmember
rest
rest facility (Class 1, 2 and 3)
rest period
scheduled flight time
short-call reserve
split duty
suitable accommodation
supplemental all-cargo operations
supplemental operations
Table A, B, and C (Part 117)
theater
transient fatigue
ultra-long-range (ULR) operations
unforeseen operational circumstances
Whitlow letter
window of circadian low

Chapter 7 Exam

Passenger-Carrying Operations

1. To be considered acclimated, a flight crewmember must be in a theater for _____ hours or must be given at least _____ consecutive hours free from duty.
   a. 72 hours in theater and 36 consecutive hours free from duty.
   b. 72 hours in theater or 36 consecutive hours free from duty.
   c. 30 hours in theater and 24 consecutive hours free from duty.
   d. 12 hours in theater and 10 consecutive hours free from duty.

2. Refer to 14 CFR §117.21(c)(1): The reserve availability period (RAP) for a short-call reserve may not exceed how many hours?
   a. 12 hours
   b. 14 hours
   c. 16 hours
   d. 18 hours if the number of flight attendants exceeds the minimum required by at least two.

3. If a flight crew needs to make a flight duty period (FDP) extension due to an unforeseen circumstance discovered after takeoff (e.g., a recent destination runway closure), are they allowed to exceed the cumulative FDP limits specified in Section 117.23?
   a. Yes
   b. No

4. A long-call reserve may be converted to a short call as long as they have how many hours of rest?
   a. 8 hours reduced rest
   b. 9 hours compensatory rest
   c. 10 hours rest
   d. 12 hours rest

5. A flight crewmember is scheduled for a domestic flight consisting of a 2-pilot crew on a 6-hour flight time. How much rest must this flight crewmember get prior to report time?
   a. 10 consecutive hours rest before with a 30 hour rest period in the preceding 168 hours
   b. 10 consecutive hours compensatory rest after 36 hours in theater
   c. 10 consecutive hours rest reducible to 9 hours
   d. 8 consecutive hours rest if less than 2 flight segments with a scheduled start time from 0700–1100

6. When does a flight crewmember "look back" to determine if he or she has received the proper amount of rest?
   a. At release time plus 30 minutes
   b. At block-in time after each leg
   c. At the start of a compensatory rest period
   d. At the start of a flight duty period or reserve availability period

7. A flight crewmember assigned to an augmented crew of 4 pilots with a Class 2 rest facility is not permitted to exceed which of the following cumulative limitations?
   a. 100 hours in any 672-consecutive-hour period
   b. 24 hours in a calendar day period
   c. 300 hours in any 672-consecutive-hour period
   d. 8 total flight hours over a split duty period

8. An augmented flight crew assigned a flight duty period with a split duty period built in to the flight segments that allows for just over a 3-hour rest opportunity in a suitable accommodation during the window of circadian low is allowed a flight duty period of up to 14 hours.
   a. True
   b. False

9. Is it legal for a flight crewmember to be scheduled five consecutive flight duty periods that begin at 0215 local time?
   a. No, a flight crewmember may not be scheduled more than 3 consecutive flight duty periods that infringe on the window of circadian low.
   b. Yes, a flight crewmember may be scheduled five consecutive flight duty periods that infringe on the window of circadian low if the certificate holder provides the flight crewmember with an opportunity to rest, at least 2 hours, in a suitable accommodation during each of the consecutive nighttime flight duty periods.
   c. No, a flight crewmember may not be scheduled five consecutive flight duty periods that infringe on the window of circadian low even if the certificate holder provides the flight crewmember with an opportunity to rest, at least 2 hours, in a suitable accommodation during each of the consecutive nighttime flight duty periods.
   d. Yes, a flight crewmember may be scheduled more than 3 consecutive flight duty periods that infringe on the window of circadian low if provided a Class A rest facility.

10. The maximum flight duty period hours for augmented operations with 4 pilots utilizing a Class 1 rest facility is:
    a. 17 hours
    b. 18 hours
    c. 19 hours
    d. It depends on the number of flight segments.

11. A deadhead leg that occurs after a flight segment is NOT considered part of a flight duty period (FDP).
    a. True
    b. False

12. Prior to takeoff, what is the maximum flight time extension for an unaugmented crew who has not had a flight time extension during the previous 168 hours?
    a. 2 hours
    b. 30 minutes
    c. 0 minutes; flight time limits are "hard limits"
    d. Up to 30 minutes without PIC concurrence; up to 2 hours with PIC concurrence

13. After takeoff, what is the maximum that a flight duty period (FDP) may be extended?
    a. 2 hours, with PIC concurrence
    b. 30 minutes, without PIC concurrence
    c. 0 minutes; flight duty period limits are "hard limits"
    d. When unforeseen operational circumstances occur after takeoff, the maximum flight duty period may be extended to the extent necessary to safely land at the next destination or alternate.

14. A short-call reserve pilot whose reserve availability period began at 0500 local time (acclimated) is contacted by crew scheduling at 0700 local time and assigned an unaugmented one-day trip that reports at 0900 local time and has two turns (4 flight segments) from ATL to Miami (MIA). When does the flight duty period begin and when must the flight duty period be scheduled to end for this flight crewmember?
    a. FDP begins at 0500 local time and must be scheduled to end by 2100 local time.
    b. FDP begins at 0700 local time and must be scheduled to end by 2000 local time.
    c. FDP begins at 0900 local time and must be scheduled to end by 2100 local time.
    d. FDP begins at 0900 local time and must be scheduled to end by 2200 local time.

15. A long-call reserve pilot whose reserve availability period began at 0500 local time (acclimated) is contacted by crew scheduling at 0700 local time and assigned an augmented (3 pilots) 3-day trip, reporting at 0900 local time and with one flight segment from ATL to Rome (FCO) in an aircraft equipped with a Class 3 rest facility. When does the flight duty period begin and when must the flight duty period be scheduled to end for this flight crewmember?
    a. FDP begins at 0900 local time and must be scheduled to end by 0000 local Rome time.
    b. FDP begins at 0700 local time and must be scheduled to end by 0000 local Atlanta time.
    c. FDP begins at 0900 local time and must be scheduled to end by 2200 local Atlanta time.
    d. FDP begins at 0900 local time and must be scheduled to end by 0000 local Atlanta time.

All-Cargo Operations

1. A cargo pilot is scheduled to fly for 6 consecutive days. Is it legal for that pilot to be assigned to deadhead home on the seventh day?
    a. Yes
    b. No

2. A cargo pilot is scheduled to fly for 6 consecutive days. It is legal for that pilot to be assigned a recurrent simulator training period on the seventh day.
    a. True
    b. False

3. A cargo pilot is scheduled to fly for 6 consecutive days. Could the pilot then be required to ferry an aircraft to some destination in order to position the aircraft for some future revenue service?
    a. Yes
    b. No

4. A cargo pilot is scheduled to deadhead in order to meet an aircraft in Memphis (MEM) on the first day of a trip. Is it legal for the pilot to be scheduled to fly for the next 6 days without a calendar day off?
    a. Yes
    b. No

5. The time a cargo pilot spends deadheading is considered rest.
    a. True
    b. False

6. A cargo pilot is originally scheduled for a minimum rest period of 8 hours, but because of weather delays this pilot's flight has been delayed. In this circumstance, the air carrier is allowed to schedule the pilot for less than an 8-hour rest period.
    a. True
    b. False

7. An all-cargo flight crew is scheduled for a 7:45 hour flight from ATL to Anchorage, Alaska (ANC). Prior to departure, the company wants to adjust the flight time to 8:10 to compensate for headwinds. Is this flight a legal assignment?

   a. Yes
   b. No

8. A pilot is given the minimum reduced rest the first night of a 3-day trip. How soon must the pilot be given the required compensatory rest?

   a. No later than 24 hours after the commencement of the reduced rest period
   b. Immediately following completion of the 3-day trip
   c. The pilot may choose to have the compensatory rest period waived
   d. No later than 24 hours after the beginning of the flight duty period on day one

9. An all-cargo flight crew, because of a prior reduced rest period, is scheduled to receive compensatory rest beginning at 2130 hours. The flight crew is scheduled to complete the last leg of the day at 2115 hours; because of a ground stop ATC delay, the flight crew will arrive at the final destination at 2145 hours. The flight crew may legally depart on this last leg.

   a. True
   b. False

10. A normally scheduled lineholding cargo pilot may be required to communicate with crew scheduling during a designated rest period by which means?

    a. Text message or company instant messaging
    b. Email
    c. Phone or pager
    d. None of the above

11. A cargo pilot "sitting reserve" for the month but in a designated rest period may be required to communicate with crew scheduling during a designated rest period by which means?

    a. Text message or company instant messaging
    b. Email
    c. Phone or pager
    d. None of the above

12. If during a cargo pilot's designated rest period, the company calls to notify the pilot of an adjustment to the departure time, this requires the pilot to "reset" the clock and begin a new rest period.

    a. True
    b. False

13. A cargo pilot is scheduled to fly 97 hours for this month (at fifteen 6.5-hour flight days). Due to circumstances beyond the company's control, the pilot has accumulated 96 hours prior to the last scheduled duty day of the month. The pilot is legal to fly the last 6.5 hour assignment.

    a. True
    b. False

14. A domestically assigned cargo pilot is scheduled to fly 97 hours for this month (at fifteen 6.5-hour flight days). Due to circumstances beyond the company's control, the pilot has accumulated 96 hours prior to the last scheduled duty day of the month. What is the maximum amount of time this pilot may be deadheaded?

    a. 4 hours up to the 100 hours actual flight time maximum for the month
    b. 3 hours up to the 100 hours scheduled flight time maximum for the month
    c. 6.5 hours hour maximum allowed due to the original schedule maximum
    d. No limit to the amount of hours this pilot may be scheduled to deadhead

15. What is the maximum flight time allowable for a two-pilot crew in domestic, flag, or supplemental all-cargo operations for the following time periods *(Fill in the blanks)*:

    Domestic operations limitations:
    1. Calendar year _____
    2. Calendar month _____
    3. 7 consecutive calendar days _____
    4. Between rest periods_____

    Flag operation limitations:
    1. 12 calendar months _____
    2. Calendar month _____
    3. 7-consecutive-day period _____
    4. 24 consecutive hours _____

Supplemental all-cargo operations limitations:
1. Calendar year _____
2. 30 consecutive days _____
3. Between rest periods _____

16. What is the maximum duty day for a cargo pilot in a two-pilot crew flying in supplemental all-cargo operations?
    a. 16 hours
    b. 18 hours with a Class 3 rest facility
    c. 20 hours with a Class 2 rest facility
    d. 22 hours with a Class 1 rest facility

17. Can a pilot in a two-pilot cargo flight crew flying in domestic operations exceed more than 8 hours of flying in a 24-hour period?
    a. No; 8 hours of flying in a 24-hour period is a hard limit.
    b. Yes; 8 hours of flying in a 24-hour period is legal.
    c. No; more than 8 hours of flying in a 24-hour period is only legal for augmented flight crews.
    d. No; more than 8 hours of flying in a 24-hour period is only legal with a Class 1 rest facility.

18. Is a rest period required for a cargo pilot given a domestic reserve assignment? How about an international pilot sitting reserve?
    a. No; all time sitting reserve is considered rest.
    b. No; a pilot only has to be provided with a 9-hour rest period following the first flight duty period.
    c. Yes; a domestic reserve pilot must be able to look back for a scheduled rest period of at least 8 hours; an international pilot is not protected by the look-back provision.
    d. No; the company cannot be responsible for the amount of rest opportunity a pilot receives prior to reporting for a trip.

19. What is the maximum duty day for a pilot in a domestic all-cargo operation?
    a. 8 hours
    b. 10 hours
    c. 12 hours
    d. 16 hours

20. What is the maximum amount of duty an aircraft dispatcher employed by a passenger-carrying airline may be scheduled for?
    a. 8 hours
    b. 10 hours
    c. 12 hours
    d. 14 hours with 10 hours compensatory rest to begin within 24 hours of the end of the shift

21. What is the maximum amount of duty an aircraft dispatcher employed by an all-cargo airline may be scheduled for?
    a. 8 hours
    b. 10 hours
    c. 12 hours
    d. 14 hours with 10 hours compensatory rest to begin within 24 hours of the end of the shift

22. What is the maximum number of hours a pilot in supplemental all-cargo operations, on a three-pilot crew, may be scheduled in a 24-consecutive-hour period?
    a. 8 hours
    b. 10 hours
    c. 12 hours
    d. 14 hours with 10 hours compensatory rest to begin within 24 hours of the end of the flight duty period

23. What is the maximum number of hours a pilot assigned flying in supplemental all-cargo operations may be aloft in any 30-consecutive-day period, as a member of a flight crew consisting of two pilots and one additional flight crewmember?
    a. 100 hours
    b. 100 hours or the limit found in Table C plus 4 hours
    c. 120 hours
    d. 100 hours or the lesser of the Table B limit plus 4 hours or 130 hours

24. What is the maximum number of hours an air carrier may schedule a pilot to fly in flag all-cargo operations, having two pilots and one additional flight crewmember?
    a. No more than 12 hours during any 24-consecutive-hour period
    b. No more than 14 hours during any 24-consecutive-hour period with a Class A or Class B rest facility
    c. No more than 16 hours during any 30-consecutive-hour period, allowed once in the previous 168 hour period
    d. Both b and c

25. What type of flying counts towards a cargo pilot's annual, monthly, and weekly flight time limitations?
    a. All commercial flight time, except military, in any flight crewmember position
    b. All commercial flight time and military flying, in any flight crewmember position
    c. All private, commercial and military flying totals, in any flight crewmember position
    d. All commercial flying except those hours when acting as certified flight instructor

CHAPTER 8
AIRPLANES USED IN PART 121 OPERATIONS

Scientific investigation into the possibilities [of jet propulsion] has given no indication that this method can be a serious competitor to the airscrew-engine combination.
—**British Undersecretary of State for Air**, 1934

Most of us are familiar (or will soon become familiar) with the operational provisions of 14 CFR Part 91 that prescribe general operating rules to be applied to non–air carrier operations. They are focused on basic operation of the aircraft in the national airspace system and are not very restrictive in regard to the airplanes to be used. These airplanes may be a wide variety of aircraft ranging from homebuilt, experimental aircraft to aircraft licensed in a number of different categories such as normal, limited and so forth. For non-carriage operations, these rules serve well to provide an adequate level of safety balanced against operational usage. In Part 121 operations, it is a whole different ball game. In the same way that air carriers have the highest standards imposed on them when it comes to operating rules, the aircraft used in air carrier operations are also required to meet the highest standards in terms of design, certification, and performance. In this chapter, we will examine some of the unique aspects of air carrier aircraft operated under 14 CFR Part 121.

General Aircraft Requirements

Subpart H of Part 121 sets forth the requirements for the aircraft to be used in Part 121 operations. The first of these requirements is found in Section 121.153, which requires either that the aircraft be registered as a civil aircraft in the United States or that it be a complying foreign-registered civil aircraft. To be a complying foreign-registered aircraft, it must be registered in a country that is a party to the Convention on International Civil Aviation and be leased, without crew (**dry lease**), to a U.S. carrier. In addition, it must be of a type design that is approved under a U.S. type certificate and complies with all airworthiness standards that would apply to it were it a U.S.-registered aircraft. 14 CFR §121.159 limits the aircraft used in Part 121 operations to multi-engine aircraft.

Any aircraft used in a Part 121 operation must meet appropriate certification standards. 14 CFR §121.157 serves to grandfather a number of aircraft certificated under previous versions of the FARs and the pre-1958 Civil Aeronautical Rules (CARs). If a company is involved in flying older aircraft (typically cargo and commuter operators), it should pay close attention to Section 121.157 and the exceptions created by the grandfather clauses. If we ignore those exceptions, the most important requirements for Part 121 aircraft are found in Paragraph 121.157(b), which requires that aircraft type certificated after June 30, 1942, be **transport category aircraft** and meet certain performance standards found in 14 CFR §121.173(b), (d) and (e). Transport category aircraft are certificated under **14 CFR Part 25** to the highest possible standards to ensure that the performance and safety levels required by Part 121 are achieved.

Proving Tests

Prior to being used in air carrier operations, air carrier aircraft must be shown to be suitable for the kind of operations proposed by the carrier. This is done by performing **proving tests**. These are dry runs operated by the carrier to show the suitability of the aircraft for the operations it contemplates performing. 14 CFR §121.163 requires that for a new type of aircraft that has not been previously proven for Part 121 operations, the aircraft must be operated for at least 100 hours, including a number of representative flights into airports. The FAA may reduce the 100 hours of flight time if an equivalent level of safety is shown. In addition, a minimum of 10 hours of the proving tests must be made at night. If the aircraft type has been previously proven by a carrier, then Section 121.163 allows for a minimum of 50 hours of proving tests for the kinds of operations to be conducted by the carrier. Finally, if the carrier desires to operate an aircraft that is materially altered in design (e.g., additional fuel tanks installed in the cargo compartment), the carrier must also conduct 50 hours of proving tests for each kind of operation it proposes to conduct. Generally, a carrier may not carry passengers during proving test flights.

Airplane Performance and Operating Limitations

The major distinction between aircraft operated under Part 121 and those operated under Part 91 is the level of operational performance required of the aircraft. Part 121, Subpart I, contains numerous considerations as to the performance of the aircraft to be used in air carrier operations. It is important to keep in mind that these rules for *operating* the aircraft work hand in hand with the rules found in 14 CFR Part 25 for *certificating* transport category aircraft. Part 25 certification standards ensure that the aircraft is *capable* of the performance while Part 121 ensures that it is *operated so as to comply with or achieve* the requisite performance standards required by the aircraft certification rules. Let's now examine the performance requirements for aircraft flown under Part 121.

As you study this subpart of the FAR, you may find the frequent reference to dates confusing. The reason for these dates is to recognize that performance standards have been updated and refined over the years. As this happens, older aircraft that were not certificated under the more stringent standard are frequently "grandfathered" to allow them to continue to operate for a period of time so as to allow the owners and operators to secure the economic life from their expensive assets. In our discussions, we will mostly refer to modern, turbine aircraft that meet current design standards so the dates will not be so important. This includes virtually all turbine aircraft and most (but not all) turboprop aircraft operated by Part 121 carriers. We will not discuss any reciprocating (piston) aircraft rules. If you find yourself flying these museum pieces, be sure to revisit Part 121, Subpart I, on your own and pay close attention in your initial training. In the discussions below, we will examine only aircraft certificated after August 29, 1959.

We will now turn our attention to the specific performance requirements of these modern turbine (and turboprop) transport category aircraft operated under Part 121. There is a major conceptual difference between air carrier aircraft (transport category aircraft) and other airplanes used in Part 91 operations. In air carrier operations, the FAA insists on certain minimum performance requirements that assure safe operation of the aircraft is possible even with loss of thrust at critical points in the flight envelope. The following limitations will be discussed in this chapter:

- Takeoff limitations
- En route limitations: one engine inoperative
- En route limitations: two engines inoperative
- Landing limitations: destination airports
- Landing limitations: alternate airports

Before going into the specifics of these limitations, let's establish some definitions used in Parts 1, 25, and 121 or commonly used in the industry.

Definitions

The following takeoff performance V-speed definitions are based on "balanced field length" V-speeds. This means that the V-speeds are not computed based on the amount of actual runway length available for the takeoff, but on the balanced field length (see balanced field length definition later in this chapter). In other words, the heavier the aircraft, the longer it will take to stop during a rejected takeoff (RTO). Additionally, the heavier the aircraft, the longer the takeoff roll will be after an engine failure if the decision is made to continue the takeoff. Maximum takeoff weight for a given runway is reached when the balanced field length equals the runway length available. Also note that the actual V_1 speed a flight crew uses is picked from a range between a low V_1 speed and a high V_1 speed. The low V_1 limit is the lowest speed from which the aircraft can continue and still climb to be at an altitude of at least 35 feet above the runway surface; it may not be lower than V_{MCG} speed. The high V_1 limit is the highest speed at which the aircraft can still stop on the runway, and it may not be greater than V_R. The actual V_1 can be anywhere between these depending on the air carrier's performance planning procedures. If an air carrier chooses a low V_1 speed, then V_1 will increase with weight until reaching the high V_1 for the given conditions.

V_1

V_1 is the maximum speed in the takeoff at which the pilot must take first action (e.g., apply brakes, reduce thrust, deploy speed brakes) to stop the airplane within the accelerate-stop distance. V_1 also means the minimum speed in the takeoff, following a failure of the critical engine at V_{EF}, at which the pilot can continue the takeoff and achieve the required height above the takeoff surface within the takeoff distance.

Although it is not quite accurate, this speed, V_1, is often referred to as the **takeoff decision speed** or the *Go/No Go decision speed*. The reason this term is not quite accurate is because it implies that the decision to continue or abort can be made at this speed. In reality, allowing for the reaction time of the pilot, he or she must have made the decision to stop prior to attaining this speed and first take action to execute the abort no later than this speed. In other words, the decision to continue the takeoff during an engine failure at V_1 has already been made.

In summary, if during the takeoff roll the pilot has a problem with the aircraft below V_1, he or she will reject the takeoff and stop on the remaining runway. At or above V_1, the pilot is committed to flight even in the event of an engine failure, fire, or other problem. It is safer to go than to stop because the aircraft cannot stop on the remaining runway and stopway if above V_1. The only reason a flight crew might *correctly* decide to abort above V_1 is if the flight crew believes, because of some catastrophic failure, the aircraft is unable to fly.

It is important to note that V_1 only accounts for an engine failure, not a structural failure or some other abnormal event. In addition, V_1 speed is affected by a number of variables such as aircraft weight, flap setting, density altitude, runway slope and wind conditions in the following ways:

- *Aircraft weight:* an increase in aircraft weight causes a higher V_1. V_1 speed must be increased because as weight increases, the speed required to develop enough lift to counteract the weight also increases; therefore, the speed must be increased to be able to continue the takeoff with one engine inoperative if necessary.
- *Flap setting:* An increase in flap angle will increase the lift generated by the wings. This enables the V_1 speed to be reduced.
- *Density altitude:* the higher the density altitude, the less lift the wings create and V_1 speed must be higher to compensate for the reduced lift. Or put another way, the higher the density altitude, the heavier the aircraft's apparent weight (*see* Figure 8-1).
- *Runway slope:* runway upslope increases the aircraft's weight component, in effect making the aircraft perform as if it were heavier. A higher V_1 will be needed to develop enough lift to counteract the runway upslope and to allow the option for a continued takeoff with one engine inoperative, if necessary. Runway downslope has just the opposite effect on an aircraft's performance. Takeoff performance increases with a runway downslope, so V_1 speed can be reduced.
- *Wind conditions:* a headwind increases aircraft performance, which allows for a higher V_1 speed, while a tailwind has the opposite effect.

Of all of these variables, aircraft weight, flap setting and even in many cases runway slope are the easiest for an air carrier to adjust. The aircraft weight may be lowered by limiting the amount of cargo, passengers or even fuel. Runway slope and wind conditions may be adjusted at some airports simply by choosing a different runway.

V_R

V_R is the **rotation speed** or the speed at which the nose may be raised to initial climb attitude. This is not a safety speed, *per se*, but rather is the speed to which the aircraft should be accelerated prior to establishing the takeoff/climb pitch attitude for liftoff. It is an aerodynamic consideration to achieve proper performance from the aircraft for the liftoff and climb.

While runway slope and wind conditions have no effect on V_R speed, aircraft weight, flap settings and density altitude affect V_R speed in the following ways:

- *Aircraft weight:* an increase in aircraft weight causes V_R to increase. Aircraft speed must be increased to produce the required lift.

- *Flap setting:* An increase in flap angle increases the lift generated by the wings. Therefore, for any given weight, the rotation speed will decrease with increased flap angle. Increasing flap angle for takeoff allows the aircraft a shorter takeoff distance; however, it comes at the expense of lower climb performance due to the increased drag.
- *Density altitude:* The higher the density altitude, the less lift the wings create. For any given aircraft weight, the V_R speed must be increased to produce the required lift.

V_S

V_S is the **stalling speed** or the **minimum steady flight speed** at which the airplane is controllable. It is the minimum speed at which the wing can create enough lift to support the aircraft. On a coefficient of lift curve, it is the airspeed where the wing creates its maximum coefficient of lift.

V_{SR}

V_{SR} is a **reference stalling speed** that may not be less than a 1-g stall speed.

V_2

V_2 is the single engine **takeoff safety speed**. In the event of an engine failure on takeoff, this is the minimum speed to be maintained to at least 400 feet above the takeoff surface. Maintaining V_2 will guarantee that a twin-engine aircraft is capable of a 2.4 percent (or 24 feet per 1,000 feet) single-engine climb gradient (2.7 percent for three-engine aircraft and 3.0 percent for four-engine aircraft). V_2 is analogous to the best single-engine rate of climb (V_{YSE}) for a light twin-engine aircraft. V_2 speed is affected by aircraft weight, flap setting and density altitude in a similar manner as V_1:

- *Aircraft weight:* A higher weight requires an increase in the value of V_2 because a greater speed is necessary to generate the increased lift required to counteract the increased weight and maintain the minimum climb gradient. A decrease in weight has the opposite effect.
- *Flap setting:* An increased flap angle produces greater lift, which means a lower V_2 is possible. The opposite is true for a decrease in flap angle for takeoff: V_2 speed must be increased.
- *Density altitude:* An increase in density altitude has the effect of lowering V_2 speed because a higher density altitude reduces engine thrust, so the speed needed to counteract engine thrust can be lower.

V_{EF}

V_{EF} **(engine failure speed)** is the airspeed at which the critical engine is assumed to fail. V_{EF} may not be less than V_{MCG}. This is a "reference" airspeed used in certification of the aircraft, not one which will bear on the operation of the aircraft.

V_{MC}

V_{MC} or V_{MCA}, the **minimum controllable airspeed (airborne)**, is the airspeed at which when the critical engine is suddenly made inoperative, it is possible to maintain control of the airplane with that engine still inoperative and maintain straight flight with an angle of bank of not more than 5 degrees. Additional requirements for V_{MC} may be found in 14 CFR §25.149.

V_{MC} speed is affected by density altitude in a similar manner as is V_2 speed. At high density altitudes, the engine produces less thrust so the amount of force necessary to counteract any yaw tendencies is less. Therefore V_{MC} speed will be less at higher density altitudes.

V_{FTO}

V_{FTO} **(final takeoff speed)** is the airspeed of the airplane that exists at the end of the takeoff path in the enroute configuration with one engine inoperative.

V_{LOF}

V_{LOF} **(liftoff speed)** is the airspeed at which the airplane first becomes airborne. This airspeed marks the end of the ground roll portion of the takeoff run during runway distance calculations.

V_{MCG}

V_{MCG} **(minimum control speed on the ground)** is the airspeed during the takeoff run at which when the critical engine is suddenly made inoperative, it is possible to maintain control of the airplane using the rudder control alone (without the use of nose-wheel steering). Additional requirements for V_{MCG} may be found in 14 CFR §25.149.

V_{REF}

V_{REF} is an **airspeed that is 1.3 times the stalling speed in the landing configuration** at the current aircraft weight and may not be less than 1.23 of V_{SR}. Because V_{REF} is derived from the stall speed, the V_{REF} value depends directly on aircraft gross weight. V_{REF} is the airspeed required to be flown when crossing the landing runway threshold at a height of 50 feet in landing configuration. V_{REF} is also known as the computed final approach speed or the target threshold speed. V_{REF} is usually defined in the aircraft operating manual (AOM) and the aircraft's quick reference handbook (QRH).

Accelerate-Go Distance

Accelerate-go distance is the amount of runway required to accelerate the aircraft to V_1, lose an engine, and continue the takeoff to the prescribed obstacle clearance altitude.

Accelerate-Stop Distance

Accelerate-stop distance is the amount of runway required to accelerate the aircraft to just below V_1, lose an engine, take the first action to stop the airplane, and come to a complete stop on the remaining runway and stopway.

Balanced Field Length

Balanced field length is the amount of runway and stopway that allows the aircraft either to accelerate to just below V_1, lose an engine, and then stop on the remaining runway or to accelerate to at or above V_1 and continue to the prescribed obstacle clearance altitude. Simply put, the accelerate-go performance required is exactly equal to (or "balances") the accelerate-stop performance required. Figure 8-1 illustrates how the choice of V_1 speed affects the takeoff performance in specific situations. The point at which the "rejected takeoff" line intersects the "continued takeoff" line is called the **balanced field limit**. The balanced field limit is the maximum limit for both aircraft weight (balanced field limit weight) and aircraft speed (balanced field limit V_1 speed).

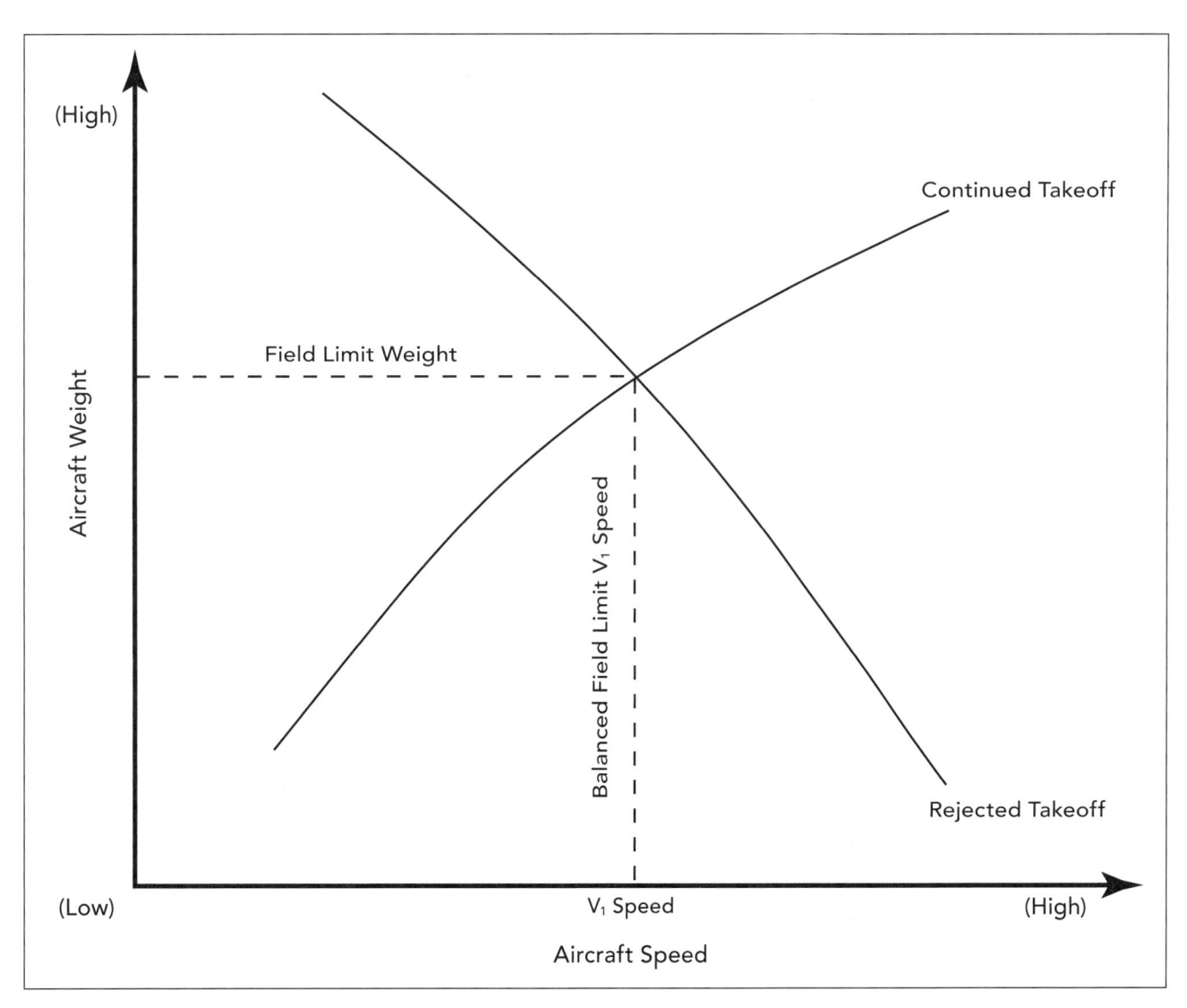

Figure 8-1. Balanced field length.

When climb limit weight is limiting but the runway length provides a significant performance margin, the planned V-speeds may be increased to improve climb performance which in turn increases the climb limit weight. Generally, the balanced field length V_2 speed is less than the speed for best angle of climb, so increasing V_2 speed by a few knots can improve the climb gradient. Takeoff flaps and V-speeds can be adjusted to give the best balance of safety and performance considering the runway limit weight and the climb limit weight, which we will discuss later in this chapter.

Clearway

Clearway (for turbine aircraft certificated after August 29, 1959) is an area beyond the runway, not less than 500 feet wide, centrally located about the extended centerline of the runway and under the control of the airport authorities. It is expressed in terms of a *clearway plane* with an upward slope not exceeding 1.25 percent, above which no object nor any terrain may protrude. (Threshold lights may protrude if they are 26 inches or less above the end of the runway and are located to the side of the runway.) In other words, it is an obstacle-free area at least 250 feet either side of the runway centerline and inclining or rising no more than 12½ feet per 1,000 feet from the runway end. The only obstacles that are permitted in this area are the runway threshold lights.

Declared Runway Distance

Declared runway distances for a runway represent the maximum distances available and suitable for meeting takeoff and landing distance performance requirements. All FAR Part 139 airports report declared distances for each runway.

Final Approach Speed

Final approach speed is defined as V_{REF} plus corrections. Airspeed corrections are based on such operational factors as weight, wind component, aircraft configuration (e.g., less than full flap landing), or use of autothrottle. The resulting final approach speed provides the best compromise between handling qualities and landing distance.

Landing Distance (Part 25)

Required **landing distance data** in the airplane flight manual (AFM) may include both **certified landing distance** and **factored landing distance**.

- Certified or "unfactored" landing distances in the manufacturer-supplied AFM reflect performance in a "flight test environment" that is not necessarily representative of the normal day-to-day flight operations. In other words, it does *not* include any safety margin and represents the best possible performance the airplane is capable of for the given conditions. The actual landing distances are determined during certification tests with a well-rested test pilot at the controls of a brand-new aircraft. These certification tests are flown with the goal of demonstrating the shortest landing distances for a given airplane weight. Therefore, the landing distances determined under 14 CFR §25.125 or §23.75 are shorter than the landing distances achieved in normal operations. This runway distance is considered the baseline landing distance from which landing performance calculations are derived.
- FAA Advisory Circular (AC) 91-79A, *Mitigating the Risks of a Runway Overrun Upon Landing*, defines the factored landing distance as the certified landing distance multiplied by 1.67, which can then be compared directly to the available landing distance. When the runway is wet, the certified distance is multiplied by 1.97 to account for the 15 percent additional runway requirement. Some manufacturers have begun to include factored landing distance in the AFM.

Landing Distance Available (LDA)

Landing distance available is the length of runway declared available for landing. This distance, also known as effective runway length, may be shorter than the full length of the runway.

Landing Field Length Requirement

Landing field length requirement prohibits the takeoff of a transport category airplane unless its weight on arrival, allowing for the normal consumption of fuel and oil in flight, will allow a full stop landing at the intended destination airport within 60 percent of the effective runway length. We will discuss this further at the end of this chapter. The intent of landing field length regulations is to ensure that a flight operation does not begin if it cannot reasonably be concluded upon reaching the destination or alternate airport, as applicable.

Net Takeoff Flight Path

Net takeoff flight path is the actual flight path of the aircraft as determined during design and certification trials reduced by a factor specified in 14 CFR §25.115(b). For twin-engine aircraft, that reduction factor is 0.8 percent, or 8 feet per 1,000 feet traveled. (For three-engine aircraft it is 0.9 percent, or 9 feet per 1,000 feet traveled, and for four-engine airplanes it is 1.0 percent, or 10 feet per 1,000 feet traveled.) This is done to create a "fudge factor" so that the actual performance a flight crew obtains from the aircraft will be at least equal to and probably better than that required. Net takeoff flight path will be compared to the climb gradients required by Part 121 to determine compliance with Part 121. For example, see Figure 8-2 for a twin-engine aircraft.

Reduced V_1

Reduced V_1 is a speed lower than the maximum V_1 and is selected to reduce the rejected takeoff stopping distance. A reduced V_1 is typically used during wet or slippery conditions in anticipation of degraded stopping capability due to poor runway conditions. The reduced V_1 speed provides additional stopping margin in the event of a rejected takeoff. However, reduced V_1 speed must also ensure the continued takeoff performance requirements are met.

Rejected Takeoff (RTO)

A **rejected takeoff (RTO)** is a takeoff that is discontinued or aborted after takeoff thrust is set and the initiation of the takeoff roll has begun. According to the FAA's *Pilot's Guide to Takeoff Safety*, there are no comprehensive worldwide records available for the total number of RTOs that have occurred throughout the jet era. However, the FAA estimates that one in 3,000 takeoff attempts ends with an RTO. During a takeoff incident study, the FAA concluded that engine failure accounted for only 21 percent of all RTOs.

Safety Margin

Safety margin is the length of runway available beyond the actual landing distance. Safety margin can be expressed in a fixed distance increment or a percentage increase beyond the actual landing distance required.

Takeoff Path

The **takeoff path**, as defined by 14 CFR §25.111, extends from a standing start on the runway to the point in the takeoff at which the airplane is 1,500 feet above the takeoff surface, *or* a point at which the transition from the takeoff to the cruise climb configuration is completed and final takeoff speed (V_{FTO}) is reached.

- The takeoff path must be based on the procedures prescribed in Section 25.101(f).
- The airplane must be accelerated on the ground to the engine failure speed (V_{EF}), *at which point the critical engine must be made inoperative and remain inoperative* for the rest of the takeoff; and
- After reaching V_{EF}, the airplane must be accelerated to V_2.
- The slope of the airborne part of the takeoff path must be positive at each point.

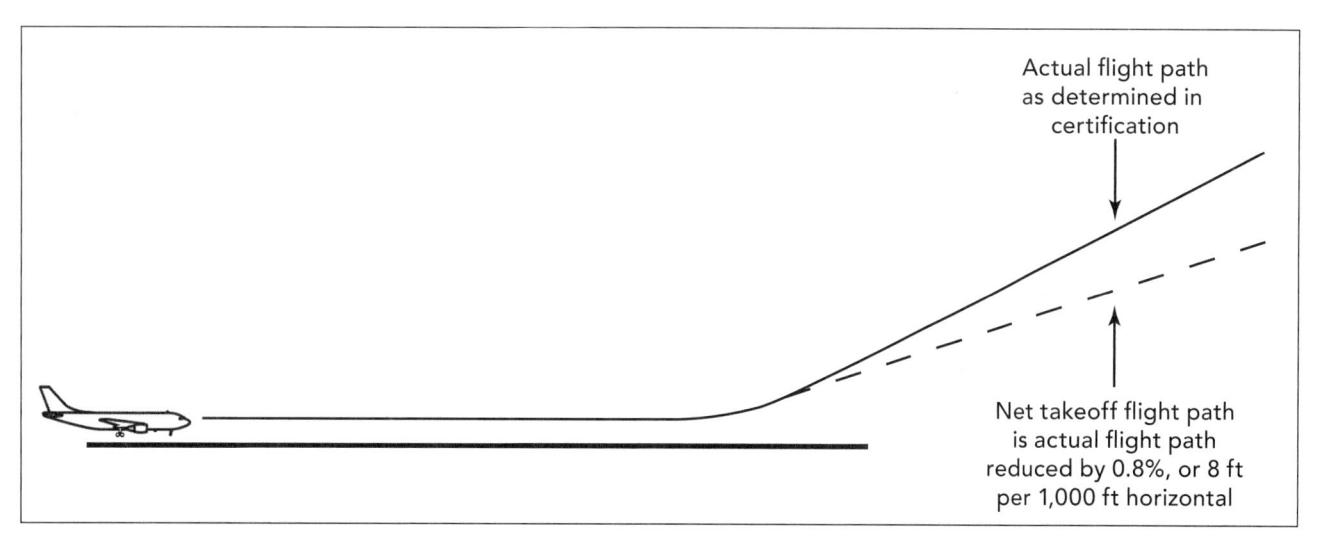

Figure 8-2. Net takeoff flight path.

- The airplane must reach V_2 before it is 35 feet above the surface and then continue at a speed as close as practical to V_2 (but not less than V_2) until it is 400 feet above the surface.
- At each point along the takeoff path, starting 400 feet above the takeoff surface, the available climb gradient may not be less than:
  – 1.2 percent for two-engine airplanes;
  – 1.5 percent for three-engine airplanes; and
  – 1.7 percent for four engine airplanes.
- No pilot action except to raise the landing gear or feather propellers may be required until the airplane is 400 feet above the takeoff surface. Other than automatic power adjustments, no change in configuration is permitted.

In other words, the takeoff path is designed to allow an aircraft to lose an engine at or above V_1. The pilot then accelerates to V_R, rotates the aircraft, accelerates to V_{LOF}, and lifts off. After liftoff at V_{LOF}, the pilot retracts the landing gear and climbs to the standard 400 feet AGL or higher altitude required by the departure procedure (sometimes called **acceleration altitude** or **cleanup altitude**); runs emergency checklists and cleans up the aircraft for climb; and then climbs to at least 1,500 feet (or higher) above the takeoff surface while maintaining the specified obstacle clearance. The takeoff path provides obstacle clearance for the entire four segment climb (discussed below) so that the takeoff and departure is obstacle-protected all the way from the surface to 1,500 feet (or sometimes higher altitude).

Takeoff Run

If the *takeoff distance* calculation does not include use of a clearway, the **takeoff run** is equal to the **takeoff distance** (*see* below).

If the *takeoff distance* includes a clearway, the *takeoff run* (on a dry runway) is the greater of the horizontal distance along the takeoff path to a point halfway between the point at which V_{LOF} **(liftoff airspeed)** is reached and the point at which the airplane is 35 feet above the takeoff surface (as determined by 14 CFR §25.111 for a dry runway), or 115 percent of the horizontal distance along the takeoff path, with all engines operating from the start of the takeoff to a point halfway between the point at which V_{LOF} is reached and the point at which the airplane is 35 feet above the takeoff surface.

If the takeoff distance includes a clearway, the takeoff run (on a wet runway) is the greater of the horizontal distance along the takeoff path from the start of the takeoff to the point at which the airplane is 15 feet above the takeoff surface, achieved in a manner consistent with the achievement of V_2 before reaching 35 feet above the takeoff surface (as determined by §25.111 for a wet runway), or 115 percent of the horizontal distance along the takeoff path, with all engines operating from the start of the takeoff to a point halfway between the point at which V_{LOF} is reached and the point at which the airplane is 35 feet above the takeoff surface.

Perhaps at the risk of oversimplifying, the *takeoff run* is the distance that allows the pilot to

- release brakes,
- accelerate to V_1,
- lose the critical engine,
- accelerate to V_R,
- accelerate to V_{LOF}, and
- proceed horizontally to a point that is halfway between the point where liftoff speed was attained and the point where the airplane reached an altitude of 35 feet above the takeoff surface.

It is somewhat analogous to the *ground roll* of a light aircraft. Alternatively, it is 115 percent of the horizontal distance (with all engines operating) from brake release to a point that is halfway between the point where liftoff speed was attained and the point at which the airplane is 35 feet above the takeoff surface.

Takeoff Distance

Takeoff distance on a **dry runway** is the greater of:

- The horizontal distance along the takeoff path from the start of the takeoff to the point at which the airplane is 35 feet above the takeoff surface, determined under Section 25.111 for a dry runway, or
- 115 percent of the horizontal distance along the takeoff path, with all engines operating, from the start of the takeoff to the point at which the airplane is 35 feet above the takeoff surface, as determined by a procedure consistent with Section 25.111.

Takeoff distance on a **wet runway** is the greater of:

- The takeoff distance on a dry runway determined in accordance with the dry runway procedures, above, or

- The horizontal distance along the takeoff path from the start of the takeoff to the point at which the airplane is 15 feet above the takeoff surface, achieved in a manner consistent with the achievement of V_2 before reaching 35 feet above the takeoff surface, determined under Section 25.111 for a wet runway.

Again, perhaps at the risk of oversimplifying, the *takeoff distance* is the distance that allows the pilot to

- release brakes,
- accelerate to V_1,
- lose the critical engine,
- accelerate to V_R,
- accelerate to V_{LOF}, and
- proceed horizontally to a point 35 feet above the takeoff surface (by which V_2 must be achieved).

Takeoff distance is somewhat analogous to the total distance to clear a 50-foot obstacle given for light aircraft. There are two alternative ways of computing the takeoff distance. On a dry runway, it is 115 percent of the horizontal distance (with all engines operating) from brake release to a point where the aircraft reaches an altitude of 35 feet above the takeoff surface (Figure 8-3). On a wet runway, it is the horizontal distance (with all engines operating) from brake release to a point where the aircraft reaches an altitude of 15 feet above the takeoff surface.

Takeoff distance with an engine failure is the distance from brake release to the point where the aircraft attains a height of 35 feet, assuming the engine fails at V_{EF} (Figure 8-3). Part 25 requires that the length of runway plus clearway be at least equal to the engine failure takeoff distance.

The foregoing has all considered the certification requirements of the aircraft used in Part 121 operations. Now, let's look at the operating limitations of Part 121.

Takeoff Limitations

The first requirement of 14 CFR §121.189(a) is quite straightforward. It simply requires that no one operating a turbine-powered airplane may take off at a weight that exceeds the maximum allowable weight permitted by the airplane flight manual considering the altitude (airport elevation) and temperature existing at the time of departure. This requirement is satisfied by referring to the **WAT limit charts** (weight-altitude-temperature limit charts). The WAT limit charts will be prepared for use for each aircraft type for each runway used by the carrier. Several limiting weights will appear on these charts.

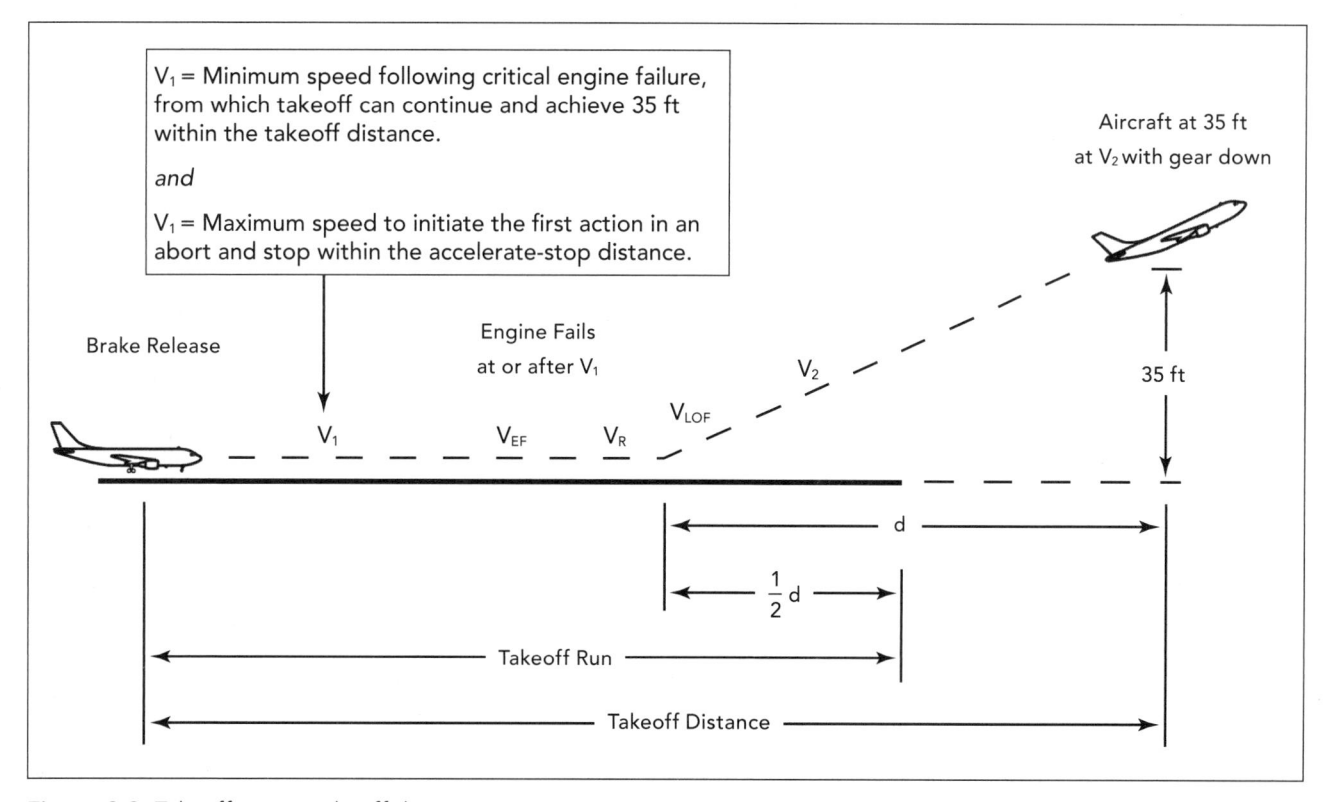

Figure 8-3. Takeoff run vs. takeoff distance

The first such limit is the **runway limit weight**. The runway limit weight is the maximum weight, at existing conditions, that will guarantee that the aircraft meets the balanced field length requirements. In other words, it is the maximum weight at which the aircraft can experience a so-called V_1 failure and still stop on the remaining runway or continue to a point 35 feet above the runway within the runway/clearway distance limits. The runway limit weight is the most restrictive weight limit.

14 CFR §121.189(c) requires that several conditions be met (Figure 8-4):

- A pilot may not take off at a weight so great that the *accelerate-stop distance* would exceed the length of the *runway and any **stopway***. That is, the weight must allow the aircraft to accelerate to engine failure speed and still be able to stop on the concrete (or improved) surface.
- The *takeoff run* must not be greater than the length of the *runway*.
- Further, the weight may not be so great that the *takeoff distance* exceeds the *length of the runway plus any clearway*. If any clearway is used to compute the takeoff distance, you may only use clearway less than or equal to one-half the length of the runway surface.

The second limiting weight is the so-called **climb limit weight**. The climb limit weight guarantees that the pilot can proceed from the point 35 feet above the runway to 1,500 feet above the runway surface (or specified higher altitude) while maintaining required climb gradients in order to achieve adequate obstacle clearance.

Another weight-limiting factor to control is V_{MC}. The **V_{MC} limit** is used in aircraft in which reduced power takeoffs are used. Reduced power takeoff techniques might be used for economy, noise abatement, or other reasons. However, in the event of an engine failure, the pilot would probably increase the power on the operating engine(s). Remember that this is permitted if it occurs automatically. V_2 protects against loss of control due to V_{MC}, but only to the original reduced power setting. When the higher power is automatically applied, that could cause loss of control due to the speed at the existing weight being below the new V_{MC} that results from the higher power setting. V_{MC} is higher at lower weights; therefore, the V_{MC} weight limit is a *minimum weight* whereas the runway limit weight and the climb limit weight are *maximum weights*.

14 CFR §121.189(d) looks at the net takeoff flight path after takeoff to ensure that pilots have increasing separation from obstacles and terrain as they work their way out of the immediate airport/runway environment. The airplane's weight must allow a *net takeoff flight path* that clears all obstacles either by a height of 35 feet vertically, or by at least 200 feet horizontally within the airport boundaries (300 feet after passing the airport boundaries).

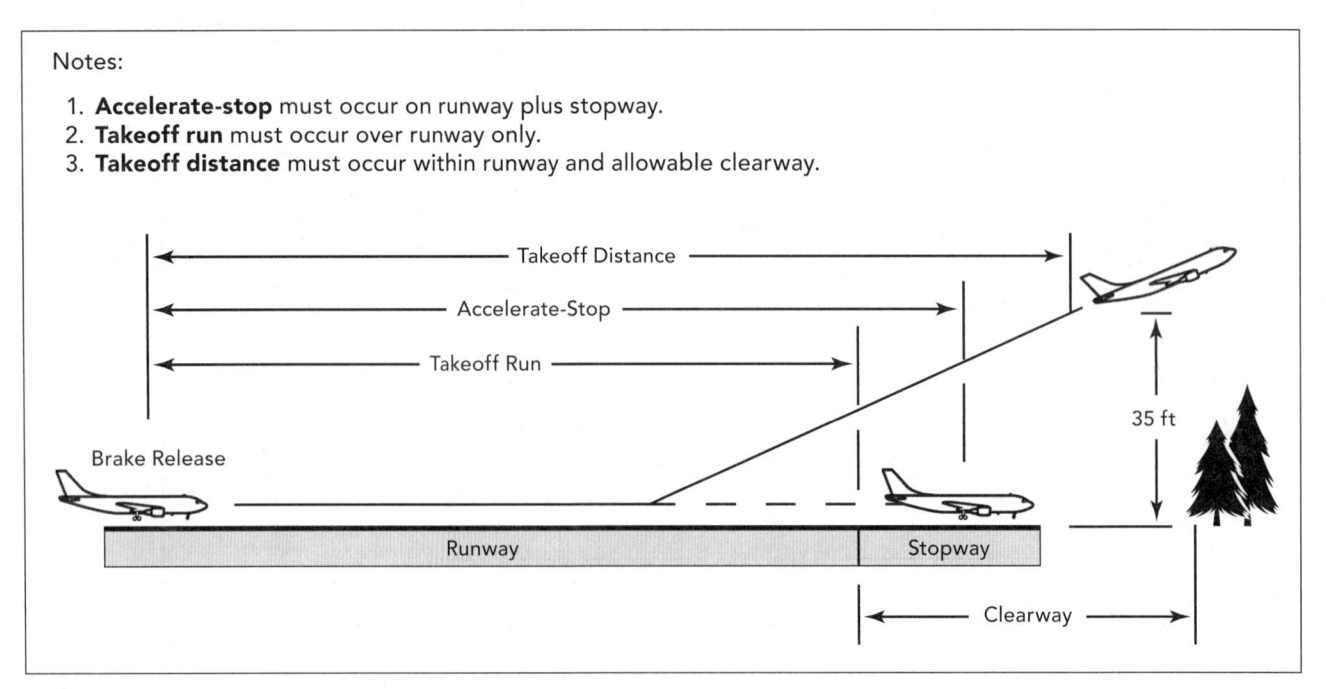

Notes:
1. **Accelerate-stop** must occur on runway plus stopway.
2. **Takeoff run** must occur over runway only.
3. **Takeoff distance** must occur within runway and allowable clearway.

Figure 8-4. Takeoff run over a clearway.

In performing maximum weight calculations for 14 CFR §121.189 flight paths, it's necessary to consider (correct for)

- the runway to be used,
- the airport elevation,
- the effective runway gradient,
- the ambient temperature (normally gotten from ATIS),
- wind component at the time of takeoff, and
- runway surface condition (wet/dry) if the airplane flight manual adjusts for this. (Note that the manual may allow a correction for grooving or porous friction courses. This correction may be used only if the runway actually has this surface.)

Therefore, as we mentioned earlier, the takeoff performance charts used by the flight crew and dispatch in calculating this information must be for each runway to be used, for any reasonable weight likely to be encountered, and for the wind and temperature conditions existing at the time of departure. That is, takeoff charts (and landing charts) are runway and condition specific.

Finally, Section 121.189 makes some assumptions about maneuvering the aircraft immediately after departure, as banking would reduce performance. First, the aircraft *may not be banked* prior to reaching a height of 50 feet as shown by the flight path or net flight path data. Second, after attaining 50 feet in height, the aircraft *may not be banked more than 15 degrees* in any additional maneuvering. The FAA acknowledges that obstacle clearance at certain airports can be enhanced by the use of bank angles greater than 15 degrees. As you might imagine, the FAA does authorize progressively greater bank angles as altitude is increased. Table 8-1 shows the bank angles and the heights at which these bank angles may be used with specific operation specification authorization. When bank angles of more than 15 degrees are used, V_2 speeds are increased or V_2 plus an additive number of knots (e.g., $V_2 + 5$ at flaps 20 degrees; $V_2 + 10$ at flaps 25 degrees) are typically used to provide for stall protection and adequate controllability.

Table 8-1. Maximum bank angles

Height (above departure end of runway, in feet)	Maximum Bank Angle (degrees)
height > 400 ft	25°
400 ft > height > 100 ft	20°
100 ft > height > 50 ft*	15°

* or ½ of the wingspan, whichever is higher

Let's now summarize the takeoff limitations in a way that simplifies and explains more clearly what they actually accomplish. To do this, we will examine the **four segment climb performance** (Figure 8-5). Four segment climb performance requirements take all of the requirements previously discussed and relate them in such a way as to ensure adequate terrain/obstacle clearance all the way from the runway up to the enroute environment. To begin with, the manufacturer's takeoff performance data assumes the aircraft is lined up and brakes held while takeoff power is selected. Takeoff thrust is expected to be achieved between 40 and 80 knots during the takeoff run.

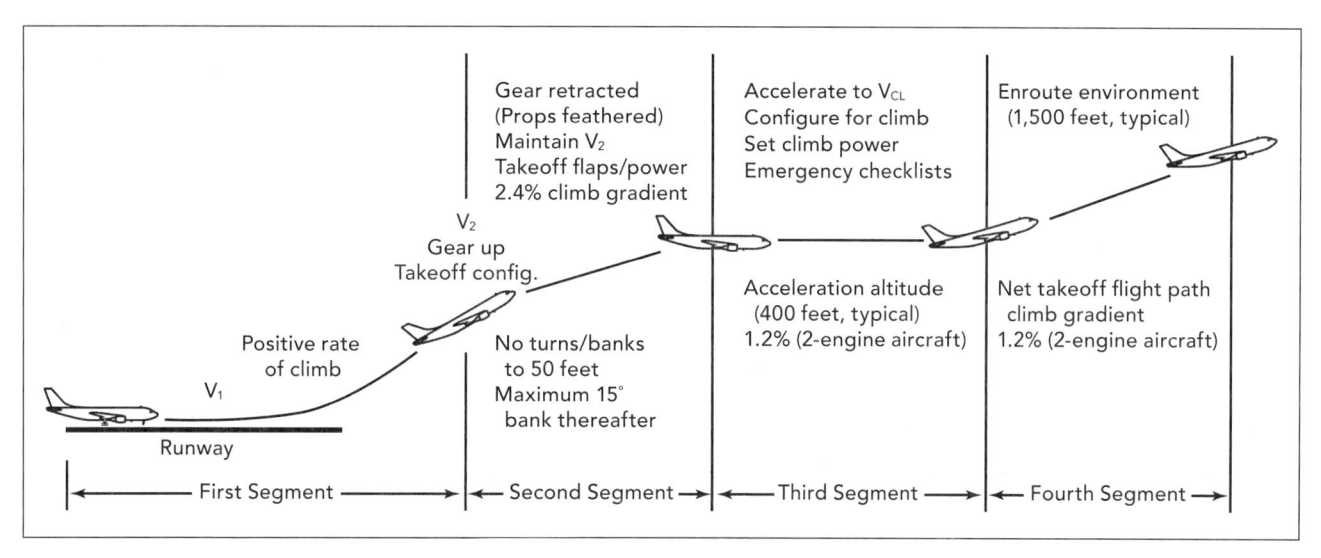

Figure 8-5. Twin engine, four segment climb.

First segment climb begins at brake release and ends at a point after takeoff where the speed is V_2 and the landing gear has finished retracting. This will be at an altitude of at least 35 feet above the runway surface and at an airspeed of V_2. During first segment climb (starting from V_{LOF}), two-engine aircraft are only required to demonstrate a *positive rate of climb* after liftoff, while three-engine aircraft must have a 0.3 percent positive gradient and four-engine aircraft must have a 0.5 percent positive gradient, all without considering ground effect. During this portion of the departure, the crew is neither expected nor required to do anything except fly the airplane and raise the landing gear.

Second segment climb begins at the point where the aircraft achieves gear retraction at a speed of V_2 and ends at *acceleration altitude* (normally 400 feet). In the event of an engine failure during this segment of the departure, the crew is only expected to do the immediate items required to fly the airplane. This would include feathering an inoperative turboprop propeller. A two-engine aircraft must maintain a *minimum climb gradient of 2.4 percent or 24 feet per 1,000 feet traveled*, while the climb gradient for three-engine airplanes is 2.7 percent and for four-engine airplanes is 3.0 percent (Figure 8-6). No turning or banking of the aircraft is permitted prior to 50 feet above the runway surface. After 50 feet, a maximum 15-degree bank is permitted.

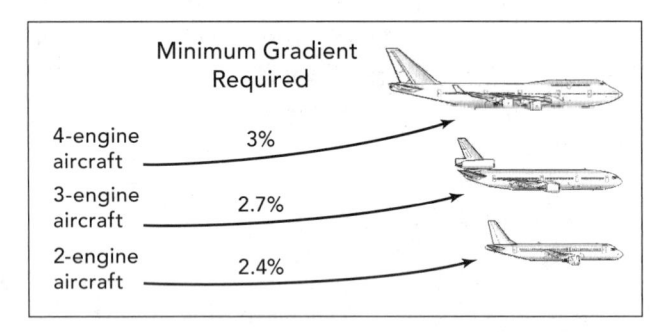

Figure 8-6. Required second segment climb performance at climb limit weight.

Third segment climb begins at acceleration altitude and continues until the aircraft is cleaned up and established in the cruise climb configuration at the cruise climb airspeed. During this segment of departure, the aircraft is accelerated, flaps are retracted, any emergency checklists are run, and maximum continuous or cruise climb power is set. The aircraft must maintain a net takeoff flight path with *minimum climb gradient of 1.2 percent for two-engine aircraft or 12 feet per 1,000 feet traveled*. The minimum gradient is 1.5 percent for three-engine aircraft (15 feet per 1,000 feet traveled) and 1.7 percent for four-engine aircraft (17 feet per 1,000 feet traveled).

Fourth segment climb begins with the climb configuration and airspeed set and ends (normally) at 1,500 feet above the surface. During fourth segment climb, a twin-engine aircraft must also be able to maintain a net takeoff flight path *minimum climb gradient of 1.2 percent or 12 feet per 1,000 feet traveled*. The minimum gradient is 1.5 percent for three-engine aircraft and 1.7 percent for four-engine aircraft.

En Route Limitations: One Engine Inoperative

The takeoff limitations of 14 CFR §121.189 provide protection in the event of an engine failure on departure from anywhere on the runway to a point nominally 1,500 feet above the surface. It does this by ensuring that the aircraft is operated so that it is able to climb out and provide an increasing separation between the aircraft and the terrain/obstacles. **En route limitations**, found in 14 CFR §121.191, are similarly designed to ensure that realistic reasonable options exist to successfully complete a flight should the aircraft lose an engine (or engines) en route, and that the aircraft has sufficient performance to clear all terrain on the way back into an airport terminal area.

The first requirement is found in 14 CFR §121.161(a). It states that a two-engine, turbine-powered airplane may not be operated over a route that contains a point farther than 60 minutes of flying time (in still air at normal cruising speed with one engine inoperative) from an adequate airport. This is commonly referred to as the "**60-minute rule.**" Turbine-engine-powered airplanes with three or more engines may not be operated over a route that contains a point farther than 180 minutes of flying time (in still air at normal cruising speed with one engine inoperative) from an adequate airport. We will see later that there are exceptions to this rule in an area known as ETOPS, or extended operations.

14 CFR §121.191(a) requires that the aircraft be operated at such a weight that for **OEI (one engine inoperative)** performance, if the aircraft loses an engine, the pilot has the ability to operate the aircraft safely to an alternate airport (en route alternate). This can be demonstrated in either of two ways. First, Paragraph

121.191(a)(1) requires that the net flight path exhibit a positive slope (meaning that the aircraft is climbing faster than the terrain is rising or the terrain is falling away at a rate greater than the descent rate) from cruise altitude all the way down to within 1,000 feet of the ground. This is measured within 5 statute miles on either side of the flight track of the aircraft. In addition, it requires a positive slope at 1,500 feet above the airport of intended emergency landing after the engine failure. The other way to comply with this en route limitation is by using the so-called **driftdown technique**.

14 CFR §121.191(a)(2) recognizes that the pilot may be operating the aircraft at a high altitude where the OEI (one engine inoperative) performance would result in a descent rate that was not a positive slope net flight path. That is, the aircraft would be descending at a faster rate than the ground is falling away. This is not necessarily dangerous. For example, the airplane may be descending at a descent gradient of 300 feet per nautical mile while the terrain is only lowering at an average of 100 feet per nautical mile. This would be a negative slope of 200 feet per nautical mile. If the aircraft were only a couple of thousand feet above the terrain, this might be a problem. On the other hand, the pilot may have begun the OEI operation at flight level 390 (approximately 39,000 ft.) over terrain that is only 3,000 feet MSL. Clearly, there is no immediate hazard even though the aircraft is descending at a greater rate than the terrain is lowering. In fact, the OEI maximum absolute ceiling may only be 12,000 feet MSL. Section 121.191(a)(2) states that you may operate in this situation so long as the net flight path allows the aircraft to clear all terrain and obstructions within 5 statute miles by at least 2,000 feet vertically and with a positive slope at 1,500 feet above the airport.

Driftdown altitude is the altitude to which, following the failure of an engine above the one-engine inoperative absolute ceiling, an airplane will descend to and maintain, while using maximum continuous power on the operating engine and maintaining the one-engine inoperative best rate of climb speed (Figure 8-7).

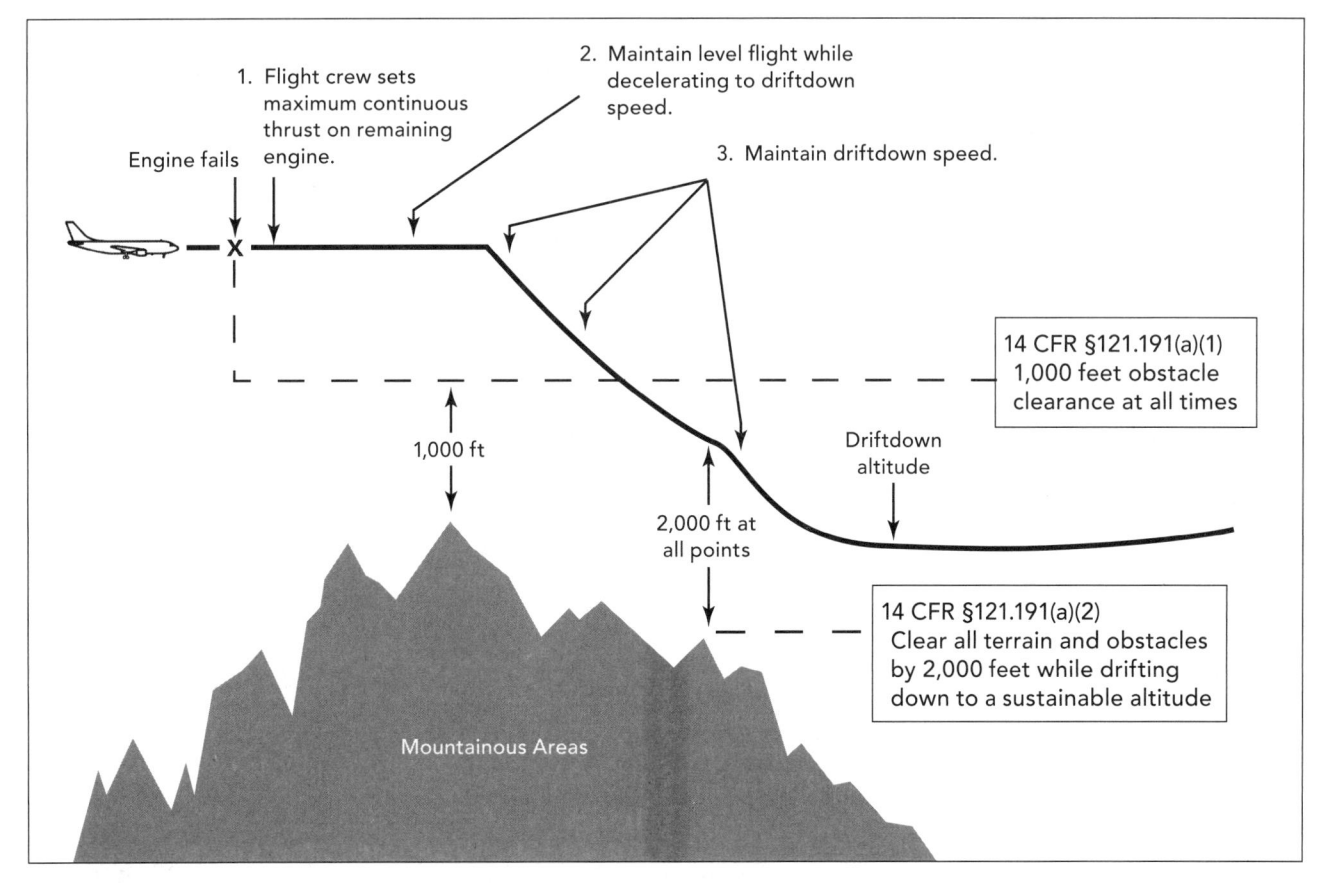

Figure 8-7. Driftdown procedure.

When calculating the ability to comply with 14 CFR §121.191, the following assumptions must be made:

- The engine fails at the most critical point en route.
- The airplane passes over the critical obstruction after engine failure at a point that is no closer to the obstruction than the nearest approved radio navigation fix (although alternatives to this may be approved).
- An approved method for considering adverse winds is employed.
- The crew may jettison fuel if the crew is trained and precautions are taken to ensure jettisoning may be performed safely.
- The alternate airport to be used must be specified in the dispatch or flight release and must meet alternate weather minimums.
- Fuel consumption is based on approved values in the approved net flight path data in the airplane flight manual (AFM).

Figure 8-7 depicts an aircraft that had an engine failure and has begun a driftdown descent. The standard air carrier emergency driftdown descent begins with the flight crew completing their emergency procedures and maintaining altitude with maximum thrust on the remaining engine. The flight crew allows the aircraft to slow from the all engine cruising speed to the best engine out climb speed (now the "target driftdown airspeed"). Once the aircraft has slowed to this target driftdown airspeed, a descent is begun at that airspeed with maximum thrust on the remaining engine until the aircraft reaches its single engine absolute ceiling. At this altitude, the aircraft will level-off; this is the highest attainable driftdown altitude for the given conditions. The steepness of the descent path may be relatively steep depending on the difference between the all-engine cruising altitude and the single engine absolute ceiling. The greater the altitude difference, the steeper the descent path.

En Route Limitations: Two Engines Inoperative

For aircraft having three or more engines, the en route limitations options in the event of a dual engine failure are twofold. The first option, found in 14 CFR §121.193(c)(1), is quite simple. It states that the operator can comply so long as there is no point on the route structure where the flight is more than 90 minutes flying time (all engines operating) from an approved alternate airport. This is commonly referred to as the "**90-minute rule**." If the operator can comply with this provision, then the two-engine inoperative driftdown analysis is not required. If the operator cannot comply with this provision, then it may use a concept similar in nature to what we saw earlier for OEI operations.

The second option is found in 14 CFR §121.193(c)(2), which states that if the aircraft can be operated at a weight allowed by the airplane flight manual that allows it to fly from a point where the two engines failed simultaneously to an authorized alternate airport and clear all terrain and obstructions within 5 statute miles of the intended track by at least 2,000 feet vertically, then it is good to go. This performance is achieved under the following assumptions:

- The two engines fail simultaneously at the most critical point en route.
- The net flight path has a positive slope at 1,500 feet above the alternate airport.
- The crew may jettison fuel if the crew is trained and precautions are taken to ensure this may be performed safely.
- The weight at the point of engine failure includes enough fuel to continue to the airport, arrive at an altitude of 1,500 feet directly over the airport, and fly for 15 additional minutes at cruise thrust.
- Fuel and oil consumption is the same as allowed in the net flight path data in the airplane flight manual.

Landing Limitations: Destination Airports

The next area to consider is the landing performance at the destination and alternate airports. 14 CFR §§121.195, 135.385, and 91.1037 cover **landing limitations for destination airports**. The first requirement in Section 121.195(a) is quite simple: an operator cannot *take off* an airplane at a weight that, allowing for normal fuel and oil consumption, would exceed the approved maximum landing weight (at the destination airport's elevation and actual ambient temperature at the time of intended landing) provided for in the airplane flight manual. Note that this rule would be violated on *takeoff*, not upon arrival at the destination airport. It is a *planning rule* and must be complied with upon takeoff. Also, note that alternate airports listed for the flight must be considered as well as the destination airports.

Next, we consider the landing distance requirements for the destination airport. 14 CFR §121.195(b) says that an aircraft must take off so as to arrive at the destination at a weight that allows the aircraft to be landed within 60 percent of the effective length of the runway. This is measured from the point 50 feet above the intersection of the obstruction clearance plane and the runway (Figure 8-8). The rule assumes that

- in still air, the operator may select the most favorable runway and the most favorable direction *(14 CFR §121.195[b][1])*; and
- if there is forecast to be winds upon arrival, the airplane is landed on the most suitable runway considering the probable wind velocity and direction, ground handling characteristics of the aircraft, and other conditions such as landing aids and terrain. *(14 CFR §121.195[b][2])*

14 CFR §121.195(c) provides some relief from the above rule. In the case of a turbopropeller aircraft that can't comply with Paragraph 121.195(b)(2), it may take off if you file an alternate airport where the aircraft can be landed within 70 percent of the effective length of the runway. If a turbojet aircraft can't comply with §121.195(b)(2), then Paragraph 121.195(e) allows it to take off if an alternate airport is filed that meets the requirements of paragraph (b) for a destination airport.

Wet runways require a further consideration. 14 CFR §121.195(d) states that unless there are approved landing distances/techniques in the AFM, if the runways are forecast to be wet or slippery at the estimated time of arrival, the available runway at the destination must be at least 115 percent of the length calculated above.

Next, it's necessary to adjust any AFM performance data with consideration for conditions such as minimum equipment list (MEL) and configuration deviation list (CDL) items. These calculations constitute the regulatory requirement for the pre-departure operational planning.

Let's put all of this together. A flight crew is about to depart for a destination airport that has a 9,000-foot-long runway (*see* Figure 8-9). To be legal, the aircraft would need to depart at a weight that (allowing for normal fuel and oil consumption during the flight) would:

1. Allow the aircraft to land at a weight that is below the maximum landing weight set forth in the AFM landing distance table for the elevation of the destination or alternate airport and the ambient temperature anticipated at the time of landing.

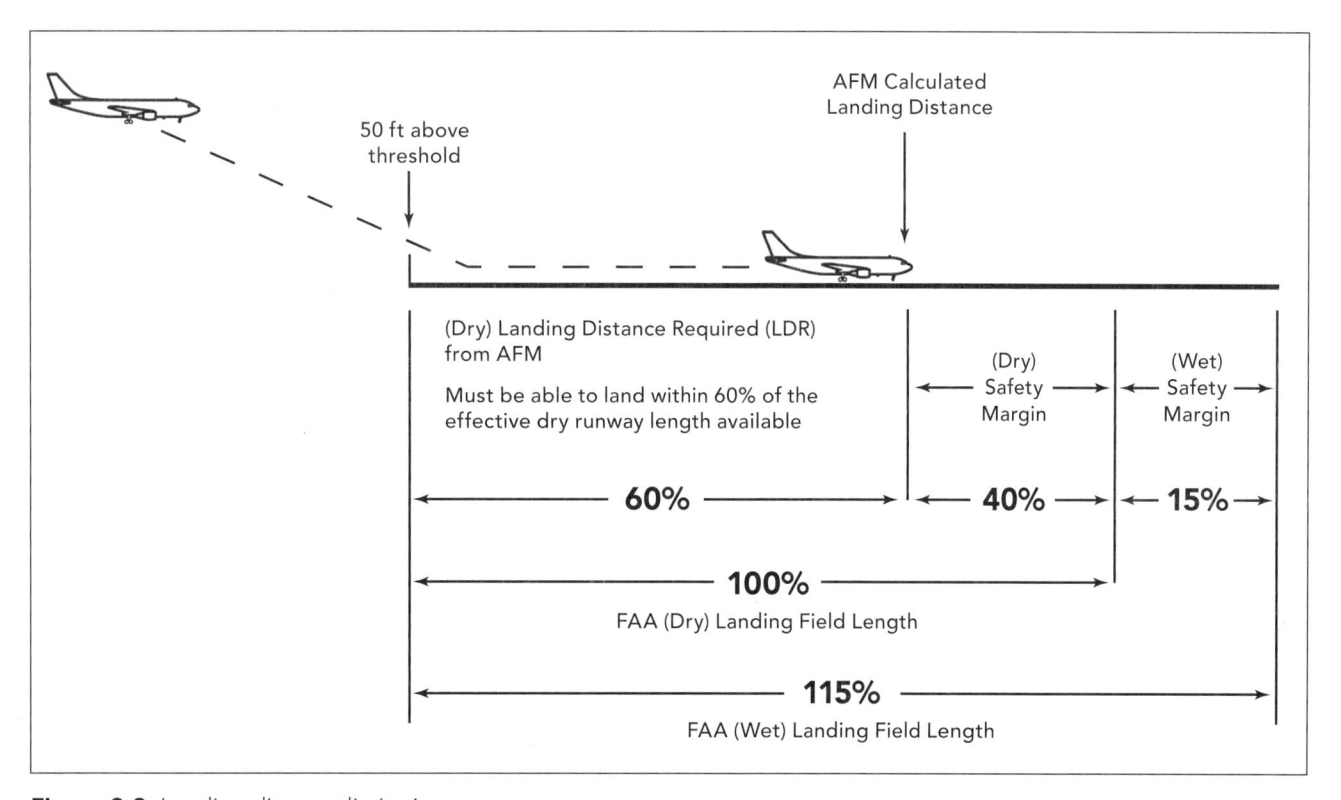

Figure 8-8. Landing distance limitations.

2. Also allow the aircraft to land to a full stop at the intended destination within 60 percent of the (dry) runway length. 60 percent of 9,000 feet is 5,400 feet of dry runway; this is called landing distance required.

To be legal to depart for this destination, the AFM landing distance table must say that the aircraft can land in 5,400 feet of runway or less.

Using the landing distance table for the current weight, airport elevation and temperature, the flight crew computes that the aircraft can land within 4,900 feet. Since this is less than 5,400 feet, the flight may legally depart for their destination.

If, however, the destination is forecasting wet runway or slippery conditions at this flight's arrival time, the flight crew needs to ensure that there is an additional 15 percent performance buffer to compensate for the anticipated reduced stopping performance of the aircraft. That is, the required ability to land within 5,400 feet of dry runway is reduced by another 15 percent for a wet runway. 15 percent of 5,400 feet is 810 feet. The flight crew completes the math: 5,400 feet − 810 feet = 4,590 feet. To be legal, the AFM performance charts must say that the aircraft will be able to stop in 4,590 feet of runway or less.

Using our current example, at our current weight, the AFM table says that 4,900 feet of runway is required to land. Therefore, this flight is *not* legal to depart for a wet runway until the aircraft's weight is reduced enough so that the aircraft will be able to land within 4,590 feet of runway or less.

Another way of working landing distance requirements is by computing the total length of the runway that will be needed. Let's use the aircraft from the previous example: If this aircraft required an AFM-calculated landing distance of 4,900 feet to land, the required effective runway length would be (4,900)/(0.60) = 8,167 feet—or put another way, 4,900 feet × 1.6667 = 8,167 feet. If it were forecast to be wet or slippery, the aircraft would require 8,167 feet × 1.15 = 9,392 feet.

Landing Limitations: Alternate Airports

The rule regarding **landing limitations for alternate airports** is similar to the landing limitations for destination airports. It says that the operator may not list an airport as an alternate airport if—based on the same assumptions as used in 14 CFR §121.195(b)—at the anticipated weight at the anticipated time of arrival the aircraft cannot be brought to a stop in 60 percent of

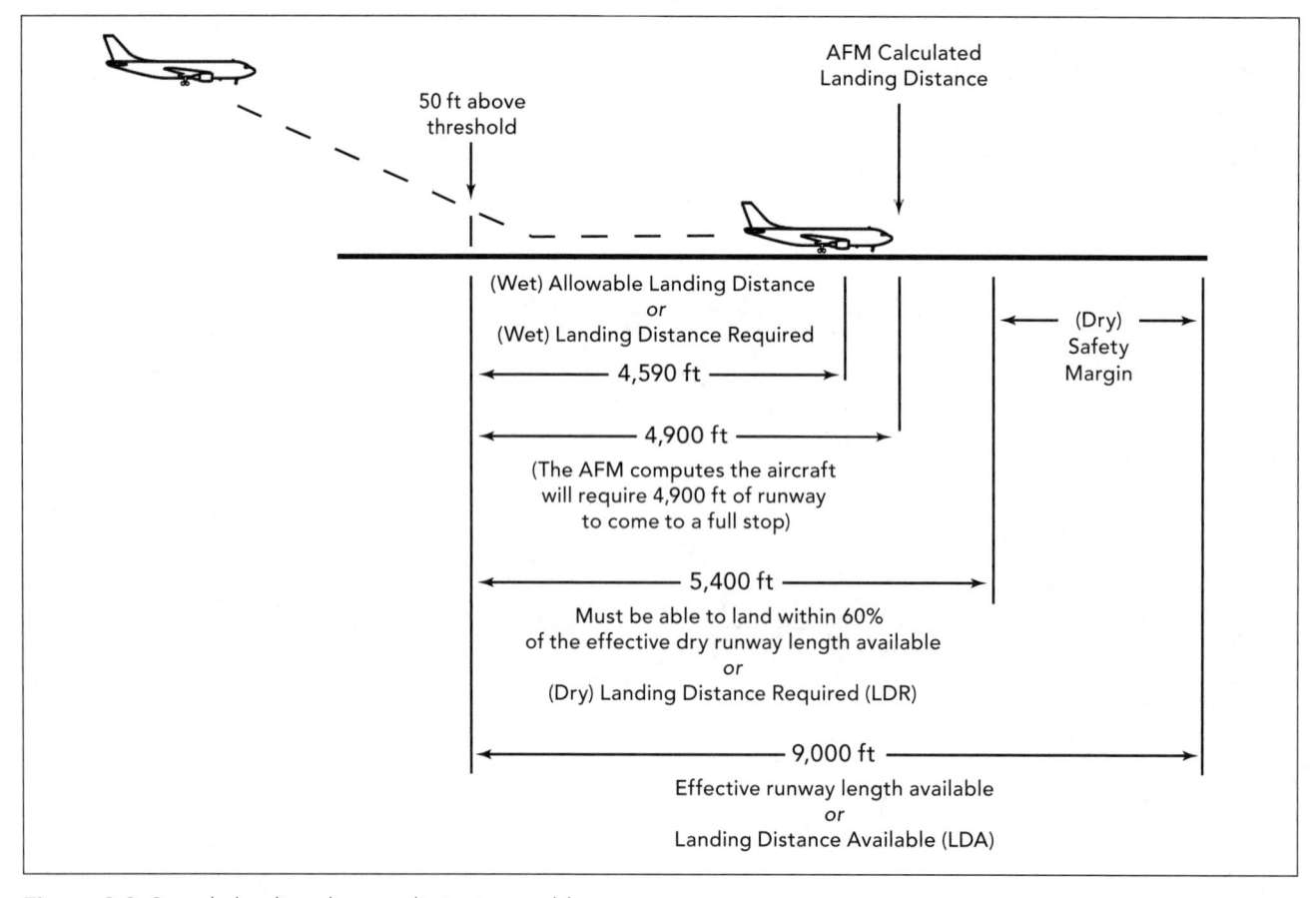

Figure 8-9. Sample landing distance limitation problem.

the effective runway length for turbojet aircraft or 70 percent of the effective runway length for turboprop aircraft. In the case of a departure airport alternate, the rule allows fuel to be jettisoned (dumped) in addition to normal consumption.

Category and Class of Aircraft

Let's briefly review the difference between a category and class of aircraft. A **category** is a classification of aircraft. The following are examples of common aircraft categories:

- Airplane
- Rotorcraft
- Glider
- Lighter-than-air (balloons and airships)

Some categories are further broken down into an aircraft **class**. Class of aircraft further distinguishes between different types of aircraft. Note, not every category has a class.

Airplane category:

- Single-engine land class (Figure 8-10)
- Multiengine land class (Figure 8-11)
- Single-engine sea class (Figure 8-12)
- Multiengine sea class

Rotorcraft category:

- Helicopter class (Figure 8-13)
- Gyroplane class

Lighter-than-air category:

- Airship class
- Balloon class

Figure 8-10. Cessna 208 Caravan: airplane, single-engine land.

Figure 8-11. British Aerospace Jetstream 41: airplane, multiengine land.

Figure 8-12. Cessna 208 Caravan: airplane, single-engine sea.

Figure 8-13. Bell 407: rotorcraft, helicopter (rotorcraft do not differentiate between single- and multiengine).

Summary

In this chapter, we have examined the performance required of transport category aircraft used in Part 121 operations. Table 8-2 summarizes the sources of dispatch rules for large, turbine-powered transport category airplanes. The requirements are designed to ensure that in the event of readily anticipated equipment failures, the flight crew will still have adequate performance to operate the aircraft safely. In the next chapter, we look in detail at the wide variety of special airworthiness standards that apply to Part 121 aircraft.

Table 8-2. Summary of dispatch rules for large, turbine-powered, transport category airplanes

Structural Limits	
Maximum Taxi Weight	AFM Limit
Maximum Takeoff Weight	AFM Limit
Zero Fuel Weight	AFM Limit

Takeoff Limits	
Accelerate-Stop	14 CFR §121.189 and 135.379
All-Engines Takeoff	14 CFR §121.189 and 135.379
Accelerate-Go	14 CFR §121.189 and 135.379
Obstacle Limit	14 CFR §121.189 and 135.379
Climb Limit	14 CFR §121.189 and 135.379

En Route Limits	
All-Engines	14 CFR §25.123
One-Engine Inoperative	14 CFR §121.191 and 135.381
Two-Engines Inoperative	14 CFR §121.193 and 135.383

Arrival Limits	
Approach Climb	14 CFR §121.195(a), 25.121(d), 135.385(a)
Landing Climb	14 CFR §121.195(a), 25.119, 135.385(a)
Maximum Landing Weight	AFM Limit

Runway Limits	
Destination Runway	14 CFR §121.195, 135.385
Alternate Runway	14 CFR §121.197, 135.387

Important Terms in Chapter 8

14 CFR Part 25
60-minute rule
90-minute rule
accelerate-go distance
accelerate-stop distance
acceleration altitude
balanced field length
balanced field limit
category of aircraft
certified landing distance
class of aircraft
clean-up altitude (or acceleration altitude)
clearway
climb limit weight
declared runway distance
driftdown altitude
driftdown technique
dry lease
en route limitations
en route limitations: one engine inoperative
en route limitations: two engines inoperative
factored landing distance
final approach speed
first segment climb
four segment climb performance
fourth segment climb
landing distance available (LDA)
landing distance data
landing field length requirement
landing limitations for alternate airports
landing limitations for destination airports
minimum steady flight speed (V_S)
net takeoff flight path
OEI (one engine inoperative)
proving tests
reduced V_1
rejected takeoff (RTO)
rotation speed (V_R)
runway limit weight
safety margin
second segment climb
stall speed (V_S)
stopway
takeoff decision speed (V_1)
takeoff distance
takeoff distance with an engine failure
takeoff distance, dry runway
takeoff distance, wet runway
takeoff limitations
takeoff path
takeoff run
third segment climb
transport category aircraft
V_1: takeoff decision speed
V_2: takeoff safety speed
V_{EF}: engine failure speed
V_{FTO}: final takeoff speed
V_{LOF}: liftoff speed
V_{MC} limit
V_{MC} or V_{MCA}: minimum controllable airspeed (airborne)
V_{MCG}: minimum control speed on the ground
V_R: rotation speed
V_{REF}: 1.3 times the stalling speed in the landing configuration
V_S: stall speed or minimum steady flight speed
V_{SR}: reference stalling speed
WAT limit charts

Chapter 8 Exam

1. All aircraft operated by Part 121 carriers must either be U.S.-registered aircraft or
   a. foreign aircraft operated under wet lease to the U.S. carrier.
   b. foreign aircraft, approved under U.S. type design and operated under dry lease to the U.S. carrier.
   c. foreign aircraft, approved under ICAO type design and operated under dry lease to the U.S. carrier.
   d. foreign aircraft may not be operated by U.S. carriers.

2. Proving tests are required of new type designs. If the design has never been proved under Part 121, it must be operated for
   a. 25 hours including 10 at night.
   b. 50 hours including 10 at night.
   c. 100 hours including 10 at night.
   d. 200 hours including 10 at night.

3. V_1, or takeoff decision speed, is the
   a. maximum speed in the takeoff at which the pilot must first take action to stop.
   b. maximum speed in the takeoff at which the pilot must decide to take action to stop.
   c. maximum speed in the takeoff where a takeoff may still be initiated.
   d. minimum speed in the takeoff where it is possible to get airborne.

4. In the event of an engine failure at or above V_1, the pilot should achieve and maintain V_2, until
   a. 35 feet above the runway surface.
   b. the landing gear is retracted.
   c. acceleration altitude.
   d. the airplane is established (configured) for enroute climb.

5. Net takeoff flight path is used in computing takeoff/climb performance capability of the aircraft. What is net takeoff flight path for a twin-engine aircraft?
   a. The climb performance of the aircraft as determined in certification testing
   b. The climb performance of the aircraft as determined in certification testing reduced by 8 feet per 1,000 feet traveled
   c. The climb performance of the aircraft as determined in certification testing reduced by the loss of performance in the event of an engine failure
   d. All of the above

6. Takeoff run must be accomplished
   a. within the length of the runway.
   b. within the length of the runway plus stopway.
   c. within the length of the runway plus stopway plus clearway.
   d. within the length of the runway plus clearway (except clearway may only be counted up to one-half the length of the runway).

7. Takeoff distance must be accomplished
   a. within the length of the runway.
   b. within the length of the runway plus stopway.
   c. within the length of the runway plus stopway plus clearway.
   d. within the length of the runway plus clearway (except clearway may only be counted up to one-half the length of the runway).

8. Runway limit weight guarantees that an aircraft may
   a. accelerate to V_1, lose an engine, and stop on the remaining runway.
   b. accelerate to V_1, lose an engine, and stop on the remaining runway plus stopway.
   c. accelerate to V_1, lose an engine, and continue the flight.
   d. None of the above.

9. The maximum weight at which an air carrier aircraft may depart is limited to
   a. the maximum weight that will assure compliance with engine out climb limits.
   b. the maximum weight that will guarantee enroute OEI terrain clearance.
   c. the maximum weight that will ensure landing below maximum landing weight.
   d. All of the above.

10. A turbine aircraft is scheduled into a runway that is 8,600 feet in length. May this aircraft (which will require 5,100 feet to land) land there on a wet day?
    a. Yes
    b. No
    c. Insufficient information to determine

11. A turbine aircraft is scheduled into a runway that is 11,000 feet in length. May this aircraft (which will, due to an anti-skid inoperative MEL, require 6,500 feet to land) land there on a dry runway? How about on a wet runway?
    a. Yes on a dry runway; no on a wet runway.
    b. Yes; at this weight the aircraft is legal to depart for both the dry or wet runway conditions.
    c. Insufficient information to determine.

12. According to an FAA study of rejected takeoffs (RTOs), statistically, one RTO occurs every _____ takeoffs.
    a. 500
    b. 1,000
    c. 3,000
    d. 4,500

13. In a situation in which the gross takeoff weight is limited by runway limit weight, in the event of an engine failure, the Go/No Go decision must be made
    a. after reaching V_1 speed.
    b. before reaching V_R speed.
    c. before reaching V_1 speed.
    d. before reaching V_{EF} speed.

14. In a situation in which the gross takeoff weight is limited by climb limit weight, in the event of an engine failure, the Go/No Go decision must be made
    a. after reaching V_1 speed.
    b. before reaching V_R speed.
    c. before reaching V_1 speed.
    d. before reaching V_{EF} speed.

15. Climb limit weight is the maximum weight that guarantees that the aircraft:
    a. at existing conditions, can complete the first segment portion of the climb and that the aircraft meets 60 percent of the balanced field length requirements.
    b. will be able to accelerate to V_1, lose an engine, and stop on the remaining runway plus stopway, including a 15-percent safety buffer for a wet runway.
    c. can proceed from a point 35 feet above the departure end of the runway to 1,500 feet above the runway surface (or specified higher altitude) while maintaining required climb gradients in order to achieve adequate obstacle clearance.
    d. can proceed from V_{LOF} to a point 50 feet above the departure end of the runway, or 35 feet if the runway has a designated stopway and clearway free of obstacles at least 200 feet either side of runway centerline.

16. Driftdown altitude is
    a. the altitude at which, following the failure of an engine, the pilot begins the driftdown procedure. This altitude must be high enough to guarantee terrain clearance of at least 2,000 feet over a mountainous terrain area.
    b. the altitude that guarantees at least 1,000 feet of terrain clearance over a non-mountainous terrain area.
    c. the altitude that guarantees at least 2,000 feet of terrain clearance over a mountainous terrain area.
    d. the altitude to which, following the failure of an engine above the one-engine inoperative absolute ceiling, an airplane will descend to and maintain, while using maximum continuous power on the operating engine and maintaining the one-engine inoperative best rate of climb speed.

17. During a normal takeoff, an aircraft may not be banked prior to reaching a height of _____ feet as shown by the flight path or net flight path data. After attaining _____ feet in height, the aircraft may not be banked more than _____ degrees in any additional maneuvering.
    a. 100, 200 and 20
    b. 50, 50 and 15
    c. 200, 400 and 50, or double the autopilot altitude loss (as specified in the AFM) above the terrain, whichever is higher.
    d. 100, 100, 10

18. A two-engine, turbine-powered airplane may not be operated over a route that contains a point farther than _____ minutes of flying time (in still air at normal cruising speed with one engine inoperative) from an adequate airport.
    a. 90
    b. 180
    c. 120
    d. 60

19. For an aircraft having three or more engines on a route that does not comply with the "90-minute rule" (a route within 90 minutes flying time, all engines operating, from an approved alternate airport), what must be done for the flight to be dispatched on the planned route?
    a. The aircraft must be operated at a weight allowed by the AFM that allows it to fly from a point where the two engines failed simultaneously to an authorized alternate airport and clear all terrain and obstructions within 5 statute miles of the intended track by at least 2,000 feet vertically. Also, the net flight path must have a positive slope at 1,500 feet above the airport where the landing is assumed to be made after the engines fail.
    b. The aircraft must be operated at a weight allowed by the AFM that allows it to fly from a point where the two engines failed simultaneously to an authorized alternate airport and clear all terrain and obstructions within 50 statute miles of the intended track by at least 1,000 feet vertically. Also, the net flight path must have a positive slope at 2,000 feet above the airport where the landing is assumed to be made after the engines fail.
    c. The aircraft must be operated at a weight allowed by the AFM that allows it to fly from a point where the two engines failed simultaneously to an authorized alternate airport and clear all terrain and obstructions within 50 statute miles of the intended track by at least 1,500 feet vertically. Also, the net flight path must have a positive slope at 1,000 feet above the airport where the landing is assumed to be made after the engines fail.
    d. The flight cannot be dispatched on the planned route. It must be flight planned on a route that is within 90 minutes of a suitable alternate airport.

20. Landing limitations for alternate airports are similar to the landing limitations for destination airports. An operator may not list an airport as an alternate airport if at the anticipated weight at the anticipated time of arrival the aircraft cannot be brought to a stop in _____ percent of the effective runway length for turbojet aircraft or _____ percent of the effective runway length for turboprop aircraft.
    a. 15, 60
    b. 50, 60
    c. 15, 50
    d. 60, 70

21. Of the following, which would be considered a category of aircraft?
    a. Airplane.
    b. Multiengine land.
    c. Helicopter.

CHAPTER 9
AIRWORTHINESS REQUIREMENTS

A commercial aircraft is a vehicle capable of supporting itself aerodynamically and economically at the same time.
—**William Stout**, Designer of the Ford Tri-Motor

In this chapter, we will examine the airworthiness standards applicable to air carrier transport category aircraft. We will begin by discussing what the FAA actually means by the term "**airworthy**." The definition of airworthy can be found in 14 CFR §3.5.

> Airworthy means the aircraft conforms to its type design and is in a condition for safe operation.

Surprisingly, the FAA had never defined the term airworthy in the Code of Federal Regulations until just a few years ago with the creation of 14 CFR Part 3, General Requirements. Prior to that, the only definitions that could be found were located in FAA *guidance* publications, such as Advisory Circulars (AC) 120-77 and 43-13-1B, but never in a *regulatory* manner. However, we've never had to look very far to find an FAA airworthiness definition as it can be found in block #5 of a **standard airworthiness certificate (FAA Form 8100-2)** on board every FAA-certified airplane (*see* Figure 9-1). To review, a standard airworthiness certificate is the FAA's official authorization allowing for the operation of a type certificated aircraft. Block #5 of a standard airworthiness certificate states:

> This aircraft conforms to its type certificate and is considered in condition for safe operation.

14 CFR Part 21 covers the conditions that must be complied with before the FAA will issue a standard airworthiness certificate. Specifically, 14 CFR §21.183 describes the issuance of standard airworthiness certificates for normal, utility, acrobatic, commuter, and transport category aircraft. Paragraphs (a) and (b) both state that, to be airworthy, the aircraft is required to be inspected by the FAA and must conform to the type design and be found in condition for safe operation. This refers to the condition of the aircraft relative to wear and deterioration—for example, skin corrosion, window delamination, fluid leaks, and tire wear.

If we look at Section 21.130, it also states the aircraft must conform to its **type certificate**. This conformity to type design is considered attained when the aircraft configuration and the components installed are consistent with the specifications, and other data that are part of the type certificate, which includes any **supplemental type certificates (STC)** and field-approved alterations incorporated into the aircraft.

If these conditions are met, the aircraft is in condition for safe operation and is considered "airworthy." Of course, keeping an aircraft in an airworthy condition is the goal of any air carrier and those persons who maintain and operate the aircraft. The FAA refers to this condition as "continued airworthiness." As the name implies, continued airworthiness is a process by which aircraft are continually kept in a condition in which they conform to the type certificate and are continually kept in a condition for safe operation. An important concept to understand when thinking of an aircraft's airworthiness is that it's not relevant whether the aircraft is "new" or "old," only whether it is airworthy or not airworthy. The age of an aircraft really only affects its commercial value, not its airworthiness. A properly maintained and inspected aircraft can be kept airworthy indefinitely (e.g., the 1930s-era DC-3 aircraft still flown in revenue service). Today an air carrier may fly an airliner profitably for as long as thirty years.

Chapter 14 will cover the maintenance and inspection programs required to ensure continuous airworthiness of an air carrier's fleet of aircraft. Now let's turn our attention toward the *special* airworthiness requirements of Subpart J of Part 121 while including some of the certification requirements of Part 25 as well.

Part 121, Subpart J

Subpart J to Part 121: **Special Airworthiness Requirements** is a good example of why it is important to read the applicability section of each subpart of Part 121 closely. Upon close reading of 14 CFR §121.211, we see that most of Subpart J is applicable only to older aircraft certificated under the CAR (Civil Aeronautics Regulations of the CAA) prior to November 1, 1946. The intent of those rules (14 CFR §121.215 through §121.283) is to bring the safety standards of older aircraft up to approximately the standards of more modern aircraft. These standards are now required as part of the certification of newer aircraft (and in some cases current standards are more stringent than those found in Subpart J). Later in this chapter, we will examine the current standards for many of these issues. All Part 121 certificate holders must comply with 14 CFR §121.285 through §121.291. Therefore, let's start with a look at those rules.

UNITED STATES OF AMERICA

DEPARTMENT OF TRANSPORTATION -- FEDERAL AVIATION ADMINISTRATION

STANDARD AIRWORTHINESS CERTIFICATE

1 NATIONALITY AND REGISTRATION MARKS	2 MANUFACTURER AND MODEL	3 AIRCRAFT SERIAL NUMBER	4 CATEGORY
N52993DL	Airbus A350	A1520893	TRANSPORT

5 AUTHORITY AND BASIS FOR ISSUANCE

This airworthiness certificate is issued pursuant to the Federal Aviation Act of 1958 and certifies that, as of the date of issuance, the aircraft to which issued has been inspected and found to conform to the type certificate therefor, to be in condition for safe operation, and has been shown to meet the requirements of the applicable comprehensive and detailed airworthiness code as provided by Annex 8 to the Convention on International Civil Aviation, except as noted herein.

Exceptions:

NONE

6 TERMS AND CONDITIONS

Unless sooner surrendered, suspended, revoked, or a termination date is otherwise established by the Administrator, this airworthiness certificate is effective as long as the maintenance, preventative maintenance, and alterations are performed in accordance with Parts 21, 43, and 91 of the Federal Aviation Regulations, as appropriate, and the aircraft is registered in the United States.

DATE OF ISSUANCE	FAA REPRESENTATIVE	DESIGNATION NUMBER
06-14-15	By: *Ted Striker* Ted Striker	DAL-PC4

Any alteration, reproduction, or misuse of this certificate may be punishable by a fine not exceeding $1,000, or imprisonment not exceeding 3 years, or both. THIS CERTIFICATE MUST BE DISPLAYED IN THE AIRCRAFT IN ACCORDANCE WITH APPLICABLE FEDERAL AVIATION REGULATIONS.

FAA Form 8100-2 (7-67) FORMERLY FAA FORM 1362

Figure 9-1. Standard airworthiness certificate.

Carrying Cargo

The first two rules in this area relate to carrying cargo aboard the aircraft either in the passenger cabin or the cargo compartment. 14 CFR §121.285 begins with the basic premise that, subject to exceptions, a carrier may not carry cargo in a passenger compartment of the aircraft. This rule is imposed in consideration of the reaction of the cargo and its containers in the event of an accident. Cargo may be carried in the passenger compartment under either of two conditions. The first condition under which it is allowed is if the cargo is carried in properly designed bins, and the second is if the cargo is carried behind a bulkhead and is properly restrained. Let's look at the specifics.

Cargo Bins

14 CFR §121.285(b) states that cargo may be carried anywhere in the passenger compartment so long as it is in an approved cargo bin that can withstand "g" forces equal to 1.15 times the load factors applicable to emergency landing conditions. The maximum weight that can be carried must be conspicuously marked on the bin along with any instructions necessary to ensure proper loading and weight distribution of the cargo. The bin must be securely anchored to either the floor or seat tracks in the aircraft. Installation of the bin cannot in any way interfere with or restrict the access to or use of any required emergency exit or aisle in the passenger compartment and it may not block the view of the "no smoking" and "fasten seat belt" signs. The bin itself must be made of material that is at least flame resistant. The bin must be designed to prevent the cargo from shifting in the bin.

Bulkheads

14 CFR §121.285(c) permits a carrier to install a bulkhead to separate the passenger and cargo compartments on the main deck of the aircraft. The cargo must be carried behind the bulkhead and must be properly secured by a safety belt or tie-down that is strong enough to eliminate the possibility of cargo shifting in all normally anticipated conditions. The cargo must be packaged or covered so as to prevent injury to the passengers. The cargo must comply with the load limitations that are imposed on the floor and seat tracks (if used). Location of the main deck cargo compartment cannot restrict or limit access to any required emergency or regular exit or the aisle in the passenger compartment. The cargo compartment cannot restrict the passenger's view of the "fasten seat belt" and "no smoking" signs unless alternative signs are installed.

Access to Cargo Compartments

If the cargo compartment is designed to require crewmembers to enter the compartment to extinguish fires in flight, then Section 121.287 requires that the cargo be loaded in such a manner as to allow the crewmember to effectively reach all parts of the compartment with the contents of a hand fire extinguisher.

Landing Gear Aural Warning Device

Current Part 25 regulations require a **landing gear aural warning device**:

> The flight crew must be given an aural warning that functions continuously, or is periodically repeated, if a landing is attempted when the landing gear is not locked down. *(14 CFR §25.729[e][2])*

Older regulations required only that the warning system test the throttle position. 14 CFR §121.289 therefore applies to aircraft certificated prior to January 6, 1992, that only tested the throttle position. Now, those aircraft systems must also test the flap position. If the system detects the flaps in a position normally used for landing and the landing gear is not down, the warning must sound.

Evacuation Demonstrations

14 CFR §121.291 requires operators of aircraft with 44 or more seats to conduct **evacuation demonstrations** prior to placing an aircraft in service. This demonstration requires that the carrier be able to evacuate the entire aircraft in 90 seconds or less. If the manufacturer has demonstrated this in certification under Part 25 since December 1, 1978, then the carrier may dispense with the full evacuation demonstration. In that case, the carrier may perform the partial evacuation demonstration required by Section 121.291(b). This partial evacuation demonstration is required when the carrier initially places the aircraft in service. Note that the carrier must also perform partial evacuation tests any time it alters the aircraft by changing the number, location, type of exits, or type of opening mechanism on emergency exits available for evacuation.

Part 25 Airworthiness Requirements

14 CFR Part 25 airworthiness requirements impose a large number of airworthiness standards on transport category aircraft. For the balance of this chapter we will explore some of these requirements that make air carrier aircraft quite different from the light, general aviation aircraft with which you may be familiar.

Flight Control Systems

14 CFR §25.671 pertains to flight controls and contains some interesting requirements. First, each control and control system must operate with the ease, smoothness, and "positiveness" appropriate to its function. Each element of each **flight control system** must be designed, or distinctively and permanently marked, to minimize the probability of incorrect assembly that could result in the malfunctioning of the system. The airplane must be shown to be capable of continued safe flight and landing after any of the following failures or jamming in the flight control system and surfaces (including trim, lift, drag, and feel systems), within the normal flight envelope, without requiring exceptional piloting skill or strength:

(1) Any single failure, excluding jamming (for example, disconnection or failure of mechanical elements, or structural failure of hydraulic components, such as actuators, control spool housing, and valves).
(2) Any combination of failures not shown to be extremely improbable, excluding jamming (for example, dual electrical or hydraulic system failures, or any single failure in combination with any probable hydraulic or electrical failure).
(3) Any jam in a control position normally encountered during takeoff, climb, cruise, normal turns, descent, and landing unless the jam is shown to be extremely improbable, or can be alleviated. A runaway of a flight control to an adverse position and jam must be accounted for if such runaway and subsequent jamming is not extremely improbable.

(14 CFR §25.671[c])

Probable malfunctions can have only minor effects on control system operation and must be capable of being readily counteracted by the pilot. The requirement that the aircraft be able to be flown in the event of a control jam leads to a major difference between many air carrier aircraft and light general aviation aircraft. Since the aircraft must be controllable even in the event of a control jam, many transport category aircraft have split controls. That means that one side (left ailerons, for example) is controlled by the pilot's control yoke and the other side (right ailerons in this example) is controlled by the copilot's control yoke. In normal operations the two systems are interconnected and flown as a single unit as on light aircraft. In the event of a jam, the crew can disconnect the two sets of controls, identify the jammed side (or *circuit*), and continue control of the aircraft using the operating control system.

Control Systems Gust Locks

While some light aircraft have **control systems gust locks**, which are installed or operated by the pilot, many others do not. In transport category aircraft this is not an option. 14 CFR §25.679 requires that there must be a device to prevent damage to the control surfaces (including tabs) and to the control system from gusts striking the airplane while it is on the ground. If the device, when engaged, prevents normal operation of the control surfaces by the pilot, it must

(1) Automatically disengage when the pilot operates the primary flight controls in a normal manner; or
(2) Limit the operation of the airplane so that the pilot receives unmistakable warning at the start of takeoff.

(14 CFR §25.679[a])

Further, the device must have means to preclude the possibility of it becoming engaged inadvertently in flight.

Takeoff Warning System

Transport category aircraft must have a **takeoff warning system** installed that meets the requirements of 14 CFR §25.703. These requirements state that the system must provide an aural warning that is automatically activated during the initial portion of the takeoff roll if the airplane is in a configuration that would not allow a safe takeoff. That includes the following erroneous configurations:

(1) The wing flaps or leading edge devices are not within the approved range of takeoff positions.
(2) Wing spoilers (except lateral control spoilers meeting the requirements of §25.671), speed brakes, or longitudinal trim devices are in a position that would not allow a safe takeoff.

(14 CFR §25.703[a])

Once the takeoff warning is given, it must continue to sound until

(1) The configuration is changed to allow a safe takeoff;
(2) Action is taken by the pilot to terminate the takeoff roll;
(3) The airplane is rotated for takeoff; or
(4) The warning is manually deactivated by the pilot.

(14 CFR §25.703[b])

Flight Crew Emergency Exits

All airplanes having a passenger seating capacity greater than 20 seats are required by 14 CFR §25.807 to have **flight crew emergency exits** that are located in the flight crew area. These exits must be of sufficient size and located so as to permit rapid evacuation by the crew. One exit must be provided on each side of the airplane; or, alternatively, a top hatch must be provided. Each exit must encompass an unobstructed rectangular opening of at least 19 by 20 inches unless satisfactory exit utility can be demonstrated by a typical crewmember.

Emergency Lighting and Signs

14 CFR §25.812 requires that an **emergency lighting system** that is independent of the main lighting system be installed in transport category airplanes. The sources of general cabin illumination may be common to both the emergency and the main lighting systems if the power supply to the emergency lighting system is independent of the power supply to the main lighting system. The emergency lighting system must include illuminated emergency exit marking and locating signs, sources of general cabin illumination, interior lighting in emergency exit areas, and floor proximity escape path marking. It must also include exterior emergency lighting.

Emergency Exit Signs

14 CFR §25.812 also states that each passenger **emergency exit locator sign** required and each passenger *emergency exit marking sign* required must have red letters on an illuminated white background. These signs must be internally electrically illuminated. The floor of the passageway leading to each floor-level passenger emergency exit, between the main aisles and the exit openings, must be provided with illumination centered on the passenger evacuation path. *Floor proximity emergency escape path marking* must provide emergency evacuation guidance for passengers when all sources of illumination more than 4 feet above the cabin aisle floor are totally obscured. 14 CFR §25.812(e) requires that at night, the floor proximity emergency escape path marking must enable each passenger to:

(1) After leaving the passenger seat, visually identify the emergency escape path along the cabin aisle floor to the first exits or pair of exits forward and aft of the seat; and
(2) Readily identify each exit from the emergency escape path by reference only to markings and visual features not more than 4 feet above the cabin floor.

Emergency Lighting Controls

Part 25 aircraft must have appropriate **emergency lighting controls**. Generally, but not always, the lights must be operable manually from the flight crew station and from a point in the passenger compartment that is readily accessible to a normal flight attendant seat. There must be a flight crew warning light, which illuminates when power is on in the airplane and the emergency lighting control device is not armed. The cockpit control device must have an "on," "off," and "armed" position so that when armed in the cockpit or turned on at either the cockpit or flight attendant station, the lights will either light or remain lighted upon interruption of the airplane's normal electric power. There must be a means to safeguard against inadvertent operation of the control device from the "armed" or "on" positions. The energy supply to each emergency lighting unit must provide the required level of illumination for at least 10 minutes at the critical ambient conditions after emergency landing. (14 CFR §25.812 [h][2])

Emergency Lighting Energy Supply

If storage batteries are used as the **emergency lighting system energy supply**, 14 CFR §25.812(j) allows them to be recharged from the airplane's main electric power system, provided that the charging circuit is designed to preclude inadvertent battery discharge into charging circuit faults. Components of the emergency lighting system, including batteries, wiring relays, lamps, and switches, must be capable of normal operation after being subjected to the inertia forces typical of a crash landing. The emergency lighting system must be designed so that after any single transverse vertical separation of the fuselage during crash landing, not more than 25 percent of all electrically illuminated emergency lights (in addition to the lights that are directly damaged by the separation) are rendered inoperative. In addition, each required electrically illuminated exit sign must remain operative (again, exclusive of those that are directly damaged by the separation) and at least one exterior emergency light for each side of the airplane must remain operative.

Pressurized Cabins

Pressurized cabins and compartments are required by 14 CFR §25.841 to be equipped to provide a cabin pressure altitude of not more than 8,000 feet at the maximum operating altitude of the airplane under normal operating conditions. If certification for operation above 25,000 feet is requested, the airplane must be designed so that occupants will not be exposed to cabin pressure altitudes in excess of 15,000 feet after any probable failure condition in the pressurization system. Further, the airplane must be designed so that occupants will not be exposed to a cabin pressure altitude that exceeds the following after decompression from any failure condition not shown to be extremely improbable:

- 25,000 feet for more than 2 minutes, or
- 40,000 feet for any duration.

Interior Fire Protection and Flammability Standards

Part 25 sets rigorous **interior fire protection and flammability standards** for everything that goes into a transport category airplane interior. 14 CFR §25.853 provides that for each interior compartment occupied by the crew or passengers, the following apply:

(a) Materials (including finishes or decorative surfaces applied to the materials) must meet the applicable test criteria prescribed in part I of appendix F of this part, or other approved equivalent methods, regardless of the passenger capacity of the airplane.

(b) [Reserved]

(c) In addition to meeting the requirements of paragraph (a) of this section, seat cushions, except those on flight crewmember seats, must meet the test requirements of part II of appendix F of this part, or other equivalent methods, regardless of the passenger capacity of the airplane.

(d) Except as provided in paragraph (e) of this section, the following interior components of airplanes with passenger capacities of 20 or more must also meet the test requirements of parts IV and V of appendix F of this part, or other approved equivalent method, in addition to the flammability requirements prescribed in paragraph (a) of this section:

  (1) Interior ceiling and wall panels, other than lighting lenses and windows;
  (2) Partitions, other than transparent panels needed to enhance cabin safety;
  (3) Galley structure, including exposed surfaces of stowed carts and standard containers and the cavity walls that are exposed when a full complement of such carts or containers is not carried; and
  (4) Large cabinets and cabin stowage compartments, other than underseat stowage compartments for stowing small items such as magazines and maps.

Smoking Regulations

The smoking of lit cigarettes or anything else that produces smoke or flame is currently prohibited on all scheduled passenger flights. Prior to 1988, there was little prohibition from "lighting-up" on airliners other than a few non-smoking rows on some flights. Due to health concerns after decades of debate between tobacco companies and health advocates, Congress phased in what would eventually become a total smoking ban. Initially, the inflight smoking ban only affected domestic flights with a scheduled time enroute of two hours or less. In 1990, the inflight smoking ban was expanded to include all domestic flights of six hours or less. Finally in 2000, a total inflight smoking ban was implemented. Refer to 14 CFR Part 252, "Smoking Aboard Aircraft."

14 CFR §252.1—Purpose.

This part implements a ban on smoking of tobacco products on air carrier and foreign air carrier flights in scheduled intrastate, interstate and foreign air transportation, as required by 49 U.S.C. 41706. It also addresses smoking on charter flights. Nothing in this regulation shall be deemed to require air carriers or foreign air carriers to permit the smoking of tobacco products aboard aircraft.

14 CFR §252.3—Smoking ban: air carriers.

Air carriers shall prohibit smoking on all scheduled passenger flights.

While we are on the subject of smoking, battery-powered vaporizing nicotine delivery systems, also known as electronic cigarettes, have become more popular in recent years. It is expected that the FAA will eventually include these e-cigarettes in the smoking ban due to the fact that most airlines do not allow their use inflight for various reasons. However, the FAA has not yet issued a regulation regarding e-cigarettes, instead leaving the decision to allow their inflight use up to individual airlines. It is important to note that current versions of e-cigarettes utilize a lithium battery to vaporize the nicotine mixture. To date, lithium batteries in e-cigarettes have been the cause of multiple inflight cargo compartment fires. For this reason, the FAA and the TSA require all e-cigarettes to be carried on board the aircraft and not placed in "checked" baggage placed in the aircraft's cargo compartment.

Lavatory Fire Protection

Because the United States has banned smoking on all U.S. air carrier aircraft, **lavatory fire protection** receives special attention: There is a real concern that nicotine addicts will adjourn to the rest rooms and smoke. A major problem with this is that the trash bins (full of lightweight paper) become the most likely place to dispose of cigarette butts. To protect against the possibility of a serious fire in the lavatories, each lavatory must be equipped with a smoke detector system or equivalent that provides either a warning light in the cockpit or a warning light or audible warning in the passenger cabin that would be readily detected by a flight attendant. In addition, each lavatory must be equipped with a built-in fire extinguisher for each disposal receptacle for towels, paper, or waste located within the lavatory. The extinguisher must be designed to discharge automatically into each disposal receptacle upon occurrence of a fire in that receptacle. (14 CFR §25.854)

Cargo Compartment Classification

The FAA has classified the cargo and baggage spaces aboard aircraft into four classes as defined in 14 CFR §25.857: A, B, C, and E. (A **Class D compartment** is no longer permitted by the FAA.) This is done to provide distinctions for these spaces as related to fire detection and protection. Class A, B, and C compartments are found on passenger and cargo aircraft while Class E compartments are found only on all-cargo aircraft. Following are the definitions that apply to each class

Class A

A **Class A cargo or baggage compartment** is one in which:

(1) The presence of a fire would be easily discovered by a crewmember while at his station; and
(2) Each part of the compartment is easily accessible in flight.

(14 CFR §25.857[a])

Class B

A **Class B cargo or baggage compartment** is one in which:

(1) There is sufficient access in flight to enable a crewmember to effectively reach any part of the compartment with the contents of a hand fire extinguisher;
(2) When the access provisions are being used, no hazardous quantity of smoke, flames, or extinguishing agent will enter any compartment occupied by the crew or passengers;
(3) There is a separate approved smoke detector or fire detector system to give warning at the pilot or flight engineer station.

(14 CFR §25.857[b])

Class C

A **Class C cargo or baggage compartment** is one not meeting the requirements for either a Class A or B compartment but in which:

(1) There is a separate approved smoke detector or fire detector system to give warning at the pilot or flight engineer station;
(2) There is an approved built-in fire extinguishing or suppression system controllable from the cockpit;
(3) There are means to exclude hazardous quantities of smoke, flames, or extinguishing agent from any compartment occupied by the crew or passengers;
(4) There are means to control ventilation and drafts within the compartment so that the extinguishing agent used can control any fire that may start within the compartment.

(14 CFR §25.857[c])

Class D

Class D cargo or baggage compartments are not currently defined (or allowed) by the FAA. In older aircraft, Class D cargo compartments were those that were not accessible during flight and were designed to choke out fires due to lack of oxygen rather than detect or extinguish the fire. These were eliminated after the ValuJet Flight 592 accident in 1996.

Class E

A **Class E cargo compartment** is one on airplanes used only for the carriage of cargo and in which:

(1) [Reserved]
(2) There is a separate approved smoke or fire detector system to give warning at the pilot or flight engineer station;
(3) There are means to shut off the ventilating airflow to, or within, the compartment, and the controls for these means are accessible to the flight crew in the crew compartment;
(4) There are means to exclude hazardous quantities of smoke, flames, or noxious gases from the flight crew compartment; and

(5) The required crew emergency exits are accessible under any cargo loading condition.

(14 CFR §25.857[e])

Cargo or Baggage Stowage Compartments

14 CFR §25.855 establishes rules for the design and use of **cargo and baggage storage compartments**. Each compartment for the stowage of cargo, baggage, carry-on articles, and equipment (such as life rafts) must be designed for its placarded maximum weight of contents considering the maximum load factors corresponding to flight and ground load conditions and to the emergency landing conditions. The loads applied in the emergency landing conditions need not be applied to compartments located below or forward of all occupants in the airplane. Except for underseat and overhead passenger convenience compartments, each stowage compartment in the passenger cabin must be completely enclosed.

There must be a means to prevent the contents in the compartments from becoming a hazard by shifting under load. For stowage compartments in the passenger and crew cabin, if the means used to prevent shifting is a latched door, the design must take into consideration the wear and deterioration expected in service. If cargo compartment lamps are installed, each lamp must be installed so as to prevent contact between lamp bulb and cargo.

The definitions of the various classes of cargo compartments were discussed above. Now let's turn our attention to some specific requirements for the construction of these compartments. First, 14 CFR §25.855(b) requires any compartment classified as a Class B through Class E cargo or baggage compartment to have a liner, and the liner must be separate from (but may be attached to) the airplane structure. The ceiling and sidewall liner panels and other materials used in the construction of the compartments must meet the flammability test requirements of Part 25. Class C compartments have to meet the higher standards found in a separate section of the flammability test standards.

> No compartment may contain any controls, wiring, lines, equipment, or accessories whose damage or failure would affect safe operation, unless those items are protected so that—
> (1) They cannot be damaged by the movement of cargo in the compartment, and
> (2) Their breakage or failure will not create a fire hazard.
>
> *(14 CFR §25.855[e])*

In the design of the compartments, there must be means to prevent cargo or baggage from interfering with the functioning of the fire protective features of the compartment. Sources of heat within the compartment must be shielded and insulated to prevent igniting the cargo or baggage. Flight tests must be conducted to show compliance with the provisions concerning

- compartment accessibility,
- the entries of hazardous quantities of smoke or extinguishing agent into compartments occupied by the crew or passengers, and
- the dissipation of the extinguishing agent in Class C compartments.

In these tests, it must be shown that no inadvertent operation of smoke or fire detectors in any compartment would occur as a result of fire contained in any other compartment, either during or after extinction, unless the extinguishing system floods each such compartment simultaneously. In other words, any alarms have to be limited only to the protected area unless all areas are subject to extinguishing actions.

Cargo or Baggage Compartment Smoke or Fire Detection Systems

If the aircraft is certificated with **cargo or baggage compartment smoke or fire detection equipment**, the following must be met for each cargo or baggage compartment:

(a) The detection system must provide a visual indication to the flight crew within one minute after the start of a fire.
(b) The system must be capable of detecting a fire at a temperature significantly below that at which the structural integrity of the airplane is substantially decreased.
(c) There must be means to allow the crew to check, in flight, the functioning of each fire detector circuit.
(d) The effectiveness of the detection system must be shown for all approved operating configurations and conditions.

(14 CFR §25.858)

Fire Extinguishers

Each airplane must have a minimum number of hand **fire extinguishers** conveniently located and evenly distributed in passenger compartments. The number of required fire extinguishers depends on the airplane's passenger capacity, as shown in Table 9-1.

Table 9-1. Number of required fire extinguishers

Passenger capacity	No. of fire extinguishers
7 through 30	1
31 through 60	2
61 through 200	3
201 through 300	4
301 through 400	5
401 through 500	6
501 through 600	7
601 through 700	8

These extinguishers must be distributed around the airplane so that at least one hand fire extinguisher is conveniently located in the pilot compartment and one is readily accessible for use in each Class A or Class B cargo or baggage compartment. One must be available to use in each Class E cargo or baggage compartment that is accessible to crewmembers in flight. At least one hand fire extinguisher must be located in, or readily accessible for use in, each galley located above or below the passenger compartment. All hand fire extinguishers must be approved.

The quantity of extinguishing agent used in each extinguisher required must be appropriate for the kinds of fires likely to occur where used. Each extinguisher intended for use in a personnel compartment must be designed to minimize the hazard of toxic gas concentration.

If a built-in fire extinguisher is provided, it must be installed so that no extinguishing agent likely to enter personnel compartments is hazardous to the occupants, and discharge of the agent cannot cause structural damage. The capacity of each required built-in fire extinguishing system must be adequate for any fire likely to occur in the compartment where used, considering the volume of the compartment and the ventilation rate.

Designated Fire Zones

Designated fire zones are areas inside an engine cowling or auxiliary power unit compartment where a fire is most likely to occur. This includes areas such as:

(1) The engine power section;
(2) The engine accessory section;
(3) Except for reciprocating engines, any complete power plant compartment in which no isolation is provided between the engine power section and the engine accessory section;
(4) Any auxiliary power unit compartment;
(5) Any fuel-burning heater and other combustion equipment installation described in §25.859;
(6) The compressor and accessory sections of turbine engines; and
(7) Combustor, turbine, and tailpipe sections of turbine engine installations that contain lines or components carrying flammable fluids or gases.

(14 CFR §25.1181)

Fire Protection: Flight Controls, Engine Mounts, and Other Flight Structures

Fire protection for essential flight controls, engine mounts, and other flight structures located in designated fire zones or in adjacent areas which would be subjected to the effects of fire in the fire zone requires that these items be constructed of fireproof material or shielded so that they are capable of withstanding the effects of fire. (14 CFR §25.865)

Fire Protection: Other Components

Fire protection for other components (other than tail surfaces to the rear of the nacelles that could not be readily affected by heat, flames, or sparks coming from a designated fire zone or engine compartment of any nacelle) require that surfaces to the rear of the nacelles, within one nacelle diameter of the nacelle centerline, must be at least fire resistant. (14 CFR §25.867)

Fire Extinguishing Systems

Except for combustor, turbine, and tail pipe sections of turbine engine installations that contain lines or components carrying flammable fluids or gases for which it is shown that a fire originating in these sections can be controlled, 14 CFR §25.1195 requires that there must be a fire extinguisher system serving each designated fire zone. The **fire extinguishing system**, the quantity of the extinguishing agent, the rate of discharge, and the discharge distribution must be adequate to extinguish fires. It must be shown by either actual or simulated flights tests that under critical airflow conditions in flight, the discharge of the extinguishing agent in each designated fire zone will provide an agent concentration capable of extinguishing fires in that zone and of minimizing the probability of reigniting.

An individual "one-shot" system may be used for auxiliary power and other combustion equipment. For each other designated fire zone, two discharges must be provided, each of which produces adequate agent concentration. The fire extinguishing system for a nacelle must be able to simultaneously protect each zone of the nacelle for which protection is provided.

Fire Detector Systems

For **fire detector systems**, each aircraft is required by 14 CFR §25.1203 to have approved, quick-acting fire or overheat detectors in each designated fire zone and in the combustion, turbine, and tailpipe sections of turbine engine installations, in sufficient numbers and in locations that will ensure prompt detection of fire in those zones. The fire detector system must be constructed and installed so that it will withstand the vibration, inertia, and other loads to which it may be subjected in operation.

There must be a means to warn the crew in the event that the sensor or associated wiring within a designated fire zone is severed unless the system continues to function as a satisfactory detection system after the severing. The fire detection system must also warn the crew in the event of a short circuit in the sensor or associated wiring within a designated fire zone unless the system continues to function as a satisfactory detection system after the short circuit. The fire or overheat detector may not be affected by any oil, water, other fluids, or fumes that might be present. The crew must be able to check, in flight, the functioning of each fire or overheat detector electric circuit.

The wiring and other components of each fire or overheat detector system in a fire zone must be at least fire resistant. No fire or overheat detector system component for any fire zone may pass through another fire zone, unless it is protected against the possibility of false warnings resulting from fires in zones through which it passes or else each zone involved is simultaneously protected by the same detector and extinguishing system. Each fire detector system must be constructed so that when it is in the configuration for installation it will not exceed the alarm activation time approved for the detectors using the response time criteria specified in the appropriate standards for the fire detector.

PBE: Protective Breathing Equipment

If there is a Class A, B, or E cargo compartment on the airplane, **protective breathing equipment (PBE)** must be installed for the use of appropriate crewmembers. In addition, protective breathing equipment must be installed in each isolated separate compartment in the airplane, including the upper and lower lobe galleys, in which crewmember occupancy is permitted during flight for the maximum number of crewmembers expected to be in the area during any operation.

For required protective breathing equipment, the following apply:

(1) The equipment must be designed to protect the appropriate crewmember from smoke, carbon dioxide, and other harmful gases while on flight deck duty or while combating fires.
(2) The equipment must include—
  (i) Masks covering the eyes, nose, and mouth; or
  (ii) Masks covering the nose and mouth, plus accessory equipment to cover the eyes.
(3) Equipment, including portable equipment, must allow communication with other crewmembers while in use. Equipment available at flightcrew assigned duty stations must also enable the flightcrew to use radio equipment.
(4) The part of the equipment protecting the eyes shall not cause any appreciable adverse effect on vision and must allow corrective glasses to be worn.
(5) The equipment must supply protective oxygen of 15 minutes duration per crewmember at a pressure altitude of 8,000 feet with a respiratory minute volume of 30 liters per minute BTPD....BTPD refers to body temperature conditions (that is, 37° C., at ambient pressure, dry).

(14 CFR §25.1439)

Flight Crew Alerting: Warning, Caution, and Advisory Lights and Aural Annunciators

As a result of recommendations made by an Aviation Rulemaking Advisory Committee (ARAC), the long-standing standards for alerting crews of current or impending issues were updated in 2010 to recognize the tremendous advances in cockpit automation and displays since the rule was last revised in 1976. If **warning, caution or advisory lights** are installed in the cockpit, they must, unless otherwise approved by the Administrator, be *red* for warning lights (lights indicating a hazard which may require immediate corrective action); *amber* for caution lights (lights indicating the possible need for future corrective action); *green* for safe operation lights; and any other color, including white, for lights not described above. These other colors must differ sufficiently from the colors above to avoid possible confusion. *(14 CFR §25.1322)*

Cockpit Voice Recorders

Air carrier, transport category aircraft must have **cockpit voice recorders (CVRs)**. These are the recorders that record the cockpit communications and noises from the airplane. They must be approved and must be installed so that they will record the following:

(1) Voice communications transmitted from or received in the airplane by radio.
(2) Voice communications of flight crewmembers on the flight deck.
(3) Voice communications of flight crewmembers on the flight deck, using the airplane's interphone system.
(4) Voice or audio signals identifying navigation or approach aids introduced into a headset or speaker.
(5) Voice communications of flight crewmembers using the passenger loudspeaker system, if there is such a system and if the fourth channel is available in accordance with the requirements of paragraph (c)(4)(ii) of this section.
(6) If datalink communication equipment is installed, all datalink communications, using an approved data message set. Data link messages must be recorded as the output signal from the communications unit that translates the signal into usable data.

(14 CFR §25.1457[a])

Each cockpit voice recorder must be installed so that it receives its electric power from the bus that provides the maximum reliability for operation of the cockpit voice recorder without jeopardizing service to essential or emergency loads. There must be an automatic means to simultaneously stop the recorder and prevent each erasure feature from functioning, within 10 minutes after crash impact, and there must be an aural or visual means for preflight checking of the recorder for proper operation.

The CVR is required to record continuously for a minimum of 30 minutes, though many newer CVRs record for longer periods of time. By union/management agreement, in most cases the CVR recording may only be used for accident/incident investigation by the National Transportation Safety Board (NTSB). Most cockpit voice recorders, therefore, have the ability to bulk erase the recording. This erasure feature is provided so that the crew may, upon termination of a "routine" flight, erase the cockpit voice recording. If the CVR has this erasure device, the installation must be designed to minimize the probability of inadvertent operation and actuation of the device during crash impact.

Flight Data Recorders (FDRs) or Digital Flight Data Recorders (DFDRs)

Air carrier transport category aircraft must also carry **flight data recorders (FDRs)** in a separate container from the cockpit voice recorder. The flight data recorder records a wide variety of parameters concerning the ongoing operation of the aircraft, such as airspeed, attitude, control inputs, switch positions, and so on. Many union/management agreements limit the use of the flight data recorder information to either accident/incident investigation by the NTSB or **flight operational quality assurance (FOQA)** analytical purposes, where the data is de-identified as to flight number or crew and used to develop statistical models of aircraft operations. Air carriers then use the captured data to identify and correct deficiencies in all areas of flight operations.

Each flight data recorder is required to be carried in a container that must:

(1) Be either bright orange or bright yellow;
(2) Have reflective tape affixed to its external surface to facilitate its location under water; and
(3) Have an underwater locating device, when required by the operating rules of this chapter, on or adjacent to the container which is secured in such a manner that they are not likely to be separated during crash impact.

(14 CFR §25.1459[d])

Summary

In this chapter, we have examined a number of airworthiness issues that affect the certification of transport category airplanes. The next chapter will look at the Part 121 rules relating to the use of the equipment and instruments that must be aboard the airplane due to Part 25.

Important Terms in Chapter 9

advisory light
airworthy
cargo and baggage storage compartments
cargo compartment classification
cargo or baggage compartment smoke or fire detection systems
caution light
Class A cargo or baggage compartment
Class B cargo or baggage compartment
Class C cargo or baggage compartment
Class D compartment (no longer permitted)
Class E cargo compartment
cockpit voice recorder (CVR)
control systems gust locks
designated fire zones
digital flight data recorders (DFDR)
emergency exit locator sign
emergency lighting controls
emergency lighting system
emergency lighting system energy supply
evacuation demonstrations
fire detector systems
fire extinguishers
fire extinguishing systems
fire protection for essential flight controls, engine mounts and other flight structures
flight control system
flight crew emergency exits
flight data recorders (FDRs)
flight operational quality assurance (FOQA)
interior fire protection and flammability standards
landing gear aural warning device
lavatory fire protection
mandatory smoking regulations
Part 25 airworthiness requirements
pressurized cabins
protective breathing equipment (PBE)
special airworthiness requirements
standard airworthiness certificate (FAA Form 8100-2)
supplemental type certificate (STC)
takeoff warning system
type certificate
warning lights

Chapter 9 Exam

1. In order to carry cargo on the passenger level in a passenger aircraft, the cargo
   a. must be approved by the ramp services agent responsible for the flight.
   b. must be on pallets that are securely strapped to the flooring of the aircraft.
   c. must be secured in bins that can withstand 1.15 times the emergency landing g loads or, alternatively, the cargo may be properly restrained behind a bulkhead.
   d. must be smaller than 15 pounds.

2. Landing gear aural warning devices must sound a warning if
   a. a landing is attempted with the gear not locked down.
   b. throttles are reduced for landing with the gear not locked down (only).
   c. flaps are set for landing with the gear not locked down (only).
   d. None of the above.

3. To be used in Part 121 operations, aircraft with more than 44 seats must be shown to be able to conduct an evacuation in
   a. 60 seconds or less.
   b. 90 seconds or less.
   c. 120 seconds or less.
   d. No time is specified for conducting evacuations.

4. Transport category aircraft elevators typically
   a. are interconnected but may be operated separately in an emergency.
   b. are rigidly interconnected and operate together as a unit.
   c. are only connected to the control columns by electrical circuits.
   d. are a single unit that may be operated from either the pilot or copilot seat.

5. The takeoff warning system of a transport category aircraft must operate from the initial portion of the takeoff (application of takeoff power) until
   a. the aircraft passes the takeoff decision speed.
   b. the aircraft passes through 500 feet on the takeoff.
   c. the aircraft is rotated for takeoff.
   d. the aircraft is properly configured.

6. Under normal operating conditions, the pressurized cabin of a Part 121 aircraft must maintain a maximum cabin pressure altitude of
   a. 8,000 feet.
   b. 10,000 feet.
   c. 12,500 feet.
   d. 15,000 feet.

7. Which cargo compartment on a passenger airplane has fire extinguishing equipment built into the compartment that is controllable from the cockpit?
   a. Class A
   b. Class B
   c. Class C
   d. Class D

8. An aircraft with 254 passenger seats would require
   a. 1 fire extinguisher.
   b. 2 fire extinguishers.
   c. 3 fire extinguishers.
   d. 4 fire extinguishers.

9. A blue cockpit annunciator light would indicate
   a. warning.
   b. caution.
   c. status.
   d. exit.

10. Cockpit voice recorders are required to continuously record the
    a. last 15 minutes of each flight.
    b. last 30 minutes of each flight.
    c. last 45 minutes of each flight.
    d. last 1 hour of each flight.

11. To be used in Part 121 operations, aircraft must have flight crew emergency exits located in the flight area if they have a passenger seating capacity greater than
    a. 9 seats.
    b. 20 seats.
    c. 44 seats.
    d. Required for any passenger-carrying aircraft.

12. The inflight use of cigarettes or cigars is allowed only on flights with a scheduled time en route of greater than six hours.
    a. True
    b. False

13. If there is a Class A, B, or E cargo compartment on the airplane, what must be installed for the use of appropriate crewmembers?
    a. A crash axe
    b. A portable crew oxygen bottle for each required crewmember
    c. At least one, two-phase, timed fire suppression nozzle in each cargo compartment
    d. Protective breathing equipment (PBE)

14. If the aircraft is certificated with cargo or baggage compartment smoke or fire detection equipment, the following must be met for each cargo or baggage compartment:
    a. The detection system must provide a visual warning indication to the flight crew within one minute after the start of a fire.
    b. The detection system must be powered by an isolated independent lithium battery pack.
    c. The detection system must provide a visual warning indication to the flight crew within thirty seconds after the start of a fire.
    d. The detection system must be powered by an isolated independent NiCad battery pack.

15. Class D cargo compartments are not accessible during flight and are designed with a protective liner allowing the compartment to be used to ship cargo containing lithium or NiCad batteries.
    a. True
    b. False

CHAPTER 10
INSTRUMENT AND EQUIPMENT REQUIREMENTS

First, by the figurations of art there be made instruments of navigation without men to row them, as great ships to brooke the sea, only with one man to steer them, and they shall sail far more swiftly than if they were full of men.

—**Roger Bacon**, thirteenth-century Franciscan friar

In the last chapter, we explored some of the equipment required for certification of aircraft in the transport category. Those rules assure that the airplane is designed and built to the much more exacting standards demanded of aircraft to be used in public transportation. In this chapter, we will look at the interaction between the certification rules found in Part 25 and the operational rules found in Part 121. Most of the rules covered in this chapter are contained in Part 121, Subpart K.

Airplane Instruments and Equipment

The instrument and equipment requirements of this subpart apply to all operations under Part 121. Any of the instruments and equipment required by 14 CFR §121.305 through §121.359 must be approved and installed in accordance with the Part 25 airworthiness requirements that are applicable to them. Airspeed indicators must be calibrated in knots, and each airspeed limitation and item of related information in the airplane flight manual and pertinent placards must be expressed in knots.

No person may *take off* any airplane unless the following instruments and equipment are in operable condition:

- Instruments and equipment required to comply with airworthiness requirements under which the airplane is type certificated. (Slightly different rules are applicable to the older aircraft; remember, we are limiting our discussions to aircraft certificated since August 29, 1959.)
- Instruments and equipment specified in Sections 121.305 through 121.321, 121.359, and 121.360 for all operations, and the instruments and equipment specified in Sections 121.321 through 121.351 for the kind of operation indicated. These latter rules apply to issues such as night operations, operations over-the-top or in IFR (IMC) conditions, overwater operations, and flight in icing conditions.

Notice that this rule is violated on *takeoff*. If any of the specified equipment is inoperative and the carrier hasn't complied with the relief provision discussed below, it is in violation as soon as the airplane leaves the ground. On the other hand, if the equipment breaks in flight, different rules will apply. The relief provisions mentioned above are found in 14 CFR §121.627 and 121.628. Section 121.627 covers enroute failures and Section 121.628 covers equipment failure prior to departure. This last provision is commonly referred to as the minimum equipment list provisions or, simply, MELs. This is discussed in more detail in Chapter 11.

Flight and Navigational Equipment

The following **flight and navigational equipment** and instruments are required to be installed and operational:

(a) An airspeed indicating system with heated pitot tube or equivalent means for preventing malfunctioning due to icing.
(b) A sensitive altimeter. *[That means adjustable for variable pressure.]*
(c) A sweep-second hand clock (or approved equivalent *[such as a digital clock]*).
(d) A free-air temperature indicator.
(e) A gyroscopic bank and pitch indicator (artificial horizon).
(f) A gyroscopic rate-of-turn indicator combined with an integral slip-skid indicator (turn-and-bank indicator) except that only a slip-skid indicator is required when a third attitude instrument system usable through flight attitudes of 360° of pitch and roll is installed in accordance with paragraph (k) of this section.
(g) A gyroscopic direction indicator (directional gyro or equivalent).
(h) A magnetic compass.
(i) A vertical speed indicator (rate-of-climb indicator).
(j) On the airplane described in this paragraph *[see 14 CFR §121.305(j), (1)–(4)]*, in addition to two gyroscopic bank and pitch indicators (artificial horizons) for use at the pilot stations, a third such instrument is installed in accordance with paragraph (k) of this section:…
(k) When required by paragraph (j) of this section, a third gyroscopic bank-and-pitch indicator (artificial horizon)…*[This third artificial horizon must be powered from a source independent of the electrical generating system and continue reliable operation for a minimum of 30 minutes after total failure of the electrical generating system. It must operate independently of any other attitude indicating system. Its use can't require any crew selection after total failure of the electrical generating system. It must be lighted and plainly visible to and usable by each pilot at his or her station.]*
(14 CFR §121.305)

Portable Electronic Devices

A **portable electronic device (PED)** is any piece of lightweight, electrically powered equipment. These devices, covered in 14 CFR §121.306, range from typical consumer electronic devices such as tablets, e-readers, and smartphones to small devices such as MP3 players and electronic toys.

Recently, the Federal Aviation Administration recognized the increasing consumer interest in the expanded use of personal electronic devices on airplanes and decided to reconsider when passengers can use the latest technologies safely during a flight.

The FAA determined that airlines could safely expand passenger use of portable electronic devices during all phases of flight. The decision is based on input from the PED Aviation Rulemaking Committee (ARC), which concluded that most commercial airplanes can tolerate radio interference signals from PEDs.

Current FAA regulations require an aircraft operator to determine that radio frequency interference from PEDs is not a flight safety risk before the operator authorizes them for use during certain phases of flight. As you might expect, PEDs that do not intentionally transmit signals can still emit unintentional radio energy. This energy may affect aircraft safety because the signals can occur at the same frequencies used by the plane's highly sensitive communications, navigation, flight control and electronic equipment. This has been a safety concern for years. An airline must now show it can prevent potential interference that could pose a safety hazard.

The FAA did not consider changing the regulations regarding the use of cell phones for voice communications during flight because the issue is under the jurisdiction of the Federal Communications Commission (FCC). The ARC did recommend that the FAA consult with the FCC to review its current rules. Cell phones differ from most PEDs in that they are designed to send out signals strong enough to be received at great distances. For this reason, cell phone voice-call use during flight remains prohibited.

14 CFR §121.306—Portable electronic devices.

(a) Except as provided in paragraph (b) of this section, no person may operate, nor may any operator or pilot in command of an aircraft allow the operation of, any portable electronic device on any U.S.-registered civil aircraft operating under this part.
(b) Paragraph (a) of this section does not apply to:
 (1) Portable voice recorders;
 (2) Hearing aids;
 (3) Heart pacemakers;
 (4) Electric shavers;
 (5) Portable oxygen concentrators that comply with the requirements in §121.574 or
 (6) Any other portable electronic device that the part 119 certificate holder has determined will not cause interference with

the navigation or communication system of the aircraft on which it is to be used.

(c) The determination required by paragraph (b)(6) of this section shall be made by that part 119 certificate holder.

Emergency Equipment

Air carriers must be equipped to deal with a number of different emergency situations. For this reason, the carrier must equip the aircraft with the **emergency equipment** listed below (14 CFR 121.309):

- **Hand fire extinguishers** for crew, passenger, cargo, and galley compartments of an approved type in accordance with the following:

  (1) The type and quantity of extinguishing agent must be suitable for the kinds of fires likely to occur in the compartment where the extinguisher is intended to be used and, for passenger compartments, must be designed to minimize the hazard of toxic gas concentrations.
  (2) *Cargo compartments*. At least one hand fire extinguisher must be conveniently located for use in each Class E cargo compartment that is accessible to crewmembers during flight.
  (3) *Galley compartments*. At least one hand fire extinguisher must be conveniently located for use in each galley located in a compartment other than a passenger, cargo, or crew compartment.
  (4) *Flight crew compartment*. At least one hand fire extinguisher must be conveniently located on the flight deck for use by the flightcrew.
  (5) *Passenger compartments*. Hand fire extinguishers for use in passenger compartments must be conveniently located and, when two or more are required, uniformly distributed throughout each compartment. Hand fire extinguishers shall be provided in passenger compartments *[in numbers as shown in the table in 121.309 (c)(5)]*.
  (6) ...*[If there is a galley located in the passenger compartment]* at least one hand fire extinguisher must be conveniently located and easily accessible for use in the galley.
  (7) At least two of the required hand fire extinguishers installed in passenger-carrying airplanes must contain Halon 1211 or equivalent as the extinguishing agent. At least one hand fire extinguisher in the passenger compartment must contain Halon 1211 or equivalent.

(14 CFR §121.309)

- **Crash ax**.
- **Portable battery-powered megaphones**. There must be one megaphone on each airplane with a seating capacity of more than 60 and less than 100 passengers, and two megaphones in the passenger cabin on each airplane with a seating capacity of more than 99 passengers.

Of course it would make no sense to require a carrier to have this emergency equipment unless it was "current," that is, inspected according to the required schedules. Therefore, each item of emergency and flotation equipment listed must be inspected regularly in accordance with inspection periods established in the operations specifications to ensure its condition for continued serviceability and immediate readiness to perform its intended emergency purposes. When carried in a compartment or container, the compartment or container must be marked both as to its contents and as to the date of last inspection.

Additional Emergency Equipment

Chapter 9 covered some of the certification requirements in regard to emergency escape and lighting equipment required for aircraft certification. 14 CFR §121.310 applies requirements specifically to Part 121 carriers. First, if the airplane's emergency exit (other than over the wing) is more than 6 feet from the ground with the airplane on the ground and the landing gear extended, it must have an **approved means to assist the occupants in descending to the ground**. An assisting means that deploys automatically must be armed during taxiing, takeoffs, and landings. If the FAA finds that the design of the exit makes compliance impractical, it may grant a deviation from the requirement of automatic deployment if the assisting means automatically erects upon deployment.

Next, the airplane must have **interior emergency exit markings**. For passenger airplanes, each passenger emergency exit, its means of access, and its means of opening must be conspicuously marked. The identity and location of each passenger emergency exit must be recognizable from a distance equal to the width of the cabin. A sign visible to occupants must indicate the location of each passenger emergency exit approaching along the main passenger aisle. There must be locating signs in the following locations:

(i) Above the aisle near each over-the-wing passenger emergency exit, or at another ceiling location if it is more practical because of low headroom;

(ii) Next to each floor level passenger emergency exit, except that one sign may serve two such exits if they both can be seen readily from that sign; and

(iii) On each bulkhead or divider that prevents fore and aft vision along the passenger cabin, to indicate emergency exits beyond and obscured by it, except that if this is not possible the sign may be placed at another appropriate location.

(14 CFR §121.310[b][1])

No passenger emergency exit shall be more than 60 feet from any adjacent passenger emergency exit on the same side of the same deck of the fuselage, as measured parallel to the airplane's longitudinal axis between the nearest exit edges.

Each passenger-carrying airplane (except for non-transport category airplanes type certificated after December 31, 1964) must have an **emergency lighting system**, *for interior emergency exit markings*. This system must be independent of the main lighting system. The sources of general cabin illumination may be common to both the emergency and the main lighting systems if the power supply to the emergency lighting system is independent of the power supply to the main lighting system.

The emergency lighting system must:

- illuminate each passenger exit marking and locating sign,
- provide a specified level of general lighting in the passenger cabin, and
- include floor proximity emergency escape path marking which meets the requirements of Section 25.812(e).

Emergency light operation: Each emergency light required for interior exit lights or exterior exit lighting must comply with the following:

(i) Be operable manually both from the flightcrew station and, for airplanes on which a flight attendant is required, from a point in the passenger compartment that is readily accessible to a normal flight attendant seat;

(ii) Have a means to prevent inadvertent operation of the manual controls; and

(iii) When armed or turned on at either station, remain lighted or become lighted upon interruption of the airplane's normal electric power.

(14 CFR §121.310[d][1])

These lights must be armed or turned on during taxiing, takeoff, and landing. Each light must provide the required level of illumination for at least 10 minutes at the critical ambient conditions after emergency landing. These lights must have a cockpit control device that has an "on," "off," and "armed" position.

Emergency exit operating handles: For a passenger-carrying airplane for which the application for the type certificate was filed on or after May 1, 1972, the location of each passenger emergency exit operating handle and instructions for opening the exit must be shown in accordance with the requirements under which the airplane was type certificated. On these airplanes, no operating handle or operating handle cover may continue to be used if its luminescence (brightness) decreases to below 100 microlamberts.

Emergency exit access must be provided as follows for each passenger-carrying transport category airplane:

(1) Each passageway passing between individual passenger areas, or leading to a Type I or Type II emergency exit, must be unobstructed and at least 20 inches wide.

(2) For each Type I or Type II emergency exit equipped with an assist means, there must be enough space next to the exit to allow a crewmember to assist in the evacuation of passengers without reducing the unobstructed width of the passageway below that required in paragraph (f)(1) of this section....

(3) There must be access from the main aisle to each Type III and Type IV exit. The access from the aisle to these exits must not be obstructed by seats, berths, or other protrusions in a manner that would reduce the effectiveness of the exit....

(4) If it is necessary to pass through a passageway between passenger compartments to reach any required emergency exit from any seat in the passenger cabin, the passageway must not be obstructed. However, curtains may be used if they allow free entry through the passageway.

(5) No door may be installed in any partition between passenger compartments.

(6) No person may operate an airplane manufactured after November 27, 2006, that incorporates a door installed between any passenger seat occupiable for takeoff and landing and any passenger emergency exit, such that the door crosses any egress path (including aisles, crossaisles and passageways).

(7) If it is necessary to pass through a doorway separating the passenger cabin from other areas to reach a required emergency exit from any passenger seat, the door must have a means to latch it in open position, and the door must be latched open during each takeoff and landing....

(14 CFR §121.310[f])

14 CFR §25.811 and §121.310(g) and (h) discuss the requirements for the placement of additional emergency equipment, exterior markings and exterior emergency lighting.

Exterior exit markings: Each passenger emergency exit and the means of opening that exit from the outside must be marked on the outside of the airplane. There must be a two-inch colored band outlining each passenger emergency exit on the side of the fuselage. Each outside marking, including the band, must be readily distinguishable from the surrounding fuselage area by contrast in color. Exits that are not in the side of the fuselage must have external means of opening and applicable instructions marked conspicuously in red (or, if red is inconspicuous against the background color, in bright chrome yellow). In addition, when the opening means for such an exit is located on only one side of the fuselage, a conspicuous marking to that effect must be provided on the other side.

Exterior emergency lighting: Each passenger-carrying airplane must be equipped with exterior emergency lighting.

Slip resistant escape route: Each passenger-carrying airplane must be equipped with a slip resistant escape route that meets the requirements of Part 25.

Paragraphs 121.310(i), (j), and (k) discuss the requirements for various types of emergency exits.

Floor level exits: Each floor level door or exit in the side of the fuselage (other than those leading into a cargo or baggage compartment that is not accessible from the passenger cabin) that is 44 or more inches high and 20 or more inches wide, but not wider than 46 inches; each passenger ventral exit; and each tail cone exit must meet the requirements of this section for floor level emergency exits.

Additional emergency exits: Approved emergency exits in the passenger compartments in excess of the minimum number of required emergency exits must meet all of the applicable provisions of 14 CFR §121.310 except for the minimum access-way requirements and must be readily accessible.

Ventral exits and tailcone exits: On each large passenger-carrying turbojet-powered airplane, each ventral exit and tailcone exit must be:

- designed and constructed so that it cannot be opened during flight and
- marked with a placard readable from a distance of 30 inches and installed at a conspicuous location near the means of opening the exit, stating that the exit has been designed and constructed so that it cannot be opened during flight.

Portable lights: No person may operate a passenger-carrying airplane unless it is equipped with flashlight stowage provisions accessible from each flight attendant seat.

Seats, Safety Belts, and Shoulder Harnesses

Seats, safety belts, and shoulder harnesses: No person may operate an airplane unless there are available during the takeoff, en route flight, and landing phases of flight an approved seat or berth for each person (over the age of two) on board the airplane. Each person (over the age of two) on board the airplane must have an approved safety belt for his or her separate use. Two people occupying a berth may share one approved safety belt, and two persons occupying a multiple lounge or divan seat may share one approved safety belt during the en route phase of flight only.

Each person on board an air carrier airplane must occupy an approved seat or berth with a separate safety belt properly secured about him or her during movement on the surface, takeoff, and landing. A safety belt provided for the occupant of a seat may not be used by more than one person (over the age of two).

Carriage of infants and children under 2 years of age: A child (under the age of two) may be held by an adult who is occupying an approved seat or berth provided the child does not occupy or use any restraining device. A child under 2 years of age may occupy an approved child restraint system furnished by the certificate holder, a parent, guardian, or attendant designated by the child's parent or guardian to attend to the safety of the child during the flight. The child must be accompanied by a parent, guardian, or attendant designated by the child's parent or guardian. The restraint system must be approved and bear one or more of the following labels:

(A) Seats manufactured to U.S. standards between January 1, 1981, and February 25, 1985, must bear the label: "This child restraint system conforms to all applicable Federal motor vehicle safety standards."
(B) Seats manufactured to U.S. standards on or after February 26, 1985, must bear two labels:
   (1) "This child restraint system conforms to all applicable Federal motor vehicle safety standards"; and
   (2) "THIS RESTRAINT IS CERTIFIED FOR USE IN MOTOR VEHICLES AND AIRCRAFT" in red lettering.
(C) Seats that do not qualify under paragraphs (B)(2)(ii)(A) and (b)(2)(ii)(B) of this section must bear a label or markings showing:
   (1) That the seat was approved by a foreign government;
   (2) That the seat was manufactured under the standards of the United Nations;
   (3) That the seat or child restraint device furnished by the certificate holder was approved by the FAA through Type Certificate or Supplemental Type Certificate; or
   (4) That the seat or child restraint device furnished by the certificate holder [or other approved party has labeling indicating current approval by the FAA or other authorized certification authorities].

(14 CFR §121.311[b][2][ii])

The restraint system must be properly secured to an approved forward-facing seat or berth, the child must be properly secured in the restraint system and must not exceed the specified weight limit for the restraint system, and the restraint system must bear the appropriate label(s). A certificate holder may not allow a child in an aircraft to occupy a booster-type child restraint system, a vest-type child restraint system, a harness-type child restraint system, or a lap held child restraint system during takeoff, landing, or movement on the surface.

Sideward facing seats: Each sideward facing seat must comply with the applicable requirements of Part 25.

No certificate holder may take off or land an airplane unless each passenger seat back is in the upright position. Each passenger shall comply with instructions given by a crewmember in compliance with 14 CFR §121.311(e). An exception is made for persons who are unable to sit erect for a medical reason and are carried in accordance with procedures in the certificate holder's manual if the seat back does not obstruct any passenger's access to the aisle or to any emergency exit. In aircraft that don't require a flight attendant, the certificate holder may take off or land as long as the flight crew instructs each passenger to place his or her seat back in the upright position for takeoff and landing.

Crew seat belts/shoulder harnesses: Part 121 aircraft flight crew seats must be equipped with a combined safety belt and shoulder harness. This harness must meet the applicable requirements specified in Part 25 (except that shoulder harnesses and combined safety belt and shoulder harnesses that were approved and installed before March 6, 1980, may continue to be used).

Flight attendant seats: Each flight attendant that is a required part of the crew must have a seat for takeoff and landing in the passenger compartment that meets the requirements of Part 25. Nonrequired flight attendants placed aboard the aircraft for customer service may occupy a passenger seat.

Each crewmember with a shoulder harness or with a combined safety belt and shoulder harness must have the shoulder harness or combined safety belt and shoulder harness properly secured during takeoff and landing. If a shoulder harness is not combined with a safety belt, it may be unfastened if the occupant cannot perform the required duties with the shoulder harness fastened.

At each unoccupied seat, the safety belt and shoulder harness, if installed, must be secured so as not to interfere with crewmembers in the performance of their duties or with the rapid egress of occupants in an emergency.

Miscellaneous Equipment

As the name suggests, various items of miscellaneous equipment are required by Part 121 (14 CFR §121.313).

(a) If protective fuses are installed on an airplane, the number of spare fuses approved for that airplane and appropriately described in the certificate holder's manual.
(b) A windshield wiper or equivalent for each pilot station.
(c) A power supply and distribution system… [that meets the requirements of Part 25] or that is able to produce and distribute the load for the required instruments and equipment, with use of an external power supply if any one power source or component of the power distribution system fails. The use of common elements in the system may be approved if the Administrator finds that they are designed to be reasonably protected against malfunctioning. Engine-driven sources of energy, when used, must be on separate engines.

(d) A means for indicating the adequacy of the power being supplied to required flight instruments.

(e) Two independent static pressure systems, vented to the outside atmospheric pressure so that they will be least affected by air flow variation or moisture or other foreign matter, and installed so as to be airtight except for the vent. When a means is provided for transferring an instrument from its primary operating system to an alternate system, the means must include a positive positioning control and must be marked to indicate clearly which system is being used.

(14 CFR §121.313)

Following the events September 11, 2001, the FAA mandated improved flightdeck security by making flight deck doors more secure, as well as other operational changes to prevent unauthorized access to the flightdeck on passenger-carrying aircraft and some cargo aircraft. (A complete description of the required security considerations may be found in 14 CFR §25.795.)

(f) A door between the passenger and pilot compartments (i.e., **flightdeck door**), with a locking means to prevent passengers from opening it without the pilot's permission, except that nontransport category airplanes certificated after December 31, 1964, are not required to comply with this paragraph. For airplanes equipped with a crew rest area having separate entries from the flightdeck and the passenger compartment, a door with such a locking means must be provided between the crew rest area and the passenger compartment.

(g) A key for each door that separates a passenger compartment from another compartment that has emergency exit provisions. Except for flightdeck doors, a key must be readily available for each crewmember. Except as provided below, no person other than a person who is assigned to perform duty on the flightdeck may have a key to the flightdeck door. Before April 22, 2003, any crewmember may have a key to the flightdeck door but only if the flightdeck door has an internal flightdeck locking device installed, operative, and in use. Such "internal flightdeck locking device" has to be designed so that it can only be unlocked from inside the flightdeck.

(h) A placard on each door that is the means of access to a required passenger emergency exit, to indicate that it must be open during takeoff and landing.

(i) A means for the crew, in an emergency to unlock each door that leads to a compartment that is normally accessible to passengers and that can be locked by passengers.

(j) After April 9, 2003, for airplanes required by paragraph (f) of this section to have a door between the passenger and pilot or crew rest compartments, and for transport category, all-cargo airplanes that have a door installed between the pilot compartment and any other occupied compartment on January 15, 2002;
   (1) After April 9, 2003, for airplanes required by paragraph (f) of this section to have a door between the passenger and pilot or crew rest compartments,
      (i) Each such door must meet the requirements of §25.795(a)(1) and (2) in effect on January 15, 2002; and
      (ii) Each operator must establish methods to enable a flight attendant to enter the pilot compartment in the event that a flightcrew member becomes incapacitated. Any associated signal or confirmation system must be operable by each flightcrew member from that flightcrew member's duty station.
   (2) After October 1, 2003, for transport category, all-cargo airplanes that had a door installed between the pilot compartment and any other occupied compartment on or after January 15, 2002, each such door must meet the requirements of §25.795(a)(1) and (2) in effect on January 15, 2002; or the operator must implement a security program approved by the Transportation Security Administration (TSA) for the operation of all airplanes in that operator's fleet.

(k) Except for all-cargo operations as defined in §110.2 of this chapter, for all passenger-carrying airplanes that require a lockable flightdeck door in accordance with paragraph (f) of this section, a means to monitor from the flightdeck side of the door the area outside the flightdeck door to identify persons requesting entry and to detect suspicious behavior and potential threats.

(14 CFR §121.313)

Flight Deck Check Procedure

Paragraph 121.315 requires each certificate holder to provide flight crews with an approved **flight deck check** procedure/checklist for each type of aircraft that it operates. The approved procedures must include each item necessary for flight crewmembers to check for safety before starting engines, taking off, or landing, and in engine and systems emergencies. The procedures must be designed so that a flight crewmember will not need to rely upon his or her memory for items to be checked. (Remember this rule when you go for your initial equipment training!) The approved procedures must be readily usable in the cockpit of each aircraft and the flight crew shall follow them when operating the aircraft.

Passenger Information

In accordance with 14 CFR §121.317 and §25.791, each carrier must equip its aircraft with **passenger information signs** regarding no smoking and fastening seat belts. The "Fasten Seat Belt" sign shall be turned on during any movement on the surface, for each takeoff, for each landing, and at any other time considered necessary by the pilot-in-command. Additionally, a "Fasten Seat Belt While Seated" sign must be visible from each passenger seat. If smoking is prohibited, the "No Smoking" passenger information signs must be lighted during the entire flight segment, or one or more "No Smoking" placards must be posted during the entire flight segment. If both the lighted signs and the placards are used, the signs must remain lighted during the entire flight segment. Smoking is prohibited on scheduled flight segments.

Of note, some aircraft manufacturers include an automatic Fasten Seat Belt sign selection. When the flight crew selects the automatic function, the Fasten Seat Belt signs turn on or off automatically with reference to cabin altitude, flap position, landing gear configuration and passenger oxygen use. Some aircraft even come equipped with an automatic pre-recorded "Please fasten your seat belt" audio message that plays over the cabin PA system every time the Fasten Seat Belt sign is selected on or comes on automatically.

A sign must be placed in each lavatory that reads: "Federal law provides for a penalty of up to $2,000 for tampering with the smoke detector installed in this lavatory." Not surprisingly, no person may smoke in any airplane lavatory nor may any person tamper with, disable, or destroy any smoke detector installed in any airplane lavatory.

Public Address System

Airplanes with a seating capacity of more than 19 passengers are required by 14 CFR §121.318 to be equipped with a **public address system** (PA) that is capable of operation independent of the required crewmember interphone system (except for handsets, headsets, microphones, selector switches, and signaling devices). The PA system must be accessible for immediate use from each of two flight crewmember stations in the pilot compartment. For each required floor-level passenger emergency exit that has an adjacent flight attendant seat, there must be a microphone that is readily accessible to the seated flight attendant. One microphone may serve more than one exit, provided the proximity of the exits allows unassisted verbal communication between seated flight attendants. The PA must be capable of being operated within 10 seconds by a flight attendant at each position in the passenger compartment where it is accessible.

Crewmember Interphone System

14 CFR §121.319 requires aircraft with more than 19 passenger seats to be equipped with a **crewmember interphone system** that is capable of operation independent of the public address system. The interphone system must provide a means of two-way communication between the pilot compartment and each passenger compartment and between the pilot compartment and each galley located on other than the main passenger deck level. It must be accessible for immediate use by flight crewmembers and from at least one normal flight attendant station in each passenger compartment. Like the PA system, it must be capable of operation within 10 seconds by a flight attendant at those positions from which its use is accessible.

Large turbojet-powered airplanes have additional interphone requirements. The interphone system must be accessible for use at enough flight attendant stations so that all floor-level emergency exits (or entryways to those exits in the case of exits located within galleys) in each passenger compartment are observable from one or more of the positions equipped with an interphone. It must have an alerting system incorporating aural or visual signals for use by flight crewmembers to alert flight attendants and for use by flight attendants to alert flight crewmembers. The alerting system must have a means for the recipient of a call to determine whether it is a normal call or an emergency call. When the airplane is on the ground, it must provide a means of two-way communication between ground personnel and either of at least two flight crewmembers in the pilot compartment. The interphone system station for use by ground personnel must be located so that personnel using the system may avoid visible detection from within the airplane.

Operations in Icing

No person may operate an airplane with a certificated maximum takeoff weight less than 60,000 pounds in conditions conducive to airframe icing unless it complies with the following equipment requirements:

(1) The airplane must be equipped with a certificated **primary airframe ice detection system**.
 (i) The airframe ice protection system must be activated automatically, or manually by the flightcrew, when the primary ice detection system indicates activation is necessary.
 (ii) When the airframe ice protection system is activated, any other procedures in the Airplane Flight Manual for operating in icing conditions must be initiated.
(2) Visual cues of the first sign of ice formation anywhere on the airplane and a certificated advisory airframe ice detection system must be provided.
 (i) The airframe ice protection system must be activated when any of the visual cues are observed or when the advisory airframe ice detection system indicates activation is necessary, whichever occurs first.
 (ii) When the airframe ice protection system is activated, any other procedures in the Airplane Flight Manual for operating in icing conditions must be initiated.

(14 CFR §121.321)

If the airplane is not equipped to comply with the provisions of the first part of this section, then when operating in icing conditions, the airframe ice protection system must be activated prior to, and operated during, critical phases of flight such as takeoff, climbing maneuvers, holding, and approach and landings. During other phases of flight, the flight crew must activate and operate the airframe ice protection system at the first sign of ice formation anywhere on the airplane in accordance with aircraft flight manual guidance.

Instruments and Equipment for Operations at Night

To conduct **operations at night** under Part 121, an airplane must be equipped with the following additional instruments and equipment:

(a) Position lights.
(b) An anti-collision light.
(c) Two landing lights…
(d) Instrument lights providing enough light to make each required instrument, switch, or similar instrument, easily readable and installed so that the direct rays are shielded from the flight crewmembers' eyes and so that no objectionable reflections are visible to them…
(e) An airspeed-indicating system with heated pitot tube or equivalent means for preventing malfunctioning due to icing.
(f) A sensitive altimeter.

(14 CFR §121.323)

The specifics of the type of exterior and interior lighting, color specifications, distribution and intensities may be found in 14 CFR §§25.1381–25.1401.

Instruments and Equipment for Operations under IFR or Over-the-Top

Operations under IFR: For IFR operations, the aircraft must be equipped with the following instruments and equipment in addition to all previously mentioned equipment except the required night operations equipment:

(a) An airspeed indicating system with heated pitot tube or equivalent means for preventing malfunctioning due to icing.
(b) A sensitive altimeter.
(c) Instrument lights providing enough light to make each required instrument, switch, or similar instrument, easily readable…

(14 CFR §121.325)

Supplemental Oxygen for Sustenance: Turbine Engine Powered Airplanes

14 CFR §121.329, **supplemental oxygen for sustenance**, covers the oxygen requirements for continuing operations in an unpressurized or partially pressurized airplane. Turbine engine powered airplanes must be equipped with oxygen and dispensing equipment. The amount of oxygen to be provided depends on the person, the altitude, and the time spent at that altitude.

Crewmember Oxygen

Above cabin pressure altitudes of 10,000 feet, flight deck crewmembers must be provided with and use oxygen. At cabin pressure altitudes above 10,000 feet, up to and including 12,000 feet, oxygen must be provided for other crewmembers for the portion of the flight at those altitudes in excess of 30 minutes duration. At cabin pressure altitudes above 12,000 feet, oxygen must be provided for and used by each member of the flight crew on flight deck duty, and must be provided for other crewmembers during the entire flight at those altitudes. When a flight crewmember is required to use oxygen, he or she must use it continuously except when necessary to remove the oxygen mask or other dispenser in connection with his or her regular duties. Standby crewmembers that are on call or are definitely going to have flight deck duty before completing the flight must be provided with an amount of supplemental oxygen equal to that provided for crewmembers who are on duty other than on flight duty. If a standby crewmember is not on call and will not be on flight deck duty during the remainder of the flight, that crewmember is considered to be a passenger for the purposes of supplemental oxygen requirements.

Passenger Oxygen

From 10,001 feet up to and including 14,000 feet, 10 percent of the passengers must be supplied oxygen for that part of the flight that exceeds 30 minutes duration (at those altitudes). For flights at cabin pressure altitudes from 14,001 feet up to and including 15,000 feet, enough oxygen must be supplied for that part of the flight at those altitudes for 30 percent of the passengers. For flights at cabin pressure altitudes above 15,000 feet, enough oxygen must be provided for each passenger carried during the entire flight at those altitudes.

Other Considerations

In determining how much sustaining and first aid oxygen is required for a particular operation, the cabin pressure altitudes, the flight duration, and the operating procedures of the carrier will be considered. In pressurized airplanes, the assumption is made that a cabin pressurization failure will occur at the altitude or point of flight that is most critical from the standpoint of oxygen need. After the failure, the airplane will descend in accordance with the emergency procedures specified in the airplane flight manual without exceeding its operating limitations. It will descend to a flight altitude that will allow successful termination of the flight. Following the failure, the cabin pressure altitude is considered to be the same as the flight altitude unless it is shown that no probable failure of the cabin or pressurization equipment will result in a cabin pressure altitude equal to the flight altitude. Under those circumstances, the maximum cabin pressure altitude attained may be used as a basis for certification or determination of oxygen supply or both.

Supplemental Oxygen for Emergency Descent and for First Aid; Turbine Engine Powered Airplanes with Pressurized Cabins

This rule on supplemental oxygen for emergency descent and first aid provides for an emergency descent after a loss of pressurization.

Crewmember Oxygen

In the event of a cabin pressurization failure at flight altitudes above 10,000 feet, crewmembers must be supplied enough oxygen to comply with 14 CFR §121.329, but not less than a two-hour supply for each flight crewmember on flight deck duty. The required two-hour supply is that quantity of oxygen necessary for a constant rate of descent from the airplane's maximum certificated operating altitude to 10,000 feet in 10 minutes, followed by 110 minutes at 10,000 feet. The oxygen required for protective breathing equipment (PBE) may be included in determining the supply required for flight crewmembers on flight deck duty.

When operating at flight altitudes above flight level 250, each flight crewmember on flight deck duty must be provided with an oxygen mask that can be rapidly placed on his or her face from its ready position, properly secured, sealed, and supplying oxygen upon demand. It must be designed so that after being placed on the face, it does not prevent immediate communication between the flight crewmember and other crewmembers over the airplane intercommunication system. When it is not being used at flight altitudes above flight level 250, the oxygen mask must be kept ready for use and located so as to be within the immediate reach of the flight crewmember while at his or her duty station.

Unless each flight crewmember on flight deck duty has a quick-donning type of oxygen mask, when operating at flight altitudes above flight level 250, one pilot at the controls of the airplane must wear and use an oxygen mask at all times. It must be secured, sealed, and supplying oxygen. If both pilots have quick-donning type masks, neither pilot needs to wear an oxygen mask at or below the following flight levels:

(A) For airplanes having a passenger seat configuration of more than 30 seats, excluding any required crewmember seat, or a payload capacity of more than 7,500 pounds, at or below flight level 410.
(B) For airplanes having a passenger seat configuration of less than 31 seats, excluding any required crewmember seat, and a payload capacity of 7,500 pounds or less, at or below flight level 350.

(14 CFR §121.333[c][2][i])

Whenever a quick-donning type of oxygen mask is to be used, the carrier must show that the mask can be put on without disturbing eyeglasses and without delaying the flight crewmember from proceeding with his or her assigned emergency duties. After being put on, the oxygen mask must not prevent immediate communication between the flight crewmember and other crewmembers over the airplane intercommunication system.

If for any reason at any time it is necessary for one pilot to leave his or her station at the controls of the airplane when operating at flight altitudes above flight level 250, the remaining pilot at the controls shall put on and use his or her oxygen mask until the other pilot has returned to his or her duty station.

Before the takeoff of a flight, each flight crewmember must personally preflight his or her oxygen equipment to ensure that the oxygen mask is functioning, fitted properly, and connected to appropriate supply terminals and that the oxygen supply and pressure are adequate for use.

Each flight attendant shall, during flight above flight level 250, carry portable oxygen equipment with at least a 15-minute supply of oxygen. This is not required if it is shown that enough portable oxygen units with masks or spare outlets and masks are distributed throughout the cabin to ensure immediate availability of oxygen to all flight attendants, regardless of their location at the time of cabin depressurization.

Passenger Oxygen

When the airplane is operating at flight altitudes above 10,000 feet, emergency oxygen must be provided for the use of passenger cabin occupants. First consider airplanes certificated to operate at flight altitudes up to and including flight level 250. If an airplane can (at any point along the route to be flown) descend safely to a flight altitude of 14,000 feet or less within four minutes, oxygen must be available for a 30-minute period for at least 10 percent of the passenger cabin occupants. If an airplane is operated at flight altitudes up to and including flight level 250 and cannot descend safely to a flight altitude of 14,000 feet within four minutes, or when an airplane is operated at flight altitudes above flight level 250, oxygen must be available for at least 10 percent of the passenger cabin occupants for the entire flight after cabin depressurization, at cabin pressure altitudes above 10,000 feet up to and including 14,000 feet and, as applicable, to allow compliance with Section 121.329. There must be not less than a 10-minute supply for the passenger cabin occupants.

For first aid treatment of occupants who, for physiological reasons, might require undiluted oxygen following descent from cabin pressure altitudes above flight level 250, a supply of oxygen must be provided for two percent of the occupants for the entire flight after depressurization. An appropriate number of acceptable dispensing units, but in no case less than two, must be provided, with a means for the cabin attendants to use this supply.

Before a flight is operated above flight level 250, a crewmember must instruct the passengers on the necessity of using oxygen in the event of cabin depressurization and shall point out to them the location and demonstrate the use of the oxygen dispensing equipment.

Equipment Standards (Oxygen Equipment)

With minor exceptions, operators of turbine engine powered airplanes are required by 14 CFR §121.335 to show that the oxygen apparatus, the minimum rate of oxygen flow, and the supply of oxygen necessary to comply with Sections 121.329 and 121.333 meet the standards established in Section 4b.651 of the Civil Air Regulations as in effect on September 1, 1958. 14 CFR §25.1443 gives specific minimum oxygen mass flow rates measured in liters per minute with a corresponding pressure measured in millimeters of mercury (mmHg).

Protective Breathing Equipment

Operators of air carrier aircraft must furnish approved **protective breathing equipment (PBE)** to their flight crews. Protective breathing equipment with a fixed or portable breathing gas supply must be conveniently located on the flight deck and be easily accessible for immediate use by each required flight crewmember at his or her assigned duty station. In addition, PBE will be located at other points in the cabin. This equipment protects crewmembers from the effects of smoke, carbon dioxide, or other harmful gases or an oxygen-deficient environment caused by something other than an airplane depressurization. It must protect crewmembers from these effects while they combat fires on board the airplane.

This equipment is typically in the form of a "smoke hood" or device that covers the entire head and shoulders of the crewmember. That part of the equipment protecting the eyes can't impair the wearer's vision to the extent that a crewmember's duties cannot be performed. The hood must allow corrective glasses to be worn without impairment of vision or loss of protection. In addition to protecting the crew from smoke and other gases, the hood must allow at least two flight crewmembers to communicate using the airplane radio equipment and to communicate by interphone with each other and at least one flight attendant station while at their assigned duty stations. The PBE or smoke hood may also be used to meet the supplemental oxygen requirements for the flight crew. Protective breathing gas duration and supply system equipment requirements are as follows:

(i) The equipment must supply breathing gas for 15 minutes at a pressure altitude of 8,000 feet for the following:
   (A) Flight crewmembers while performing flight deck duties; and
   (B) Crewmembers while combating an in-flight fire.
(ii) The breathing gas system must be free from hazards in itself, in its method of operation, and in its effect upon other components.
(iii) For breathing gas systems other than chemical oxygen generators, there must be a means to allow the crew to readily determine, during the equipment preflight..., that the gas supply is fully charged.
(iv) For each chemical oxygen generator, the supply system equipment must [deliver the required oxygen flow and contain cautions regarding excess heat generation].

(14 CFR §121.337[b][7])

One PBE is required for each hand fire extinguisher located for use in a galley other than a galley located in a passenger, cargo, or crew compartment. One PBE must be located on the flight deck, except that the Administrator may authorize another location for this PBE if special circumstances exist that make compliance impractical. There must be a PBE in each passenger compartment, one for each hand fire extinguisher required by 14 CFR §121.309 and §25.1439, to be located within three feet of each required hand fire extinguisher (or other location as allowed by the FAA).

Flight crewmembers must perform a preflight inspection of their PBE. In addition, each item of PBE located at other than a flight crewmember duty station must be checked by a designated crewmember to ensure that each is properly stowed and serviceable, and, for other than chemical oxygen generator systems, the breathing gas supply is fully charged. Each certificate holder must designate in its operations manual at least one crewmember to perform those checks before taking off in that airplane for his or her first flight of the day.

Emergency Equipment for Extended Overwater Operations

Unless otherwise authorized by the FAA, a carrier may not operate an airplane in **extended overwater operations** without having the following emergency equipment on the airplane:

(1) A life preserver equipped with an approved survivor locator light, for each occupant of the airplane.
(2) Enough life rafts (each equipped with an approved survivor locator light) of a rated capacity and buoyancy to accommodate the occupants of the airplane. Unless excess rafts of enough capacity are provided, the buoyancy and seating capacity beyond the rated capacity of the rafts must accommodate all occupants of the airplane in the event of a loss of one raft of the largest rated capacity.
(3) At least one pyrotechnic signaling device for each life raft.
(4) An approved survival type emergency locator transmitter....

(14 CFR §121.339[a])

In addition, according to Paragraph 121.339(c):

(c) A survival kit, appropriately equipped for the route to be flown, must be attached to each required life raft.

Batteries used in the emergency locator transmitter must be replaced (or recharged, if the battery is rechargeable) when the transmitter has been in use for more than one cumulative hour or when 50 percent of their useful life (or for rechargeable batteries, 50 percent of their useful life of charge) has expired, as established by the transmitter manufacturer under its approval. The new expiration date for replacing (or recharging) the battery must be legibly marked on the outside of the transmitter. The battery useful life (or useful life of charge) requirements of this paragraph do not apply to batteries (such as water-activated batteries) that are essentially unaffected during probable storage intervals.

The required life rafts, life preservers, and survival type emergency locator transmitter must be stored in compartments that protect the equipment from inadvertent damage and be easily accessible in the event of a ditching without appreciable time for preparation. This equipment must be installed in conspicuously marked, approved locations. Additionally, life rafts are required to have a trailing line and static line designed to hold the raft near the airplane and must have a way for the line to be released in the event the aircraft becomes submerged.

Emergency Flotation Means

Unless the FAA approves the operation of an airplane over water without life preservers or **emergency flotation means**, a carrier is prohibited by 14 CFR §121.340 from operating an airplane in any overwater operation unless it is equipped with a FAA-approved life preserver for each occupant. This life preserver must be within easy reach of each seated occupant and must be readily removable from the airplane.

Equipment for Operations in Icing Conditions

Unless an airplane is type certificated under the transport category airworthiness requirements relating to ice protection, a carrier is prohibited by 14 CFR §121.341 from operating an airplane in icing conditions without appropriate **equipment for operations in icing conditions**. This equipment must provide means for the prevention or removal of ice on windshields, wings, empennage, propellers, and other parts of the airplane where ice formation will adversely affect the safety of the airplane. At night, means must be provided for illuminating or otherwise determining the formation of ice on the parts of the wings that are critical from the standpoint of ice accumulation. Any illumination device that is used must be of a type that will not cause glare or reflection that would handicap crewmembers in the performance of their duties.

Pitot Heat Indication Systems

In accordance with 14 CFR §121.342, a carrier may not operate a transport category airplane or, after December 20, 1999, a nontransport category airplane type certificated after December 31, 1964, that is equipped with a flight instrument **pitot heating system** unless the airplane is also equipped with an operable pitot heat indication system.

A pitot heat indicating system warns the flight crew when the pitot heating system is not operating. In order to comply with Section 25, the indication must incorporate an amber light or something equivalent that is in clear view of a flight crewmember.

The indication provided must be designed to alert the flight crew if either of the following conditions exist:

(1) The pitot heating system is switched "off".
(2) The pitot heating system is switched "on" and any pitot tube heating element is inoperative.

(14 CFR §25.1326)

Flight Data Recorders

Aircraft certificated for operations above 25,000 feet altitude or turbine engine powered aircraft are required by 14 CFR §§121.343, 121.344, and 121.346 to be equipped with one or more approved **flight data recorders (FDR and DFDR)**. As we saw earlier, these are required to assist the NTSB in performing accident/incident investigations of air carrier aircraft. Over the years, the flight data recorders have been developed and expanded from recorders that record perhaps as few as six variables in an analog medium to modern recorders that digitally record several hundred parameters. Modern air carrier aircraft (manufactured since May 1989) must have digital flight data recorders (DFDR) and record as many as 88 parameters.

The flight data recorder must be operated continuously from the instant the airplane begins its takeoff roll until it has completed the landing roll at an airport. The recorded data must be kept until the airplane has been operated for at least 25 hours of operating time. Each flight recorder must have an approved device to assist in locating that recorder under water. A total of one hour of recorded data may be erased for the purpose of testing the flight recorder or the flight recorder system. Any erasure made in accordance with this paragraph must be of the oldest recorded data accumulated at the time of testing. In the event of an accident or occurrence that requires immediate notification of the National Transportation Safety Board and that results in termination of the flight, the carrier shall remove the recording media from the airplane and keep the recorded data for at least 60 days (or for a longer period upon the request of the NTSB or the FAA).

Radio Equipment

Air carrier aircraft are required by 14 CFR §121.345 to be equipped with radio equipment required for the kind of operation being conducted. Where two independent (separate and complete) radio systems are required, each system must have an independent antenna installation except that, where rigidly supported non-wire antennas or other antenna installations of equivalent reliability are used, only one antenna is required.

Radio Equipment for Operations under VFR over Routes Navigated by Pilotage

Operations under VFR: The minimum radio equipment requirements for aircraft flown under VFR state that the communications equipment must be able to:

(1) Communicate with at least one appropriate ground station from any point on the route;
(2) Communicate with appropriate traffic control facilities from any point within Class B, C, D, or E airspace, and
(3) Receive meteorological information from any point en route by either of two independent systems....

(14 CFR §121.347[a])

If the airplane is to be flown under VFR at night, then it requires the radio equipment necessary to receive navigational signals applicable to the route to be flown. A marker or ILS receiver is not required.

Communication and Navigation for Operations under VFR over Routes Not Navigated by Pilotage or for Operations under IFR or Over-the-Top

For **operations under IFR**, the enroute navigation aids necessary along the route of flight from departure, en route and arrival (including missed approach) must be available and suitable for use by the aircraft navigation systems required by 14 CFR §121.349. The aircraft must be equipped with the radio equipment necessary to fulfill the functions required for VFR operations and to receive satisfactorily, by either of two independent systems, radio navigational signals from all primary enroute and approach navigational facilities intended to be used. Only one marker beacon receiver providing visual and aural signals and one ILS receiver need to be provided and any RNAV system used to meet the navigation equipment requirements of this section is authorized in the certificate holder's operations specifications.

Any aircraft operating under IFR must have at least two independent communications systems required by 14 CFR §121.347 and one of these radios must have two-way voice communication capability.

If VOR navigation equipment is to be used to comply with 14 CFR §121.349, the aircraft must be equipped with at least one approved DME or suitable RNAV system. An airplane may be equipped with a single independent navigation system suitable for navigating the airplane along the route to be flown within the degree of accuracy required for ATC if:

(1) It can be shown that the airplane is equipped with at least one other independent navigation system suitable, in the event of loss of the navigation capability of the single independent navigation system permitted by this paragraph at any point along the route, for proceeding safely to a suitable airport and completing an instrument approach; and
(2) The airplane has sufficient fuel so that the flight may proceed safely to a suitable airport by use of the remaining navigation system, and complete an instrument approach and land.

(14 CFR §121.349[c])

Carriers operating airplanes having a configuration of 10 to 30 passenger seats and a payload of 7,500 pounds or less in IFR or in extended overwater operations must have, in addition to any other required radio communications and navigational equipment, facilities to communicate with at least one ground facility. The aircraft must be equipped with at least:

1. two microphones and
2. two headsets, or one headset and one speaker.

Radio Equipment for Extended Overwater Operations and for Certain Other Operations

When the aircraft is used for **extended overwater operations**, it is required by 14 CFR §121.351 to be equipped with at least two independent long-range navigation systems and at least two independent long-range communication systems necessary under normal operating conditions to communicate with any station along the intended route. The airplane must also be equipped to receive meteorological information from any point on the route by either of the two independent communication systems, and at least one of the communication systems must have two-way voice communication capability.

The FAA may also require that this same combination of equipment be installed for flag or supplemental operations or for domestic operations within the state of Alaska. This would be required if the FAA finds that equipment is necessary for search and rescue operations because of the nature of the terrain to be flown over.

If the carrier has installed and uses a single long-range navigation system (LRNS) and a single long-range communications system (LRCS), it may be authorized by the FAA to use this equipment in lieu of the dual long-range systems mentioned above. This relief provision will apply to operations and routes in certain geographic areas. The following are among the operational factors the FAA may consider in granting this relief authorization:

(1) The ability of the flight crew to navigate the airplane along the route within the degree of accuracy required by ATC,
(2) The length of the route being flown, and
(3) The duration of the very high frequency communications gap.

(14 CFR §121.351[c])

Emergency Equipment for Operations over Uninhabited Terrain Areas: Flag, Supplemental, and Certain Domestic Operations

Operations over uninhabited terrain: Flag or supplemental operations and domestic operations within the states of Alaska or Hawaii over an uninhabited area or any other area that the FAA specifies in the carrier's **operations specifications** (Ops Specs) must use aircraft that have the following required equipment for search and rescue in case of an emergency:

(a) Suitable pyrotechnic signaling devices *[flares]*.
(b) An approved survival type emergency locator transmitter. Batteries used in this transmitter must be replaced (or recharged, if the battery is rechargeable) when the transmitter has been in use for more than 1 cumulative hour, or when 50 percent of their useful life (or for rechargeable batteries, 50 percent of their useful life of charge) has expired, as established by the transmitter manufacturer under its approval....
(c) Enough survival kits, appropriately equipped for the route to be flown for the number of occupants of the airplane.

(14 CFR §121.353)

Terrain Awareness and Warning System

Terrain awareness and warning system (TAWS) is a warning system designed to prevent controlled flight into terrain (CFIT). TAWS is a relatively new term used inclusively to describe older ground proximity warning systems (GPWS) and enhanced ground proximity warning systems (EGPWS), as well as newer terrain awareness and warning systems. The following sections of 14 CFR Parts 91, 121 and 135 require TAWS:

- 14 CFR §91.223 states that no person may operate a turbine-powered, U.S.-registered airplane configured with 6 or more passenger seats, excluding any pilot seat, unless that airplane is equipped with an approved terrain awareness and warning system that meets the requirements of Class B equipment in TSO-C151a.
- 14 CFR §121.354 states that no person may operate a turbine-powered airplane unless that airplane is equipped with an approved terrain awareness and warning system, including a terrain awareness display, that meets the requirements for Class A equipment in TSO-C151a.
- 14 CFR §135.154 states that no person may operate a turbine-powered U.S.-registered airplane configured with 6 to 9 passenger seats, excluding any pilot seat, unless that airplane is equipped with an approved terrain awareness and warning system that meets the requirements of Class B equipment in TSO-C151a.

Again, Part 121 turbine-powered aircraft must be equipped with an approved terrain awareness and warning system. This system must include an approved terrain situational awareness display. The airplane flight manual must contain the flight crew procedures for the use of the terrain awareness and warning system and the proper flight crew reaction in response to a TAWS audio and visual warning. As we've seen in Sections 91.223, 121.354 and 135.154, there are currently two levels of TAWS systems: Class A for Part 121, and Class B for Part 91 and Part 135 operations. FAA Advisory Circular 25-23, *Airworthiness Criteria for the Installation Approval of a Terrain Awareness and Warning System (TAWS) for Part 25 Airplanes*, details the differences between each class:

Class A TAWS Equipment

1. As a minimum, it will provide alerts for the following circumstances
   - Reduced required terrain clearance
   - Imminent terrain impact
   - Premature descent
   - Excessive rates of descent
   - Excessive closure rate to terrain
   - Negative climb rate or altitude loss after take-off
   - Flight into terrain when not in landing configuration
   - Excessive downward deviation from an ILS glideslope
   - Descent of the airplane to 500 feet above the terrain or nearest runway elevation (voice callout "Five Hundred") during a non-precision approach
2. This class of TAWS equipment also must provide a terrain awareness display of the surrounding terrain and/or obstacles relative to the airplane. See TSO C151a.

Class B TAWS Equipment

1. As a minimum, it will provide alerts for the following circumstances
   - Reduced required terrain clearance
   - Imminent terrain impact
   - Premature descent
   - Excessive rates of descent
   - Negative climb rate or altitude loss after take-off
   - Descent of the airplane to 500 feet above the terrain or nearest runway elevation (voice callout "Five Hundred") during a non-precision approach
2. This class of TAWS equipment does not require a terrain awareness display of the surrounding terrain and/or obstacles relative to the airplane

Equipment for Operations on Which Specialized Means of Navigation Are Used

There is equipment required when **specialized means of navigation** are used. Many aircraft operating over oceans or large unsettled areas where ground-based navigation signals are not available rely on specialized navigation systems such as inertial navigation systems (INS), or in some older aircraft, Doppler radar navigation. 14 CFR §121.355 prohibits air carriers from conducting these operations using Doppler radar or an inertial navigation system outside the 48 contiguous states and the District of Columbia unless such systems have been approved. For use of these systems within the 48 contiguous states and the District of Columbia, any specialized means of navigation must be shown to be an adequate airborne system for the specialized navigation authorized for the particular operation.

Traffic Alert and Collision Avoidance System

All turbine-powered aircraft that have a maximum certificated takeoff weight of more than 33,000 pounds are required by 14 CFR §121.356 to be equipped with an approved **traffic alert and collision avoidance system II (TCAS II)** and the appropriate class of Mode S transponder. This equipment provides traffic alerts (TAs) of conflicting traffic. In case of a collision threat, it also issues resolution advisories (RAs) that give the crew specific guidance as to the maneuvers required to avoid collision.

In addition, no one may operate a passenger or combination cargo/passenger (combi) airplane that has a passenger seat configuration of 10 to 30 seats unless it is equipped with an approved traffic alert and collision avoidance system.

Airborne Weather Radar Equipment Requirements

Air carrier aircraft (other than those operating solely within Alaska, Hawaii, and parts of Canada) are required by 14 CFR §121.357 to have an approved **airborne weather radar** unit installed in the aircraft. The following must be complied with when operating the radar:

(1) No person may dispatch an airplane…under IFR or night VFR conditions when current weather reports indicate that thunderstorms, or other potentially hazardous weather conditions that can be detected with airborne weather radar, may reasonably be expected along the route to be flown, unless the airborne weather radar equipment is in satisfactory operating condition.

(2) If the airborne weather radar becomes inoperative en route, the airplane must be operated in accordance with the approved instructions and procedures specified in the operations manual for such an event.

(14 CFR §121.357[c])

Low-Altitude Windshear System Equipment Requirements

Low-altitude windshear system: There have been a number of serious, fatal air carrier accidents resulting from wind shear. Technology has become available to allow the hazardous conditions to be detected and for warnings of wind shear danger to be issued. Newer aircraft (airplanes manufactured after January 2, 1991) and specific models of older airplanes (those manufactured before January 3, 1991) are required by 14 CFR §121.358 to be equipped with either an approved airborne wind shear warning and flight guidance system, an approved airborne detection and avoidance system, or an approved combination of these systems. As a minimum requirement, all other turbine-powered (excluding turboprop) airplanes that are not specifically listed must be equipped with an approved airborne wind shear warning system. These airplanes may be equipped with an approved airborne wind shear detection and avoidance system, or an approved combination of these systems.

Cockpit Voice Recorders

The FAA has for many years required, in 14 CFR §121.359, air carrier and turbine aircraft to be equipped with **cockpit voice recorders (CVRs)**. These devices record the words of each flight crewmember, the radio communications (including datalink), and the general ambient cockpit noise and speech. They have been invaluable in assisting in accident investigations. However, their appearance in the commercial airline cockpits was not without debate. There was a widespread resentment among pilots of the "spying" or monitoring of all communications, and as a result, the use of the cockpit voice recorder has been limited by union contracts. In most airlines, the recorders may only be "read out" in the event of a reportable accident or incident. The CVR must be operated continuously from the start of the use of the checklist (before starting engines for the purpose of flight) to completion of the final checklist at the termination of the flight. At the conclusion of a "routine" flight, the crew usually has the right to erase the recording. Like the FDR, the CVR must be either bright orange or bright yellow and have reflective tape affixed to the external surface to facilitate its location under water. It must have an approved underwater locating device on or adjacent to the container that is secured in such a manner that they are not likely to be separated during crash impact. The recorder must record information for at least two hours. Earlier information may be erased or otherwise obliterated. 14 CFR §25.1457 details exactly what must be recorded:

(a) Each cockpit voice recorder required by the operating rules of this chapter must be approved and must be installed so that it will record the following:
   (1) Voice communications transmitted from or received in the airplane by radio.
   (2) Voice communications of flight crewmembers on the flight deck.
   (3) Voice communications of flight crewmembers on the flight deck, using the airplane's interphone system.
   (4) Voice or audio signals identifying navigation or approach aids introduced into a headset or speaker.
   (5) Voice communications of flight crewmembers using the passenger loudspeaker system, if there is such a system and if the fourth channel is available in accordance with the requirements of paragraph (c)(4)(ii) of this section.
   (6) If datalink communication equipment is installed, all datalink communications, using an approved data message set. Datalink messages must be recorded as the output signal from the communications unit that translates the signal into usable data.

(14 CFR §25.1457)

Summary

Transport category aircraft used in Part 121 air carrier operations have extensive requirements for the equipment and instruments that must be installed. We have not covered many of these requirements that are familiar to the reader from previous training. This list would include items such as attitude indicators, heading indicators, and airspeed indicators. Rather, we have gone through the list unique to Part 121 and provided an indication of the specialized equipment that must be carried by Part 121 carriers.

In the next chapter, we will examine the dispatching and flight release rules found in 14 CFR Part 121, Subpart U.

Important Terms in Chapter 10

additional emergency exits
airborne weather radar
approved means to assist the occupants in descending to the ground
carriage of infants and children under 2 years of age
cockpit check procedure/checklist
cockpit voice recorders (CVRs)
crew seat belts/shoulder harnesses
crewmember interphone system
crewmember oxygen
emergency equipment
emergency equipment: extended overwater operations
emergency equipment: operations over uninhabited terrain
emergency exit access
emergency exit operating handles
emergency flotation means
emergency light operation
emergency lighting system
equipment for operations in icing conditions
extended overwater operations
exterior emergency lighting
exterior exit markings
flight and navigational equipment
flight attendant seats
flight data recorders (FDR and DFDR)
flightdeck door
floor level exits
hand fire extinguishers
interior emergency exit markings
low-altitude windshear system
operations at night
operations over uninhabited terrain
operations under IFR
passenger oxygen
pitot heating system
portable electronic device (PED)
portable lights
primary airframe ice detection system
protective breathing equipment (PBE)
public address (PA) system
seats, safety belts, and shoulder harnesses
sideward facing seats
slip resistant escape route
specialized means of navigation
supplemental oxygen for sustenance
terrain awareness and warning system (TAWS)
traffic alert and collision avoidance system (TCAS II)
ventral exits and tailcone exits

Chapter 10 Exam

1. The rule requiring all required, installed equipment to be operative is violated when
   a. the aircraft is started.
   b. the aircraft is taxied.
   c. the aircraft takes off.
   d. the aircraft lands.

2. In passenger-carrying airplanes, at least two of the fire extinguishers must
   a. be of the Halon 1211 (or equivalent) type.
   b. be of the CO_2 type.
   c. be of the water/pressure type.
   d. be of the dry chemical type.

3. In considering the need for escape slides or similar evacuation means, the aircraft is assumed to be
   a. on the ground with collapsed landing gear.
   b. on the ground with a single collapsed landing gear.
   c. on the ground with the nose gear collapsed.
   d. on the ground with all landing gear extended.

4. Emergency lighting for interior or exterior use must be able to be controlled at
   a. the flight crew's station in the cockpit.
   b. a position in the passenger compartment.
   c. both (a) and (b).
   d. neither (a) nor (b) is correct.

5. During ground operations, it is
   a. suggested, but not required, that each passenger be seated with his seat belt fastened.
   b. required that each passenger be seated and belts fastened only when taking the runway.
   c. required that each passenger be seated and belts fastened only when taking off.
   d. required that each passenger be seated and belts fastened during all movement on the surface.

6. The crew uses checklist procedures that are provided by the
   a. FAA.
   b. manufacturer of the aircraft.
   c. operator of the aircraft.
   d. pilots union.

7. Flight crewmembers must be provided and use oxygen when
   a. the cabin pressure altitude exceeds 10,000 feet.
   b. the cabin pressure altitude exceeds 12,500 feet.
   c. the cabin pressure altitude exceeds 14,000 feet.
   d. the cabin pressure altitude exceeds 15,000 feet.

8. If one pilot leaves his station at the controls, it is necessary for the other pilot to don his or her oxygen mask if the aircraft is above
   a. 12,500 feet.
   b. flight level 250.
   c. flight level 350.
   d. flight level 410.

9. In the event of cabin pressurization failure, each flight crewmember must be provided with oxygen that allows for a total of
   a. 10 minutes operation allowing descent to 10,000 feet altitude.
   b. 110 minutes total operation.
   c. 120 minutes total operation.
   d. None of the above.

10. The flight data recorder must continuously record
    a. 30 minutes of continuous data.
    b. 1 hour of continuous data.
    c. 24 hours of continuous data.
    d. 25 hours of continuous data.

11. Traffic alert and collision avoidance system II (TCAS II) equipment is required for
    a. all turbine-powered aircraft with a maximum certificated takeoff weight of more than 33,000 pounds.
    b. all large Part 121 aircraft with a maximum certificated takeoff weight of 12,500 pounds.
    c. Part 121 aircraft with more than 10 seats.
    d. Part 121 aircraft with more than 30 seats.

12. The cockpit voice recorder (CVR) is required to operate starting
    a. at engine start.
    b. at application of ground or aircraft power to the aircraft.
    c. at first use of a checklist (before starting engines for the purpose of flight).
    d. from the time the crew is seated in the cockpit.

13. An air carrier may not dispatch an airplane under IFR or night VFR conditions when current weather reports indicate that thunderstorms or other potentially hazardous weather conditions that can be detected with airborne weather radar may reasonably be expected along the route to be flown, unless the airborne weather radar is working.
    a. True
    b. False

14. Airplanes with_____ must be equipped with a public address system that is capable of operation independent of the required crewmember interphone system.
    a. a seating capacity of 9 passengers
    b. a seating capacity of more than 9 but less than 19 passengers
    c. a seating capacity of more than 19 passengers
    d. All of the above.

15. _____ must have an emergency lighting system, *for interior emergency exit markings.* This system must be independent of the main lighting system.
    a. All transport category airplanes
    b. All transport category passenger-carrying airplanes
    c. Only airplanes with a seating capacity of more than 19 passengers
    d. Only airplanes with a seating capacity of more than 30 passengers

CHAPTER 11
DISPATCHING AND FLIGHT RELEASE RULES

Where am I?

—**Charles Lindbergh**, upon his arrival in Paris

In this chapter we'll examine the air carrier dispatching and release requirements that must be considered prior to a flight's departure. 14 CFR Part 121, Subpart U, contains the rules applicable to **dispatching** domestic and flag operations and **releasing** supplemental operations. The requirements to dispatch domestic, flag, and supplemental operations are found in 14 CFR §§121.593, 121.595, and 121.597, respectively. These rules are very clear and unambiguous.

A *domestic or flag* flight must be authorized by a dispatcher or *dispatch released*. In the case of domestic flights, *each* flight must be dispatched, unless the flight was originally included in the dispatch of a multi-leg flight and the aircraft doesn't spend more than one hour on the ground. In that case, the dispatch may cover multiple legs. In the case of flag operations, the rule is similar in concept, but the times are different. In this case, each flight must be dispatched except that a flight involving a stop (layover) may be conducted on a single dispatch so long as the aircraft doesn't remain on the ground for more than six hours.

The **flight release** of *supplemental* operations is addressed in Section 121.597 and contains a couple of interesting allowances not offered to domestic and flag operators. The first allowance is that there exists no requirement to have an aircraft dispatcher release each flight, hence there is no requirement to employ a certified aircraft dispatcher. The only requirement under Paragraph 121.597(a) is that a flight may not depart under a flight following system without specific authority from the person authorized by the operator to exercise operational control over the flight. Secondly, the pilot-in-command or the person authorized by the operator to exercise operational control over the flight is allowed to execute a flight release for the flights to be conducted. The pilot-in-command may sign the flight release only when he and the person authorized by the operator to exercise operational control believe that the flight can be made safely. Also, as in the flag operators' multi-leg dispatch provision, no person operating under a supplemental flight release may continue a flight from an intermediate airport without a new flight release if the aircraft has been on the ground more than six hours.

Dispatch Release (Domestic and Flag) and Flight Release Document (Supplemental)

14 CFR §121.663 requires that a **dispatch release document** be prepared by the dispatcher. Both the pilot-in-command and the dispatcher must sign this document, although the dispatcher may delegate authority to sign the document. However, note that Section 121.663 makes it clear that the dispatcher is only delegating his authority to *sign* the dispatch release, not his authority to dispatch the flight.

The required contents of the dispatch release document for domestic and flag operations are spelled out in Section 121.687. (A sample release is shown in Figure 11-1.) The release must include the:

- identification number of the aircraft;
- flight number (trip number);
- departure airport, intermediate stops, destination airport and alternate(s);
- type of operation (IFR/VFR);
- minimum required fuel supply;
- for an ETOPS flight, the ETOPS diversion time for which the flight is dispatched; and
- latest weather reports and forecasts at time of departure.

14 CFR §121.599(a) requires that both domestic and flag dispatchers be familiar with the weather reports and forecasts along the route(s) to be flown. Since there may not be an aircraft dispatcher assigned to a supplemental operator's flight, Paragraph 121.599(b) assigns to the pilot-in-command the responsibility for becoming familiar with reported and forecast weather conditions on the route to be flown.

14 CFR §121.601 addresses what information the dispatcher must provide to the pilot-in-command for both domestic and flag operations. The dispatcher must provide current information on the airports' conditions and the navigation facilities to be used. The dispatcher must also provide the pilot-in-command with all available weather reports and forecasts that may affect the safety of the flight, such as clear air turbulence, thunderstorms, and wind shear, for each airport to be used and route to be flown. During the conduct of the flight, the dispatcher must update the pilot-in-command on any changes to any of this information as changes occur.

A **flight release document** rather than a dispatch release is used by supplemental operators. Instead of an aircraft dispatcher, supplemental operators are allowed by Section 121.603 to assign the pilot-in-command the preflight duty of obtaining all available current reports or information on airport conditions and irregularities of navigation facilities that may affect the safety of the flight. Like the aircraft dispatcher in domestic and flag operations, the pilot-in-command in supplemental operations is required during a flight to obtain any additional available information of meteorological conditions and irregularities of facilities and services that may affect the safety of the flight.

Finally, in order for a flight to be either dispatched or flight released, Section 121.605 requires the aircraft to be airworthy and equipped as prescribed in Subpart K: Instrument and Equipment Requirements (*see* Chapter 10).

Load Manifest

Another document that must be prepared is the **load manifest**. 14 CFR §121.693 requires both domestic and flag operators to prepare a load manifest (*see* Figure 11-2) containing the following information:

- Weight of the loaded aircraft
- Maximum allowable weight that must not exceed the least of:
  – Max takeoff weight for runway to be used
  – Max takeoff weight that allows compliance with en route limitations
  – Max takeoff weight (considering fuel/oil consumption) that allows compliance with the max landing weight limitations
  – Max takeoff weight (considering fuel/oil consumption) that allows compliance with landing distance limitations on arrival at destination/alternate airports
- Total weight computed under approved procedures
- Evidence the aircraft is loaded within center of gravity limits
- Names of passengers unless that list is maintained by the carrier (e.g., in a reservations systems).

14 CFR §121.695 requires the pilot-in-command of a domestic or flag flight to carry aboard the aircraft a copy of:

1. the load manifest,
2. the dispatch release, and
3. the flight plan.

Supplemental carriers, on the other hand, may carry the original or a copy of the load manifest, flight release, and flight plan and are additionally required by Section 121.697 to carry the

- pilot route certification and
- aircraft's airworthiness release certificate.

```
********************************************************************************
*Flight 580/02JUL          Aircraft N2202DL         CAE-ATL         Release #1 *
********************************************************************************
Flight Dispatch Release-Captain Copy
Dispatcher: Higgins #73  ph#999-715-4473

Delta Flt. 580/02JUL    Release #1 CAE-ATL   Alternate: CAE
Aircraft:N2202DL   Type of Flt.:IFR
                                       Block Fuel:15,800 lbs
                              Minimum Fuel for Takeoff:14,630 lbs

By signing the attached flight release document I consider all factors including my own
physical condition satisfactory for this flight.

Delta 580/02 RLS 1 CAE/ATL ALTN CAE

         Scheduled          Planned         Actual
KCAE     2030z/1630L        2030z            ....
Taxi                        0012             ....
OFF                         2042z            ....
ETE                         0037             ....
ON                          2119z            ....
Taxi                        0010             ....
KATL     2140z/1740z        2129z            ....

DOT On-time arvl limit is sked plus 14 minutes or 2154z/1754z-applies only to flight
within 50 states/Puerto Rico/U.S. Virgin Isles

Ship 2202 T/ Airbus A319 /F  DMCS  Type:ECON   Filed Alt:260 Company Route: 2   Miles: 188
Elev. KCAE: 236 Ft.   KATL: 1026 Ft.

Route: KCAE..CAE.J4.IRQ.SINCA3.KATL     ETE: 37 min.

Ramp Wt.: 103,519 LWT: 099,290  Payload 066/013,753
MPTW: 109,135  Flight Plan includes cargo  000,421
Target Arrival Fuel: 11,300 lbs. Gate: B14 Ramp#2 (131.85)

Trip Time/Burn CAE ATL      37/004230-Taxi 12/00380
IFR/ALTN  CAE  FL230        33/003470
PLND Contingency Fuel       45/003310 see remarks
UNPLND CNTNGNCY Fuel        10/000790
Reserve Fuel                   004000
Block Fuel                     015800
Minimum Fuel for T/O           014630

Dispatcher and Maintenance Remarks:
-Dispatcher-
Fuel Added for:
01 Anticipated Weather
02 Traffic
Smooth rides reported at 260                         222    98
-Maintenance-
-MEL/CDL:
M22-00-04  Autothrottle System
    MEL Expiration Date-06JUL15 at 0400z
M49-00-01B Auxiliary Power Unit
    MEL Expiration Date-11JUL15 at 0400z
Aircraft Remarks:      Please note cost indexes-15OCT15**ECON 62/LRC 00/OTA 183

Descent LNDG Rnwy 27L Cross CANUK at 12,000 ft. 250 KIAS
Descent LNDG Rnway 09R Cross HUSKY at 14,000 ft.

Computed En Route winds
Fix   TROP SAT  CRZ FL
TOC   -47  -26  280/018
IRQ   -47  -26  280/022
TOD   -45  -26  280/017

Airport/Notams/Navigational Remarks
CAE/Caution Terminal construction...at night ramp area not well lit.
CAE/11 ALS OTS
ATL/TACAN OTs
```

Figure 11-1. Sample flight plan and dispatch release.

```
*****************************************************************************
*Flight 580/02JUL          Aircraft N2202DL         CAE-ATL           Release #1 *
*****************************************************************************
FLT 0580/02 CAE-ATL                              Load Planner M-EVANS  A69c789
Final   Weight Data Record                              Date/Time 02JUL  2023z
Flight Plan Release Number 01

Passenger Configuration: 8 FC/114 YC

 074025   OEW    A319  A/C 2202 Includes 3 Flight Attendants W/Bags
   1000   ADD 4 PAX/260lbs -or- SUB 2 PAX

   1440   8 FC
  10440   58 YC

      0   Bin 1 Cargo
    175   Bin 2 Cargo
   1500   Bin 3 Cargo
    110   Bin 4 Cargo

  88690   Zero Fuel Weight    MAX 105000
          88719.0  Adjusted ZFW       CG 18.8 pct MAC
  15670   Fuel/1- 7580/2- 7440/C-650
   -380   Less Taxi Fuel

 103980   Actual Takeoff Weight   Aft Index 45  16.6 pct MAC
*****************************************************************************
 104017.0 Adjusted Takeoff Weight                   CAE Takeoff Weather/ NWS
                                                       Temp 93 F  Alt 30.07
                                                       Wind 006/005 kts


 109135   Max Takeoff WT this flight limited by flight planning restrictions

Max Takeoff Wt.   Ldg. ATL   Max Ldg. Wt.   Burnoff      Forcast Temp
  117850          Flap full    114000        3850            85

130000 Maximum Structural Takeoff Weight
*****************************************************************************
CAE RWY 29                              / 8602 ft.    93F/34C      1 HW/5 XW
Standard Profile
Rwy Condition    Thrust/Flap    Climb Limit    RATOW    STAB Trim   V1    VR    V2

Dry              AT50/1          105793        123965     4.9      127   128   134
Dry              AT45/1          110698        127280     4.9      127   127   134
Dry              AT40/1          115418        130474     4.9      126   126   134
Dry              AT35/1          120048        133349     4.9      126   126   135
Dry              Norm/1          120965        134091     4.9      126   126   135
SLWET            Norm/1          120965        132893     4.9      126   126   135
ICY              Norm/1          120965        125354     4.9      122   126   135
*****************************************************************************
CAE RWY 11                              / 8602 ft.    93F/34C      1 HW/5 XW
Standard Profile
Rwy Condition    Thrust/Flap    Climb Limit    RATOW    STAB Trim   V1    VR    V2

Dry              AT50/1          105793        104464     4.9      127   128   134
Dry              AT45/1          110698        107250     4.9      127   127   134
Dry              AT40/1          115418        111680     4.9      126   126   134
Dry              AT35/1          120048        115670     4.9      126   126   135
Dry              Norm/1          120965        116552     4.9      125   126   135
SLWET            Norm/1          120965        114614     4.9      124   126   135
ICY              Norm/1          120965        107652     4.9      122   126   135
*****************************************************************************
Performance Notes:
Tailwind: -1000 lbs/knot from RATOW
Temp Inc: -495 lbs/deg F-up to 94 F From Climb Limit and RATOW
Headwind - ADD 100 lbs/knot to RATOW

Bleed Air Corrections - Engine Anti-ice
   Subtract 500 lbs. from climb limit and RATOW
Cutback Correction - Normal Power Required
   Subtract 10 lb/ft from RATOW
```

Figure 11-2. A sample load manifest.

IFR Dispatching Rules

Next, we see that 14 CFR §121.613 states that no person may dispatch an airplane under Part 121 unless the weather reports and forecasts indicate that at the time of arrival at the destination airport it is forecast to be at or above the authorized **IFR landing minimums**. This provision is much more restrictive than the rules of Part 91 under which you may depart for a destination that is forecast below landing minimums so long as a suitable alternate airport is available. There is a commonly granted exemption to this provision called the "**People's Express Exemption**," which we'll discuss a little bit later in this chapter.

The next set of rules of concern to the dispatcher are those that help assure that no matter what situations are encountered, the flight will always have an available "out" to ensure that the trip can be completed safely. In Chapter 8, we briefly mentioned the requirements to have en route alternate airports. These requirements were part of the single engine inoperative and two engine inoperative rules discussed earlier. Now, we will introduce some additional situations that may require filing alternate airports in the flight plan. These additional alternate airport requirements are the *departure airport alternate airport, extended operations (ETOPS) alternate airport, en route alternate airport, and destination airport alternate airport.*

Extended Operations (ETOPS) Alternate and En Route Alternate Airports

An **extended operations (ETOPS) alternate airport or en route alternate airport** (often referred to as a **driftdown alternate**) is an airport at which an aircraft would be able to land after experiencing an engine failure or some other abnormal or emergency condition while en route. It goes without saying that the availability of en route alternates along the planned route of flight is an important part of flight planning. For this reason, the FAA provides regulatory guidance detailing what airports qualify as safe alternate airports, the required alternate weather minimums, the required flight planned route in relation to the distance to the filed alternate, and more. Review Sections 121.624, 121.625, 121.631 and 121.633 for the specific requirements when choosing an alternate airport for flight planning purposes.

We will discuss in the next chapter the requirement that in the event of an engine failure, the pilot-in-command must land the airplane at the nearest suitable airport, in point of time (14 CFR §121.565). However, if a diversion is due to a system failure (e.g., pressurization failure), the PIC may be able to choose a more favorable alternate instead of the nearest suitable alternate. In other words, the PIC and that flight's dispatcher are allowed to take into consideration which airports are more convenient for the air carrier.

When choosing an alternate airport, an air carrier may prefer one of its hubs or regular destinations where mechanics are available and adequate support to the crew and passengers can be provided. Some companies call these alternates **operational alternates** or **on-line alternates** and they are generally better equipped with the necessary facilities than are **non-operational alternates** or **off-line alternate airports**. Think of a large Boeing 787 or Airbus 350 landing at what might be the "nearest" non-operational alternate or off-line alternate airport. It might have good weather, sufficient runway, and instrument approaches available for a successful landing. However, once parked on the ramp, the crew might find this airport has no jetway or airstairs able to reach the aircraft boarding doors, or the airport doesn't have refueling equipment able to reach the height of a large airliner's fuel nozzles, effectively stranding the passengers and aircraft. Unfortunately these problems happen around the globe a few times per year.

In Chapter 15, we will discuss extended operations regulations in more detail, but for now let's look at the basic types of extended operations (ETOPS) alternates and en route alternate airports.

Adequate Alternate Airport *(Marginally acceptable choice of alternate)*

An adequate alternate airport is an airport that is expected to be available during the time period the aircraft will be in proximity to it. The landing performance requirements on an adequate airport are required to be met and that particular airport must have the necessary facilities and services such as ATC, airport lighting, communications, meteorological services, navigation aids, rescue and firefighting services, and one suitable instrument approach procedure.

14 CFR §121.7 provides the following definitions that are useful here:

> *Adequate Airport* means an airport that an airplane operator may list with approval from the FAA because that airport meets the landing limitations of §121.197 and is either—
>
> (1) An airport that meets the requirements of part 139, subpart D of this chapter, excluding those that apply to aircraft rescue and firefighting service, or
>
> (2) A military airport that is active and operational.

Extended Operations (ETOPS) or Suitable Alternate Airport *(Better choice of alternate)*

An adequate alternate airport is declared as an ETOPS alternate or suitable alternate when:

1. The appropriate weather reports or forecasts of that planned alternate airport is equal to or better than the ETOPS-required weather minima specified in the certificate holder's operations specifications for a defined period of time.
2. The field condition reports indicate that a safe landing can be made. That is, applicable NOTAMs ensure the required en route alternate airport is and will remain available for the same period of time.
3. Surface crosswind forecasts and runway conditions are within acceptable limits to allow a safe approach and landing with one engine inoperative.

14 CFR §121.7 defines an ETOPS alternate airport as

> an adequate airport listed in the certificate holder's operations specifications that is designated in a dispatch or flight release for use in the event of a diversion during ETOPS. This definition applies to flight planning and does not in any way limit the authority of the pilot-in-command during flight.

An ETOPS aircraft may operate in remote areas of the world where few diversionary alternate airports are available. For this reason, it is important to know whether the alternate airports available are well equipped with all the necessary facilities. Whether an adequate alternate is an ETOPS alternate is decided prior to departure. This decision is based on the weather conditions forecast for the adequate alternate at the time it might be used (from the earliest to the latest possible landing time).

Additional information regarding ETOPS operations is found in FAA Advisory Circular 120-42B, *Extended Operations (ETOPS and Polar Operations)*.

Departure Airport Alternate Airport

The requirement for a **departure airport alternate airport** is found in 14 CFR §121.617 and is addressed in Part C: IFR Takeoff Minimums of an air carrier's ops specs. This provision protects the operator when weather conditions are such that an aircraft departs an airport with takeoff minimums below the departure airport's landing minimums. But how can that happen? How can the takeoff be at less than landing minimums when 14 CFR §91.175(f) prescribes takeoff minimums in excess of most landing minimums? Standard takeoff minimums are ½ statute mile visibility or 2,400 feet **RVR (runway visual range)** for airplanes with three or more engines, and 1 statute mile visibility or 5,000 feet RVR for twin-engine aircraft. Before answering that question, let's take a look at RVR.

Runway visual range (RVR) is an essential system used to calculate an estimate of how far down a runway a pilot can see objects such as runway lights or runway markings. It is an instrumentally derived value calculated using standardized equations from measurements of three parameters: (1) extinction coefficient (a measure of the ability of particles or gases to absorb and scatter photons from a beam of light); (2) ambient light level; and (3) the intensity of the runway lights. The RVR distance values are reported in feet. Because of operational decisions, sometimes with legal implications, that are taken on the basis of RVR reported, some precision in the reporting scale is essential. Too fine a scale is not justified, since RVR values cannot be completely representative of viewing conditions from the cockpit because of variations in time and space and the limitations of observing techniques.

For these reasons, the raw data is not reported; rather RVR is derived from the raw data. ICAO specifies that a reporting increment of 25 meters shall be used up to 400 meters RVR, a reporting increment of 50 meters used between 400 and 800 meters RVR, and a reporting increment of 100 meters used for RVR values above 800 meters. Any observed RVR value that does not fit the reporting scale in use should be rounded down to the nearest lower reporting step in the scale. The FAA has adapted the ICAO metric increments concept into an RVR table expressed in feet. RVR values are displayed in rounded 100-foot values and are reported as follows: 100-foot increments for products below 800 feet, 200-foot increments for products between 800 and 3,000 feet, and 500-foot increments for products between 3,000 and 6,500 feet. That results in values of 100 FT/200 FT/.../700 FT/800 FT/1,000 FT/1,200 FT/.../2,800 FT/3,000 FT/3,500 FT/4,000 FT/.../5,500 FT/6,000 FT. RVR is not reported for values greater than 6,000 FT.

Now that we have a better understanding of what and how RVR is measured let's return to the question of how takeoff minimums can be less than landing minimums. The answer is found in Section 121.651 (takeoff minimums). The certificate holder may be authorized to use lower than standard takeoff minimums in its ops specs. These lower than standard takeoff minimums may be much lower than the required landing minimums. Let's take a look at a large air carrier's lower than standard takeoff minimums as authorized in its ops specs Paragraph C.078.

U.S. Department of Transportation Federal Aviation Administration	Operation Specifications Paragraph C.078

Delta Air Lines Ops Specs	**Paragraph C.078**

IFR Lower Than Standard Takeoff Minimums, 14 CFR Part 121
Airplane Operations: All Airports

The certificate holder is authorized to use lower than standard takeoff minimums in accordance with the limitations and provisions of this operations specification as follows.

- a. Runway visual range (RVR) reports, when available for a particular runway, shall be used for all takeoff operations on that runway. All takeoff operations, based on RVR, must use RVR reports from the locations along the runway specified in this paragraph.
- b. When takeoff minimums are equal to or less than the applicable standard takeoff minimum, the certificate holder is authorized to use the lower than standard takeoff minimums described below:
  - (1) Visibility or runway visual value (RVV) 1/4 statute mile or touchdown zone RVR 1,600, provided at least one of the following visual aids is available. The touchdown zone RVR report, if available, is controlling. The mid-RVR report may be substituted for the touchdown zone RVR report if the touchdown zone RVR report is not available.
    - (a) Operative high intensity runway lights (HIRL).
    - (b) Operative runway centerline lights (CL).
    - (c) Serviceable runway centerline marking (RCLM).
    - (d) In circumstances when none of the above visual aids are available, visibility or RVV 1/4 statute mile may still be used, provided other runway markings or runway lighting provide pilots with adequate visual reference to continuously identify the takeoff surface and maintain directional control throughout the takeoff run.
  - (2) Touchdown zone RVR 1,000 (beginning of takeoff run) and rollout RVR 1,000, provided all of the following visual aids and RVR equipment are available.
    - (a) Operative runway centerline lights (CL).
    - (b) Two operative RVR reporting systems serving the runway to be used, both of which are required and controlling. A mid-RVR report may be substituted for either a touchdown zone RVR report if a touchdown zone report is not available or a rollout RVR report if a rollout RVR report is not available.
  - (3) Touchdown zone RVR 500 (beginning of takeoff run), mid-RVR 500, and rollout RVR 500, provided all of the following visual aids and RVR equipment are available.
    - (a) Operative runway centerline lights (CL).
    - (b) Runway centerline markings (RCLM).
    - (c) Operative touchdown zone and rollout RVR reporting systems serving the runway to be used, both of which are controlling, or three RVR reporting systems serving the runway to be used, all of which are controlling. However, if one of the three RVR reporting systems has failed, a takeoff is authorized, provided the remaining two RVR values are at or above the appropriate takeoff minimum as listed in this subparagraph.

1. The Certificate Holder applies for the Operations in this paragraph.
2. Support information reference: JAR-OPS changes.
3. These Operations Specifications are approved by direction of the Administrator.

(continued)

ORIGINAL SIGNED BY:
Ms. F. Faye Phisdo
Principal Operations Inspector

4. Date Approval is effective: 01/17/2015 Amendment Number: 0
5. I hereby accept and receive the Operations Specifications in this paragraph.

ORIGINAL SIGNED BY:
Al B. Phlying
System Manager Quality Assurance & Compliance Date: 01/17/2015

This air carrier is authorized in its ops specs to perform takeoffs when the visibility in the touchdown zone (beginning of takeoff run) RVR is as low as 500 feet, mid-portion of the runway as low as 500 feet RVR, and rollout (departure end of runway) as low as 500 feet RVR, provided all of the stated visual aids and RVR equipment are available. This is less than the standard Category I landing minimums of ½ statute mile or 1,800 feet RVR. What would happen if the aircraft took off and then suffered an emergency of some sort and couldn't return to the airport of departure because the weather was below that field's *landing minimums*?

14 CFR §121.617 specifies that if the conditions at the takeoff airport are below the landing minimums, a *departure airport alternate airport* must be specified in the dispatch release. For two-engine aircraft, that airport must be no more than 1 hour (at normal cruising speed in still air with one engine inoperative) away from the departure airport (e.g., the takeoff alternate must be within one hour or 340 NM of the departure airport for an Airbus 320). For three or more engine airplanes, the departure airport alternate airport must be no more than 2 hours from the departure airport at normal cruising speed with one engine inoperative. Keep in mind that even though an aircraft might be certified for Category II and/or Category III landings, a departure airport alternate airport is still required in many cases when the weather at the departure airport is below Category I landing minimums. The reason is that many aircraft, though certificated for all-engine Category II or Category III landing minima, are only certified to Category I landing minimums with one engine inoperative!

Let's take a look at a sample aircraft dispatcher's quick reference table (Table 11-1) for varied fleets of airliners.

Table 11-1. Flight time to takeoff alternate

Aircraft	Mileage (NM)	Time with One Engine Inoperative in Still Air
A319	325	One hour
A320	340	One hour
A330-300	345	One hour
A340-600	800	Two hours
B777	380	One hour
B747	790	Two hours

Destination Alternate

The third type of alternate airport required by the FAA is called a **destination alternate airport**. This type of alternate airport comes into play when the forecast for the destination airport is less than "perfect" weather. In that case, as we will see, the rules require you to have a "contingency plan" in the form of a destination alternate airport. 14 CFR §121.619 covers this for domestic operations, while §121.621 contains the destination alternate airport rules for flag operations.

In domestic operations, the rule is the same as that used in Part 91 operations (14CFR §91.167) and is as simple as 1-2-3. That is:

From *1 hour* before scheduled arrival until *1 hour* after, we require:

2,000 foot ceiling and *3 statute miles visibility*.

If the weather is not forecast to be at least this good, then we must file a destination alternate airport. In other words, this **1-2-3 rule** answers the question: Do I need a destination alternate airport?

Do I Need a Destination Alternate Airport?

If an alternate is needed, then again look to 14 CFR §121.625 to find what weather conditions the alternate airport must be forecasting. Furthermore, an additional alternate may also be required. When weather conditions at the destination airport and the first alternate airport are marginal, §121.619(a) requires that at least one additional alternate airport be designated.

Notice that in 14 CFR §121.621, alternate airport for destination for flag operations, the rules for determining the need for an alternate airport are similar in concept but differ in the numbers involved. First, if the flight is over 6 hours, an alternate must be filed, period. If the flight is 6 hours or less in duration, then in order not to file an alternate airport, the weather must be better than 1,500 feet above the lowest circling minimum descent altitude (MDA) if a circling approach is required, or at least 1,500 feet higher than the lowest published instrument minimums or 2,000 feet above airport elevations, whichever is greater. The visibility must be at least 3 miles, or 2 miles added to the lowest published minimum visibility, whichever is greater. If you compare this with the Part 135 rules for determining the need for an alternate airport (Section 135.223), you'll notice they are the same as Part 121 flag operations.

Supplemental operators must list a destination alternate airport on the flight release unless the air carrier meets FAA fuel load stipulations covered in 14 CFR §121.645. Paragraph 121.645(b) requires that a flight may not depart (flight released) unless, considering wind and other weather conditions expected, it has enough fuel:

(1) To fly to and land at the airport to which it is released;
(2) After that, to fly for a period of 10 percent of the total time required to fly from the airport of departure to, and land at, the airport to which it was released;
(3) After that, to fly to and land at the most distant alternate airport specified in the flight release, if an alternate is required; and
(4) After that, to fly for 30 minutes at holding speed at 1,500 feet above the alternate airport (or the destination airport if no alternate is required) under standard temperature conditions.

(14 CFR 121.645[b])

At a minimum, a turbojet powered airplane in flag operations may not depart for an airport for which an alternate is not specified in the flight release unless it has enough fuel, considering wind and other weather conditions expected, to fly to the destination airport and thereafter fly for at least 2 hours at normal cruising fuel consumption. The FAA reserves the right to require more fuel than any of the **fuel minimums** stated in Section 121.645 if it finds that additional fuel is necessary on a particular route in the interest of safety. This additional fuel requirement will appear in that air carrier's ops specs.

The destination and en route alternate airport rules are intended to ensure that no matter what situations are encountered, there will always be sufficient fuel aboard the aircraft to complete the trip safely. Let's see how this works. To begin with, 14 CFR §121.647 contains all of the factors for computing fuel required by the FAA. Each person computing fuel required must consider the following:

(a) Wind and other weather conditions forecast.
(b) Anticipated traffic delays.
(c) One instrument approach and possible missed approach at destination.
(d) Any other conditions that may delay landing of the aircraft.

(14 CFR §121.647)

Section 121.647 also includes a brief definition of required fuel. Required fuel is in addition to unusable fuel.

Alternate Airport Weather Minimums

14 CFR §121.625 specifies the weather conditions that must exist at the alternate airport in order to file it as an alternate. **Alternate airport weather forecast conditions** must meet or exceed whatever weather conditions are specified in the carrier's ops specs. The **standard alternate airport (weather) minimums** are found in 14 CFR §91.169 and are **600-2** for *precision (ILS)* approaches and **800-2** for *nonprecision (VOR, NDB, GPS, etc.)* approaches. This means the forecast ceiling must be at least 600 feet or 800 feet while the forecast visibility must be in excess of 2 miles to use an airport as an alternate *of any kind*.

It is common, however, for a carrier to have approval of an alternative method of computing the alternate weather minimums required. This method will often result in lower than standard alternate airport minimums. Let's take a look at typical lower than standard alternate airport weather minimums (often called **derived alternate weather minimums**), which are permitted by approval in an air carrier's ops specs.

U.S. Department of
Transportation
Federal Aviation
Administration

Operation Specifications

Paragraph C.055

JetBlue Airways Ops Specs

Paragraph C.055

Alternate Airport IFR Weather Minimums

a. The certificate holder is authorized to derive alternate airport weather minimums from the "Alternate Airport IFR Weather Minimums" table listed below.

b. Special limitations and provisions.

(1) In no case shall the certificate holder use an alternate airport weather minimum other than any applicable minimum derived from this table.

(2) In determining alternate airport weather minimums, the certificate holder shall not use any published instrument approach procedure which specifies that alternate airport weather minimums are not authorized.

(3) Credit for alternate minima based on CAT II or CAT III capability is predicated on authorization for engine inoperative CAT III operations for the certificate holder, aircraft type, and qualification of flightcrew for the respective CAT II or CAT III minima applicable to the alternate airport.

Alternate Airport IFR Weather Minimums
(sm = statute mile)

Approach Facility Configuration	Ceiling	Visibility
For airports with at least one operational navigational facility providing a straight-in nonprecision approach procedure, or a straight-in precision approach procedure, or when applicable, a circling maneuver from an instrument approach procedure.	A ceiling derived by adding 400 ft to the authorized Category I HAT or, when applicable, the authorized HAA.	A visibility derived by adding 1 sm to the authorized Category I landing minimum.
For airports with at least two operational navigational facilities, each providing a straight-in nonprecision approach procedure or a straight-in precision approach procedure to different, suitable runways. (However, when an airport is designated as an ETOPS En Route Alternate Airport in these operation specifications, the approach procedures used must be to separate, suitable runways).	A ceiling derived by adding 200 ft to the higher Category I HAT of the two approaches used.	A visibility derived by adding ½ sm to the higher authorized Category I landing minimums of the two approaches.
For airports with a published CAT II or CAT III approach, and at least two operational navigational facilities, each providing a straight-in precision approach procedure to different suitable runways.	CAT II procedures, a ceiling of at least 300 ft HAT, or for CAT III procedures, a ceiling of at least 200 ft HAT.	CAT II procedures, a visibility of at least RVR 4,000, or for CAT III procedures, a visibility of at least RVR 1,800.

(continued)

1. The Certificate Holder applies for the Operations in this paragraph.
2. Support information reference: JAR-OPS changes.
3. These Operations Specifications are approved by direction of the Administrator.

ORIGINAL SIGNED BY
Mr. Turner A. Rench
Principal Operations Inspector

4. Date Approval is effective: 01/17/2014 Amendment Number: 0
5. I hereby accept and receive the Operations Specifications in this paragraph.

ORIGINAL SIGNED BY
Mr. I. L. Phly
System Manager Quality Assurance & Compliance Date: 01/17/2014

The purpose of Paragraph C055 of an air carrier's ops specs is to specify what minimum weather conditions must exist at a particular airport in order for its dispatchers to file it as an alternate. The dispatcher must check the ceiling and visibility information in the weather report and compare that information to the approaches available at the desired airport. Let's look at an example.

A dispatcher desires to use XYZ airport for an alternate. First, the dispatcher will look up the navigational charts for that field. XYZ airport is located near sea level with a field elevation of 80 feet. Let's say XYZ has two different suitable runways: one offers a straight-in VOR approach with a minimum descent altitude (MDA) of 800 feet with a height above touchdown (HAT) of 720 feet; the other runway offers a straight-in ILS approach with a decision altitude (DA) of 280 feet and a HAT of 200 feet.

Next, the dispatcher will refer to the *Alternate Airport IFR Weather Minimums* table to determine what minimum required ceiling and visibility is allowed for filing XYZ as an alternate airport. Since XYZ has two different straight-in instrument approaches to two different suitable runways, the ceiling and visibility minimums are derived by adding 200 feet to the HAT for the VOR approach and adding ½ statute mile (SM) to VOR's minimum visibility requirement. Note that in this example the VOR approach has the highest HAT *and* the higher visibility requirement of the two approaches. *This might not always be the case*; in some cases you might use the HAT from one approach and the visibility from another.

The ceiling is derived by adding 200 feet to the higher Category I approach HAT of the two approaches. Since the VOR approach has a higher HAT, then we are required to add 200 feet to the HAT of 720 feet, for a required ceiling of at least 920 feet. To derive the visibility, we again look at both the VOR and ILS approaches (Table 11-2). The VOR has the higher visibility requirement of ¾ statute mile, so we are required to add ½ statute mile to the published visibility requirement of ¾ statute mile for a total required visibility of 1¼ statute miles. If the ceiling is higher than 920 feet and the visibility is better than 1¼ statute miles, then XYZ may be filed as an alternate.

Intuitively, one might think since an airport offering two straight-in approaches offers a lower alternate minimum additive (+200 feet and +½ statute mile), it might also offer the lowest derived alternate minimum. However, it is possible to have higher alternate minimums when using two operational navigational facilities than when using an airport with only one navigational facility. For instance, an airport with one straight-in nonprecision approach with a HAT of 400 feet and 1 statute mile visibility would have alternate minimums of 800 feet and 2 statute miles visibility (e.g., minimums derived by adding 400 feet + 400 feet and 1 statute mile + 1 statute mile).

Table 11-2. Published approach minimums for XYZ airport

	Straight-in ILS Precision Approach	Straight-in VOR Nonprecision Approach
	DA(H) 280 ft (200 ft)	MDA (H) 800 ft (720 ft)
A		
B	RVR 1,800 FT or ½ sm	RVR 4,000 FT or ¾ sm
C		
D		

However, if an airport offers two straight-in approaches, one a precision ILS with HAT of 280 feet and ½ statute mile visibility and the other a nonprecision VOR approach with an HAT of 800 feet and 1 statute mile visibility, it would have alternate minimums of 1,000 feet and 1½ statute mile visibility. That is, 200 feet + 800 feet = 1,000 feet, and ½ statute mile + 1 statute mile = 1½ statute miles. Since the air carrier's ops specs will require that the higher ceiling and visibility be used, the minimums for the airport with two straight-in approaches are higher than for the airport with only one straight-in approach. In this case the dispatcher may elect to file an alternate to an airport offering only one straight-in approach. So even though it requires that higher alternate additives be used, it provides the dispatcher with the lowest possible ceiling and visibility requirements.

This seems like a lot of work for the aircraft dispatcher to go through every time a flight is dispatched. In the real world, the dispatch department figures out in advance what the minimum ceiling and visibility requirements are for every airport the air carrier may ever desire to use as an alternate. These figures are then placed in a reference manual and on computer. The dispatcher simply refers to the manual or a computer template for the minimum weather requirements and then compares that information with the weather reports for that airport.

People's Express Exemption 3585

FAA Exemption 3585 was a petition People's Express Airlines filed in 1982 with the FAA to gain some relief from the restrictive requirements of 14 CFR §§121.613 and 121.625. Because People's Express Airlines was a "low cost" start-up airline, it could not afford to maintain its own meteorology department or even contract weather reporting services. It therefore relied solely on the National Weather Service (NWS) for the weather reports needed to dispatch flights. Other major airlines employed their own licensed meteorologists to provide up-to-date weather reports and forecasts, which enabled those carriers to rely on more immediate information rather than on historic (up to 6 hours old) NWS reports. Many times, this would allow other airlines to depart for a destination, while People's Express flights would cancel due to destination weather forecasts that were below minimums.

Let's review the structure of the terminal area forecast (TAF) for a moment. The TAF can be broken down into two parts. The first is the main body that contains the prevailing weather for a specified time period. The second section is the remarks section. The remarks section contains restrictions and modifications to the NWS's weather forecast in the main body (e.g., "becoming," "probability of 40 percent," or "temporarily").

The requested exemption from Section 121.619(a) allowed People's Express to dispatch, under IFR, an aircraft to a destination airport, even though weather reports or forecasts contain such conditional words as "becoming," "temporarily," etc., so long as there is at least one alternate airport for which weather reports or forecasts indicate that weather conditions will be at or above authorized minimums.

Included in the People's Express petition was a list of what it felt were some major flaws in Part 121 dispatching regulations. They charged the FAA had informally (by non-rulemaking) interpreted the words "will be at or above" to mean that whenever a forecast or report includes such *conditional remarks* as "becoming," "temporarily," etc., at the destination airport, the flight couldn't be dispatched even though the weather reports indicated that weather conditions may be at or above minimums at the ETA. People's Express believed this interpretation ignored the reality of NWS forecasting and gave too much operational significance to terms that were, at best, vague and uncertain. People's Express concluded that because the NWS reports are too infrequently issued and the conditional remarks so vague and uncertain, it was inappropriate for the FAA to rely on the conditional remarks section of a weather forecast as a basis for permitting or not permitting an airline to dispatch flights. The FAA agreed.

The FAA granted People's Express and other qualifying air carriers an exemption to Sections 121.613, 121.619(a), and 121.625 of the FARs, to the extent necessary to permit them to dispatch an airplane, under IFR, to a destination airport when the weather forecast for that airport indicates by the use of conditional words such as "occasionally," "intermittently," "briefly," or "a chance of," in the remarks section of that report, that the weather could be below authorized weather minimums at the time of arrival. The Exemption was subject to the following conditions and limitations:

Exemption 3585

1. Each certificate holder shall apply for and obtain approval from the FAA certificate-holding office having jurisdiction over its operations before commencing operations in accordance with this exemption.
2. Each certificate holder shall list one additional alternate airport in the dispatch release whenever the weather reports or forecasts, or any combination thereof, for the destination airport and first alternate airport indicate, by the use of conditional words in the remarks section of such reports or forecasts, that the forecast weather conditions for the destination and first alternate airport might be as low as one-half the visibility value established for the lowest visibility minimum of the instrument approach procedure expected to be used for an instrument approach at the destination or first alternate. For the additional alternate to be listed in the dispatch release, the weather reports or forecasts, or any combination thereof, for this additional alternate, shall not contain any conditional words, including but not limited to "occasionally," "intermittently," "briefly," and "a chance of," in either the main body or the remarks section of such reports.
3. No person may dispatch or take off an airplane, when operating under this exemption, unless it has enough fuel
   a. To fly to the airport to which it is dispatched;
   b. Thereafter, to fly to and land at the most distant alternate airport for the airport to which dispatched, taking into account the anticipated air traffic control routing; and
   c. Thereafter, to fly for 45 minutes at normal cruising fuel consumption.
4. Each certificate holder's pilot in command, while en route, shall ensure by way of air-ground voice communication with their company's Dispatch Center and other appropriate facilities, that he/she is in receipt of the most current relevant weather reports and forecasts for the destination and the alternate airport(s). This current weather information shall be used when making a decision to proceed to an alternate airport for landing.

To be dispatched under Exemption 3585, a flight is now required to file two alternates. Keep in mind that when using Exemption 3585, the main body of the forecast must always be above minimums for the destination *and* the alternate. Only the conditional remarks portion of the forecast can be below the published minimums. Earlier in this chapter we discussed how to determine a *derived alternate weather minimum*. Again, this process is spelled out in Paragraph C055 of an air carrier's operations specifications. When using Exemption 3585, this process is altered slightly (*see* Table 11-3):

- *First alternate minimums:* The main body *and* conditional phrases of the forecast weather (METAR or TAF) for the first filed alternate airport must not be less than one-half of the derived alternate weather minimum visibility values and a ceiling as low as the published ceiling minimums specified in the air carrier operations specifications for that airport at the ETA. In most cases, this means the weather at the first alternate can't be forecast to be lower than 200 foot ceiling and ½ SM mile visibility (most common Category I minimums).
- *Second alternate minimums:* The forecast weather (METAR or TAF) for a filed second alternate must call for weather equal to, or better than, the approved ceiling and visibility minimums (even with conditional phrases) used for the specified approach. In order for this to be possible, the main body of the forecast would have to be nearly visual conditions. So the weather at the second alternate must be pretty good and enough fuel must be carried to reach the furthest alternate plus the required 45-minute reserve.

Now, let's take a look at an example of what the weather might look like when using Exemption 3585 on a flight from San Diego (SAN) to Los Angeles (LAX). Under this exemption, we must file two alternates for our flight. Our dispatcher has picked Orange County (SNA) and Ontario, California (ONT). All three airports have at least two ILS approaches and at least two operational navigational facilities, each providing a straight-in approach procedure to different runways.

Our destination weather:

Destination: LAX TAF
For ETA: 31004KT 1/2SM -SHRA OVC002 TEMPO* 30002KT 1/4SM -SHRA OVC001 RMK NXT FCST BY 00Z

* at our ETA
(Exemption 3585 Destination Minimums = ½ landing minimum visibility in conditional statement.)

First Alternate: SNA TAF
For ETA: 30003KT 1SM -SHRA OVC004 TEMPO* 30002KT 1/2SM -SHRA OVC002 RMK NXT FCST BY 00Z

* at our ETA
(Exemption 3585 First Alternate Minimum = ½ derived alternate visibility and/or ceiling in conditional.)

Second Alternate: ONT TAF
For ETA: 290004KT 1SM -SHRA OVC004 RMK NXT FCST BY 00Z

(Exemption 3585 Second Alternate Minimums = No lower than derived alternate visibility and/or ceiling.)

Most air carriers use Exemption 3585 today, although the exemption must be renewed periodically (usually every 2 years). The airline trade association, Airlines for America (A4A), on behalf of all the member airlines, has undertaken that task. In granting this exemption, the FAA stated it believed it had preserved the safety objectives of the applicable sections of the FARs, while at the same time allowed air carriers to avoid canceling flights on the basis of vague, speculative, and ultimately unfulfilled NWS weather forecasts. Over time this exemption has allowed many carriers to realize enormous efficiencies and economic benefits without denigrating safety to any extent.

Table 11-3. Alternate restrictions under Exemption 3585

	Criteria	Terminal Forecast Main Body	Terminal Forecast Remarks Section
Destination Requirements	Visibility Minimum Only	All needed for landing on suitable runway	½ of ceiling and visibility needed for landing on the suitable runway
First Alternate Requirements	Ceiling *and* Visibility Minimums Required	All needed to designate as an alternate per Ops Specs Paragraph C055	½ of ceiling and visibility needed for landing on the suitable runway
Second Alternate Requirements	Ceiling *and* Visibility Minimums Required	All needed to designate as an alternate per Ops Specs Paragraph C055	All needed for landing on suitable runway

CHAPTER 11: DISPATCHING AND FLIGHT RELEASE RULES

Domestic Fuel Requirements: All Aircraft

14 CFR §121.639 states that for domestic operations, the flight can't depart unless it has enough fuel

a. to fly to the airport to which it is dispatched, then
b. to fly to the most distant alternate (if required), then
c. fly for 45 minutes at normal cruising fuel consumption rates.

A good way to work these problems is to use this worksheet:

a. Destination fuel   _____ hours = _____ lbs
b. Alternate fuel   _____ hr/min = _____ lbs
c. Reserve fuel   :45 min   = _____ lbs
   Total fuel   _____ hours = _____ lbs

For example:

> A turboprop aircraft is operating in domestic service from ABC to QRS airport and requires a destination alternate of TUV. The flight times are as stated below:
> ABC ————>QRS   (1:12 hours)
> QRS ————>TUV   (:36 minutes)
>   (to alternate airport)

How much fuel is required if this turboprop aircraft burns an average of 1,500 lbs/hour?

In flight planning, fuel is referred to both by weight of the fuel and by the amount of time that a given quantity of fuel will last for a specific set of operating conditions. Using planning data, we can estimate the time the aircraft will be en route. This is called the **estimated time enroute**, or **ETE**. ETE is the planned flight time from takeoff to touchdown at the destination airport. It does not include taxi or ground holding fuel or any of the airborne additional fuel requirements.

In this problem, the ETE is 1:12 (1 hour and 12 minutes). Then, using the given hourly rate of fuel consumption (fuel burn), we can compute the total fuel consumed:

1. Convert hours and minutes to decimal hours—1:12 hours = 1 + 12/60 hrs = 1.2 hrs
2. 1.2 hours × 1,500 lbs/hour = 1,800 lbs

With this information, we can calculate the total fuel required to operate the flight:

a. Destination fuel   1:12 hours = 1,800 lbs
b. Alternate fuel   :36 min   =   900 lbs
c. Reserve fuel   :45 min   = 1,125 lbs
   Total fuel   2:33 hours = 3,825 lbs

Flag Operation Fuel Requirements: Nonturbine and Turboprop Aircraft

14 CFR §§121.641 and 121.645 state the requirements for flag operators. Note that Section 121.641 covers nonturbine and turboprop flag operations and Section 121.645 covers turbojet powered flag operations.

14 CFR §121.641 requires nonturbine and turboprop operators to ensure that at the time of departure, the aircraft has enough fuel to

a. Fly and land at the airport to which it is dispatched, then
b. Fly and land at the most distant alternate airport, plus
c. fly for 30 minutes of fuel, plus
d. have 15 percent of the total required in a and b above or 90 minutes, whichever is less.

A good way to work these problems is to use this worksheet:

a. Destination fuel   _____ hours   = _____ lbs
b. Alternate fuel   _____ hours   = _____ lbs
c. 15% of a+b or 90 min   _____ min   = _____ lbs
d. 30 minutes holding fuel :30 min   = _____ lbs
   Total fuel required   _____ hrs/min = _____ lbs

For example:

> A turboprop aircraft is operating in flag service from ABC to XYZ airport and requires a destination alternate of MNO. The flight times are as stated below:
> ABC ————>XYZ   (6:54 hours)
> XYZ ————>MNO   (2:13 hours)
>   (to alternate airport)

How much fuel is required if this turboprop aircraft burns an average of 1,500 lbs/hour?

a. Destination fuel   6:54 hours = 10,350 lbs
b. Alternate fuel   2:13 hours = 3,325 lbs
c. 15% of a+b or 90 min   1:22 hours = 2,050 lbs
d. 30 minutes holding fuel :30 min   =   750 lbs
   Total fuel required   10:59 hours = 16,475 lbs*

*This entry is the sum of the individual fuel consumption calculations. The sum of the individual calculations is slightly different than the result of calculating total fuel consumption by multiplying the total flight time by the hourly fuel consumption due to rounding error in both the individual fuel burn and total fuel required calculations.

Flag Operation Fuel Requirements: Turbojet Powered Aircraft

As we discussed in alternate airport requirements for supplemental operators, 14 CFR §121.645 covers the operation of turbine engine powered airplanes (other than turboprops). The requirements are similar in concept to the turboprop rules of Section 121.641, just with different numbers. For jet aircraft in flag operations, the requirements are to have enough fuel to

a. fly to the destination airport, plus
b. have 10% of the fuel required to the destination, plus
c. fly to and land at the most distant alternate, plus
d. fly for 30 minutes at 1,500 feet above the alternate airport.

If there is no alternate required, then the airplane must have enough fuel to get to the destination plus 2 hours of reserve fuel. A good worksheet for this problem would look like this:

a. Destination fuel _____ hours = _____ lbs
b. 10% of (a) _____ min = _____ lbs
c. Alternate fuel _____ hours = _____ lbs
d. 30 minutes holding fuel :30 min = _____ lbs
   Total fuel required _____ hours = _____ lbs

If we had exactly the same problem as above, except with a turbojet powered aircraft, let's see what fuel is required:

> A turbojet aircraft is operating in flag service from ABC to XYZ airport and requires a destination alternate of MNO. The flight times are as stated below:
>
> ABC ———>XYZ   (6:54 hours)
> XYZ ———>MNO (2:13 hours)
>   (to alternate airport)

What fuel is required if the turbojet powered aircraft burns 12,000 lbs/hour?

a. Destination fuel   6:54 hours = 82,800 lbs
b. 10% of (a)   :42 min   = 8,400 lbs
c. Alternate fuel   2:13 hours = 26,600 lbs
d. 30 minutes holding fuel :30 min   = 6,000 lbs
   Total fuel required   10:19 hours = 123,800 lbs

Rerelease Rules

Earlier we have seen references to a flight that is released or *rereleased*. Just what is a **redispatch/rerelease**? This is simply a situation in which the flight was originally dispatched and released to one destination, and during the course of the flight the destination was changed and the flight was sent on to a different destination. Why would this occur? Well, there are several reasons. One would be in a situation in which due to extensive air traffic delays, which were not forecast, the aircraft no longer has sufficient fuel to get to its destination. In conjunction with the dispatcher, the pilot-in-command would decide to proceed to an alternate airport to put on more fuel before continuing to the destination.

Another, more interesting, use of the rerelease occurs (particularly in international operations) where the amount of fuel required on long legs may be limiting as to the ability to perform the flight. Let's take a look at the problem first and then the solution.

Suppose the following trip is being planned:

> A turbojet powered aircraft with an average fuel burn of 14,500 lbs/hour:
>
> Schedule: ATH———>JFK—alternate———>BGR
>   Dep: ATH   1000Z
>   Arr: JFK   2113Z
>   ETE: ATH———>JFK (11:13 hours)
>   JFK ———>BGR (1:38 hours)
>   (time to alternate airport)

Calculated Fuel Requirements:

a. Destination fuel   11:13 hours = 162,646 lbs
b. 10% of (a)   1:08 hours = 16,436 lbs
c. Alternate fuel   1:38 hours = 23,696 lbs
d. 30 minutes holding fuel :30 min   =   7,250 lbs
   Total fuel required   14:29 hours = 210,028 lbs

This is all well and good if the aircraft has an adequate fuel supply. But suppose the airplane's fuel tanks only have the capacity for 200,000 lbs of fuel, which would be just about 14:00 hours of flying time. Could we still do the trip? A rerelease can often solve this problem. Instead of releasing the flight to JFK, let's try the following:

```
Schedule: ATH——>BGR—alternate——>JFK
    Dep:  ATH   1000Z
    Arr:  BGR   1935Z
    ETE:  ATH——>BGR (11:13 hours)
          JFK——>BGR (1:38 hours)
                    (time to alternate airport)
```

Notice that the flight time to JFK is still the same as before (11:13 hours), but the primary destination of JFK is shown as our alternate.

Fuel Requirements:

a.	Destination fuel	9:35 hours	=	138,970 lbs
b.	10% of (a)	:58 min	=	14,036 lbs
c.	Alternate fuel	1:38 hours	=	23,696 lbs
d.	30 minutes holding fuel	:30 min	=	7,250 lbs
	Total fuel required	12:41 hours	=	183,952 lbs

So this flight is legal (with 14:00 hours of fuel) to dispatch/release to BGR with a JFK alternate.

Once in flight, as we approach BGR, the flight crew performs a "How Goes It" check and find we are operating exactly on this schedule. That means we will arrive over BGR having consumed 9:35 hours (or 138,970 lbs) of fuel. Let's see what a BGR to JFK flight would require. We have the choice of using domestic or flag rules here, but let's stick with the flag rules for the sake of clarity. (If it helps to use domestic rules, remember that in this situation you may do so since the flight is entirely within the 48 contiguous United States.)

The "new flight" would be a BGR to JFK with a BGR alternate. We'll assume 1:38 each way.

a.	Destination fuel	1:38 hours	=	23,696 lbs
b.	10% of (a)	:10 min	=	2,420 lbs
c.	Alternate fuel	1:38 hours	=	23,696 lbs
d.	30 minutes holding fuel	:30 min	=	7,250 lbs
	Total fuel	3:56 hours	=	57,062 lbs

At this point, we have burned 9:35 hours (or 138,970 lbs) of fuel getting to Bangor (BGR) and require 3:56 hours (or 57,062 lbs) of additional fuel on board to release from BGR to JFK and return to BGR as the alternate airport. The following shows the calculation of the total fuel required to be on board leaving Athens in this scenario:

```
  9:35  hours (actual ATH to BGR)
 +3:56  hours (minimum dispatch fuel:
              BGR—>JFK—>BGR)
 13:31  hours of fuel on board at Athens
```

So our example requires 13:31 hours = 195,750 lbs of fuel. Since the tanks hold 14:00 hours (or 200,000 lbs), we would be legal to make this flight. The "savings," if you will, come from the reduced "10% fuel" needed if we compute the trip this way. So, as we approach BGR, as long as we have 3:56 in the tanks, we're good to go. This type of redispatch is commonly used in extending the planned range of a long-range flight. For a graphical view of this redispatch, refer to Figure 11-3.

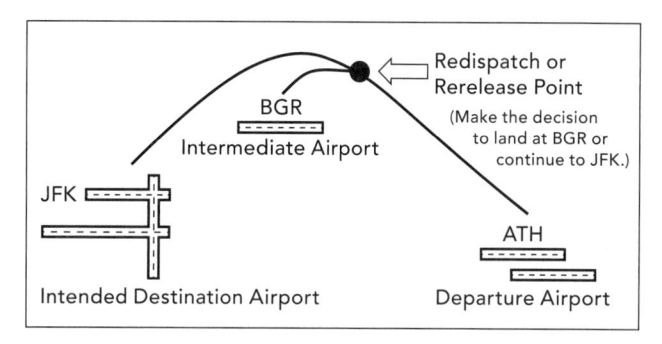

Figure 11-3. Redispatch flight planning.

IFR Landing Minimums

IFR landing minimums can be found in a number of locations. For example, 14 CFR §§91.175, 91.176, 135.225, and 121.651 all address minimum approach and landing weather conditions. The landing minimums an air carrier is authorized to use are those specified in its ops specs and are dependent on a few criteria. First, the certificate holder is only authorized to conduct the types of instrument approach procedures contained in Paragraph C.052 of its ops specs. The air carrier may not conduct any other types of approach procedures. Let's take a look at a sample of an air carrier's basic instrument approach procedure authorizations found in its ops specs (see next page).

This air carrier is authorized to do a number of non-precision and precision approaches. Would an Aero-Mech Airlines flight crew be legal to conduct a localizer backcourse (LOC/BC) approach or simplified directional finder (SDF) approach at a destination airport? The answer is no, because LOC/BC approaches or SDF approaches do not appear in the air carrier's ops specs.

| U.S. Department of Transportation Federal Aviation Administration | Operation Specifications Paragraph C.052 |

AeroMech Airlines, Inc.
Basic Instrument Approach Procedure Authorizations: All Aiports

The certificate holder is authorized to conduct the following types of instrument approach procedures and shall not conduct any other types.

Instrument Approach Procedures Nonprecision Approaches Without Vertical Guidance	Instrument Approach Procedures (Other Than ILS) Precision-Like Approaches With Vertical Guideance	Precision Approach Procedures (ILS, GLS)
ASR	LDA wtih Glide Slope	ILS
GPS	RNAV (GPS)	ILS/PRM
LDA/DME	RNAV (GNSS)	ILS/DME
LOC	LDA PRM	PAR B777/787/A350 (only Pacific Operations)
LOC/DME	RNAV (GPS) PRM	GLS
VOR		
VOR/DME		
RNAV (GPS)		

b. Conditions and Limitations.

(1) All the approaches approved by this Operations Specification must be published in accordance with Title 14 of the Code of Federal Regulations (14 CFR) Part 97.

(2) Approach procedures listed in column 1 of this Operations Specification must be trained and conducted in accordance with an approved procedure that assures descent will not go below Minimum Descent Altitude (MDA) unless the required visual references for continuing the approach are present.

(3) Approach procedures listed in column 2 of this Operations Specification authorize the certificate holder to conduct instrument approach procedures approved with vertical guidance that provides a precision-like approach and are to be trained using an approved method that allows descent to a published decision altitude (DA).

1. The Certificate Holder applies for the Operations in this paragraph.
2. These Operations Specifications are approved by direction of the Administrator.
   Original signed by: Hantla, Becky J., Principal Operations Inspector
4. Date Approval is effective: 11/07/2015 Amendment Number: 3
5. I hereby accept and receive the Operations Specifications in this paragraph.

Original signed by: Wakning, Rudy
Senior Vice President, Flight Operations Date: 11/07/2015

Paragraph C of an air carrier's ops specs contains specific ceiling and visibility minimums for each type of approach. 14 CFR §121.651 states that the certificate holder shall not use any IFR landing minimum lower than that prescribed by the applicable published instrument approach procedure and the carrier's ops specs. If we look at Paragraph 121.651(b), we see a big difference between Part 121 and the Part 91 landing minimums. Instrument approaches conducted under Part 91 regulations are allowed to continue an approach to minimums even if the weather reports indicate the weather is below minimums. This type of approach is sometimes called a "look-see" approach. That is, the Part 91 operators may continue the approach to take a "look-see" of the actual weather conditions for themselves. Instrument approaches conducted under Part 121 regulations are prohibited by Paragraph 121.651(b) from continuing an approach past the final approach fix or final approach segment or continuing an instrument procedure if an approved weather source reports the visibility to be less than the authorized visibility minimums prescribed for that procedure. These authorized landing minimums take into account the available ground-based equipment and lighting, as well as operative aircraft equipment and the airspeed at which the approach will be flown (i.e., circling approaches). Table 11-4, shown below, is contained in paragraph C.074 as it appears in the Delta Air Lines ops specs.

High Minimums Captain

Now that we've covered air carrier landing weather minimums for IFR operations, let's take a look at an interesting provision contained in the FARs concerning captains with less than 100 hours as pilot-in-command in operations under Parts 121 and 135 or in the type of airplane the captain is operating. 14 CFR §121.652, §135.225, and Paragraph C.054 of their ops specs restrict these captains to higher landing weather minimums. These **"high minimums" captains** must add 100 feet to the minimum descent altitude (MDA) or decision altitude (DA) and ½ mile (or the RVR equivalent) to the visibility landing minimums in the certificate holder's ops specs. This is done to allow the captain a chance to become comfortable with the new airplane before flying approaches to the normal minimums. Let's look again at the published approach minimums for XYZ Airport (Table 11-5) to see how high minimums are applied to a typical ILS approach or VOR approach.

Table 11-5. Published approach minimums for XYZ airport

Straight-in ILS Precision Approach	Straight-in VOR Nonprecision Approach
DA(H) 280 ft (200 ft)	MDA (H) 800 ft (720 ft)
A	
B	
C	RVR 1,800 FT or ½ sm	RVR 4,000 FT or ¾ sm
D	

A high minimums captain would need to increase the ILS DA to 380 feet and the visibility to 1 statute mile or an RVR of 4,500 feet. The VOR approach minimums would need to be increased to a MDA of 900 feet and a visibility of 1¼ statute miles (*see* Table 11-6).

Remember the high minimums captain we discussed in chapter 6? As you can imagine, a captain looks forward to logging the required amount of flight time to be allowed to fly to the lower published minimums. It's not much fun having to divert to your alternate because the weather conditions didn't meet your high minimums while other aircraft are successfully landing at your destination airport. Fortunately, the FAA does not require use of the higher minimums over the alternate airport published approach minimums; however, the lowest minimums allowed are 1 statute mile visibility (5,000 RVR) and a 300 foot HAT.

Table 11-4. Precision approaches requiring lateral and vertical guidance

Approach Light Configuration	HAT	Visibility in Statute Miles	TDZ RVR in Feet[1]
No Lights or ODALS	200	3/4	4,000
MALS or SALS	200	5/8	3,000
MALSR, or SSALR, or ALSF-1 or ALSF-2	200	1/2	2,400
MALSR with TDZ and CL, or SSALR with TDZ and CL, or ALSF-1/ALSF-2 with TDZ and CL	200	Visibility not Authorized[2]	1,800
MALS, or MALSR, or SSALR, or ALSF-1/ALSF-2, or REILS and HIRL, or RAIL, and HIRL	200	Visibility not Authorized	1,800

[1] The mid-RVR and rollout RVR reports (if available) provide advisory information to pilots. The mid-RVR report may be substituted for the TDZ RVR report if the TDZ RVR is not available.
[2] Visibility values below ½ statute mile are not authorized and shall not be used.

Table 11-6. Sample Ops Specs Paragraph C054, Limitations and Provisions for Instrument Approach Procedures and Instrument Flight Rules Landing Minimums: 14 CFR Part 121

a. High Minimum PIC Provisions. PICs who have not met the requirements of 14 CFR Part 121, §121.652, shall use the high minimum pilot RVR landing minimum equivalents as determined from the following table.

RVR Landing Minimum as published	RVR Landing Minimum Equivalent Required for High Minimum Pilots
RVR 1800	RVR 4500
RVR 2000	RVR 4500
RVR 2400	RVR 5000
RVR 3000	RVR 5000
RVR 4000	RVR 6000
RVR 5000	RVR 6000

So far we've discussed only increased landing minimums; what about the published takeoff minimums? The FAA does allow a high minimums captain to use an airport's published takeoff minimums for departure. However, since the need for a takeoff alternate is dependent upon the landing weather minimums at the departure airport, there is a greater chance a departure airport alternate airport will be required.

Many air carriers have been granted an exemption from the higher landing minimums provided certain weather conditions (e.g., crosswind <15 knots) and aircraft equipment exist (e.g., autopilot/flight director with approach coupler used to DA). This **Special Exemption 5549** allows the authorized air carrier's high minimums captains to fly to published landing minimums.

Inoperable Instruments and Equipment

So far, we've discussed the alternate airport and fuel supply requirements covered in Subpart U. Now we'll focus on what procedures must be followed for a flight to legally depart with certain inoperable instruments and equipment. 14 CFR §§121.628 and 135.179 both contain guidance for operating an aircraft with inoperative instruments and equipment. To begin with, unless an FAA-approved **minimum equipment list (MEL)** exists for that airplane *and* the certificate holder is authorized to use a minimum equipment list, no person may take off an airplane with inoperable instruments or equipment installed. Authorization for the use of a MEL is found in Paragraph D.095 of a Part 121 or 135 certificate holder's ops specs.

The MEL is a list that provides for the operation of aircraft, under specified conditions, with certain instruments, items of equipment or functions inoperative at the commencement of the flight. The MEL determines what instruments, items, or equipment may be temporarily inoperative while maintaining an acceptable level of safety. The MEL is prepared by the air carrier or operator for a specific aircraft. An aircraft's MEL is based on the FAA's approved aircraft type **master minimum equipment list (MMEL)** and may be more restrictive than the MMEL, but can never be less restrictive.

14 CFR §91.213(b) lists criteria for instruments and equipment that may not be included in an MEL. Section 91.213 also covers specific situations and conditions that must be met to fly with inoperative instruments and equipment *without* an approved MEL.

The MEL must always be on board the airplane and located so as to allow the flight crew direct access to it at all times prior to flight. Procedures and records for identifying the inoperable instruments and equipment must be listed in the air carrier's general operating manual and must be available to the pilot. The certificate holder may not use an MEL for any type of aircraft that is not specifically authorized in its ops specs Paragraph D.095. Also, the airplane must be operated under all applicable conditions and limitations contained in the MEL and the operations specifications authorizing use of the MEL (Figure 11-4). 14 CFR §§121.628 and 135.179 both require that the approved minimum equipment list:

Provide for the operation of the airplane with certain instruments and equipment in an inoperable condition. *(14 CFR 121.628[a][3][ii])*

The following instruments and equipment may not be included in the minimum equipment list:

(1) Instruments and equipment that are either specifically or otherwise required by the airworthiness requirements under which the airplane is type certificated and which are essential for safe operations under all operating conditions.
(2) Instruments and equipment required by an airworthiness directive to be in operable condition unless the airworthiness directive provides otherwise.
(3) Instruments and equipment required for specific operations by this part.

(14 CFR 121.628[b])

L1011 Minimum Equipment List

MEL ITEM NO.	MEL Name/Description	Flight Crew May Placard	Number Installed	Number Required for Dispatch	Repair Category	Limitations/Procedures
29-11-71A	Air Turbine Motor (ATM) Driven Pumps (B-2) ATM		1	0	A	(M)(O): May be inoperative provided: (a) All engine driven pumps are operative (b) C-2 ATM is operative (29-11-71 B), and (c) Repairs are made within 25 flight hours. (M): Refer to M.M. 19-11-71. (O): Refer to provisos (a,b) above.
29-11-71B	Air Turbine Motor (ATM) Driven Pumps (C-2) ATM **Dispatcher Approval Required**		1	0	A	(M)(O) May be inoperative provided: (a) All engine driven pumps are operative, (b) B-2 ATM is operative (29-11-71A), (c) Operation is conducted in accordance with Landing Gear Extended Performance Calculations, and (d) Repairs are made within 25 flight hours. (M): Refer to M.M. 29-11-71. (O): Refer to provisos (a,b, c) above
29-21-01	Ram Air Turbine (RAT) Deployment Sys. (Auto and Manual) **Dispatcher Approval Required**		2	0	B	(M)(O): May be inoperative provided: (a) Ram Air Turbine (RAT) is extended, and (b) Operations are conducted in accordance with Ops Manual Limitations Section, Hydraulics (M): Refer to M.M. 29-21-01. (O): Refer to provisos (a,b) above.
29-31-04	Hydraulic Fluid Temperature Indicator (Cockpit)	**YES**	1	0	C	
77-12-07A	N_3 RPM Indicating System	**YES**	3	2	B	(M)(O): May be inoperative provided associated EPR, N_1, N_2 and Fuel Flow Indicating Systems are operative. (M): Refer to M.M. 77-12-07. (O): Refer to proviso above.

Figure 11-4. Minimum equipment list.

Take a look at a sample of a page from a L-1011 minimum equipment list (Figure 11-4). Reading from left to right, you'll see that the first two columns contain the *MEL number* and the *name and/or description* of the inoperative component. Notice that under the second MEL item's name and description (for the Air Turbine Motor deferral), the note "Dispatcher Approval Required" appears. This notation will be added if the deferral of this item affects the performance of the aircraft. Any time an item affecting aircraft performance is deferred, the dispatcher (the person completing the performance calculations) must be notified so he or she may take the performance limitation(s) into consideration for flight planning purposes. Also, this note will be included if the item is a critical safety of flight item. If the dispatcher does not agree that flight with that item deferred can be completed with the highest level of safety, then the dispatcher may refuse to dispatch the flight.

The next two columns are fairly self-explanatory: the *number of installed* equipment vs. the *number required for dispatch*. In the last row of Figure 11-4, the deferral for the N_3 RPM gauge, notice that the number of installed N_3 gauges is three (the L-1011 has three engines), but the number of gauges required for dispatch is two. So according to this MEL, a flight may depart if one N_3 gauge is inoperative, but may not depart with more than one N_3 gauge inoperative.

Next let's look at the *Flight Crew May Placard* column. If there is a "YES" in this column, it means the inoperative component does not need to be deferred by a mechanic. The flight crew may write up the item, placard it, and continue with the flight. If the word "YES" does not appear in the column, then a mechanic must be called out and the inoperative item written up and deferred by the mechanic.

When a certificate holder is authorized to use an approved minimum equipment list, Paragraph D.095 of the ops specs requires inoperative items to be repaired within the time intervals specified for the **repair category** of items listed below:

- Category A. Items in this category shall be repaired within the *time interval specified* in the remarks column of the certificate holder's approved MEL.
- Category B. Items in this category shall be repaired within *3 consecutive calendar days (72 hours)* excluding the calendar day the malfunction was recorded in the aircraft maintenance log and/or record.
- Category C. Items in this category shall be repaired within *10 consecutive calendar days (240 hours)* excluding the calendar day the malfunction was recorded in the aircraft maintenance log and/or record.
- Category D. Items in this category shall be repaired *within 120 consecutive calendar days (2,880 hours)* excluding the day the malfunction was recorded in the aircraft maintenance log and/or record.

Equipment with little redundancy and/or items more critical to the safety of flight (e.g., electric standby hydraulic pumps) will be categorized as either "A" or "B." Equipment that is part of highly redundant systems and not as critical to the safety of flight (e.g., auxiliary power unit) will be classified category "C." Equipment that, if inoperative, poses little hazard to flight safety (e.g., Freon air conditioner) will be categorized as "D." Referring again to Figure 11-4, under the repair category, the N_3 gauge is listed as a Category B item, which means the gauge must be repaired or replaced within 3 calendar days after the day the item was written up in the logbook.

The certificate holder's ops specs are required to contain a program to manage the process of repairing the items listed in the approved MEL. This MEL management program is required to accomplish the following:

- Track the date and the time an item was deferred and subsequently repaired.
- Maintain a current record of the number of deferred items per aircraft and a supervisory review of each deferred item to determine the reason for any delay in repair, length of delay, and the estimated date the item will be repaired.
- Contain a plan for bringing together parts, maintenance personnel, and aircraft at a specific time and place for repair.
- Continually review the items deferred because of the unavailability of parts to ensure that a valid back order exists with a firm delivery date.

A few important things must be kept in mind when using a minimum equipment list. All equipment not listed in the MEL and related to the aircraft's airworthiness must be operative (e.g., the aircraft's wings must be in good condition, not damaged). The aircraft may not be dispatched with any inoperative equipment not specifically listed in the MEL or items that have been deferred longer than the MEL repair category allows. The air carrier must comply with any special limitations or procedures contained in the MEL.

Summary

This chapter has examined the rules under which flight dispatch works. The rules are primarily centered around assuring that the dispatcher has properly planned the flight so that in the event of any unforeseen contingency, there is an alternative plan that guarantees the safety of the flight. This planning deals with three major issues. The first issue is the procurement of weather information and operational data on the airports and NAVAIDs and other pertinent information for the routes to be flown. The second is the assurance that sufficient fuel is available to conduct the flight. The third is that the aircraft be airworthy and have the requisite performance under the existing conditions to successfully perform the flight.

In the next chapter, we will move from the planning stage of dispatch to the operational rules of Part 121 Subpart T: Flight Operations.

Important Terms in Chapter 11

1-2-3 rule
600-2 standard alternate weather minimums
800-2 standard alternate weather minimums
adequate alternate airport
alternate airport weather forecast conditions
alternate airport weather minimums
departure airport alternate airport
derived alternate (weather) minimums
destination alternate airport
dispatch release document
dispatching
en route alternate airport
estimated time en route (ETE)
extended operations (ETOPS) alternate
flight release
flight release document
fuel minimums
high minimums captain
IFR landing minimums
load manifest
master minimum equipment list (MMEL)
minimum equipment list (MEL)
on-line vs. off-line alternate
operational vs. non-operational alternate
People's Express Exemption
redispatch/rerelease
releasing
repair category
RVR (runway visual range)
Special Exemption 5549
standard alternate (weather) minimums
suitable alternate airport

Chapter 11 Exam

1. In the case of domestic flights, *each* flight must be dispatched, unless the flight was originally included in the dispatch of a multi-leg flight and the aircraft doesn't spend more than how many hours on the ground?
   a. 4 hours
   b. 3 hours
   c. 2 hours
   d. 1 hour

2. What information is required to appear on a Part 121 domestic or flag operator's dispatch release form?
    a. Company or organization name, make and model of aircraft, aircraft VIN number, flight number, name of each flight crewmember, departure airport, destination airport and alternate airports, minimum fuel supply, and weather reports and forecasts
    b. Identification number of the aircraft, trip number, departure airport, intermediate stops, destination airport and alternate airports, a statement about the type of operation (e.g., VFR, IFR), minimum fuel supply, and weather reports and forecasts
    c. Aircraft VIN number, air carrier name, make and model of aircraft, trip number, name of the pilot-in-command, departure airport, destination airport and alternate airports, minimum fuel supply, and weather reports and forecasts
    d. Air carrier name, trip number, departure airport, intermediate stops, destination airport and alternate airports, a statement about the type of operation (e.g., VFR, IFR), and weather reports and forecasts

3. What is the main difference between the load manifest used in domestic and flag operations and the load manifest used in supplemental operations?
    a. Domestic load manifests do not require passenger names, while flag and supplemental load manifests must contain passenger names.
    b. Load manifests used in supplemental international operations may use metric measurements for weight and balance calculations.
    c. Load manifests used in supplemental international operations may use metric measurements for the calculation of fuel load only.
    d. No difference. Domestic, flag, and supplemental load manifests must contain identical information.

4. 14 CFR §121.613 states that an air carrier may not dispatch an IFR flight under Part 121 unless the weather reports and forecasts indicate that at the time of arrival at the destination airport,
    a. the ceiling will be at least 1,500 feet above the lowest published instrument approach minimum for at least 1 hour before and 1 hour after the estimated time of arrival at the destination airport.
    b. the visibility and RVR will be greater than the standard takeoff minimums of ½ statute mile visibility or 2,400 feet RVR (runway visual range) for three or more engine airplanes and 1 statute mile visibility or 5,000 feet RVR for twin-engine aircraft.
    c. conditions will be at or above the authorized landing minimums.
    d. conditions will be at or above the authorized landing minimums for at least 1 hour before and 1 hour after the estimated time of arrival at the destination airport.

5. When is a departure airport alternate airport required prior to the departure of a flight operating under Part 121?
    a. When weather conditions are greater than the standard takeoff minimums of ½ statute mile visibility or 2,400 feet RVR (runway visual range) for three or more engine aircraft.
    b. When weather conditions are such that an aircraft departs an airport with takeoff minimums below the departure airport's landing minimums in the certificate holder's ops specs.
    c. When weather conditions are forecast to be, for at least 1 hour before and 1 hour after the estimated time of arrival at the destination airport, at or above the authorized landing minimums.
    d. When the appropriate weather reports or forecasts indicate the ceiling will be at least 1,500 feet above the lowest published instrument approach minimum or lowest circling MDA.

6. How are alternate airport weather minimums derived for an airport with one operational navigational facility providing a straight-in nonprecision approach procedure, or a straight-in precision approach procedure, or a circling maneuver from an instrument approach procedure?

   a. A ceiling is derived by adding 200 feet to the authorized Category I HAT or HAA, and a visibility is derived by adding 1 statute mile to the authorized Category I landing minimum.
   b. A ceiling is derived by adding 400 feet to the authorized Category I HAT or HAA, and a visibility is derived by adding 1 statute mile to the authorized Category I landing minimum.
   c. A ceiling is derived by adding 200 feet to the authorized Category I HAT or HAA, and a visibility is derived by adding ½ statute mile to the authorized Category I landing minimum.
   d. A ceiling is derived by adding 400 feet to the authorized Category I HAT or HAA, and a visibility is derived by adding ½ statute mile to the authorized Category I landing minimum.

7. How are alternate airport weather minimums derived for an airport with at least two operational navigational facilities, each providing a straight-in nonprecision approach procedure or a straight-in precision approach procedure to different, suitable runways?

   a. A ceiling is derived by adding 200 feet to the authorized Category I HAT or HAA, and a visibility is derived by adding 1 statute mile to the authorized Category I landing minimum.
   b. A ceiling is derived by adding 400 feet to the authorized Category I HAT or HAA, and a visibility is derived by adding 1 statute mile to the authorized Category I landing minimum.
   c. A ceiling is derived by adding 200 feet to the authorized Category I HAT or HAA, and a visibility is derived by adding ½ statute mile to the authorized Category I landing minimum.
   d. A ceiling is derived by adding 200 feet to the higher Category I HAT of the two approaches used, and a visibility is derived by adding ½ statute mile to the higher authorized Category I landing minimum of the two approaches used.

8. In Part 121 domestic operations, when is a destination alternate airport required?

   a. When the destination weather is not forecast to be, from 1 hour before until 1 hour after scheduled arrival time, at least ½ statute mile visibility or 2,400 feet RVR (runway visual range) for three or more engine airplanes and 1 statute mile visibility or 5,000 feet RVR for twin-engine aircraft.
   b. When the weather is not forecast to be better than 1,500 feet higher than the lowest published instrument minimums or 2,000 feet above airport elevations, whichever is greater. The visibility must be at least 3 miles or at least 2 miles added to the lowest published minimum visibility, whichever is greater.
   c. When the destination weather is not forecast to be, from 1 hour before scheduled arrival until 1 hour after, a ceiling of 2,000 feet and 3 statute miles visibility.
   d. When the destination weather is not forecast to be, from 1 hour before scheduled arrival until 1 hour after, a ceiling of 3,000 feet and 2 statute miles visibility.

9. What are the mandatory fuel requirements for Part 121 domestic operations?

   a. A flight may not depart unless it has enough fuel to fly to the airport to which it is dispatched, then fly to the most distant alternate (if required), then fly for 45 minutes at normal cruising fuel consumption rates.
   b. A flight may not depart unless it has enough fuel to fly to the airport to which it is dispatched, then fly to the closest alternate (if required), then fly for 30 minutes at normal cruising fuel consumption rates.
   c. A flight may not depart unless it has enough fuel to fly to and land at the airport to which it is dispatched plus an additional 15 percent of the required fuel load (from departure airport to destination airport).
   d. A flight may not depart unless it has enough fuel to fly to and land at the airport to which it is dispatched plus 90 minutes of contingency fuel, if no destination alternate is required.

10. Repair "B" on a minimum equipment list requires inoperative items to be repaired within what time interval?
    a. Repair category "B" shall be repaired within the *time interval specified* in the remarks column of the certificate holder's approved MEL.
    b. Repair category "B" inoperative items shall be repaired within *3 consecutive calendar days (72 hours)* **excluding** the calendar day the malfunction was recorded in the aircraft maintenance log and/or record.
    c. Repair category "B" inoperative items shall be repaired before midnight on the *third consecutive calendar day (72 hours)* **including** the calendar day the malfunction was recorded in the aircraft maintenance log and/or record.
    d. Repair category "B" inoperative items shall be repaired within *10 consecutive calendar days (240 hours)* **excluding** the calendar day the malfunction was recorded in the aircraft maintenance log and/or record.

11. A JetBlue flight crew flying a CAT I ILS approach, on glidepath, and just inside the final approach fix (FAF), is told by the tower that the weather for the intended runway has just dropped below minimums. What must this flight crew do?
    a. Immediately execute the published missed approach procedure and report to tower they are flying the missed approach procedure.
    b. This flight crew may continue the approach to DA/DH or MDA. In order to land the aircraft, the flight visibility must not be less than the visibility prescribed in the standard instrument approach procedure being used.
    c. Because this flight is Part 121, they are allowed to fly a "look-see" approach to the DA/DH or MDA, however they must execute a missed approach at the missed approach point.
    d. None of the above.

12. Under what conditions must a second alternate be filed prior to a flight departing for its destination?
    a. A second alternate is required when the first alternate weather is forecast to be, from one hour before to one hour after ETA, a ceiling of less than 2,000 feet and visibility of less than 3 SM (1-2-3 rule).
    b. A second alternate is needed if using Exemption 5549.
    c. A second alternate is needed if using Exemption 3585.
    d. A second alternate is needed if the first alternate is farther than one hour flying time, in still air from the departure airport, with one engine inoperative.

13. A "high minimums" captain is planning on flying a LDA/DME approach to ABC airport. If the published minimums for the LDA/DME approach are MDA(H) 650 feet and ¾ SM visibility, what would be this captain's minimums to fly this approach?
    a. A high minimums captain would need to increase the minimums to a MDA of 750 feet and a visibility of 1¼ SM.
    b. A high minimums captain may actually reduce the approach minimums by half because they've just completed a thorough instrument training course and they are really sharp when flying instruments.
    c. A high minimums captain would need to increase the minimums to a MDA of 1,000 feet and a visibility of 1¾ SM.
    d. None of the above.

14. What adjustment must be made for a high minimums captain's takeoff minimums?
    a. None; the FAA allows a high minimums captain to use the normal published takeoff minimums for the airport.
    b. The takeoff minimums must be increased by adding ½ SM to the lowest allowable published takeoff visibility minimums.
    c. None. The FAA allows the high minimums captain to use the normal published takeoff minimums for the airport; however, a takeoff alternate must be filed for every high minimums departure.
    d. None of the above.

15. A dispatch release document is used by supplemental operators while a flight release document is used by domestic and flag operators.
    a. True
    b. False

CHAPTER 12
PART 121, SUBPART T: FLIGHT OPERATIONS

Ladies and gentlemen, this is your captain speaking. We have a small problem. All four engines have stopped. We are doing our damnedest to get them all going again. I trust you are not in too much distress.

—**Capt. Eric Moody**, British Airways, after flying through volcanic ash in a Boeing 747

In this chapter we'll discuss Subpart T, which covers the FAA requirements for flight operations for all Part 121 air carriers. These requirements are, as we'll see, broad in nature and cover many aspects of flight operations, from who controls an air carrier's flight movements to the required passenger safety briefings and carry-on bag programs. The flight operations requirements found in Subpart T are addressed throughout an air carrier's ops specs and company operations manuals.

Operational Control (Domestic and Flag Operations)

A Part 121 air carrier is required by the FAA to spell out in its ops specs the system and procedures for the operational control of all flight movements, including training flights, charter flights, and the ferrying of aircraft. As we've discussed previously, **operational control** means the *exercise of authority over initiating, conducting or terminating a flight.* In practice, an air carrier exercises operational control by making the necessary decisions and performing the required procedures to operate flights safely and in compliance with the FARs and the air carrier's ops specs.

Operational control may be centralized in one position or delegated to many different individuals throughout the flight operations organization. Typically, the authority to dispatch or release flights is held by an air carrier's director of operations (DO) or the vice president of operations. The authority to dispatch or release flights is then delegated to aircraft dispatchers (domestic and flag operations) or flight followers (supplemental operations). While operational control functions may be delegated, the **responsibility for operational control** may not, and it rests with the certificate holder. The system and/or procedures used to establish and maintain operational control at an air carrier must be clearly defined in Paragraph A.008 of an air carrier's ops specs and the air carrier's general operations manual (GOM).

The person responsible for operational control must ensure that the air carrier's flight crews and operational control employees (aircraft dispatchers or flight followers) comply with company policies and procedures. For this reason, an air carrier's operating manuals must contain guidance on the conditions that must be met before a flight is dispatched. Let's take a look at Paragraph A.008 in the Delta Air Lines ops specs.

U.S. Department of
Transportation
Federal Aviation
Administration

Operation Specifications

Paragraph A.008

Delta Air Lines Ops Specs **Paragraph A.008**

Operational Control

A. The certificate holder provides operational control of flight operations through the use of the system described or referenced in this paragraph:

Flight Control—Flight Evaluation: *Flight Operations Manual—Chapter 33 Dispatcher Supplement*

Flight Control—Training Program: *Flight Control Training Manual*

Flight Operations—Department Organization: *Flight Operations Administrative Manual (FOAM)*

Flight Control—Duties Sabotage Threat: *Bomb Threat—Delta's Bomb Threat Procedures, Hijack—Delta Emergency Operations Manual*

Flight Control—Radio Transmissions: *Flight Operations Administrative Manual (FOAM) and Flight Operations Manual (FOM) Chapter 30*

Flight Control—Responsibility Aircraft Accident: *Emergency Operations Manual and Flight Operations Manual Chapter 10*

Flight Control—Aircraft Emergency: *Emergency Operations Manual and Flight Operations Manual Chapter 10*

1. Issued by the Federal Aviation Administration.
2. These Operations Specifications are approved by direction of the Administrator.

Principal Operations Inspector

3. Date Approval is effective: 05/24/2015 Amendment Number: 1
4. I hereby accept and receive the Operations Specifications in this paragraph.

Hantla, Becky J.
Senior Vice President, Flight Operations Date: 05/24/2015

We can see from ops specs Paragraph A.008 that a major aspect of operational control consists of developing and publishing flight control policies and procedures for flight operations personnel to follow in the performance of their duties. Specific operational control duties are covered in 14 CFR §121.533 and 121.535. The pilot-in-command (PIC) and the aircraft dispatcher are jointly responsible for the preflight planning, delay, and dispatch release of a flight in compliance with applicable FARs and operations specifications. This means that both the pilot-in-command and the aircraft dispatcher must consider all FARs and ops specs rules applicable to airworthiness, crew legality, duty/flight time, and operating rules before dispatching a flight. Their respective responsibilities can be broken down by position.

The aircraft dispatcher is responsible for:

- monitoring the progress of each flight,
- issuing necessary information for the safety of the flight, and
- canceling or redispatching a flight if, in his opinion or the opinion of the pilot-in-command, the flight cannot operate or continue to operate safely as planned or released.

The pilot-in-command is, during a flight, responsible for:
- the safety of the passengers, crewmembers, cargo, and aircraft.

Prior to flight, one of the pilot-in-command's most important responsibilities is determining whether the aircraft is airworthy. Since the pilot-in-command cannot track airworthiness directives (AD) or participate in overhaul and inspection activities, the PIC relies upon the aircraft logbook's airworthiness release. Review of the aircraft logbook and the preflight "walk-around" inspection are the approved means by which the pilot-in-command determines an aircraft's airworthiness.

Finally, the pilot-in-command has full control and authority in the operation of the aircraft. This authority is granted by Paragraphs 121.533(e) and 121.535(e), without limitation, over other crewmembers and their duties during flight time, even if the pilot-in-command does not hold a valid certificate authorizing him or her to perform the duties of those crewmembers (e.g., flight engineer certificate).

Operational Control (Supplemental Operations)

For supplemental operations, the responsibility for operational control differs due to the nature of supplemental operations, and as we've discussed previously, a supplemental air carrier is not required to employ an aircraft dispatcher. 14 CFR §121.537 places the responsibility for the operational control of supplemental carriers with the director of operations and the pilot-in-command. A supplemental air carrier must list in its general operations manual each person authorized to exercise operational control because there may be different individuals exercising operational control at various times (e.g., director of operations, flight follower, or even the pilot-in-command). Like domestic and flag operations, the system and/or procedure for establishing operational control at a supplemental carrier must be clearly defined in Paragraph A.008 of the air carrier's ops specs.

Section 121.537 gives the certificate holder the power to delegate the functions for the initiation, continuation, diversion, and termination of a flight, but like domestic and flag operations, the certificate holder may not delegate the responsibility for those functions.

The pilot-in-command and the director of operations are jointly responsible for the initiation, continuation, diversion, and termination of a supplemental flight in compliance with the applicable FARs and the operations specifications.

The director of operations is responsible for

- canceling,
- diverting, or
- delaying a flight, and
- assuring that each flight is monitored from
  - departure of the flight from the place of origin to arrival at the place of destination, including intermediate stops and any diversions.
  - maintenance and mechanical delays encountered at places of origin and destination and intermediate stops.
  - any known conditions that may adversely affect the safety of flight.

It is the responsibility of both the director of operations and the pilot-in-command to determine if, in their opinion, the supplemental flight cannot operate or continue to operate safely as planned or released. This responsibility is covered in Paragraph 121.537(c). Note that because there might not be an aircraft dispatcher assigned to the flight, the duties typically performed by a dispatcher are now the responsibility of the pilot-in-command.

The pilot-in-command is, during a flight, in command of the aircraft and crew and is responsible for the following:

- The safety of the passengers, crewmembers, cargo, and aircraft
- The preflight planning and the operation of the flight in compliance with 14 CFR Chapter 1 and the operations specifications
- Not operating an aircraft in a careless or reckless manner, so as to endanger life or property

Paragraph 121.537(d) grants the pilot-in-command full control and authority in the operation of the aircraft, without limitation, over other crewmembers and their duties during flight time, whether or not the PIC holds valid certificates authorizing him to perform the duties of those crewmembers.

Airplane Security

The Transportation Security Administration, Department of Homeland Security and the FAA require each air carrier to develop and maintain an **aviation security program** that provides for the safety of passengers and property traveling in air transportation against acts of criminal violence and air piracy. An air carrier must maintain at least one complete copy of its approved security program at its principal business office and the pertinent portions of its approved security program or appropriate implementing instructions at each airport where security screening is being conducted. All carriers conducting operations under Part 121 are required by Section 121.538 to comply with the security requirements found in the **Transportation Security Administration (TSA)** and **Department of Homeland Security (DHS)** regulations: 49 CFR, Chapter XII, Parts 1500–1562. The rules contained in Parts 1500–1562 also govern:

- each person aboard a Part 121 air carrier's aircraft,
- each person on an airport at which the operations of Part 121 air carriers are being conducted, and
- any certificate holder, if that carrier provides deplaned passengers access to an airport area where access is controlled by the inspection of persons and property in accordance with an approved security program.

A security program must provide for the following, as detailed in the Sections of 49 CFR, Chapter XII, Part 1544 listed below:

CFR 49, Chapter XII, Part 1544—Aircraft Operator Security: Air Carriers and Commercial Operators

Subpart C—Operations

§1544.201	Acceptance and screening of individuals and accessible property.
§1544.202	Persons and property onboard an all-cargo aircraft.
§1544.203	Acceptance and screening of checked baggage.
§1544.205	Acceptance and screening of cargo.
§1544.207	Screening of individuals and property.
§1544.209	Use of metal detection systems.
§1544.211	Use of X-ray systems.
§1544.213	Use of explosives detection systems.
§1544.215	Security coordinators.
§1544.217	Law enforcement personnel.
§1544.219	Carriage of accessible weapons.
§1544.221	Carriage of prisoners under the control of armed law enforcement officers.
§1544.223	Transportation of Federal Marshals.
§1544.225	Security of aircraft and facilities.
§1544.227	Exclusive area agreement.
§1544.228	Access to cargo and cargo screening: Security threat assessments for cargo personnel in the United States.
§1544.229	Fingerprint-based criminal history records checks (CHRC): Unescorted access authority, authority to perform screening functions, and authority to perform checked baggage or cargo functions.
§1544.230	Fingerprint-based criminal history records checks (CHRC): Flightcrew members.
§1544.231	Airport-approved and exclusive area personnel identification systems.
§1544.233	Security coordinators and crewmembers, training.
§1544.235	Training and knowledge for individuals with security-related duties.
§1544.237	Flight deck privileges.
§1544.239	Known shipper program.

Section 1544.215 provides that prior to flight, the **ground security coordinator (GSC)** is responsible for airplane security. The GSC is an employee of the air carrier, typically a gate agent with additional security training, whose job it is to inform the pilot-in-command of any pertinent security issues that may affect the flight. The GSC brings security issues such as any irregularities or occurrences within the local community that may affect security to the attention of the pilot-in-command. The GSC will also brief the pilot-in-command about any passengers that may be boarding that may increase the security risk during routine operations (e.g., armed law enforcement officers, prisoners). Before any domestic or flag departure, the GSC must signify on the dispatch release paperwork that all pertinent security issues have been brought to the attention of the pilot-in-command. Once airborne, the pilot-in-command assumes responsibility for airplane security.

Operations Notices

All air carriers are required by 14 CFR §121.539 to *notify their appropriate operations personnel of each change in equipment and operating procedures*. These **operations notices** are similar in concept to NOTAMs or SIGMET, and contain information such as the status of navigation aids, airport facilities, special air traffic control procedures and regulations, local airport traffic control rules (e.g., Washington's Ronald Reagan National Airport), and weather reports, including icing and other potentially hazardous meteorological conditions.

The method an air carrier uses to accomplish this task must be contained in its ops specs. Typically, most of this information can be found in an air carrier's flight plan, flight operations bulletins, or the carrier's airway manual. To supplement this, some companies publish a detailed brief of each individual airport served by the carrier. This airport brief is updated regularly and includes such information as local navigation facilities, obstacles such as terrain or towers, single engine departure procedures, noise abatement procedures, typical arrival gates, company radio frequencies, and so on.

Operations Schedules

As we discussed in Chapter 7, a scheduled air carrier—that is, a domestic and flag carrier—is required by 14 CFR §121.541 to establish realistic operations schedules. In establishing flight operations schedules, air carriers must allow enough time for the proper servicing of aircraft at intermediate stops and must consider the prevailing winds en route and the cruising speed of the type of aircraft used. These requirements are placed on air carriers for a couple of reasons. The first is to prevent them from developing "creative schedules" that would allow one carrier an unfair competitive advantage over another carrier (e.g., scheduling shorter flight times to attract more passengers). The second reason is to prevent an air carrier from altering a flight schedule to avoid the provisions of other FARs (e.g., flight and duty time limitations or number of required cockpit crewmembers). Normally, average or median flight times are used to determine if a schedule is realistic. If the destination is one that has never been served by the air carrier, then the flight time is determined by using the planned cruising speed of the aircraft. To further clarify cruising speed, Section 121.541 also requires that the cruising speed used in flight planning *may not be more than that resulting from the output of the engines* (the FAA thinks of everything).

Air carriers do have an inherent desire to use realistic flight schedules because their customers demand it. For this reason, most air carriers do query flight crews for analytical help in determining the causes of repeated delays for a particular flight segment. Airlines typically ask a flight crewmember to fill out some type of a "delay report" for flights that they identify as being frequently delayed or flown over scheduled block time. The flight crew states, in the delay report, what reasons they believe cause a particular flight to be delayed. These reports are then turned in to the chief pilot, who in turn forwards them to the director of operations office for analysis.

Flight Crewmember Duties

An overwhelming majority of air carrier incidents (e.g., altitude violations, runway incursions, etc.) over the years have been attributed to the distractions caused by flight crewmembers performing duties other than those required for the safe operation of the aircraft during some critical phase of flight. For example, many altitude violations have occurred during descent into a destination when one crewmember was "off" the ATC radio and "on" the aircraft's intercom discussing passenger requirements such as connecting gate information or required wheelchairs with a flight attendant. Obviously, anytime one pilot is "out of the loop" performing other duties, the chances of a mistake not being caught go up. For this reason, the FAA has established, in 14 CFR §121.542, **critical phase of flight** periods during which only duties required for the safe operation of the aircraft are allowed. This is usually referred to as the **sterile cockpit rule**.

The FAA has established *critical phases of flight* to include all ground operations involving taxi, takeoff, and landing and all other flight operations conducted below 10,000 feet, unless in level cruise flight. Section 121.542 states that *no certificate holder shall require, nor may any flight crewmember perform, any duties during a critical phase of flight except those duties required for the safe operation of the aircraft*. Duties such as "in-range" radio calls, company required position reports, passenger gate information, passenger special requests (e.g., wheelchairs), eating meals, and routine passenger convenience PAs (announcements) are not required for the safe operation of the aircraft and are not allowed during a critical phase of flight.

Another aspect of flight crewmember duties is the conduct of crewmembers during critical phases of flight. A good portion of crew resource management (CRM) training is devoted to instructing crewmembers how to best function during a critical phase of flight. Crewmembers are not allowed to engage in any activity during a critical phase of flight that could distract any flight crewmember from or interfere with the performance of his or her duties. Activities such as eating meals, engaging in nonessential conversations within the cockpit and nonessential communications between the cabin and cockpit crews, or reading publications not related to the proper conduct of the flight are not required for the safe operation of the aircraft and are therefore not allowed.

Prohibition on the Personal Use of Electronic Devices on the Flight Deck

Several incidents over the last decade involving a breakdown of cockpit discipline prompted Congress to address the use of **personal electronic devices (PEDs)** in the cockpit via legislation. In one instance, two commercial airline pilots were using their personal laptop computers during cruise flight and lost situational awareness, leading to a 150-mile fly-by of their planned destination. In another instance, during a post-accident investigation, it was discovered a pilot had sent text messages on her personal cell phone during the taxi phase of the flight after the aircraft pushed back from the gate and before the takeoff sequence. These incidents illustrate the potential for such PEDs to create a hazardous distraction during critical phases of flight.

For this reason, the FAA amended Section 121.542 in 2014 to include a prohibition of the use of PEDs during flight unless the use is directly related to the operation of the aircraft, or for emergency, safety-related, or certain employment-related communication. "PED" is a somewhat broad and technologically evolving category; it includes, but is not limited to, devices such as cell phones, smartphones, personal digital assistants, tablets, e-readers, gaming systems, iPods and MP3 players, as well as netbooks and notebook computers. This rule was created with the aim of ensuring that certain nonessential activities do not contribute to the challenge of task management on the flight deck and do not contribute to a loss of situational awareness due to attention to non-essential activities. The PED prohibition, which commences at taxi and ends when the aircraft is parked at the gate at the end of the flight segment, reflects the familiar provisions in the "sterile cockpit" rule. Let's look at the actual language of the rule, 14 CFR §121.542(d):

> (d) During all flight time as defined in 14 CFR 1.1, no flight crewmember may use, nor may any pilot in command permit the use of, a personal wireless communications device (as defined in 49 U.S.C. 44732(d)) or laptop computer while at a flight crewmember duty station unless the purpose is directly related to operation of the aircraft, or for emergency, safety-related, or employment-related communications, in accordance with air carrier procedures approved by the Administrator.

The FAA was quick to clarify in the amended ruling that "emergency" communications are those related to the safe operation of the aircraft and its occupants, not a flight crewmember's personal emergency.

Notice that while the FAA prohibits the "personal use" of wireless communications devices and laptop computers, it does allow for their "approved operational use." That is, the FAA does allow the use of PEDs in approved air carrier programs regarding "approved operational use" (e.g., electronic flight bags [EFB], digitized charts or manuals) of personal wireless communications devices and laptop computers.

Flight Crewmembers at Controls

14 CFR §121.543 dictates that all required flight crewmembers on flight deck duty must remain at the assigned duty station with seat belt fastened while the aircraft is taking off or landing and for the duration of the flight. A required flight crewmember may leave an assigned duty station for only three reasons:

- In connection with duties in operation of the aircraft (e.g., visual check for ice on wings).
- In connection with physiological needs, including personal relief and movement to ensure mental and physical alertness.
- If the required flight crewmember is beginning an assigned rest period and an authorized and qualified relief pilot is provided. The specifics of the required qualifications of a relief pilot have been recently amended in Section 121.543:

(3) If the crewmember is taking a rest period, and relief is provided—
   (i) In the case of the assigned pilot in command during the en route cruise portion of the flight, by a pilot who holds an airline transport pilot certificate not subject to the limitations in §61.167 of this chapter and an appropriate type rating, is currently qualified as pilot in command or second in command, and is qualified as pilot in command of that aircraft during the en route cruise portion of the flight. A second in command qualified to act as a pilot in command en route need not have completed the following pilot in command requirements: The 6-month recurrent flight training required by §121.433(c)(1)(iii); the operating experience required by §121.434; the takeoffs and landings required by §121.439; the line check required by §121.440; and the 6-month proficiency check or simulator training required by §121.441(a)(1); and
   (ii) In the case of the assigned second in command, by a pilot qualified to act as second in command of that aircraft during en route operations. However, the relief pilot need not meet the recent experience requirements of §121.439(b).

(14 CFR §121.543[b][3])

Pilot Monitoring

14 CFR §121.544 requires the **non-flying pilot (NFP)** to accomplish **pilot monitoring (PM)** duties that are designated in the air carrier's standard operating procedures (SOP) manual. As you would expect, both pilots are responsible for maintaining their own "big picture" by cross-checking each other's activities. The **pilot flying (PF)** is responsible for flying the aircraft in accordance with the approved operational procedures while the PM is tasked with the observation of the PF and comparing the current flight path with the intended flight path, automation modes and levels, and configuration status. The primary duty of the PM is to call attention to any deviations and, if required, the timely intervention in the event of a serious deviation.

Manipulation of Controls

Anyone familiar with the crash of Aeroflot Airlines Flight 593 knows what can happen if an unqualified person is allowed to manipulate the controls of an airliner. Flight 593 was an Airbus 310 flight from Moscow to Hong Kong, operated by Aeroflot Airlines, that crashed after the pilot allowed his 16-year-old son to fly the aircraft. The son had unknowingly disabled the A310 autopilot's control while seated at the controls. The end result was that the aircraft rolled into a steep bank and near-vertical dive from which the pilots were unable to regain control.

That brings us to 14 CFR §121.545, which specifies who is allowed to manipulate the controls of an aircraft during flight. To be authorized to manipulate an aircraft's controls, a person must be:

(a) A qualified pilot of the certificate holder operating that aircraft. *[i.e., the designated captain or first officer]*
(b) An authorized pilot safety representative of the Administrator or of the National Transportation Safety Board who has the permission of the pilot in command, is qualified in the aircraft, and is checking flight operations.
(c) A pilot of another certificate holder who has the permission of the pilot in command, is qualified in the aircraft, and is authorized by the certificate holder operating the aircraft.

(14 CFR §121.545)

Admission to Flight Deck

Due to the events of September 11, 2001, the prevalent decision-making philosophy regarding flight deck access is one of a restrictive nature. The FAA is judicious when determining which persons qualify for flight deck access. 14 CFR §121.547 and air carrier policy govern admission to the flight deck. The flight deck is defined as the area forward of the cockpit-to-cabin door. Notice that Section 121.547 does not limit the emergency authority of the pilot-in-command to exclude any person from the flight deck in the interest of safety. Both 14 CFR §91.3 and §121.547(a)(4) provide the PIC with final authority regarding the operation of the aircraft and, as such, the PIC may exclude any person from the flight deck in the interest of safety. So if in the opinion of the PIC, the presence of a person on the flight deck jeopardizes the safety of flight, the pilot-in-command may remove that person.

According to Paragraph 121.547(a), no person may be admitted to the flight deck unless that person is:

(1) A crewmember;
(2) An FAA air carrier inspector, a DOD commercial air carrier evaluator, or an authorized representative of the National Transportation Safety Board, who is performing official duties;

(3) Any person who—
   (i) Has permission of the pilot in command, an appropriate management official of the part 119 certificate holder, and the Administrator; and
   (ii) Is an employee of—
      (A) The United States, or
      (B) A part 119 certificate holder and whose duties are such that admission to the flightdeck is necessary or advantageous for safe operation; or
      (C) An aeronautical enterprise certificated by the Administrator and whose duties are such that admission to the flightdeck is necessary or advantageous for safe operation.
(4) Any person who has the permission of the pilot in command, an appropriate management official of the part 119 certificate holder and the Administrator. Paragraph (a)(2) of this section does not limit the emergency authority of the pilot in command to exclude any person from the flightdeck in the interests of safety.

(14 CFR §121.547[a])

For a brief listing of persons permitted admission to the flight deck and the authorization documentation required, see Table 12-1.

No person may admit any person to the flight deck unless there is a seat available for that person's use in the passenger compartment, except:

(1) An FAA air carrier inspector, a DOD commercial air carrier evaluator, or authorized representative of the Administrator or National Transportation Safety Board who is checking or observing flight operations;
(2) An air traffic controller who is authorized by the Administrator to observe ATC procedures;
(3) A certificated airman employed by the certificate holder whose duties require an airman certificate;
(4) A certificated airman employed by another part 119 certificate holder whose duties with that part 119 certificate holder require an airman certificate and who is authorized by the part 119 certificate holder operating the aircraft to make specific trips over a route;
(5) An employee of the part 119 certificate holder operating the aircraft whose duty is directly related to the conduct or planning of flight operations or the in-flight monitoring of aircraft equipment or operating procedures, if his presence on the flightdeck is necessary to perform his duties and he has been authorized in writing by a responsible supervisor, listed in the Operations Manual as having that authority; and
(6) A technical representative of the manufacturer of the aircraft or its components whose duties are directly related to the in-flight monitoring of aircraft equipment or operating procedures, if his presence on the flightdeck is necessary to perform his duties and he has been authorized in writing by the Administrator and by a responsible supervisor of the operations department of the part 119 certificate holder, listed in the Operations Manual as having that authority.

(14 CFR §121.547[c])

Table 12-1. Admission to flight deck

Person Seeking Admission to Flight Deck of U.S. Registered Aircraft	Required Authorization
FAA Air Safety Inspector	ID: FAA Form 110A and provides Form 8430-13 to air carrier personnel.
NTSB Investigator	NTSB ID Card (Form 1660.2) and NTSB Form 7000-5.
DOD Commercial Carrier Evaluator	S&A Form 110B or Form 8430-6
Federal Air Marshal (FAM)	ID Issued by Department of Homeland Security (DHS)
U.S. Air Traffic Controller (ATC)	Evaluation staff, FAA Form 7010-2 and 7000-1
	FAA Form 3120-28 in accordance with Air Traffic Procedures
U.S. Secret Service Agents	U.S. Secret Service credentials
Other authorized personnel. May require a seat in cabin.	Authorization letter from FAA and FAA Admission to Flight Deck form 8430-6

Note: Title 14 CFR Part 91, 91.3 and 121.547(a)(4) provide the PIC with "final authority" regarding the operation of the aircraft and as such, may exclude any person from the flight deck in the interest of safety.

The FAA and the **Transportation Security Administration (TSA) Security Directives (SD)** may further restrict access to the flight deck. The onus is on the air carrier to remain current with any pertinent TSA approvals or authorizations for any associated policies or procedures when determining who may have access to the flight deck.

How does an air carrier expeditiously verify who may be allowed access to the flight deck? There are currently two verification programs available for air carrier use:

1. **Cockpit Access Security System (CASS).** The CASS verification program is a network of databases hosted by participating Part 121 air carriers that contains employment and security information for individuals authorized by the FAA to occupy an aircraft's flight deck jump seat during normal operations. The information and process used for the CASS is intended to verify a person's identity, eligibility for access to the jump seat, and their employment status at the time of check in. CASS was developed by Airlines for America (A4A), in coordination with the FAA, the TSA, Part 121 certificated air carriers, and labor unions.

2. **Flight Deck Access Restriction (FDAR) Program.** The FDAR is a separate database similar to CASS, and serves the same purpose in confirming a requester's identity, employment status, and jump seat eligibility. Similar to the CASS, each air carrier must develop procedures that are incorporated in their operations manual required by 14 CFR §121.133. The FDAR may employ methods similar to CASS through a direct access computerized database system, or through the more conventional methods of telephone, email, and fax verification. The TSA may further restrict the use of the FDAR through an air carrier's TSA-approved security program.

Each air carrier must develop its own verification procedures and then incorporate them into the operations manual required by 14 CFR §121.133 (discussed in Chapter 4).

Observer's Seat: En Route Inspections

Now that we've discussed what credentials a person must have to gain admission to the flight deck, let's take a look at the requirement for an observer's seat on the flight deck of an air carrier's aircraft. All carriers are required by 14 CFR §121.581 to provide *and* make available a seat on the flight deck of each airplane for the occupancy by the Administrator (or his designee) while conducting en route inspections. The Administrator determines the location and equipment of the seat, with respect to its suitability for use in conducting en route inspections.

The only exception to this rule is for aircraft type certificated before December 20, 1995, for not more than 30 passengers. Many of these smaller aircraft were never manufactured with an observer's seat on the flight deck because prior to December 1995 these aircraft were governed by Part 135 regulations. With the implementation of Part 119, transferring the majority of these smaller aircraft to Part 121 regulations, the forward observer seat was then a requirement for all newly type certificated aircraft. For aircraft without a forward observer's seat, the air carrier must provide a forward passenger seat with headset or speaker for occupancy by the Administrator while conducting en route inspections.

So regardless of what some airline pilots (those who jumpseat to and from work) jokingly may tell you, the real reason airliners have a cockpit observer's jumpseat is to allow the FAA Administrator's designee, the FAA air carrier inspector, to conduct en route inspections. For this reason, FAA air carrier inspectors are issued FAA Form 110A, which is the identification credential for use in performance of official duties and presented when credentialed identification is requested by airline or airport security personnel. FAA inspectors must prominently display the **FAA Form 110A** on their outermost garment. In the United States, Form 110A has universal recognition as an FAA air carrier inspector's authority for unescorted movement in secure areas in and around an airport in order to perform official inspection duties. Inspectors may access aircraft or the airport operations areas through any access point used by the air carrier such as its boarding gates, operations office and any other access points used by the airline. In such cases, the FAA air carrier inspector who presents Form 110A is not subject to random screening at the aircraft boarding gate and should be permitted to board the aircraft at any time.

Closing and Locking of Flight Crew Compartment Door

In chapter 10 we discussed 14 CFR §121.313(f), which required a door between the passenger and pilot compartments for aircraft certificated after 1964. This door must have a locking means to prevent anyone from opening it without the pilot's permission. Sections 121.584 and 121.587(a) require the pilot-in-command of an airplane equipped with such a door to ensure that the door separating the flight crew compartment from the passenger compartment is closed and locked at all times when the aircraft is being operated. The exception to this requirement is:

> (b) The provisions of paragraph (a) of this section do not apply at any time when it is necessary to permit access and egress by persons authorized in accordance with §121.547 and provided the part 119 operator complies with FAA approved procedures regarding the opening, closing and locking of the flightdeck doors.
>
> (14 CFR §121.587[b])

Personal Flying Equipment (Flight Kit)

Flight crews are required by air carrier policy and 14 CFR §121.549 to carry certain personal and company issued flying equipment while on duty. An air carrier may require all flight crewmembers to maintain a "flight kit bag" containing company manuals, airway manuals, copies of checklists, passports, and a flashlight.

As far as Section 121.549 is concerned, the only flying equipment required of both crewmembers is an operative flashlight, which must be readily available. Additionally, the pilot-in-command is required to ensure the appropriate aeronautical charts containing adequate information concerning navigation aids and instrument approach procedures are aboard the aircraft for each flight. These charts are contained in a company airway manual issued to all flight crewmembers.

In addition to the equipment requirements discussed in Section 121.549, each flight crewmember must also carry:

- A current airman's certificate for the pilot's position
- A FCC radiotelephone operator permit
- A current FAA medical certificate of the appropriate class for the pilot's position

A current trend in the industry is for air carriers to go "paperless," that is, the carrier supplies an electronic "flight bag" (EFB) in the form of a laptop computer or tablet device. This computer is either supplied to each flight crewmember or is installed in a convenient location on each of the carrier's aircraft. The computer contains all required company manuals and airway manuals (including approach charts), plus a variety of other reference manuals for use by the flight crews. Advisory Circular (AC) 120-76B, *Guidelines for the Certification, Airworthiness, and Operational Use of Electronic Flight Bags*, contains guidance on the operational use of electronic flight bags for all operators conducting flight operations under Part 121, 125, 135, or Part 91 Subpart F and Part 91 Subpart K who want to replace required paper information with an EFB. There are a number of benefits for using an EFB, the most obvious being the incredible weight savings and therefore fuel savings by replacing the traditional flight bag (which included some thirty pounds of paper manuals and other company manuals previously stored in the cockpit) with an EFB. Other benefits include the ease with which a flight crew is able to access required information stored in the manuals and the ability for the company to "push" the revision of old material with the most current data.

Restriction or Suspension of Operation

When a certificate holder conducting domestic or flag operations knows of conditions, including airport and runway conditions, that are a hazard to safe operations, Section 121.551 and 121.553 require **restriction or suspension of operations** by the air carrier until those conditions are corrected. This authority to restrict or suspend air carrier operations is delegated to an air carrier's aircraft dispatchers and pilots-in-command. Whenever a pilot-in-command or aircraft dispatcher comes into knowledge that a situation exists dictating the need to restrict or suspend operations, their decision to do so is supported by the director of operations.

A good example of this is when a pilot-in-command and aircraft dispatcher deem weather or runway conditions are such that aircraft control and braking action might adversely affect safety; in such a case, they may suspend that air carrier's service to the airport. Service will only be resumed when in the opinion of the pilot-in-command, with the concurrence of the aircraft dispatcher, weather conditions improve to a level allowing safe operations.

Compliance with Approved Routes and Limitations

As discussed in Chapter 1, unlike flying under Part 91, an air carrier cannot simply fly anywhere it wishes to fly. 14 CFR §121.555 makes it clear that an air carrier's pilots are only authorized to conduct en route operations in the areas specified in its ops specs. Specifically, this is found in Paragraph B.050 of a carrier's ops specs. We've seen that Subparts E and F provide the basis for certificating every route or area the carrier intends to fly. This certification process looks at how the aircraft is equipped and at the adequacy of airports and other facilities and then approves those routes and airports for use. Sections 121.93 and 121.95 set up the requirements for approving routes, and Section 121.97 sets the requirements for airport approvals. A small airline may only be approved to operate in the 48 contiguous states, while a large airline might be approved for the 48 contiguous states and dozens of other areas. Let's take a look at a couple of examples of a carrier's ops specs Paragraph B.050, Authorized Areas of En Route Operations, on the following pages. The first Paragraph B.050 shown is from the JetBlue Airways ops specs, and the second is from the Delta Air Lines ops specs. (Note: The Delta Air Lines Paragraph B.050 has been abbreviated for simplicity.)

Finally, anytime a carrier would like to provide service to a destination in an area not appearing in Paragraph B.050 of their ops specs, the carrier must complete the entire route approval process for that route.

U.S. Department of Transportation
Federal Aviation Administration

Operation Specifications

Paragraph B.050

JetBlue Airways

a. The certificate holder is authorized to conduct en route operations in the areas of en route operation specified in this paragraph. The certificate holder shall conduct all en route operations in accordance with the provisions of the paragraphs referenced for each area of en route operation. The certificate holder shall not conduct any en route operation under these operations specifications unless those operations are conducted within the areas of en route operation authorized by this paragraph.

Authorized Areas of Operation	Referenced Op Specs Paragraphs
Atlantic—The North Atlantic Ocean west of the western boundary of NAT/MNPS airspace, between 45 degrees N and 24 degrees N, but excluding Bermuda and the Caribbean Islands	A005, B031, B032, B034, B036, B045, C077
USA—The 48 contiguous United States and the District of Columbia	A005, B031, B032, B034, B035, C077

1. The Certificate Holder applies for the Operations in this paragraph.
2. Support information reference: Added RVSM B046 for European operations.
3. These Operations Specifications are approved by direction of the Administrator.

Original signed by:
Gann, Ernest K.
Principal Operations Inspector

4. Date Approval is effective: 02/23/2015 Amendment Number: 3
5. I hereby accept and receive the Operations Specifications in this paragraph.

Original signed by:
Tyler O'Conner
Vice President, Flight Operations Date: 02/23/16

U.S. Department of
Transportation
Federal Aviation
Administration

Operation Specifications

Paragraph B.050

Delta Air Lines Ops Specs   **Paragraph B.050**

Authorized Area of En Route Operations

a. The certificate holder is authorized to conduct en route operations in the areas of en route operation specified in this paragraph. The certificate holder shall conduct all en route operations in accordance with the provisions of the paragraphs referenced for each area of en route operation. The certificate holder shall not conduct any en route operation under these operations specifications unless those operations are conducted within the areas of en route operation authorized by this paragraph.

Authorized Areas of Operation	Referenced Op Specs Paragraphs
The 48 contiguous United States and the District of Columbia	None
Africa—excluding Libya, Somalia, and Angola	B031, B032, B034, B043, B044
Asia	B031, B032, B034, B036, B043, B044
Australia	B031, B032, B044
Canada, including Canadian MNPS airspace and the Area of Magnetic Unreliability as established in the Canadian AIP	B031, B032, B034, B036, B039, B040, B042, B043, B044
Europe and the Mediterranean Sea Including Albania	B031, B032, B034, B036, B044, B046
Japan	B031, B032, B034, B044
Mexico and Central America	B031, B032, B034
Moscow-Karmanovo via direct	None
New Zealand	B031, B032, B044
Singapore	B031, B032, B034, B044
South America	B031, B032, B044
Thailand	B031, B032, B034, B044
The Atlantic Ocean and the islands of Greenland and Iceland	B031, B032, B036, B041, B042, B043, B044, B046
The Caribbean Sea and the Gulf of Mexico	B031, B032, B034, B036, B043, B044
The Indian Ocean	B031, B032, B043, B044
The State of Alaska	B031, B032, B034, B035
The State of Hawaii	B031, B032, B034, B036

1. The Certificate Holder applies for the Operations in this paragraph.
2. Support information reference: Added RVSM B046 for European operations.
3. These Operations Specifications are approved by direction of the Administrator.

Original signed by:
Gann, Ernest K.
Principal Operations Inspector

4. Date Approval is effective: 04/12/2015 Amendment Number: 2
5. I hereby accept and receive the Operations Specifications in this paragraph.

Original signed by:
Mr. Alfred Kahn II
Senior Vice President, Flight Operations Date: 04/18/2015

Use of Certificated Land Airports

Now that we've discussed what routes an air carrier is authorized to fly, let's turn our attention to **certificated land airports** and the regulations governing the airports that a Part 121 air carrier may serve. For aircraft larger than 30 seats, 14 CFR §121.590 prohibits operations to or from an airport unless that airport is federally certificated under Part 139; the only exception is that an air carrier may designate *and* use as a required alternate airport for departure or destination an airport that is not certificated under Part 139 of this chapter. Part 139 governs the certification and operations of land airports. Let's take a look at some of the major sections of Part 139:

§139.301	Records.
§139.303	Personnel.
§139.305	Paved areas.
§139.307	Unpaved areas.
§139.309	Safety areas.
§139.311	Marking, signs, and lighting.
§139.313	Snow and ice control.
§139.315	Aircraft rescue and firefighting: Index determination.
§139.317	Aircraft rescue and firefighting: Equipment and agents.
§139.319	Aircraft rescue and firefighting: Operational requirements.
§139.321	Handling and storing of hazardous substances and materials.
§139.323	Traffic and wind direction indicators.
§139.325	Airport emergency plan.
§139.327	Self-inspection program.
§139.329	Pedestrians and ground vehicles.
§139.331	Obstructions.
§139.333	Protection of NAVAIDS.
§139.335	Public protection.
§139.337	Wildlife hazard management.
§139.339	Airport condition reporting.
§139.341	Identifying, marking, and lighting construction and other unserviceable areas.
§139.343	Noncomplying conditions.

Paragraph A.070 of an air carrier's ops specs addresses the airports that carrier is authorized to use. Let's take a look at Paragraph A.070 of the Delta Air Lines ops specs.

U.S. Department of Transportation Federal Aviation Administration	Operation Specifications Paragraph A.070
Delta Air Lines Ops Specs	**Paragraph A.070**

Airports Authorized for Scheduled Operations

a. The certificate holder is authorized to conduct scheduled passenger and cargo operations between the regular, refueling, and provisional airports specified in the following table. Except for alternate airports, the certificate holder shall not use any other airport in the conduct of scheduled passenger and cargo operations. The certificate holder shall maintain a list of alternate airports which can be used and shall not use any alternate airport unless it is suitable for the type of aircraft being used and the kind of operation being conducted.

b. The following definitions shall apply:

Regular Airport. An airport approved under scheduled service to a community as the regular stop to that community.

Refueling Airport. An airport approved as an airport to which flights may be dispatched only for refueling.

Provisional Airport. An airport approved for use by an air carrier for the purpose of providing scheduled service to a community when the regular airport serving that community is not available.

Alternate Airport. An airport at which an aircraft may land if a landing at the intended airport becomes inadvisable.

NOTE: Refueling and provisional airports are not applicable to Part 135 operations.
R = Regular, F = Refueling, A = Alternate, and P = Provisional

Airports Authorized for Scheduled Operations

Airport	Aircraft Authorized				
Airport Name:	Provisional Airport:	MD90	B-737	B-757/767	B-777
Anchorage, AK	Fairbanks, AK	N/A	N/A	R	A
Albany, NY		R	R	R	A
Baltimore, MD		R	R	R	A
Paris, France		N/A	N/A	N/A	R
Shannon, Ireland		N/A	N/A	N/A	R
Cork, Ireland		N/A	N/A	N/A	A
Pasco, WA		N/A	R	A	N/A
Yuma, AZ		A	R	A	N/A

(Delta Air Lines paragraph A.070 abbreviated for simplicity.)

Emergencies: Domestic, Flag, and Supplemental Operations

14 CFR §91.3(b) grants a pilot-in-command the authority to deviate from any FAR during an emergency situation to whatever extent necessary to meet that emergency. In 14 CFR §121.557(a), we see this is also the case in domestic and flag air carrier operations; however, Part 121 takes this "emergency authority" a step further. That step is to allow for the inclusion of the aircraft dispatcher. Section 121.557 states that a pilot-in-command may in an emergency *take any action that he or she considers necessary under the circumstances to the extent required in the interests of safety*. This includes deviations not only from FARs, but also from ops specs limitations or company procedures. If an emergency situation arises during flight that requires immediate decision and action by an aircraft dispatcher, that person is required by Paragraph 121.557(b) to advise the pilot-in-command of the emergency (e.g., bomb threat) and ascertain and record any decision by the captain. If the aircraft dispatcher cannot make contact with the pilot-in-command, *he shall declare an emergency and take any action that he considers necessary under the circumstances*. Once emergency authority has been exercised, the pilot-in-command or dispatcher must keep the appropriate ATC facility and that air carrier's dispatch center fully informed of the progress of the flight.

Anytime emergency authority is exercised by either the pilot-in-command or dispatcher, the person declaring the emergency is required by §121.557(c) to send in a written report to the Administrator within 10 days after the date of the emergency (aircraft dispatcher) or within 10 days of returning to that pilot's home base (pilot-in-command). Typically, an air carrier will require the dispatcher or the pilot-in-command to first send the report to the director of operations. The DO will review it and forward it to the principal operations inspector (POI) on behalf of the Administrator.

Emergency authority for supplemental operators is virtually identical to that of the domestic and flag operators. The only difference is the allowance for operations without an aircraft dispatcher. In this case the duties required of the dispatcher in domestic and flag operations are the responsibility of the appropriate management personnel under supplemental operations.

Reporting Potentially Hazardous Meteorological Conditions and Irregularities of Ground and Navigation Facilities

Whenever a pilot-in-command encounters a meteorological condition (e.g., wind shear, in-flight icing, turbulence, etc.) or an irregularity of ground and navigation facilities (e.g., VOR outage, inoperative approach lights, etc.), the knowledge of which he considers essential to the safety of other flights, that person is required by Section 121.561 to notify an appropriate ground station as soon as practicable. This ground station is then required to notify the agency directly responsible for the operation of that facility.

Reporting Mechanical Irregularities

Prior to flight, the pilot-in-command is required by 14 CFR §121.563 to ascertain the status of any irregularity entered in the aircraft logbook at the end of the preceding flight. Either an authorized mechanic must sign off any "write-ups" or flight crews must comply with any applicable minimum equipment list provisions. Furthermore, the pilot-in-command must enter any maintenance mechanical irregularities occurring during flight time in the maintenance log of the airplane at the end of that flight time. Chapter 13 contains a more detailed discussion of the aircraft logbook.

Engine Inoperative: Landing and Reporting

When an aircraft engine fails or is shut down in flight as a precautionary measure to prevent possible damage, the pilot-in-command is required by 14 CFR §121.565 to do two things:

- Land the airplane at the nearest suitable airport, *in point of time*, at which a safe landing can be made (unless the airplane has three or more engines; see below).
- Notify the appropriate air traffic control (ATC) facility as soon as practicable after the engine failure or in flight shutdown.

If an aircraft has three or more engines and not more than one has failed, the FAA allows the pilot-in-command either to select the nearest suitable airport or to select another airport after considering the following:

(1) The nature of the malfunction and the possible mechanical difficulties that may occur if flight is continued.
(2) The altitude, weight, and usable fuel at the time that the engine is shutdown.
(3) The weather conditions en route and at possible landing points.
(4) The air traffic congestion.
(5) The kind of terrain.
(6) His familiarity with the airport to be used.

(14 CFR §121.565[b])

If the pilot-in-command elects to land at an airport other than the nearest suitable airport, the PIC is then required to send a written report to that carrier's director of operations (DO). The report must contain the reasons for determining that the selection of the chosen airport, other than the nearest airport, was as safe a course of action as landing at the nearest suitable airport.

The director of operations is then required by Paragraph 121.565(d) to forward this report with his or her comments to the certificate holding district office within 10 days after the pilot returns to his or her home base.

Instrument Approach Procedures and IFR Landing Minimums

As we discussed in the last chapter, an air carrier's instrument approach procedures are covered in its flight operations manual (FOM), airway manual, training manuals, and ops specs. A carrier's particular IFR landing minimums are covered in its ops specs, specifically in Part C, Terminal Instrument Procedures, paragraphs C.051–C.063. In Part C, the carrier lists exactly how it will conduct IFR approach procedures and what approaches its pilots are authorized to conduct (e.g., many operators do not authorize circling approaches if conditions are less than basic VFR). Air carrier pilots are only allowed to make those instrument approaches using weather minimums found in Part C of their ops specs.

Equipment Interchange: Domestic and Flag Operations

Air carriers from time to time have engaged in **equipment interchange agreements** or temporary "**dry leases**" of aircraft from one airline to another. These agreements are commonly used to meet specific market demands and/or seasonal fluctuations. While a "**wet lease**" is a leasing agreement involving the aircraft *and* at least one crewmember, a dry lease is an aircraft leased without the crew. An equipment interchange agreement is a dry lease of an aircraft from one carrier to another for short periods of time.

During the late 1980s, American Airlines entered an equipment interchange agreement with Alaska Airlines. This agreement involved a dry lease of five Alaska Airlines B-727s, painted in Alaska Airlines colors, and flown by American Airlines crewmembers on certain routes in the western United States. These five aircraft were operated from HOU-DFW-SEA-ANC-FAI and the return trip. Since American only flew in the lower 48 states, the aircraft were flown with American crewmembers for each direction of the HOU-DFW-SEA legs of the trip, while Alaska pilots flew each direction on the SEA-ANC-FAI legs. On return to SEA from Alaska, the Alaska crewmembers would literally walk off the airplane and the American Airlines crewmembers would board for the leg to DFW. During each exchange of crews, the aircraft was signed over and operational control responsibilities transferred to the receiving airline. American flight crews had to use a special call sign to help avoid as much confusion as possible with tower, ground control, and other aircraft expecting to see an airplane painted in American Airlines colors (e.g., American Flight 71 in an Alaska Airlines aircraft). Braniff International was the sole U.S. operator of the Concorde through a similar arrangement with British Airways where control was passed at Dulles Airport. Braniff operated the aircraft subsonic from Dulles to Dallas. The aircraft were painted in Braniff colors on one side and British Airways colors on the other, with two different registration numbers.

14 CFR 121.569 governs the procedures for entering into and gaining approval for an interchange agreement between air carriers. Before a domestic or flag air carrier can gain approval to operate under an interchange agreement, the carrier must show:

(1) The procedures for the interchange operation conform… [with the applicable FARs] and with safe operating practices;
(2) Required crewmembers and dispatchers meet approved training requirements for the airplanes and equipment to be used and are familiar with the communications and dispatch procedures to be used;
(3) Maintenance personnel meet training requirements for the airplanes and equipment, and are familiar with the maintenance procedures to be used;
(4) Flight crewmembers and dispatchers meet appropriate route and airport qualifications; and
(5) The airplanes to be operated are essentially similar to the airplanes of the certificate holder with whom the interchange is effected with respect to the arrangement of flight instruments and the arrangement and motion of controls that are critical to safety unless the Administrator determines that the certificate holder has adequate training programs to insure that any potentially hazardous dissimilarities are safely overcome by flight crew familiarization.

(14 CFR §121.569[a])

Airplane Evacuation Capability

In chapter 10, we discussed some of the certification requirements in regard to emergency escape and lighting equipment required for Part 121 aircraft certification. Specifically, we looked at 121.310, which states that *if the airplane's emergency exit (other than over the wing) is more than 6 feet from the ground with the airplane on the ground and the landing gear extended, the airplane must have an approved means to assist the occupants in descending to the ground.* 14 CFR §121.570(a) requires this *automatically deployable emergency evacuation assisting means* to be ready for evacuation before an airplane carrying passengers may be moved on the ground, take off, or land.

Paragraph 121.570(b) requires at least one floor-level exit be available that can provide for the evacuation of passengers through normal or emergency means during the time passengers are on board the aircraft prior to its movement on the surface. Note that to satisfy the requirement of 121.570(a), this floor level door must be *available* for use. This requirement may restrict certain aircraft servicing operations from being conducted while passengers are on board the aircraft. For instance, some aircraft may not fuel the left side of the aircraft while passengers are on board because the fueling operation blocks the *availability* of the one floor-level exit.

The Briefing of Passengers Before Takeoff

Each air carrier is required by 14 CFR §121.571 to ensure that all passengers, prior to takeoff, are orally briefed by the appropriate crewmember on the following:

- Smoking policy
- The location of emergency exits
- The use of safety belts
- The location and use of any required emergency flotation means

Paragraph 121.571(a)(2) addresses the required "after takeoff safety briefing," which states that passengers should keep their seat belts fastened, while seated, even when the seat belt sign is off.

An individual briefing is required by 121.571(a)(3) for persons who may need the assistance of another person to move expeditiously to an exit in the event of an emergency. This briefing must occur prior to every takeoff unless that person has been given a briefing before a previous leg on the same flight in the same aircraft. In the individual briefing, the required crewmember shall

(i) Brief the person and his attendant, if any, on the routes to each appropriate exit and on the most appropriate time to begin moving to an exit in the event of an emergency; and

(ii) Inquire of the person and his attendant, if any, as to the most appropriate manner of assisting the person so as to prevent pain and further injury.

(14 CFR §121.571[a][3])

All air carriers must carry on each passenger-carrying airplane, in convenient locations for use of each passenger, printed cards supplementing the oral briefing and containing:

(1) Diagrams of, and methods of operating, the emergency exits
(2) Other instructions necessary for use of emergency equipment

(14 CFR §121.571[b])

Each card required by this paragraph must contain information that is pertinent only to the type and model airplane used for that flight.

Finally, the air carrier is required by Paragraph 121.571(c) to describe in its manual the procedure to be followed in the before takeoff briefing. Usually this will be addressed in both the flight operations manual and the flight attendant's manual.

Briefing Passengers: Extended Overwater Operations

In addition to the oral briefing previously discussed in 121.571(a), 14 CFR §121.573 requires each air carrier operating an airplane in extended overwater operations (more than 50 nautical miles from the nearest shoreline) to ensure all passengers are orally briefed by the appropriate crewmember on the location of life rafts. This includes a demonstration of the method of donning and inflating a life preserver. This briefing is not required to be given before takeoff unless the aircraft will be flying over water immediately after takeoff (e.g., departing New York's JFK airport for London Heathrow). If the aircraft does not fly over water immediately after takeoff, then the briefing is not required to be given until before entering the overwater segment of the flight (e.g., departing Dallas's DFW airport for London). Paragraph 121.573(c) requires that the extended overwater briefing be described in the air carrier's operations manual. Like the before takeoff briefing, this briefing will usually be addressed in both the flight operations manual and the flight attendant's manual.

Oxygen for Medical Use by Passengers

Chapter 10 covered the "first aid" passenger oxygen requirements for passengers. This applies to cases in which a passenger develops the need for oxygen while on a flight (e.g., chest pains, asthma, unconsciousness), not prior to boarding. 14 CFR §121.574 governs the carriage of *oxygen for medical use* by passengers who know of their need for oxygen in advance of the flight. Paragraph 121.574(a) prohibits passengers from using their own oxygen bottles on board an air carrier's aircraft. An air carrier must provide the oxygen bottles, tubing, and mask/nasal cannula, except that a person may be allowed to use their own mask/cannula provided the equipment is shown to be compatible with the oxygen bottles supplied by the air carrier. So if any medical oxygen is to be used on a flight, the bottles must be ordered from that air carrier in advance of the flight. The reason for this is simply to assure the quality control of the oxygen bottles.

Section 121.574 allows for only two types of oxygen storage systems: gaseous oxygen bottles (compressed gas) and liquid oxygen bottles. When a gaseous oxygen system is used, the equipment must have been under the air carrier's approved maintenance program since it was purchased new or since the last hydrostatic test of the storage cylinder, and the pressure in any oxygen cylinder must not exceed the rated cylinder pressure. A hydrostatic test is simply a test to see if an oxygen bottle (filled with water) can withstand a pressure that is greater than the pressure of the gas that will be carried in the bottle. Also, when using a gaseous oxygen system, no air carrier may allow any person to connect or disconnect oxygen-dispensing equipment from the oxygen bottle while any passenger is aboard the airplane. When liquid oxygen bottles are used, the equipment must have been under the air carrier's approved maintenance program since it was purchased new or since the storage container was last purged.

Passengers needing oxygen for medical use must order the oxygen in advance of the flight; usually this must be done at least 48 hours prior to departure time. Any person requesting oxygen is required by §121.574(a)(4) to have in their possession a licensed physician's written statement that specifies the maximum quantity of oxygen needed each hour and the maximum flow rate needed for the pressure altitude corresponding to the pressure in the cabin of the airplane under normal operating conditions. Paragraph 121.574(a)(4) does allow passengers to use their own oxygen bottles during a flight if that aircraft is carrying only persons who may have a medical need for oxygen during flight (e.g., medical transport or Red Cross flight).

Whenever oxygen is used for medical reasons on board the aircraft, the pilot-in-command must be advised of its presence on the aircraft and of when the oxygen is to be used. Oxygen equipment must be properly secured in the cabin, and the passenger must be seated in such a way as to allow access to or use of any required emergency or regular exit or of the aisle in the passenger compartment.

An additional type of oxygen delivery device commonly used on board aircraft is a portable oxygen concentrator (POC). As the name implies, an oxygen concentrator is a device that concentrates the oxygen from the surrounding air, compressing it to the required density and then delivering purified medical-grade oxygen directly to the patient through a mask or nasal canula. The big advantage of portable oxygen concentrators is a passenger may bring their own FAA-approved device on board the aircraft. Another advantage is that while liquid or gaseous oxygen systems require passengers to order from the air carrier in advance of the flight, POCs may be brought aboard without prior approval. Airlines will check the POC for the FAA label that identifies the device approval. The label must include the following statement in red text: "The manufacturer of this portable oxygen concentrator has determined this device conforms with all applicable FAA requirements for portable oxygen concentrator carriage and use on board aircraft." Airline personnel can look for this label to determine whether the POC may be used on the aircraft.

As you might expect, during aircraft movement on the surface, takeoff, and landing, the device must be stowed under the seat in front of the user or in another approved stowage location so that it does not block the aisle way or the entryway to the row. If the device is to be operated by the user, it must be operated only at a seat location that does not restrict any passenger's access to, or use of, any required emergency or regular exit, or the aisle(s) in the passenger compartment. For this reason, no person operating a portable oxygen concentrator is permitted to occupy an exit row seat.

Paragraph 121.574(a)(7)(b) and (c) covers additional important safety regulations concerning the use of onboard medical oxygen such as:

(b) No person may smoke or create an open flame and no certificate holder may allow any person to smoke or create an open flame within 10 feet of oxygen storage and dispensing equipment carried in accordance with paragraph (a) of this section or a portable oxygen concentrator carried and operated in accordance with paragraph (e) of this section.

(c) No certificate holder may allow any person to connect or disconnect oxygen dispensing equipment, to or from a gaseous oxygen cylinder while any passenger is aboard the airplane.

As we discussed earlier, it is important to point out the medical oxygen and portable oxygen concentrators covered in §121.574 do not apply to the carriage of supplemental or first-aid oxygen covered by §121.333, discussed in Chapter 10. The distinction here is §121.574 deals with prior to flight and pre-planned passenger oxygen use, while §121.333 covers the storage and use of onboard oxygen for first aid during an unplanned medical event that occurs during the flight.

Alcoholic Beverages

14 CFR §121.575 contains a number of prohibitions (pun intended) concerning the use of alcoholic beverages on board an aircraft. They are as follows:

(a) No person may drink any alcoholic beverage aboard an aircraft unless the certificate holder operating the aircraft has served that beverage to him.

(b) No certificate holder may serve any alcoholic beverage to any person aboard any of its aircraft who—
  (1) Appears to be intoxicated;
  (2) Is escorting a person or being escorted in accordance with 49 CFR 1544.221; or
  (3) Has a deadly or dangerous weapon accessible to him while aboard the aircraft in accordance with 49 CFR 1544.219, 1544.221, or 1544.223.

(c) No certificate holder may allow any person to board any of its aircraft if that person appears to be intoxicated.

(d) Each certificate holder shall, within five days after the incident, report to the Administrator the refusal of any person to comply with paragraph (a) of this section, or of any disturbance caused by a person who appears to be intoxicated aboard any of its aircraft.

(14 CFR §121.575)

Retention of Items of Mass in Passenger and Crew Compartments

When we talk of items of mass stored in the cabin or crew compartments, the first thing that comes to mind is cargo. However, considering the average fully stocked galley cart weighs more than 200 pounds, it is easy to see the need to secure these items. For this reason, Section 121.576 requires air carriers to provide and use means to prevent each item of galley equipment and each serving cart, when not in use, and each item of crew baggage that is carried in a passenger or crew compartment from becoming a hazard by shifting under the appropriate load factors corresponding to the emergency landing conditions under which the airplane was type certificated.

Stowage of Food, Beverage, and Passenger Service Equipment During Airplane Movement on the Surface, Takeoff, and Landing

Now that we've covered the requirement to have a means of securing galley equipment and crew baggage in the passenger cabin, let's take a look at the requirements for the stowage of food, beverage, and passenger service equipment during airplane movement. No certificate holder may move an airplane on the surface, take off, or land:

- When any food, beverage, or tableware furnished by the certificate holder is located at any passenger seat.
- Unless each food and beverage tray and seat-back tray table is secured in its stowed position.
- Unless each passenger serving cart is secured in its stowed position.
- Unless each movie screen that extends into an aisle is stowed.

To facilitate accomplishment of this task by the flight attendants, Section 121.577 requires all passengers to comply with instructions given by a crewmember with regard to the stowage of tray tables and food and beverage items.

Prohibition against Interference with Crewmembers

In response to an increase of air rage incidents occurring throughout the airline industry, the FAA, in 1999, added a provision protecting air carrier crewmembers from interference with their duties. 14 CFR §121.580 governs the behavior of persons aboard an aircraft and may look familiar to you because it is identical to the language used in 14 CFR §91.11, Prohibition on Interference with Crewmembers.

> No person may assault, threaten, intimidate, or interfere with a crewmember in the performance of the crewmember's duties aboard an aircraft being operated under this part. *(14 CFR §121.580)*

As you might imagine, the most common form of interference towards crewmembers occurs in the cabin of an air carrier flight. Typically these air rage cases involve an intoxicated passenger(s) being verbally abusive to flight attendants or other passengers. Extreme cases have involved passengers physically striking flight attendants or attempting to break down the cockpit door. As you might imagine, in a post-9/11 world, there is little tolerance for these types of behaviors. In many cases fellow passengers overpower the offending passenger and help the cabin crew handcuff and strap down the passenger to any available passenger seat for the remainder of the flight.

Means to Discreetly Notify a Flight Crew

While we are on the subject of inflight of disturbances, 14 CFR §121.582 requires an air carrier to have an approved means by which the cabin crew can discreetly notify the flight crew in the event of suspicious activity or security breaches in the cabin. This is generally accomplished through the use of the standard onboard cabin interphone system, although each air carrier has developed their own FAA-approved procedures and devices to comply with this requirement.

Carriage of Persons without Compliance with the Passenger-Carrying Requirements of This Part

Throughout this text we have discussed a variety of aircraft equipment and personnel requirements necessary for Part 121 operations (e.g., emergency equipment, number of flight attendants, emergency exits, etc.). These requirements are all based on the passenger-carrying capacity of the aircraft. 14 CFR §121.583 covers the carriage of certain persons without compliance with the passenger-carrying requirements of Part 121.

The following persons may be carried aboard an airplane without complying with the passenger-carrying airplane requirements:

(a) (1) A crewmember.
 (2) A company employee.
 (3) An FAA air carrier inspector, a DOD commercial air carrier evaluator, or an authorized representative of the National Transportation Safety Board, who is performing official duties.
 (4) A person necessary for—
   (i) The safety of the flight;
   (ii) The safe handling of animals;
   (iii) The safe handling of hazardous materials whose carriage is governed by regulations in 49 CFR part 175;
   (iv) The security of valuable or confidential cargo;
   (v) The preservation of fragile or perishable cargo;
   (vi) Experiments on, or testing of, cargo containers or cargo handling devices;
   (vii) The operation of special equipment for loading or unloading cargo; and
   (viii) The loading or unloading of outsize cargo.
 (5) A person described in paragraph (a)(4) of this section, when traveling to or from his assignment.
 (6) A person performing duty as an honor guard accompanying a shipment made by or under the authority of the United States.
 (7) A military courier, military route supervisor, military cargo contract coordinator, or a flight crewmember of another military cargo contract air carrier or commercial operator, carried by a military cargo contract air carrier or commercial operator in operations under a military cargo contract, if that carriage is specifically authorized by the appropriate armed forces.
 (8) A dependent of an employee of the certificate holder when traveling with the employee on company business to or from outlying stations not served by adequate regular passenger flights.
(b) No certificate holder may operate an airplane carrying a person covered by paragraph (a) of this section unless—
 (1) Each person has unobstructed access from his seat to the pilot compartment or to a regular or emergency exit;
 (2) The pilot in command has a means of notifying each person when smoking is prohibited and when safety belts must be fastened; and
 (3) The airplane has an approved seat with an approved safety belt for each person. The seat must be located so that the occupant is not in any position to interfere with the flight crewmembers performing their duties.
(c) Before each takeoff, each certificate holder operating an airplane carrying persons covered by paragraph (a) of this section shall ensure that all such persons have been orally briefed by the appropriate crewmember on—
 (1) Smoking;
 (2) The use of seat belts;
 (3) The location and operation of emergency exits;
 (4) The use of oxygen and emergency oxygen equipment; and
 (5) For extended overwater operations, the location of life rafts, and the location and operation of life preservers including a demonstration of the method of donning and inflating a life preserver.
(d) Each certificate holder operating an airplane carrying persons covered by paragraph (a) of this section shall incorporate procedures for the safe carriage of such persons into the certificate holder's operations manual.
(e) The pilot in command may authorize a person covered by paragraph (a) of this section to be admitted to the crew compartment of the airplane.

(14 CFR §121.583[a]–[e])

Even though these persons are exceptions to the Part 121 passenger-carrying requirements, the FAA does require that certain safety measures be taken. For instance, all of the standard safety briefings must be accomplished before takeoff (e.g., use of oxygen, emergency exits, and seat belts). Also, there must be an approved seat with an approved safety belt for each person, and if that seat is located on the flight deck it must be in a position so that the occupant will not interfere with the flight crewmembers performing their duties. Regardless of where this person is seated, he or she must have unobstructed access to a regular or emergency exit. Finally, the procedures for the safe carriage of such persons without compliance with the passenger-carrying requirements must be addressed in the air carrier's operations manual.

Security of the Flightdeck Door

From the time the airplane moves in order to initiate a flight segment through the end of that flight segment, no person may unlock or open the flightdeck door unless:

(a) A person authorized to be on the flightdeck uses an approved audio procedure and an approved visual device to verify that:
 (1) The area outside the flightdeck door is secure, and;
 (2) If someone outside the flightdeck is seeking to have the flightdeck door opened, that person is not under duress, and;
(b) After the requirements of paragraph (a) of this section have been satisfactorily accomplished, the crewmember in charge on the flightdeck authorizes the door to be unlocked and open.

(14 CFR §121.584)

Exit Seating

The procedures an air carrier follows for the assignment of exit row seating must be in accordance with 14 CFR §121.585. As in the carry-on bag provisions, each passenger is required to comply with exit seating restrictions and/or instructions given by a crewmember or other employee of the carrier. First let's define the term exit seat. An exit seat means a seat that

- provides access to an exit, including all the seats in a row from the fuselage to the aisle inboard of the exit, and
- has direct access to an exit (i.e., a passenger can proceed directly to the exit without entering an aisle or passing around an obstruction).

A carrier is authorized to use FAA-approved selection criteria to determine the suitability of each person it permits to occupy an exit seat. These criteria must be included in its operations manual. Typically, an air carrier will only allow those passengers who are able to activate an emergency exit and take whatever additional actions may be necessary to ensure the safe use of that exit in an emergency to be seated in the exit seat. Paragraph 121.585(b) prohibits an air carrier from seating a person in an exit seat if:

- It is likely the person would be unable to perform the required functions because of the lack of physical or mental capacity.
- The person is less than 15 years of age.
- The person is caring for small children, which might prevent them from performing the required functions.
- The person does not wish to be seated in an exit seat.

If a passenger seated in an exit row seat is deemed not suitable for exit row seating, the flight attendant is required by Paragraph 121.585(l) to attempt a seat trade with a passenger who is willing and able to assume the required evacuation functions.

Section 121.585 requires a carrier to make available for inspection by the public, at ticket counters, gates, or other passenger operations areas, written procedures used for determining a person's suitability to be seated in an exit seat. Paragraph 121.585(d) requires these procedures to be included on the passenger information cards on board the aircraft and to include written procedures, in the form of passenger information cards at each exit seat. Included are the procedures for determining a passenger's suitability to be seated in an exit seat. There must also be a printed request that a passenger identify himself or herself to allow reseating if he or she cannot meet that carrier's selection criteria or does not choose to sit there. The passenger information cards must present information that a passenger may use in the event of an emergency to:

(1) Locate the emergency exit;
(2) Recognize the emergency exit opening mechanism;
(3) Comprehend the instructions for operating the emergency exit;
(4) Operate the emergency exit;
(5) Assess whether opening the emergency exit will increase the hazards to which passengers may be exposed;
(6) Follow oral directions and hand signals given by a crewmember;
(7) Stow or secure the emergency exit door so that it will not impede use of the exit;
(8) Assess the condition of an escape slide, activate the slide, and stabilize the slide after deployment to assist others in getting off the slide;
(9) Pass expeditiously through the emergency exit; and
(10) Assess, select, and follow a safe path away from the emergency exit.

(14 CFR §121.585[d])

Finally, no carrier may allow taxi or pushback unless at least one required crewmember has verified that no exit seat is occupied by a person the crewmember determines is likely to be unable to perform the required functions.

Authority to Refuse Transportation

14 CFR §121.586 addresses the issue of *if* and *when* an air carrier may refuse to transport a person with a disability. A disabled passenger is generally considered to be a person with a physical or mental impairment, disability, or condition of such nature that the individual may need the assistance of another individual to move to an exit in the event of an emergency on board the aircraft. The FAA does not allow an air carrier to refuse transportation to a disabled individual solely because that person's disability may cause him or her to need the assistance of another individual to move to an exit in the event of an emergency. An air carrier may not refuse transportation to a disabled person on the basis of safety unless:

(1) The certificate holder has established procedures (including reasonable notice requirements) for the carriage of passengers who may need the assistance of another person to move expeditiously to an exit in the event of an emergency; and
(2) At least one of the following conditions exist:
   (i) The passenger fails to comply with the notice requirements in the certificate holder's procedures.
   (ii) The passenger cannot be carried in accordance with the certificate holder's procedures.

(14 CFR §121.586[a])

Additionally, as a result of a number of legal actions, a carrier may not refuse to provide transportation to

- a disabled individual solely because the person's disability results in appearance or involuntary behavior that may offend, annoy, or inconvenience crewmembers or other passengers.
- disabled individuals by limiting the number of such persons who are permitted to travel on a given flight.

Finally, a carrier may not require a disabled person to preboard an aircraft. It may be offered, but the disabled person may if they so choose proceed to board the aircraft at any time during the boarding process.

Closing and Locking of Flightcrew Compartment Door

FAR 121.587 requires that the pilot-in-command of an airplane that has a lockable flightcrew compartment door, required by 121.313 (discussed in chapter 10), and that is carrying passengers ensure that the door separating the flightcrew compartment from the passenger compartment is closed and locked at all times when the aircraft is being operated.

Carry-on Baggage

Probably one of the most contentious issues for airline passengers these days is the regulation governing carry-on bags. Nothing frustrates a passenger more than having to "gate check" a carry-on bag for the following reasons (listed in descending order of the most common occurrences):

- The passenger would like to carry on more than the allowable limit (the usual limit is one bag).
- The passenger would like to carry on a bag that is larger than the allowable size (a carry-on item must be of such dimensions that it may be stowed under a seat or in an overhead compartment). Typical dimensions range from 22 × 14 × 9 inches to 26 × 18 × 12 inches.
- The airplane is full and there is no longer any carry-on bag space available for the last few remaining passengers to board the aircraft.

14 CFR §121.589 governs an air carrier's carry-on baggage program *and* requires the compliance of each passenger with instructions given by crewmembers regarding that carrier's approved carry-on bag program. This program must be approved by the FAA and will be found in Paragraph A.011 of the carrier's ops specs. Normally, an air carrier restricts passengers to two carry-on items, one to be stowed in an overhead compartment and the other stowed under the seat in front of the passenger. This depends of course on the airline and the type of airplane. Regardless of the allowable amount and size of the carry-on items, Section 121.589 primarily addresses the stowage of carry-on items. It states that no air carrier may allow:

1. the boarding of carry-on baggage on an airplane unless each passenger's baggage has been scanned to control the size and amount carried on board in accordance with an approved carry-on baggage program in its operations specifications;

2. a passenger to board an airplane if his/her carry-on baggage exceeds the baggage allowance prescribed in the carry-on baggage program in the certificate holder's operations specifications;
3. all passenger entry doors of an airplane to be closed in preparation for taxi or pushback unless at least one required crewmember has verified that each article of baggage is properly stowed; or
4. an airplane to take off or land unless each article of baggage is stowed either in a suitable closet or stowage compartment placarded for its maximum weight and providing proper restraint for all baggage or cargo stowed within, and in a manner that does not hinder the possible use of any emergency equipment, or under a passenger seat.

Summary

In this chapter we discussed Subpart T, which covers the FAA requirements ranging from who controls an air carrier's flight movements to the required passenger safety briefings and carry-on bag programs. Most importantly, we have seen that the operational control rules are primarily centered around assuring that the dispatcher has properly planned the flight to ensure that in the event of any unforeseen contingency, there is an alternative plan that guarantees the safety of the flight.

In the next chapter, we will move from the operational rules of Part 121, Subpart T: Flight Operations to the air carrier regulatory requirements for FAA-required reports and record keeping under Part 121, Subpart V and Part 135, Subpart B.

Important Terms in Chapter 12

aviation security program
certificated land airports
Cockpit Access Security System (CASS)
critical phase of flight
Department of Homeland Security (DHS)
dry lease
equipment interchange agreements
Flight Deck Access Restriction (FDAR) Program
Form 110A (aviation safety inspector's credentials)
ground security coordinator (GSC)
manipulation of controls
non-flying pilot (NFP)
operational control
operations notices
personal electronic device (PED)
pilot flying
pilot monitoring (PM)
responsibility for operational control
restriction or suspension of operations
sterile cockpit rule
Transportation Security Administration (TSA)
Transportation Security Administration (TSA) Security Directives (SD)
wet lease

Chapter 12 Exam

1. Operational control may be defined as
   a. the supervision of the dispatching of flight crew by the crew scheduling department.
   b. the exercise of the FAA's inspection authority over U.S. certificated air carriers.
   c. the exercise of authority over initiating, conducting, or terminating a flight.
   d. the exercise of an air carrier's maintenance inspection authority granted under Part 145.

2. To whom may the person designated by the certificate holder as responsible for operational control delegate the functions of operational control such as initiating, conducting or terminating a flight?
   a. The flight control department
   b. A contractor such as another air carrier
   c. Both (a) and (b) are correct.
   d. None of the above.

3. To whom may the director of operations, designated by the certificate holder as responsible for operational control, delegate the responsibility for assuring operational control over issues such as initiating, conducting or terminating a flight?
    a. The flight control department
    b. A contractor such as another air carrier
    c. Both (a) and (b) are correct.
    d. None of the above.

4. Typically, the authority to dispatch or release a flight is held by which position(s)?
    a. An air carrier's director of operations (DO), aircraft dispatcher, and/or pilot-in-command
    b. An air carrier's chief financial officer, chief flight instructor, or principal operations inspector (POI)
    c. The pilot-in-command, who may delegate this authority to the aircraft dispatcher
    d. An air carrier's crew scheduling supervisor

5. Prior to flight, who is responsible for airplane security?
    a. the air carrier security marshal
    b. the ground security coordinator
    c. the airport security marshal
    d. the ramp supervisor

6. Since it is a given that passengers prefer the shortest time in flight, can a carrier publish schedules that are shorter than the competition for competitive advantage knowing that the actual flight will take longer than schedule?
    a. Yes, it can publish false schedules shown with shorter than realistic flight times, as that is just advertising hype like "new and improved" or the "very best value."
    b. Yes, it can publish schedules that show shorter than realistic flight times as it alone controls its flight schedules.
    c. No, it can't because 14 CFR §121.541 requires the airline to publish realistic schedules based on realistic evaluation of aircraft performance and prevailing winds. It must also allow reasonable time for aircraft servicing.
    d. No, it can't because both anti-trust regulations and state unfair trade practices laws prevent such actions.

7. What is the definition of a critical phase of flight?
    a. That period during ground or flight operations anytime the cockpit-to-cabin door is closed
    b. That period of flight involving takeoff, landing, and all flight operations conducted below 10,000 feet
    c. That period of flight including all ground operations involving taxi, takeoff, landing, and all other flight operations conducted below 10,000 feet, unless in level cruise
    d. That period of flight or ground operations involving taxi, takeoff, landing, and all other flight operations

8. Which crew activity would be allowed by the "sterile cockpit rule" (assuming the aircraft is in a critical phase of flight)?
    a. While descending for landing, getting a weather update for the departure on the next leg of the flight
    b. While descending for landing, discussing whether the next leg is going to be delayed due to bad weather
    c. While descending, discussing the abnormal procedure dealing with the fact that the flaps are not deploying
    d. None. The sterile cockpit rule would prohibit each of these discussions.

9. What credential(s) must an FAA air carrier inspector possess to gain access to the flight deck?
    a. Two forms of government photo ID, FAA Form 110A (FAA inspector's ID card), and a driver's license or military ID
    b. FAA Form 121-548 jumpseat authorization letter, and a photo ID
    c. An air carrier's standard jumpseat authorization Form (DOT Form 121-548)
    d. FAA Form 110A (FAA inspector's ID card) and FAA Form 8430-13 jumpseat form

10. When may a pilot use his or her personal electronic device (PED) while on duty?
    a. Only when not in a critical phase of flight.
    b. Only when during a break or rest period and not during a critical phase of flight.
    c. Only when its use is directly related to the operation of the aircraft or for emergency, safety-related or certain employment-related communications.
    d. The pilot may never use a PED (personal electronic device) while on duty in the cockpit.

11. When may a required flight deck crewmember leave the assigned duty station?
    a. In conjunction with operating the aircraft; for example, to check the cabin for a report of fumes in the cabin.
    b. To speak with a very important customer/passenger about a problem they had with their flight connections.
    c. To stretch his or her legs after a period at the controls on a transatlantic flight.
    d. (a) and (c) are both correct.

12. What is the primary responsibility of the pilot flying (PF)?
    a. The PF is primarily responsible for flying the aircraft in accordance with the approved operational procedures.
    b. The PF is primarily responsible for flying the aircraft and the overall supervision of the crew.
    c. The PF is primarily responsible for observation of the non-flying pilot (NFP) and, among other tasks, comparing the current flight path with the intended flight path.
    d. None of the above are the primary responsibility of the PF.

13. The pilot-in-command of a passenger-carrying airplane that has a lockable cockpit-to-cabin door must ensure the door is closed and locked during which period of aircraft operations?
    a. The cockpit-to-cabin door must be closed during taxi, takeoff, and landing.
    b. The cockpit-to-cabin door must be closed prior to aircraft pushback and for the duration of aircraft operations.
    c. The cockpit-to-cabin door must be closed and locked during flight.
    d. The cockpit-to-cabin door must be closed and locked prior to any aircraft movement.

14. Which document is not required to be carried by a pilot in Part 121 operations?
    a. FCC radiotelephone operator permit
    b. English language demonstrated proficiency card
    c. Current FAA medical certificate of the appropriate class
    d. Current FAA-issued airman certificate appropriate to the position he or she is working

15. Where could a dispatcher or flight crewmember look to determine that the carrier is authorized to fly to a certain area?
    a. The worldwide Official Airline Guide
    b. The company system timetable
    c. The appropriate ops specs paragraph
    d. None of these choices are correct.

16. May a Part 121 air carrier use other than Part 139 certificated airports?
    a. Not for destination airports, but it may file (and use, if needed) a Part 139 airport as a takeoff or destination alternate airport.
    b. Not for takeoff or destination alternates, but it may file a Part 139 airport as a destination if the runway lengths are determined to be suitable for the expected arrival conditions.
    c. Yes, but only when that airport is allowed in the ops specs for use as a destination airport.
    d. Yes, there is no restriction to the use of non-Part 139 airports so long as the flight plan identifies the airport as a non-Part 139 airport on the flight plan.

17. What precautions must an air carrier take when transporting a passenger that requires medical oxygen?
    a. The carrier must ensure the passenger's personal oxygen canisters were manufactured in accordance with DOT 4166 oxygen safety requirements.
    b. The carrier must inspect the passenger's personal oxygen canisters to ensure they comply with the approved types authorized in the carrier's ops specs.
    c. An air carrier may allow a passenger to carry and operate oxygen equipment as long as that carrier supplies the necessary equipment.
    d. The carrier must ensure the passenger's personal oxygen canisters were manufactured after December 31, 1999.

18. When a twin-engine aircraft suffers engine failure or an engine is shut down in flight as a precautionary measure to prevent possible damage, the pilot-in-command is required to do what two things?
    a. Inform air traffic control of the engine failure or in flight shutdown and contact the person responsible for operational control for instructions.
    b. Land the airplane at the nearest suitable airport, in nautical miles, at which a safe landing can be made and notify the appropriate ATC facility as soon as practicable after the engine failure or in flight shutdown.
    c. Inform air traffic control of the engine failure or in flight shutdown and request immediate clearance to the nearest airport with appropriate maintenance facilities.
    d. Land the airplane at the nearest suitable airport, in point of time, at which a safe landing can be made, and notify the appropriate ATC facility as soon as practicable after the engine failure or in flight shutdown.

19. The verification program that contains the employment and security information for determining if an individual is authorized by the FAA to occupy an aircraft's flight deck jump seat operations is called?
    a. CARPT
    b. FFDO
    c. CASS
    d. CREEP

20. From the time the airplane moves in order to initiate a flight segment through the end of that flight segment, no person may unlock or open the flightdeck door.
    a. True
    b. False

CHAPTER 13
PART 121, SUBPART V: RECORDS AND REPORTS AND PART 135, SUBPART B: RECORDKEEPING REQUIREMENTS

*No aircraft is considered airworthy by the FAA
until the weight of its paperwork exceeds its maximum certificated takeoff weight.*

—**anonymous**

This chapter contains the air carrier regulatory requirements for recordkeeping under Part 121, Subpart V, and Part 135, Subpart B. As a certificate holder, an air carrier is subject to visits and inspections by officials of many different government agencies. These agencies include the Federal Aviation Administration (FAA), the National Transportation Safety Board (NTSB), the Department of Transportation (DOT), the Department of Homeland Security (DHS), the Transportation Security Agency (TSA), the Federal Communications Commission (FCC), and U.S. Customs as well as a variety of state and local government agencies. As an employer, an air carrier must also expect oversight by the Occupational Safety and Health Administration (OSHA) and, if the air carrier serves food, the Food and Drug Administration (FDA). Each of these agencies has regulatory requirements that must be followed by the air carrier. Most of these regulatory requirements begin with the need to maintain adequate documentation. The primary reason for this requirement is to allow these agencies to better verify regulatory compliance.

In this chapter, we will discuss the FAA-required records and reports that must be created and maintained by Part 121 and 135 air carriers. The FAA requires air carriers to maintain vast amounts of documentation. Some records must be kept indefinitely, while others may be discarded after 30 days. This documentation covers records ranging from employee training records, dispatch releases, load manifests, flight plans, and maintenance reports to aircraft logbook entries and even en route aircraft-to-company communications. Before we start, what exactly is a required record? The FAA defines a record as *an account which preserves evidence of the occurrence of an event*. In general, a record must show what event occurred, to whom, by whom, when, and proof of the event's occurrence, such as a certification by signature or by an approved electronic means. The reason for recordkeeping is simple: the air carrier uses records to show that its personnel have accomplished a particular event, have met certain criteria, or have fulfilled specific conditions required by the regulations.

FAR 121, Subpart V: Records and Reports

Crewmember and Dispatcher Records

14 CFR §121.683(a) requires certificate holders conducting domestic or flag operations to maintain current records of each crewmember and each aircraft dispatcher. These **crewmember and dispatcher records** must show whether each crewmember or aircraft dispatcher is qualified and proficient with regard to route checks, route qualifications, airplane qualifications, currency training, and any required physical examinations. These records must also include flight, duty, and rest time records.

A record must also be kept for each action taken concerning the release from employment for professional disqualification of any flight crewmember or aircraft dispatcher or physical disqualification for any flight crewmember. This record must be maintained for a minimum of 6 months (14 CFR §121.683). Notice that the employment records are the only records stated here that must be maintained for a specific period of time. The crewmember and dispatcher qualification records are kept in a permanent file during the period that person is employed by the company. Following are examples of the records a pilot's permanent file may include:

- Basic indoctrination training records
- Initial qualification training records
- Transition and/or upgrade training records
- Operation experience line checks by FAA inspectors

Air carriers involved in supplemental operations are required by 14 CFR §121.683(b) to maintain the records required by §121.683(a) either at their principal operations base or at another location approved by the FAA. This is different than the domestic or flag recordkeeping requirement. The reason is that since supplemental operations are typically transient in nature, the FAA requires an established approved location for the maintenance of records. As we'll see later in this chapter, this is also true for Part 135 operators. 14 CFR §135.63 requires that operators keep certain records at either the principal business office or another place approved by the Administrator.

A relatively recent advance in recordkeeping for Part 121 and 135 air carriers has been the ability for air carriers to maintain the required air carrier records on an approved electronic recordkeeping system. An electronic recordkeeping system is a system of record processing in which records are entered, stored, and retrieved electronically by a computer system rather than in the traditional hard copy format. Computer-based recordkeeping systems offer more flexible and efficient access and maintenance of records. This provides benefits for both the operator and the FAA. To gain approval to use an electronic recordkeeping system, an air carrier must:

- Maintain manuals that fully describe the system and actions necessary to input and retrieve data stored within the system.
- Maintain an electronic recordkeeping system sufficient to allow verification of regulatory compliance with applicable sections of the FARs.
- Not make changes to the electronic record system without FAA approval.
- Maintain any hard copy paper files for a minimum of 30 days following completion of a flight.

For Part 121 and 135 certificate holders, the approval for the use of electronic recordkeeping systems can be found in Paragraph A.025 of the carrier's operations specifications. Let's again look at the operations specifications for Delta Air Lines (see next page).

Aircraft Records

A Part 121 certificate holder conducting domestic or flag operations is required by 14 CFR §121.685 to maintain and supply the FAA's certificate-holding district office with a current list of each aircraft that it operates in scheduled air transportation. See Figure 13-1 for a sample **aircraft listing record**. If the air carrier operates airplanes of another certificate holder under an equipment interchange agreement, like the interchange agreement discussed in Chapter 12, those aircraft may be incorporated by reference into the aircraft listing record.

Additionally, 14 CFR Part 205 (specifically §205.4[b]) states that aircraft shall not be listed in the carrier's aircraft listing record, found in its operations specifications with the FAA, and shall not be operated unless liability insurance coverage is in force. All air carrier certificate holders are required to have continuous, effective liability insurance coverage that is in effect to ensure that the public is protected in the event of an accident.

U.S. Department of
Transportation
Federal Aviation
Administration

Operation Specifications

Paragraph A.025

Delta Air Lines Ops Specs   **Paragraph A.025**

Approved Computer-based Record Keeping System

    a. The certificate holder is authorized to use the approved computer-based record keeping system, described and/or referenced in this paragraph.

The Delta Air Lines computer-based record system for all crew members includes the following:

- The Aircrew Records Tracking System (ARTS) for pilot and flight engineer personnel.
- The Flight Attendant Training Records System (FATRS) for flight attendant personnel.
- The Crew Member Duty and Flight Time Record System (CDFTRS) for all crewmembers.

The continued use of this system is contingent upon adherence to the following stipulations:

- Delta Air Lines will maintain manuals which fully describe the system and the actions necessary to input and retrieve data stored within the system.
- Delta Air Lines will maintain a computerized record system which is sufficient to determine compliance with applicable sections of FAR Part 121.
- Delta Air Lines will not make changes to the computerized record system without FAA approval. Change requests will be submitted to the Certificate Management Office (CMO-27) a minimum of 60 days prior to the proposed implementation date.
- Source documents (hard copy paper files and magnetic tape records of ACARS messages) utilized for data will be maintained a minimum of 60 days following the completion of an event.

1. Issued by the Federal Aviation Administration.
2. These Operations Specifications are approved by direction of the Administrator.

ORIGINAL SIGNED BY: Mr. Drew U. Reed, Principal Operations Inspector

3. Date Approval is effective: 05/25/2015 Amendment Number: 1
4. I hereby accept and receive the Operations Specifications in this paragraph.

ORIGINAL SIGNED BY: Capt. Neil A. Armstrong, Senior Vice President, Flight Operations Date: 05/25/2015

U.S. Department of Transportation		Federal Aviation Administration
	Operations Specifications	

D085. Aircraft Listing: The certificate holder is authorized to conduct operations under Part 121 using the aircraft identified on this operations specification.

Registration No.	Aircraft Manufacturer Serial No.	Aircraft Make/Model
N001	23070	ATR-72-600
N002	23071	ATR-72-600
N003	23072	ATR-72-600
N004	23073	ATR-72-600
N005	23074	ATR-72-600
N006	23075	ATR-72-600
N007	23076	ATR-72-600
N1001	221	EMB-170
N1002	222	EMB-170
N1003	223	EMB-170
N1004	224	EMB-170
N1005	225	EMB-170
N1006	226	EMB-170
N1007	227	EMB-170
N1008	228	EMB-170
N1009	229	EMB-170
N1010	230	EMB-170
N2010	11-901	Airbus 319 LR
N2011	11-902	Airbus 319 LR
N2012	11-903	Airbus 319 LR
N2013	11-904	Airbus 319 LR
N2014	12-905	Airbus 319 LR
N7380	05-9801	Boeing 737-800
N7381	05-9802	Boeing 737-800
N7382	05-9803	Boeing 737-800
N333	14-1000	Airbus 321-200
N334	14-1001	Airbus 321-200
N335	14-1002	Airbus 321-200
N336	15-1003	Airbus 321-200

1. Issued by the Federal Aviation Administration
2. These Operations Specifications are approved by direction of the Administrator.
3. Date Approval is effective: 4/01/13

Figure 13-1. Sample aircraft listing record.

Dispatch or Flight Release Forms

For domestic and flag operations, an air carrier is required by 14 CFR §121.695(a) to carry a **dispatch release** (Figure 13-2) on every flight. As we discussed in Chapter 11, 14 CFR §121.687(a) states that this dispatch release may be organized in any manner but must contain at least the following information:

1. Identification number of the aircraft
2. Trip or flight number
3. Departure and destination airport, as well as any alternate airports and any intermediate stops, if applicable
4. A statement concerning the type of flight (e.g., IFR, VFR)
5. Minimum fuel supply
6. For each flight dispatched as an ETOPS flight, the ETOPS diversion time for which the flight is dispatched

The dispatch release must also contain at a minimum the latest available weather reports and forecasts for the destination airport, alternate airport, and intermediate stop, if applicable. The dispatch release must be signed by both the pilot-in-command and the aircraft dispatcher assigned to the flight (121.687[b]). Additionally, the FAA requires the certificate holder to keep records of the dispatch release on file for a period of at least three months (121.695[b]).

The pilot-in-command or dispatcher has the authority to change any aspect of the release provided there is communication and agreement between both people. This agreement is documented by the dispatch release. In most cases, the dispatcher signs the dispatch release electronically, while the pilot-in-command signs the dispatch release and returns it to the gate agent. At select carriers, the FAA has approved procedures for the pilot-in-command to sign the dispatch release electronically.

FLIGHT DISPATCH RELEASE   Dispatcher Neil-Armstrong #323-222-11xx

Flight: 112/29MAY15   ETE = 03:05   JFK-MIA   Alternate(s): none   Domestic

Ship: 222   IFR   ICAO   FLIGHT PLAN   BLOCK FUEL   40,000
                                              MINIMUM FUEL FOR TAKEOFF   36,000

Scheduled Departure time: KJFK: 1200 (Local) /1600Z
Scheduled Arrival time: KMIA: 1505 (Local) /1905Z

I hereby acknowledge receipt of the dispatch release including weather reports for the destination and any required alternate airports, and I believe that the flight can be completed safely as planned. I consider my physical condition satisfactory for this flight:

_____
Captain Signature/Printed Name/Domicile

_____
(Additional) Captain Signature/Printed Name/Domicile

I consider my physical condition satisfactory for this flight:

_____
First Officer Signature/Printed Name/Domicile

_____
(Additional) First Officer Signature/Printed Name/Domicile

Figure 13-2. Dispatch release.

Supplemental air carriers conducting domestic or flag operations are required by 14 CFR §121.689(c) to comply with the dispatch or flight release required for scheduled domestic or flag operations covered in 14 CFR §121.687. For supplemental operations *not* conducting domestic or flag operations, 14 CFR §121.697(a) requires an air carrier to carry a flight release on every flight. 14 CFR §121.689(a) states that this flight release may be organized in any manner but must contain at least the following information:

(1) Company or organization name.
(2) Make, model, and registration number of the aircraft being used.
(3) Flight or trip number, and date of flight.
(4) Name of each flight crewmember, flight attendant, and pilot designated as pilot in command.
(5) Departure airport, destination airports, alternate airports, and route.
(6) Minimum fuel supply (in gallons or pounds).
(7) A statement of the type of operation (e.g., IFR, VFR).
(8) For each flight released as an ETOPS flight, the ETOPS diversion time for which the flight is released.

(14 CFR §121.689[a])

The **flight release**, like the domestic and flag operator's dispatch release, must contain at a minimum the latest available weather reports and forecasts for the destination airport, alternate airport, and intermediate stop, if applicable. The flight release must be signed by both the pilot-in-command and the aircraft dispatcher assigned to the flight (14 CFR §121.689[b]). Also, supplemental operators, like domestic and flag operators, are required to keep these records on file for a period of at least three months. These records must be kept at its principal base of operation.

Aircraft Load Manifests/Composition and Disposition

Air carriers are required by 14 CFR §121.693 to create a **load manifest** for each flight they operate. As we discussed in Chapter 11, this load manifest must contain the following weight and balance and performance information at time of takeoff:

(a) The planned aircraft weight, including fuel and oil, cargo and baggage, passengers and crewmembers.
(b) The maximum allowable weight for that flight that must not exceed the least of the following weights:
  (1) Maximum allowable takeoff weight for the runway intended to be used (including corrections for altitude and gradient, and wind and temperature conditions existing at the takeoff time).
  (2) Maximum takeoff weight considering anticipated fuel and oil consumption that allows compliance with applicable enroute performance limitations.
  (3) Maximum takeoff weight considering anticipated fuel and oil consumption that allows compliance with the maximum authorized design landing weight limitations on arrival at the destination airport.
  (4) Maximum takeoff weight considering anticipated fuel and oil consumption that allows compliance with landing distance limitations on arrival at the destination and alternate airports.
(c) The total weight computed under approved procedures.
(d) Evidence that the aircraft is loaded according to an approved schedule that ensures that the center of gravity is within approved limits.
(e) Names of passengers, unless such information is maintained by other means by the certificate holder.

(14 CFR §121.693)

Section 121.693(e), as shown above, requires that air carriers include as part of the load manifest, *the names of the passengers, unless such information is maintained by other means by the air carrier.* Other means could be a computer source or other electronic means. The reason for this part of the regulation is to aid in the rapid and accurate determination of how many passengers are on board an aircraft, and who they are, in the event of an emergency situation. Not having an accurate record would hamper the efforts of emergency crews during an accident or of identifying passengers during an illness or even a hijacking situation. The word "passenger," as used throughout the FARs, means any passenger regardless of age (e.g., infants or lap children). The passenger names list would also include any air carrier employees who are deadheading, other employees not assigned duties during the flight time, and non-revenue passengers.

The load manifest, like the dispatch release and flight plan, is required by Section 121.695 to be carried to the

C038902			Delta							Airworthiness Release
A/C No. **222**	Serial No. C038902		0412-40205/ Log 6-01 TOPP 50-10-05							Ref. TOPP 50-10-05 By: R.J. Simpson ID No. 9195057 Sta.: ATL

From	To	Date	Flt. No.	T/O Power	Arrival Fuel	Arrival Oil	APU Oil	Hyd. Fluid	Type Check	Mechanics Signature
ATL	MEM	08/08/10	946	Norm	11.5					
MEM	DFW	08/10/10	946	Norm	8.9					
DFW	LIT	08/10/10	302	35	7.9					
LIT	MEM	08/10/10	302	35	10.0	3.5/3.2				
MEM	CVG	08/11/10	717	45	11.1					
CVG	LEX	08/11/10	311	35	8.5					
LEX	ATL	08/11/10	311	Norm	9.1					

Item No. 1   Maintenance Code: 432-55   Irregularity: Hydraulic leak in right main wheel well notified maintenance 1743 local time/DH

Corrective Action: Found main landing gear control valve supply line leaking. Cleared area and retorqued B-nut Pressurized hyd. system-Leak Check Good. Hyd. System Quantity O.K.

Mechanic signature: Russell Levy   ID No. 99789411   Sta. DFW

Item No. 1   Maintenance Code: N/A   Irregularity: Max Power Takeoff ATL

Corrective Action: Info noted + Recorded

Mechanic signature: Russell Levy   ID No. 99789411   Sta. DFW

Use Black Ball Point Pen-Ensure Both Copies Are Legible-See Coding Instructions

Figure 13-3. Aircraft maintenance log.

aircraft's destination by the pilot-in-command. Domestic, flag, and supplemental operators are then required to keep the load manifest for a period of at least 3 months.

Aircraft Maintenance Logs

Sections 121.563, 121.701 and 135.65 require each certificate holder to provide an **aircraft maintenance logbook** for recording or deferring mechanical irregularities, and the subsequent corrective maintenance actions performed. The air carrier's general operations manual provides a method by which the flight crew will record and inform the operator of mechanical irregularities or defects that appear before, during, and after a flight. Not surprisingly, the FAA requires in Section 121.701 that each aircraft used in Part 121 domestic, flag, or supplemental operations carry aboard a FAA-approved aircraft maintenance logbook. The PIC is then required by Sections 121.563 and 135.65 to ensure any maintenance difficulties or irregularities and any deferred maintenance items from an observed or reported failure or malfunction of airframe, engine, propeller, or other component critical to the safety of flight are entered into the maintenance log at the end of that particular flight. The air carrier then uses this information to let the maintenance personnel know of any suspected problems so they can perform the appropriate corrective action. This logbook must be kept in a location easily accessible to the flight crew and is ultimately used to record aircraft status (e.g., airworthy, non-airworthy). All maintenance items as well as any corrective action, once maintenance has been accomplished, must be written in the logbook by either a flight crewmember or a mechanic (*see* Figure 13-3). Verbal reports—i.e., simply speaking with a mechanic about an aircraft malfunction—are not allowed. Everything must be documented because the FAA and most air carriers use these logbooks not only to verify compliance with FARs but to develop a historical record for each aircraft. This historical data is ultimately used to determine mechanical reliability, which brings us to 14 CFR §121.703.

Aircraft Service Difficulty Reports

In order to keep a close eye on the mechanical reliability of aircraft under the jurisdiction of the FAA, air carriers are required to report certain aircraft equipment malfunctions, failures, or structural defects to the FAA. This report is called a **service difficulty report** (Figure 13-4). The report helps the FAA determine if an aircraft's malfunction or failure was a random occurrence or whether there is some equipment or structural defect that could be improved upon and that requires an airworthiness directive (AD) issued in the hopes of avoiding another malfunction or failure.

First, let's look at 14 CFR §121.703 and what service difficulty reports cover. The FAA categorizes malfunctions, failures, or defects in three ways:

- Malfunctions, failures, or defects that occur *during flight*
- Malfunctions, failures, or defects occurring or detected *on the ground*
- Malfunction, failure, or defect in an aircraft *at any time that in the opinion of the certificate holder has endangered or may endanger the safe operation of the aircraft used by it*

Let's look at each malfunction category a little more closely. Malfunctions, failures, or defects that occur during flight are defined by 14 CFR §121.703(b) as events that occur during the period from the moment the aircraft leaves the surface of the earth on takeoff until it touches down on landing. Specifically, the FAA requires in Section 121.703 that each certificate holder report the occurrence or detection of each failure, malfunction, or defect *during flight* concerning:

1. Any fire and, when monitored by a related fire warning system, whether the fire warning system functioned properly;
2. Any fire that occurs during flight and that is not protected by a related fire-warning system;
3. Any false warning of fire or smoke;
4. An engine exhaust system that causes damage to the engine, adjacent structure, equipment, or components;
5. An aircraft component that causes the accumulation or circulation of smoke, vapor, or toxic or noxious fumes;
6. Any engine flameout or shutdown during flight operations;
7. Any engine shutdown during flight when external damage to the engine or airplane structure occurs;
8. Any engine shutdown during flight due to foreign object ingestion or icing;
9. Engine shutdown during flight of more than one engine;
10. A propeller feathering system or ability of the system to control overspeed during flight;
11. A fuel or fuel-dumping system that affects fuel flow or causes hazardous leakage;

Service Difficulty Report

DEPARTMENT OF TRANSPORTATION
FEDERAL AVIATION ADMINISTRATION

AERONAUTICAL EQUIPMENT

FORM APPROVED
OMB No. 2120-008

RIS-WS 8070-1
Control No. USAA201502100016
ATA | Code

MAJOR EQUIPMENT IDENTITY

Enter pertinent date 2015-02-09	MANUFACTURER	MODEL/SERIES	SERIAL NUMBER	N- 704US
AIRCRAFT	AIRBUS	319-112	06141999	
POWERPLANT				
PROPELLER				

PROBLEM DESCRIPTION

| DATE 2015-02-09 | STATUS | CARRIER ALLEGHENY | ATA | AIRCRAFT TYPE AIRBUS 319-112 | N- 704US | CONTROL NO. |

TEXT
AIRCRAFT DIVERTED AFTER LOSING GREEN HYDRAULIC SYSTEM REPLACED LEFT ENGINE GREEN SYSTEM HYDRAULIC PUMP IN ACCORDANCE WITH AIRBUS 319 AIRCRAFT MAINTENANCE MANUAL 29-11-51. AFTER INSPECTION PUMP WAS FOUND WITH NO FAULTS

SPECIFIC PART CAUSING PROBLEM

PART NAME HYDRAULIC PUMP	MFG. PART NUMBER 05291993	PART CONDITION GOOD	PART/DEFECT LOCATION LEFT ENGINE
COMPONENT/APPLIANCE ABOVE PART INSTALLED ON		Report whole hours	PART TT 45,902	PART TSO
COMP/APPL NAME	MANUFACTURER EATON AERO.	MFG. MODEL/NUMBER 3031863001	SERIAL NO. 3124287804

SUBMITTED BY

| SUBMITTER (Check one) | A CARRIER [X] | B REP STA | C OPER | D MECH | E AIR TAXI | F MFG | G FAA | H OTHER | I Spec. | P.S.L. | ALERT | OPER/D.O. |

PREC. PROC. | NATURE | STAGE | STAT | ROLL | Frame | SYS. | SYS.

ADDITIONAL COMMENTS

FAA Form 8070-1 (11-15) SUPERSEDES PREVIOUS EDITION

Shaded Areas are for FAA USE ONLY

Figure 13-4. Service difficulty report.

12. An unwanted landing gear extension or retraction, or the unwanted opening or closing of landing gear doors during flight;
13. Any brake system component that results in any detectable loss of brake actuating force when the aircraft is in motion on the ground;
14. Aircraft structure that requires major repair;
15. Cracks, permanent deformation, or corrosion of aircraft structures, if more than the maximum acceptable to the manufacturer or the FAA;
16. Aircraft components or systems that result in taking emergency actions during flight (except action to shut down an engine); and
17. Any emergency evacuation system or component including any exit door, passenger emergency evacuation lighting system, or evacuation equipment found to be defective or that fails to perform the intended function during an actual emergency or during training, testing, maintenance, demonstrations, or inadvertent deployments;

The FAA also requires in Section 121.703(a) that each certificate holder report the occurrence or detection of each failure, malfunction, or defect that occurred or was detected on the ground. Specifically 121.703(a) requires reports for the following:

1. Brake system components that result in loss of brake actuating force when the airplane is in motion on the ground;
2. Cracks, permanent deformation, or corrosion of aircraft structures, if more than the maximum acceptable to the manufacturer or the FAA;
3. Emergency evacuation systems or components including all exit doors, passenger emergency evacuation lighting systems, or evacuation equipment that are found defective, or that fail to perform the intended functions during an actual emergency or during training, testing, maintenance, demonstrations, or inadvertent deployments.

The catchall paragraph is 121.703(c), which states a report is required for *any malfunction, failure, or defect in an aircraft at any time that, in the opinion of the certificate holder, has endangered or may endanger the safe operation of the aircraft used by it.*

Paragraphs 121.703(d) and (e) cover when and how these reports are to be sent to the FAA. If a certificate holder has had a malfunction, failure, or defect and a report is required by Paragraphs 121.703(a) and (c), then the air carrier is required to send a report, in writing, to that air carrier's certificate-holding district office within 96 hours of the occurrence. This report must be sent within the 96 hour limit even though all required information might not be available. If additional information necessary to complete the report becomes available after the initial report was filed, the air carrier must expeditiously submit that additional information to the FAA. Also, each air carrier must make the report data available for 30 days for examination by the certificate-holding district office in a form and manner acceptable to the FAA Administrator or designated representative. The reports are required by 121.703(e) to include the following information:

(1) Type and identification number of the aircraft.
(2) The name of the operator.
(3) The date, flight number, and stage during which the incident occurred (e.g., preflight, takeoff, climb, cruise, descent, landing, and inspection).
(4) The emergency procedure effected (e.g., unscheduled landing and emergency descent).
(5) The nature of the failure, malfunction, or defect.
(6) Identification of the part and system involved, including available information pertaining to type designation of the major component and time since overhaul.
(7) Apparent cause of the failure, malfunction, or defect (e.g., wear, crack, design deficiency, or personnel error).
(8) Whether the part was repaired, replaced, sent to the manufacturer, or other action taken.
(9) Whether the aircraft was grounded.
(10) Other pertinent information necessary for more complete identification, determination of seriousness, or corrective action.

(14 CFR §121.703[e])

In order to avoid duplicate service difficulty reports being sent for the same event, the FAA does not require a report if a malfunction, failure, or defect has already been reported by the certificate holder under the provision of 14 CFR §21.3, which addresses certification procedures for products and parts, or under the provisions of 49 CFR Part 830 (commonly known as "NTSB Part 830") concerning the notification and reporting of aircraft accidents or incidents.

Service difficulty reports are important because they provide the FAA and the aviation industry with airworthiness statistical data which can be studied and used to improve safety-related programs. These reports can be used to rapidly identify defective component trends that could cause future aviation safety problems. The database for these reports is easily accessible online to the public for study and research.

Additionally, an air carrier's maintenance department is required by 14 CFR §145.221 to submit a maintenance report to the Administrator within 96 hours after it discovers any serious defect in, or other recurring unairworthy condition of, an aircraft, powerplant or propeller, or any of their components. If the defect or malfunction could result in an imminent hazard to flight, the repair station is required to inform the Administrator in the most "expeditious manner" possible. The repair station need not report the defect, failure or malfunction if it has already been reported by 14 CFR §121.703, §121.705 or §135.417.

Mechanical Interruption Summary Report

Every month, an air carrier must submit a **mechanical interruption summary report** to the FAA. A mechanical interruption summary report is a detailed report of occurrences during the previous month that caused an interruption of an air carrier's normal service. The following events are discussed in Sections 121.705(a) and 135.417, and require a mechanical interruption summary report:

- Interruption to a flight, unscheduled change of aircraft en route.
- Unscheduled stop or diversion from a route.
- Unscheduled engine removal caused by known or suspected mechanical difficulties or malfunctions that are not required to be reported as service difficulty reports (14 CFR §121.703).

Mechanical summary reports are to be submitted to the FAA before the tenth of every month for the previous month's mechanical interruptions. Analysis of the events in these reports is one of the air carrier's most effective means of determining the effectiveness of their continuous airworthiness maintenance programs (CAMP), which we will cover in the next chapter.

Alteration and Repair

Whenever an air carrier performs a **major alteration** or **major repair** of an aircraft's airframe, engine, propeller, or other aircraft system, it is required by Sections 121.707 and 119.59 to promptly submit an **alteration and repair report** of the work accomplished to the FAA principal maintenance inspector (PMI) assigned to the Part 121 air carrier. The air carrier must also maintain a copy of this report available for inspection by the air carrier's principal maintenance inspector. What does the FAA consider as a major alteration or major repair?

14 CFR Part 1 defines a *major alteration* as an alteration not listed in the aircraft, aircraft engine, or propeller specifications that might appreciably affect weight, balance, structural strength, performance, powerplant operation, flight characteristics, or other qualities affecting airworthiness or that is not done according to accepted practices or cannot be done by elementary operations.

There are three types of alterations that the FAA considers major alterations:

1. **Airframe major alterations:** Alterations to the main parts of an aircraft such as wings, tail surfaces, fuselage, control system and landing gear and major systems changes.
2. **Propeller major alterations:** Alterations of an aircraft's propellers such as changes in blade or hub design, adding or changing a propeller governor, or even installing a propeller de-ice system.
3. **Appliance major alterations:** Alterations of the basic design not made in accordance with recommendations of the appliance manufacturer or in accordance with an FAA airworthiness directive.

14 CFR Part 1 defines a *major repair* as a repair that, if improperly done, might appreciably affect weight, balance, structural strength, performance, powerplant operation, flight characteristics, or other qualities affecting airworthiness, or a repair that is not done according to accepted practices or cannot be done through elementary operations.

There are four types of repairs that the FAA considers major repairs:

1. **Airframe major repairs:** Repairs involving the strengthening, reinforcing, splicing, and manufacturing of primary structural members or their replacement, when replacement is by fabrication such as riveting or welding (e.g., box beams, spars, parts of control systems, engine mounts, or wing brace struts).
2. **Powerplant major repairs:** Separation or disassembly of crankcase/crankshaft or repairs to structural engine parts of an engine by welding, plating, metalizing, or other methods.
3. **Propeller major repairs:** Any repairs to deep cuts, nicks or dents, or the straightening or shortening, of steel blades; retipping, lamination replacement or repairing of elongated bolt holes

in the hub of fixed pitch wood propellers; or repair of propeller governors.

4. **Appliance major repairs:** Repairs to calibration and repair of instruments or radio equipment, the disassembly of complex hydraulic power valves, or the overhaul of pressure type carburetors, fuel, oil and hydraulic pumps.

Appendix A of 14 CFR Part 43, entitled Major Alterations, Major Repairs, and Preventive Maintenance, contains the complete regulatory definition of what constitutes a major alteration or major repair.

Airworthiness Release or Aircraft Log Entry

14 CFR §121.709(a) and §135.443 require that after maintenance, preventive maintenance, or alterations are performed on an aircraft, an **airworthiness release** logbook entry (Figure 13-5) must be completed before an aircraft can be returned to service. The FAA allows only authorized certificated mechanics or repairmen to sign an airworthiness release, *except a certificated repairman may sign the release or entry only for the work for which he is employed and certificated* (121.709[b][3]). An air carrier must have procedures set forth in the approved certificate holder's manual for preparing the airworthiness release or logbook entry. Paragraphs 121.709(b) and (d) specify that the signing of the airworthiness release by a qualified person's signature certifies that:

(i) The work was performed in accordance with the requirements of the certificate holder's manual;
(ii) All items required to be inspected were inspected by an authorized person who determined that the work was satisfactorily completed;
(iii) No known condition exists that would make the airplane unairworthy; and
(iv) So far as the work performed is concerned, the aircraft is in condition for safe operation.

(14 CFR §121.709[b][2])

Once an airworthiness release is completed and signed, the certificate holder must give a copy to the pilot-in-command. The way most air carriers comply with this provision is by including the airworthiness release in the aircraft maintenance logbook. Since the aircraft logbook is required to be on board the aircraft at all times, the pilot-in-command has access to the airworthiness release. The pilot-in-command must ensure that the airworthiness release entry has been completed correctly in accordance with the air carrier's prescribed procedures *before* the flight is dispatched. Finally, Paragraph 121.709(d) requires the air carrier to keep a record of that particular airworthiness release for at least 2 months.

Communication Records

Air carriers must comply with the two-way radio communication provision addressed in 14 CFR §121.99, which states:

(a) Each certificate holder conducting domestic or flag operations must show that a two-way communication system, or other means of communication approved by the FAA certificate holding district office, is available over the entire route. The communications may be direct links or via an approved communication link that will provide reliable and rapid communications under normal operating conditions between each airplane and the appropriate dispatch office, and between each airplane and the appropriate air traffic control unit.

(14 CFR §121.99[a])

The communication system used to comply with this regulation is required by Paragraph 121.99(b) to be independent of any system operated by the U.S. government. An air carrier can maintain communication with each flight it operates via different means depending on

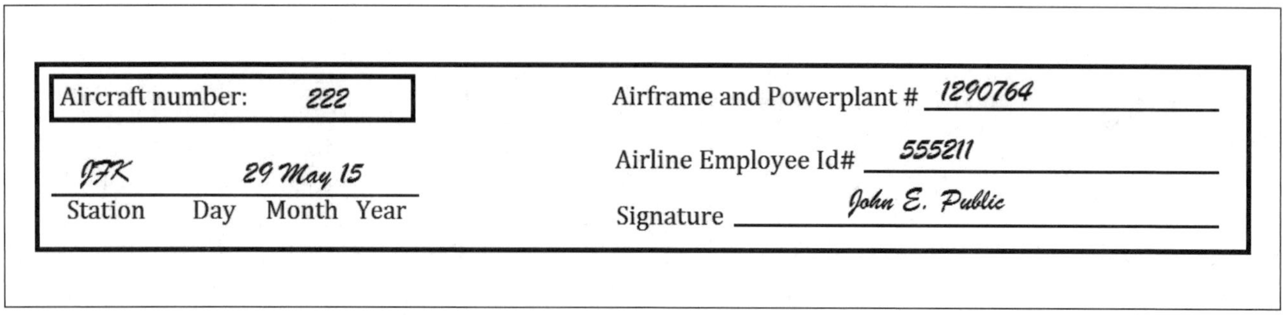
Aircraft number: 222
JFK 29 May 15
Station Day Month Year
Airframe and Powerplant # 1290764
Airline Employee Id# 555211
Signature John E. Public

Figure 13-5. Airworthiness release.

where the aircraft may be situated (i.e., on the ground or in flight) and how the aircraft may be equipped. In the past, flight crews maintained a "listening watch" on a second or third VHF radio dedicated to a "company frequency" or commercially subscribed radio frequency (ARINC) in order to maintain contact with their company. While this satisfied the requirements of 14 CFR §121.99, it was inefficient and often distracting to the crewmember whose duty it was to listen to the company frequency and monitor simultaneously the air traffic control frequency. Some older aircraft still use this method of remaining in contact with the dispatch office.

Over the last 20 years, air carriers have adopted a variety of methods by which they can maintain communications between the company dispatch office and the flight crews. One of the most popular is the *Automated Communication And Reporting System*, known as **ACARS**. This communication system is an aircraft-to-dispatcher data link transmitting over an assigned VHF frequency. ACARS Datalink transmission has been around since the late 1970s when Piedmont Airlines first began using it on their Boeing 737s. The flight crew or the dispatcher uses a keypad to type a message, and with a push of a button that message is sent from the aircraft to the dispatcher or from the dispatcher to the aircraft. The goal of the ACARS system was to reduce cockpit workload and improve operational reliability by capturing and moving data more efficiently than is possible with voice communication. Another method of ACARS transmission is via a satellite communication system or SATCOM. For obvious reasons, this is particularly well suited to flying over remote regions especially extended overwater operations. Speaking of flying over remote regions, ETOPS operation beyond 180 minutes is required by Paragraph 121.99(d) to have a second independent communication system that offers immediate satellite-based voice communications of landline-telephone fidelity. This system must be able to communicate between the flight crew and air traffic control, and the flight crew and the air carrier.

This brings us to the **communication record** requirements for domestic and flag operations, which are covered in 14 CFR §121.711. An air carrier conducting domestic or flag operations is required to record each enroute radio contact between the certificate holder and its pilots. To do this, all radio and telephone call communication between pilots, dispatchers, and maintenance personnel may be recorded. Air carriers utilizing ACARS communications simply maintain an electronic record of every message sent or received and may store the communication information electronically. Whichever method is approved for retaining communications is used, these records are required by 14 CFR §121.711(d) to be kept for at least 30 days.

Part 135 Recordkeeping Requirements

Now let's take a look at the recordkeeping requirements for Part 135 operators. The bulk of the Part 135 recordkeeping requirements is covered in 14 CFR §135.63. The first requirement is that the following records must be kept at the certificate holder's principal business office or at other places approved by the FAA and shall be made available for inspection by the Administrator:

- The certificate holder's operating certificate
- The certificate holder's operations specifications
- A current list of aircraft used for Part 135 operations
- A record of each pilot
- A record of each flight attendant
- A completed aircraft load manifest (multi-engine aircraft only)

(14 CFR §135.63)

Aircraft Records

As are Part 121 air carriers, Part 135 certificate holders are required by 14 CFR §135.63(a) to maintain a current list of aircraft used or available for use and the operations for which each is equipped. Furthermore, the certificate holder must keep this record for at least 6 calendar months.

Alteration and Repair

Unlike Part 121 operators, an air carrier conducting operations under Part 135 is not required to submit reports of major alterations or major repairs. However, while a report is not required, the records of aircraft maintenance or alteration are required and must be made available to the FAA if requested.

Crewmember and Flight Attendant Record

Each certificate holder is required to keep an individual record of each pilot used in Part 135 operations for a period of at least 12 calendar months. This record must include the following information:

(i) The full name of the pilot.
(ii) The pilot certificate (by type and number) and ratings that the pilot holds.
(iii) The pilot's aeronautical experience in sufficient detail to determine the pilot's qualifications to pilot aircraft in operations under this part.

(iv) The pilot's current duties and the date of the pilot's assignment to those duties.
(v) The effective date and class of the medical certificate that the pilot holds.
(vi) The date and result of each of the initial and recurrent competency tests and proficiency and route checks required by this part and the type of aircraft flown during that test or check.
(vii) The pilot's flight time in sufficient detail to determine compliance with the flight time limitations found in this part.
(viii) The pilot's check pilot authorization, if any.
(ix) Any action taken concerning the pilot's release from employment for physical or professional disqualification.
(x) The date of the completion of the initial phase and each recurrent phase of the training required by this part.

(14 CFR §135.63[a][4])

An individual record for each flight attendant who is required under the applicable Part 135 regulations must also be maintained for a period of at least 12 months. This record must be of sufficient detail to determine compliance with the applicable portions of 14 CFR §135.273(a) concerning duty period limitations and rest requirements.

Load Manifest Record

14 CFR §135.63(c) requires a certificate holder operating multi-engine aircraft to prepare an accurate load manifest in duplicate containing information concerning the loading of the aircraft. The pilot-in-command of an aircraft for which a load manifest must be prepared shall carry a copy of the completed load manifest in the aircraft to its destination. The certificate holder shall keep copies of completed load manifests for at least 30 days at its principal operations base or at another location used by it and approved by the FAA. The required load manifest must be prepared before each takeoff and must include the following:

(1) The number of passengers;
(2) The total weight of the loaded aircraft;
(3) The maximum allowable takeoff weight for that flight;
(4) The center of gravity limits;
(5) The center of gravity of the loaded aircraft, except that the actual center of gravity need not be computed if the aircraft is loaded according to a loading schedule or other approved method that ensures that the center of gravity of the loaded aircraft is within approved limits. In those cases, an entry shall be made on the manifest indicating that the center of gravity is within limits according to a loading schedule or other approved method;
(6) The registration number of the aircraft or flight number;
(7) The origin and destination; and
(8) Identification of crew members and their crew position assignments.

(14 CFR §135.63[c])

Reporting of Mechanical Irregularities

Each Part 135 certificate holder, like their Part 121 counterparts, is required by Section 135.65 to carry an aircraft maintenance log on board each aircraft for recording or deferring mechanical irregularities and their correction. The pilot-in-command must ensure that each mechanical irregularity that comes to the pilot's attention during flight time is entered into the aircraft maintenance log. If a previous maintenance irregularity is detected prior to flight, the pilot-in-command is required to determine the status of the irregularity entered in the maintenance log at the end of the previous flight.

As we've seen with the Part 121 maintenance logbook, the FAA requires a written record of any maintenance action made on the aircraft. If any mechanic or pilot completes a maintenance corrective action or defers maintenance concerning a reported or observed failure or malfunction of an airframe, powerplant, propeller, rotor, or other aircraft equipment, that person is required by Section 135.65 to record the action taken in the aircraft maintenance log. Furthermore, each certificate holder's manual, which is required by Section 135.21 (policies and procedures), must include an approved procedure for keeping copies of the aircraft maintenance log in the aircraft for access by the appropriate personnel.

Summary

In this chapter, we've discussed what records and reports the FAA requires Part 121 air carriers to create and maintain. As we've seen, records and reports are required to be kept for everything from employee training records, dispatch release forms, load manifests, flight plans, and aircraft service difficulty reports to aircraft logbook entries and even en route aircraft-to-company communications. The FAA's primary reason for requiring these records is to allow it to better monitor and verify regulatory compliance.

In the next chapter, we will discuss the maintenance requirements placed on 14 CFR Part 121 air carriers.

Important Terms in Chapter 13

ACARS
aircraft listing record
aircraft maintenance logbook
airframe major alteration
airframe major repair
airworthiness release
alteration and repair report
appliance major alteration
appliance major repair
communication record
crewmember and dispatcher records
dispatch release
flight release
load manifest
major alteration
major repair
mechanical interruption summary report
powerplant major repairs
propeller major alteration
propeller major repair
service difficulty report

Chapter 13 Exam

1. Air carriers operating under Part 121 are required to maintain current employee records of
   a. certified airframe and powerplant mechanics and flight crewmembers.
   b. mechanics and repairmen authorized to complete an airworthiness release certificate.
   c. aircraft dispatchers and security screening personnel.
   d. aircraft dispatchers and crewmembers.

2. Air carriers operating under Part 121 must maintain a current list of each aircraft that
   a. the certificate holder operates domestically and/or internationally.
   b. the certificate holder owns; leased aircraft are not required to appear on the list.
   c. the certificate holder operates in scheduled air transportation.
   d. the certificate holder operates in revenue operations.

3. What information is required to appear on a Part 121 domestic or flag operator's dispatch release form?
   a. Identification number of the aircraft, trip number, departure airport, intermediate stops, destination airport and alternate airports, a statement about the type of operation (e.g., VFR, IFR), minimum fuel supply, weather reports and forecasts
   b. Company or organization name, make and model of aircraft, aircraft VIN number, flight number, name of each flight crewmember, departure airport, destination airport and alternate airports, minimum fuel supply, weather reports and forecasts
   c. Aircraft VIN number, air carrier name, make and model of aircraft, trip number, name of the pilot-in-command, departure airport, destination airport and alternate airports, minimum fuel supply, weather reports and forecasts
   d. Air carrier name, trip number, departure airport, intermediate stops, destination airport and alternate airports, a statement about the type of operation (e.g., VFR, IFR), weather reports and forecasts

4. What is the main difference between the load manifest used in domestic and flag operations and the load manifest used in supplemental operations?
   a. Domestic, flag, and supplemental load manifests must contain identical information.
   b. Load manifests used in supplemental international operations may use metric measurements for weight and balance calculations.
   c. Load manifests used in supplemental international operations may use metric measurements for the calculation of fuel load only.
   d. None of the above.

5. What paperwork is the pilot-in-command required by Part 121, Subpart V, to carry aboard an airplane to its destination for domestic and flag operations?
   a. Completed load manifest, minimum fuel load calculations, flight plan
   b. Completed load manifest, dispatch release, communications logbook
   c. Completed load manifest, dispatch release, flight plan
   d. Dispatch release, service interruption report, flight plan, crewmember records

6. What additional paperwork items is the pilot-in-command required by Part 121, Subpart V, to carry aboard an airplane to its destination for supplemental operations?
   a. Pilot route certification, airworthiness release and a flight release instead of a dispatch release
   b. Flight following paperwork, airworthiness release, and international route authority
   c. Airworthiness release
   d. None of the above

7. The FAA requires an air carrier to maintain a record of each dispatch release or flight release for a period of
   a. 60 days
   b. 30 days
   c. 6 months
   d. 3 months

8. Air carriers are required to maintain a record of service difficulty reports for a period of
   a. 30 days
   b. 3 months
   c. 6 months
   d. 10 days

9. Who is allowed to sign an aircraft's airworthiness release certificate?
   a. Only the pilot-in-command or a certificated mechanic
   b. The authorized certificated mechanic or repairman
   c. A certificated repairman and the pilot-in-command
   d. The air carrier's operations inspector or designated principal operations inspector

10. An air carrier is required to maintain a record of each en route radio contact between the certificate holder and its pilots for what period of time?
    a. 90 days
    b. 60 days
    c. 2 years
    d. 30 days

11. A Part 135 certificate holder must maintain a current list of aircraft used or available for use and the operations for which each is equipped for how long?
    a. For a period of 90 days
    b. For a period of 6 calendar months
    c. For a period of 2 years
    d. For a period of 30 days

12. Each certificate holder is required to keep an individual record of each pilot or required flight attendant used in Part 135 operations for a period of
    a. at least 3 calendar months.
    b. at least 60 days.
    c. at least 12 calendar months.
    d. at least 24 calendar months.

13. An air carrier must keep a record of each airworthiness release for a period of at least how many months?
    a. 2 months
    b. 90 days
    c. 6 months
    d. 24 calendar months

14. A mechanical interruption summary report is required to be submitted to the FAA how often?
    a. Every two weeks
    b. Every month before the 10th of the month for the previous month's mechanical interruptions
    c. Every month before the end of the month for the previous month's mechanical interruptions
    d. Every 90 days

15. For how long must a copy of each flight's load manifest be kept on file?
    a. One year
    b. 6 months
    c. 3 months
    d. 30 calendar days

CHAPTER 14
MAINTENANCE

No flying machine will ever fly from New York to Paris…
[because] no known motor can run at the requisite speed for four days without stopping.
—**Orville Wright,** 1908

Airworthiness Responsibility

In this chapter, we will examine the requirements for maintenance that Part 121 places on air carriers. This is another area that is quite different for air carriers than what you may be familiar with from your previous exposure to Part 91 civilian training and operations. For the most part in Part 91 operations, airworthiness is primarily the responsibility of a certificated airframe and powerplant mechanic and the pilot flying the aircraft. In the case of an annual inspection or major repairs, a certificated airworthiness inspector must also be involved. In Part 121 operations, the FAA is very much concerned about **process control**. That is: how does the air carrier maintain control of the maintenance procedures for which it is responsible?

Subpart L of Part 121 concerns maintenance, preventive maintenance, and alterations. It applies to all Part 121 certificate holders. With the "globalization" of the airline industry, it applies to carriers that have work done outside the United States by persons that do not hold U.S. airmen certificates. In that case, it puts the specific responsibility on the carrier to ensure that the foreign maintenance service providers or suppliers are subject to the same degree of surveillance that the FAA would perform within the United States. Furthermore, the carrier is specifically responsible for assuring that all work performed is done in accordance with the carrier's maintenance and inspection manuals. This concept is very similar to that of operational control, except applied to maintenance instead of flight operations.

The FARs are very clear that the certificate holder is responsible for the airworthiness of its aircraft and component parts. It must ensure that the processes used are those approved in its maintenance manual. In 1979, an American Airlines DC-10 aircraft was lost when the left engine separated from the aircraft. Subsequent investigation of the accident by the National Transportation Safety Board (NTSB) revealed that the carrier was using a procedure for removing the engine for maintenance that was not the one approved by the FAA and included in the carrier's maintenance manual. Although the procedures seemed similar in intent and result, an apparently minor difference in procedure repeatedly stressed the attach flange on the engine pylon, eventually causing it to break. In this case, the carrier was held responsible for violating its own procedures in its own maintenance shop.

The same problem can arise in a different context. In 1996, ValuJet Flight 592 crashed in the Florida Everglades near Miami. The NTSB investigation revealed that this accident was directly caused by expired oxygen canisters that were improperly shipped in the aircraft's cargo hold; these canisters ignited and caused a major fire and loss of control of the aircraft. During the NTSB hearing, an interesting question was posed to the senior ValuJet official in charge of maintenance. He was asked if he thought that the carrier could delegate the responsibility for compliance with FARs to the contract maintenance company that had worked on another of the carrier's DC-9s and shipped the expired canisters on a ValuJet aircraft. The answer stunned the hearing when he stated that yes, responsibility for compliance with FAR's could be delegated. That clearly is *not* the correct answer; and that answer largely sealed the fate of ValuJet's demise as an air carrier.

14 CFR §121.363 and §135.413 make it clear that a carrier may delegate the performance of any maintenance, preventive maintenance, or alteration to an outside contractor. However, this delegation of the work does not relieve the carrier of the responsibility to ensure the airworthiness of its aircraft. That responsibility includes ensuring that the maintenance provider has the capability to do the work on the carrier's behalf, directing their work, and determining if their work was done satisfactorily in compliance with the air carrier's maintenance manual procedures and company policies relating to airworthiness. This **airworthiness responsibility**, like operational control, may never be delegated. Only the actual "wrench turning" can be delegated; all responsibility for ensuring that the work was properly done and documented remains with the carrier. If the contractor makes a mistake in maintenance procedures or fails to properly document the work performed, it is the *carrier* that the FAA will hold accountable.

14 CFR §121.363—Responsibility for airworthiness.

(b) A certificate holder may make arrangements with another person for the performance of any maintenance, preventive maintenance, or alterations. However, this does not relieve the certificate holder of the responsibility specified in paragraph (a) of this section.

In order to ensure that the company can actually do this, the FAA requires that the carrier have an adequate organization that is actually able to perform the required maintenance. This requirement is also extended to any contractors or subcontractors doing work for the carrier. The same organizational requirement is placed on the carrier or its contractors for the **inspection function** as well as the maintenance function. This inspection function brings us to one of the key differences between maintenance performed for Part 91 operators and Part 121 airlines.

Maintenance of Part 121 aircraft includes two interrelated components. First, the aircraft must be *maintained*. For this, think of the actual wrench turning.

Then, the maintenance must be taken one step further. The aircraft must be inspected by an independent organization. The *inspection* of the work assures that whatever was to be done has actually been accomplished correctly and completely. It is this independent inspection that is designed to make sure things don't slip by or get overlooked. The airline must have separate maintenance functions and inspection functions. These two organizations must be separated (organizationally) at the operational level (Figure 14-1). That is, it must be separated at the level of the persons doing the actual work. The separation must occur below the level of administrative control at which overall responsibility for the required inspection functions and other maintenance and alteration functions is exercised.

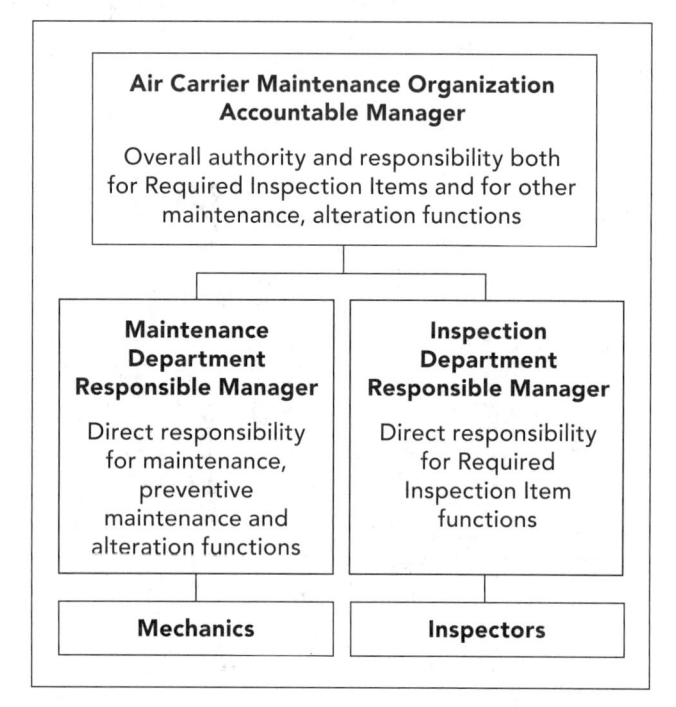

Figure 14-1. Maintenance and inspection organizational chart.

When a carrier delegates the performance of any maintenance, preventive maintenance, or alteration to an outside contractor, this is called "outsourced" or "contract maintenance." 14 CFR §121.368 spells out what requirements must be met in order to use this contract maintenance. The main requirement is that regardless of who actually performs the work, the responsibility of the airworthiness of the aircraft is placed squarely on the air carrier. No maintenance provider may perform work unless that work is carried out under the supervision and control of the certificate holder. For this reason, a representative of the air carrier, while not required to constantly and physically observe and direct each maintenance provider, he or she must be available for consultation on matters requiring instruction or decision.

14 CFR §121.368 Contract Maintenance

(b) Each certificate holder must be directly in charge of all covered work done for it by a maintenance provider.
[Directly in charge means having responsibility for covered work performed by a maintenance provider.]

(c) Each maintenance provider must perform all covered work in accordance with the certificate holder's maintenance manual.
[Covered work means either regularly scheduled maintenance or essential maintenance that could result in a failure, malfunction, or defect endangering the safe operation of an aircraft if not performed properly or if improper parts or material are used.]

(e) Each certificate holder who contracts for maintenance, preventive maintenance or alterations must develop and implement policies, procedures, methods and instructions for the accomplishment of all contracted maintenance, preventive maintenance, and alterations to be performed in accordance with the certificate holder's maintenance program and maintenance manual.

The most frequently outsourced tasks include engine maintenance, component overhaul and heavy maintenance D-Check inspections (discussed later in this chapter). Cost savings is the primary motivating factor in the decision to use contract maintenance. This decision must take into account the personnel, training, and tools and test equipment necessary to complete the maintenance task. Contract maintenance is an attractive option for air carriers for a number of reasons. For example, an operator may not have a sufficient number of aircraft in a particular fleet type to justify the expense of trained personnel, facilities, tooling and test equipment required to perform the maintenance function themselves. In this situation, substantial savings are realized when the maintenance is performed externally.

As you might imagine, the Federal Aviation Administration oversight of the air carrier will also include the contract maintenance station that completes the work for the certificate holder. For this reason, each air carrier who contracts for maintenance, preventive maintenance or alterations must provide the FAA with a list that includes the name and physical (street) address, or addresses, where the work is carried out for each maintenance provider that performs work for the certificate holder, and a description of the type of maintenance, preventive maintenance, or alteration that is to be performed at each location, The list must be updated with any changes, including additions or deletions, and the updated list provided to the FAA in a format acceptable to the FAA by the last of each calendar month.

Part 121 Maintenance Manual Requirement

As we've seen above, the Part 121 carrier's maintenance program is vested in a properly organized and staffed facility that ensures that the carrier is able to exercise its airworthiness responsibility. To that end, 14 CFR §121.367 requires that the carrier must have in place the previously described programs that ensure maintenance is performed in accord with its **maintenance manual**. It must have adequate facilities and equipment to carry out the maintenance and it must ensure that each aircraft that has been **released to service** has been properly maintained. Being released to service means that the carrier has assured that all required maintenance, repairs, and inspections have been performed and the documentation (records) prepared that ensures the continuing airworthiness of the aircraft.

To ensure that all personnel involved with maintenance have the information needed to perform their functions, the FAA requires that the carrier have a maintenance manual (discussed above and previously in Chapter 4). This manual must contain an organization chart (or description) for the maintenance and inspection functions as well as a list of any contractors or subcontractors that the carrier uses to perform maintenance or inspections. It must contain descriptions and details of the programs of maintenance, inspection, and continuing airworthiness that must be used by the carrier. These programs are normally drawn up starting with the aircraft manufacturer's maintenance manual and then adapted to the specific needs of the carrier. The maintenance program must include:

- The method of performing routine and nonroutine maintenance (other than required inspections), preventive maintenance, and alterations.
- A designation of the items of maintenance and alteration that must be inspected (**required inspections**), including at least those that

could result in a failure, malfunction, or defect endangering the safe operation of the aircraft if not performed properly or if improper parts or materials are used.
- The method of performing required inspections and a designation by occupational title of personnel authorized to perform each required inspection.
- Procedures for the reinspection of work performed pursuant to previous required inspection findings (**buy-back procedures**).
- Procedures, standards, and limits necessary for required inspections and acceptance or rejection of the items required to be inspected and for periodic inspection and **calibration of precision tools**, measuring devices, and test equipment.
- Procedures to ensure that all required inspections are performed.
- Instructions to prevent any person who performs any item of work from performing any required inspection of that work.
- Instructions and procedures to prevent any decision of an inspector, regarding any required inspection, from being countermanded by persons other than supervisory personnel of the inspection unit, or a person at that level of administrative control that has overall responsibility for the management of both the required inspection functions and the other maintenance, preventive maintenance, and alterations functions.
- Procedures to ensure that required inspections, other maintenance, preventive maintenance, and alterations that are not completed as a result of shift changes or similar work interruptions are properly completed before the aircraft is released to service.

Part 135 Maintenance Manual Requirement

Depending on the seating configuration, Part 135 operators may or may not be required to have a company-specific maintenance manual. If we look at 14 CFR §135.411, the *Applicability* section, it specifies that aircraft that are type certificated with a passenger seating configuration of nine or less are allowed to be maintained using the maintenance manual provided by the aircraft manufacturer. Those aircraft that are type certificated with a passenger seating configuration of 10 or more seats must be maintained in accordance with a FAA-approved maintenance manual written by the air carrier.

Maintenance Recordkeeping

The FAA views the recordkeeping as being as important as the actual maintenance work. To that end, the carrier must provide (in its manual) for a suitable system, as required by 14 CFR §121.369 and §135.427, that provides for preservation and retrieval of maintenance information (records) in an acceptable manner. This system of **maintenance records** must contain the following:

- A description of the work performed (this can be by way of a coding system)
- The name of the person performing the work if the work is performed by a person outside the organization of the certificate holder
- The name or other positive ID of the individual approving the work

These records are primarily kept to show that the air carrier is in compliance with all pertinent regulations and that each aircraft to be flown is airworthy and capable of safe flight. The records of each required maintenance task must include:

(1) All the records necessary to show that all requirements for the issuance of an airworthiness release under §121.709 have been met. *[See chapter 13.]*
(2) Records containing the following information:
   (i) The total time in service of the airframe.
   (ii) …the total time in service of each engine and propeller.
   (iii) The current status of **life-limited parts** of each airframe, engine, propeller, and appliance.
   (iv) The time since last overhaul of all items installed on the aircraft which are required to be overhauled on a specified time basis.
   (v) The identification of the current inspection status of the aircraft, including the times since the last inspections required by the inspection program under which the aircraft and its appliances are maintained.
   (vi) The current status of applicable airworthiness directives **[ADs]**, including the date and methods of compliance, and, if the airworthiness directive involves recurring action **[recurring AD]**, the time and date when the next action is required.
   (vii) A list of current major alterations to each airframe, engine, propeller, and appliance.

(14 CFR §121.380[a])

These records must be maintained by the carrier and kept available for inspection by the FAA or the NTSB at the location(s) specified in its ops specs. Section 121.380 requires the carrier to retain the required records for the following periods:

(1) Except for the records of the last complete overhaul of each airframe, engine, propeller, and appliance, the records... *[required to show that all requirements for issuing an airworthiness release have been met]* shall be retained until the work is repeated or superseded by other work or for one year after the work is performed.
(2) The records of the last complete overhaul of each airframe, engine, propeller, and appliance shall be retained until the work is superseded by work of equivalent scope and detail.

(14 CFR §121.380[c])

These records must be retained and transferred with the aircraft at the time the aircraft is sold. The purchaser of the aircraft may allow the seller to retain the records (for example, if the seller is going to continue to perform the maintenance for the purchaser), but the purchaser is still responsible to provide these records to the FAA and NTSB if required for surveillance or an investigation. As you might expect, because reviewing maintenance records is often the only direct means of determining the accomplishment of required maintenance, the FAA treats the act of intentionally failing to make and keep—as well as the act of intentionally falsifying, mutilating, or altering—air carrier aircraft records as a criminal act subject to substantial fines or imprisonment.

Who can perform the maintenance? The carrier may set up its own maintenance and inspection departments. If it does so under 14 CFR §121.379, then §121.378 requires each person *directly in charge* of maintaining or altering the carrier's aircraft to have an appropriate airman certificate. "Directly in charge of" means any person assigned to a position in which he or she is responsible for the work of a shop or station that performs the maintenance or alteration or any other function that affects airworthiness. This person who is directly in charge of a shop or station does not have to physically observe and direct each worker at that shop or station. Rather, the person must be available for consultation and decision on matters that require instructions or decisions from a higher authority than that of the person actually performing the work. Further, any inspector must have an appropriate airman certificate.

An alternative method of certificating the operation is to rely on a certificate issued under 14 CFR Part 145. This part covers certification of repair stations (facilities). If the **maintenance repair organization (MRO)** is certificated under Part 145, then the FAA will look to that organization *as an organization* for the authority which allows it to perform maintenance and inspections for a carrier. In other words, a carrier may perform maintenance and alterations for itself or other carriers. In addition, it may contract out work to maintenance repair organizations certificated under Part 145. In any event, it may not contract out *responsibility* for maintaining the continuous airworthiness of its aircraft.

14 CFR §121.371 sets forth the requirements for the inspection personnel that are required for a carrier's inspection program. Inspectors must be appropriately certificated, properly trained, qualified, and authorized by the carrier to perform the inspections. The inspectors don't work individually on their own authority. Rather, the person performing inspections must be under the supervision and control of an inspection unit. This management unit will be held accountable by the FAA for any irregularities that occur. Of course, the inspector may also be held accountable. A basic concept of inspection and one required by the FAA is that no person may perform a required inspection if he or she performed the item of work required to be inspected.

The FAA wants to be able to tell exactly who is responsible for inspections. Therefore, the inspection unit must maintain a current listing of persons who have been trained, qualified, and authorized to conduct required inspections. The persons authorized to perform inspections must be identified by name, occupational title, and the inspections that they are authorized to perform. If the inspections are contracted to third parties, then the carrier must assure that those third parties maintain this same information. The carrier (or person with whom it arranges to perform its required inspections) must give written information to each person authorized to perform inspections describing the extent of his or her responsibility and authority, and limits on his or her inspection authority. This information must be made available to the FAA upon request.

Once the maintenance and inspection programs have been set up, the FAA expects the carrier to perform continuing surveillance (or audits) of both its maintenance and its inspection programs. 14 CFR §121.373 requires this **continuing analysis and surveillance system (CASS)**. Introduction of the CASS requirement resulted from an FAA industry study of a series of maintenance-related air carrier accidents occurring in the 1950s. The study found that, in many cases, the primary cause of an accident was a weakness in the maintenance program. The study also found that in some cases maintenance personnel failed to accomplish required maintenance tasks or failed to complete the tasks correctly. Responding to this industry study, the FAA introduced Sections 121.373 and 135.431 requiring air carriers to establish and maintain a CASS system for their maintenance programs. Section 121.373 also requires each air carrier to include a process in its CASS to correct any deficiency identified in its maintenance program, regardless of whether a contracted maintenance provider did the work or the work was completed by its own maintenance personnel.

The continuing analysis and surveillance system (CASS) monitors the following elements of an air carrier's maintenance program:

- The air carrier's airworthiness responsibility
- Maintenance manual
- Maintenance organization
- Accomplishment and approval of maintenance and alterations
- Maintenance schedule
- Required inspection items (RII)
- Recordkeeping system
- Contract maintenance providers
- Maintenance personnel training program

The purpose of these programs is to ensure that if the programs start to produce unacceptable results, that fact will be picked up and corrected before any serious maintenance issues arise. It is the carrier's responsibility to continuously monitor its maintenance and inspection programs for the purposes of quality control. If the FAA finds that either of these programs is not adequately assuring that the requirements of Part 121 are being met, it may make any changes in the program(s) that it deems necessary to bring the program(s) back into compliance with Part 121. This process is subject to appeal by the carrier. Unless an emergency situation requiring immediate action exists, the carrier must be given a hearing to allow it to show that the programs were working as required.

14 CFR §121.375 requires that each carrier or person performing maintenance or preventive maintenance functions for it shall have a **maintenance or inspection training program** to ensure that each person (including inspection personnel) who determines the adequacy of work done is fully informed about procedures and techniques and new equipment in use and is competent to perform his duties.

As we saw earlier with pilots, flight attendants, and dispatchers, the FAA is concerned that safety-sensitive workers such as mechanics are sufficiently rested so as not to be prone to fatigue-related errors. Section 121.377 states that within the United States, each carrier (or contractor performing maintenance functions for it) must relieve each person performing maintenance from duty for a period of at least 24 consecutive hours during any 7 consecutive days, or the equivalent thereof within any single calendar month. Note that due to jurisdictional issues, this provision only applies within the United States. This is one of the areas in Part 121 where serious conflict of national objectives occurs. On the one hand, the United States supports increased competition in the global marketplace by allowing maintenance work to be contracted to cheaper facilities outside the United States. On the other hand, these facilities are not subject to U.S. labor law and regulations, so the United States can't dictate the rest provisions. That makes these shops cheaper to operate and more competitive, but does it allow for the same level of safety as required for U.S. MROs?

Continuous Airworthiness Maintenance Program (CAMP)

When we think of an aircraft's continued airworthiness, it is important to remember that we don't think of aircraft as "old" or "new" but rather in terms of whether the aircraft is airworthy or unairworthy. The **continuous airworthiness maintenance program (CAMP)**, first introduced in 1964, is a compilation of the individual maintenance functions utilized by an air carrier to fulfill its regulatory maintenance requirements. The functions that are included are shown in Figure 14-2. The goal of any continuous airworthiness maintenance program is to maintain an air carrier's fleet in an airworthy condition. Section 121.367 requires an air carrier to have an inspection program and a program covering scheduled maintenance, preventive maintenance, and alterations to ensure that each aircraft released to service is airworthy and properly maintained for operations in air transportation. To do this, the air carrier must provide competent personnel, adequate facilities, and equipment. Also, everyone who works on an aircraft must follow the air carrier's maintenance manual and maintenance program. The continuous airworthiness maintenance program is derived from the approved requirements stated in the operations specifications. Let's look at how an air carrier ensures continuous airworthiness for its fleet of aircraft.

Under the watchful eye of the FAA, each air carrier prepares a CAMP under its operations specifications. The CAMP includes both routine and detailed scheduled maintenance checks. These scheduled checks are called **maintenance event letter checks**, or simply **letter checks**. Letter checks are inspections labeled "A," "B," "C," or "D."

A-Checks and B-Checks are simple, relatively quick and inexpensive inspections, while the C-Checks and D-Checks are more intrusive, time-consuming and expensive inspections.

> **Continuous Airworthiness Maintenance**
>
> The general rules for air carrier maintenance, including its organization and personnel involved in continuous maintenance airworthiness programs, can be found in **Part 43: Maintenance, Preventive Maintenance, Rebuilding, and Alteration**.
>
> The certification of personnel involved in maintenance operation is regulated by **Part 65: Certification of Airmen other than Flight Crewmembers**.
>
> Approval of organizations involved in maintenance can be found in **Part 145: Repair Stations**.
>
> The certification of an organization seeking approval to conduct training of maintenance personnel is covered in **Part 147: Aviation Maintenance Technician Schools**.

Figure 14-2. Continuous airworthiness maintenance (CAMP).

- **A-Checks** are typically weekly or biweekly general inspections of the interior and exterior of an aircraft with selected areas to be checked. This includes checking hydraulic, engine oil and cockpit oxygen levels as well as other basic operational inspections. This inspection is performed while the aircraft is still considered to be in service. 14 CFR §121.374 addresses the requirement for maintenance inspections prior to ETOPS flights. These ETOPS pre-departure checks are similar to and may even be identical to a particular air carrier's A-Check depending on the operations specifications.
- **B-Checks** are more thorough bi-monthly inspections of the aircraft system fluid levels, emergency equipment, aircraft placards, etc. Select inspection panels are removed and aircraft systems are checked. B-checks are usually performed at a hangar or remote maintenance ramp area with the aircraft out of service for a short period of time (i.e., one or two days).
- **C-Checks** are usually performed every two years or after a specific amount of flight hours and are a much more thorough type of maintenance inspection. A C-Check takes place in a maintenance hangar, takes up to two weeks, and involves extensive inspection and overhaul. A C-Check includes aircraft systems checks, and thorough cleaning and servicing of the entire aircraft. These checks also include fairly minor structural inspections and compliance with any manufacturer's service bulletin requirements.
- **D-Checks**, also called heavy maintenance visits (HMV), are required generally once every decade of service and are an extensive overhaul of the airframe and most of the aircraft's systems. D-Checks are restrictively time consuming and expensive, usually taking close to two months to complete. During a D-Check, the aircraft is stripped down to the supporting structure of the airframe. All systems are overhauled and inspected. The aircraft is usually painted and functionally checked before going back into line service.

Continuous Airworthiness Maintenance Program (CAMP) for Two-Engine ETOPS

In order to conduct an ETOPS flight using a two-engine airplane, each certificate holder is required by 14 CFR §121.374 to develop and comply with the ETOPS continuous airworthiness maintenance program (CAMP), as authorized in the certificate holder's operations specifications, for each airplane-engine combination used in ETOPS. The certificate holder must develop this ETOPS CAMP by supplementing the manufacturer's maintenance program or the CAMP currently approved for the certificate holder. This ETOPS CAMP must include the following elements, as detailed in Section 121.374:

- *ETOPS maintenance document.* The certificate holder must have an ETOPS maintenance document for use by each person involved in ETOPS.

- *ETOPS pre-departure service check.* Except as provided in Appendix P of 14 CFR Part 121, the certificate holder must develop a pre-departure check tailored to their specific operation. This pre-departure service check (PDSC) must be performed before each ETOPS flight by an appropriately trained maintenance person, who is ETOPS qualified, and who must accomplish and certify by signature ETOPS-specific tasks.
- *Limitations on dual maintenance.* Except in certain circumstances discussed in Paragraph 121.374(c)(2), the certificate holder may not perform scheduled or unscheduled maintenance during the same maintenance visit on a substantially similar ETOPS Significant System listed in the ETOPS maintenance document, if the improper maintenance could result in the failure of an ETOPS Significant System.
- *Verification program.* The certificate holder must develop and maintain a program for the resolution of discrepancies that will ensure the effectiveness of maintenance actions taken on ETOPS Significant Systems. The verification program must identify potential problems and verify satisfactory corrective action.
- *Task identification.* The certificate holder must identify all ETOPS-specific tasks. An appropriately trained mechanic who is ETOPS qualified must accomplish and certify by signature that the ETOPS-specific task has been completed.
- *Centralized maintenance control procedures.* The certificate holder must develop and maintain procedures for centralized maintenance control for ETOPS.
- *Parts control program.* The certificate holder must develop an ETOPS parts control program to ensure the proper identification of parts used to maintain the configuration of airplanes used in ETOPS.
- *Reliability program.* The certificate holder must have an ETOPS reliability program. This program must be the certificate holder's existing reliability program or its Continuing Analysis and Surveillance System (CASS) supplemented for ETOPS. This program must be event-oriented and include procedures to report certain events within 96 hours of the occurrence to its **certificate holding district office (CHDO)**.
- *Propulsion system monitoring.* If the **inflight shutdown (IFSD)** rate (computed on a 12-month rolling average) for an engine installed as part of an airplane-engine combination exceeds the values listed in Paragraph 121.374(i), the certificate holder must do a comprehensive review of its operations to identify any common cause effects and systemic errors. The IFSD rate must be computed using all engines of that type in the certificate holder's entire fleet of airplanes approved for ETOPS.
- *Engine condition monitoring.* The certificate holder must have an engine condition monitoring program to detect deterioration at an early stage and to allow for corrective action before safe operation is affected. This is to ensure that in the event of a prolonged engine-inoperative diversion the remaining engine is in good condition.
- *Oil-consumption monitoring.* The certificate holder must have an engine oil consumption monitoring program to ensure that there is enough oil to complete each ETOPS flight. APU oil consumption must be included if an APU is required for ETOPS.
- *APU in-flight start program.* If the airplane type certificate requires an APU but does not require the APU to run during the ETOPS portion of the flight, the certificate holder must develop and maintain a program acceptable to the FAA for cold soak in-flight start-and-run reliability.
- *Maintenance training.* For each airplane-engine combination, the certificate holder must develop a maintenance training program that provides training adequate to support ETOPS. It must include ETOPS specific training for all persons involved in ETOPS maintenance that focuses on the special nature of ETOPS. This training must be in addition to the operator's maintenance training program used to qualify individuals to perform work on specific airplanes and engines.
- *Configuration, maintenance, and procedures (CMP) document.* If an airplane-engine combination has a CMP document, the certificate holder must use a system that ensures compliance with the applicable FAA-approved document.
- *Procedural changes.* Each substantial change to the maintenance or training procedures that were used to qualify the certificate holder for ETOPS must be submitted to the CHDO for review. The certificate holder cannot implement a change until its CHDO notifies the certificate holder that the review is complete.

Airworthiness Directive (AD)

In addition to the normal actions designed to maintain continued airworthiness of an air carrier's fleet of aircraft, it is occasionally necessary, in the interest of safety, for the FAA to intervene by extraordinary means. If the FAA becomes aware of an unsafe condition in an aircraft model, engine, avionics or other system installed on an aircraft that has the potential to develop into a problem on similar types of aircraft, then the FAA issues an **airworthiness directive (AD)**. Airworthiness directives are made up of two parts, *the preamble* and *the rule*. The preamble provides the basis and the purpose of the AD. The rule portion provides regulatory requirements for correcting the unsafe condition. Airworthiness directives are part of the Code of Federal Regulations and require certain mandatory actions be complied with in order for the aircraft to be considered airworthy. The FAA's airworthiness directives are legally enforceable rules that must be complied with by a certain date or flight hour period or the aircraft becomes unairworthy. The FAA typically becomes aware of the need for an airworthiness directive by review of the service difficulty reports we discussed in Chapter 13.

The regulations contained in Part 39 provide a legal framework for the FAA's system of airworthiness directives. The FAA makes it clear that anyone who operates an aircraft that does not meet the requirements of an applicable airworthiness directive is in violation of Part 39.

The FAA issues three types of airworthiness directives:

1. **Notice of proposed rulemaking (NPRM):** The standard process is to issue an NPRM followed by a final rule. After an unsafe condition is discovered, a proposed solution is published as an NPRM, which solicits public comment on the proposed action. After the comment period closes, the final rule is prepared, taking into account all the comments received, with the rule perhaps being changed as warranted by the comments. The preamble of the final rule AD will state if no changes were made or if no comments were received.
2. **Final rule** (with request for comments): In certain cases, the critical nature of an unsafe condition may warrant the immediate adoption of a rule without prior notice and solicitation of comments. However, this is not normally the case. If the time by which the terminating action must be accomplished is too short to allow public comment (that is, less than 60 days), then a "finding of impracticability" is justified for the terminating of the action, and this can be issued as an immediately adopted rule. The immediately adopted rule is then published in the *Federal Register* with a request for comments. The final rule AD may be changed later if substantive comments are received.
3. **Emergency AD:** An Emergency AD is issued when an unsafe condition exists that requires immediate action by an owner/operator prior to further flight. The intent of an Emergency AD is to rapidly correct an urgent safety of flight situation.

The FAA Aircraft Certification Directorates write ADs using a standard template that includes the following (*see* Figure 14-3):

- The AD reference number
- A description of the unsafe condition
- The product to which the AD applies
- The required corrective action or operating limitations, or both
- The effective date
- Compliance time limit

Compliance requirements in ADs are specified in different ways. Most ADs specify compliance in terms of hours of operation, number of landings, or number of cycles (start of flight operation to completion of flight). Some ADs are so serious in nature that they require compliance before further flight. An AD is considered obsolete when it is superseded by a new AD. The superseding AD identifies the AD that is no longer in effect. There are no compliance requirements for an AD that has been superseded.

Different approaches or techniques that are not specified in an AD can, after FAA approval, be used to correct an unsafe condition on an aircraft or aircraft product. Although the alternative procedure or limitation may not have been known at the time the AD was issued, **an alternative method of compliance (AMOC)** for an AD could be acceptable to accomplish the intent of the AD. A compliance time that differs from the requirements of the AD can also be approved if the revised time period provides an acceptable level of safety that is at least equivalent to that of the requirements of the AD.

FAA Aviation Safety

Sample Emergency Airworthiness Directive

www.faa.gov/aircraft/safety/alerts/

DATE: January 16, 2013
AD#: 2013-02-51

Emergency airworthiness directive **(AD) 2013-02-51** is sent to owners and operators of: The Boeing Company Model 787-8 airplanes.

Background

This emergency AD was prompted by recent incidents involving lithium ion battery failures that resulted in release of flammable electrolytes, heat damage, and smoke on two Model 787-8 airplanes. The cause of these failures is currently under investigation. These conditions, if not corrected, could result in damage to critical systems and structures, and the potential for fire in the electrical compartment.

FAA's Determination

We are issuing this AD because we evaluated all the relevant information and determined the unsafe condition described previously is likely to exist or develop in other products of the same type design.

AD Requirements

This AD requires modification of the battery system, or other actions, in accordance with a method approved by the Manager, Seattle Aircraft Certification (ACO), FAA.

AD 2013-02-51: The Boeing Company

(a) Effective Date: This Emergency AD is effective upon receipt.

(b) Affected AD's: None

(c) Applicability: This AD applies to all The Boeing Company Model 787-8 airplanes, certificated in any category.

(d) Subject: Joint Aircraft System Componenet (JASC)/Air Transport Association (ATA) of America Code 24, Electrical Power.

(e) Unsafe Condition: This AD was prompted by recent incidents involving lithium ion battery failures that resulted in release of flammable electrolytes, heat damage, and smoke on two Model 787-8 airplanes. The cause of these failures is currently under investigation. We are issuing this AD to prevent damage to critical systems and structures, and the potential for fire in the electrical compartment.

(f) Compliance: Comply with this AD within the compliance times specified, unless already done.

(g) Modification or Other Action: Before further flight, modify the battery system, or take other actions, in accordance with a method approved by the Manager, Seattle Aircraft Certification Office (ACO), FAA.

(h) Alternative Method of Compliance (AMOC's): The FAA has the authority to approve AMOC's for this AD, if requested using the procedures found in 14 CFR 39.19. In accordance with 14 CFR 39.19, send your request to your principal inspector or local Flight Standards District Office, as appropriate.

Figure 14-3. Emergency airworthiness directive.

Summary

In this chapter, we have examined the structure of Part 121 air carrier maintenance. We have seen how it differs from the maintenance performed in Part 91, particularly in the organization, structure, inspections, and training required. These requirements are to ensure that the highest level of safety is achieved by air carriers.

In the next chapter, we will review several of the appendices that are most likely to be encountered by air carrier employees in day-to-day operations.

Important Terms in Chapter 14

A, B, C and D checks
airworthiness directive (AD)
airworthiness responsibility
alternative method of compliance (AMOC)
buy-back procedures
calibration of precision tools
certificate holding district office (CHDO)
continuing analysis and surveillance system (CASS)
continuous airworthiness maintenance program (CAMP)
emergency AD
final rule
inflight shutdown (IFSD)
inspection function
life-limited parts
maintenance event letter checks
maintenance manual
maintenance or inspection training program
maintenance records
maintenance repair organization (MRO)
notice of proposed rulemaking (NPRM)
process control
recurring airworthiness directive (AD)
released to service
required inspection

Chapter 14 Exam

1. If repair work is "farmed out" to an outside maintenance repair organization under an approved contract, who is responsible for the airworthiness of the repair?
    a. The maintenance repair organization
    b. The air carrier certificate holder
    c. The FAA
    d. Both (a) and (b) are jointly responsible.

2. The air carrier certificate holder may delegate the responsibility for the repair of its aircraft to:
    a. Another Part 121 certificate holder repair station.
    b. A Part 145 FAA-authorized repair station.
    c. Both (a) and (b) are permitted.
    d. Neither (a) nor (b) is permitted.

3. The air carrier certificate holder may delegate the responsibility for airworthiness of its aircraft to:
    a. Another Part 121 certificate holder repair station.
    b. A Part 145 FAA authorized repair station.
    c. Both (a) and (b) are permitted.
    d. Neither (a) nor (b) is permitted.

4. Organizationally, the maintenance function and inspection function of a carrier
    a. must be combined into a single department under the director of maintenance to ensure control of the program.
    b. must place the maintenance department under the inspection department to emphasize the relative importance of inspection vis-à-vis maintenance.
    c. may be placed wherever is most feasible for the company operations.
    d. must be placed in separate organizations at the operational level of the company.

5. The maintenance program for each aircraft is described in the carrier's
    a. ops specs.
    b. maintenance manual.
    c. management manual.
    d. flight operations manual.

6. Records to show that all requirements for issuing a maintenance release have been met must be kept available for inspection for how long?
   a. 30 days
   b. 90 days
   c. 1 year
   d. Forever, and transferred with the aircraft if it is sold

7. Records to show that the aircraft was overhauled must be kept for how long?
   a. 30 days
   b. 90 days
   c. 1 year
   d. Forever, and transferred with the aircraft if it is sold

8. The mechanic for an airline (that has set up its maintenance under Section 121.379) that changes a DC generator on an engine must hold which of the following?
   a. An airframe certificate
   b. A powerplant certificate
   c. An airframe and powerplant certificate
   d. The mechanic needn't hold any airman's certificate.

9. Maintenance and inspection training
   a. is required at all Part 121 carriers.
   b. is required only if the carrier has contracted its maintenance to a Part 145 maintenance repair facility.
   c. is only suggested for Part 121 carriers but required for Part 145 facilities.
   d. None of the above.

10. If a Part 121 carrier contracts its maintenance work out to a foreign Part 145 maintenance facility, then that facility must provide its workers
    a. 1 day off every 7 days.
    b. 4 days off every calendar month.
    c. 1 week off every calendar year.
    d. It is not required to provide its workers any time off.

11. What Part provides a legal framework for the FAA's system of airworthiness directives?
    a. Part 39
    b. Part 45
    c. Part 147
    d. Part 139

12. Depending on the seating configuration, Part 135 operators may or may not be required to have a company-specific maintenance manual. Part 135 operators using aircraft type certificated for a passenger seating configuration, excluding any pilot seat, of _____ seats or more, shall maintain those aircraft in accordance with a FAA-approved maintenance manual written by the air carrier.
    a. 19 seats
    b. 21 seats
    c. 10 seats
    d. 15 seats

13. While a continuing analysis and surveillance system (CASS) is required for a Part 121 air carrier maintenance program, Part 135 operators are not required to have CASS for their maintenance program.
    a. True
    b. False

14. An FAA Airworthiness Directive (AD) is an advisory message only and is not a legally enforceable rule that must be complied with by a certain date or flight hour period, otherwise the aircraft becomes unairworthy.
    a. True
    b. False

15. If the inflight shutdown (IFSD) rate (computed on a 12-month rolling average) for an engine installed as part of an airplane-engine combination exceeds the values listed in Paragraph 121.374(i), the certificate holder must do a comprehensive review of its operations to identify any common cause effects and systemic errors. The IFSD rate must be computed using all engines of that type in the certificate holder's entire fleet of airplanes approved for ETOPS.
    a. True
    b. False

CHAPTER 15
SELECTED PART 121 APPENDICES AND PART 120

FAA regulations forbid drinking within 8 feet of the aircraft and smoking within 50 hours of flight. Or is it the other way around?
—anonymous

At the conclusion of the numbered sections of Part 121, there are several appendices to Part 121 found in Subpart DD, Special Federal Aviation Regulations. These are supplemental materials to specific regulations and provide detail on how these things are to be done. For example, 14 CFR §121.803 states that no Part 121 aircraft may be operated unless it is equipped with the emergency medical equipment that meets the specifications and requirements of appendix A of this part: So the rule (§121.803[c]) requiring first aid kits makes an external reference to **Appendix A: First Aid Kits and Emergency Medical Kits**, which details exactly what must be in the first aid kits. There are a number of these rules that make this sort of external reference to the appendices of Part 121. This final chapter will review several of the appendices that are most likely to be encountered by air carrier employees in day-to-day operations.

Appendix A: First Aid Kits and Emergency Medical Kits

Let's look a little closer at the first appendix found in Part 121, Subpart DD. Appendix A provides guidance about the required content of onboard emergency medical equipment, including first-aid kits, emergency medical kits (EMK) and automated external defibrillators (AED). It is intended to guide air carriers when establishing protocols for emergency medical equipment.

The FAA expects and anticipates some variation among the programs that air carriers establish for emergency medical equipment. Appendix A contains a number of tables listing the types, content and minimum number of required onboard medical equipment.

Appendix A to Part 121—First Aid Kits and Emergency Medical Kits

Approved first-aid kits, at least one approved emergency medical kit, and at least one approved automated external defibrillator required under §121.803 of this part must be readily accessible to the crew, stored securely, and kept free from dust, moisture, and damaging temperatures.

First Aid Kit (FAK): The first aid kit must meet the requirements of 14 CFR §121.803(c)(1). This kit contains basic bandaging supplies, splints, antiseptic swabs, etc. The first aid kit may also be supplemented by a passenger service kit: This is an additional first aid kit that has extra adhesive bandages, aspirin, Tylenol, antacid, etc. (Air carriers usually carry this kit in a galley compartment or galley cart so crewmembers do not have to open the "safety-sealed" kits that are required for aircraft operation for simple/common-need items.)

Emergency Medical Kit (EMK): The emergency medical kit must meet the requirement of 14 CFR §121.803(c)(3). The EMK includes prescription medications and is intended for use by medical professionals or by crew under the direction of the captain or a remote-assistance medical MedLink doctor via airphone/radio communications.

Automated external defibrillator (AED): At least one approved automated external defibrillator, legally marketed in the United States in accordance with Food and Drug Administration requirements, must be stored in the passenger cabin. The AED must have a power source that meets FAA Technical Standard Order requirements for power sources for electronic devices used in aviation.

A good follow-up to Appendix A are two FAA advisory circulars that cover these requirements: AC 121-33B, *Emergency Medical Equipment,* and AC 121-34B, *Emergency Medical Equipment Training.*

Appendix B: Airplane Flight Recorder Specifications

Appendix B specifies exactly what parameters are included in an airplane flight data recorder (FDR) and the technical specifications applicable to that data. You may recall from our previous discussions about required equipment that the NTSB has been calling on the FAA to expand the number of data channels required to be recorded on the flight data recorders. Appendix B contains approximately 50 parameters that may be recorded on the flight data recorder. It is important to note that Appendix B doesn't set forth the requirement to have the flight data recorder or what data must be recorded. That was done in Sections 121.343 and 121.344. But Appendix B does set forth the specific technical standards applicable to that parameter. For example, the first parameter is time. Time must be recorded in GMT (UTC) or on a frame counter as you would see on a camcorder or cell phone video recorder. The range must be a 24 hour period and is required to be accurate to plus or minus 0.125 percent per hour. Time must be sampled (recorded) once every 4 seconds and resolvable down to 1 second.

Some items will refer to the range as being "as installed." This means that the system installation standards can recognize the inherent differences of different systems. For example, groundspeed readout calls for the range to be as installed. If one aircraft has a groundspeed potential of 0–300 knots and another aircraft a potential of 0–600 knots, the FDR channel may record this differing range.

Appendix E: Flight Training Requirements

Appendix E contains an extensive "Flight Training Requirements" table that lists the maneuvers and procedures required by Section 121.424, discussed in Chapter 6, for pilot **initial training**, **transition training** and **upgrade training** and the maneuvers that are in the carrier's approved low altitude windshear flight training program. The appendix indicates whether these maneuvers must be performed in flight or, as in the case of windshear maneuvers and procedures, in an authorized airplane simulator. Certain other maneuvers and procedures may be performed in an airplane visual simulator, a nonvisual airplane simulator, a training device, or a static airplane as indicated by the appropriate symbol in the table of maneuvers. Whenever a maneuver or procedure is authorized to be performed in a nonvisual simulator, it may be performed in a visual simulator; when it is authorized to be performed in a training device, it may be performed in a visual or nonvisual simulator, and in some cases, a static airplane. The appendix indicates whether the requirement may be performed in either a training device or a static airplane.

If you refer to the table in Appendix E, you will find that it is broken into three vertical sections. These sections are applicable to initial, transition, and upgrade training, respectively. Within each column, it indicates where the maneuver may be performed and for which crewmembers it is required. Appendix E should be particularly helpful to new hires going for initial training as it is a clear, unambiguous roadmap of what is going to be done in training. At the conclusion of training, you will be evaluated using the proficiency check requirements of Appendix F.

Appendix F: Proficiency Check Requirements

Once pilots or flight engineers are qualified on an operation and continue to fly, the regulations require that they be monitored fairly frequently as to training and proficiency.

14 CFR §121.441 requires that all captains receive a proficiency check within the preceding 12 calendar months in the aircraft type in which the person is to serve and, within the preceding 6 calendar months, either a proficiency check or the approved simulator course of training. These are commonly referred to as "PC Checks" or "6 checks." Second-in-command pilots and flight engineers need to undergo either a proficiency

check or line-oriented simulator training every 24 months and a proficiency check and any other simulator course within 12 months. The content of the proficiency check is spelled out in Part 121 Appendix F and 14 CFR §121.409, covering training courses using airplane simulators and other training devices.

Appendix H: Advanced Simulation

The FAA has encouraged, and now even mandated, the use of advanced flight simulators in air carrier training. In the Part 91 world, the word simulator is widely misused to mean any device that is a cockpit mock-up—realistic or not—that is in some way able to mimic some actions of an airplane. This is actually a misnomer. The FAA has three classes of devices used for pilot training that use varying degrees of replicating cockpit appearance, function and control. In a 2014 notice of policy change, the terminology describing these devices has once again changed. There are now three levels of cockpit emulation approved for use in pilot training. These are **advanced aviation training devices (AATDs), flight training devices (FTDs)**, and **full flight simulators (FFSs)**. Taken together, FTDs and FFSs are referred to as **flight simulation training devices (FSTDs)**. These three classes are further divided into subcategories:

- **AATDs** are what were formerly referred to as personal computer aviation training devices (PCATDs), Level 1 through Level 3 flight training devices and aviation training devices. These machines represent fairly basic, usually personal computer generated cockpit displays, flight performance models, and computer visual displays or projected graphics if visual capability is included. The most recent of these devices are a far cry from the original PCATDs that were, literally, a computer display sitting atop a personal computer. Many current ATDs have full, operational cockpit panels, and most if not all have operational controls and a somewhat realistic aircraft performance model. Some have a very basic motion capability. These devices are authorized through letters of authorization from AFS-800 Commercial and General Aviation Division of FAA Flight Standards.
- **FTDs** are what were formerly referred to as Level 4 through Level 7 flight training devices and Level A non-visual full flight simulation equipment. 14 CFR Part 60, Appendix F, states that FTDs are "a replica of aircraft instruments, equipment, panels, and controls in an open flight deck area or an enclosed aircraft flight deck replica. It includes the equipment and computer programs necessary to represent aircraft (or set of aircraft) operations in ground and flight conditions having the full range of capabilities of the systems installed in the device." FTDs include everything from cockpit procedures trainers (CPTs) to non-motion, aircraft-specific, flight training devices.
- **FFSs** are true flight simulators of the type you will encounter in your airline training program. They are classified from Level B to Level D and must be approved by the FAA for use in the training program. A full flight simulator is: "a replica of a specific type, make, model, or series aircraft. It includes the equipment and computer programs necessary to represent aircraft operations in ground and flight conditions, a visual system providing an out-of-the-flight deck view, a system that provides cues at least equivalent to those of a three-degree-of-freedom motion system, and has the full range of capabilities of the systems installed in the device as described in part 60 of this chapter and the QPS for a specific FFS qualification level." (14 CFR Part 60, Appendix F) Approval oversight of FTDs and FFSs is conducted by the Aviation Simulation Office (AFS-205) based in Atlanta.

In the primary and instrument training a pilot receives to obtain an initial commercial pilot certificate with an instrument rating (the minimum for employment in any entry-level job), a student is likely to encounter an array of and, on occasion, perhaps brief exposure to a higher class of FSTD. In the air carrier world, a pilot in training will spend most of the training time in Level B through D although, especially in initial training, he or she may encounter from Level 6 FTDs through Level D FFSs with additional, non-regulated devices called part task trainers. These are used to teach very narrow skills such as programming and use of a flight management system or certain emergency procedures.

The use of the simulator in training and checking at an air carrier is determined by the level of simulation, that is, Level B through Level D. To be used under **Appendix H training**, the simulator must be a Level B through Level D simulator. What are the differences in the levels of simulation? The differences are outlined below.

Level B Simulators

Level B simulators must provide the following performance features.

Aerodynamic modeling and electromechanical performance requirements

- Aerodynamic programming to include:
  - Ground effect—for example, roundout, flare, and touchdown. This requires data on lift, drag, and pitching moment in ground effect.
  - Ground reaction—Reaction of the airplane upon contact with the runway during landing, including strut deflections, tire friction, and side forces.
  - Ground handling characteristics—steering inputs to include crosswind, braking, thrust reversing, deceleration, and turning radius.
- Minimum of three-axis freedom of motion systems.
- Level B landing maneuver test guide to verify simulator data with actual airplane flight test data, and provide simulator performance tests for Level B initial approval.
- Multichannel recorders capable of recording Level B performance tests.

Visual System Requirements

- Visual system compatibility with aerodynamic programming.
- Visual system response time from pilot control input to visual system output shall not exceed 300 milliseconds more than the movement of the airplane to a similar input. Visual system response time is defined as the completion of the visual display scan of the first video field containing different information resulting from an abrupt control input.
- A means of recording the visual response time for comparison with airplane data.
- Visual cues to assess sink rate and depth perception during landings.
- Visual scene to instrument correlation to preclude perceptible lags.

Level C Simulators

Level C simulators must provide the following performance features.

Aerodynamic modeling and electromechanical performance requirements

- Representative crosswind and three-dimensional windshear dynamics based on airplane-related data.
- Representative stopping and directional control forces for at least the following runway conditions based on airplane-related data:
  - Dry
  - Wet
  - Icy
  - Patchy wet
  - Patchy icy
  - Wet on rubber residue in touchdown zone
- Representative brake and tire failure dynamics (including antiskid) and decreased brake efficiency due to high brake temperatures based on airplane-related data.
- A motion system which provides motion cues equal to or better than those provided by a six-axis freedom of motion system.
- Operational principal navigation systems, including electronic flight instrument systems, FMS, RNAV, and GPS, if applicable.
- Means for quickly and effectively testing simulator programming and hardware.
- Expanded simulator computer capacity, accuracy, resolution, and dynamic response to meet Level C demands. Resolution equivalent to that of at least a 32-bit word length computer is required for critical aerodynamic programs.
- Timely permanent update of simulator hardware and programming subsequent to airplane modification.
- Sound of precipitation and significant airplane noises perceptible to the pilot during normal operations and the sound of a crash when the simulator is landed in excess of landing gear limitations.
- Aircraft control feel dynamics shall duplicate the airplane simulated. This shall be determined by comparing a recording of the control feel dynamics of the simulator to airplane measurements in the takeoff, cruise, and landing configuration.

- Relative responses of the motion system, visual system, and cockpit instruments shall be coupled closely to provide integrated sensory cues. These systems shall respond to abrupt pitch, roll, and yaw inputs at the pilot's position within 150 milliseconds of the time, but not before the time, when the airplane would respond under the same conditions. Visual scene changes from steady state disturbance shall not occur before the resultant motion onset but within the system dynamic response tolerance of 150 milliseconds. The test to determine compliance with these requirements shall include simultaneously recording the analog output from the pilot's control column and rudders, the output from an accelerometer attached to the motion system platform located at an acceptable location near the pilots' seats, the output signal to the visual system display (including visual system analog delays), and the output signal to the pilot's attitude indicator or an equivalent test approved by the Administrator. The test results will compare a recording of the simulator's response to actual airplane response data in the takeoff, cruise, and landing configuration.

Visual System Requirements

- Dusk and night visual scenes with at least three specific airport representations, including a capability of at least 10 levels of occulting, general terrain characteristics, and significant landmarks.
- Radio navigation aids properly oriented to the airport runway layout.
- Test procedures to quickly confirm visual system color, RVR, focus, intensity, level horizon, and attitude as compared to the simulator attitude indicator.
- For the approach and landing phase of flight, at and below an altitude of 2,000 feet height above the airport (HAA) and within a radius of 10 miles from the airport, weather representations including the following:
  - Variable cloud density
  - Partial obscuration of ground scenes; that is, the effect of a scattered to broken cloud deck
  - Gradual break out
  - Patchy fog
  - The effect of fog on airport lighting
  - Category II and III weather conditions
- Continuous minimum visual field of view of 75 degrees horizontal and 30 degrees vertical per pilot seat. Visual gaps shall occur only as they would in the airplane, simulated or as required by visual system hardware. Both pilot seat visual systems shall be able to be operated simultaneously.
- Capability to present ground and air hazards such as another airplane crossing the active runway or converging airborne traffic.

Level D Simulators

Level D simulators must provide the following performance features.

Aerodynamic modeling and electromechanical performance requirements

- Characteristic buffet motions that result from operation of the airplane (for example, high speed buffet, extended landing gear, flaps, nose-wheel scuffing, stall) and that can be sensed at the flight deck. The simulator must be programmed and instrumented in such a manner that the characteristic buffet modes can be measured and compared to airplane data. Airplane data are also required to define flight deck motions when the airplane is subjected to atmospheric disturbances such as rough air and cobblestone turbulence. General purpose disturbance models that approximate demonstrable flight test data are acceptable.
- Aerodynamic modeling for aircraft for which an original type certificate is issued after June 1, 1980, including low-altitude, level-flight ground effect, mach effect at high altitude, effects of airframe icing, normal and reverse dynamic thrust effect on control surfaces, aeroelastic representations, and representations of nonlinearities due to side slip based on airplane flight test data provided by the manufacturer.
- Realistic amplitude and frequency of cockpit noises and sounds, including precipitation, static, and engine and airframe sounds. The sounds shall be coordinated with the weather representations required in the visual requirements for special weather representations (see below).

- Self-testing for simulator hardware and programming to determine compliance with Level B, C, and D simulator requirements.
- Diagnostic analysis printout of simulator malfunctions sufficient to determine MEL compliance. These printouts shall be retained by the operator between recurring FAA simulator evaluations as part of the daily discrepancy log required under Section 121.407(a)(5).

Visual System Requirements

- Daylight, dusk, and night visual scenes with sufficient scene content to recognize a specific airport, the terrain, and major landmarks around that airport and to successfully accomplish a visual landing. The daylight visual scene must be part of a total daylight cockpit environment that at least represents the amount of light in the cockpit on an overcast day. For the purpose of this rule, daylight visual system is defined as a visual system capable of producing, as a minimum, full-color presentations, scene content comparable in detail to that produced by 4,000 edges or 1,000 surfaces for daylight and 4,000 light points for night and dusk scenes, 6 foot lamberts of light at the pilot's eye (highlight brightness), 3 arc minutes resolution for the field of view at the pilot's eye, and a display which is free of apparent quantization and other distracting visual effects while the simulator is in motion. The simulation of cockpit ambient lighting shall be dynamically consistent with the visual scene displayed. For daylight scenes, such ambient lighting shall neither wash out the displayed visual scene nor fall below 5 foot lamberts of light as reflected from an approach plate at knee height at the pilot's station and/or 2 foot lamberts of light as reflected from the pilot's face.
- Visual scenes portraying representative physical relationships that are known to cause landing illusions in some pilots, including short runway, landing over water, runway gradient, visual topographic features, and rising terrain.
- Special weather representations that include the sound, visual, and motion effects of entering light, medium, and heavy precipitation near a thunderstorm on takeoff, approach, and landings at and below an altitude of 2,000 feet HAA and within a radius of 10 miles from the airport.
- Level C visual requirements in daylight as well as dusk and night representations.
- Wet and, if appropriate for the operator, snow-covered runway representations, including runway lighting effects.
- Realistic color and directionality of airport lighting.
- Weather radar presentations in aircraft where radar information is presented on the pilot's navigation instruments.

The differences between the levels of flight simulation are summarized in Table 15-1, which is taken from FAA Advisory Circular 120-40B, *Airplane Simulator Qualification*.

Table 15-1 General requirements for simulators by level.

				Flight Simulators (AC 120-40 B)					
Simulator Level	Control Loading	Visual Scenes	Motion	Visual Field of View (Note 1)	Ground Handling Package	Runway Contaminates	Sound	Buffets	Radar
A	Static	Night	3 Axis	45 x 30					
B	Static	Night	3 Axis	45 x 30	Yes			Yes	
C	Static & Dynamic	Night & Dusk	6 Axis	75 x 30	Yes	Feel	Cockpit Noise	Yes	
D	Static & Dynamic	Night, Dusk, & Day	6 Axis	75 x 30	Yes	Feel & See	Realistic Cockpit Noise	Characteristic, Compliance Statement, & Test Required	Operating Radar (Note 2)

Notes: (1) Per pilot simultaneously; (2) When display is on pilot's navigation display.

Training and Checking Permitted

Part 121, Appendix H, also specifies the training and checking that may be accomplished in each level of simulation under an approved simulator training program.

Level B

- Regency of experience (§121.439).
- Night takeoffs and landings (Part 121, Appendix E).
- Except for EFVS operations, landings in a proficiency check without the landing on the line requirements (§121.441).

Level C

- For all pilots, *transition training* between airplanes in the same group, and for a pilot-in-command, the certification check required by Section 61.153(g).
- Upgrade to pilot-in-command training and the certification check when the pilot
  - has previously qualified as second-in-command in the equipment to which the pilot is upgrading;
  - has at least 500 hours of actual flight time while serving as second-in-command in an airplane of the same group; and
  - is currently serving as second-in-command in an airplane in this same group.
- Initial pilot-in-command training and the certification check when the pilot
  - is currently serving as second-in-command in an airplane of the same group;
  - has a minimum of 2,500 flight hours as second-in-command in an airplane of the same group; and
  - has served as second-in-command on at least two airplanes of the same group.
- For all second-in-command pilot applicants who meet the aeronautical experience requirements of 14 CFR §61.159 in the airplane, the initial and upgrade training and checking required by 14 CFR Part 121, and the certification check requirements of 14 CFR §61.153.
- For all pilots, the extended envelope training required by 14 CFR §121.423

Level D

Except for the line check required by Section 121.440, the static airplane requirements of Appendix E to Part 121, and the operating experience requirements of Section 121.434, all pilot flight training and checking required by Part 121 and the certification check requirements of Section 61.153(g) may be done in a Level D simulator. The exceptions must be performed in an actual airplane.

Simulation Qualification, Operation and Maintenance

A simple way to keep all of these training devices and simulator classifications straight is to remember: if the training device or simulator has a letter in its name, it has been *certified* by the FAA for full motion. If the training device has a number, it is *not certified* for full motion. Also, the higher the classification number or farther down the alphabet for a letter-designated simulator, the more sophisticated the training device or simulator. For instance, Level C or Level D simulators have more realistic visual presentations than Level B simulators. In fact, the visuals are so good that circle-to-land currency requirements can be met in a Level C or D simulator (memory aid: C stands for circle-to-land approaches). Only Level C or D simulators are authorized for air carrier instrument proficiency checks. This is because the FAA requires, in Appendix F to Part 121 (Proficiency Checks), that landings be accomplished during the proficiency check. Only Level C and D simulators are deemed sophisticated and realistic enough by the FAA to be approved for landing credit during a proficiency check.

In 2009, the FAA established a new Federal Aviation Regulation, **14 CFR Part 60: Flight Simulation Training Device Initial and Continuing Qualification and Use**. Part 60 prescribes the rules governing the initial and continuing qualification and use of all aircraft flight simulation training devices (FSTD) that are Level 6 or higher that are used for meeting training, evaluation, or flight experience requirements found in 14 CFR, Chapter I, for flight crewmember certification or qualification. The Flight Standards Service—General Aviation and Commercial Division, AFS-800, oversees the requirements for and use of all devices certificated Level 5 FTD and below. These are the typical devices found in most private, instrument and commercial pilot training programs.

Part 60 also includes the mandatory use of a FAA-approved quality assurance program for the Level 6 and higher devices, while the lower level devices must comply with FAA Advisory Circular 61-136B, *FAA Approval of Aviation Training Devices and Their Use for Training and Experience*, dated 11-17-2014. The quality assurance program requires pilot schools and training centers using Level 6 and above devices to adopt certain flight simulation device maintenance plans, recurrent inspections and maintenance evaluations, operating procedures, recordkeeping and reporting, all of which must be approved by the FAA's National Simulator Program Office. Level 5 devices and below must comply with the continuing performance standards outlined in FAA AC 61-136B. The quality assurance program also requires the development of comprehensive procedures that are designed to identify and correct any deficiencies identified by way of internal and external audits. Part 60 also requires the development of all-inclusive manuals that fully describe the procedures to be followed.

Appendix O: Hazardous Materials Training Requirements for Certificate Holders

Appendix O to Part 121 contains two extensive tables illustrating the requirements for **hazardous materials training** found under 14 CFR Part 121, Subpart Z, and Part 135, Subpart K. Training requirements for certificate holders authorized in their operations specifications to transport hazardous materials (will-carry) are prescribed in Table 1 of Appendix O. Those certificate holders with a prohibition in their operations specifications against carrying or handling hazardous materials (will-not-carry) must follow the curriculum prescribed in Table 2.

The training requirements for the proper handling and preparation for handling hazardous materials, limitations, packing requirements, required recordkeeping and emergency procedures are found under this provision. The training requirements for various categories of persons are defined by job function or responsibility, as listed at the top of the tables. An "X" in a box under a category of persons indicates that the specified category must receive the noted training. All training requirements listed in Tables 1 and 2 of Appendix O apply to direct supervisors as well as to persons actually performing the job function. The regulations requiring the hazardous materials training are found in paragraphs 14 CFR §§121.433(a), 121.1001–1007 and 135.501–507.

Appendix P: Requirements for ETOPS and Polar Operations

(It will be helpful to refer to Figure 15-1 in the discussion on ETOPS and Polar Operations.)

The FAA approves ETOPS in accordance with the requirements and limitations of Part 121 Appendix P: Requirements for ETOPS (Extended Operations) and Polar Operations. When discussing Appendix P, it is helpful to review Section 121.161 and FAA Advisory Circular (AC) 120-42B, *Extended Operations (ETOPS and Polar Operations)*, which provide air carriers with guidance for obtaining approval to conduct ETOPS under 14 CFR §121.161. Section 121.161 defines what is considered an ETOPS route of flight.

> (a) ...unless approved by the Administrator in accordance with Appendix P of this part and authorized in the certificate holder's operations specifications, no certificate holder may operate a turbine-engine-powered airplane over a route that contains a point—
> (1) Farther than a flying time from an Adequate Airport (at a one-engine-inoperative cruise speed under standard conditions in still air) of 60 minutes for a two-engine airplane or 180 minutes for a passenger-carrying airplane with more than two engines;
> (2) Within the North Polar Area; or
> (3) Within the South Polar Area.

(14 CFR §121.161)

14 CFR §121.161 has its origins as far back as the mid-1930s. During this time period, an air carrier operating an airliner with less than three engines was required to plan routes so that diversionary fields were located at no more than 100-mile intervals along the proposed route. Over the years, the acronym **ETOPS** has had several different but related meanings. As it has been generally defined since the mid-1980s, Extended Twin-Engine Operations has referred to flight in airspace where a planned route places an airliner more than 60 minutes from a diversionary airfield. It is important to note that Section 121.161 applies to all areas of operations, not just overwater operations. ETOPS regulations are an important part of flight planning over remote landmasses (e.g., north and south polar areas, parts of Africa) as well as flight over the world's oceans. Since the early 1950s, FAA regulations required that for both two-engine and three-engine airliners, the aircraft must be able to fly to a diversionary airport with one engine inoperative, and land within 60 minutes. As you might imagine, this regulation severely limited the routes two- or three-engine airliners were allowed to fly across large bodies of water or remote rural areas. For this reason, the airlines lobbied for relief from this limitation and three-engine airliners were exempted from this restriction by the mid-1960s. By the 1980s and the development of airliners like the Airbus 310 and Boeing 767—both with improved range, aircraft technology and engine reliability—it was recognized that the old extended range flight regulations

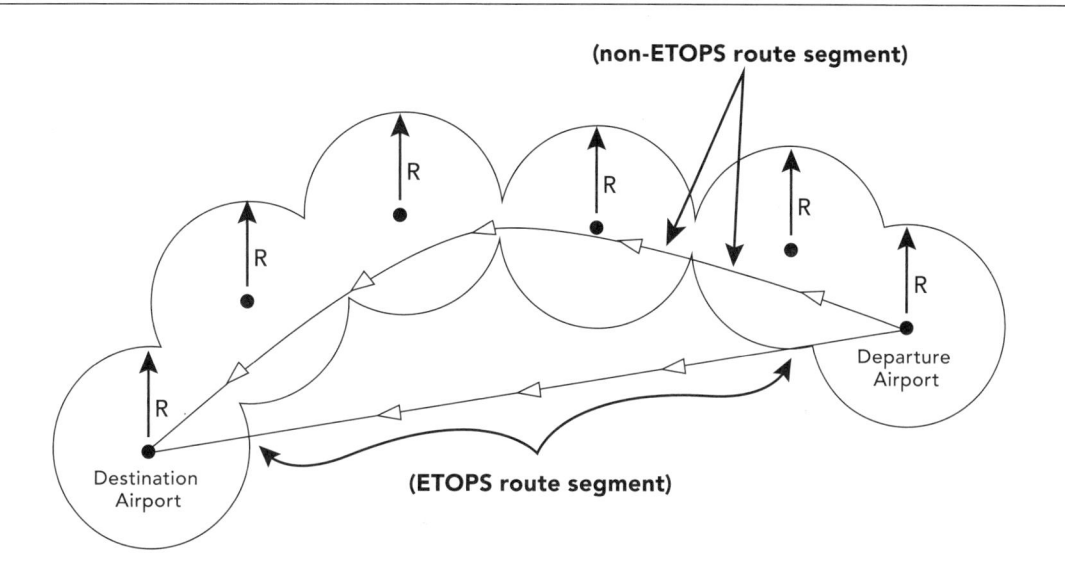

R = the distance travelled with one-engine-inoperative cruise speed under standard conditions in still air.

○ = Typical Twin 60 Minute Radius Area (400 NM)
Typical Four-engine 180 Minute Radius Area (1,500 NM)

• = Adequate Airport (Alternate)

ETOPS Route Planning

1. Determine the Adequate Airports along intended route.
2. Draw circles centered on each Adequate Airport with a radius area equal to the distance travelled (e.g., for 60 or 180 min)
for the particular type of aircraft.
3. If the intended route goes outside of the drawn circles, the flight is flown under ETOPS regulations.

FAR 121.161

Except as provided in paragraph (e) of this section, unless approved by the Administrator in accordance with Appendix P of this part and authorized in the certificate holder's operations specifications,

No certificate holder may operate a turbine-engine-powered airplane
over a route that contains a point—
Farther than a flying time from an Adequate Airport

(at a one-engine-inoperative cruise speed under standard conditions in still air) of:

   60 minutes for a two-engine airplane or,

   180 minutes for a passenger-carrying airplane with more than two engines.

Figure 15-1. Determining area of ETOPS Operations.

for twin-engine aircraft were inadequate and ETOPS regulations needed to be updated. The FAA published AC 120-42 and the first ETOPS regulations to address 120-minute operations in 1985. The new ETOPS rule allowed twin-engine airliners to fly long-distance routes that were previously off-limits to twin-engine, passenger-carrying airliners. The first FAA-approved ETOPS flight occurred in February of that year when a TWA Boeing 767-200 flew from Boston to Paris.

In 1988, the FAA used the statistical data gathered from the previous three years' experience with 120-minute ETOPS to publish AC 120-42A and new rules for 180-minute ETOPS. For many years thereafter, 120 minute ETOPS (narrowbody) and 180 minute (widebody) was the international standard. After the first decade of twin-engine ETOPS, the reliability of these operations improved to the point that they were on par with three- and four-engine airliners.

With the latest generation of airliners, engine reliability and aircraft technology have improved to the point that airlines are now gaining approval for flights well over 180-minute ETOPS. The current limit of 240-minute ETOPS has been extended to 330-minute ETOPS for the 787 and the A350 is planned to have approval for 370-minute ETOPS! ETOPS flights have become more commonplace with over one thousand flights per day worldwide. Current ETOPS requirements are now applied more broadly to embrace all extended operations, regardless of number of engines; the ETOPS acronym is now defined as **Extended Operations**. This is to address the common issues that impact operations regardless of the number of engines. Under the current definition, ETOPS flying begins when the airplane is more than 60 minutes (for twinjets) or 180 minutes (for three- and four-engine jets) flying time from an adequate diversionary airport at an approved one-engine-inoperative cruise speed under standard conditions in still air.

So how does an air carrier get approval to fly routes that would be outside the applicable restrictions found in 14 CFR §121.161? ETOPS authorizations, including Part 121 operations in polar areas, are guided by FAA AC 120-42B, various FAA policy letters, and granted through the provisions of the air carrier's operations specifications in accordance with the requirements and limitations of Appendix P. Let's look at ETOPS approvals for twin-engine airliners first. In order to gain ETOPS approval from the FAA for twin-engine airliners, an air carrier must first demonstrate the ability to achieve and maintain the level of propulsion system reliability required by 14 CFR §21.4(b) for the engines the air carrier intends to use in ETOPS operations. The FAA requires the holder of a type certificate for an ETOPS-approved airplane-engine combination to report monthly to their respective FAA type certificate holding office on the reliability of those airplanes and engines. The FAA may approve quarterly reporting if the airplane-engine combination demonstrates an **IFSD (in-flight shutdown) rate** at or below those specified in 14 CFR §21.4(b)(2) for a period acceptable to the FAA. The air carrier must investigate any cause of an IFSD resulting from an occurrence attributable to the design of its product and report the results of that investigation to its FAA office responsible for administering its type certificate.

Let's put the IFSD (inflight shutdown) into a historical perspective. Early jet engines were somewhat unreliable; initially they had an IFSD rate of 0.9 shutdowns per 1,000 engine hours. The latest generation of jet engines is capable of an incredibly low IFSD rate of 0.001 per 1,000 hours! That is the equivalent of about two IFSDs over the entire operating life (some 20-plus years) of a present-day airliner.

The minimum 12-month rolling average IFSD rates are specified in 14 CFR §21.4(b)(2):

(2) World fleet IFSD rate for two-engine airplanes. The holder of a type certificate for an airplane approved for ETOPS and the holder of a type certificate for an engine installed on an airplane approved for ETOPS must issue service information to the operators of those airplanes and engines, as appropriate, to maintain the world fleet 12-month rolling average IFSD rate at or below the following levels:
- (i) A rate of 0.05 per 1,000 world-fleet engine-hours for an airplane-engine combination approved for up to and including 120-minute ETOPS. When all ETOPS operators have complied with the corrective actions required in the configuration, maintenance and procedures (CMP) document as a condition for ETOPS approval, the rate to be maintained is at or below 0.02 per 1,000 world-fleet engine-hours.
- (ii) A rate of 0.02 per 1,000 world-fleet engine-hours for an airplane-engine combination approved for up to and including 180-minute ETOPS, including airplane-engine combinations approved for 207-minute ETOPS in the North Pacific operating area under appendix P, section I, paragraph (h), of part 121 of this chapter.

(iii) A rate of 0.01 per 1,000 world-fleet engine-hours for an airplane-engine combination approved for ETOPS beyond 180 minutes, excluding airplane-engine combinations approved for 207-minute ETOPS in the North Pacific operating area under appendix P, section I, paragraph (h), of part 121 of this chapter.

(14 CFR 21.4[b][2])

Airplane certification guidance for ETOPS can be found in primarily in 14 CFR §§121.161, 121.162, 25.3, and 25.1535. As with all other operations, a certificate holder requesting any route approval must first show that it is able to satisfactorily conduct operations between each required airport as defined for that route or route segment, and any required enroute alternate airport. Certificate holders must show that the facilities and services specified in Sections 121.97 through 121.107 (domestic and flag operations) and Sections 121.113 through 121.127 (supplemental and commercial operations) are available and adequate for the proposed operation. In addition, the certificate holder must be approved for ETOPS under Part 121. Each air carrier must develop and comply with the ETOPS continuous airworthiness maintenance program (CAMP) for each type of aircraft-engine combination to be used in ETOPS. Following ETOPS operational approval, the operator must then monitor the propulsion system reliability for the airplane-engine combination used in ETOPS, and take action as required by Section 121.374(i) for the specified Inflight Shutdown (IFSD) rates.

(i) Propulsion system monitoring.
   (1) If the IFSD rate (computed on a 12-month rolling average) for an engine installed as part of an airplane-engine combination exceeds the following values, the certificate holder must do a comprehensive review of its operations to identify any common cause effects and systemic errors. The IFSD rate must be computed using all engines of that type in the certificate holder's entire fleet of airplanes approved for ETOPS.
     (i) A rate of 0.05 per 1,000 engine hours for ETOPS up to and including 120 minutes.
     (ii) A rate of 0.03 per 1,000 engine hours for ETOPS beyond 120-minutes up to and including 207 minutes in the North Pacific Area of Operation and up to and including 180 minutes elsewhere.
     (iii) A rate of 0.02 per 1,000 engine hours for ETOPS beyond 207 minutes in the North Pacific Area of Operation and beyond 180 minutes elsewhere.

(14 CFR 121.374[i])

The bulk of Appendix P lists current FAA ETOPS approvals ranging from 75 minutes to 330 minutes. The greater the approved distance from a diversionary field, the stricter the standards for FAA approval. Appendix P begins with the two different 75-minute ETOPS approvals, one for use in the Caribbean and Western Atlantic and a somewhat stricter approval for use in other parts of the world. The 75-minute ETOPS approval used for the Caribbean and Western Atlantic routes of flight is the least restrictive. For this approval the FAA is mainly concerned with the propulsion system reliability and ensuring that time-limited systems (e.g., cargo fire suppression systems) will operate long enough to safely get the aircraft to the diversionary field. For 75-minute ETOPS approval in areas other than the Caribbean and Western Atlantic routes, the FAA adds the requirement that the certificate holder must comply with the MEL in its operations specifications for 120-minute ETOPS. For gaining approval to fly routes progressively farther from diversionary airports requires incrementally more stringent requirements for aircraft, engines, diversionary airfield, flight crew training, dispatching, MEL, communication, and operational control. The first section of Appendix P lists these requirements for the following twin-engine ETOPS approvals:

- 90-minute ETOPS
- 120-minute ETOPS
- 138-minute ETOPS
- 180-minute ETOPS
- Greater than 180-minute ETOPS
- 207-minute ETOPS in the North Pacific Area of Operations.
- 240-minute ETOPS in the North Polar Area, in the area north of the NOPAC, and in the Pacific Ocean north of the equator
- 240-minute ETOPS in areas south of the equator
- Greater than 240-minute ETOPS. (The FAA grants approval to conduct ETOPS with diversion times beyond 240 minutes for operations between specified city pairs and routing on a case-by-case basis.)

The second section of Appendix P covers ETOPS approval for passenger-carrying airplanes with *more than* two engines. Since ETOPS do not technically begin for these aircraft until flight beyond 180 minutes from a diversionary airfield, the FAA spells out the requirements for only the following conditions:

- 240-minute ETOPS
- Greater than 240-minute ETOPS

The third and final section of Appendix P lists additional requirements for operations in which airplane routes are planned to traverse either the North Polar or South Polar areas. These additional requirements are to help mitigate the risks of operating in those extreme climatic conditions of the polar regions. For example, the air carrier must provide at least two cold weather anti-exposure suits in the aircraft to protect crewmembers during outside activity at a diversion airport with extreme climatic conditions.

14 CFR Part 120: Drug and Alcohol Testing Program

The objective of a drug and alcohol testing program is to prevent accidents and injuries resulting from the use of prohibited drugs or the misuse of alcohol by employees who perform safety-sensitive functions in aviation. The drug testing required for Part 121 carriers is found in 14 CFR Part 120. This provision sets the requirements and standards for all drug testing of air carrier and other employees.

Who must be tested? Here is a big surprise for some Part 91 operators, who probably aren't even aware of the existence of Part 120. Why should they be? That applies to airlines, right? Well, not completely. To find the applicability of Part 120 to Part 91 operators, we must look not to Part 91 but to Part 135! 14 CFR §135.1, the applicability section for Part 135, states the following:

> (a)(5) Nonstop Commercial Air Tour flights conducted for compensation or hire in accordance with §119.1(e)(2) of this chapter that begin and end at the same airport and are conducted within a 25-statute-mile radius of that airport; provided further that these operations must comply only with the drug and alcohol testing requirements in §§120.31, 120.33, 120.35, 120.37, and 120.39 of this chapter; and with the provisions of part 136, subpart A, and §91.147 of this chapter…
>
> (14 CFR §135.1[a][5])

So the excluded activities from Part 135 for nonstop sightseeing flights are placed back under Part 135 for drug and alcohol testing. Where do you find the requirements for the testing? 14 CFR §135.1(a)(5) directs you to Part 120. Therefore, the individual or small flight school that conducts sightseeing flights without a drug and alcohol testing program is in violation of Part 120!

Other than these sightseeing flights, air carrier employees who perform a **safety-sensitive function** directly or by contract for an air carrier (including Part 135 carriers) must be tested pursuant to an FAA-approved drug and alcohol testing program. Section 120.105 covers which employees must be tested. These safety-sensitive positions include:

- Flight crewmembers
- Flight attendants
- Flight instructors
- Aircraft dispatchers
- Aircraft maintenance and preventive maintenance personnel
- Ground security coordinators
- Aviation screening
- Air traffic control personnel
- Operations control specialist duties

Subpart E: Drug Testing Program Requirements

The drug testing must be done in accordance with approved DOT procedures as outlined in 49 CFR Part 40, Procedures for Transportation Workplace Drug and Alcohol Testing Programs. The laboratory used to perform the analysis must be a Department of Health and Human Service (HHS) approved laboratory and comply with all procedures required by HHS and the DOT. The program must be approved by the FAA prior to implementation and is subject to annual review. The program must accomplish seven types of testing. These are:

1. **pre-employment testing,**
2. **periodic testing,**
3. **random testing,**
4. **post-accident testing,**
5. **testing based on reasonable cause,**
6. **return to duty testing, and**
7. **follow-up testing.**

Pre-Employment Testing
Under paragraph 120.109(a), pre-employment drug testing, an applicant/employee must be drug tested (screened) prior to the first time he or she performs a

safety-sensitive function for an employer. The employer must advise each individual applying to perform a safety-sensitive function at the time of application that he will be required to undergo a pre-employment test to determine the presence of marijuana, cocaine, opiates, phencyclidine (PCP), and amphetamines, or a metabolite of those drugs in the individual's system. An employer must not allow an individual required to undergo pre-employment testing to perform a safety-sensitive function unless the employer has received a verified negative drug test result for the individual. Pre-employment also applies to employees that previously performed safety-sensitive functions and are now returning to perform a safety-sensitive function.

Periodic Testing

Each employee, such as a pilot, that is required to undergo a medical examination under 14 CFR Part 67 shall submit to a periodic drug test. The employee shall be tested for the presence of marijuana, cocaine, opiates, phencyclidine (PCP), and amphetamines, or a metabolite of those drugs, during the first calendar year of implementation of the employer's anti-drug program. The tests shall be conducted in conjunction with the first medical evaluation of the employee or in accordance with an alternative method for collecting periodic test specimens detailed in an employer's approved anti-drug program. An employer may discontinue periodic testing of its employees after the first calendar year of implementation of the employer's anti-drug program when the employer has implemented an unannounced testing program based on random selection of employees.

Random Testing

The basic rule for random testing is that the minimum annual percentage rate for random drug testing must be 50 percent of covered employees. However, the airline industry has shown that the incidence of drug use is so low among the employees in the industry that it has successfully gotten the FAA to lower the actual random testing rate. This reduction of the percentage rate for random drug testing is based on the reported positive rate for the entire industry. All information used for this determination is drawn from the statistical reports required of the airlines. Each year, the FAA publishes in the *Federal Register* the minimum annual percentage rate for random drug testing of covered employees for the next year. When the minimum annual percentage rate for random drug testing is 50 percent, the Administrator may lower this rate to 25 percent of all covered employees if the Administrator determines that the data received under the reporting requirements for 2 consecutive calendar years indicate that the reported positive rate is less than 1.0 percent. When the minimum annual percentage rate for random drug testing is 25 percent and the data received under the reporting requirements for any calendar year indicate that the reported positive rate is equal to or greater than 1.0 percent, the Administrator will increase the minimum annual percentage rate for random drug testing to 50 percent of all covered employees.

As the name suggests, this is a random selection of employees for random drug testing. It must be made by a scientifically valid method, such as a random-number table or a computer-based random number generator that is matched with employees' Social Security numbers, payroll identification numbers, or other comparable identifying numbers. Under the selection process used, each covered employee shall have an equal chance of being tested each time selections are made. These tests must ensure that the random drug tests are unannounced and that the dates for administering random tests are spread reasonably throughout the calendar year. Under random testing, employees should expect one day to be returning from a flight and be invited to "make a deposit" before leaving the terminal building.

Post-Accident Testing

Post-accident testing is required of each employee who performs a safety-sensitive function if that employee's performance either contributed to an accident or cannot be completely discounted as a contributing factor to the accident. The employee shall be tested as soon as possible but not later than 32 hours after the accident. The decision not to administer a test under this appendix must be based on a determination, using the best information available at the time of the determination, that the employee's performance could not have contributed to the accident. The employee must submit to post-accident testing under this section.

Testing Based on Reasonable Cause

Testing based on reasonable cause is required of each employee who performs a safety-sensitive function and who is reasonably suspected of using a prohibited drug. An employer may test an employee's specimen for the presence of other prohibited drugs or drug metabolites only in accordance with 14 CFR Part 120 and the DOT Procedures for Transportation Workplace Drug Testing Programs (49 CFR Part 40). At least two of the employee's supervisors, one of whom is trained in detection of the symptoms of possible drug use, shall substantiate and concur in the decision to test an employee who is reasonably suspected of drug use. (In the case of an employer other than a Part 121 certificate holder who employs 50 or fewer employees who perform safety-sensitive functions, one supervisor who is trained in detection of symptoms of possible drug use may substantiate the decision to test an employee who is reasonably suspected of drug use.) The decision to test must be based on a reasonable and articulable belief that the employee is using a prohibited drug on the basis of specific contemporaneous physical, behavioral, or performance indicators of probable drug use.

Return to Duty Testing

Each employer must ensure that before an individual is returned to duty to perform a safety-sensitive function after refusing to submit to a drug test or receiving a verified positive drug test result, the individual shall undergo a drug test. No employer shall allow an individual required to undergo return-to-duty testing to perform a safety-sensitive function unless the employer has received a verified negative drug test result for the individual.

Follow-up Testing

Follow-up drug testing is required for any individual that has been hired to perform or who has been returned to the performance of a safety-sensitive function after refusing to submit to a required drug test or after receiving a verified positive drug test result. The number and frequency of these tests will be established by the employer's **medical review officer (MRO)**. (The medical review officer is a person qualified in accordance with 49 CFR Part 40 who performs the functions set forth in 14 CFR Part 120. If the employer does not have a qualified individual on staff to serve as MRO, then it may contract for the provision of MRO services as part of its drug testing program.)

In the case of a person who is evaluated under 14 CFR Part 120 and determined to be in need of assistance in resolving problems associated with illegal use of drugs, follow-up testing shall consist of at least six tests in the first 12 months following the employee's return to duty. The employer may direct the employee to undergo testing for alcohol, in addition to drugs, if the medical review officer determines that alcohol testing is necessary for the particular employee. Any such alcohol testing must also be conducted in accordance with the provisions of 49 CFR Part 40. This follow-up testing may not exceed 60 months after the date the individual begins to perform or returns to the performance of a safety-sensitive function. The medical review officer may terminate the requirement for follow-up testing at any time after the first six tests have been conducted, if he or she determines that such testing is no longer necessary.

Finally, let's note the harshness of penalties for violations of this program. An employee who has verified positive drug test results on two required drug tests is *permanently precluded* from performing for any employer the safety-sensitive duties that he or she performed prior to the second drug test. Also, an employee who has engaged in prohibited drug use during the performance of a safety-sensitive function is also permanently precluded from performing that safety-sensitive function for any employer.

Employee Assistance Plan (EAP)

Each employer is required by 14 CFR §120.115 to provide an **employee assistance plan (EAP)** for its employees. The employer may establish the EAP as a part of its internal personnel services or the employer may contract with an entity that will provide EAP services to an employee. The program includes education and training on drug use for employees and training for supervisors making determinations for testing of employees based on reasonable cause. The program must include a **drug education program** that includes at least the following elements: display and distribution of informational material; display and distribution of a community service hotline telephone number for employee assistance; and display and distribution of the employer's policy regarding drug use in the workplace. The employer's policy shall include information regarding the consequences under the rule of using drugs while performing safety-sensitive functions, receiving a verified positive drug test result, or refusing to submit to a drug test required under the rule.

The employee assistance program must also include a **drug training program**. This must be a reasonable program of initial training for employees. The employee training program must include at least the following elements: the effects and consequences of drug use on personal health, safety, and work environment; the manifestations and behavioral cues that may indicate drug use and abuse; and documentation of training given to employees and the employer's supervisory personnel.

The employer's supervisory personnel who will determine when an employee is subject to testing based on reasonable cause must receive specific training on specific, contemporaneous physical, behavioral, and performance indicators of probable drug use in addition to the training specified above. The employer shall ensure that supervisors who will make reasonable cause determinations receive at least 60 minutes of initial training. The employer shall implement a reasonable recurrent training program for supervisory personnel making reasonable cause determinations during subsequent years. The employer shall identify the employee and supervisor EAP training in the employer's drug testing plan submitted to the FAA for approval.

Subpart F: Alcohol Testing Program Requirements

The FAA also requires an **alcohol abuse prevention program**, described in 14 CFR Part 120, Subpart F, which is somewhat similar to the drug testing program of Subpart E. This program is to help prevent accidents and injuries resulting from the misuse of alcohol by employees who perform safety-sensitive functions in aviation. The same employees are covered as are covered by the drug testing provisions of Subpart E. Section 120.217 lists seven types of alcohol testing performed:

1. pre-employment testing,
2. post-accident testing,
3. random testing,
4. reasonable suspicion testing,
5. return to duty testing,
6. follow-up testing, and
7. **retesting of covered employees with an alcohol concentration of 0.02 or greater but less than 0.04.**

Pre-Employment Testing

An employer may, but is not required to, conduct pre-employment alcohol testing under this part. If it chooses to conduct pre-employment alcohol testing, it must comply with the following requirements:

- It must conduct a pre-employment alcohol test before the first performance of safety-sensitive functions by every covered employee (whether a new employee or someone who has transferred to a position involving the performance of safety-sensitive functions).
- It must treat all safety-sensitive employees performing safety-sensitive functions the same for the purpose of pre-employment alcohol testing (i.e., it must not test some covered employees and not test others).
- It must conduct the pre-employment tests after making a contingent offer of employment or transfer, subject to the employee passing the pre-employment alcohol test.
- It must conduct all pre-employment alcohol tests using the alcohol testing procedures of 49 CFR Part 40.
- It must not allow a covered employee to begin performing safety-sensitive functions unless the result of the employee's test indicates an alcohol concentration of less than 0.04.

Post-Accident Testing

Post-accident testing is required as soon as practicable following an accident. The employer must test each surviving covered employee for alcohol if that employee's performance of a safety-sensitive function either contributed to the accident or cannot be completely discounted as a contributing factor to the accident. The decision not to administer a test under this section shall be based on the employer's determination, using the best available information at the time of the determination, that the covered employee's performance could not have contributed to the accident.

If a required post-accident alcohol test is not administered within 2 hours following the accident, the employer shall prepare and maintain on file a record stating the reasons the test was not promptly administered. If a test required by this section is not administered within 8 hours following the accident, the employer shall cease attempts to administer an alcohol test and shall prepare and maintain the same record. Records shall be submitted to the FAA upon request of the Administrator or his or her designee.

A covered employee who is subject to post-accident testing shall remain readily available for such testing or may be deemed by the employer to have refused to submit to testing. However, this doesn't require the employee to delay receipt of necessary medical attention for injured people following an accident, or prohibit a covered employee from leaving the scene of an accident for the period necessary to obtain assistance in responding to the accident or to obtain necessary emergency medical care.

Random Testing

The rules for random testing for alcohol are essentially the same as the rules for random drug testing. The selections must be on a statistically sound basis and cover a specified percentage of employees.

Reasonable Suspicion Testing

The alcohol testing provisions for reasonable suspicion are very similar to those for reasonable cause testing for drugs. The most significant difference between the two is the recognition of the fact that alcohol metabolizes much more quickly, so there are time limits set on when the testing may be performed. The employer must require a covered employee to submit to an alcohol test when the employer has reasonable suspicion to believe that the employee has violated the alcohol misuse prohibitions. The employer's determination that reasonable suspicion exists to require the covered employee to undergo an alcohol test shall be based on specific, contemporaneous, articulable observations concerning the appearance, behavior, speech, or body odors of the employee. The required observations must be made by a supervisor who is trained in detecting the symptoms of alcohol misuse. The supervisor who makes the determination that reasonable suspicion exists cannot conduct the breath alcohol test on that employee.

Alcohol testing is authorized if the observations required above are made during, just preceding, or just after the period of the work day that the covered employee is required to be in compliance with this rule. An employee may be directed by the employer to undergo reasonable suspicion testing for alcohol only while the employee is performing safety-sensitive functions, just before the employee is to perform safety-sensitive functions, or just after the employee has ceased performing such functions.

If a test required by this part is not administered within 2 hours following the determination of reasonable suspicion, the employer shall prepare and maintain a record stating the reasons the test was not promptly administered. If a test required by this appendix is not administered within 8 hours following the determination of reasonable suspicion, the employer shall cease attempts to administer an alcohol test and shall state in the record the reasons for not administering the test. Even in the absence of a reasonable suspicion alcohol test, no covered employee shall report for duty or remain on duty requiring the performance of safety-sensitive functions while the employee is under the influence of or impaired by alcohol, as shown by the behavioral, speech, or performance indicators of alcohol misuse. The employer may not permit the covered employee to perform or continue to perform safety-sensitive functions until

- an alcohol test is administered and the employee's alcohol concentration measures less than 0.02; or
- the start of the employee's next regularly scheduled duty period, but not less than 8 hours following the determination that there was reasonable suspicion that the employee had violated the alcohol misuse provisions.

Return to Duty Testing

An employer must ensure that before a covered employee returns to duty requiring the performance of a safety-sensitive function after engaging in conduct that constitutes misuse of alcohol, the employee shall undergo a return-to-duty alcohol test with a result indicating an alcohol concentration of less than 0.02.

Follow-up Testing

Following a determination that a covered employee is in need of assistance in resolving problems associated with alcohol misuse, the employer must ensure that the employee is subject to unannounced **follow-up alcohol testing** as directed by a substance abuse professional. A covered employee must be tested under this paragraph only while the employee is performing safety-sensitive functions, just before the employee is to perform safety-sensitive functions, or just after the employee has ceased performing such functions.

Retesting of Covered Employees with an Alcohol Concentration of 0.02 or Greater but Less than 0.04

Each employer must retest a covered employee to ensure that the employee has an alcohol concentration of less than 0.02 if the employer chooses to permit the employee to perform a safety-sensitive function within 8 hours following the administration of an alcohol test indicating an alcohol concentration of 0.02 or greater but less than 0.04.

The provisions of 14 CFR Part 120 provide for the establishment of an employee assistance plan and training for supervisors in identifying the symptoms of alcohol misuse.

Summary

This chapter has covered several of the appendices to Part 121 as well as the Part 120 Drug and Alcohol Testing Program. These are developed to be incorporated by reference into the regulations in the subparts of Part 121. An employee of a Part 121 carrier must at least be aware of the existence of these appendices, and in some cases, even Part 91 operators and employees need to be aware of the rules found in Part 121.

Important Terms or Concepts in Chapter 15

14 CFR Part 60: Flight Simulation Training Device Initial and Continuing Qualification and Use
14 CFR Part 120: Drug and Alcohol Testing Program
alcohol abuse prevention program
Appendix A to Part 121: First Aid Kits and Emergency Medical Kits
Appendix B to Part 121: Airplane Flight Recorder Specification
Appendix E to Part 121: Flight Training Requirements
Appendix F to Part 121: Proficiency Check Requirements
Appendix H to Part 121: Advanced Simulation
aviation training device (ATD)
drug education program
(drug) testing based on reasonable cause
drug training program
employee assistance plan (EAP)
Extended Operations (ETOPS)
flight training device (FTD)
flight simulation training device (FSTD)
follow-up alcohol testing
follow-up drug testing
full flight simulator (FFS)
hazardous materials training
IFSD (inflight shutdown) rate
initial training
Level B simulator
Level C simulator
Level D simulator
medical review officer (MRO)
Part 120 Drug and Alcohol Testing Program
periodic (drug) testing
post-accident (drug) testing
pre-employment (drug) testing
random (drug) testing
retesting of covered employees with an alcohol concentration of 0.02 or greater but less than 0.04
return to duty (drug) testing
safety-sensitive function
transition training
upgrade training

Chapter 15 Exam

1. If a new-hire pilot wished to know what maneuvers would be covered in his initial aircraft training, which of the following would be a good place to look?
   a. The relevant provisions of Part 61: Certification of Airmen
   b. The relevant provisions of Part 121, Subpart N: Air Carrier Training Requirements
   c. The relevant provisions of Part 121, Subpart O: Crewmember Qualification
   d. Part 121 Appendix E: Flight Training Requirements

2. Which level of simulation has the greatest degree of fidelity to the aircraft?
   a. Level B
   b. Level C
   c. Level D
   d. None of the above

3. Which level of simulation may be used to meet the training requirements for landings?
   a. Level B
   b. Level C
   c. Level D
   d. All of the above

4. If you are a flight instructor for a small flight school and it conducts sightseeing flights for hire, must you have a drug testing program?
   a. Yes
   b. No
   c. Insufficient information to determine

5. Which of the following require drug testing at a Part 121 carrier?
   a. Flight attendants
   b. Ground security coordinators
   c. Pilots
   d. All of the above

6. Pre-employment drug testing is required by the FAA of
   a. all newly hired pilots.
   b. all newly hired customer service agents.
   c. airport ticket office manager.
   d. All of the above.

7. Reasonable cause drug testing
   a. can be instituted at any time by the carrier.
   b. requires at least two of the employee's supervisors to concur in the testing decision.
   c. requires a medical review officer to concur in the testing decision.
   d. is unavailable unless the employee has a documented history of drug abuse.

8. If a pilot fails two drug tests,
   a. the pilot must undergo drug rehabilitation for at least 1 year before returning to duty.
   b. the pilot must undergo 6 months of rehabilitation and peer counseling and review.
   c. the pilot is forbidden to act as pilot-in-command until he has been drug free for 6 months.
   d. the pilot is forever barred from acting as a commercial pilot for any company.

9. At what blood alcohol concentration is a covered employee prohibited from performing any safety-sensitive function?
   a. 0.04
   b. 0.4
   c. 0.8
   d. 1.0

10. After an accident, the employer must administer an alcohol test to any relevant employees within
    a. 1 hour after the accident.
    b. 2 hours after the accident.
    c. 4 hours after the accident.
    d. 8 hours after the accident.

APPENDIX: ANSWERS TO CHAPTER EXAMS

Is this going to be on the test?

—**Students**, from time immemorial.

Chapter 1

1. Answer (c): British common law.

   Common carriage derives from the early application of British common law to the transportation and hospitality (hotel/inn) industries. It has carried into United States legal concepts through American common law.

2. Answer (d): transportation (carriage) of only one or a very small number of parties.

   Private carriage is that transportation (carriage) arranged between one party (or some other small number of parties) and the carrier. As the number of parties being provided carriage increases, the likelihood of common carriage increases.

3. Answer (a): Having a license or certificate.

   It is not necessary that the carrier be licensed or certificated in order to be determined to be a common carrier. It is only necessary that it hold out to the public that it is willing to perform carriage for anyone from place to place for compensation or hire.

4. Answer (d): All of the above.

   Holding out as an air carrier can be done in any of a number of ways. The key element is an indication to the public at large of a willingness to perform transportation.

5. Answer (b): Had an independent interest in taking the trip.

   While there are tests that partially involve prorating fuel, oil, rental, and airport fees, and determining whether the pilot held out to the public, answers (a) (was paid only for the fuel, oil, and aircraft rental) and (c) (had a commercial pilot certificate) are both incomplete statements of the tests applied to determine if the pilot was acting as a common carrier, and it is irrelevant that the pilot owned or rented the aircraft. The independent interest test looks specifically at whether the pilot had an independent interest in taking the trip or was only interested in going if he or she received money for the trip.

6. Answer (c): charge a gas company to perform pipeline aerial spotter patrols.

   Answers (a), (b), and (d) all involve carrying people for hire. Without an air carrier certificate (or meeting one of the small exceptions allowed for private pilots) you would not be legal to perform these missions. Pipeline patrol is one of the specific activities excluded from certification requirements by operation of 14 CFR 119.1(e)(4)(vi).

7. Answer (a): a domestic operation.

   A domestic, flag, or supplemental operation must be conducted under Part 121 rules. Commuter and on-demand operations are conducted under Part 135 rules.

8. Answer (d): a Part 135 operating certificate (which allows on-demand operations).

   Scheduled operations using other than turbojet aircraft with nine or fewer passenger seats and a 7,500 pound or less payload capacity on fewer than five roundtrips per week according to published schedule(s) fall under the purview of Part 135 of the regulations.

9. Answer(c): each provision of Part 135 applicable to each flight conducted.

   The rules applicable to unauthorized operators act as if to give you a certificate for the sole purpose of holding you responsible for all things a certificate holder is responsible for. You would then be fined for every section you were not complying with for each and every flight conducted. This could easily amount to hundreds of thousands of dollars (or more) of potential fines.

10. Answer (a): The carrier, not the crew, is the final determinant of how the aircraft is operated.

    The carrier, not the crew, determines how its flights are to be operated. It is a collaborative process, but ultimately, the company controls its operations through personnel authorized to exercise operational control.

11. Answer (a): A supplemental operation is one that conducts charter type (nonscheduled) operations using aircraft having more than 30 seats and/or with more than 7,500 pounds payload capacity.

12. Answer (b): A commuter operation is one that conducts scheduled operations (five or more round trips per week) in non-turbojet aircraft which have nine or fewer passenger seats or a payload capacity of 7,500 pounds or less.

13. Answer (d): A flag carrier must use weather sources approved by the Administrator of the FAA.

14. Answer (c): Part 121 air carriers must have the ability to communicate with a flight crew at any point in the route structure in a rapid and reliable fashion (14 CFR §121.99).

15. Answer (c): a flight follower is not required to be a certificated airman.

Chapter 2

1. Answer (a): The purpose of the operations specifications (ops specs) is for the company to identify to the FAA and itself how it intends to comply with specific provisions of the FARs. It is available as guidance to all affected employees, management, and the FAA.

2. Answer (c): 14 CFR Part 119.

   14 CFR Part 119 was created to effectuate the idea of "One Level of Safety," meaning that the FAA sought to narrow the gap in safety standards between Part 121 large airplane operators and smaller charter and on-demand operators regulated under 14 CFR Part 135.

3. Answer (c): Requires the carrier to comply with Part 91 as well as Part 121 unless the requirements under Part 121 are more stringent than the Part 91 requirements.

   All operators must comply with the general operating rules contained in Part 91. In addition, air carriers must also comply with the much more stringent rules contained in Part 121.

4. Answer (d): All of the above.

   14 CFR §119.49(a) sets forth the required contents of the operations specifications. The list is very specific as to what must be included. Items to be included are authorizations for various activities, limitations tied to airports, time between maintenance limits, and procedures for accomplishing various tasks.

5. Answer (c): 14 CFR Part 119. (14 CFR§119.49)

6. Answer (a): Names and addresses of the five largest shareholders.

   14 CFR §119.49(a) sets forth the required contents of the operations specifications. The list is very specific as to what must be included; however, it does not include the names and addresses of any of the shareholders of the company.

7. Answer (b): Standard in form and language but tailored to suit the individual, specific needs of each carrier.

   The automated ops specs program is intended to provide uniformity to the ops specs of various carriers while, at the same time, allowing the ops specs to be "custom fit" to the specific needs of each carrier. There will be uniformity for similar provisions, but each carrier can decide what provisions it will need in order to operate.

8. Answer (c): Volume 3 of the flight crew operations manual (FCOM).

   (Refer to Aeromech Ops Specs E096, page 29.)

9. Answer (a): First contact a representative of the national certification team.

   The first step for a new Part 121 domestic carrier in setting up ops specs is to contact the national air carrier certification team.

10. Answer (d): Its principal base of operations.

    14 CFR §119.43(a) requires that the carrier keep a copy of its approved ops specs at its principal base of operations. It must also place the material into its manual and indicate that the material comes from the ops specs and that therefore compliance is mandatory.

11. Answer (c): Until the carrier fails to conduct the kind of approved operation for 30 days and doesn't give the FAA 5 days' notice before resuming operations.

    Ops specs, once issued, are generally valid until suspended, surrendered, or revoked by the FAA. The one exception to this is if a carrier fails to conduct the kind of operation approved by the ops specs for 30 days. If that happens, 14 CFR §119.63 requires that the carrier give the FAA at least 5 working days' notice and make itself available for a full inspection before resuming service.

12. Answer (d): A safety issue required by the FAA

    The air carrier operating certificate is no longer required for economic reasons. It is now only required for safety issues and is issued by the FAA.

Chapter 3

1. Answer (b): Director of safety, director of operations, chief pilot, director of maintenance and chief inspector.

   Certificate holders conducting operations under Part 121 are required to have qualified personnel serving in these five specific management personnel positions (14 CFR §119.65).

2. Answer (d): Director of operations, chief pilot and director of maintenance.

   As per the Part 135 requirements found in 14 CFR §119.69, these are the three specific management positions required for operations conducted under Part 135.

3. Answer (c): Director of operations and the chief pilot.

   The positions of chief pilot and the director of operations must be filled by a pilot holding an air transport pilot certificate. (14 CFR §119.67[a] and [b] for Part 121, and 14 CFR §119.71[a] and [c] for Part 135)

4. Answer (a): Director of maintenance and the chief inspector.

   The director of maintenance and the chief inspector positions must be filled by a mechanic holding an airframe and powerplant (A&P) certificate. (14 CFR §119.67[a] and [b] for Part 121, and 14 CFR §119.71[e] for Part 135)

5. Answer (b): Director of operations.

   The director of operations provides operational control of all flight operations for the air carrier.

6. Answer (a): The dispatch center, flight control or flight following center.

   The dispatch center serves to specifically implement the concept of operational control. Dispatchers have the responsibility to plan the details of each specific flight and maintain communications with the flight at all times to keep it appraised of things such as weather, NOTAMs, operational limitations, and so forth.

7. Answer (d): None.

   There is no requirement for the director of safety to hold an ATP or A&P certificate.

8. Answer (c): The exercise of authority over initiating, conducting, and terminating a flight. (14 CFR §1.1)

9. Answer (c): Under routine operations, the flight is conducted under control and through consensus with the appropriate authority within the company. In emergency situations, it is conducted in this manner to the extent possible, subject to the captain's emergency authority.

(continued)

Operational control means that someone other than the pilot-in-command is involved in the decision making as to whether a flight starts, how it is conducted, and how and where it terminates. The pilot-in-command retains emergency authority to act independently, but under routine operations, the flight is conducted under control and through consensus with the appropriate authority within the company.

10. Answer (b): Active flight control is the part of the airline organization that oversees the tactical operation of the airline.

    Active control is the tactical operation of the airline flight operations. It consists of making those decisions and performing those actions necessary to operate a specific flight such as crew scheduling, accepting charter flights from the public, reviewing weather and NOTAMs, and flight planning.

Chapter 4

1. Answer (c): The carrier should contact the FAA office that it will deal with and work collaboratively with the assigned inspectors.

   While the actual production of an acceptable manual is the sole responsibility of the air carrier, it is strongly suggested that it be a collaborative effort between representatives of appropriate airline departments and the FAA Operations Inspector assigned to the airline. The FAA encourages its inspectors to offer guidance and advice to air carriers in the crafting of their manuals and this guidance should be welcomed by the carrier.

2. Answer (a): The flight operations manual required by 14 CFR §121.133.

   The flight operations manual required by 14 CFR §121.133 must contain procedures for operating in periods of ice, hail, thunderstorms, turbulence, or any potentially hazardous meteorological condition. Since the issues of icing and turbulence are not applicable to just one aircraft type, the planning for such flights would be found in the flight operations manual. There may be unique systems of operational issues with a particular aircraft type and the information about specific flight operations procedures for that aircraft would be found in the airplane flight manual (AFM) or company flight manual (CFM) as applicable to an individual airline. Dispatchers and flight crew would need to be familiar with both sources of information.

3. Answer (c): The airplane flight manual or company flight manual and the certificate holder's Section 121.133 manual parts pertaining to flight operations.

   14 CFR §121.141 requires either the AFM or the FAA-approved company flight manual to be carried aboard all aircraft during Part 121 operations. Also, 14 CFR §121.137 requires that crewmembers have the specific parts of the manual required in §121.133 pertaining to flight operations easily accessible while performing their duties (e.g., flight operations manual including weight and balance information, performance analysis, minimum equipment lists, etc.).

4. Answer (a): The AFM or CFM and the entire 14 CFR §121.133 manual including all of its subparts.

   14 CFR §121.141 requires that the AFM or CFM be aboard all Part 121 aircraft. In addition, Section 121.139 requires supplemental air carriers to carry the entire 14 CFR §121.133 manual. That includes all parts and or subparts.

5. Answer (b): The general operations manual.

   14 CFR §121.137 requires that the ground operations portion of the manual be furnished to ground operations personnel.

6. Answer (b): At the carrier's principal base of operations.

   14 CFR §121.135(c) requires that each certificate holder shall maintain at least one complete copy of the manual at its principal base of operations. In addition, it shall provide duplicate manual(s) to representatives of the Administrator which will be kept at the FAA certificate holding district office.

7. Answer (b): The manual(s) must contain a revision control page that shows the applicable effective dates of every page.

   Whenever a manual revision page is issued, it will be accompanied by a revised revision control log that shows the effective dates of all pages in the manual. In this way a user can always determine that he or she is using the current information.

8. Answer (d): None of the above.

   The Federal Aviation Administration (FAA) issued a legal interpretation in which it clarified that an electronic version of a manual is satisfactory. This interpretation also clarified that if a manual is provided in electronic form, the certificate holder must provide sufficient technological resources to permit crewmembers "to review effectively the applicable portions of the manual while performing their duties."

9. Answer (a): A compatible reading device that produces a legible image of the maintenance information and instructions.

   14 CFR §121.139(a) requires that if the certificate holder carries aboard an airplane all or any portion of the maintenance part of its manual in other than printed form, it must carry a compatible reading device that produces a legible image of the maintenance information and instructions or a system that is able to retrieve the maintenance information and instructions in the English language.

10. Answer (c): exercising authority over initiating, conducting or terminating a flight.

    14 CFR §1.1: Operational control, with respect to a flight, means the exercise of authority over initiating, conducting or terminating a flight.

11. Answer (c): Ground operations manual.

    The GOM includes non-aircraft specific information such as policies, procedures, and guidance covering the entire airline operation. Information such as policies and procedures pertaining to passenger handling would be found here.

12. Answer (d): 14 CFR §121.139 requires supplemental air carriers to have a copy of the entire manual aboard the aircraft for use by the contract personnel at those locations. By the nature of supplemental operations, these air carriers don't operate to the same locations on a repetitive basis, so this ensures a manual will be accessible to maintenance personnel.

Chapter 5

1. Answer (c): Cockpit crewmembers, dispatchers, and mechanics require an FAA certificate. (14 CFR §§121.383, 63.3, 65.5, 65.111)

2. Answer (c): Cockpit crewmembers, mechanics, and dispatchers are required to carry, on their person, the appropriate FAA certificate when engaged in operations covered under 14 CFR Parts 121 or 135. (14 CFR §§121.383, 63.3, 65.5, 65.111)

3. Answer (c): No person may serve as a pilot on an airplane engaged in operations under Part 121 if that person has reached his/her sixtieth-fifth birthday. (14 CFR §121.383[c])

4. Answer (b): 2

   The minimum pilot crew is two pilots and the certificate holder shall designate one pilot as pilot-in-command and the other second-in-command. (14 CFR §121.385[c])

5. Answer (d): Either a restricted airline transport pilot certificate or an airline transport pilot certificate. (14 CFR §§61.160[g][h], 121.436[a])

6. Answer (d): Depending upon where the training was obtained, (a), (b) or (c) may be correct.

   Section 61.160(a) allows military-trained and qualified pilots to get their ATP with 750 hours of total flight time and the remaining requirements found in paragraph (a). For a graduate of a four-year institution with an aviation program who has received a commercial certificate and instrument rating from a Part 141 program affiliated with that institution and who meets the remaining requirements of §61.160(b), an ATP certificate can be achieved after 1,000 hours. Similarly, a graduate who holds an associate's degree with an aviation major and meets the remaining requirements of §61.160(c) will be able to hold an R-ATP with a total time of 1,250 hours.

7. Answer (a): 1

   An aircraft equipped with less than 10 passenger seats may be flown under Part 135 without a second-in-command under the following conditions:

   - The aircraft is equipped with an operative approved autopilot system and the use of that system is authorized by the appropriate operations specifications. (14 CFR §135.105 [a])
   - The pilot-in-command must have at least 100 hours PIC time in the make and model of aircraft to be flown and have met all other applicable requirements of this part. (14 CFR §135.105 [a])
   - The certificate holder must apply for an amendment of its operation specifications to authorize the use of an autopilot system in place of a second-in-command. (§135.105[b], [c][1])

(continued)

- The certificate holder demonstrates, to the satisfaction of the Administrator, that operations using the autopilot system can be conducted safely and in compliance with this part. (§135.105[c][2])
- The aircraft is not operated in a Category II operation. (§135.111)

8. Answer (b): Six flight attendants are required. (14 CFR §121.391)

9. Answer (d): Zero flight attendants are required. (14 CFR §121.391)

10. Answer (c): The FAA minimum number of flight attendants required for dispatch must be onboard the aircraft during boarding and deplaning. (14 CFR §121.393)

11. Answer (b): False.

    Flight attendants are required to hold but not required to carry a FAA certificate of demonstrated proficiency.

12. Answer (c): The Fair Treatment for Experienced Pilots Act.

13. Answer (a): be at least 21 years old and hold a commercial pilot certificate with an instrument rating.

14. Answer (c): be at least 23 years old and hold a commercial pilot certificate with an instrument rating.

15. Answer (b): hold an R-ATP certificate, with type rating for the aircraft flown; and hold at least a second-class medical certificate.

    To serve as a first officer (SIC) in Part 121 air carrier operations, a pilot must hold either an Airline Transport Pilot certificate (ATP) or a Restricted Airline Transport Pilot certificate (R-ATP), a type rating for the aircraft to be flown, and at least a second-class medical certificate.

16. Answer (c): Each pilot is responsible for their own record.

Chapter 6

1. Answer (c): piston aircraft, turboprop aircraft, and turbojet aircraft.

   For the purpose of the training regulations, airplanes are broken down into three categories of aircraft: piston, turboprop, and turbojet. (14 CFR §121.400)

2. Answer (d): transition training.

   The type of training required for crewmembers who have qualified and served in the same capacity on another airplane in the same group is called transition training. (14 CFR §121.400)

3. Answer (c): Recurrent training.

   Recurrent training ensures each crewmember or dispatcher is adequately trained and currently proficient with respect to the type of airplane and crewmember position involved. (14 CFR §121.427)

4. Answer (c): Recurrent must be completed before the end of April of the next year.

   A crewmember may complete recurrent training anytime from the beginning of the calendar month before recurrent is due to be completed through the end of the month after the calendar month in which that training or check is required. (14 CFR §121.401[b])

5. Answer (b): The required training may be conducted by either the Part 121 certificate holder or a company holding a Part 142 flight training certificate. (14 CFR §121.402)

6. Answer (a): A flight engineer must have at least 50 hours of flight engineer time in the same make/model aircraft within the preceding 6 months. (14 CFR §121.453)

7. Answer (d): the preceding 12 calendar months.

   No person may serve as a pilot-in-command unless that pilot has satisfactorily completed a line check within the preceding 12 calendar months. (14 CFR §121.440)

8. Answer (b): When the visibility is below ¾ statute mile or RVR 4,000 FT for the runway to be used.

   If the second-in-command has fewer than 100 hours of flight time as second-in-command in operations under this part in the type airplane to be flown and the pilot-in-command is not a check airman, the pilot-in-command must make all takeoffs and landings when the visibility is below ¾ statute mile or RVR 4,000 FT for the runway to be used. (14 CFR §121.438)

9. Answer (a): 5 hours, reducible to 2½ hours by the substitution of additional takeoff and landing for an hour of flight; yes.

   An aircraft dispatcher must have, within the preceding 12 calendar months, observed flight operations from the flight deck for at least 5 hours in one of the types of aircraft in each group to be dispatched. The requirement may be satisfied by observing 5 hours of simulator training. (14 CFR §121.463[c])

10. Answer (d): A pilot-in-command must satisfactorily complete a proficiency check within the preceding 12 calendar months and must also complete either simulator training or a proficiency check within the preceding 6 calendar months. (14 CFR §121.441)

11. Answer (c): Circling approach—VMC only.

Chapter 7

Passenger-Carrying Operations

1. Answer (b): 72 hours in theater or 36 consecutive hours free from duty.

   Acclimated means a condition in which a flight crewmember has been in a theater for 72 hours or has been given at least 36 hours free from duty. (14 CFR §117.3)

2. Answer (b): 14 hours. (14 CFR §117.21[c][1])

3. Answer (a): Yes.

   The cumulative FDP limits specified in Section 117.23 may be exceeded after takeoff, with an FDP extension due to an unforeseen circumstance. (14 CFR §117.19[b][3])

4. Answer (c): 10 hours rest.

   A long-call reserve may be converted to a short-call if the flight crewmember is given a rest period of at least 10 consecutive hours. (14 CFR §117.21[e], §117.25[e])

5. Answer (a): 10 consecutive hours rest before with a 30 hour rest period in the preceding 168 hours. (14 CFR §117.25[a],[b],[c])

6. Answer (d): At the start of a flight duty period or reserve availability period.

   The Whitlow letter established that a flight crewmember must "look back" to see if all rest requirements are met at the start of each flight duty period or reserve availability period.

7. Answer (a): 100 hours in any 672-consecutive-hour period. (14 CFR §117.23[b][1])

8. Answer (b): False.

   Split duty periods are only allowed for an unaugmented operation. (14 CFR §117.15)

9. Answer (b): Yes, a flight crewmember may be scheduled five consecutive flight duty periods that infringe on the window of circadian low if the certificate holder provides the flight crewmember with an opportunity to rest, at least 2 hours, in a suitable accommodation during each of the consecutive nighttime flight duty periods. (14 CFR §117.27)

10. Answer (c): 19 hours.

    The maximum flight duty period hours for augmented operations with 4 pilots utilizing a Class 1 rest facility is 19 hours. (Table C to Part 117)

11. Answer (a): True.

    A deadhead leg that occurs after a flight segment is not considered part of a flight duty period (FDP).

12. Answer (c): 0 minutes, flight time limits are "hard limits."

    All Part 117 flight time limits are both scheduling and actual limits. So, unlike the previous Part 121 rules, Part 117 does not allow an extension to be made to the maximum flight time limits. Therefore, they may not be exceeded prior to takeoff. (14 CFR §117.11[b])

13. Answer (d): When unforeseen operational circumstances occur after takeoff, the maximum flight duty period may be extended to the extent necessary to safely land at the next destination or alternate. (14 CFR §117.19[b][1])

14. Answer (c): FDP begins at 0900 local time and must be scheduled to end by 2100 local time.

    The reserve availability period (RAP) begins at 0500 local time. The flight duty period (FDP) begins at 0900 local time. Using §117.21(c)(3) for unaugmented crews: the total number of hours a flight crewmember may spend in a flight duty period and a reserve availability period may not exceed the lesser of the maximum applicable flight duty period in Table B (13 hours) plus 4 hours (total of 17 hours), or 16 hours, as measured from the beginning of the reserve availability period. Therefore, the *reserve availability period* begins at 0500 local time and may run until 16 hours later, ending at 2100 local time.

15. Answer (d): FDP begins at 0900 local time and must be scheduled to end by 0000 local Atlanta time.

    The reserve availability period (RAP) begins at 0500 local time. The flight duty period (FDP) begins at the report time of 0900 local time. Using §117.21(c)(4) for augmented crews: the total number of hours a flight crewmember may spend in a flight duty period and a reserve availability period may not exceed the flight duty period in Table C (15 hours) plus 4 hours, as measured from the beginning of the reserve availability period. So the reserve availability period begins at 0500 local time and may run until 19 hours later, ending at 0000 local time.

All-Cargo Operations

1. Answer (a): Yes.

    The 7 day rest requirement, or "1 in 7 rule," exists as a scheduled flight time limitation only. There is no restriction placed on consecutive days of duty. The air carrier is only required to assure a 24-consecutive-hour rest period is granted before the pilot may again be used in scheduled air transportation.

2. Answer (a): True.

    The 7 day rest requirement, or "1 in 7 rule," exists as a scheduled flight time limitation only. There is no restriction placed on consecutive days of duty (e.g., simulator training period). The air carrier is only required to assure a 24-consecutive-hour rest period is granted before the pilot may again be used in scheduled air transportation.

3. Answer (a): Yes.

    The 7 day rest requirement, or "1 in 7 rule," exists as a scheduled flight time limitation only. There is no restriction placed on consecutive days of duty. The air carrier is only required to assure a 24-consecutive-hour rest period is granted before the pilot may again be used in scheduled air transportation. Regarding the ferry flight, as long as the ferry flight is conducted under 14 CFR Part 91, the Part 121 7-day rest limitation does not apply.

4. Answer (a): Yes.

    It is legal for that pilot to be scheduled to fly for the next 6 days without a calendar day off, as long as there is a 24-consecutive-hour rest period in the pilot's schedule prior to the seventh day on duty.

5. Answer (b): False.

    The time spent deadheading is not considered rest. (14 CFR §121.471[f], §121.491, §121.519)

6. Answer (b): False.

    The minimum 8 hour reduced rest period may not be further reduced. In this case, the pilot's next departure time must be delayed in order to provide an 8 hour period free from duty. A pilot must always be able to look back 24 hours and find at least an 8 hour rest period.

7. Answer (a): Yes.

    Weather conditions are beyond the control of the air carrier and the FAA does give the all-cargo air carrier relief from the 8 hour schedule limitation.

8. Answer (a): No later than 24 hours after the commencement of the reduced rest period.

    14 CFR §121.471(c)(1) states: A required compensatory rest period must begin no later than 24 hours after the commencement of the reduced rest period.

9. Answer (b): False.

    The flight crew may not depart. The FAA offers no relief from the time the compensatory rest period is required to begin. If the historic block time plus any anticipated delays will have the crew arrive at the destination after 2130 hours, the flight crew may not depart.

10. Answer (d): None of the above.

    The FAA defines a rest period in 14 CFR §121.471(e). The FAA has determined rest as a continuous period of time a flight crewmember is free from all duty requirements. These duty requirements include answering the phone, pager, or email or in any way remaining in contact with the company for the reason of being available for assignment if the need arises. (14 CFR §121.471[f], domestic operations; §121.491, flag operations; §121.519, supplemental operations)

11. Answer (d): None of the above.

    The FAA defines a rest period in 14 CFR §121.471(e). The FAA has determined rest as a continuous period of time a flight crewmember is free from all duty requirements. These duty requirements include answering the phone, pager, or email or in any way remaining in contact with the company for the reason of being available for assignment if the need arises. (14 CFR §121.471[f], domestic operations; §121.491, flag operations; §121.519, supplemental operations)

12. Answer (b): False.

    The pilot is not required to answer the phone during his rest period but may choose to answer the phone. This, however, is not deemed to interrupt the pilot's rest period and therefore, would not require the company to alter the pilot's schedule by starting a new rest period.

13. Answer (b): False.

    The pilot is not legal to begin the last scheduled flight day. The company would be required to alter the pilot's schedule to keep the pilot from exceeding the 100 hour per month limitation. In this example, the pilot could be scheduled for a 3 hour flight day. If during the last day the pilot was delayed again and was projected to go over the scheduled 3 hours, this would then be legal. Remember the "legal to start, legal to finish" rule.

14. Answer (d): No limit to the amount of hours this pilot may be scheduled to deadhead.

    Since deadhead time does not count as flight time, any amount of deadhead time would be legal.

15. Domestic operations limitations:

    1. Calendar year—1,000 flight hours maximum
    2. Calendar month—100 flight hours maximum
    3. 7 consecutive calendar days—30 flight hours maximum
    4. Between rest periods—8 flight hours maximum

    Flag operation limitations:

    1. 12 calendar months—1,000 flight hours maximum
    2. Calendar month—100 flight hours maximum
    3. 7 consecutive day period—32 flight hours maximum
    4. 24 consecutive hours—8 flight hours maximum (without a rest period)

    Supplemental all-cargo operations limitations:

    1. Calendar year—1,000 flight hours maximum
    2. 30 consecutive days—100 flight hours maximum
    3. Between rest periods—8 to 10 flight hours maximum

16. Answer (a): 16 hours.

    The maximum on duty limit is 16 hours in a 24-hour period. A pilot must always be able to look back over the last 24-hour period and find at least 8 hours of rest. Therefore, a pilot cannot exceed a 16-hour duty day.

17. Answer (b): Yes; 8 hours of flying in a 24-hour period is legal.

    The 8 hour limitation is based on rest periods; a pilot may not fly more than 8 hours between rest periods.

18. Answer (c): Yes, a domestic reserve pilot must be able to look back for a scheduled rest period of at least 8 hours; an international pilot is not protected by the look-back provision.

    Since December 1999, the FAA has required a reserve pilot to be able to look back for a scheduled rest period of at least 8 hours. If the pilot cannot find a scheduled rest period of at least 8 hours, the flight assignment is not legal. International pilots are not protected by the look-back provision.

19. Answer (d): 16 hours.

    The maximum on duty limit is 16 hours in a 24-hour period. A pilot must always be able to look back over the last 24 hour period and find at least 8 hours of rest. Therefore, a pilot cannot exceed a 16 hour duty day.

20. Answer (b): 10 hours.

    No air carrier may schedule an aircraft dispatcher for more than 10 hours of duty.

21. Answer (b): 10 hours.

    No air carrier may schedule an aircraft dispatcher for more than 10 hours of duty.

22. Answer (a): 8 hours.

    No air carrier conducting supplemental operations may schedule a pilot for more than 8 hours in any 24-consecutive-hour period.

23. Answer (c): 120 hours.

    No air carrier conducting supplemental operations may schedule a pilot for more than 120 hours aloft during any 30-consecutive-day period.

24. Answer (a): No air carrier conducting flag operations may schedule a pilot to fly for more than 12 hours during any 24-consecutive-hour period.

25. Answer (a): All commercial flight time, except military, in any flight crewmember position.

Chapter 8

1. Answer (b): foreign aircraft, approved under U.S. type design and operated under dry lease to the U.S. carrier.

    Airplanes operated by U.S. carriers must either be U.S.-registered aircraft or foreign aircraft registered in an ICAO country and of a type design that is approved under a U.S. type certificate. Furthermore, it must comply with all airworthiness standards that would apply if it were a U.S.-registered aircraft. (14 CFR §121.153)

2. Answer (c): 100 hours including 10 at night.

    If the aircraft type has never been proven in Part 121 operations, then the carrier must perform at least 100 hours of proving flights into representative destinations and operations. The proving flights must include at least 10 hours of night flights and the total number may be reduced in some instances where an equivalent level of safety may be demonstrated to the FAA. (14 CFR §121.163)

3. Answer (a): maximum speed in the takeoff at which the pilot must first take action to stop.

    V_1, takeoff decision speed, is the speed by which the pilot must have first taken action to stop the aircraft and still be able to do so in the remaining runway. The name is a bit misleading as it implies the decision to stop may be made anytime up to that speed and the pilot will still be able to stop. This does not consider the reaction time and would result in not being able to stop on the remaining runway. (14 CFR §1.1)

4. Answer (c): acceleration altitude.

    Part 25 requires that on takeoff, in the event of an engine failure, the crew must be able to achieve a 2.4 percent climb gradient from the point the aircraft landing gear is retracted (and airspeed is at V_2) until it reaches acceleration altitude, normally 400 feet above the takeoff surface. At that point the aircraft is accelerated to allow the flaps to be retracted and the aircraft configured for en route climb. (14 CFR §1.1)

5. Answer (b): The climb performance of the aircraft as determined in certification testing reduced by 8 feet per 1,000 feet traveled.

    The net takeoff flight path of a twin-engine aircraft for performance planning is the actual climb performance of the airplane reduced by a "fudge factor" of 0.8 percent, or 8 feet per 1,000 feet. This gives an extra margin of safety in the climb as the actual climb is slightly better than the minimum required and is increasing throughout the climb. For three-engine aircraft it is 0.9 per cent and four-engine aircraft require a 1.0 per cent factor. (14 CFR §25.111)

6. Answer (a): within the length of the runway.

    The takeoff run is somewhat analogous to the takeoff roll for light aircraft and must be accomplished within the confines of the runway surface.

7. Answer (d): within the length of the runway plus clearway (except clearway may only be counted up to one-half the length of the runway).

   The takeoff distance is analogous to the total distance to clear a 50 foot obstacle for light aircraft and must be accomplished within the confines of the runway surface plus any clearway, except you may only consider clearway up to one-half the runway length. (14 CFR §121.189)

8. Answer (c): Accelerate to V_1, lose an engine, and continue the flight.

   Runway limit weight is the maximum weight that allows for stopping the aircraft if an engine failure occurs below V_1, and allows flight to continue if the engine failure occurs at or above V_1.

9. Answer (d): All of the above.

   It is important to understand that the maximum takeoff weight must consider a number of variables, any one of which may be controlling (limiting). For example, on a short runway and a hot day, the runway limit may be controlling; on a hot day, the climb limit might control; and on an IFR day with a short stage length and a quite distant alternate, landing weight limits may control.

10. Answer (b): No.

    If the runway is 8,600 feet in length, in accordance with 14 CFR §121.195, the aircraft must be able to come to a complete stop within 60% of the effective length of the runway. 8,600 feet × 0.6 = 5,160 feet of runway. If the AFM landing distance table says the aircraft can land in 5,100 feet, it is legal to fly to this (dry) runway. The aircraft would be unable to legally fly to this runway if it was wet: 5,160 feet (60% of full length) × 0.15 = 774 feet (wet additional 15% reduction); 5,160 feet – 774 feet = 4,386 feet. We would be unable to stop in 4,386 feet of wet runway.

    Another way of computing this same problem: If our turbine aircraft has an AFM calculated landing distance of 5,100 feet, the runway must be a minimum of 8,500 feet (5,100 ÷ 0.60). Or put another way, multiply AFM calculated landing distance of 5,100 by 1.667 to get the landing distance required, 8,501 feet. On a dry day, this would be sufficient. On a wet day, we must multiply the landing distance of 8,500 feet by 1.15 for a total distance required of 9,775 feet.

11. Answer (a): Yes on a dry runway; no on a wet runway.

    If the runway is 11,000 feet in length, in accordance with 14 CFR §121.195, the aircraft must be able to come to a complete stop within 60% of the effective length of the runway: 11,000 feet × 0.6 = 6,600 feet of runway. If the AFM landing distance table says our aircraft can land in 6,500 feet, we are legal to fly to this (dry) runway. We would be unable to legally fly to this runway if it was wet: 6,600 feet (60% of full length) × 0.15 = 990 feet (wet additional 15% reduction); 6,600 feet – 990 feet = 5,510 feet. We would be unable to stop in 5,510 feet of wet runway.

    Another way of computing this same problem: If our turbine aircraft has an AFM calculated landing distance of 6,500 feet, the runway must be a minimum of 6,500 ÷ 0.60 = 10,833 feet. Or put another way, multiply AFM calculated landing distance of 6,500 feet by 1.667 to get the landing distance required, 10,835 feet. On a dry day, this would be sufficient. On a wet day, we must multiply the landing distance of 10,835 feet by 1.15 for a total distance required of 12,460 feet.

12. Answer (c): 3,000.

    According to an FAA study of rejected takeoffs (RTOs), statistically, one RTO occurs every 3,000 takeoffs.

13. Answer (c): before reaching V_1 speed.

    In a situation in which the gross takeoff weight is limited by runway limit weight, in the event of an engine failure, the Go/No Go decision must be made before reaching V_1 speed.

14. Answer (c): before reaching V_1 speed.

    In a situation in which the gross takeoff weight is limited by climb limit weight, in the event of an engine failure, the Go/No Go decision must be made before reaching V_1 speed.

15. Answer (c): Climb limit weight is the maximum weight that guarantees that the aircraft can proceed from the point 35 feet above the runway to 1,500 feet above the runway surface (or specified higher altitude) while maintaining required climb gradients in order to achieve adequate obstacle clearance.

16. Answer (d): the altitude to which, following the failure of an engine above the one-engine inoperative absolute ceiling, an airplane will descend to and maintain, while using maximum continuous power on the operating engine and maintaining the one-engine inoperative best rate of climb speed.

17. Answer (b): During a normal takeoff, an aircraft may not be banked prior to reaching a height of **50** feet as shown by the flight path or net flight path data. After attaining **50** feet in height, the aircraft may not be banked more than **15** degrees in any additional maneuvering.

18. Answer (d): A two-engine, turbine-powered airplane may not be operated over a route that contains a point farther than **60** minutes of flying time (in still air at normal cruising speed with one engine inoperative) from an adequate airport. (14 CFR §121.161)

19. Answer (a): The aircraft must be operated at a weight allowed by the AFM that allows it to fly from a point where the two engines failed simultaneously to an authorized alternate airport and clear all terrain and obstructions within 5 statute miles of the intended track by at least 2,000 feet vertically. Also, the net flight path must have a positive slope at 1,500 feet above the airport where the landing is assumed to be made after the engines fail. (14 CFR §121.193)

20. Answer (d): Landing limitations for alternate airports are similar to the landing limitations for destination airports. An operator may not list an airport as an alternate airport if at the anticipated weight at the anticipated time of arrival the aircraft cannot be brought to a stop in **60** percent of the effective runway length for turbojet aircraft or **70** percent of the effective runway length for turboprop aircraft. (14 CFR §121.197)

21. Answer (a): Airplane.

Chapter 9

1. Answer (c): Must be secured in bins that can withstand 1.15 times the emergency landing g loads or, alternatively, the cargo may be properly restrained behind a bulkhead.

   14 CFR §121.285(b) requires that passenger-carrying aircraft that are used to carry cargo as well as passengers must have the cargo in approved bins that can withstand "g" forces equal to 1.15 times the load factors applicable to emergency landing conditions. Alternatively, the cargo may be properly restrained behind a bulkhead.

2. Answer (a): a landing is attempted with the gear not locked down.

   The present regulations require that the aural warning be given at any time a landing is attempted and the gear is not locked down. The old regulation required only that the throttle position be tested.

3. Answer (b): 90 seconds or less.

   14 CFR §121.291 requires that Part 121 passenger aircraft with more than 44 seats be capable of being evacuated in 90 seconds or less.

4. Answer (a): are interconnected but may be operated separately in an emergency.

   This is one of the major design differences of Part 25 aircraft and Part 23 aircraft. The transport category aircraft must preclude the possibility of a control circuit jam. One way of doing this is to use separate controls for each half of the elevator structure (ailerons and rudder as well) and allow, in emergency conditions, for these controls to be separated and operated independently.

5. Answer (c): the aircraft is rotated for takeoff.

   The takeoff warning system must sound an alarm that is automatically activated if a takeoff is attempted and the aircraft is not properly configured for takeoff. It sounds from application of takeoff power until the configuration is changed to allow for a safe takeoff, the takeoff is terminated, the warning is deactivated by the pilot, or the airplane is rotated for takeoff.

6. Answer (a): 8,000 feet.

   Part 25 requires that pressurized compartments and cabins maintain a maximum cabin pressure altitude of 8,000 feet at the maximum operating altitude of the aircraft.

7. Answer (c): Class C.

   A Class C compartment must have both an approved smoke/fire detector system and a built-in fire extinguishing or suppression system. It is the only class of compartment to require extinguishing equipment.

8. Answer (d): 4 fire extinguishers.

   Aircraft with seating capacity of 7 to 30 require one fire extinguisher; those with 31 through 60 seats require two extinguishers; those with 61 to 200 seats require three extinguishers; and those with 201 through 300 passenger seats require four fire extinguishers.

9. Answer (c): Status.

   A warning light is red, a caution light is yellow, a safe light is green, and other colors may be used (if there is no chance of confusion) for other purposes such as status of a system.

10. Answer (b): last 30 minutes of each flight.

    Cockpit voice recorders (CVRs) are required to record continuously for 30 minutes.

11. Answer (b): 20 seats.

    All airplanes having a passenger seating capacity greater than 20 seats are required by 14 CFR §25.807 to have flight crew emergency exits that are located in the flight crew area.

12. Answer (b): False.

    Air carriers shall prohibit smoking on all scheduled passenger flights. (14 CFR §252.3)

13. Answer (d): Protective breathing equipment (PBE).

    Protective breathing equipment must be installed for the use of the flight crew, and at least one portable protective breathing equipment shall be located at or near the flight deck for use by a flight crewmember. (14 CFR §25.1439)

14. Answer (a): The detection system must provide a visual warning indication to the flight crew within one minute after the start of a fire. (14 CFR §25.858)

15. Answer (b): False.

    Class D cargo or baggage compartments are not currently defined (or allowed) by the FAA. In older aircraft, Class D cargo compartments were those that were not accessible during flight and were designed to choke out fires due to lack of oxygen rather than detect or extinguish the fire. (14 CFR §25.857)

Chapter 10

1. Answer (c): the aircraft takes off.

   The rule reads that no person may take off an aircraft with inoperative instruments or equipment installed. Of course in air carrier operations this is substantially modified by the availability of minimum equipment list relief provisions.

2. Answer (a): be of the Halon 1211 (or equivalent) type.

   14 CFR §121.309 requires that at least two fire extinguishers aboard passenger-carrying aircraft be of the Halon 1211 type.

3. Answer (d): on the ground with all landing gear extended.

   14 CFR §121.310 requires that an approved means of evacuating the passengers be available if the emergency exit (other than over-the-wing exits) are more than 6 feet above ground with the airplane on the ground and the landing gear extended.

4. Answer (c): Both (a) and (b).

   14 CFR §121.310 provides that each emergency light required for interior exit lights or exterior exit lighting be operable manually from both the flight crew station and a point in the passenger compartment that is readily accessible to a normal flight attendant seat.

5. Answer (d): required that each passenger be seated and belts fastened during all movement on the surface.

    14 CFR §121.311 requires that each person on board an air carrier airplane must occupy an approved seat or berth with a separate safety belt properly secured about him or her during movement on the surface, takeoff, or landing.

6. Answer (c): operator of the aircraft.

    14 CFR §121.315 provides that each certificate holder must provide flight crews with an approved cockpit check procedure for each type of aircraft that it operates.

7. Answer (a): the cabin pressure altitude exceeds 10,000 feet.

    14 CFR §121.329 provides that anytime the aircraft is above 10,000 feet, the flight crew must be provided and use oxygen. Answers (b), (c) and (d) are the various altitudes regarding oxygen use in Part 91 operations.

8. Answer (b): flight level 250.

    14 CFR §121.333 provides that if for any reason at any time it is necessary for one pilot to leave his station at the controls of the airplane when operating at flight altitudes above flight level 250, the remaining pilot at the controls shall put on and use his oxygen mask until the other pilot has returned to his duty station.

9. Answer (c): 120 minutes total operation.

    14 CFR §121.333 provides for the emergency descent after loss of pressurization. It requires that the pilots be supplied enough oxygen to comply with 14 CFR §121.329 but not less than a 2 hour supply. This consists of enough oxygen to descend from the maximum certificated altitude to 10,000 feet in 10 minutes and then to fly at 10,000 feet for 110 minutes thereafter.

10. Answer (d): 25 hours of continuous data.

    14 CFR §121.343 requires that aircraft certificated for flight above 25,000 feet be equipped with flight recorders. The flight data recorder must operate continuously from the instant the aircraft begins its takeoff roll until it has completed its landing roll at an airport. The data must be kept until the aircraft has operated for at least 25 hours of operating time.

11. Answer (a): all turbine-powered aircraft with a maximum certificated takeoff weight of more than 33,000 pounds must be equipped with a TCAS II. (14 CFR §121.356)

12. Answer (c): at first use of a checklist (before starting engines for the purpose of flight).

    14 CFR §121.359 requires that the cockpit voice recorder (CVR) be operated continuously from the start of the first use of the checklist until the completion of the final checklist at the termination of the flight.

13. Answer (a): True.

    An air carrier may not dispatch an airplane under IFR or night VFR conditions when current weather reports indicate that thunderstorms or other potentially hazardous weather conditions that can be detected with airborne weather radar may reasonably be expected along the route to be flown, unless the airborne weather radar is working. (14 CFR §121.357)

14. Answer (c): Airplanes with a seating capacity of more than 19 passengers must be equipped with a public address system that is capable of operation independent of the required crewmember interphone system. (14 CFR §121.318)

15. Answer (b): All transport category passenger-carrying airplanes.

    Each passenger-carrying airplane must have an emergency lighting system for interior emergency exit markings. (14 CFR §121.310)

Chapter 11

1. Answer (d): 1 hour.

    In the case of domestic flights, each flight must be dispatched, unless the flight was originally included in the dispatch of a multi-leg flight and the aircraft doesn't spend more than 1 hour on the ground.

2. Answer (b): The information that is required to appear on a Part 121 domestic or flag operator's dispatch release form is identification number of the aircraft, trip number, departure airport, intermediate stops, destination airport and alternate airports, a statement about the type of operation (e.g., VFR, IFR), minimum fuel supply, and weather reports and forecasts.

3. Answer (d): No difference. Domestic, flag, and supplemental load manifests must contain identical information. (14 CFR §121.693)

4. Answer (c): conditions will be at or above the authorized landing minimums.

   14 CFR §121.613 states that no flight may be dispatched unless appropriate weather reports or forecasts, or any combination thereof, indicate that the weather conditions will be at or above the authorized landing minimums at the estimated time of arrival at the airport or airports to which the flight is dispatched or released.

5. Answer (b): When weather conditions are such that an aircraft departs an airport with takeoff minimums below the departure airport's landing minimums in the certificate holder's ops specs. (14 CFR §121.617)

6. Answer (b): A ceiling is derived by adding 400 feet to the authorized Category I HAT or HAA, and a visibility is derived by adding 1 statute mile to the authorized Category I landing minimum. (Paragraph C.055 of an air carrier's ops specs)

7. Answer (d): A ceiling is derived by adding 200 feet to the higher Category I HAT of the two approaches used, and a visibility is derived by adding ½ statute mile to the higher authorized Category I landing minimum of the two approaches used. (Paragraph C.055 of an air carrier's ops specs)

8. Answer (c): When the destination weather is not forecast to be, from 1 hour before scheduled arrival until 1 hour after, a ceiling of 2,000 feet and 3 statute miles visibility.

   Remember the "1-2-3 rule"—14 CFR §121.619 requires that from 1 hour before scheduled arrival until 1 hour after, the weather shall be forecast to be at least a 2,000 foot ceiling and 3 statute miles visibility.

9. Answer (a): A flight may not depart unless it has enough fuel to fly to the airport to which it is dispatched, then fly to the most distant alternate (if required), then fly for 45 minutes at normal cruising fuel consumption rates. (14 CFR §121.619)

10. Answer (b): Repair category "B" inoperative items shall be repaired within 3 consecutive calendar days (72 hours) excluding the calendar day the malfunction was recorded in the aircraft maintenance log and/or record. (Paragraph D.095 of an air carrier's ops specs)

11. Answer (b): This flight crew may continue the approach to DA/DH or MDA: In order land the aircraft, the flight visibility must not be less than the visibility prescribed in the standard instrument approach procedure being used.

    No pilot may continue an approach past the final approach fix unless the visibility is equal to or better than the visibility minimums prescribed for that procedure. If past the FAF when the flight crew receives a weather report indicating below-minimum conditions, the flight crew may continue to DA/DH or MDA. (14 CFR §121.651[c])

12. Answer (c): A second alternate is needed if using Exemption 3585.

    A second alternate is needed anytime a flight is filed under FAA Exemption 3585.

13. Answer (a): A high minimums captain would need to increase the minimums to a MDA of 750 feet and a visibility of 1¼ SM.

    A high minimums captain must add 100 feet to the MDA and ½ SM to the visibility requirements.

14. Answer (a): None, the FAA allows a high minimums captain to use the normal published takeoff minimums for the airport.

15. Answer (b): False.

    A dispatch release document is required to be used for domestic and flag operators, while supplemental operators are allowed to use a flight release document. (14 CFR §121.663)

Chapter 12

1. Answer (c): the exercise of authority over initiating, conducting, or terminating a flight. (14 CFR §1.1)

2. Answer (c): Both (a) and (b) are correct.

    An air carrier employee designated in the ops specs as responsible for operational control may delegate the *functions* of operational control to its own internal divisions or departments of the Part 121 air carrier or even to another carrier or contract service provider.

3. Answer (d): None of the above.

    An air carrier, or the position stated in the ops specs as responsible for operational control, may never delegate the *responsibility for* operational control to anyone. That responsibility is always on the person designated in the ops specs.

4. Answer (a): An air carrier's director of operations (DO), aircraft dispatcher, and/or pilot-in-command.

    The authority to dispatch or release a flight is held by an air carrier's director of operations, who typically delegates this duty to both the aircraft dispatcher and pilot-in-command. (14 CFR §§121.533, 121.535, 121.537)

5. Answer (b): The ground security coordinator.

    Prior to flight, the ground security coordinator (GSC) is responsible for airplane security. (49 CFR §1544.215)

6. Answer (c): No, it can't because 14 CFR §121.541 requires the airline to publish realistic schedules based on realistic evaluation of aircraft performance and prevailing winds. It must also allow reasonable time for aircraft servicing.

    14 CFR §121.541 requires airlines to publish realistic schedules that take into consideration all factors such as typical congestion delays, realistic wind effects, and true and typical aircraft performance.

7. Answer (c): That period of flight including all ground operations involving taxi, takeoff, and landing, and all other flight operations conducted below 10,000 feet, unless in level cruise flight. (14 CFR §121.542[c])

8. Answer (c): While descending, discussing the abnormal procedure dealing with the fact that the flaps are not deploying.

    14 CFR §121.542 states that during a critical phase of flight, a crewmember may not perform any duties or partake in any activities except those required for safe operation of the aircraft. Dealing with stuck flaps is the only choice that meets that criteria.

9. Answer (d): FAA Form 110A (FAA inspector's ID card) and FAA Form 8430-13 jumpseat form.

    An FAA air carrier inspector on official duty must present FAA Form 110A (FAA inspector's ID card) and FAA Form 8430-13 (jumpseat form). (14 CFR §121.548)

10. Answer (c): Only when its use is directly related to the operation of the aircraft or for emergency, safety-related or certain employment-related communications.

    14 CFR §121.542 states that a pilot may not use a PED during flight unless the use is directly related to operation of the aircraft or for emergency, safety-related or certain employment-related communications.

11. Answer (d): (a) and (c) are both correct.

    14 CFR §121.543 states that a flight crewmember may leave his or her assigned station in connection with duties related to the operation of the aircraft, to meet physiological needs including personal relief and movement to ensure mental and physical alertness, and to begin an assigned rest period (assuming a qualified relief pilot is provided).

12. Answer (a): The PF is primarily responsible for flying the aircraft in accordance with the approved operational procedures.

    The pilot flying (PF) is primarily responsible for flying the aircraft in accordance with the approved operational procedures. The captain is responsible for overall supervision of the crew whether PF or non-flying pilot (NFP). The NFP's role is to monitor flight path, avionics and instrument settings and to check that actual operational actions match those that were actually intended.

13. Answer (c): The cockpit-to-cabin door must be closed and locked during flight.

    The pilot-in-command of a passenger-carrying airplane that has a lockable flight crew compartment door must ensure that the door is closed and locked during flight. (14 CFR §121.587[a])

14. Answer (b): English language demonstrated proficiency card.

    A pilot must carry an FCC radiotelephone operator permit and current FAA medical and FAA-issued airman certificates appropriate to the position flown. While there is a requirement to show English proficiency, that is not a separate certificate but rather an endorsement on the airman certificate.

15. Answer (c): The appropriate ops specs paragraph.

    While the Official Airline Guide and company system timetables are useful documents for determining schedules, there may be many areas that the company is authorized to fly but to which it does not currently have (or maybe has never had) flights scheduled. The only certain place to look to determine where the company is authorized to fly is in the ops specs.

16. Answer (a): Not for destination airports, but it may file (and use, if needed) a Part 139 airport as a takeoff or destination alternate airport.

    Part 121 carriers are restricted to using Part 139 airports in all cases except when required as a takeoff or destination airport. Other than that, use of non-Part 139 airports is prohibited.

17. Answer (c): An air carrier may allow a passenger to carry and operate oxygen equipment as long as that carrier supplies the necessary equipment. (14 CFR §121.574[a][1][i])

18. Answer (d): Land the airplane at the nearest suitable airport, in point of time, at which a safe landing can be made, and notify the appropriate ATC facility as soon as practicable after the engine failure or in flight shutdown.

19. Answer (c): CASS.

    The Cockpit Access Security System (CASS) verification program is a network of databases hosted by participating Part 121 air carriers that contains employment and security information for individuals authorized by the FAA to occupy an aircraft's flight deck jump seat during normal operations. The information and process used for the CASS is intended to verify a person's identity, eligibility for access to the jump seat, and their employment status at the time of check in.

20. Answer (b): False.

    An authorized person may open the flightdeck door as long as an approved audio procedure and an approved visual device is used to verify that: (1) the area outside the flightdeck door is secure, and (2) if someone outside the flightdeck is seeking to have the flightdeck door opened, that person is not under duress.

Chapter 13

1. Answer (d): aircraft dispatchers and crewmembers.

    Air carriers operating under Part 121 are required to maintain current records of aircraft dispatchers and crewmembers. (14 CFR §121.683)

2. Answer (c): the certificate holder operates in scheduled air transportation.

    Air carriers operating under Part 121 must maintain a current list of each aircraft that the certificate holder operates in scheduled air transportation. (14 CFR §121.685)

3. Answer (a): The information that is required to appear on a Part 121 domestic or flag operator's dispatch release form is identification number of the aircraft, trip number, departure airport, intermediate stops, destination airport and alternate airports, a statement about the type of operation (e.g., VFR, IFR), minimum fuel supply, and weather reports and forecasts.

4. Answer (a): Domestic, flag, and supplemental load manifests must contain identical information. (14 CFR §121.693)

5. Answer (c): Completed load manifest, dispatch release, flight plan.

   The pilot-in-command is required by Part 121, Subpart V, to carry aboard an airplane to its destination a dispatch release, flight plan, and a completed load manifest. (14 CFR §121.695)

6. Answer (a): Pilot route certification, airworthiness release and a flight release instead of a dispatch release.

   The pilot-in-command of an aircraft in supplemental operations is required by Part 121, Subpart V, to carry aboard an airplane to its destination pilot route certification paperwork, airworthiness release, and a flight release instead of a dispatch release. (14 CFR §121.697)

7. Answer (d): 3 months.

   Certificate holders are required by 14 CFR §121.695(b) and §121.697(e) to maintain copies of the dispatch release or flight release, flight plan, and load manifest for a period of 3 months.

8. Answer (a): 30 days.

   Air carriers are required to maintain a record of service difficulty reports for a period of 30 days. (14 CFR §121.703[d])

9. Answer (b): The authorized certificated mechanic or repairman.

   An airworthiness release may be signed by an authorized certificated mechanic or repairman except that a certificated repairman may sign the release or entry only for the work for which he or she is employed and certificated.

10. Answer (d): 30 days.

    An air carrier is required to maintain a record of each en route radio contact between the certificate holder and its pilots for a period of 30 days. (14 CFR §121.711)

11. Answer (b): For a period of 6 calendar months.

    As are Part 121 air carriers, Part 135 certificate holders are required by 14 CFR §135.63(a) to maintain a current list of aircraft used or available for use and the operations for which each is equipped. Furthermore, the certificate holder must keep this record for at least 6 calendar months.

12. Answer (c): at least 12 calendar months.

    Each certificate holder is required to keep an individual record of each pilot used in Part 135 operations for a period of at least 12 calendar months. An individual record for each flight attendant who is required under the applicable Part 135 regulations must also be maintained for a period of at least 12 months. (14 CFR §135.63[a])

13. Answer (a): 2 months.

    When an airworthiness release form is prepared, the certificate holder must give a copy to the pilot-in-command and must keep a record thereof for at least 2 months. (14 CFR §121.709)

14. Answer (b): Every month before the 10th of the month for the previous month's mechanical interruptions.

    Each certificate holder shall submit to the Administrator, before the end of the 10th day of the following month, a summary report for the previous month. (14 CFR §121.705)

15. Answer (c): 3 months.

    The certificate holder shall keep copies of the records required in this section (14 CFR §121.695) for at least three months.

Chapter 14

1. Answer (b): The air carrier certificate holder.

   The FARs are very clear that the certificate holder is responsible for the airworthiness of its aircraft and, further, that this responsibility may not be delegated.

2. Answer (c): Both (a) and (b) are permitted.

   While the carrier may not delegate the responsibility for assuring airworthiness of its aircraft, it may delegate the actual maintenance work to be done. It may delegate the work to either another Part 121 certificate holder repair station or to an FAA-approved Part 145 maintenance facility.

3. Answer (d): Neither (a) nor (b) is permitted.

   As stated previously, the carrier may not delegate the responsibility for airworthiness to any other party.

4. Answer (d): must be placed in separate organizations at the operational level of the company.

   The maintenance and inspection functions must be separated (organizationally) at the operational level. The separation must occur below the level of administrative control at which overall responsibility for the required inspection functions and other maintenance and alteration functions is exercised.

5. Answer (b): maintenance manual.

   The ops specs provide the general outline of responsibility for the maintenance program while the approved maintenance manual of the airline provides the detailed information of how specific tasks are to be performed.

6. Answer (c): 1 year.

   Minor repairs such as those needed to return an aircraft to service (issue a maintenance release) must be retained until the work is repeated or 1 year, whichever is longer.

7. Answer (d): Forever, and transferred with the aircraft if it is sold.

   Records of major repairs such as an airframe overhaul must be kept forever and must be transferred with the aircraft when it is sold.

8. Answer (d): The mechanic needn't hold any airman's certificate.

   Since the carrier has set up its maintenance under 14 CFR §121.379, it is operating as a repair station. In that case, the individual person doing the work need not hold an airman certificate. Rather, the person supervising the maintenance must hold the appropriate airman certificate. In this case we are relying on the certificate of the carrier for accountability.

9. Answer (a): is required at all Part 121 carriers.

   Maintenance and inspection training is part of the ongoing quality assurance programs required by the FAA.

10. Answer (d): It is not required to provide its workers any time off.

    The foreign repair station is subject to the U.S. FAA's aviation regulations but is not subject to U.S. labor laws. There is no specific requirement under U.S. law that the repair station provide days off. Of course, the facility is subject to its own local labor laws.

11. Answer (a): Part 39.

    The regulations contained in Part 39 provide a legal framework for FAA's system of airworthiness directives.

12. Answer (c): 10 seats.

    Part 135 operators that operate aircraft type certificated for a passenger seating configuration, excluding any pilot seat, of ten seats or more, shall maintain those aircraft in accordance with a FAA-approved maintenance manual written by the air carrier. (14 CFR §135.411)

13. Answer (b): False.

    14 CFR §135.431 requires Part 135 operators to establish and maintain CASS for their maintenance programs.

14. Answer (b): False.

    The FAA's airworthiness directives are legally enforceable rules that must be complied with by a certain date or flight hour period or the aircraft becomes unairworthy. FAA regulations contained in Part 39 provide a legal framework for the FAA's system of airworthiness directives. The FAA makes it clear that anyone who operates an aircraft that does not meet the requirements of an applicable airworthiness directive is in violation of Part 39.

15. Answer (a): True.

    If the inflight shutdown (IFSD) rate (computed on a 12-month rolling average) for an engine installed as part of an airplane-engine combination exceeds the values listed in 14 CFR §121.374(i), the certificate holder must do a comprehensive review of its operations to identify any common cause effects and systemic errors. The IFSD rate must be computed using all engines of that type in the certificate holder's entire fleet of airplanes approved for ETOPS.

Chapter 15

1. Answer (d): Part 121 Appendix E: Flight Training Requirements.

   Appendix E to Part 121 contains all of the required training for pilot initial, upgrade, and transition training. It is a very useful document for the newly hired pilot to use to become familiar with the scope of training to be performed.

2. Answer (c): Level D.

   Referring to Figure 15-1, you can see that the highest level of fidelity available in a certificated flight simulator is found in a Level D simulator.

3. Answer (d): All of the above.

   Refer to Appendix H to Part 121. This appendix specifies all of the training and checking that can be performed in a simulator. Levels B, C, and D may all be used for some (or all) of the required landings.

4. Answer (a): Yes.

   This is one of the most surprising requirements in the FARs! 14 CFR §135.1 requires small, Part 91 operators that give sightseeing rides (using the 25 mile exception to Part 135) to perform Part 120 drug testing. In other words, Part 91 pilots are held to a Part 135 standard that is nowhere mentioned in Part 91! You really must read the regulations carefully and seek advice from more experienced personnel, legal counsel and/or FAA Air Safety Inspectors if you have any questions or concerns about the FARs.

5. Answer (d): All of the above.

   All safety-sensitive positions require drug and alcohol testing. Flight attendants, ground security coordinators, and pilots are all positions that are included on the list of safety-sensitive employees found in 14 CFR §120.105.

6. Answer (a): All newly hired pilots.

   Of the listed positions, only the pilots are carried as safety sensitive for the purposes of Appendix I. While a company may elect to test the other individuals, it may do so only as permitted by local law. It is not exempt from local laws for non–safety related employees.

7. Answer (b): requires at least two of the employee's supervisors to concur in the testing decision.

   Reasonable cause drug testing may be performed only after at least two of the employee's supervisors have seen acts leading to suspicion of drug usage. At least one of these supervisors must have been trained in detection in the symptoms of drug use.

8. Answer (d): the pilot is forever barred from acting as a commercial pilot for any company.

   This is the capital punishment for airline employees, especially pilots. If a pilot fails two drug tests, that pilot can never again work for any employer in the same safety-sensitive position.

9. Answer (a): 0.04.

   Refer to 14 CFR §120.37. The level of blood alcohol concentration that bars an employee from performing a safety sensitive function is 0.04.

10. Answer (b): 2 hours after the accident.

    14 CFR §120.217 gives the employer up to 2 hours to test an employee for alcohol after an accident. If it doesn't do so, it must establish and maintain records that show why the testing was not performed.

GLOSSARY OF TERMS

The following glossary defines terms used in this book. Other definitions may be found in 14 CFR §1.1, General Definitions; the *Aeronautical Information Manual*; and FSIMS 8900.1 Volume 1, Chapter 1, Section 2, or other appropriate sources. Official acronyms and abbreviations may be found in the 14 CFR §1.2 and FSIMS Volume 1, Chapter 1, Sections 3 and 4.

1-2-3 rule. A rule for determining the destination alternate requirement. From 1 hour before scheduled arrival until 1 hour after, a domestic operator must have at least a 2,000 foot ceiling and 3 statute miles visibility.

1 in 7 rule. The rule requiring an air carrier to give a pilot 1 day (24 consecutive hours) free from all duty in each 7-day period.

14 CFR Part 1. FARs: Definitions and abbreviations.

14 CFR Part 25. FARs governing airworthiness standards for transport category airplanes.

14 CFR Part 60. FARs governing the initial and continuing qualification and use of all aircraft flight simulation training devices (FSTDs) used for meeting training, evaluation, or flight experience requirements for flight crewmember certification or qualification.

14 CFR Part 61. FARs governing certification of pilots, flight instructors and ground instructors.

14 CFR Part 63. FARs governing certification of flight crewmembers other than pilots.

14 CFR Part 65. FARs governing certification of airmen other than flight crewmembers.

14 CFR Part 91. FARs governing general operating and flight rules.

14 CFR Part 110. FARs governing general requirements of all operations conducted under CFR Title 1, Chapter 14, Subchapter G—Air Carriers and Operators for Compensation or Hire: Certification and Operations.

14 CFR Part 117. The section of the Code of Federal Regulations that governs the flight and duty limitations and rest requirements of Part 121 passenger-carrying flight crewmembers.

14 CFR Part 119. FARs that define, for air carriers and commercial operators, which operating rule will apply to the operation of their aircraft. Part 119 references passenger seat configuration and payload capacity to determine the applicable operating rules.

14 CFR Part 120. FARs governing the FAA Drug and Alcohol Testing Program.

14 CFR Part 121. FARs detailing the operating requirements for domestic, flag and supplemental air carrier operations.

14 CFR Part 125. FARs prescribing rules governing the operations of U.S.-registered airplanes that have a seating configuration of 20 or more passenger seats, or a maximum payload capacity of 6,000 lbs or more when common carriage is not involved.

14 CFR Part 135. FARs covering the operating requirements for commuter and on-demand operations and rules governing persons on board such aircraft.

14 CFR Part 142 Flight Training Certificate. Implemented in 1996, Part 142 provides the regulatory basis to enable training centers to become FAA certified and use approved curriculums, qualified instructors, and authorized evaluators to conduct the training, testing, and checking of airmen in qualified simulators and flight training devices (FTDs). Prior to the implementation of Part 142, regulations did not permit organizations other than certificated air carriers to use qualified simulators or FTDs to conduct the training, checking, or testing to qualify flight crewmembers. To acknowledge the advantages of modern simulation technology, the FAA issued various regulatory exemptions to training organizations that enabled them to conduct required training, checking, or testing in flight simulation devices.

14 CFR Part 145. Contains the rules a certificated repair station must follow related to its performance of maintenance, preventive maintenance, or alterations of an aircraft, airframe, aircraft engine, propeller, appliance, or component part to which Part 43 applies. It also applies to any person who holds, or is required to hold, a repair station certificate issued under this part.

30 in 7 rule. The rule, set out in 14 CFR §121.471, that limits the flight time of flight crewmembers flying in domestic all-cargo operations to 30 hours in any 7-day period.

50 in 6 requirements. The requirement in 14 CFR §121.453 that flight engineers must have acquired at least 50 hours of flight time as flight engineers in the preceding 6 months in the airplane type in which they are to serve. An FE who has not met this requirement must reestablish recency of experience by completing a basic qualification module (flight check) conducted by either a check FE or an FAA inspector. The check may be conducted in an airplane in nonrevenue operations, or in an "engineer simulator."

600-2 standard alternate weather minimums. Represents the minimum forecast ceiling (600 feet) and visibility (2 statute miles) required to use an airport equipped with a precision approach as an alternate airport on an IFR flight plan. *See* standard alternate (weather) minimums.

60-minute rule. A flight planning rule contained in 14 CFR §121.161(a) that, unless otherwise approved by the Administrator, prohibits a carrier from planning to operate a twin turbine-engine-powered airplane over a route within either the North or South Polar Areas that contains a point farther than 60 minutes flying time (at a one-engine-inoperative cruise speed under standard conditions in still air) from an adequate airport.

800-2 standard alternate weather minimums. Represents the minimum forecast ceiling (800 feet) and visibility (2 statute miles) required to use an airport equipped with a non-precision approach as an alternate airport on an IFR flight plan. *See* standard alternate (weather) minimums.

90-minute rule. A flight planning rule contained in 14 CFR §121.193(c) that provides flight planners with several options for aircraft with three or more engines. First, the rule allows a three- or four-engine airplane to operate anywhere on the airline's route structure so long as the aircraft is always within 90 minutes flying time (all engines operating) from an approved alternate airport. If it can, the flight dispatcher need not do a two engine inoperative driftdown analysis for the flight. If the flight route does not meet this requirement, then the airline may conduct the flight using the driftdown analysis technique and procedures for two engines inoperative.

ACARS. An automated communication and reporting system allowing an aircraft-to-company automated data link. This system enables data transmissions between the airplane and a ground station using a VHF network.

accelerate-go distance. The amount of runway required to accelerate the aircraft to V_1, lose an engine, and continue the takeoff to the prescribed obstacle clearance altitude.

accelerate-stop distance. The amount of runway distance required to accelerate the aircraft to a point *immediately prior* to V_1, lose an engine, take the first action to stop the airplane and come to a complete stop on the remaining runway and stopway.

accelerate-stop distance available (ASDA). The runway plus stopway length declared available and suitable for the acceleration and deceleration of an airplane aborting a takeoff.

acceleration altitude (or clean-up altitude). The minimum altitude during departure (usually 400 feet above the takeoff surface) to which the airplane must be climbed before pitch may be lowered for the purpose of accelerating to a speed at which takeoff flaps may be raised.

acclimated. A condition in which a flight crewmember has been in a theater for 72 hours or has been given at least 36 hours free from duty and is considered adjusted to the new time zone.

A-Check. A general inspection of the interior and exterior of an aircraft with selected areas to be checked, typically conducted weekly or biweekly. This includes checking hydraulic, engine oil and cockpit oxygen levels as well as other basic operational inspections. This inspection is performed while the aircraft is still considered to be in service. ETOPS pre-departure checks are similar to and may even be identical to a particular air carrier's A-Check depending on the operations specifications. *See also* maintenance event letter checks.

active control. In the context of operational control, consists of making those tactical decisions and performing those actions necessary to operate a specific flight such as crew scheduling, accepting charter flights from the public, reviewing weather and NOTAMs, and flight planning. Operational control is exercised through both active and passive means. *See also* operational control; passive control.

actual flight time. The actual time it takes to get from departure airport to destination airport. In the context of discussing flight time limitations, Part 121 limitations are based primarily on scheduled amounts of flight time (i.e., historic block hours) not the actual flight time. In Part 117, on the other hand, the flight time limits are both scheduled and actual flight hour limits.

additional emergency exits. Approved emergency exits in the passenger compartments in excess of the minimum number of required emergency exits must meet all of the applicable provisions found in 14 CFR Part 25, except for the minimum access-way requirements, and must be readily accessible.

adequate alternate airport. An airport that is expected to be available during the time period the aircraft will be in proximity to it. The landing performance requirements on an adequate airport are required to be met and that particular airport must have the necessary facilities and services such as ATC, airport lighting, communications, meteorological services, navigation aids, rescue and firefighting services and one suitable instrument approach procedure. *See also* suitable alternate airport.

Administrator. The Federal Aviation Administration Administrator or any person to whom he has delegated his authority.

ADS-B. Automatic Dependent Surveillance–Broadcast equipment, an advanced surveillance technology that combines an aircraft's positioning source, aircraft avionics, and a ground infrastructure to create an accurate surveillance interface between aircraft and ATC.

advanced qualification program (AQP). A type of voluntary training program that offers an alternative to the traditional Part 121 crewmember training and checking requirements. AQP curriculum covers indoctrination, qualification, and continuing qualification training.

advisory circulars (ACs). Issued by the FAA to inform the aviation public in a systemic way of nonregulatory material. An AC is issued to provide guidance and information in a designated subject area or to show a method acceptable to the Administrator for complying with a related 14 CFR part.

advisory light. A status light indicating conditions that require flight crew awareness and may require subsequent flight crew response. If advisory lights are installed in the cockpit, they may be any color except red or green.

age 65 rule. The rule that prohibits the use of pilots in Part 121 operations after they reach the age of 65 years old.

airborne weather radar. A type of radar used to provide an indication to the flight crew of the position and intensity of active convective weather. Part 121 air carriers may not dispatch an airplane under IFR or night VFR conditions when current weather reports indicate that thunderstorms, or other potentially hazardous weather conditions that can be detected with airborne weather radar, may reasonably be expected along the route to be flown, unless the airborne weather radar equipment is in satisfactory operating condition.

air carrier. A person who undertakes directly by lease, or other arrangement, to engage in air transportation.

air carrier certificate. An FAA certification process to ensure that the applicant is to design, document, implement, and audit safety critical processes that do two things: (1) Comply with regulations and safety standards; and (2) Manage hazard-related risks in its operating systems and environment. The process is designed to preclude the certification of applicants who are unwilling or unable to comply with regulations or to conform to safe operating practices. In addition, there is a separate air carrier economic certificate of fitness to conduct air transportation that is issued by the U.S. Department of Transportation that is not directly safety related. A certificate authorizing interstate air transportation may be issued after a finding by the Department that the applicant is "fit, willing, and able" to perform the proposed service. The award of a certificate for foreign authority must also be found to be "consistent with the public convenience and necessity."

air commerce. Interstate, overseas, or foreign air commerce or the transportation of mail by aircraft or any operation or navigation of aircraft within the limits of any federal airway, or any operation or navigation of aircraft which directly affects or which may endanger safety in interstate, overseas, or foreign air commerce.

Air Commerce Act of 1926. The first federal statute imposing regulations on the nascent aviation industry in the United States by establishing the Aeronautics Branch of the Department of Commerce with regulatory authority over safety and the certification of pilots and aircraft.

aircraft listing record. A reference list of the specific aircraft registration numbers an air carrier intends to operate contained in a section of the air carrier's operations specifications.

aircraft maintenance logbook. A logbook used to record any maintenance difficulties or irregularities and any deferred maintenance items for an observed or reported failure or malfunction of airframe, engine, propeller, or other component critical to the safety of flight.

airframe major alterations. Alterations of the following parts and types, when not listed in the aircraft specifications issued by the FAA: wings; tail surfaces; fuselage; engine mounts; control system; landing gear; hull or floats; elements of an airframe including spars, ribs, fittings, shock absorbers, bracing, cowling, fairings, and balance weights; hydraulic and electrical actuating system of components; rotor blades; changes to the empty weight or empty balance that result in an increase in the maximum certificated weight or center of gravity limits of the aircraft; changes to the basic design of the fuel, oil, cooling, heating, cabin pressurization, electrical, hydraulic, de-icing, or exhaust systems; and changes to the wing or to fixed or movable control surfaces which affect flutter and vibration characteristics.

airframe major repairs. Repairs to the parts of an airframe and repairs of the types listed in 14 CFR Part 43, Appendix A (Major Alterations, Major Repairs, and Preventive Maintenance), Paragraph (b), involving the strengthening, reinforcing, splicing, and manufacturing of primary structural members or their replacement, when replacement is by fabrication such as riveting or welding.

Airline Safety and Federal Aviation Administration Extension Act of 2010 (49 USC 40101). This Act, passed by U.S. Congress and signed into law on August 1, 2010, requires first officers in 14 CFR Part 121 operations to hold an Airline Transport Pilot (ATP) certificate. This bill, signed into law as Public Law 111-216, included sweeping regulatory changes (e.g., the creation of Part 117 and significant changes to Part 121 affecting flight crew scheduling).

Airline Transport Pilot Certificate Training Program (ATP CTP). A training program designed to bridge the knowledge gap between a pilot holding a commercial pilot certificate and a pilot operating in an air carrier environment. This requires training in essential subject areas, including aerodynamics, automation, adverse weather conditions, air carrier operations, transport airplane performance, professionalism, and leadership and development. The ATP CTP is designed to ensure an ATP applicant receives the baseline knowledge and experience to prepare them for the duties, responsibilities, and challenges of an air carrier environment.

airplane flight manual or approved flight manual (AFM). A manual prepared by the manufacturer and approved by the FAA, designed to give a flight crew all of the operational and performance information it needs in order to operate the aircraft safely.

airport/standby reserve (ASR). A defined duty period during which a flight crewmember is required by a certificate holder to be at an airport for a possible assignment.

air transportation. Interstate, overseas, or foreign air commerce or the transportation of mail by aircraft.

airways navigation facilities. Those ICAO standard navigation aids (VOR, VOR/DME, and/or NDB) that are used to establish the en route airway structure. These facilities are also used to establish the degree of navigation accuracy required for air traffic control and Class I navigation.

airworthiness certificate. *See* standard airworthiness certificate.

airworthiness directive (AD). A form of communication used by the FAA to notify aircraft owners and operators of unsafe conditions that may exist because of design defects, maintenance, or other cases and to specify the conditions under which the product may continue to be operated. An AD is a regulatory requirement, just like any FAR.

airworthiness release. A required logbook entry returning an aircraft to service after maintenance, preventive maintenance, or alterations were performed on the aircraft.

airworthiness responsibility. Responsibility by an air carrier for assuring compliance with manual procedures and company policies relating to airworthiness. This responsibility may not be delegated by the air carrier.

airworthy. An aircraft that conforms to its type design and is in condition for safe operation.

alcohol abuse prevention program. A FAA required program, described in 14 CFR Part 120, Subpart F, which is somewhat similar to the drug testing program of Subpart E. This program is designed to help prevent accidents and injuries resulting from the misuse of alcohol by employees who perform safety-sensitive functions in aviation.

all-cargo operation. Flight operations that do not include passenger-carrying operations. Regarding flight time and duty time regulations, all-cargo operators are exempt from Part 117 regulations, which apply to all passenger-carrying operations conducted by 14 CFR Part 121 certificate holders regardless of whether the kind of operation being conducted is domestic, flag, or supplemental. For those Part 121 certificate holders conducting all-cargo operations, the operations must be conducted under the provisions prescribed in Part 121, Subparts Q (domestic), R (flag), or S (supplemental), as applicable. However, a Part 121 certificate holder conducting all-cargo operations may opt to conduct its operations under the provisions prescribed in Part 117.

alteration and repair report. A report that must be submitted to the FAA principal maintenance inspector (PMI) assigned to the Part 121 air carrier any time that air carrier performs a major alteration or major repair of an aircraft's airframe, engine, propeller, or other aircraft system. The air carrier must also maintain a copy of this report available for inspection by the air carrier's principal maintenance inspector.

alternate airport. An airport that the aircraft dispatcher, flight follower, or captain may designate to be used if weather conditions at the departure or intended destination are less than required or if a landing at the intended airport becomes inadvisable. When an alternate is required for a flight, that airport designated as an alternate for destination or as a takeoff alternate must meet the requirements for alternate airports in the operations specifications Paragraph C055.

alternate airport weather forecast conditions. The official weather conditions forecast by an authorized weather forecaster to exist at an alternate airport for a specified period of time before and after scheduled arrival at that alternate, if used.

alternate airport weather minimums. The minimum forecast ceiling and visibility required to permit an airport to be listed (filed) as an alternate airport in a flight plan. *See* standard alternate (weather) minimums; derived alternate (weather) minimums.

alternate fuel. The fuel necessary for a flight to make a missed approach at the destination airport, fly from the destination to the most distant alternate airport, make an IFR approach (if available forecasts indicate conditions will be below VFR minimums), and make a landing.

alternative method of compliance (AMOC). The FAA requires operators to comply with all regulations. However, recognizing that there is often more than one way to accomplish something, it will very often approve a method of compliance different than the method required in the regulation. The standard required to be met in evaluating requests for alternative methods of compliance is that the method provide an equivalent level of safety. If it does, then the FAA may (but is not required to) approve the request.

annual line check (also called line check). A routine evaluation of a crewmember's skills while operating live, line flights. These checkrides are conducted in the normal course of business by company check airmen and consist of observations of one or more legs.

annual recurrent ground and flight training. The objective of required recurrent training is to ensure that flight crewmembers continue to be knowledgeable of, and proficient in, their specific aircraft type and duty assignment. Periodic recurrent training also provides operators with an opportunity to introduce flight crewmembers to changes in company operating procedures, in crewmember duties and responsibilities, and in developments within the operating environment and aviation industry.

Appendix A to Part 121: First Aid Kits and Emergency Medical Kits. Provides guidance about the required content of onboard emergency medical equipment, including first-aid kits, emergency medical kits (EMK) and automated external defibrillators (AED). Appendix A contains a number of tables listing the types, content and minimum number of required onboard medical equipment.

Appendix B to Part 121: Airplane Flight Recorder Specification. Specifies exactly what performance parameters are recorded in an airplane flight data recorder (FDR) and the technical specifications applicable to that data. Appendix B contains approximately 50 parameters that may be recorded on the flight data recorder and sets forth the specific technical standards applicable to each parameter.

Appendix E to Part 121—Flight Training Requirements. Appendix E covers the maneuvers and procedures required for pilot initial, transition, and upgrade flight training, which are also set forth in the certificate holder's approved low-altitude windshear flight training program (required by §121.424) and extended envelope training (required by §121.423).

Appendix F to Part 121—Proficiency Check Requirements. Appendix F covers the maneuvers and procedures required for pilot proficiency checks (by §121.441). All required maneuvers and procedures must be performed inflight except to the extent that certain maneuvers and procedures may be performed in an airplane simulator with a visual system (visual simulator), an airplane simulator without a visual system (nonvisual simulator), or a training device.

Appendix H to Part 121: Advanced Simulation. This appendix provides guidelines and a means for achieving flight crew training in advanced airplane simulators. The requirements in this appendix are in addition to the simulator approval requirements in §121.407.

appliance major alteration. Alterations of the basic design not made in accordance with recommendations of the appliance manufacturer or in accordance with an FAA airworthiness directive. In addition, changes in the basic design of radio communication and navigation equipment approved under type certification or a Technical Standard Order that have an effect on frequency stability, noise level, sensitivity, selectivity, distortion, spurious radiation, AVC characteristics, or ability to meet environmental test conditions and other changes that have an effect on the performance of the equipment are also appliance major alterations.

appliance major repair. Repairs of the following types of appliances: calibration and repair of instruments, calibration of avionics or computer equipment, rewinding of the field coil of an electrical accessory, complete disassembly of complex hydraulic power valves, and overhaul of pressure type carburetors and pressure type fuel, oil and hydraulic pumps.

approved means to assist the occupants in descending to the ground. In regards to emergency escape equipment required for aircraft certification, 14 CFR §121.310 requires that if the airplane's emergency exit (other than over the wing) is more than 6 feet from the ground with the airplane on the ground and the landing gear extended, it must have an approved means to assist the occupants in descending to the ground (e.g., inflatable escape slide). An assisting means that deploys automatically must be armed during taxiing, takeoffs, and landings.

approved repair station. A maintenance facility certificated under 14 CFR Part 145 to perform maintenance functions.

augmented flight crew. A flight crew that has more than the minimum number of flight crewmembers required by the airplane type certificate to operate the aircraft, to allow a flight crewmember to be replaced by another qualified flight crewmember for in-flight rest.

auto flight guidance system (AFGS). Aircraft systems, such as an autopilot, autothrottles, displays, and controls, that are interconnected in such a manner so as to allow the crew to automatically control the aircraft's lateral and vertical flight path and speed. A flight management system is sometimes associated with an AFGS.

available landing distance (ALD). The portion of a runway available for landing and roll-out for aircraft cleared for land and hold short operations (LAHSO). This distance is measured from the landing threshold to hold-short point.

aviation safety inspector's credentials: Form 110A. The credentials issued to qualified aviation safety inspectors by the FAA for use in the performance of official duties. Whenever, in performing the duties of conducting an inspection, an inspector of the Federal Aviation Administration presents Form FAA 110A to the pilot-in-command of an aircraft operated by a certificate holder, the inspector must be given free and uninterrupted access to the pilot's compartment of that aircraft.

aviation security program. A program that provides for the safety of passengers and property traveling in air transportation against acts of criminal violence and air piracy.

aviation training device (ATD). A training device, other than a full flight simulator (FFS) or flight training device (FTD), that has been evaluated, qualified, and approved by the Administrator. An ATD includes the equipment and computer programs necessary to represent aircraft (or set of aircraft) operations in ground and flight conditions having the full range of capabilities of the systems installed in the device as described in FAA AC 61-136 for a specific Basic or Advanced qualification level.

bailment. The temporary placement of control over or possession of personal property by one person (the bailor) into the hands of another (the bailee) for a designated purpose upon which the parties have agreed. This can be either a gratuitous bailment (meaning no form of compensation is paid) or a bailment for hire.

bailment for hire. The temporary placement of control over or possession of personal property by one person (the bailor) into the hands of another (the bailee) for a designated purpose upon which the parties have agreed, in exchange for money, services or other compensation.

balanced field length. The amount of runway and stopway that allows an aircraft to accelerate to V_1, lose an engine, and then either stop on the remaining runway or continue with guaranteed obstacle clearance.

balanced field limit. The point at which the rejected takeoff line intersects the continued takeoff line. The balanced field limit is the maximum limit for both aircraft weight (balanced field limit weight) and aircraft speed (balanced field limit V_1 speed).

base month. In regard to recurrent training, the month in which training or a renewal of a medical certificate (FAA physical) is due. The FAA uses a three-month "eligibility period" comprised of the month before the base month (called "month early"), the base month, and the month after the base month (called the "grace month"). Recurrent training performed at any time during the three-month eligibility period is considered to have been done during the base month.

Basic FAR Part 135 operator. A certificate holder who will use more than one pilot-in-command and will be authorized, because of the operator's limited size and scope, certain deviations from the manual content, management personnel, and training program curriculum requirements of 14 CFR Part 135. Normally, a deviation will not be granted to operators intending to use more than five pilots, including seconds-in-command; more than five aircraft; or more than three different types of aircraft; or who intend to use check airmen or aircraft type-certificated for more than nine passenger seats; conduct Category II or III approach operations; or conduct operations outside the United States, Canada, Mexico, and the Caribbean.

basic indoctrination ground training (indoc). The first training a new crewmember or dispatcher receives. This training includes such things as duties and responsibilities of crewmembers or dispatchers, FARs, ops specs, and company manuals.

B-Check. A bi-monthly inspection of the aircraft system fluid levels, emergency equipment, aircraft placards, etc. Select inspection panels are removed and aircraft systems are checked. B-checks are usually performed at a hangar or remote maintenance ramp area with the aircraft out of service for a short period of time (i.e., one or two days). *See also* maintenance event letter checks.

Bureau of Air Commerce. In 1934, the Department of Commerce renamed the Aeronautics Branch the Bureau of Air Commerce to reflect the growing importance of aviation to the nation. In one of its first acts, the Bureau encouraged a group of airlines to establish the first air traffic control centers.

buy-back procedures (inspections). During an inspection, each defect is written up as a non-routine repair (NRR) record, which is translated into a set of work cards which is used by the maintenance crew to rectify the defect. Once the defect is rectified, it may also generate additional inspections—typically referred to as buy-back inspections (or buy-back procedures)—to ensure that the work meets necessary standards.

calendar day. A 24-hour period from 0000 through 2359 using Coordinated Universal Time or local time.

calibration of precision tools. Many tools that are used in aircraft maintenance and other fields requiring precision measurements and tolerances must periodically be calibrated to a measurement standard. The FAA requires a maintenance operation to have the calibration done by a certificated, approved facility that can trace the measurements back to the National Institute of Standards and Technology (NIST), a manufacturer, or an accepted international standard. These include items such as torque wrenches and scales for mechanical tools and multimeters and frequency meters for electronic equipment.

cargo and baggage compartment smoke or fire detection systems. Several different fire protection schemes are used with respect to cargo and baggage compartments. The difference in detection methods used depends primarily upon the access to the particular type of compartment. *See* Class A cargo or baggage compartment *through* Class E cargo compartment.

cargo and baggage storage compartments. A compartment designed and intended for the stowage of cargo, baggage, carry-on articles, and equipment (such as life rafts).

cargo compartment classification. A system of classifying cargo compartments according to the fire detection and protection capabilities installed. The FAA currently lists four compartment classifications: Class A, Class B, Class C and Class E. Class D is no longer permitted on U.S.-certificated aircraft. *See* Class A cargo or baggage compartment *through* Class E cargo compartment.

carriage. In the context of transportation, carriage is the act of transporting persons or property between two or more places.

carriage of all comers. In the context of air transportation, when a carrier has indicated a willingness to carry (transport) anyone or anything that is within a class of people or property, for which a tariff is paid. While the carriage may be so limited in scope that it does not apply to "all," the FAA will view a very small, indefinite number, such as four or five persons, to be a willingness to carry anyone.

carriage of infants and children under 2 years of age. A child (under two) may be held by an adult who is occupying an approved seat or berth provided the child does not occupy or use any restraining device. A child under 2 years of age may occupy an approved child restraint system furnished by the certificate holder, a parent, guardian, or attendant designated by the child's parent or guardian to attend to the safety of the child during the flight. The child must be accompanied by a parent, guardian, or attendant designated by the child's parent or guardian.

CASS. *See* Cockpit Access Security System; continuing analysis and surveillance system.

Category I instrument approach. Any authorized precision or nonprecision instrument approach which is conducted with a minimum height for IFR flight not less than 200 feet above the touchdown zone and a minimum visibility of not less than ½ statute mile.

caution light. For airplanes certificated prior to 2010, annunciator lights were required for certain types of events. An event which wasn't immediately critical but could become so with the passage of time would be annunciated with an amber-colored light called a caution light.

C-Check. A type of maintenance inspection usually performed every two years or after a specific number of flight hours. A C-Check, performed in a maintenance hangar, takes up to two weeks and involves extensive inspection and overhaul, including aircraft systems checks, thorough cleaning and servicing of the entire aircraft, minor structural inspections, and compliance with any manufacturer's service bulletin requirements. *See* maintenance event letter checks.

ceiling. The height above the ground or water of the base of the lowest layer of clouds that is reported as broken, overcast, or obscuration, and not classified as "thin" or "partial." Partial obscuration (-X), thin broken (-BKN), and thin overcast (-OVC) do not constitute a ceiling.

certificated land airports. A land airport meeting the requirements of and certified under Part 139. Part 139 prescribes rules governing the certification and operation of airports in any state of the United States, the District of Columbia, or any territory or possession of the United States. It requires the FAA to issue airport operating certificates to airports that serve scheduled and unscheduled air carrier aircraft with more than 30 seats or that the FAA Administrator requires to have a certificate. For aircraft larger than 30 seats, 14 CFR §121.590 prohibits operations to or from an airport unless that airport is a federally certificated land airport under Part 139.

certificate holder. A person holding an FAA operating certificate when that person engages in scheduled passenger or public charter passenger operations, or both.

certificate holding district office (CHDO). The flight standards district office that has responsibility for administering the certificate and is charged with the overall inspection of the certificate holder's operations.

certificate of demonstrated proficiency. A certificate issued by the FAA to persons who have successfully completed flight attendant training to serve on a Part 121 or Part 135 aircraft that has 20 or more seats. No person may serve as a flight attendant aboard an aircraft of an air carrier unless that person holds a certificate of demonstrated proficiency issued by the FAA. *See also* flight attendant.

certified landing distance. Certified or "unfactored" landing distances in the manufacturer-supplied AFM reflect performance in a "flight test environment" that is not necessarily representative of the normal day-to-day flight operations (i.e., it does *not* include any safety margin, and represents the best possible performance the airplane is capable of for the given conditions).

check airman. A check airman (airplane) is a person who is qualified, and permitted, to conduct flight checks or instruction in an airplane, in a flight simulator, or in a flight training device for a particular type airplane.

check pilot. *See* check airman.

chief executive officer (CEO). The CEO's primary duty is the relationship between the air carrier and the board of directors of the company and the oversight of senior financial matters.

chief inspector. A Part 121-required maintenance position. A chief inspector supervises all company inspectors and auditors in the performance of their duties and ensures all work performed on company aircraft conforms with the approved company maintenance manual and all applicable federal regulations. A chief inspector also conducts air carrier maintenance program audits and supervises the scheduling and conduct of all maintenance training.

chief operating officer (COO). Ensures a successful working relationship is maintained between various top air carrier management positions.

chief pilot. Position responsible for the supervision of all the air carrier's pilots.

circadian fatigue. The reduced performance during nighttime hours, particularly during an individual's window of circadian low (WOCL) (typically between 2:00 a.m. and 05:59 a.m.).

circadian rhythms. A daily alteration in a person's behavior and physiology controlled by an internal biological clock located in the brain. Examples of circadian rhythms include body temperature, melatonin levels, cognitive performance, alertness levels, and sleep patterns.

Civil Aeronautics Act of 1938. Reorganized federal regulation of aviation by creating a new organization called the Civil Aeronautics Authority and transferring the responsibilities of the Bureau of Air Commerce to it.

Civil Aeronautics Administration (CAA). A U.S. federal agency established in 1940 with the reorganization of the Civil Aeronautics Authority (also CAA). The Civil Aeronautics Administration was given the responsibility for operation of the air traffic control system, airman and aircraft certification, safety enforcement, and airway development. In 1958 the responsibilities of the CAA were folded into the newly established Federal Aviation Agency (now Administration).

Civil Aeronautics Authority (CAA). A U.S. federal agency established in 1938 by the Civil Aeronautics Act, which transferred from the Bureau of Air Commerce the responsibilities for the air traffic control system, and regulatory authority over safety and the certification of pilots and aircraft.

Civil Aeronautics Board (CAB). A U.S. agency created as part of the 1940 reorganization of federal oversight and regulation of commercial aviation. The CAB was created and given the former CAA's authority to issue air carrier route certificates and to regulate airline fares. From 1940 onward, the CAA was responsible for safety-related activities and the CAB was charged with regulation of the economics of the airline industry in the United States.

Class A cargo or baggage compartment. A cargo or baggage compartment in which the presence of a fire would be easily discovered by a crewmember while at his station, and each part of the compartment is easily accessible in flight.

Class B cargo or baggage compartment. A compartment in which there is sufficient access in flight to enable a crewmember to effectively reach any part of the compartment with the contents of a hand fire extinguisher; when the access provisions are being used, no hazardous quantity of smoke, flames, or extinguishing agent will enter any compartment occupied by the crew or passengers; and there is a separate approved smoke detector or fire detector system to give warning at the pilot or flight engineer station.

Class C cargo or baggage compartment. A compartment not meeting the requirements for either a Class A or B compartment but in which there is a separate approved smoke detector or fire detector system to give warning at the pilot or flight engineer station; there is an approved built-in fire extinguishing or suppression system controllable from the cockpit; there are means to exclude hazardous quantities of smoke, flames, or extinguishing agent from any compartment occupied by the crew or passengers; and there are means to control ventilation and drafts within the compartment so that the extinguishing agent used can control any fire that may start within the compartment.

Class D cargo or baggage compartment. No longer defined or allowed by the FAA. Previously allowed in older aircraft, they were eliminated after the ValuJet Flight 592 accident in 1996. Class D compartments were not accessible during flight and had no fire suppression systems, but instead were designed to extinguish fires by allowing the theoretically limited oxygen to be consumed and subsequently smother the fire.

Class E cargo compartment. A compartment on airplanes used only for the carriage of cargo and in which there is a separate approved smoke or fire detector system to give warning at the pilot or flight engineer station; there are means to shut off the ventilating airflow to, or within, the compartment, and the controls for these means are accessible to the flight crew in the crew compartment; there are means to exclude hazardous quantities of smoke, flames, or noxious gases from the flight crew compartment; and the required crew emergency exits are accessible under any cargo loading condition.

Class I navigation. Any enroute flight operation or portion of an operation that is conducted entirely within the operational service volumes of ICAO standard airway navigation facilities. Class I navigation also includes enroute flight operations over routes designated with an "MEA GAP" (or the ICAO equivalent).

Class II navigation. Any en route flight operation that is not defined as Class I navigation. It is any enroute operation that takes place outside the service volume of ICAO standard airway navigation facilities; it does not include operations within an "MEA GAP."

clean-up altitude (or acceleration altitude). The minimum altitude during departure (usually 400 feet above the takeoff surface) to which the airplane must be climbed before pitch may be lowered for the purpose of accelerating to a speed at which takeoff flaps may be raised.

clearway. An area beyond the runway, not less than 500 feet wide, centrally located about the extended centerline of the runway and under the control of the airport authorities.

climb limit weight. The maximum weight that still guarantees an aircraft can proceed from the point 35 feet above the runway to 1,500 feet above the runway surface (or specified higher altitude) while maintaining required climb gradients in order to achieve adequate obstacle clearance.

Cockpit Access Security System (CASS) A set of required procedures combined with the use of a computer database system that the certificate holder's employees who are assigned cockpit access verification tasks (e.g., gate agents) can use to positively confirm the identity, employment status, and flight deck eligibility of the person requesting cockpit access. CASS is most commonly used to verify a pilot's eligibility to ride on the cockpit jump seat.

cockpit check procedure/checklist. A list in either printed or electronic form that provides a detailed list of items to be checked with regard to any critical or important procedures or process utilized in flying, controlling or managing an aircraft in flight or on the ground.

cockpit voice recorder (CVR). Devices that are able to record multiple channels of audio from within the cockpit of an aircraft. In older models, the recordings were on 30-minute continuous audio tapes, whereas more modern devices use electronic media for storage. Cockpit audio is recorded from several microphones placed near each flight crewmember and other locations. The design and installation must provide for the survivability of the data in the worst of crashes and post-accident fires. *See also* flight data recorders.

Code of Federal Regulations (CFR). A codification (arrangement of) the general and permanent rules published in the *Federal Register* by the executive departments and agencies of the federal government. These rules provide for the safe and orderly conduct of flight operations and prescribe airman privileges and limitations.

commercial flying. In the context of flight and duty time regulations, any flying done for compensation or hire. There are two aspects to this: Either the pilot is being compensated for any flying that he or she does, and/or the entity arranging the flight has been hired, regardless if the pilot is compensated.

commercial operator. A person who, for compensation or hire, engages in the carriage by aircraft in air commerce of persons or property.

common carriage. Any operation for compensation or hire in which an operator holds itself out (by advertising or any other means) as willing to furnish transportation for any member of the public who seeks the services that the operator is offering. The operator openly offers service for a fee to any member of the public.

common carrier. Any entity performing common carriage.

common type rating. A common type rating allows pilot-in-command (PIC) operations in all models covered in the type rating. When a type rating covers multiple aircraft models, the term common type rating is used to describe this authorization. *See also* type rating.

communication record. An air carrier conducting domestic or flag operations is required to record each enroute radio voice or ACARS contact between the certificate holder and its pilots. These communication records are required to be kept for at least 30 days. *See also* ACARS.

commuter operation. A common carriage, passenger-carrying operation using aircraft having a maximum passenger-seat configuration of 9 seats or less, excluding any crewmember seat, and a maximum payload capacity of 7,500 pounds or less, with a frequency of operations of at least five round trips per calendar week on at least one route between two or more points.

company flight manual (CFM). An airplane flight manual (AFM) developed by and/or for a specific operator.

compensation or hire. The entity providing the flight has been hired and/or the pilot(s) are being compensated for their flight time duty.

composition of flight crews. The number and type of flight crewmembers who operate an aircraft while in flight. The composition of a flight crew depends on the type of aircraft, the duration of the flight and the kind of operation being conducted. The minimum number of flight crewmembers is stated in the airworthiness certificate or the airplane flight manual approved for that type airplane and required by the kind of operation being conducted. For all Part 121 operations, the minimum pilot crew is two pilots and the certificate holder shall designate one pilot as pilot-in-command and the other second-in-command. If the aircraft certification requires a flight engineer, then the flight crew must be a minimum of three people.

computer-based training. A type of interactive education in which the student learns by executing special self-paced, hands-on training programs on a computer.

configuration deviation list (CDL). Similar to an aircraft's minimum equipment list (MEL), an FAA-approved CDL contains allowances and limitations for aircraft to operate without secondary airframe or engine parts while still being considered airworthy.

configuration, maintenance, and procedures (CMP) document. A document approved by the FAA that contains minimum configuration, operating, and maintenance requirements, hardware life-limits, and master minimum equipment list (MMEL) constraints necessary for an airplane-engine combination to meet ETOPS type design approval requirements.

consecutive nighttime operations. Consecutive flight duty periods that infringe on the window of circadian low (WOCL). *See also* window of circadian low.

contingency fuel. The increment of fuel necessary for a flight to compensate for any known traffic delays and to compensate for any other condition that may delay the landing of the flight.

continuing analysis and surveillance system (CASS). An air carrier quality assurance system, which must consist of the following functions: surveillance, controls, analysis, corrective action, and follow-up. Together, these functions form a closed-loop system that allows the air carrier to monitor the quality of its maintenance.

continuous airworthiness maintenance program (CAMP). A system of continuing surveillance, investigation, data collection, analysis, corrective action, and corrective action follow-up that ensures all parts of the maintenance program are effective and are being performed in accordance with a particular air carrier's maintenance manual. Introduced by the FAA on May 20, 1964, this program was created in response to safety concerns and discoveries of weaknesses in the maintenance programs of some air carriers discovered during accident investigations and surveillance of operator maintenance activities. CAMP strengthens requirements for air carrier maintenance safety management activities.

Contract Air Mail Act of 1925. The first significant step in the federal regulation and support of the developing airline and aviation industries. It provided for contracting of carriage of U.S. mail by certificated airlines, thus beginning the commercial phase of aviation development in the United States.

control systems gust locks. Mechanical locking mechanisms that can be placed upon or incorporated into the design of the primary flight control surfaces (i.e., elevators, ailerons or rudders) to prevent damage from being blown back and forth in gusty wind conditions. With the gust lock installed or activated, the surfaces will remain in place and undamaged in heavy, gusty winds.

crewmember. A person assigned to perform duty in an aircraft during flight time.

crewmember and dispatcher records. Records of each crewmember and each aircraft dispatcher (domestic and flag operations only). This record must show whether each crewmember or aircraft dispatcher complies with the applicable sections of the regulations, including, but not limited to, proficiency and route checks; airplane and route qualifications; training; required physical examinations; and flight, duty, and rest time records. These records must also include each action taken concerning the release from employment or physical or professional disqualification of any flight crewmember or aircraft dispatcher. This record must be kept for at least six months.

crewmember interphone system. An interphone system for use by aircraft crewmembers that provides a means of two-way communication between the pilot compartment and each passenger compartment and between the pilot compartment and each galley located on other than the main passenger deck level. 14 CFR §121.319 requires aircraft with more than 19 passenger seats to be equipped with such a system capable of operation independent of the public address system.

crewmember oxygen. A required emergency equipment system installed on pressurized aircraft to supply crewmembers with oxygen, intended for use when the cabin pressurization system has failed and the cabin pressure altitude has climbed above 10,000 feet.

crew resource management (CRM) training. Training that focuses on the interrelationships between crewmembers, dispatch, maintenance, the FAA, and other agencies. It is especially designed to help crewmembers learn to communicate effectively and to use all available resources when dealing with in-flight problems or emergencies.

crew seat belts/shoulder harnesses. Protective multipoint harness restraint systems that must be worn by flight crew at specified times in flight that prevent the pilot from being thrown from his or her seat in normal operations or in an accident.

critical phase of flight. The phases of flight that include all ground operations involving taxi, takeoff, and landing, and all other flight operations conducted below 10,000 feet, except cruise flight.

cumulative fatigue. A "sleep debt" caused by long periods of time on duty across a series of days that infringe upon an individual's opportunity to sleep.

cumulative flight time limitations. "Rolling" flight time limitations that include all flying performed for any certificate holder or Part 91K Program manager during the applicable periods. 14 CFR §117.23(b) stipulates that a flight crewmember's total flight time may not exceed 100 hours in the last 672 hours or 1,000 hours in the last 365 calendar days. The cumulative flight time limits are hard limits and could only be exceeded after a flight takes off.

curriculum. A FAA approved curriculum for each type of airplane and each crewmember or dispatcher training course. This curriculum must specify things such as the content of the course, the training devices and pictorials to be used, the maneuvers to be taught, and the number of programmed hours (or reduced programmed hours) that are approved.

D-Check. Also called a heavy maintenance visit (HMV). An extensive overhaul of the airframe and most of the aircraft's systems, generally required once every decade of service. D-Checks are restrictively time consuming and expensive, usually taking close to two months to complete. During a D-Check the aircraft is stripped down to the supporting structure of the airframe. All systems are overhauled and inspected. The aircraft is usually painted and then functionally checked before going back into line service. *See also* maintenance event letter checks.

deadhead transportation. Transportation of a flight crewmember as a passenger or non-operating flight crewmember, by any mode of transportation (i.e., ground or air), as required by a certificate holder, excluding transportation to or from a suitable accommodation. All time spent in deadhead transportation is duty and is not rest.

decision altitude/decision height (DA/DH). The specified missed approach point on a precision approach decision altitude (DA), expressed in feet above mean sea level, or ILS approach (DH), expressed in feet above ground level, to either continue the approach or execute a missed approach.

declared runway distance. The maximum runway distance available and suitable for meeting takeoff and landing distance performance requirements. All FAA Part 139 airports report declared distances for each runway.

deferred maintenance item (DMI). A deferred maintenance discrepancy or maintenance carry-over item to be repaired within an approved time period.

Department of Homeland Security (DHS). A cabinet-level department of the U.S. federal government, created in response to the September 11, 2001 attacks, and with the primary responsibilities of protecting the territory of the United States and protectorates from and responding to terrorist attacks, man-made accidents, and natural disasters.

Department of Transportation (DOT). Cabinet-level department in the executive branch of the United States. It is charged with overall transportation policy setting for all modes of interstate transportation in the United States.

departure airport alternate airport. (Also known as a takeoff alternate.) Required when weather conditions are such that an aircraft departs an airport with takeoff minimums below the departure airport's landing minimums.

derived alternate (weather) minimums. A method by which the weather minimums required to file an airport as an alternate airport may be reduced from the standard requirements of 600 feet and 2 statute miles for a precision approach and 800 feet and 2 miles for a nonprecision approach.

designated fire zones. Areas on an aircraft susceptible to fire, which include the engine power and accessory section and auxiliary power unit (APU) compartment. Additional designated fire zones are listed in 14 CFR §25.1181.

destination alternate airport. A type of alternate airport used when the forecast for the destination airport is less than "perfect" weather. In that case, the FAA requires air carriers to have a "contingency plan" in the form of a destination alternate airport in case weather conditions at the destination airport require a diversion.

deviation authority. The authority granted by the FAA to operate an aircraft outside of FAR compliance in order to perform operations under a military contract or in an emergency circumstance.

differences training. The training required for crewmembers and dispatchers who have qualified and served on a particular type airplane when the FAA determines that additional training is necessary before that crewmember/dispatcher serves in the same capacity on a particular variation of that airplane. (For example, a pilot qualified on the 767-200 for a given company must receive training on the differences of a 767-400 before flying that new model.)

digital flight data recorders (DFDR). *See* flight data recorders (FDR and DFDR).

direct air carrier. A person who provides or offers to provide air transportation and who has operational control over the operational functions performed in providing that transportation.

director of maintenance (DM). Position responsible for all air carrier maintenance and inspection personnel.

director of operations (DO). Position responsible for ensuring all flight operations are conducted safely and in compliance with all FARs, ops specs, and company policies.

director of safety. Position responsible for the overall safety functions required of a Part 121 air carrier. Conducts safety reviews of all functions including public safety, security, maintenance, and flight operation.

dispatch. The flight planning function performed by Part 121 carriers. Dispatch is a department in the airline that is responsible for all flight planning and control.

dispatcher. An airline employee who is responsible for authorizing the departure of an aircraft. The dispatcher must ensure, among other things, that the aircraft's crew has all the proper information necessary for the flight and that the aircraft is in proper mechanical condition. The dispatcher shares responsibility with the pilot-in-command for the dispatch of every flight.

dispatcher initial training. Introductory airline dispatcher training. 14 CFR §121.422 requires that initial and transition aircraft dispatcher ground training curriculum segments include instruction in at least general dispatch subjects, aircraft characteristics, operations procedures, and emergency procedures.

dispatcher resource management (DRM) training. Training that focuses on the interrelationships between crewmembers, dispatch, maintenance, the FAA, and other agencies. It is especially designed to help dispatchers learn to communicate effectively and to use all available resources when dealing with in-flight problems or emergencies.

dispatching. A domestic or flag flight must be authorized by a dispatcher or "dispatch released." 14 CFR Part 121, Subpart U, contains the rules applicable to dispatching domestic and flag operations.

dispatch release document. A document required to be prepared by an air carrier's licensed dispatcher and carried on board a flight for domestic and flag operations. The dispatch release document includes the identification number of the aircraft, flight number, departure airport, intermediate stops, destination airport, alternate airports, and minimum fuel supply. It also must list whether the flight will be a VFR or IFR operation, ETOPS, and contain the latest weather reports and forecasts at the time of departure. Both the pilot-in-command and the dispatcher must sign the dispatch release; this may be done electronically.

domestic all-cargo operations. Domestic flight operations that do not include passenger-carrying operations. Regarding flight time and duty time regulations, all-cargo operators are exempt from Part 117 regulations, which apply to all passenger-carrying operations conducted by 14 CFR Part 121 certificate holders regardless of whether the kind of operation being conducted is domestic, flag, or supplemental. For Part 121 certificate holders conducting all-cargo operations, the certificate holder conducts its operations under the provisions prescribed in Part 121, Subparts Q (domestic), R (flag), or S (supplemental), as applicable. However, a Part 121 certificate holder conducting all-cargo operations may opt to conduct its operations under the provisions prescribed in Part 117.

domestic operation. Any scheduled passenger-carrying operation conducted between any points within the 48 contiguous states of the United States and the District of Columbia by any U.S. citizen engaged in common carriage using airplanes having a passenger seating configuration of more than 30 seats, excluding any required crewmember seat, or a payload capacity of more than 7,500 pounds.

driftdown altitude. The lowest altitude at which an aircraft can maintain a net flight path that allows the aircraft to clear all terrain and obstructions within 5 statute miles by at least 2,000 feet vertically and with a positive slope at 1,500 feet above the airport.

driftdown technique. Driftdown technique is used after an aircraft experiences an engine failure and begins a driftdown descent. The standard air carrier emergency driftdown descent procedure begins with the flight crew completing their emergency procedures and maintaining altitude with maximum thrust on the remaining engine(s). The flight crew allows the aircraft to slow from the all engine cruising speed to the best engine out climb speed (now the "target driftdown airspeed"). Once the aircraft has slowed to this target driftdown airspeed, a descent is begun at that airspeed with maximum thrust on the remaining engine until the aircraft reaches its single engine absolute ceiling.

drug education program. The FAA sets drug and alcohol education and training requirements for safety-sensitive employees and supervisors who will make reasonable suspicion testing decisions. Air carriers must implement an employee drug and alcohol education program that at a minimum includes the effects and consequences of drug use on individual health, safety, and work environment; the manifestations and behavioral cues that may indicate drug use and abuse; and the consequences for covered employees found to have violated the prohibitions in Part 120, including the requirement that the employee be removed immediately from performing safety-sensitive functions.

drug testing based on reasonable cause. An air carrier must test each employee who performs a safety-sensitive function and is reasonably suspected of having used a prohibited drug. The decision to test must be based on a reasonable and articulable belief that the employee is using a prohibited drug on the basis of specific contemporaneous physical, behavioral, or performance indicators of probable drug use.

drug training program. *See* drug education program.

dry lease. An aircraft leased without a crew.

duty. Any task that a flight crewmember performs as required by the certificate holder, including but not limited to flight duty period, flight duty, pre- and post-flight duties, administrative work, training, deadhead transportation, aircraft positioning on the ground, aircraft loading, and aircraft servicing.

duty aloft. Duty time aloft. It is restricted for Part 121 Subpart S supplemental operations with more than two pilots. This includes all time spent aloft in an aircraft (i.e., all time while serving on the flightdeck plus any time spent during rest breaks).

duty day. Begins from the "sign-in" or first duty assignment and continues until the beginning of a rest period.

duty period. A period of duty that begins when a flight crewmember is required to report for duty with the intention of conducting a flight, a series of flights, or positioning or ferrying flights, and ends when the aircraft is parked after the last flight and there is no intention for further aircraft movement by the same flight crewmember. A duty period includes deadhead transportation before a flight segment without an intervening required rest period; training conducted in an aircraft, flight simulator or flight training device; and airport/standby reserve.

duty to care. The level of responsibility that a person (or company) has toward others to protect them from harm.

e-CFR. The electronic Code of Federal Regulations, the Office of the Federal Register's online version of the Code of Federal Regulations.

electronic flight bag (EFB). An electronic display and information storage device intended primarily for flight crewmember use that includes the hardware and software necessary to support all the functions of paper-based manuals and charts.

emergency airworthiness directive (EAD). An airworthiness directive issued when an unsafe condition exists that requires immediate action by an owner/operator. The intent of an Emergency AD is to rapidly correct an urgent safety of flight situation. *See also* airworthiness directive.

emergency equipment. Equipment an aircraft must carry to deal with a number of different emergency situations. Emergency equipment includes such items as hand fire extinguishers, first aid kits, a crash ax, flotation devices and a megaphone.

emergency equipment: extended overwater operations. Additional emergency equipment required for extended overwater operations, including items such as life preservers, life rafts, survival kits, pyrotechnic signaling devices, and an emergency locator transmitter.

emergency equipment: operations over uninhabited terrain. Emergency equipment required for flag, supplemental, and certain domestic operations over uninhabited terrain to facilitate search and rescue in remote areas. This includes such items as suitable pyrotechnic signaling devices, an approved survival type emergency locator transmitter, and suitable survival kits.

emergency evacuation demonstration. For aircraft with more than 44 passenger seats, each air carrier must perform a full or partial (as applicable) actual emergency evacuation demonstration, proving the ability to evacuate the aircraft in 90 seconds or less.

emergency exit access. Unobstructed access to emergency exits must be provided for each passenger-carrying transport category airplane. The number, size and type of emergency exits are strictly regulated.

emergency exit locator sign. An electrically illuminated sign required for each emergency exit to clearly direct passengers to the emergency exit location.

emergency exit operating handles. The handles that open the emergency exit doors. The location of each passenger emergency exit operating handle and instructions for opening the exit must be shown in accordance with the requirements under which the airplane was type certificated.

emergency flotation means. For overwater operations, each aircraft must be equipped with life preservers or approved flotation devices for each occupant. The life preservers or flotation devices must be within easy reach of each seated occupant and must be readily removable from the airplane.

emergency lighting controls. The control device that switches emergency lighting on or off. The control device in the cockpit is required by regulation to have an "on," "off," and "armed" position.

emergency lighting system. A lighting system for use during emergency situations, independent of the main lighting system. The sources of general cabin illumination may be common to both the emergency and the main lighting systems if the power supply to the emergency lighting system is independent of the power supply to the main lighting system.

emergency lighting system energy supply. The power supply to the emergency lighting system. This power supply must be independent of the power supply to the main lighting system. The energy supply to each emergency lighting unit must provide the required level of illumination for at least 10 minutes at the critical ambient conditions after emergency landing.

emergency light operation. Regulations relating to the operation of emergency lights (14 CFR §121.310[d]), which requires that interior exit lights or exterior exit lighting must be operable manually both from the flight crew station or flight attendant station (as applicable); have a means to prevent inadvertent operation of the manual controls; and when armed or turned on at either station, remain lighted or become lighted upon interruption of the airplane's normal electric power. Each light must provide the required level of illumination for at least 10 minutes at the critical ambient conditions after emergency landing.

employee assistance plan (EAP). A voluntary, work-based program that offers free and confidential assessments, short-term counseling, referrals, and follow-up services to employees who have personal and/or work-related problems.

en route alternate airport. An en route airport that meets stated requirements for planned diversion use and at which the weather conditions are at or above operating minimums specified for a safe landing.

en route alternate weather (ETOPS) operations. At dispatch, an en route alternate must meet ETOPS alternate weather requirements in 14 CFR§§121.624 and 121.625 and in the certificate holder's ops specs. Because of the natural variability of weather conditions with time, as well as the need to determine the suitability of a particular en route alternate before departure, such requirements are higher than the weather minimums required to initiate an instrument approach.

enroute fuel. The fuel necessary for a flight to reach the airport to which it is dispatched and to conduct one instrument approach.

en route limitations. Limitations designed to ensure that realistic reasonable options exist to successfully complete a flight should the aircraft lose an engine (or engines) en route, and that the aircraft has sufficient performance to clear all terrain on the way back into an airport terminal area.

en route limitations: one engine inoperative. Requirements stating that a two-engine, turbine-powered airplane may not be operated over a route that contains a point farther than 60 minutes of flying time from an adequate airport. This is commonly referred to as the "60-minute rule."

en route limitations: two engines inoperative. En route requirements for aircraft having three or more engines, stating that the operator is in compliance so long as there is no point on the route structure where the flight is more than 90 minutes flying time (all engines operating) from an approved alternate airport. This is commonly referred to as the "90-minute rule."

equipment for operations in icing conditions. Equipment that provides a means for the prevention or removal of ice on windshields, wings, empennage, propellers, and other parts of the airplane where ice formation will adversely affect the safety of the airplane.

equipment interchange agreement. Any agreement in which the operational control of an aircraft is transferred for short periods of time from one air carrier to another air carrier and in which the latter air carrier assumes responsibility for the operation of the aircraft at the time of transfer. An interchange agreement is a form of a dry lease agreement. An interchange agreement permits two air carriers to connect two or more points on a route using the same aircraft but each operator's crewmembers.

Essential Air Service. Government-subsidized airline service to rural areas of the United States, which continued after the Airline Deregulation Act of 1978.

estimated time en route (ETE). The estimated flying time from departure point to destination (lift-off to touchdown).

ETA. The estimated time of arrival of a flight at its intended destination.

ETOPS. *See* Extended Operations.

evacuation demonstration. A requirement for operators of aircraft with 44 or more seats to demonstrate that the carrier is able to evacuate the entire aircraft in 90 seconds or less.

exemption. Approval to be free from current regulations in Title 14 of the Code of Federal Regulations (14 CFR).

Extended Operations (ETOPS). An airplane flight operation, other than an all-cargo operation in an airplane with more than two engines, during which a portion of the flight is conducted beyond a time threshold identified in 14 CFR Part 121 or Part 135 that is determined using an approved one-engine-inoperative cruise speed under standard atmospheric conditions in still air.

Extended Operations (ETOPS) alternate airport. An adequate airport listed in the certificate holder's operations specifications that is designated in a dispatch or flight release for use in the event of an engine failure or some other abnormal or emergency condition requiring a diversion during ETOPS.

extended overwater operations. Those flights conducted at a horizontal distance of more than 50 nautical miles from the nearest shoreline.

exterior emergency lighting. Exterior lighting required on each passenger-carrying airplane, designed to illuminate the exterior area nearby emergency exit doors. Exterior lights must be bright enough to sufficiently illuminate the descent path from the emergency to the ground.

exterior exit markings. Each passenger emergency exit and the means of opening that exit from the outside must be marked conspicuously on the outside of the airplane. Exits that are not in the side of the fuselage must have external means of opening and applicable instructions marked in red (or, if red is inconspicuous against the background color, in bright chrome yellow) and, when the opening means for such an exit is located on only one side of the fuselage, a conspicuous marking to that effect must be provided on the other side.

factored landing distance. The certified landing distance multiplied by 1.67, which can then be compared directly to the available landing distance.

Fair Treatment for Experienced Pilots Act. Signed into law on December 13, 2007, this Act is officially recorded as Public Law 110-135. Also known as the "Age 65" rule, it raised the mandatory retirement age of U.S. airline pilots from age 60 to age 65.

FARs. A colloquial expression very commonly used by the aviation industry (and abhorred by the FAA) referring to Title 14 of the U.S. Code of Federal Regulations. *See* Federal Aviation Regulations; Title 14 of the Code of Federal Regulations.

fatigue. A physiological state of reduced mental or physical performance capability resulting from lack of sleep or increased physical activity that can reduce a flight crewmember's alertness and ability to safely operate an aircraft or perform safety-related duties.

fatigue risk management plan. An air carrier's management plan outlining policies and procedures for reducing the risks of flight crewmember fatigue and improving flight crewmember alertness.

fatigue risk management system (FRMS). A management system for a certificate holder to use to mitigate the effects of fatigue in its particular operations. It is a data-driven process and a systematic method used to continuously monitor and manage safety risks associated with fatigue-related error. An FRMS is largely developed as an alternative method of compliance to the current FAA limitations based upon objective performance standards. A certificate holder may be authorized to apply an FRMS to any part or all of its operation, provided that the certificate holder demonstrates an effective alternative method of compliance.

Federal Aviation Act of 1958. A reorganization of the federal responsibilities for aviation regulation in the United States under the newly created Federal Aviation Agency. The reorganization was primarily a response to three tragic airline accidents, two of which involved midair collisions between airliners and military aircraft. The act's major impacts were the establishment of a unified air traffic control system under civilian control, including implementation of universal radar coverage within the continental United States above 6,000 feet above ground level (AGL), and establishing the FAA as an independent agency reporting to the President of the United States.

Federal Aviation Administration (FAA). A federal government agency created in 1966 as a result of the reorganization of the regulatory structure of the entire transportation sector of the United States. The major change with respect to the previous FAA was that it was downgraded from an agency directly reporting to the president to that of a subordinate organization within the newly created Department of Transportation. The responsibilities of the FAA were largely unchanged.

Federal Aviation Agency (FAA). An independent federal agency which reported directly to the President that had authority to regulate and oversee all aspects of civil aviation. It was created as a result of the reorganization of the CAA and CAB in 1958. The Federal Aviation Agency was replaced in 1966 by the Federal Aviation Administration. *See* Federal Aviation Administration.

Federal Aviation Regulations (FARs). The colloquial but almost universally used term describing the body of federal regulations concerning aviation found in Title 14 of the U.S. Code of Federal Regulations—Aviation and Aerospace.

Federal Register Act of 1935. Mandates a specific and universal set of regulations as to the development and issuance of federal regulations. This allows the public far greater access to the federal regulatory process and notice of impending regulations than previously available.

final approach speed. V_{REF} plus corrections. Airspeed corrections are based on such operational factors as weight, wind component, aircraft configuration (e.g., less than full flap landing), or use of autothrottle. The resulting final approach speed provides the best compromise between handling qualities and landing distance.

final rule. Sets out new or revised regulatory requirements and their effective date, and may remove certain requirements. *See also* notice of proposed rulemaking.

fire detector systems. A system that signals the flight crew of the presence of an onboard fire. Units of the system are installed in locations where there are greatest possibilities of a fire.

fire extinguishers (portable). Used by flight crewmembers to extinguish fires in the cabin or flight deck.

fire extinguishing systems (fixed). A system used in most engine fire and cargo compartment fire protection systems designed to dilute the atmosphere with an inert agent that does not support combustion.

fire protection for essential flight controls, engine mounts and other flight structures. Fire protection for these items located in designated fire zones, or in adjacent areas which would be subjected to the effects of fire in the zone, requires that these items be constructed of fireproof material or shielded so that they are capable of withstanding the effects of fire.

first segment climb. The segment of a departure that begins at brake release and ends at a point after takeoff where the speed is V_2 and the landing gear has finished retracting. This will be at an altitude of more than 35 feet above the runway surface and at an airspeed of V_2. During first segment climb, the aircraft is only required to demonstrate a *positive rate of climb* after liftoff. During this portion of the departure, the crew is not expected nor required to do anything except fly the airplane. *See also* four segment climb performance.

fitness for duty. Physiologically and mentally prepared and capable of performing assigned duties at the highest degree of safety.

flag all-cargo operations. Pertaining to a flight crew's flight and duty time limitations when conducting flag all-cargo operations. 14 CFR Part 121, Subpart R, covers limitations for flight crews in flag all-cargo operations. *See also* all-cargo operations

flag operation. Operations between any point within the State of Alaska or the State of Hawaii or any territory or possession of the United States and any point outside the State of Alaska or the State of Hawaii or any territory or possession of the United States, respectively; or between any point within the 48 contiguous States of the United States or the District of Columbia and any point outside the 48 contiguous States of the United States and the District of Columbia; or between any point outside the U.S. and another point outside the U.S. The name derives from the treaty obligations to display the national flag emblem on the country of the registry on the outside of the aircraft when used in international operations.

flight and duty time limitations. Regulatory limitations placed on the amount of flight or duty time a flight crewmember, flight attendant or aircraft dispatcher is allowed during a "work-day." *See also* flight time; duty time.

flight and navigational equipment. Instruments and equipment in the cockpit of an aircraft that provide the flight crew with information about the flight situation of that aircraft (i.e., airspeed indicating system, altimeter, horizontal situation indicator, vertical speed indicator, magnetic compass and free-air temperature gauge, etc.).

flight attendant. An individual who works in the cabin of an aircraft that has 20 or more seats and is used by a Part 121 or Part 135 air carrier to provide air transportation.

flight attendant minimum staffing levels. The minimum number of FAA-required flight attendants, which is determined by aircraft seating configuration and not by the actual number of passengers on board. The minimum staffing level is to ensure safety standards can be met in emergency situations.

flight attendant seat. A dedicated seat for flight attendant use during takeoff and landing placed in the passenger compartment and that meets the requirements of Part 25.

flight attendant training. FAA-approved training that satisfies the requirements of 14 CFR §121.401 and ensures that each flight attendant is adequately trained to perform his or her assigned duties.

flight control. A department, similar to a dispatch office, responsible for operational control of all aircraft, including monitoring the status and activity of each individual airplane.

flight control system. The system in an aircraft consisting of components to control its flightpath. The primary control system consists of ailerons, elevator (or stabilizer), and rudder, which are required to control an aircraft safely during flight. The secondary control system consists of wing flaps, leading edge devices, spoilers, and trim systems, and improves the performance characteristics of the airplane or relieves the pilot of excessive control forces.

flight crew emergency exits. A moveable door or hatch, in the external walls of the fuselage, allowing flight crew egress during an emergency evacuation where exit through the cockpit door is impossible.

Flight crewmember. A pilot, flight engineer, or flight navigator assigned to duty in an aircraft during flight time.

flight crew operations manual (FCOM). A document developed by a manufacturer that describes, in detail, the characteristics and operation of the airplane or its systems.

flight data monitoring (FDM). A program air carriers use to collect and analyze digital flight data of actual line aircraft operations. Also known as flight operations quality assurance (FOQA).

flight data recorders (FDR and DFDR). A flight data recorder (FDR) is an instrument or device that records information about the performance of an aircraft or conditions encountered in flight, monitoring parameters such as altitude, airspeed and heading. Older analog units used one-quarter-inch magnetic tape as a storage medium and the newer digital flight data recorder (DFDR) units use digital technology and memory chips. Both recorders are installed in the most crash-survivable part of the aircraft, usually the tail section.

Flight Deck Access Restriction (FDAR) Program. A set of required procedures combined with the use of a computer database system that the certificate holder's employees assigned cockpit access verification tasks (i.e., gate agents) can use to positively confirm the identity, employment status, and flight deck eligibility of the person requesting cockpit access.

flight deck door. A door between the passenger and pilot compartments with a locking means to prevent passengers from opening it without the pilot's permission.

flight deck duty. The time spent "on duty" in the cockpit. The FAA distinguish between flight deck duty time and duty aloft time when computing flight crew duty time limits.

flight dispatcher. *See* dispatcher.

flight duty period (FDP). A period that begins when a flight crewmember is required to report for duty with the intention of conducting a flight, a series of flights, or positioning or ferrying flights, and ends when the aircraft is parked after the last flight and there is no intention for further aircraft movement by the same flight crewmember. A flight duty period includes the duties performed by the flight crewmember on behalf of the certificate holder that occur before a flight segment or between flight segments without a required intervening rest period (including tasks such as deadhead transportation, training conducted in an aircraft or flight simulator, and airport/standby reserve).

flight duty period extensions. An extension of a flight crewmember's maximum flight duty period. The pilot-in-command and the certificate holder may extend the maximum flight duty period permitted in Tables B or C of Part 117 up to 2 hours. The pilot-in-command and the certificate holder may also extend the maximum combined flight duty period and reserve availability period limits by up to 2 hours.

flight engineers. A technical expert who must be thoroughly familiar with the operation and function of various airplane systems and components. The principal function of the flight engineer is to assist the pilots in the operation of the airplane. Specific duties vary with different airplanes and operators.

flight follower. A person who performs the duties required to exercise operational control over a supplemental air carrier or Part 135 operator's flight.

flight following. The exercise of performing operational control over a Part 121 supplemental air carrier or Part 135 operator's flight.

Flight Information Service – Broadcast (FIS-B). A ground broadcast service provided through the FAA's Universal Access Transceiver (UAT) ADS-B Broadcast Services Network. The FAA FIS-B system provides pilots and flight crews of properly equipped aircraft with a cockpit display of certain aviation weather and flight operational information.

flight navigators. Assist pilots in aircraft operations by determining, planning, and performing the navigational aspects of the flight.

flight management system (FMS). An integrated system used by flight crews for flight planning, navigation, performance management, aircraft guidance, and flight progress monitoring. Also called a flight management computer system (FMCS).

flight operations manual. A manual providing amplified and detailed guidance as well as standard operating procedures for flight crewmembers. The standard operating procedures systematically cover crewmember duties and responsibilities, flight planning requirements, and passenger-handling issues, among many other operational elements.

flight operational quality assurance (FOQA). A program air carriers use to collect and analyze digital flight data of actual line aircraft operations. Also known as flight data monitoring (FDM).

flight plan. A planning document required for air carriers that covers the expected operational details of a flight such as destination, route, fuel onboard, etc. It is filed with the appropriate FAA air traffic control facility.

flight release. A required document, used in supplemental air carrier operations, allowing the pilot-in-command to start a flight in a flight following system under the specific authority of the person authorized by the operator to exercise operational control over the flight. Supplemental operators are not required to have an aircraft dispatcher *dispatch release* each flight, but instead use a *flight release document*. The flight release authority of supplemental operations is addressed in 14 CFR §121.597.

flight simulation training device (FSTD). A flight training device as defined in Part 60 that has a replica of an airplane cockpit's instruments, equipment, panels, and controls. It includes the equipment and computer programs necessary to represent airplane operations in ground or flight conditions having the full range of capabilities of the systems installed in the device as described in 14 CFR Part 60, or the qualification performance standard for a specific FTD qualification level (6 or 7).

Flight Standards. The Flight Standards organization of the FAA promotes safe air transportation by setting the standards for certification and oversight of airmen, air operators, air agencies, and designees. FAA Flight Standards also promotes safety of flight of civil aircraft and air commerce.

Flight Standards District Office (FSDO). An FAA field office serving an assigned geographical area and staffed with Flight Standards personnel who serve the aviation industry and general public on matters relating to the certification and operation of air carrier and general aviation aircraft.

flight time. Pilot time that commences when an aircraft moves under its own power for the purpose of flight and ends when the aircraft comes to rest at the next point of landing.

flight training device (FTD). A class of flight simulation devices that previously covered a broad array of synthetic trainers. With the advent of FAA Advisory Circular 61-136B, FTDs only cover a small number of Level 1 through 5 devices (mostly obsolete or no longer approved) and Level 6 and Level 7 devices that are administered (along with all FSTDs) by the National Simulation Program, AFS-205.

floor level exits. A floor level door or exit in the side of the fuselage (other than those leading into a cargo or baggage compartment that is not accessible from the passenger cabin) that is at least 44 inches high and 20 inches wide, but is not wider than 46 inches, and that is not part of a passenger ventral exit or tail cone exit.

flying pilot (FP). *See* pilot flying (PF); pilot monitoring (PM).

follow-up alcohol testing. An employer's unannounced alcohol testing of a covered employee, as directed by a substance abuse professional, following a determination that the employee is in need of assistance in resolving problems associated with alcohol misuse. A covered employee must be tested under Part 120 only while the employee is performing safety-sensitive functions, just before the employee is to perform safety-sensitive functions, or just after the employee has ceased performing such functions.

follow-up drug testing. Testing required for any individual who has been hired to perform or who has been returned to the performance of a safety-sensitive function after refusing to submit to a required drug test or after receiving a verified positive drug test result.

foreign air carrier. Any person, other than a citizen of the United States, who undertakes directly, by lease or other arrangement, to engage in air transportation.

Form 110A. *See* aviation safety inspector's credentials.

four segment climb performance. A summary of the takeoff and climb limitations that simplifies and explains more clearly what the performance requirements actually accomplish. Each segment's requirements are in place to ensure adequate terrain/obstacle clearance from the runway all the way up to the enroute environment.

fourth segment climb. The fourth segment climb begins with the climb configuration and airspeed set and ends (normally) at 1,500 feet above the surface. During fourth segment climb, a twin-engine aircraft must be able to maintain a net takeoff flight path minimum climb gradient of 1.2 percent or 12 feet per 1,000 feet traveled. *See also* four segment climb performance.

fuel minimums. The minimum allowable fuel for an aircraft's release on a particular flight segment. This includes fuel to destination, then to the most distant required alternate, required reserves, contingency, and fuel for start and taxi. Known delays, diversions, and so forth are considered in this figure. Also included is fuel for acceleration, climb, cruise, descent, one instrument approach and missed approach, and the landing.

free flight. A flight capability in which operators have the freedom to select a path and speed in real time. Air traffic restrictions are imposed only to ensure separation, to preclude exceeding airport capacity, to prevent unauthorized flight through special use airspace, and to ensure safety of flight. Restrictions are limited in extent and duration to correct the identified problem.

fuel burn. The total burnoff of fuel from the departure airport to the destination airport and to land. Included in this figure is precomputed fuel for taxi to and from a given runway. An air carrier uses some precomputed fuel burns for frequently flown routes.

full flight simulator (FFS). A replica of a specific type, make, model, and series airplane cockpit. It includes the equipment and computer programs necessary to represent airplane operations in ground and flight conditions, a visual system providing an out-of-the-cockpit view, a system that provides cues at least equivalent to those of a three-degrees-of-freedom-motion system, and the full range of capabilities of the systems installed in the device.

general maintenance manual (GMM). A manual prepared by the air carrier or aircraft manufacturer that covers the airworthiness information for a particular model of aircraft.

general operations manual (GOM). A company manual that contains flight operations material not related specifically to a particular aircraft's operation. The GOM includes information such as policies, procedures, and guidance necessary for flight operations personnel to perform their duties with the highest degree of safety.

global positioning system (GPS) landing system (GLS). A differential GPS-based landing system providing both vertical and lateral position fixing capability.

grace month. In regard to recurrent training, the month after the month in which a flight crewmember's training is due. The FAA uses a three-month "eligibility period" that allows the recurrent training to be accomplished a month before the base month ("month early"), during the base month, or in the grace month. *See also* base month.

gratuitous bailment. A type of bailment in which the bailee receives no compensation (e.g., borrowing a friend's car). A gratuitous bailee is liable for loss of the property only if the loss is caused by the bailee's gross negligence. Therefore, a lower standard of care is imposed upon the bailee in a gratuitous bailment. Gratuitous bailment is also referred to as naked bailment or bailment for sole benefit of bailor.

ground proximity warning system (GPWS). A device that can detect certain hazardous conditions and warn the crew. Conditions such as too rapid closure to the ground (sink rate), being too close to the ground (terrain), or going below the approach flight path (glide slope) will be called to the crew's attention through a verbal annunciator.

ground security coordinator (GSC). An employee of the air carrier, typically a gate agent with additional security training, whose job it is to inform the pilot-in-command of any pertinent security issues that may affect the flight.

Group I airplanes. For the purposes of 14 CFR Part 121, Subpart N, piston or turboprop airplanes.

Group II airplanes. For the purposes of 14 CFR Part 121, Subpart N, turbofan or turbojet airplanes.

guidance material. The direction provided by a guide; these are FAA policy and advisory materials.

hand fire extinguishers. *See* fire extinguishers (portable).

hazardous materials (HAZMAT) training. Training in marking, identifying, handling, and storing of hazardous materials.

HAZMAT. Hazardous materials.

high minimums captain. A captain with less than 100 hours of pilot-in-command time in the type of aircraft he or she is operating. A high minimums captain must add 100 feet and ½ statute mile to the landing minimums appearing in the operator's ops specs.

holding out. Offering to the public the carriage of persons and property for hire either intrastate or interstate (e.g., advertising, using a booking agent).

home base. The location designated by a certificate holder where a flight crewmember normally begins and ends his or her duty periods.

IFR landing minimums. FAA regulated minimum approach and landing weather conditions (i.e., instrument approach minimum altitude and visibility requirements) an air carrier is authorized to use. Minimum allowable landing minimums are those specified in an air carrier's ops specs.

IFSD (inflight shutdown) rate. For ETOPS only, the rate at which an engine ceases to function (when the airplane is airborne) and is shutdown, whether self-induced, flight-crew initiated, or caused by an external influence. The FAA considers IFSD for all causes, including flameout, internal failure, flight-crew initiated shutdown, foreign object ingestion, icing, inability to obtain or control desired thrust or power, and cycling of the start control, however briefly, even if the engine operates normally for the remainder of the flight. This definition excludes the airborne cessation of the functioning of an engine when immediately followed by an automatic engine relight and when an engine does not achieve desired thrust or power but is not shutdown.

independent interest. One of the tests the FAA uses to determine if a flight is common carriage or not.

inflight shutdown. *See* IFSD.

indoc. *See* basic indoctrination training.

initial operating experience (IOE). A period of time that a new crewmember (new to the operation, not necessarily to the company) flies while under the direct supervision of a qualified check pilot.

initial training. The training required for crewmembers and dispatchers who have not qualified and served in the same capacity on another airplane of the same group.

inspection function. The FAA requirement that an air carrier's maintenance department must have separate maintenance functions and inspection functions. The inspection of the work assures that whatever was to be done has actually been accomplished correctly and completely. This independent inspection function is designed to make sure things don't slip by or get overlooked.

installed EFB. An electronic flight bag "hard-wired" or installed in an aircraft and considered part of the aircraft, covered by the aircraft airworthiness approval. Installed EFBs are fully certified as part of the aircraft avionics system and are integrated with aircraft systems such as the FMS and GPS.

insurer. Someone who has responsibility to make sure or secure, to guarantee, to ensure safety to anyone covered by a policy. This is done is by financial compensation for loss. An insurer is completely responsible financially for the liability for breeches of safety and security of anyone with whom it has a contract.

interior emergency exit markings. Required for passenger airplanes to conspicuously mark each passenger emergency exit, its means of access, and its means of opening. The identity and location of each passenger emergency exit must be recognizable from a distance equal to the width of the cabin. A sign visible to occupants must indicate the location of each passenger emergency exit approaching along the main passenger aisle.

interior fire protection and flammability standards. Rigorous fire protection and flammability standards, specified in 14 CFR Part 25, for everything that goes into a transport category airplane interior.

interstate air transportation. The carriage by aircraft of persons or property as a common carrier for compensation or hire, or the carriage of mail by aircraft in commerce, between a place in a state or the District of Columbia and another place in another state; between places in the same state through the airspace over any place outside that state; or between places in the same possession of the United States.

intrastate air transportation. The carriage of persons or property as a common carrier for compensation or hire, by turbojet-powered aircraft capable of carrying 30 or more persons, wholly within the same state of the United States.

JAA JAR-OPS-1. European Joint Aviation Authorities (JAA) Joint Aviation Requirements (JAR) operational agreements (OPS). The European JAA adopted common operational guidance for all member states in order to harmonize the rules within those states. JAR-OPS-1 is Part 1 of the operational agreement applicable to commercial air transportation fixed-wing aircraft.

kind of operation. One of the various operations a certificate holder is authorized to conduct, as specified in its operations specifications (e.g., domestic, flag, supplemental, commuter, or on-demand operations).

landing distance available (LDA). The runway length declared available and suitable for a landing airplane. The LDA may be less than the physical length of the runway or the length of the runway remaining beyond a displaced threshold if necessary to satisfy runway design standards (for example, in a case where the airport operator uses a portion of the runway to achieve the runway safety area requirement).

landing distance data. The required landing distance data in the airplane flight manual (AFM), which may include both certified landing distance and factored landing distance.

landing field length requirement. A requirement which prohibits the takeoff of a transport category airplane unless its weight on arrival, allowing for the normal consumption of fuel and oil in flight, will allow a full stop landing at the intended destination airport within 60 percent of the effective runway length. The intent of landing field length regulations is to ensure that a flight operation does not begin that cannot reasonably be concluded upon reaching the destination or alternate airport, as applicable.

landing gear aural warning device. An aural warning device that functions continuously or is periodically repeated if a landing is attempted when the landing gear is not locked down.

landing limitations for alternate airports. The rule stating that an operator may not list an airport as an alternate airport if (based on the same assumptions as used in 14 CFR §121.195[b]) at the anticipated weight at the anticipated time of arrival the aircraft cannot be brought to a stop in 60 percent of the effective runway length for turbojet aircraft or 70 percent of the effective runway length for turboprop aircraft. In the case of a departure airport alternate, the rule allows fuel to be jettisoned (dumped) in addition to normal consumption.

landing limitations for destination airports. The requirement that a flight crew cannot take off an airplane at a weight that, allowing for normal fuel and oil consumption, would exceed the approved maximum landing weight (at the destination airport's elevation and actual ambient temperature at the time of intended landing) provided for in the airplane flight manual. Note that this is a planning rule and would be violated on takeoff, not upon arrival at the destination airport. Alternate airports listed for the flight must be considered as well as the destination airports.

landing minimums. The necessary visibility for an instrument approach for a particular runway. This value controls whether an air carrier may initiate or complete an instrument approach under existing weather conditions.

large aircraft. Aircraft of more than 12,500 pounds maximum certificated takeoff weight.

lavatory fire protection. Regulations that require each lavatory to be equipped with a smoke detector system or equivalent that provides either a warning light in the cockpit or a warning light or audible warning in the passenger cabin that would be readily detected by a flight attendant. Each lavatory must be equipped with a built-in fire extinguisher, designed to discharge automatically upon occurrence of a fire, for each disposal receptacle for towels, paper, or waste located within the lavatory.

letter of authorization (LOA). A letter of authorization allowing an institution of higher education to certify its graduates for an airline transport pilot certificate under the academic and aeronautical experience requirements in 14 CFR §61.160. An institution of higher education that is accredited, as defined in §61.1, may apply for an LOA. This authorization allows the institution to certify its graduates to take the FAA ATP Knowledge and Practical tests with less than the required 1,500 total flight hours.

Level A, B, C or D simulator. Classifications of aircraft training simulators. The later in the alphabet the letter, the more sophisticated the device. For example, a Level D simulator is more capable than a Level A simulator.

life-limited parts. Any part for which a mandatory replacement time limit is specified in the type design or maintenance manual.

line check. *See* annual line check.

lineholder. A flight crewmember who has an assigned flight duty period and is not acting as a reserve flight crewmember.

line operating flight time. The time spent serving as a flight crewmember during regular flight and ground airline operations. A minimum amount of line operating flight time is required by Section 121.434 in order to facilitate the consolidation of knowledge and skills learned during training on a new aircraft or new flight crew position.

line-oriented flight training (LOFT). Flight training designed to instill a team attitude on the flight deck and evaluate an entire crew's performance instead of performance of individual crewmembers.

load manifest. A document containing the weight of a loaded aircraft, total weight computed under approved procedures, evidence the aircraft is loaded within center of gravity limits, and names of passengers (unless that list is maintained by the air carrier).

long-call reserve. When a flight crewmember, prior to beginning the rest period required by §117.25, is notified by the certificate holder to report for a flight duty period following the completion of the rest period.

"look-back" requirements. A requirement that before each flight segment, a flight crewmember look back at the number of flight and flight duty period hours he or she has actually accumulated to determine if the flight can be operated within the cumulative limits. If cumulative limits have been exceeded, the flight crewmember cannot operate the flight. The same holds true for determining if a flight crewmember has accumulated the proper amount of rest prior to beginning a flight duty period.

low-altitude windshear flight training. Required as part of pilots' initial, transition, and upgrade training, this training must include flight training and practice in the maneuvers and procedures set forth in the certificate holder's approved low-altitude windshear flight training program and Part 121 Appendix E.

low-level windshear advisory system. Airborne wind shear detection, warning, and avoidance equipment. A system may include either an approved airborne wind shear warning and flight guidance system, an approved airborne detection and avoidance system, or an approved combination of these systems.

maintenance. The inspection, overhaul, repair, preservation, and replacement of parts, excluding preventive maintenance.

maintenance event letter checks. Both routine and detailed scheduled maintenance checks included in the continuous airworthiness maintenance program (CAMP) prepared by an air carrier under its operations specifications. Also known as letter checks, these inspections are labeled "A," "B," "C," or "D." *See also* A-Check; B-Check; C-Check; D-Check.

maintenance ferry flight. A ferry flight operating under the authority of the director of maintenance or his representative and applicable FARs. Such a flight must be issued a maintenance ferry flight authorization specifying the limitations and conditions under which it is to operate. A maintenance ferry flight is not to be confused with a repositioning flight.

maintenance manual. A manual that describes the necessary procedures to follow when performing maintenance tasks and the interval at which these tasks are to be completed, taking into account the operating environment of the aircraft.

maintenance or inspection training program. A training program that each air carrier or person performing maintenance or preventive maintenance functions is required to have to ensure that each person (including inspection personnel) who determines the adequacy of work done is fully informed about procedures and techniques and new equipment in use and is competent to perform his duties.

maintenance records. Records of maintenance kept by an air carrier, in a recordkeeping system that provides for the preservation and retrieval of maintenance information in an acceptable manner. Maintenance records must contain a description of the work performed; the name of the person performing the work if it was performed by a person outside the certificate holder's organization; and the name or other positive ID of the individual approving the work.

maintenance repair organization (MRO) An air carrier repair station certificated under Part 145, allowing it to perform maintenance and alterations for itself or other carriers.

major alteration. An alteration not listed in the aircraft, aircraft engine, or propeller specifications that might appreciably affect weight, balance, structural strength, performance, powerplant operation, flight characteristics, or other qualities affecting airworthiness; or one that is not done according to accepted practices or cannot be done by elementary operations. *See also* airframe major alteration; appliance major alteration; propeller major alteration.

major repair. A repair that, if improperly done, might appreciably affect weight, balance, structural strength, performance, powerplant operation, flight characteristics, or other qualities affecting airworthiness or that is not done according to accepted practices or cannot be done by elementary operations. *See also* airframe major repair; appliance major repair; powerplant major repair; propeller major repair.

management policy and procedures manual. A manual detailing the functions of the complex organization of the many divisions and departments that are needed behind the scenes to run an airline but that are not structured within the operational frameworks of flight operations, ground (airport) operations, or maintenance. The manual is primarily used by the staff and support organizations in administering the business aspects of the carrier.

mandatory smoking regulations. Implements a ban on smoking of tobacco products on air carrier and foreign air carrier flights in scheduled intrastate, interstate and foreign air transportation, as required by 49 U.S.C. 41706. It also addresses smoking on charter flights.

manipulation of controls. Pertains to who is allowed, by regulation, to manipulate the controls of an aircraft during flight.

master minimum equipment list (MMEL). A list of items of equipment and instruments that may be inoperative on a specific type of aircraft (e.g., BE-200, Beechcraft Model 200). Whereas the minimum equipment list (MEL) is the specific inoperative equipment document for a particular make and model aircraft by serial and registration number, the MMEL is for a particular type of aircraft.

mechanical interruption summary report. A detailed report of occurrences during flight that cause a disruption of an air carrier's normal service.

medical certificate. Acceptable evidence of physical fitness on a form prescribed by the Administrator.

medical review officer (MRO). A person qualified in accordance with 49 CFR Part 40 who performs the functions set forth in 49 CFR Part 40. If an employer does not have a qualified individual on staff to serve as MRO, then it may contract for the provision of MRO services as part of its drug testing program.

minimum descent altitude (MDA). The lowest altitude, expressed in feet above mean sea level, to which descent is authorized on final approach or during circle-to-land maneuvering in execution of a standard instrument approach procedure where no glide slope is provided.

minimum equipment list (MEL). A FAA-approved list of aircraft equipment that are not essential to an aircraft's airworthiness and may be deferred for limited periods of time. Whereas the master minimum equipment list (MMEL) is for a particular type of aircraft, the MEL is the specific inoperative equipment document for a particular make and model aircraft by serial and registration numbers.

minimum navigation performance standards (MNPS). *See* required navigation performance.

minimum number of flight attendants required for dispatch. *See* flight attendant minimum staffing levels.

minimum steady flight speed (Vs). Stall speed. The minimum steady flight speed at which the airplane is controllable. It is the minimum speed that the wing can create enough lift to support the aircraft. On a coefficient of lift curve, it is the airspeed where the wing creates its maximum coefficient of lift.

MRO. *See* maintenance repair organization; medical review officer.

National Transportation Safety Board (NTSB). The federal government agency charged with investigating the factual basis for aviation, highway, railroad, maritime and pipeline transportation accidents, determining the probable cause of those accidents and, where appropriate, issuing safety recommendations. It is an independent board composed of five members appointed by the president and supported by a staff of technical experts and investigators. It possesses no regulatory or legal enforcement power except as related to compliance with its own regulations as to its procedures and processes for investigating accidents.

net takeoff flight path. The actual flight path of the aircraft as determined during design and certification trials reduced by a factor specified in 14 CFR §25.115(b).

non common carriage. An aircraft operation for compensation or hire that does not involve holding out to others. Non common carriage operations require the issuance of an operating certificate, and would be conducted under 14 CFR Part 125 or Part 135, depending on the type of aircraft, seating configuration, and payload capacity.

non-flying pilot (NFP). In a multi-pilot cockpit crew operation, the pilot who is manipulating the aircraft controls is considered the flying pilot (FP) and the other pilot is designated as the non-flying pilot (NFP). The NFP's role is to monitor the aircraft control actions and flight management of the flying pilot and manage the support duties such as reading checklists, communicating with ATC and making PAs to the passengers. *See also* pilot flying (PF); pilot monitoring (PM).

nonscheduled on-demand operation. An operation utilizing an airplane with 30 or fewer passenger seats *and* a 7,500 pound or less payload capacity, or any rotorcraft. Though called nonscheduled operations, they are permitted to operate aircraft of 9 seats or less on schedules of no more than 5 roundtrips per week between any city pair.

nonscheduled operation. Any passenger-carrying operation that is other than a scheduled operation, or any all-cargo operation, including on-demand and supplemental operations.

notice of proposed rulemaking (NPRM). Issued as part of the standard process of rulemaking, followed by a final rule. After an unsafe condition is discovered, a proposed solution is published as an NPRM, which solicits public comment on the proposed action. *See also* final rule.

OEI. *See* one engine inoperative.

off-line alternate airport. *See* operational (on-line) alternate vs. non-operational (off-line) alternate airport.

on-demand operation. An on-demand operation can be either a scheduled operation or non-scheduled operation. *See* scheduled on-demand operation; nonscheduled on-demand operations.

one engine inoperative (OEI). 14 CFR §121.191(a) requires that aircraft be operated at such a weight that for one engine inoperative (OEI) performance, if the aircraft loses an engine, the pilot has the ability to operate the aircraft safely to an alternate airport (en route alternate).

on-line alternate airport. *See* operational (on-line) alternate vs. non-operational (off-line) alternate airport.

operational alternate airport. *See* operational (on-line) alternate vs. non-operational (off-line) alternate airport.

operational control. With respect to a flight, the exercise of authority over initiating, conducting, or terminating a flight.

operational (on-line) alternate vs. non-operational (off-line) alternate airport. An operational or on-line alternate is an alternate airport that is one of an air carrier's hubs or regular destinations, and thus is generally better equipped with necessary facilities at which mechanics are available and adequate support to the crew and passengers can be provided. A non-operational or off-line alternate airport is not assured of having the necessary facilities to handle a particular type of aircraft.

operations at night. For flight crew time logging requirements, night operations are those operations taking place between the end of evening civil twilight and the beginning of morning civil twilight, as published in the Air Almanac, converted to local time. For certain equipment requirements (e.g., position lights) night operations are defined as being from sunset to sunrise. For flight crew logging of takeoff and landings, the FAA defines night operations as being from one hour after sunset to one hour before sunrise.

operational service volume. The volume of airspace surrounding a NAVAID which is available for operational use and within which a signal of usable strength exists and where that signal is not operationally limited by co-channel interference.

operations notices. Notices required to be issued by air carriers to notify their appropriate operations personnel of each change in equipment and operating procedures. Operations notices contain information such as the status of navigation aids, airport facilities, special air traffic control procedures and regulations, local airport traffic control rules, and weather reports, including icing and other potentially hazardous meteorological conditions.

operations over uninhabited terrain. Flag or supplemental operations and domestic operations within the states of Alaska or Hawaii over an uninhabited area or any other area that the FAA specifies in the ops specs must use aircraft that has the equipment required by FAR 121.353, for search and rescue in case of an emergency.

operations specifications (ops specs). The document created by the carrier and FAA wherein the carrier specifically explains (or identifies) how it will conduct operation of its aircraft in accordance with Federal Aviation Regulations.

operations under IFR. For operations under IFR flight rules, aircraft must be equipped with the instruments and equipment listed in 14 CFR §121.325 (e.g., a sensitive altimeter and an airspeed indicating system with heated pitot tube or equivalent means for preventing malfunctioning due to icing).

outsourced training. Any training, testing, or checking activity that an air carrier certificate holder provides by way of a contract arrangement with another party.

overwater operations. Those flights conducted over any body of water beyond that point at which an aircraft is then unable to glide to the shoreline of land when all engines fail.

pairing limitations. Limitations placed by the FAA on air carriers in regards to the pairing of flight crewmembers for a particular flight. Generally these limitations are based on the age (e.g., over age 60) or the individual experience levels of each crewmember.

paperless cockpit. A cockpit that has completely transitioned from paper manuals, aeronautical charts, checklists, or other data required by the operating rules to displaying the required information electronically. An air carrier may use either installed or portable electronic flight bags (tablet or other electronic display device) to display this information, and the FAA requires at least two operational EFBs be available in the cockpit.

passenger-carrying operation. Any aircraft operation carrying any person other than a crewmember, company employee, authorized government representative, or person accompanying a shipment.

passenger oxygen. A system designed to store or to generate a supply of pure oxygen and to regulate, dilute as required, and then distribute that oxygen to passengers. This oxygen system may be used for normal operations, to provide supplemental oxygen for specific situations, or for provision of emergency oxygen in the event of smoke, fire, fumes or loss of pressurization.

passive control. In the context of operational control, consists of developing and publishing policies and procedures for operational control personnel and flight crew to follow in the performance of their duties and assuring adequate information and facilities are available to conduct the planned operation. Operational control is exercised through both active and passive means. *See also* active control; operational control.

People's Express Exemption 3585. An exemption People's Express Airlines received after filing a petition with the FAA in 1982 to gain some relief from the restrictive requirements of 14 CFR §§121.613 and 121.625. It allows Part 121 carriers to dispatch to destinations in certain cases when conditional language in a one-time increment of the weather forecast states that the weather at the destination airport, alternate airport, or both airports could be below the authorized weather minimums when other time increments of the weather forecast state the weather conditions will be at or above the authorized weather minimums.

performance objectives. A statement describing the behavior a crewmember must demonstrate to be able to successfully perform a crewmember's task.

periodic (drug) testing. Drug testing of employees at various time intervals. Each employee that is required to undergo a medical examination under 14 CFR Part 67 shall submit to a periodic drug test, which includes testing for the presence of marijuana, cocaine, opiates, phencyclidine (PCP), and amphetamines, or a metabolite of those drugs, during the first calendar year of implementation of the employer's anti-drug program.

physiological night's rest. Ten hours of rest that encompasses the hours of 0100 and 0700 at the flight crewmember's home base, unless the individual has acclimated to a different theater, in which case the rest must encompass the hours of 0100 and 0700 at the acclimated location.

pilot flying (PF). In a multi-pilot cockpit crew operation the pilot who is manipulating the aircraft controls is considered the pilot flying (PF). The other pilot is designated as the pilot monitoring (PM). *See also* pilot monitoring.

pilot-in-command (PIC). The person who has final authority and responsibility for the operation and safety of the flight; has been designated as pilot-in-command before or during the flight; and holds the appropriate category, class, and type rating, if appropriate, for the conduct of the flight.

pilot monitoring (PM). In a multi-pilot cockpit crew operation, the pilot who is manipulating the aircraft controls is considered the pilot flying (PF) and the other pilot is designated as the pilot monitoring (PM). The PM's role is to monitor the aircraft control actions and flight management of the flying pilot and manage support duties such as reading checklists, communicating with ATC and making PAs to the passengers. *See also* pilot flying; non-flying pilot.

pitot heating system. A heated pitot tube or equivalent means for preventing malfunctioning due to icing; an aircraft must be equipped with a pitot heating system for operations under IFR flight rules and/or at night.

place to place. Relating to the idea of carriage: taking people or goods to a place other than the place where you started (i.e., from place to place).

planned redispatch (rerelease en route). Any flag operation (or international supplemental operation) that is planned, before takeoff, to be redispatched or rereleased while in flight to a destination airport other than the original destination airport.

portable EFB. A portable electronic flight bag (e.g., tablet) mounted in the cockpit using suction cups or other type of mount (e.g., kneeboard). The FAA requires the EFB to be easily removable from its mounting device without the use of tools, and it must not block emergency egress out of the cockpit.

portable electronic device (PED). Any piece of lightweight, portable, electrically powered equipment. These devices, covered in 14 CFR §121.306, range from typical consumer electronic devices such as tablets, e-readers, and smartphones to small devices such as MP3 players and electronic toys.

portable lights. Portable flashlights, which are required to be stowed in a location accessible from each flight attendant seat on passenger-carrying airplanes.

post-accident (drug) testing. Post-accident drug testing that is required of each employee who performs a safety-sensitive function if that employee's performance either contributed to an accident or cannot be completely discounted as a contributing factor to the accident.

powerplant major repairs. Separation or disassembly of crankcase/crankshaft or repairs to structural engine parts of an engine by welding, plating, metalizing, or other methods.

pre-employment (drug) testing. Drug testing (screening) required of an applicant or employee prior to the first time he or she performs a safety-sensitive function for an employer.

pressurized cabins. An aircraft cabin that uses some of the air compressed by the plane's engines to increase cabin air pressure as the aircraft gains altitude. As the aircraft changes altitude the pressurization system uses outflow valves to adjust the cabin pressure to a programmed amount.

primary airframe ice detection system. A system used to determine when inflight ice protection systems must be activated. The ice detection system annunciates the presence of ice accretion or icing conditions, and may also provide information to other aircraft systems.

principal base of operations. The primary operating location of a certificate holder as designated by the Administrator.

principal maintenance inspector (PMI). An FAA maintenance inspector assigned the regulatory oversight of a particular air carrier's maintenance activities.

principal operations inspector (POI). An FAA safety inspector assigned the regulatory oversight of a particular air carrier's flight operations.

private carriage. Carriage arranged between two parties—the carrier and the carried (or between some other small numbers of parties and the carrier). Private carriage involves the carriage of persons or property for compensation or hire, with limitations on the number of contracts, under a contractual business arrangement between the operator and another person or organization, which did not result from the operator's holding out or offering service. (In this situation, the customer seeks an operator to perform the desired service and enters into an exclusive, mutual agreement as opposed to the operator seeking customers). Private carriage operations require the issuance of an operating certificate. Operations are conducted under Part 125 or Part 135, depending on the type of aircraft, seating configuration, and payload capacity. *See also* holding out.

private charter. Any charter for which the entity chartering the airplane engages the total capacity of an airplane for the carriage of passengers in civil or military air movements conducted under contract with the government of the United States or the government of a foreign country; or for passengers invited by the charterer, the cost of which is borne entirely by the charterer and not directly or indirectly by the individual passengers.

Procedures for Air Navigation Services—Aircraft Operations (PANS-OPS). ICAO document outlining procedure standards for terminal instrument procedures. In the United States, these procedures are covered in the United States Standard for Terminal Instrument Procedures (TERPS).

process control. The control of maintenance procedures required by the air carrier.

proficiency check. The basic flight crew checking module required in Part 121. For pilots, a proficiency check consists of the written or oral test elements and the flight test events specified in Appendix F of Part 121.

proficiency objectives. A statement describing the behavior a crewmember must demonstrate to be considered as successful in performing a task. Proficiency objectives are developed by each air carrier and must be approved by the FAA, after which they become regulatory requirements for that particular carrier.

programmed hours. Training hours specified in Part 121 for certain categories of training (e.g., initial new hire, transition, requalification, and recurrent).

progressive inspection. The approach of breaking down the large task of conducting a major inspection into smaller tasks that can be accomplished periodically without taking the aircraft out of service for an extended period of time.

propeller major alteration. Alterations of an aircraft's propellers, such as changes in blade or hub design, adding or changing a propeller governor, or installing a propeller de-ice system.

propeller major repair. Any repairs to deep cuts, nicks or dents, or the straightening or shortening, of steel blades; retipping, lamination replacement, or repairing of elongated bolt holes in the hub of fixed-pitch wood propellers; or repair of propeller governors.

protective breathing equipment (PBE). A portable, protective, self-contained breathing unit conveniently located on the flight deck or at other points throughout the aircraft. A PBE protects against the effects of smoke, carbon dioxide, or other harmful gases or an oxygen-deficient environment caused by other than an airplane depressurization.

proving tests. A "dry run" operated by an air carrier to show the suitability of the aircraft for the operations it contemplates performing.

public address (PA) system. A system of microphones, amplifiers, and loudspeakers used to amplify the speech of a crewmember.

public carriage. Carriage that implies a willingness to deal with many people who have a need to have something or someone taken someplace. An air carrier is engaged in public carriage if it "holds out" to the public (by advertising or other means) to transport persons or property for compensation or hire. *See also* holding out.

public charter. A one-way or round trip charter flight to be performed by one or more direct air carriers that is arranged and sponsored by a charter operator.

Public Law 111-216, Section 216—Flight Crewmember Screening and Qualification. Part of the sweeping Airline Safety and Federal Aviation Administration Extension Act (49 USC 40101) signed into law on August 1, 2010. Section 216 of the Act requires each flight crewmember for a Part 121 air carrier to hold an airline transport pilot certificate under 14 CFR Part 61. Previously, only the pilot-in-command was required to hold an ATP certificate.

Public Law 111-216, Section 217—Air Transport Pilot Certification. A section of the Airline Safety and Federal Aviation Administration Extension Act of 2010. Section 217 required the FAA to modify the requirements of an ATP certificate, as issued under Part 61, and also significantly raised the bar on standards for obtaining the airline transport pilot certificate.

qualified local observer. A person who provides weather, landing area, and other information as required by the carrier and who has been trained by the carrier under an approved training program.

random (drug) testing. Random selection of employees for drug testing. The selection must be made by a scientifically valid method, and each covered employee shall have an equal chance of being tested each time selections are made. The random drug tests must be unannounced and the dates for administering random tests must be spread reasonably throughout the calendar year.

recency of experience. FAA requirements intended to help maintain a crewmember's proficiency. For example, the requirements specify that a pilot must have made at least three takeoffs and landings, in the preceding 90 days, in the type airplane in which that pilot is to serve. Flight engineers must have had at least 50 hours of flight time within the preceding 6 calendar months as a flight engineer on that type airplane.

recurrent training. Training specified in 14 CFR 121.427 that ensures each crewmember or dispatcher is adequately trained and currently proficient with respect to the type of airplane he or she is crewing or dispatching.

recurring airworthiness directive (AD). An airworthiness directive that requires repetitive or periodic inspections. In order to provide for flexibility in administering such ADs, the AD may provide for adjustment of the inspection interval to coincide with inspections required by Part 91 or other regulations. The conditions and approval requirements under which adjustments may be allowed are stated in the AD.

redispatch/rerelease. A situation in which a flight is originally dispatched or released to one destination, and during the course of the flight the destination is changed and the flight is sent to a different destination. The term "redispatch" applies to certificate holders conducting flag operations; "rerelease" applies to certificate holders who are only authorized to conduct supplemental operations. A redispatch/rerelease may be planned (e.g., international operations) or unplanned (e.g., destination airport closure).

reduced minimums takeoff. Although Part 91 establishes IFR takeoff visibility minimums for Part 121 and Part 135 operators, an air carrier may be authorized to conduct takeoffs at reduced minimums. If so, the method of computing the amount of reductions and the applicable conditions will be given in an approved flight operations manual.

reduced programmed hours. The programmed hours of training prescribed in Part 121, Subpart M, reduced by the Administrator upon a showing by the certificate holder that circumstances justify a lesser amount.

reduced V_1. A speed lower than the maximum V_1, selected to reduce the rejected takeoff stopping distance. It is typically used during wet or slippery conditions in anticipation of degraded stopping capability due to poor runway conditions.

rejected takeoff (RTO). A takeoff that is discontinued or aborted after takeoff thrust is set and the initiation of the takeoff roll has begun.

released to service. A document that contains a certification confirming that the maintenance work to which it relates has been completed in a satisfactory manner, either in accordance with the approved data and the procedures described in the maintenance organization's procedures manual, or under an equivalent system.

releasing. Refers to the releasing of a supplemental air carrier flight within a flight following system (as compared to *dispatching* a flight in a scheduled domestic or flag operations dispatching system). No person may start a flight under a flight following system without specific authority, in the form of a flight release, from the person authorized by the operator to exercise operational control over the flight.

reliable fix. With respect to air navigation, the passage of a VOR, VORTAC, or NDB. It also includes a VOR/DME fix or a VOR intersection, an NDB intersection, and a VOR/NDB intersection.

repair category. A classification of inoperative items on board an aircraft; each repair category contains the time interval within which inoperative items must be repaired.

report time. The time that the certificate holder requires a flight crewmember to report for an assignment.

repositioning flight. The movement of an aircraft on which no payload is carried, the purpose of which is to locate the aircraft at a point where passengers and/or cargo are to be boarded for revenue service. The aircraft may carry a full crew complement and other nonrevenue passengers, as approved, but will not carry revenue payload under this classification. A repositioning flight may be operated under 14 CFR Part 91. A repositioning flight is not to be confused with a maintenance ferry flight. The only correct reference to a ferry flight is when the authorization to operate is in accordance with a special ferry permit.

requalification training. Training required for crewmembers previously trained and qualified, but who have become unqualified due to not having had the recurrent training required under 14 CFR §121.427 or not having taken a proficiency check required by §121.441.

required inspections. A maintenance program designation of the items of maintenance and alteration that must be inspected, including at least those that could result in a failure, malfunction, or defect endangering the safe operation of the aircraft if not performed properly or if improper parts or materials are used.

required navigation performance (RNP). A statement of navigation performance necessary for operations within a defined airspace such as the North Atlantic Minimum Navigation Performance Standards (MNPS) Airspace.

reserve availability period. A duty period during which a certificate holder requires a flight crewmember on short call reserve to be available to receive an assignment for a flight duty period.

reserve flight crewmember. A flight crewmember that a certificate holder requires to be available to receive an assignment for duty.

responsibility for operational control. 14 CFR §§121.533, 121.535, and 121.537 place the operational control responsibility with the certificate holder, who must ensure that anyone in a position to exercise control over operations is qualified through training, experience, and expertise in accordance with Part 119. *See also* operational control.

rest facility (Class 1, 2 and 3). A bunk or seat accommodation installed in an aircraft that provides a flight crewmember with a sleep opportunity. Rest facilities are categorized as Class 1, Class 2, or Class 3, based on the sleeping space provided, separation from the flight deck and passengers, and other environmental conditions.

rest period. A continuous period determined prospectively during which the flight crewmember is free from all restraint by the certificate holder, including freedom from present responsibility for work should the occasion arise.

rest records. Records showing how much rest a crewmember or dispatcher has received during the previous 24-hour period.

Restricted ATP (R-ATP). A restricted privileges ATP Certificate. The holder of a R-ATP certificate may not serve as a pilot-in-command (PIC) in any operation where an ATP certificate is required by regulation (14 CFR 61.167[b]). A holder of a restricted privileges ATP certificate may serve as a SIC in Part 121 operations, with the exception of Part 121 flag or supplemental operations requiring three or more pilots. While an applicant for an ATP certificate must be at least 23 years of age, an applicant for a R-ATP certificate must be at least 21 years of age.

restriction or suspension of operations. Regulations require a restriction or suspension of operations when a certificate holder conducting domestic or flag operations knows of conditions, including weather or airport and runway conditions, that are a hazard to safe operations, until those conditions are corrected. The authority to restrict or suspend air carrier operations is delegated by an air carrier's director of operations to the carrier's aircraft dispatchers and pilots-in-command.

retesting of covered employees with an alcohol concentration of 0.02 or greater but less than 0.04%. Alcohol testing required to be conducted by an employer of a covered employee to ensure that the employee has an alcohol concentration of less than 0.02 if the employer chooses to permit the employee to perform a safety-sensitive function within 8 hours following the administration of an alcohol test indicating an alcohol concentration of 0.02 or greater but less than 0.04.

return to duty (drug) testing. Drug testing that an individual is required to undergo, after refusing to submit to a drug test or receiving a verified positive drug test result, before an employer allows the individual to return to duty to perform a safety-sensitive function. No employer shall allow an individual required to undergo return to duty testing to perform a safety-sensitive function unless the employer has received a verified negative drug test result for the individual.

rotation speed (V_R). *See* V_R.

route and airport qualifications. Requirements that the air carrier establish a system for disseminating information to each pilot concerning the routes and airports to be served by that pilot. 14 CFR §121.443 requires that the captain must be route qualified and airport qualified.

runway limit weight. The maximum weight, at existing conditions, that will guarantee the aircraft meets the balanced field length requirements.

RVR (runway visual range). A specific measurement of visibility taken by a device placed alongside a runway for the purpose of measuring runway visibility. Measurements are expressed in hundreds of feet. Devices may be placed at the approach end of the runway (touchdown RVR), in the middle of the runway (mid-RVR), or at the far end of the runway (rollout RVR), or at all three locations.

safety management system. An FAA safety initiative with a top-down, business-like approach to managing safety risk. It includes a systemic approach to managing safety, including the necessary organizational structures, accountabilities, policies and procedures.

safety margin. The length of runway available beyond the actual landing distance, expressed in either a fixed distance increment or a percentage increase beyond the actual landing distance required.

safety-sensitive functions. Those functions performed by employees in safety-sensitive positions (e.g., aircraft dispatchers, aircraft maintenance and preventive maintenance personnel, air traffic control personnel, aviation screening, ground security coordinators, flight crewmembers, flight attendants, flight instructors).

scheduled flight time. The planned amount of flight time prior to the actual flight. Part 121 pilot flight time limitations, unlike Part 117, are based primarily on scheduled flight time, not actual flight time.

scheduled on-demand operations. On-demand operations that utilize airplanes, other than turbojets, with nine or fewer passenger seats *and* a 7,500-pound or less payload capacity, or any rotorcraft, used in scheduled passenger-carrying operations with a frequency less than five round trips per week on at least one route between two or more points according to the published flight schedules.

scheduled passenger operations. The holding out to the public of air transportation service for passengers from identified air terminals at a set time announced by timetable or schedule published in a newspaper, magazine, or other advertising medium.

seats, safety belts, and shoulder harnesses. Approved seats, safety belts, and shoulder harnesses or berths are required for each person (over the age of two) on board the airplane. For flight crewmembers, Part 121 aircraft flight crew seats must be equipped with a combined safety belt and shoulder harness that meets the applicable requirements specified in Part 25.

second-in-command. A pilot that is designated to be second-in-command of an aircraft during flight time.

second segment climb. The segment of a departure that begins at the point where the aircraft achieves gear retraction at a speed of V_2 and ends at acceleration altitude (normally 400 feet). *See also* four segment climb performance.

service difficulty reports. A report of certain aircraft equipment malfunctions, failures, or structural defects that must be sent to the FAA.

short-call reserve. A period of time in which a flight crewmember is assigned to a reserve availability period.

sideward facing seats. Flight crew or passenger seats which do not face forward or aft.

single pilot operator. A certificate holder who uses only one pilot in 14 CFR Part 135 operations.

single-pilot type rating. A type rating allowing a single pilot to fly certain aircraft that are above the small aircraft takeoff weight threshold that the FAA has determined to be safe when flown by one properly trained pilot (*see* type rating).

single-visit training program (SVT). A program that allows air carriers to place all flight crewmembers on the same recurrent training cycle.

slip resistant escape route. On each passenger-carrying aircraft that has an overwing emergency exit, each exit must have an escape route that is covered with a slip-resistant surface (except for flap surfaces suitable as slides). The slip-resistant surface must meet the requirements of Part 25.

small aircraft. Aircraft of 12,500 pounds or less, maximum certificated takeoff weight.

special airport qualifications. Airports requiring that each pilot-in-command make an actual entry into that airport within the last 12 months or qualify using pictorial means to train for the unusual circumstances affecting that airport.

special airworthiness requirements. Rules in Subpart J to Part 121: Special Airworthiness Requirements, applicable to older aircraft certificated under the CAR (Civil Aeronautics Regulations of the CAA) prior to November 1, 1946. The intent of these rules is to bring the safety standards of older aircraft up to approximately the standards of more modern aircraft.

Special Exemption 5549. This exemption allows authorized air carrier's high minimums captains to fly to published landing minimums when they would otherwise have to fly to higher minimums (i.e., published minimums plus 100 feet to DA or MDA, and plus ½ mile to visibility minima). Many air carriers have been granted an exemption from the higher landing minimums provided certain weather conditions and aircraft equipment exist.

specialized means of navigation. Refers to equipment required when specialized means of navigation are used. A dwindling number of older aircraft operating over oceans or large unsettled areas where ground based navigation signals are not available rely on specialized means of navigation systems, such as an inertial navigation system (INS), or Doppler Radar Navigation.

specialized navigational equipment. Instead of utilizing human flight navigators, modern air carrier aircraft are operated under a specialized navigation equipment provision. The cost considerations make it much more efficient to make a one-time investment in specialized navigation equipment and not have the recurring labor costs of live navigators.

split duty. A flight duty period that has a scheduled break in duty that is less than a required rest period.

stall speed (V_S). The minimum steady flight speed at which the airplane is controllable. It is the minimum speed that the wing can create enough lift to support the aircraft. On a coefficient of lift curve, it is the airspeed at which the wing creates its maximum coefficient of lift.

standard airworthiness certificate (FAA form 8100-2). A certificate displayed in the aircraft that is the FAA's official authorization allowing for the operation of type certificated aircraft in the following categories: normal, utility, acrobatic, commuter, transport, manned free balloons, and special classes. It remains valid as long as the aircraft meets its approved type design, is in a condition for safe operation, and has maintenance, preventative maintenance, and alterations performed in accordance with 14 CFR Parts 21, 43, and 91.

standard alternate (weather) minimums. The standard minimum ceiling and visibility that must be forecast in order to list an airport as an alternate airport. Standard minimums are 600-2 for precision approaches and 800-2 for nonprecision approaches. These minimums apply unless a carrier has received approval in its ops specs to use lower than standard derived alternate minimums. *See also* 600-2; 800-2; derived alternate (weather) minimums.

sterile area. An airport area to which access is controlled by the inspection of persons and property in accordance with an approved security program.

sterile cockpit rule. The rule that requires flight crews to refrain from nonessential tasks and conversation during defined critical phases of flight.

stopway. An area beyond the takeoff runway, no less wide than the runway and centered upon the extended centerline of the runway, able to support the airplane during an aborted takeoff without causing structural damage to the airplane and designated by the airport authorities for use in decelerating the airplane during an aborted takeoff.

suitable accommodations. A temperature-controlled facility with sound mitigation and the ability to control light that provides a flight crew member with the ability to sleep either in a bed, bunk or in a chair that allows for flat or near flat sleeping position. (Only applies to ground facilities and does not apply to aircraft onboard rest facilities.)

suitable alternate airport. An adequate alternate airport that also has acceptable weather and field conditions available during the time period the field is to be flight-planned as an alternate airport. *See also* adequate alternate airport.

supplemental all cargo operations. Part 121 nonscheduled all-cargo operations with airplanes having a passenger seat configuration of more than 30 seats, excluding each crewmember seat, and a payload capacity of more than 7,500 pounds.

supplemental operations. Any nonscheduled passenger-carrying operation or any all-cargo operation conducted under 14 CFR Part 121.

supplemental oxygen for sustenance. Sustaining oxygen and dispensing equipment required for continuing operations in an unpressurized or partially pressurized airplane. When operating a turbine engine powered airplane, each certificate holder must equip the airplane with such equipment. The amount of oxygen to be provided depends on the amount of passengers and crew, the altitude, and the time spent at that altitude.

supplemental type certificate (STC). A type certificate (TC) issued when an applicant has received FAA approval to modify an aeronautical product such as an aircraft, engine, propeller or appliance (e.g., alternator) from its original design. The STC, which incorporates by reference the related TC, approves not only the modification but also how that modification affects the original design.

Table A, B, C (Part 117). Tables A, B and C are found in 14 CFR Part 117, which regulates flight and duty limitations and rest requirements for flight crewmembers. Flight crews must verify that the flight can be completed within the applicable flight time and flight duty period limit for each crewmember (including any extension agreed to by the PIC).

Table A covers flight time limits for unaugmented operations, which restricts a flight crewmember's time on task (flight time) to either 8 or 9 hours based on the time the flight crewmember reports for duty.

Table B is used for unaugmented operations (2-pilot crews) and limits the maximum flight duty period (hours) for lineholders based on number of flight segments.

Table C is used for augmented operations (3 and 4-pilot crews) and limits the maximum flight duty period (hours) based on rest facility and number of pilots.

takeoff decision speed. *See* V_1.

takeoff distance. *See* takeoff distance, dry runway; takeoff distance, wet runway.

takeoff distance, dry runway. The greater of: (1) The horizontal distance along the takeoff path from the start of the takeoff to the point at which the airplane is 35 feet above the takeoff surface, determined under §25.111 for a dry runway, or (2) 115 percent of the horizontal distance along the takeoff path, with all engines operating, from the start of the takeoff to the point at which the airplane is 35 feet above the takeoff surface, as determined by a procedure consistent with Section 25.111.

takeoff distance, wet runway. The greater of (1) the takeoff distance on a dry runway determined in accordance with the dry runway procedures, or (2) the horizontal distance along the takeoff path from the start of the takeoff to the point at which the airplane is 15 feet above the takeoff surface, achieved in a manner consistent with the achievement of V_2 before reaching 35 feet above the takeoff surface. *See also* takeoff distance, dry runway.

takeoff distance available (TODA). The takeoff run available plus the length of any remaining runway or clearway beyond the far end of the takeoff run available. TODA is the distance declared available for satisfying takeoff distance requirements for airplanes where the certification and operating rules and available performance data allow for the consideration of a clearway in takeoff performance computations.

takeoff distance with an engine failure. The distance from brake release to the point where the aircraft attains a height of 35 feet, assuming the engine fails at V_{EF}. Part 25 requires that the length of runway plus clearway be at least equal to the engine failure takeoff distance.

takeoff limitations. The requirement that no one operating a turbine-powered airplane may take off at a weight that exceeds the maximum allowable weight permitted by the airplane flight manual considering the altitude (airport elevation) and temperature existing at the time of departure. This requirement is satisfied by referring to the WAT limit charts.

takeoff path. A conditional distance that extends from the point of brake release on the runway to a point in the takeoff at which the airplane is 1,500 feet above the takeoff surface, *or* a point at which the transition from the takeoff to the cruise climb configuration is completed and a speed in compliance with §25.111(c) is shown.

takeoff run. When a clearway is present, the takeoff run is the greater of the horizontal distance along the flight path to a point halfway between where liftoff airspeed is reached and the point at which the airplane is 35 feet above the takeoff surface, or 115% of the horizontal distance along the flight path (all engines operating) from the start of the takeoff to a point halfway between the point at which liftoff airspeed is reached and the point at which the airplane is 35 feet above the takeoff surface. With no clearway, the takeoff run is equal to the takeoff distance.

takeoff warning system. A warning system providing an aural warning that is automatically activated during the initial portion of the takeoff roll if the airplane is in a configuration that would not allow a safe takeoff. Also known as takeoff configuration warning system (TOCWS).

TERPS. The United States Standard for Terminal Instrument Procedures, which outlines the methods for certifying terminal procedures (approaches) in the United States. The TERPS is similar in concept to the ICAO PANS-OPS and the JAA-JAR-OPS-1 documents.

terrain awareness and warning system (TAWS). A warning system designed to prevent controlled flight into terrain (CFIT). TAWS is a relatively new term used inclusively to describe older GPWS and EGPWS systems as well as newer terrain awareness and warning systems.

tests for common carriage. The FAA will determine if an aircraft operator is acting as a common carrier (and thereby falling within the air carrier regulations) by determining if it is (1) holding itself out to the general public, (2) involved in the transportation of people or cargo (3) from place to place (4) for compensation. If it is found to be doing so it is acting as a common carrier.

theater. A geographical area in which the distance between the flight crewmember's flight duty period departure point and arrival point differs by no more than 60 degrees longitude.

third segment climb. The segment of a departure that begins at acceleration altitude and continues until the aircraft is cleaned up and established in the cruise climb configuration at the cruise climb airspeed. During this segment, the aircraft is accelerated, flaps are retracted, any emergency checklists are run, and maximum continuous or cruise climb power is set. *See also* four segment climb performance.

Title 14 of the Code of Federal Regulations (14 CFR). The codification of all regulations promulgated (issued) under Title 49 of the United States Code (USC).

Title 49 of United States Code (49 USC). The title of the United States Code that contains U.S. statutes (laws) related to aviation and space.

Title 49 of USC, Section 40101. *See* Airline Safety and Federal Aviation Administration Extension Act of 2010

tort. In law, a civil wrong for which a court may provide monetary or injunctive relief. Injunctive relief simply means the court may order a person or company to do or to refrain from doing something.

traffic alert and collision avoidance system (TCAS). Equipment that provides traffic alerts of conflicting traffic. In the case of collision threat, it also issues resolution advisories.

Traffic Information Service – Broadcast (TIS-B). ADS-B service broadcasts relevant traffic position reports to appropriately equipped aircraft. TIS-B information is available to aircraft that utilize 978 MHz (UAT), 1090MHz (1090ES) or both. The aircraft must be within coverage of an ADS-B ground station and an FAA radar or multilateration system to receive the target information.

transient fatigue. An acute form of fatigue brought on by extreme sleep restriction or extended hours awake within 1 or 2 days.

transition training. The training required for crewmembers and dispatchers who have qualified and served in the same capacity on another airplane in the same group.

transport category aircraft. Airplanes for which a type certificate is applied for under Part 21 in the transport category and that meet the transport category airworthiness requirements. Multi-engine airplanes with more than 19 seats or a maximum takeoff weight greater than 19,000 lbs must be certificated in the transport category

Transportation Security Administration (TSA). The federal agency created after 9/11 to provide security to all transportation modes. It performs all passenger, baggage and cargo security clearance for aircraft operations in Part 121.

Transportation Security Administration (TSA) Security Directives (SD). Security requirements that all air carriers conducting operations under Part 121 must comply with. These security requirements may be found in the Transportation Security Administration and Department of Homeland Security regulations.

type certificate. Issued to signify the airworthiness of an aircraft manufacturing design. The type certificate reflects a determination made by the FAA that the aircraft is manufactured according to an approved design, and that the design ensures compliance with airworthiness requirements.

type rating. An FAA authorization stating an airman's particular privileges and limitations pertaining to certain aircraft type and listed directly on a pilot's license. The FAA has determined certain airplanes are so complicated they require training above and beyond initial license and aircraft class training. Large aircraft, turbojet-powered airplanes, and other aircraft specified by the Administrator require an aircraft type rating.

ultra-long-range (ULR) operations. Air carrier operations with flight segments of greater than 12 hours in length, with duty periods of 16 to 22 hours.

unauthorized operator. Someone who operates an aircraft in operations that require an air carrier certificate but doesn't possess one.

unforeseen operational circumstances. An unplanned event of insufficient duration to allow for adjustments to schedules, including unforecast weather, equipment malfunction, or air traffic delay that could not be reasonably expected.

Universal Access Transceiver (UAT). A broadcast data link supporting ADS-B, TIS-B, and FIS-B. Allows aircraft equipped with "out" broadcast capabilities so they can be seen by other aircraft using ADS-B In technology as well as FAA ground stations. Aircraft equipped with ADS-B In technology will be able to see detailed altitude and vector information from ADS-B Out equipped aircraft as well as FIS-B and TIS-B broadcasts.

upgrade training. The training required for crewmembers that have qualified and served as second-in-command or flight engineer on a particular airplane type, before they serve as a pilot-in-command or second-in-command, respectively, on that airplane.

V_1. The maximum speed in the takeoff at which the pilot must take first action to stop the airplane within the accelerate-stop distance. V_1 also means the minimum speed in the takeoff, following a failure of the critical engine at V_{EF}, at which the pilot can continue the takeoff and achieve the required height above the takeoff surface within the takeoff distance. V_1 is the end of the go/no-go decision process.

V_2. The single-engine takeoff safety speed. In the event of an engine failure on takeoff, this is the minimum speed to be maintained to at least 400 feet above the takeoff surface. V_2 is analogous to the best single engine rate of climb (V_{YSE}) for a light twin-engine aircraft.

V_{EF}. The reference airspeed at which the critical engine is assumed to fail. The aircraft continues to accelerate from the instant an engine fails until the instant the pilot recognizes and reacts to the engine failure by activating the first deceleration device.

V_{FTO}. Final takeoff speed: the airspeed of the airplane that exists at the end of the takeoff path in the enroute configuration with one engine inoperative.

V_{LOF}. Liftoff speed: the speed at which the aircraft will leave the ground if rotation is begun at V_R and the correct rate of rotation is used.

V_{MC} or V_{MCA}. Minimum controllable airspeed (airborne). The airspeed at which, when airborne, the critical engine is suddenly made inoperative, it is possible to maintain control of the airplane with that engine still inoperative and maintain straight flight with an angle of bank of not more than 5 degrees.

V_{MC} limit. A minimum weight limit used in aircraft where reduced power takeoffs are used. This minimum weight is designed to control V_{MC} from being too high on takeoff.

V_{MCG}. The minimum control speed on the ground. The airspeed during the takeoff run at which, when the critical engine is suddenly made inoperative, it is possible to maintain control of the airplane using rudder control alone (without the use of nose-wheel steering).

V_R. The rotation speed, or the speed at which the nose may be raised to initial climb attitude.

V_{REF}. The airspeed that is 1.3 times the stalling speed in the landing configuration

V_S. Stall speed or minimum steady flight speed. *See* stall speed; minimum steady flight speed.

V_{SR}. The reference stall speed is a calibrated airspeed defined by the applicant. V_{SR} may not be less than a 1-g stall speed.

ventral and tailcone exits. An exit door and airstair that allows egress through the belly of an aircraft is called a ventral exit. A door and airstair allowing egress through the tailcone of the aircraft is called a tailcone exit.

Vision 100—Century of Aviation Reauthorization Act. A Public Law adopted in late 2003, to coincide with the 100th Anniversary of the Wright brothers' first powered flight at Kitty Hawk.

warning light. For airplanes certificated prior to 2010, annunciator lights are required for certain types of events. An event which is deemed immediately critical is annunciated with a red-colored light called a warning light.

warning, caution and advisory lights. Cockpit lights to alert the flight crew of various aircraft systems events. For aircraft manufactured prior to 2010, they are mandatory for certain events. Since 2010, due to tremendous advancement in display technology they are not required to be used but are permitted for use if approved by the administrator. The colors of the lights must be red for emergencies (warning), amber for cautionary information, and green for safe operations. Other colors such as blue and white may be for other purposes as approved.

WAT limit charts. Weight, altitude, temperature (WAT) limit charts are takeoff performance planning charts. *See also* runway limit weight; climb limit weight.

wet lease. A form of aircraft leasing that most often occurs between two airlines or an aircraft brokerage firm that includes the leased aircraft and its operating costs such as flight and cabin crews, maintenance, insurance and fuel (hence the name). It is normally billed on the basis of flight hours used.

Whitlow letter. A letter written by James Whitlow, former Deputy Chief Counsel at the FAA, in response to some questions posed by an American Airlines captain regarding duty and rest rules for pilots on reserve status. The main focus of the letter was the clarification of what was considered duty time. Mr. Whitlow stated that the airlines could not put a pilot "on call" without considering that time to be duty time, even if the pilot was at home.

window of circadian low. A period of maximum sleepiness that occurs between 0200 and 0559 hours during a physiological night.

BIBLIOGRAPHY

14 C.F.R. Aeronautics and Space. Office of the Federal Register. Electronic Code of Federal Regulations (eCFR) updated daily at https://www.ecfr.gov/current/title-14.

American Airlines Flight Department. *Boeing 727 Operating Manual.* Fort Worth: American Airlines Flight Academy, 1971.

Black's Law Dictionary. 4th ed. St. Paul: West Publishing Company, 1968.

Brown, Greg N., and Mark J. Holt. *The Turbine Pilot's Flight Manual.* 4th ed. Newcastle, WA: Aviation Supplies & Academics, Inc., 2019.

English, Dave. *Slipping the Surly Bonds.* New York: McGraw Hill Publishing, 2000.

Federal Aviation Administration (FAA). *Flightcrew Alerting.* Advisory Circular 25.1322-1. Washington, DC: FAA, 13 December 2010.

———. *Airline Transport Pilot Certification Training Program.* Advisory Circular 61-138. Washington, DC: FAA, 02 July 2013.

———. *Advanced Qualification Program.* Advisory Circular 120-54A. Washington, DC: FAA, 23 June 2006.

———. *Air Carrier First Aid Programs.* Advisory Circular 120-44A. Washington, DC: FAA, 09 March 1995.

———. *Air Carrier Maintenance Programs.* Advisory Circular 120-16G. Washington, DC: FAA, 04 January 2016.

———. *Airplane Flight Training Device Qualification.* Advisory Circular 120-45A. Washington, DC: FAA, 05 February 1992.

———. *Airplane Simulator Qualification.* Advisory Circular 120-40B. Washington, DC: FAA, 29 July 1991.

———. *Airport Obstacle Analysis.* Advisory Circular 120-91. Washington, DC: FAA, U.S. Government Printing Office. 05 May 2006.

———. *Airworthiness Directives Manual.* Washington, DC: United States Department of Transportation, Federal Aviation Administration, Aircraft Certification Service, AIR-1, May 2010.

———. *Aviation Maintenance Technician Handbook—General.* FAA-H-8083-30. Oklahoma City: United States Department of Transportation, Federal Aviation Administration, Airman Testing Standards Branch, AFS-630, 2011.

———. *Cabin Safety Subject Index.* Scottsdale: United States Department of Transportation, Federal Aviation Administration, Scottsdale Flight Standards District Office, 05 May 2014.

———. *Developing and Implementing an Air Carrier Continuing Analysis and Surveillance System.* Advisory Circular 120-79A. Washington, DC: FAA, 07 September 2010.

———. *Emergency Medical Equipment.* Advisory Circular 121-33B. Washington, DC: FAA, 12 January 2006.

———. *Extended Operations (ETOPS and Polar Operations).* Advisory Circular 120-42B. Washington, DC: FAA, 13 June 2008.

———. *FAA Approval of Aviation Training Devices and Their Use for Training and Experience.* Advisory Circular 61-136B. Washington, DC: FAA, 12 September 2018.

———. *Fatigue Education and Awareness Training Program.* Advisory Circular 117-2. Washington, DC: FAA, 11 October 2012.

———. *Fatigue Risk Management Systems for Aviation Safety.* Advisory Circular 120-103A. Washington, DC: FAA, 06 May 2013.

———. *Flight Standards Information Management System.* FAA Order 8900.1. FAA, 2011. Retrieved from http://fsims.faa.gov

———. *Flightcrew Member Rest Facilities.* Advisory Circular 117-1. Washington, DC: FAA, 20 September 2012.

———. *Guidelines for the Certification Airworthiness, and Operational Use of Electronic Flight Bags.* Advisory Circular 120-76C. Washington, DC: FAA, 09 May 2014.

———. *Mitigating the Risks of a Runway Overrun Upon Landing.* Advisory Circular 91-79A. Washington, DC: FAA, 17 September 2014.

———. *Private Carriage Versus Common Carriage of Persons or Property.* Advisory Circular 120-12A. Washington, DC: FAA, 24 April 1986.

———. *Takeoff Safety Training Aid.* Advisory Circular 120-62. Washington, DC: FAA, 12 September 1994. Included in its entirety in Takeoff Safety Training Aid: Pilot Guide to Takeoff Safety. Washington, DC: FAA. Retrieved from http://flightsafety.org/files/RERR/TakeoffTrainingSafetyAid.pdf

Hopkins, George E. *Flying the Line.* Vol. 2. Washington DC: Airline Pilots Association, International, 2000.

Office of the Federal Register. 1988. *Air Transportation Operations Inspectors Handbook Order 8400.10*, Department of Transportation, Federal Aviation Administration, Washington DC, U.S. Government Printing Office.

Office of the Federal Register. *Special Federal Aviation Regulation 58—Advanced Qualification Program.* Federal Register, Vol. 55, No. 91. Washington DC: Federal Aviation Administration, 2 October 1990: pp. 40262–40352.

Prosser, William L. *Law of Torts*, St. Paul, MN: West Publishing Company, 1974.

U.S. Department of Transportation/FAA. *Federal Aviation Regulations for Flight Crew.* Newcastle, WA: Aviation Supplies & Academics, Inc., 2016.

INDEX

1-2-3 rule *196*
1 in 7 rule *120*
14 CFR Part 1 *3, 10*
14 CFR Part 21 *3, 4, 155*
14 CFR Part 23 *3*
14 CFR Part 25 *3, 133, 134, 138, 157–165, 169, 173*
14 CFR Part 39 *4, 265*
14 CFR Part 43 *4, 252, 263*
14 CFR Part 60 *271, 275*
14 CFR Part 61 *4, 10–11*
14 CFR Part 63 *10*
14 CFR Part 65 *4, 10, 263*
14 CFR Part 67 *4, 281*
14 CFR Part 91 *4, 10, 22, 33, 196, 206–207, 224, 257*
14 CFR Part 110 *4, 21, 22*
14 CFR Part 111 *4*
14 CFR Part 117 *4, 95–116*
14 CFR Part 119 *4, 10, 13, 21–22, 35*
14 CFR Part 120 *5, 280–284*
14 CFR Part 121 *5, 22, 31, 33, 39–42*
  composition of flight crews *64–66*
  maintenance manual requirement *259*
  operating manual requirements *51–56*
  Subpart A, General *14*
  Subpart E, Approval of Routes: Domestic and Flag Operations *14–15*
  Subpart F, Approval of Areas and Routes: Supplemental Operations *15–16*
  Subpart J, Special Airworthiness Requirements *156–157*
  Subpart M, Airman and Crewmember Requirements *63–79*
  Subpart N, Training Programs *81–85*
  Subpart O, Crewmember Qualifications *85–94*
  Subpart P *125–126*
  Subpart Q *116–120*
  Subpart R *120–122*
  Subpart S *122–124*

14 CFR Part 125 *5, 22*
14 CFR Part 129 *5*
14 CFR Part 135 *5, 14, 22, 42*
  composition of flight crews *73*
  maintenance manual requirements *260–263*
  operating manual requirements *56–58*
  recordkeeping requirements *253–254*
14 CFR Part 136 *5*
14 CFR Part 141 *5, 22*
14 CFR Part 142 *5, 22, 31*
14 CFR Part 145 *5, 10, 22, 263*
14 CFR Part 147 *6, 263*
30 in 7 *113, 116, 122*
50 in 6 requirements *88*
60-minute rule *144*
90-minute rule *146*
600-2 *32, 197*
800-2 *32, 197*

A

accelerate-go distance *137*
accelerate-stop distance *135, 137, 141, 142*
acceleration altitude *140, 143, 144*
acclimated *98, 100–101*
A-Checks *263*
active control *44*
actual flight time *115, 119*
additional emergency exits *173*
adequate alternate airport *193, 194*
Administrator *15*
  approved by *15, 55*
advanced qualification program (AQP) *89–90*
advanced simulation *271–276*
advisory circulars (ACs) *6*
advisory lights *164*
age 65 rule *63–64*

airborne weather radar *184*
air carrier *7–19, 11. See also* airline
    certification of *21–22*
air carrier certificate *12, 13, 14, 21, 35, 98*
    required to conduct training *83*
Air Commerce Act of 1926 *2*
aircraft. *See also* airplane
    en route limitations *144–146*
    landing limitations of *146–149*
    operating limitations of *134–141*
    performance of *134–141*
    requirements of *133–154*
    takeoff limitations of *141–144*
aircraft listing record *34, 242, 244*
aircraft maintenance logbook *247, 248, 252*
airframe major alterations *251–252*
airframe major repairs *251–252*
airline *21. See also* air carrier
    organization of *39–49*
Airline Safety and Federal Aviation Administration Extension Act (49 USC 40101) *3, 95*
airline transport pilot (ATP) certification *69, 72*
Airline Transport Pilot Certification Training Program (ATP CTP) *71–72*
airman requirements *63–79*
airplane. *See also* aircraft
    authorization and limitations *30*
    instruments and equipment *169*
    security *218*
airplane flight manual (AFM) *55*
airport
    aeronautical data of *30*
    and route qualifications *88*
    authorizations and limitations *27, 32–33*
    certification and operations of *15, 227–228*
    landing limitations for *146–149*
airport qualifications. *See* route and airport qualifications; special airport qualifications
airport/standby reserve *98, 109*
air rage *233*
airworthiness directive (AD) *4, 217, 248, 260, 265. See also* emergency airworthiness directive (EAD)
airworthiness release *217, 252, 260*
airworthiness requirements *155–165, 169*
airworthiness responsibility *257–259*
airworthy *47, 155, 262*
alcohol abuse prevention program *283*
alcoholic beverages, use of *232*
alcohol testing *280, 283–284*
    follow-up *284*
    post-accident *283*
    pre-employment *283*
    random *283*
    reasonable suspicion *284*
    retesting of covered employees *284*
    return to duty *284*

all-cargo operations *95, 115–126. See also* flag all-cargo operations; domestic all-cargo operations; supplemental all-cargo operations
alteration and repair report *251*
alternate airport weather minimums *197–200*
alternative method of compliance (AMOC) *265*
annual line check *87*
annual recurrent ground and flight training *86*
anti-icing requirements *31*
Appendix A (Part 121): First Aid Kits and Emergency Medical Kits *269–270*
Appendix B (Part 121): Airplane Flight Recorder Specifications *270*
Appendix E (Part 121): Flight Training Requirements *82, 270*
Appendix F (Part 121): Proficiency Check Requirements *82, 270–271*
Appendix H (Part 121): Advanced Simulation *271–276*
appliance major alterations *251*
appliance major repairs *251–252*
approach minimums *32, 207*
approach procedures *32, 33. See also* instrument approach procedures
approved means to assist the occupants in descending to the ground *171*
approved routes and limitations *225–227*
area navigation system *31, 33*
areas of operations *15, 276*
augmented flight crew *98, 103, 107–108*
augmented operations *105, 110, 111*
authority to refuse transportation *236*
auto flight guidance system (AFGS) operations *33*
automated communication and reporting system (ACARS) *253*
automatic landing operations *33*
autopilot system *33, 73*
aviation security program *218*
aviation training devices (ATDs) *275*

B

baggage, carry-on *31, 162, 235, 236*
baggage compartment. *See* cargo or baggage compartment
bailment *8*
bailment for hire *8*
balanced field length *134, 137–138*
balanced field limit *137*
base month *82*
basic indoctrination ground training (indoc) *84*
B-Checks *263*
Boeing 737, composition of flight crew *65*
borrowed parts *34*
briefing of passengers *230–231*
bulkheads *157*
Bureau of Air Commerce *2*
buy-back procedures *260*

C

cabin pressurization failure *178*
calendar day *98*
calibration of precision tools *260*
cargo bins *157*
cargo, carrying on aircraft *157*
cargo or baggage compartment *157*
    classification *161–162*
        design of *162*
        smoke or fire detection system *162–164*
carriage *7*. *See also* private carriage, public carriage, common carriage
carriage of all comers *8*
carriage of infants and children under 2 years of age *173–174*
Category I IFR landing minimums *33, 196*
caution lights *164*
C-Checks *263*
certificated land airports *227*
certificate holder *98*
    training *31*
certificate holding district office (CHDO) *264*
certificate of demonstrated proficiency *63, 74*
certification, airman. *See* pilot certification
certified landing distance *138*
check airmen, training of *83–84*
check pilot. *See* check airman
chief executive officer (CEO) *46*
chief inspector *41*
chief operating officer (COO) *46*
chief pilot *40, 43*
child restraint system *173–174*
circadian fatigue *102*
circadian rhythms *96, 97*
circling approach procedures *33, 275*
Civil Aeronautics Act of 1938 *2*
Civil Aeronautics Administration (CAA) *2*
Civil Aeronautics Authority (CAA) *2*
Civil Aeronautics Board (CAB) *2*
Class I navigation *31, 32*
Class II navigation *31, 32*
Class A cargo or baggage compartment *161*
Class B cargo or baggage compartment *161*
Class C cargo or baggage compartment *161*
Class D cargo or baggage compartment *161*
Class E cargo compartment *161*
clean-up altitude *140*
clearway *138*
climb limit weight *138, 142*
Cockpit Access Security System (CASS) *223*
cockpit check procedure/checklist *176*
cockpit voice recorders (CVRs) *165, 185*
Code of Federal Regulations (CFR) *2*
commercial flying *115*
    effects on flight time limitation *116–124*
commercial operator *11, 13*
    certification of *21–22*
commercial pilot certificate *12, 42, 43, 72, 271*
common carriage *7–9, 22. See also* tests for common carriage
common carrier *8–12*
communication records *252–253*
communications requirements *15*
communications systems *182*
commuter carrier, operations specifications of *23, 35*
commuter operation *13*
company flight manual (CFM) *55*
compensation or hire *8, 9, 11–13*
composition of flight crews *64–66*
computer-based recordkeeping system *31*
consecutive nighttime operations *113*
contact approaches *33*
continuing analysis and surveillance system (CASS) *261*
continuous airworthiness maintenance program (CAMP) *33, 262, 279*
Contract Air Mail Act of 1925 *1*
control systems gust locks *158*
coordinating agencies for suppliers evaluation *34*
copilot *64, 86*
crewmember interphone system *176*
crewmember oxygen *164, 178–179*
crewmember records *241*
crewmember requirements *63–79*
crewmembers. *See also* flight crewmembers
    interference with *233*
crew resource management (CRM) *73, 85*
    training *82, 220*
crew seat belts/shoulder harnesses *174*
critical phase of flight *219–220*
cumulative fatigue *102, 113*
cumulative flight time limitations *111–112*
curriculum *83*

D

DC-9-10 aircraft *64–65*
D-Checks *263–264*
deadhead time aloft *124*
deadhead transportation *98*
declared runway distances *138*
deicing requirements *31*
delay report *219*
Department of Homeland Security (DHS) *218*
Department of Transportation (DOT) *2, 241*
departure airport alternate airport *193, 194, 196*
derived alternate weather minimums *32, 197, 201*
destination alternate airport *196–197*
deviation authority *35, 112, 114*
differences training *81*
digital flight data recorders (DFDRs) *165, 181*
direct air carriers *21*

director of maintenance *41, 43*
director of operations *40, 42*
director of safety *41*
disabled passengers *236*
dispatch *15, 46*
dispatcher *44, 76. See also* flight dispatcher
    duty time limitations *125–126*
    records *241*
dispatcher resource management (DRM) *85*
    training *82*
dispatch function *47*
dispatching *189*
    rules *189–214, 193*
dispatch release *216*
dispatch release document *189–190, 191, 245*
domestic all-cargo operations *116–120*
domestic carrier
    operations schedules *219*
    operations specifications of *23, 35*
domestic operations *95*
    and approval of routes *14–15*
    and emergencies *228*
    and equipment interchange *229–230*
    and operational control *15, 215–217*
    communication record requirements *252*
    definition of *13*
    dispatching of *189–190*
    emergency equipment requirements *183*
    flight and duty time limitations *97, 115–120, 125–126*
    fuel requirements *203*
    operating requirements *14*
    recordkeeping requirements *241–246, 248*
    rest requirements *97*
    to airports outside 48 contiguous states *31*
Doppler radar *184*
driftdown altitude *145*
driftdown technique *145*
drug education program *282*
drug testing
    based on reasonable cause *281*
    follow-up *282*
    periodic *281*
    post-accident *281*
    pre-employment *280*
    random *281*
    return to duty *282*
drug training program *282*
dry lease *133, 229*
duty *98*
    limitations *119–120*
duty aloft time *123*
duty period *116*
duty to care *7–9*

E

e-CFR *6*
electronic flight bag (EFB) *58–59*
emergencies *228*
emergency airworthiness directive (EAD) *4, 31, 265, 266*
emergency descent *178*
emergency equipment *171–174*
    for extended overwater operations *180*
    for operations over uninhabited terrain *183*
emergency evacuation
    demonstration *74, 157*
    duties *75–76*
emergency exits *171, 230, 231*
    access *172*
    for flight crew *159*
    locator sign *159*
    markings *171, 173*
    operating handles *172*
emergency flotation means *181*
emergency lighting controls *159*
emergency lighting system *159, 172*
    energy supply *159*
emergency light operation *172*
emergency medical kits. *See* Appendix A (Part 121): First Aid Kits and Emergency Medical Kits
employee assistance plan *282*
engine failure speed *136*
engine inoperative, landing and reporting requirements *229*
en route alternate airport *193*
en route authorizations and limitations *26, 31, 144*
en route inspections *223*
en route limitations *31, 144*
    one engine inoperative *144–146*
    two engines inoperative *146*
en route operations, authorized area of *32*
equipment interchange agreements *229*
equipment requirements *169–187*
estimated time enroute (ETE) *203*
ETOPS. *See* extended operations (ETOPS)
evacuation demonstrations *75, 157*
exits. *See* emergency exits; exit seating; exterior exit markings; ventral exits; tailcone exits; *See* interior emergency exit markings; floor level exits
exit seating *31, 235–236*
extended operations (ETOPS)
    dispatch/flight release *190, 245, 246*
    maintenance requirements *263–264*
    requirements for *276–280*
extended operations (ETOPS) alternate *193–194*
extended overwater operations *32, 180, 182*
exterior emergency lighting *173*
exterior exit markings *173*

F

factored landing distance *138*
Fair Treatment for Experienced Pilots Act *63*
fatigue *98, 102*
    pilot *96–99, 101–102*
    symptoms of *102*
fatigue education and awareness training program *103*
fatigue risk management plan *96*
fatigue risk management system (FRMS) *97, 98, 102–103, 125*
Federal Aviation Act of 1958 *2*
Federal Aviation Administration (FAA) *1–3, 241*
    flight standards organization of *15*
    issuing of air carrier certificates *35*
Federal Aviation Agency (FAA) *2*
Federal Aviation Regulations (FARs) *2. See also* 14 CFR (specific Parts)
    exemptions from *30, 200–202, 208*
    governing common carriage *10–15*
Federal Register Act of 1935 *2*
ferry flight *30, 34*
final approach speed *138*
final rule *265*
fire detector system *161, 164*
fire extinguishers *162–163, 171*
fire extinguishing system *163*
fire protection for essential flight controls, engine mounts, and other flight structures *163–164*
fire protection, interior of aircraft. *See* interior fire protection
fire zones, in aircraft *163*
first aid kits. *See* Appendix A (Part 121): First Aid Kits and Emergency Medical Kits
first segment climb *143–144*
fit for duty. *See* fitness for duty
fitness for duty *98, 101, 102*
flag all-cargo operations *120–122*
flag carriers *14–15, 22. See also* flag operations
    operations schedules *219*
    operations specifications of *23, 35*
flag operations *95. See also* flag carriers
    and approval of routes *14–15*
    and emergencies *228*
    and equipment interchange *229–230*
    and local regulations *14*
    and operational control *15, 215–217*
    communication record requirements *252*
    definition of *13*
    dispatching of *189–190*
    emergency equipment requirements *183*
    flight and duty time limitations *95, 97, 115, 120–122, 125–126*
    fuel requirements *203–204*
    operations requirements *14*
    recordkeeping requirements *241–246, 248*
    rest requirements *97*

flammability standards *160*
flight and duty time limitations *95–132*
    aircraft dispatcher *125–126*
    all-cargo operations *104, 115–126*
    cumulative *111–112*
    definitions relating to *98–101*
    flight attendant *125–126*
    for emergency and government-sponsored operations *114*
    for pilots on reserve *109–110*
    Part 117 *95–116*
    rest period and *112–113*
    supplemental all-cargo operations *124*
flight and navigational equipment *170*
flight attendant
    certification requirements *63, 74–75*
    duty limitations and rest requirements *125–126*
    minimum number required for dispatch *75–76*
    minimum staffing levels *74–75*
    records *253–254*
    seats *174*
    training *82, 85, 86, 87*
flight control department *46–47*
flight controller *47*
flight control systems *33, 158*
flight crew compartment door *224*
flight crew emergency exits *159*
flight crewmembers
    at controls *220*
    composition of *64–66*
    duties *219*
    fitness for duty *101–102*
    oxygen for *178–179*
    proficiency check requirements *270–271*
    protective breathing equipment *179*
    requirements *63–79*
    screening and qualifications *65*
flight crew operations manual (FCOM) *55–56*
flight data monitoring (FDM) *90*
flight data recorders (FDR and DFDR) *165, 181*
flight deck
    admission to *221–223*
    duty time *123*
Flight Deck Access Restriction (FDAR) Program *223*
flight deck check procedure *176*
flightdeck door *175*
    security *235*
flight dispatchers *44*
flight dispatch release *245. See also* dispatch release
flight duty period (FDP) *99, 105–110*
    extensions *108*
flight duty time limitations. *See* flight and duty time limitations

flight engineer
    as crewmember *64–65*
    flight and duty time limitations *122, 124*
    recency of experience *88*
    training *84–88*
flight follower *44, 47, 215*
flight following *15, 44, 46–47*
flight instructors, training of *84*
flight kit *224*
flight navigator *73*
    flight and duty time limitations *122, 124*
flight operational quality assurance (FOQA) *90, 165*
flight operations *215–240*
flight operations manual (FOM) *55*
flight permit, special *34*
flight release document *189–190, 190, 246*
flight release rules *189–214*
flight release system *44*
flight simulation training device (FSTD) *73, 275*
flight simulators *271–276*
Flight Standards District Offices (FSDOs) *15*
flight structures, fire protection of. *See* interior fire protection
flight time *103, 116*
flight time limitations. *See* flight and duty time limitations
flight training requirements *82–83, 270*
floor level exits *173*
floor proximity emergency escape path marking *159, 172*
for compensation or hire. *See* compensation or hire
Form 110A *223*
four pilot crews, flight and duty time limitations *124*
four segment climb *143–144*
fourth segment climb *143–144*
fuel minimums *197*
fuel requirements *203–204*
full flight simulator (FFS) *71*

G

galley equipment *233*
general maintenance manual (GMM) *55*
general operations manual (GOM) *55, 215, 248*
grace month *82*
gratuitous bailment *8*
ground proximity warning systems *183*
ground security coordinator (GSC) *218*
Group I airplanes *81*
Group II airplanes *81*

H

hand fire extinguishers *162–163, 171*
hazardous materials (HAZMAT) training *82, 85, 276*
high minimums captain *32, 207–208*
holding out *8, 9*
home base *99*

I

icing conditions
    equipment for *169, 177, 181*
    operations in *31, 177, 181*
IFR approach procedures *33, 229*
IFR landing minimums *32, 193, 205, 229*
IFR operations, instruments and equipment for *177, 182*
IFR takeoff minimums *32, 194*
independent interest *11–12*
inertial navigation system *184*
infants, carriage of in aircraft. *See* carriage of infants and children under 2 years of age
inflight shutdown (IFSD) rate *264, 278*
initial operating experience (IOE) *86–87*
initial training *81, 84–86, 270*
inoperable instruments and equipment *208*
inspection. *See also* continuous airworthiness maintenance program (CAMP)
    aircraft *258–259*
    en route *223*
    personnel *258, 261*
    preflight *217*
    records *260*
    required *259, 262*
    training *262*
inspection function *258*
inspection training program. *See* maintenance or inspection training program
installed EFB *59*
instrument approach procedure *32, 229*
instrument requirements *169–187*
insurer *8*
interior emergency exit markings *171–172*
interior fire protection *160–161*
International Civil Aviation Organization *14*
international operations *120*
interphone system, for crewmembers. *See* crewmember interphone system

L

land and hold short operations (LAHSO) *31*
landing distance available (LDA) *138*
landing distance data *138*
landing field length requirement *138*
landing gear aural warning device *157*
landing limitations *146–149*
    for alternate airports *148*
    for destination airports *146*
landing minimums. *See* IFR landing minimums
lavatory fire protection *161*
letter of authorization (LOA) *22, 71*
Level B simulators *272, 275*
Level C simulators *272, 275*
Level D simulators *273, 275*

life-limited parts *260*
liftoff airspeed *140*
line checks *87*
lineholder *99*
line operating flight time *86*
line-oriented flight training (LOFT) *83, 90*
load manifest *190, 192, 246, 253, 254*
long-call reserve *99, 109*
long-range navigation system *32, 183*
look-back rule *110, 116, 119*
low-altitude windshear flight training program *83*
low-altitude windshear system *185*

M

maintenance *28, 33–34, 257–268*
    director of *41, 43*
    log *248, 254*
    program *259, 262*
    records *260–262*
    time limitations *34*
    training program *264*
maintenance event letter checks *263*
maintenance manual *55–56, 259–263*
maintenance or inspection training program *262*
maintenance provider *34, 258*
maintenance repair organization (MRO) *261*
major alteration *251–252*
major repair *251–252*
management personnel *30, 39–48*
management policy and procedures manual *55*
management positions *30, 42. See also* chief inspector, chief pilot, director of maintenance, director of operations, director of safety
    discretionary *45–46*
    required *39–49*
    required under 14 CFR Part 121 *39–42*
    required under 14 CFR Part 135 *42–44*
management specs (M specs) *22*
mandatory smoking regulations *160*
manipulation of controls *221*
master minimum equipment list (MMEL) *208*
means to assist occupants in descending. *See* approved means to assist occupants in descending to the ground
mechanical interruption summary report *251*
mechanical irregularities *254*
medical review officer (MRO) *282*
meteorological conditions *228*
minimum controllable airspeed (airborne) *136*
minimum control speed on the ground *136*
minimum equipment list (MEL) *34, 147, 169, 208–210, 229*
minimum number of flight attendants required for dispatch *75–76*.
See also flight attendant: minimum staffing levels
minimum steady flight speed *136*

N

National Transportation Safety Board (NTSB) *3, 241*
National Weather Service (NWS) *15, 200*
net takeoff flight path *139, 142*
night operations *177*
non-flying pilot (NFP) *221*
non-operational alternates *193*
notice of proposed rulemaking (NPRM) *265*

O

observer seat *223*
OEI (one engine inoperative) and en route limitations *144–145*
on-demand operation *13, 23*
One Level of Safety *21*
on-line vs. off-line alternate *193*
operating manuals *51–61*
    access and distribution of *56*
    approval of *51*
    Part 121 requirements *51–56*
    Part 135 requirements *56–58*
    periodic review of *58*
    types of *55–56*
operational alternates *193*
operational control *15, 30, 44–45, 58, 215–217*
    responsibility for *44, 215*
operational difficulty reports. *See* service difficulty report
operational vs. non-operational alternate. *See* on-line vs. off-line alternate
operations at night *177*
operations notices *219*
operations over uninhabited terrain *183*
operations schedules *219*
operations specifications (ops specs) *16, 21, 21–37*
    contents of *22–34*
    duration of *35*
    maintenance of *35*
    preparation process *34–35*
    templates *22*
operations under IFR. *See* IFR operations
operations under VFR *182*
overwater operations. *See* extended overwater operations
oxygen. *See also* supplemental oxygen
    equipment standards *179*
    for crewmembers *164, 178–179*
    for emergency descent *178*
    for medical use *231*
    for passengers *178, 179, 231*
    for sustenance *177*

P

pairing limitations *89*
paperless cockpit *59*
Part 117, Table A *104*
Part 117, Table B *105*
Part 117, Table C *107*
passenger information signs *176*
passenger oxygen *178, 179, 231*
passengers
   on board during stops *75–76*
   oxygen for *231*
   safety briefing *230*
passenger service equipment *233*
passive control *44*
People's Express Exemption *30, 193, 200–202*
periodic testing. *See* drug testing: periodic
personal flying equipment. *See* flight kit
physiological night's rest *99, 100, 101, 112, 113*
pilot. *See also* chief pilot; pilot-in-command
   and composition of flight crews *64–66*
   certification of *70–72, 95*
   flight and duty time limitations *95–132*
   maximum time on duty *119–120*
   privileges and limitations *11–12*
   recency of experience *87–88*
   rest requirements *100–101, 112–113*
   training *82–87*
pilot crews, flight and duty time limitations. *See* flight and duty time limitations
pilot flying (PF) *221*
pilot-in-command (PIC)
   and definition of common carriage *11*
   and operational control *15, 16, 44, 216–217*
   authority in emergencies *228*
   qualifications *72*
   responsibilities of *56, 189, 190, 217, 218, 224, 228–229, 252, 254*
pilot monitoring (PM) *221*
pitot heating system *181*
place to place *8–9*
portable EFB *59*
portable electronic device (PED) *170, 220*
portable lights *173*
post-accident testing. *See* drug testing: post-accident; alcohol testing: post-accident
powerplant major repairs *251*
precision tools, calibration of. *See* calibration of precision tools
pre-employment testing. *See* drug testing: pre-employment; alcohol testing: pre-employment
pressurized cabins *159*
primary airframe ice detection system *177*
principal maintenance inspector (PMI) *15, 56, 251*
principal operations inspector (POI) *15*

private carriage *7–9, 22*
private carriers *9*
private pilot privileges and limitations *11*
process control *257*
proficiency checks *82, 83, 87, 275*
proficiency objectives *89*
programmed hours *83*
propeller major alterations *251*
propeller major repairs *251*
pro rata sharing *11–12*
protective breathing equipment (PBE) *164, 179*
proving tests *134*
public address system (PA) *176*
public carriage *8*
Public Law 111-216 *65, 70, 95–116*
   Section 216, Flight Crewmember Screening and Qualifications *65, 70*
   Section 217, Air Transport Pilot Certification *69–70*

R

radar, weather. *See* airborne weather radar
radio equipment *182*
random testing. *See* drug testing: random; alcohol testing: random
recency of experience *83, 84, 87–88*
recordkeeping requirements *241–254*
recordkeeping system. *See* computer-based recordkeeping system
records. *See* crewmember: records; dispatcher: records
recurrent training *82, 87, 89*
recurring AD *260*
redispatch/rerelease *204*
reduced minimums takeoffs *32*
reduced programmed hours *83*
reduced V_1 *139*
rejected takeoff (RTO) *139*
released to service *259–260*
releasing *189*
repair category *210*
report time *99*
requalification training *82*
required inspections *259*
reserve availability period (RAP) *99, 109*
reserve flight crewmember *99, 109–110, 120*
resolution advisories (RAs) *184*
rest facility *99*
rest limitations *113*
rest period *100–101, 106, 108–110, 112–113, 116–126*
rest requirements *97–126*
restricted ATP (R-ATP) *70–71*
restriction or suspension of operations *224*
retesting of covered employees. *See* alcohol testing: retesting of covered employees

return to duty testing. *See* drug testing: return to duty; alcohol testing: return to duty
revision control log *52, 53*
RNAV instrument approach *33*
rotation speed *135*
route and airport qualifications *88*
route approval *14, 279*
runway limit weight *142*
RVR (runway visual range) *194*

S

safety belts. *See* seats, safety belts, and shoulder harnesses
safety briefing *230, 234*
safety margin *139*
safety-sensitive function *5, 280–285*
SATCOM *253*
scheduled flight time *115, 119*
seats, safety belts, and shoulder harnesses *173*
second segment climb *143–144*
Security Directives *223*
service difficulty report *248–251*
serving carts, storage of. *See* galley equipment
short-call reserve *100, 109*
short-term escalation authorization *34*
shoulder harnesses. *See* seats, safety belts, and shoulder harnesses
sideward facing seats *174*
sightseeing flights *14, 280*
simulator check airman *84*
simulator flight instructor *84*
single long-range communication system *32*
single-visit training program *90*
slip resistant escape route *173*
smoke hood *180*
smoke or fire detection system *162, 164*
smoking regulations. *See* mandatory smoking regulations
special airport qualifications *88–89*
Special Airworthiness Requirements *156*
Special Exemption 5549 *208*
specialized means of navigation *184*
specialized navigation equipment *73*
split controls *158*
split duty *100, 101, 106*
stalling speed *136*
standard airworthiness certificate (FAA Form 8100-2) *155, 156*
standard alternate airport (weather) minimums *32, 197*
sterile cockpit rule *219–220*
stopway *142*
suitable accommodation *98, 100*
suitable alternate airport *194*. *See also* adequate alternate airport
supplemental all-cargo operations *122–124*
supplemental operations *122*
   and emergencies *228*
   and operational control *217*
   approval of areas and routes *15–17*
   definition of *13*
   emergency equipment requirements *183*
   flight and duty time limitations *97, 115, 122–126*
   operating requirements *14*
   recordkeeping requirements *242, 246, 248*
   releasing of *189–190*
   rest requirements *97*
supplemental oxygen *177–178*
supplemental type certificates (STC) *155*
systems training *84*

T

tailcone exits *173*
tailwind takeoffs *33*
takeoff *139–143*
   decision speed *135*
   distance *140, 141*
   distance, on a dry runway *140*
   distance, on a wet runway *140*
   distance, with an engine failure *141*
   limitations *141–144*
   path *139*
   run *140–142*
   warning system *158*
Terminal Instrument Procedures (TERPS) *27, 32–33*
terrain awareness and warning system (TAWS) *183–184*
testing based on reasonable cause/suspicion. *See* drug testing: based on reasonable cause; alcohol testing: reasonable suspicion
tests for common carriage *11*
theater *98–101*
third segment climb *143–144*
three pilot crew plus additional flight crewmember, flight time limitations for *122, 124*
three pilot crews, flight time limitations for *123*
time zones *96–99, 101, 116*
Title 14 of the Code of Federal Regulations: Aeronautics and Space *2, 3, 10*. *See also* 14 CFR (specific Parts)
Title 49 of United States Code (49 U.S.C.) *3*
torts *7*
traffic alert and collision avoidance system II (TCAS II) *184*
traffic alerts *184*
training *81–94*. *See also* advanced qualification program; curriculum; differences training; flight simulation training device; *See also* proficiency checks; recency of experience; single-visit training program
   crew resource management *73, 82, 85, 220*
   dispatcher initial *85*
   dispatcher resource management *82, 85*
   facilities for *83*

flight *70, 82–85, 270*
flight attendant *82, 85–87*
flight engineer *87*
flight instructor *84*
HAZMAT *82, 85, 276*
indoctrination ground *84*
initial *81, 84–86, 270*
initial operating experience *86*
maintenance and inspection *262*
recurrent *82, 86, 87, 89*
requalification *82*
sequence of *84–85*
systems *84*
transition *81, 87, 270, 275*
upgrade *81, 87, 270, 275*
training specifications (training specs) *22*
transient fatigue *102*
transition training *81, 87, 270, 275*
Transportation Security Administration (TSA) *218*
transport category aircraft *133*
turbopropeller aircraft *147*
two engines inoperative. *See* en route limitations: two engines inoperative
two pilot crews
 flight time limitations for *120–121, 123*
 plus one additional flight crewmember, flight time limitations for *122, 124*
type certificate *155*

U

ultra-long-range (ULR) operations *97*
unaugmented operations *105, 110, 111*
 flight duty periods *105*
 flight time limits *104–105*
unauthorized operators *14*
unforeseen operational circumstances *101*
uninhabited terrain, emergency equipment for operations over *183*
upgrade training *81, 87, 270, 275*

V

V_1 *135*
V_2 *136*
V_{EF} *136*
ventral exits *173*
vertical navigation *33*
VFR. *See* operations under VFR
V_{FTO} *136*
Vision 100—Century of Aviation Reauthorization Act *74*
visual flight rules. *See* operations under VFR
V_{LOF} *136*
V_{MC} *136*
V_{MCG} *136*
V_{MC} limit *142*
V_R *135*
V_{REF} *136*
V_S *136*
V_{SR} *136*

W

warning, caution or advisory lights *164*
warning lights *164*
WAT limit charts *141*
weather data *31*
weight and balance control procedures *29, 34*
wet lease *229*
Whitlow letter *110*
willingness to transport *9*
window of circadian low *101*